THE
BRITISH ISLES

G.H.DURY M.A.,Ph.D.,D.Sc.,F.G.S.

The
British Isles

FIFTH EDITION

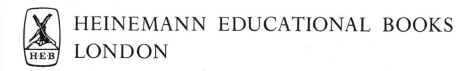

HEINEMANN EDUCATIONAL BOOKS
LONDON

Heinemann Educational Books Ltd
LONDON EDINBURGH MELBOURNE TORONTO
SINGAPORE AUCKLAND JOHANNESBURG IBADAN
HONG KONG NAIROBI NEW DELHI KUALA LUMPUR

ISBN 0 435 35260 1

Published by
Heinemann Educational Books Ltd
48 Charles Street, London W1X 8AH
Printed in Great Britain for the Publishers by
Fletcher & Son Ltd, Norwich

Contents

PART ONE

PART TWO

List of Diagrams and Maps

List of Plates

Preface to Fifth Edition

IN revising for this re-set printing, I have (as previously) welcomed the suggestions of correspondents. Information and mapping have been brought as nearly as possible up to 1970, with the aid in a few cases of slight forward projection. Some new diagrams have been introduced. The bibliography has been updated; and, where material from published papers has been directly drawn upon, bibliographic references are given. Text and diagrams have been metricated. Where possible, information subsequent to the latest industrial census has been incorporated into the text, although not always into the diagrams where that information is not comprehensive. Diagrams without acknowledged sources remain original to this book.

G. H. Dury
June 1972

Department of Geography
The University of Wisconsin
Madison, Wisconsin 53706, U.S.A.

Acknowledgments

I AM deeply grateful for the considerable help I have received in assembling material and in writing. A number of friends have kindly commented on the text in manuscript. Public bodies who have supplied information include the British Steel Corporation; the British Petroleum Company, Ltd.; the British Transport Commission; the Central Electricity Authority; the Central Office of Information; the Central Statistics Office, Dublin; Lloyd's Register of Shipping; London County Council; the Ministry of Agriculture and Ministry of Commerce, Northern Ireland; the Ministry of Housing and Local Government; the National Coal Board; the National Forestry Commission; the North of Scotland Hydro-Electricity Board; the Port of London Authority; and the United Kingdom Atomic Energy Authority. Many town clerks, public relations officers, and chambers of commerce have also been liberal with material.

The following figures are based upon Ordnance Survey maps with the sanction of the Controller of H.M. Stationery Office (Crown Copyright reserved): 4:5, 16:1, 20:3, 21:3 (based on the O.S. 1:63,360 Map); 13:3, 18:2, 24:4, 25:2, 26:4, 27:2 (based on the O.S. 1:25,000 Map); and 4:8, 13:4, 13:5, 13:10, 17:2, 17:5, 21:1, 21:2, 23:1, 27:2, 28:3 (based on the O.S. 1:10,560 Map). Figures 4:6 and 23:2 are based, by permission, on the 1:63,360 Map of the Geological Survey of England and Wales. Figure 3:23 is based, by permission, on the 1:63,360 Map of the Soil Survey Map of England and Wales, and Figure 15:2 on the corresponding Map of the Soil Survey of Scotland.

I should like to record especial gratitude to those who organised and undertook the sample land-use surveys. The relevant material was communicated by Miss M. McCririck (Figure 13:4); Mrs. M. Jones (Figure 13:5); Miss J. Roberts (Figure 13:10); Miss D. H. E. Watson (Figure 17:2); Mr. F. S. Hudson (Figure 17:5); Mr. R. S. Smith (Figure 21:1); Miss E. M. Born (Figure 21:2); Mr. W. G. S. Edwards (Figure 23:1); Mr. G. Hones (Figure 27:2); and Mr. R. H. C. Carr-Gregg (Figure 28:3). These, their helpers, and additional correspondents whose information is incorporated in the text instead of in illustrations, were most generous with time and energy, and extremely kind in acceding to my requests to make the surveys. Mr. P. T. Wheeler, with equal kindness, has allowed me to use, in Figure 14:2, information which he has collected in a survey of crofting.

Photographs have been supplied by the following, who retain the copyright: Aerofilms Ltd. (Plates 1, 7, 25, 30, 31, 33, 35, 40, 42, 45, 46, 48, 51, 52, 54, 58, 62, 66, 71, 72, 74, 76, 77); *The Belfast Telegraph* (Plate 21); Brighton Corporation (Plate 79); the British Council (Plates 2, 29); British Leyland (Plate 61); the British Petroleum Company Ltd. (Plates 34, 41, 43); British Rail, Eastern Region (Plate 17); the British Steel Corporation (Plates 14, 15, 36); the British Travel and Holiday Association (Plates 28, 32, 37, 44, 50, 68, 70); the Caterpillar Tractor Co., Ltd. (Plate 8); the Central Electricity Generating Board (Plate 60); Colin Cuff (Plate 19); Crawley Development Corporation (Plate 20); the Harris Tweed Association (Plate 38); Imperial Chemical Industries Ltd. (Plate 10); the International Wool Secretariat (Plate 57); the Irish Tourist Bureau (Plates 23, 24, 26); Kemsley Newspapers Ltd. (Plate 16); the National Coal Board (Plate 11); the Northern Ireland Government Office (Plate 22); the North of Scotland Hydro-Electricity Board (Plate 39); Photoflight Ltd. (Plates 6, 13, 53, 55, 56, 59, 63–65, 73, 78, 80, 81, 83); Sylvia Hall (Plate 75); Syndication International (Plate 82); and the United Kingdom Atomic Energy Authority (Plate 12).

PART ONE

Chapter 1

Livelihood and Land Use

In the British Isles, some 58½ million people (1970 estimate) live in an area of about 310,000 km² (121,000 mi.²). The average density of population, some 190/km² (480/mi.²) is very high. For what the comparison is worth, this value may be set against the densities of 350/km² in the Netherlands, 315/km² in Belgium, 275/km² in Japan, and 235/km² in Western Germany (respectively, about 920, 820, 720, and 635/mi.²). England as a whole is far more densely peopled than are the other parts of the British Isles, with an average density of 350/km² in England, 130 in Wales, 105 in Northern Ireland, 65 in Scotland, and about 40 in the Irish Republic (respective averages/mi.² are about 915, 340, 275, 170, and 110).

A density of 190/km² is equivalent to one person for every 5,250 m.²: that is, a plot of land about 100 m. long and about 50 m. wide (some 300 by 150 ft.). But such an average, though it only represents about 0·5 hectare, would include land of varying quality. Not much more than half the gross total is in improved farmland. Accordingly, the average extent of improved farmland per head of population comes down below 0·4 ha., less than a plot 100 by 40 m. in extent (300 by 120 ft.). Now in the cool rainy climate of the British Isles, and in the rather high latitudes in which the islands lie, there can be no question of producing from so little land enough food for so many people. Even if the standard of living fell to incredibly low levels, the British Isles could not support their present population by the unaided means of their own agricultural resources.

The high density of population sets a problem of land use and of livelihood. Within the British Isles it implies a pressure on land, a pressure reflected both in competition for space and in intensive cultivation. Externally, a high standard of living and a high density of population imply a vigorous overseas trade, which in its turn depends on a great industrial output. It is no exaggeration to say that the economy and the standard of living of the U.K. are maintained by external trade far more directly than are those of any other nation. The manifest dangers of such a condition reveal themselves fully in time of war, as when during the Napoleonic and the two World Wars a hostile blockade was imposed; they can also be severe in times of peace, as when world trade slumped during the Great Depression of the 1930s. In the later part of 1956 and during the early months of 1957, the rationing of petrol followed the blocking of the Suez Canal— a purely political matter. But it is pointless to deplore the dependence of the U.K. or of the Irish Republic on external trade. This dependence is a fact which must be recognised and accepted.

The present geographical status of the British Isles, and the nature of the geographical problem which they present, are indicated by summary statistics of employment, land use, and oversea trade. The relevant figures, showing the dominant occupations of the people, the chief goods produced and the chief services rendered, the significance of external trade in the economy, and the distribution of land among various categories of use, give a factual basis to the general statement that the British Isles are highly industrialised, intensively cultivated, and deeply committed to production for export.

LABOUR FORCE AND NATIONAL PRODUCT

As Fig. 1:1 shows, the decade of the 1970s opened with nearly half the population of the United Kingdom in paid work of some kind—work for salaries, work for wages, or (in the case of employers and the self-employed) work for direct profit. For census purposes, housewives are not automatically classed as part of the workforce, a fact which enrages numbers of them. Of the 13·5 million married women in the United Kingdom, only those who take paid employment outside their homes are included in the 26 million paid workers. At a rough estimate, these could number something like 5 million.

the remainder work in building and construction or in public utility supply. Agriculture, forestry, and fishing combined employ only 1 in 70 of the paid workers in the U.K.; mining and quarrying take an additional 1 in 50, but primary production of all types demands only about 1 in 30.

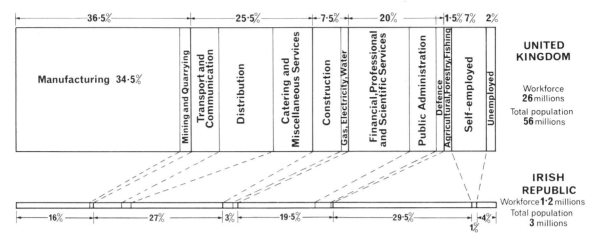

Fig. 1:1. Employment in the United Kingdom and the Irish Republic: approximate data for 1969–70

By far the largest subdivision of the total workforce belong to manufacturing, which takes rather more than one-third of the whole. About half as many, one in six of all paid workers, are engaged in transport, communication, and distribution—that is, in moving people, goods, mail, and messages. One paid worker in five is needed in the great range of professional, financial, administrative, and defensive services which a complex industrial society demands. Included here are doctors, bankers, professional scientists, and civil servants. Already nearly three-quarters of the whole workforce has been accounted for; and the fraction rises to three-quarters or above when employers and the self-employed are distributed. About half

A generally similar distribution appears in Fig. 1:2, which shows the origin of the national product. The figures from which this diagram is constructed are for the gross national product—that is, for values added during manufacture or processing and for services rendered. They represent the contributions made by the various groups of activity, after allowance has been made for costs of working and of materials. The grouping has been changed slightly from that used in Fig. 1:1, so as to bring together manufacture, mining and quarrying, and building and construction. These account for well over two-fifths of the gross national product. Buying and selling of goods, carriage of goods, mail and passengers, and the transmission of messages

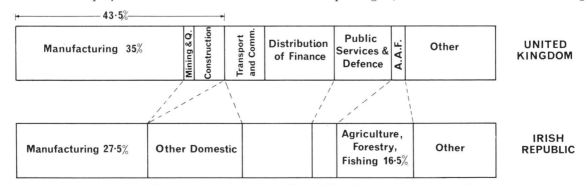

Fig. 1:2. Percentage origin of gross national product, United Kingdom and Irish Republic: approximate data for 1969–70

account for another quarter. Agriculture, forestry, and fishing yield but a thirtieth of the gross product, mostly from agriculture. Both in its contribution to the gross product, and in its demands on the labour force, manufacture predominates, and in both respects agriculture occupies a minor place.

The diagrams for the Irish Republic (Figs. 1:1, 1:2) immediately reveal a number of striking differences from the United Kingdom, even though the two sets of census data, as published, are not wholly comparable with one another. Manufacturing in the Republic takes rather less than half the proportion of the workforce taken in the United Kingdom. The agriculture–forestry–fishery group in the Republic exerts the greatest single demand, with nearly twice as many paid or independent workers as manufacturing. Farms in the Irish Republic take proportionately about as many workers as do factories in the United Kingdom, illustrating a fundamental difference in the two national economies. On the other hand, manufacturing in the Republic already takes about one

agriculture in the U.K. is running at a pitch of industrial efficiency, whereas agriculture in the Republic, for all its labour-intensive qualities, is distinctly unproductive on a comparative basis.

The visible trade of the United Kingdom at the end of the 1960s was running at about £145 of imports and £115 of exports per head of population. Food, beverages, and tobacco accounted for about one-quarter of all imports by value, and manufactured goods for about one-half. Raw materials, and mineral fuels and lubricants, accounted in roughly equal proportions for the remainder. About 40 per cent of the total weight of meat consumed in the U.K. is imported, and more than 30 per cent of the wheat flour. Not only manufacture, but also transport and communications depend on external supplies as heavily as the people depend on imported food. Ores, timber, wool, wood pulp and newsprint, and petroleum products figure prominently in the bulk list of imports.

Manufactured goods dominate the export trade

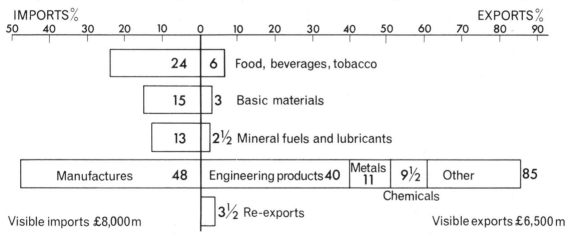

Fig. 1:3. Percentage comparison of the import and export trades of the United Kingdom, by value, 1968–69

worker in six; and the proportion, considerably increased through the 1960s, is expected to increase again in the 1970s. The large block demand illustrated for the Republic in respect of transport, communications, distribution, catering, and miscellaneous services is somewhat misleading, since the miscellaneous class includes types of workers who, in the U.K., are largely distributed among specified groups.

Manufacturing makes the largest single contribution to the gross national product of the Irish Republic. In terms of the contribution/workforce–demand ratio it compares favourably with manufacturing in the U.K. But this is mainly because

of the U.K. Their prominence in the list both of imports and of exports is in no way surprising, since the best customers of mechanised countries tend to be other mechanised countries. However, manufactures are nearly twice as prominent in the list of U.K. exports as they are in the list of imports, accounting for 85 per cent of the whole. Among manufactured exports, machinery, transport equipment, finished steel, vehicles, and aero engines all figure largely; but it is only just to point out that the international market for vehicles and aero engines is savagely competitive, and that success in this market at any given time is no guarantee of success in the future.

EXTERNAL TRADE

The *per capita* value of trade for the Irish Republic has been running for some time not greatly below that for the United Kingdom. Values corresponding to those cited for the U.K. are £135 per head of visible imports and £100 per head of visible exports. But the nature of trade differs strongly from that of the U.K. Manufactures account for 60 per cent of imports into the Republic, foodstuffs (including live meat animals), beverages, and tobacco for 60 per cent of exports from the Republic. Thus, in its external relations, the Republic acts mainly as a primary producer, even though manufactured goods account for more than a quarter of the total export value and will prospectively soon rise to one-third or more (Fig. 1:4).

Despite the demands made by towns, industry, and communication lines and installations, about three-quarters of the land area of England is in farms. Tillage, defined as excluding rotation grass, takes about one-third. Improved grassland, defined as including rotation grass and permanent pasture, takes about an equal fraction, while rough grazing amounts to about one-tenth. Tillage is far more restricted in the remaining countries—about 8 per cent in Northern Ireland and Scotland, below 8 per cent in the Irish Republic, and 6 per cent in Wales (Fig. 1:5). If an internal breakdown were made for England, the proportion of tillage would be seen to decline well below the one-third fraction in northern areas, and to rise well above this level in the east and south, as will in fact be made clear in later chapters. Total farmland (excluding rough grazing) is rather more extensive in the Irish

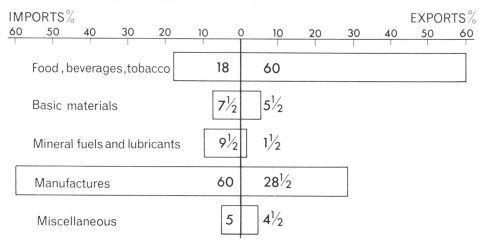

FIG. 1:4. Percentage comparison of the import trades of the Irish Republic, by value: approximate data for 1968–69

LAND USE

Since the economy of the whole of the U.K. is dominated by manufacturing industry, its component countries may suitably be grouped together in a summary account of the labour force, national product, and trade. Such a grouping is further justified by the political fact that goods passing through the ports of the U.K. are subject to a single system of regulations—for purposes of trade, prohibitions, subsidies, and tariffs, the U.K. is a single unit. But when land use is discussed, it becomes desirable to separate England, Wales, Scotland, and Northern Ireland from one another. As can be seen from Fig. 1:5, there are pronounced differences between them in the uses to which their land is put, and in the relative extent of the major categories of land use.

Republic than in England, but some contrary allowance ought probably to be made for the actual status of permanent grassland, which is classed as improved merely on account of being fenced into farms. Little more than half the area of Wales, and only about one-fifth of the area in each of Scotland and Northern Ireland, is classed as farmland. Rough grazing extends over nearly one-third of Wales, probably amounts to about one-quarter of the Irish Republic, is rather less extensive, proportionately, in Northern Ireland (one-fifth), but expands in Scotland to two-thirds of the total area. Nearly half of Wales is in rough grazing or non-agricultural use; corresponding values are 40 per cent for Northern Ireland, 30 per cent for the Irish Republic, and 80 per cent or more for Scotland.

In all the countries listed, except probably the Irish Republic, the percentage of land in agricultural use has declined through the 1950s and the 1960s. Although the decline has, in total, been more than offset by an increase in yield rates, in the long term it could be serious indeed. Currently, it amounts to about 0·1 per cent of total area per year in England and to 0·4 per cent in Northern Ireland and Scotland: Wales records an intermediate rate. That is to say, the encroachment on, or abandonment of, farming land runs at 1 to 4 per cent a decade, or 10 to 40 per cent in a century, at the minimum. Compounded rates suggest that 15 to 50 per cent in a century represents a more likely measure of loss. In so far as the losses concern land of marginal productivity, they can be borne without great difficulty. Some, however—especially in southeastern England—result from

countries. These summaries are bound to obscure the contrasts which occur within each of the countries—that is to say, between the regions into which each country can be subdivided. Regional character and regional differences are however reserved to a later section of the book. This chapter has attempted neither detailed description nor explanation: it is meant merely to present in very general terms some leading facts about the present geographical condition of the British Isles

This short account is both the starting-point and the objective of the chapters which follow. There has been nothing inevitable in the developments which have brought the British Isles to their existing geographical state—nothing, that is to say, except the fact that those developments took the course which they did. In so far as this book is an enquiry into present-day geography, it must there-

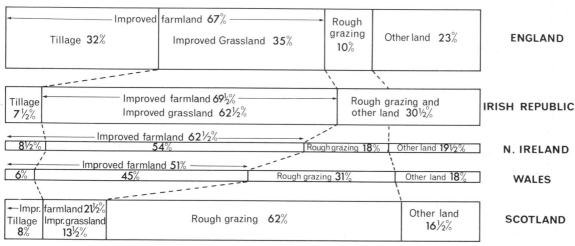

Fig. 1:5. Summaries of land use, by countries

land-use competition wherein building and construction encroach on land of the greatest farming potential.

CONCLUSION

Differences between one portion and another of the British Isles are already making themselves apparent, even in summary statistics for whole

fore attempt to be both informative and explanatory. It must seek to show the nature of the land and of the climate of the British Isles, and to indicate the ways in which the use made of the land by man has changed. Only by taking into account the resources of the land, and the way in which those resources have been exploited through the centuries, can one hope to understand the geography of the British Isles today.

Chapter 2

The Nature of the Land

THE physical environment provides, as it were, much of a country's working capital, fixed assets, and reserves. But the people are in no way obliged to exploit any particular part or property of their environment, and given elements of the environment can have different worth at different times.

A few examples will readily illustrate these principles. In Roman days, the surplus economic wealth of the British Isles was provided by food and raw materials—grain from the limestone uplands of the south and tin and lead from the mountains. During the Middle Ages fortunes were made from sheep, many of which grazed on the Cotswolds where the land had once been tilled, and where much is again under the plough today. When industry made its first beginnings, wood served for fuel and running water supplied power, so that forests and streams—instead of coalfields and seaports—influenced the location of manufacturing. The south coast of England was the sunniest part of the British Isles many centuries ago, just as it is today, but its climate did not acquire a cash value in the resort trade until quite recent times. Whereas the physical environment is, for most practical purposes, a stable one, the relationship between people and their surroundings is selective and inconstant. Changes in that relationship accompany changes in economy and in culture.

At all times, the environment sets practical limits on what people can do—limits of possibility, limits of commonsense, and limits of cost. Mineral resources are limited to certain districts; climate (among other factors) prevents the growing of wheat in the Scottish Highlands; tropical fruits could be grown in the British Isles in hot-houses, but only at great expense. Cost exerts a powerful influence on production in the competitive world of the present day. Competition tends, in a general way, to confine manufacture to those districts where

it can show a profit—districts where geographical advantages are greatest. But since production of food or of goods is promoted by the need to make a living, and not primarily by the facts of the environment, one must expect the physical environment to prove favourable in some places and in some ways, but to be adverse in others.

Adjustment to environment is most easily studied where people depend directly on the resources of the land. Very many people in the British Isles work in industry, and their dependence on the land is indirect. To this extent the influence of the physical environment on their lives is remote. On the other hand, the leading industries of the British Isles, subject to severe international competition, need to make the most of natural resources as well as of technical skill. They demand a huge and ever-growing range of raw materials. If industry is to be maintained and expanded, the resources of the British Isles must be increasingly exploited. Advantage will be taken of elements in the environment which have hitherto been neglected or little used—compare the rising output of domestic iron-ore, the recently-built hydro-electric stations in the rainy highlands, and the working of domestic oil and natural gas. Although a high state of economic development means, in one sense, a certain freedom from or command over the environment, in another sense it makes for closer links with it, complex though those links may be.

In the British Isles there is obviously some kind of association between the distribution of people, crops, and livestock on the one hand, and the qualities of landforms, soils, and climate on the other. Significantly enough, the geographical contrasts between various parts of the British land have intensified themselves in the last hundred years. It seems that the mode of adjustment between man and land is better defined today than it was a century ago. A given association may, however, reflect a complicated relationship between people and their surroundings. The connection of sheep-grazing and sparse population with certain upland districts, for instance, is by no means as simple as it looks at first sight. Even when they seem self-explanatory, existing distributions are usually the result of centuries of development. It is, moreover, impossible to say exactly how the environment produces an effect on the people. Men do not migrate from upland districts simply because the land is high, any more than they settle on coal-fields simply because coal is found there. The influence of the environment works at several removes. The best that can be done is to define and contrast the different qualities of different environments, and to describe the adjustments to them which have actually been made.

TIME-SCALES

In tracing the physical evolution of the British Isles, it is necessary to use more than one time-scale. On the scale of historical time, which is graduated in years and centuries, the physical environment appears to change very slowly indeed. The present distributions of people and of economic activity have come into being during the last two centuries—far too short a period for the physical environment to have changed. Even in the last two thousand years, changes in climate and in the form of the ground have been but slight.

The events of the Ice Age and of prehistory are measured on a coarser scale, which is divided by centuries and has a total length of nearly a million years. On this scale climatic change seems rapid, including as it does the repeated waxing and waning of ice sheets, but the evolution of the land-surface still appears slow. It is true that during the last million years the *details* of landform have been modified in many areas, but the sum total of change has amounted chiefly to a re-touching of the already-existing surface.

The scale of geological time is marked in millions of years. On it are recorded, in apparently rapid succession, profound and repeated changes in the physique of the British Isles, and the formation and deformation of the rocks which compose the land itself.

PHYSIQUE: HIGHLAND BRITAIN

The first part of the geological record relates to Highland Britain—the blocks of high ground, broken and fringed by patches of lowland, which constitute the north and west (Fig. 2:1). Most of the ground here stands above 300 m. (1,000 ft.). Its rocks are mainly of Primary age (See Appendix 1). Their sedimentary formations have been generally hardened, while in some districts crystalline rocks —both igneous and metamorphic—are wide-spread. Although some parts of the highlands have been severely dissected by rivers or deeply grooved by ice, Highland Britain is mainly plateau country. The chief physical units are rigid crustal blocks, which rise steeply from the adjacent lowlands or from the surrounding seas. Only in Central Ireland do rocks of Primary age come to the surface in a broad lowland, and even this part is more conveniently treated with the highlands than with the lowlands. Highland Britain, then, includes South-west England, Wales, Ireland, the Lake District and the Pennines, the Southern Uplands, and the Scottish Highlands.

A great deal of Highland Britain consists of the remnants of fold mountains. Two main episodes of folding occurred, separated by a vast interval of time. Each was followed by uplift and severe denudation. By the time that the fold-mountain system had been worn down, its rocks had become rigid; they were broken into blocks by faulting on a large scale, some blocks foundering and others rising. It is the latter which form the upstanding massifs visible today.

The Caledonides

The first of the two episodes of folding was responsible for the structural grain of much of Highland Britain. As can be seen on the most general geological map, the structures and out-crops in many highland areas run from northeast to southwest. This trend, emphasised by successive earth-movements, belongs to the former fold-mountains known as the *Caledonides*.

The Caledonian mountain-building began some 500 million years ago. A huge strip of the earth's crust slowly sank, forming a sedimentary basin called a geosyncline. Subsidence was intermittent but prolonged, and in the course of 150 million years the centre of the basin was depressed to a depth of miles. Great thicknesses of sediment were brought in from either side; a long and complex sequence of deposition, crumpling and uplift converted the weak sediments to firm rock and the vast basin to a system of high fold mountains.

The Hebrides and the Atlantic fringe of the Northern Highlands of Scotland represent the rigid margin of the basin; that is, they are part of

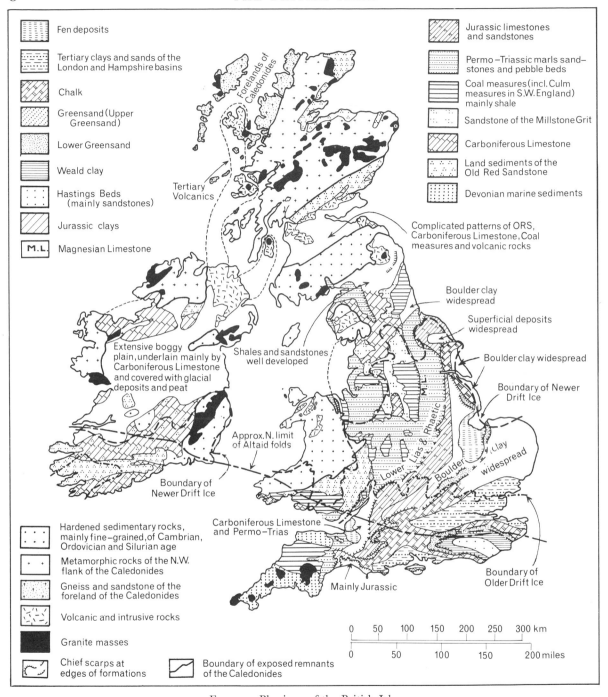

Fen deposits

Tertiary clays and sands of the London and Hampshire basins

Chalk

Greensand (Upper Greensand)

Lower Greensand

Weald clay

Hastings Beds (mainly sandstones)

Jurassic clays

M.L. Magnesian Limestone

Jurassic limestones and sandstones

Permo–Triassic marls sandstones and pebble beds

Coal measures (incl. Culm measures in S.W. England) mainly shale

Sandstone of the Millstone Grit

Carboniferous Limestone

Land sediments of the Old Red Sandstone

Devonian marine sediments

Forelands of Caledonides

Tertiary Volcanics

Complicated patterns of ORS, Carboniferous Limestone, Coal measures and volcanic rocks

Boulder clay widespread

Superficial deposits widespread

Boulder clay widespread

Boundary of Newer Drift Ice

Extensive boggy plain, underlain mainly by Carboniferous Limestone and covered with glacial deposits and peat

Shales and sandstones well developed

Approx. N. limit of Altaid folds

Boulder clay widespread

Boundary of Newer Drift Ice

Carboniferous Limestone and Permo–Trias

Lower Lias & Rhaetic

Mainly Jurassic

Boundary of Older Drift Ice

Hardened sedimentary rocks, mainly fine–grained, of Cambrian, Ordovician and Silurian age

Metamorphic rocks of the N.W. flank of the Caledonides

Gneiss and sandstone of the foreland of the Caledonides

Volcanic and intrusive rocks

Granite masses

Chief scarps at edges of formations

Boundary of exposed remnants of the Caledonides

0   50   100   150   200   250   300 km

0   50   100   150   200 miles

FIG. 2:1. Physique of the British Isles

the foreland against which the rocks in the geosyncline were folded. Northwest Ireland, the rest of the Northern Highlands of Scotland, and the Scottish Highlands south of the Great Glen were included in the flank of the folded belt itself. Their rocks are greatly disturbed and much altered; heat and pressure, operating powerfully on a regional scale, have metamorphosed them into schists and gneisses—foliated crystalline rocks. Large bodies of igneous rock, originally emplaced in the deep roots of the folded belt, have been laid bare by erosion. Nearly all the rocks of this northwestern flank of

PLATE 1. View southwestwards along the fault-guided Great Glen. The Ben Nevis group rises to more than 1,200 metres, clear above a broad summit-surface about 900 metres high.

the Caledonides are highly resistant to denudation, and valleys have been cut on lines of faulting rather than on belts of weak rock (Plate 1).

The central area of the old geosyncline is well illustrated in the Southern Uplands, the core of the Lake District, the Isle of Man, the Mourne Mountains, a large part of Wales, and the Wicklow Mountains. Here are found enormous thicknesses of sediments belonging chiefly to the Cambrian, Ordovician, and Silurian systems (Appendix 1). Most of the total bulk consists of fine-grained sediment, originally laid down as mud, and now hardened into shale or compressed into slate. Among the sediments occur the deposits of volcanoes which, strung along the axis of the geosyncline, extruded lava and showered down dust. The fine-grained sediments weather into rounded landforms, and their scenery is rarely spectacular even when the ground is high, but the lavas give rise to majestic craggy country, as in the centre of the Lake District and on Snowdon (Plates 3, 31).

Between the northwestern and the central subdivisions of the Caledonides lies a strip, some 55 km (35 mi.) wide, where the crust has been depressed between faults. In Scotland this strip is represented by the Midland Valley, but in Ireland it is largely hidden beneath the basalts of Antrim.

Little can be said about the southeastern flank of the Caledonides in the British area, for it is largely buried by later sediments. Structurally it is likely to have resembled Norway, where rocks formed in the geosyncline are crumpled and thrust southeastwards against the rigid foreland of the Baltic Shield.

Desert Sedimentation and Marine Transgression

When the Caledonides were uplifted, they bordered a lowland where the climate was dry. It is quite possible that the mountains themselves were responsible for the dryness. Sediment carried down from mountains on the northwest accumulated, in the British area, in wide but shallow lakes, forming conglomerates, sandstones, and marls with a characteristic reddish or purplish colour. These are the rocks of the Old Red Sandstone, which now appear on the fringe of older rocks on the sites of the lake-basins—along the shores of the Moray Firth, on the flanks of the Midland Valley, and along the southern Welsh Border. In this last area the thick, weak marls have been much eroded, and the terrain developed on them seems to belong to Lowland rather than to Highland Britain. In Southwest England and in the south of Ireland sediments were laid down not on land but in the sea, forming the Devonian rocks from which the whole system takes its name. They lack the bright colours of the Old Red Sandstone, being generally pale in tint and dull in tone.

By the end of Devonian times the once-lofty Caledonides had been worn down. Thirty million years of denudation had reduced them to low levels. In the British area, as in some other parts of the world, there followed a phase of subsidence. The land gently sank and was overspread by the sea and by new marine sediments. To such a marine invasion the name *transgression* is given; this transgression was that of the Carboniferous sea, in which the rocks of the Carboniferous system were formed.

Thick deposits of limestone first accumulated off the shores of the sinking land. The resulting formation is the Carboniferous Limestone, whose thick well-jointed rocks are widely exposed at the surface in the North Pennines and in the Derbyshire Dome (Plate 49). Their bare surfaces and craggy edges are unmistakable, and their underground caverns are still not fully explored. A wide expanse of Carboniferous Limestone in Central Ireland stands at a low level, and is almost wholly concealed by glacial deposits and peat. It fails therefore to display the typical features of limestone country, but these reappear round the margins of the South Wales Coalfield and in the Mendips.

Uplift of the land to the northwest caused great rivers to bring down huge loads of coarse sand. The formation of limestone ceased. Great deltas spread outwards from the shore, depositing the Millstone Grit, which now comes to the surface at the very margins of the coalfields and underlies the whole of the dark moorland of the Central Pennines. Like the Carboniferous Limestone, the Millstone Grit is generally resistant and forms high ground.

Intermittent subsidence was typical of the Millstone Grit deltas, and continued during the formation of the succeeding Coal Measures. The deltas by this time had become muddy rather than sandy, and had been colonised by flourishing associations of swamp-plants. Thick layers of peat accumulated. Every subsidence depressed the peat, which was then buried by mud or sand over which the plants spread once more. Compression changed the peat to coal, the mud to shale, and the sand to sandstone.

Without the Coal Measures, Britain might have taken a very small part in the industrial revolution and would certainly not have led it. The distribution of coalfields has of course profoundly affected the location of industry, and thereby the regional pattern of geography. The peat of the coal seams was formed at the margins of the land of Coal Measure times, so that deposits of coal now occur on the flanks of the massifs by which that land is represented. This means that some of the largest coalfields straddle the boundary between Highland and Lowland Britain, and the regional boundaries drawn round them do not coincide with the break between high ground and low—particularly on the flanks of the Pennines. Some of the coal originally formed has been destroyed by erosion, being stripped away from uplifted areas, as for instance between the Lancashire and the Yorks., Derby and Notts. coalfields. Elsewhere the seams have been carried down by subsidence and deeply buried beneath later sediments, as beneath the Lancs. Cheshire Plain.

The Carboniferous period was not free from crustal disturbance. In addition to the sinking of the basins where coal was formed, there were volcanic outbursts in the Midland Valley of Scotland. These added more lava and dust to the volcanic rocks formed in the same area in the earlier Devonian period. Today the lavas give rise to the craggy shapes of the Renfrew Hills, the Ochils, the Campsie Fells, and the Sidlaws.

The Altaides

Carboniferous times ended with an episode of mountain-building, the second of those mentioned above. The new mountains were the Altaides. Like the older Caledonides, they began with thick sedimentation in a geosyncline. Most of the British area, however, lay outside the margins of the great depressed basin and of the folded belt, acting as a foreland where crustal movements were not general but localised. The Pennines were asymmetrically uplifted, and domes were formed at their southern end and in the Lake District. Southern Ireland, South Wales, and England south of the Bristol–London line were incorporated in the mountain arcs of the Altaides, which looped across Central Europe, running westwards through the Ardennes, Northwest France, and the south of Britain. The east–west grain is still prominent where the denuded remnants of the fold mountains are exposed, and in Southwest England can be seen some of the igneous rocks which invaded the mountain roots. The folded rocks, now set firm in rigid blocks, have been broken across by subsidence, so that inlets of the sea occur between the south of Ireland and South Wales, and between the latter and Southwest England. East of the Exe, beneath the Channel, and beneath the Paris Basin, the remnants of the Altaides have foundered; where there is land today, they lie concealed by a cover of later sediments.

PHYSIQUE: LOWLAND BRITAIN

Renewed Sedimentation in Deserts

Just as the formation of the Caledonides was succeeded by a long period of dry climate, so did the rise of the Altaides introduce the desert conditions in which the rocks of the Permian and Triassic systems were laid down. These are often grouped together as the Permo-Trias. They consist of red sandstones, thick marls, breccias, pebble beds, and salt deposits which were laid down by winds and torrents, or accumulated in drying lakes, as sands, muds, scree, gravel, and evaporites. In Permo-Triassic times crustal dimples formed in parts of the British area, presumably where blocks were foundering, and provided the enclosed basins in which thick sedimentation took place.

A number of these basins are roughly oval in plan. The best-defined is that which underlies the Lancs.–Cheshire Plain, with its ends formed by the scalloped edges of the Pennines and of the Welsh Massif. Here the Coal Measures which underlie the Permo-Trias have been depressed by thousands of feet, and the faulted northeastern edge of the basin is clearly displayed. A whole complex of coalescent basins occurs in the Midland Triangle, amid the small upstanding blocks of the coalfields and of Charnwood Forest. At the angles of the Triangle the Permo-Trias merges with the Lancs.–Cheshire Plain through the Midland Gate, runs northward through the Trent valley and the Vale of York to the mouth of the Tees, and projects southwards along the Lower Severn towards the Plain of Somerset. All this is essentially lowland country, contrasting very strongly in height, texture of relief, and soil with the adjacent parts of Highland Britain.

The boundary between the two divisions is in many places formed by the exhumed edges of the massifs, for the Permo-Trias is generally weak and has been deeply eroded. Only on the eastern side of the Pennines, where the crust has been tilted rather than broken, does the Permo-Trias dip gently off the older rocks.

It seems likely that the Irish Sea is underlain by a second complex of basins filled with Permo-Trias, for rocks belonging to this group occur in northeast Ireland and project as tongues into the valleys of the Conway, Clwyd, and Eden. In these three valleys the desert sediments accumulated in long narrow depressions bounded by huge faults which have subsequently been stripped out by erosion. The Vale of Taunton between Exmoor and the Quantocks is also due to faulting, and is also partly filled by Permo-Trias.

The margins of Lowland Britain correspond generally to the lower boundary of the Permo-Trias, and in places they coincide with marked structural breaks. Highland Britain, beyond the margins, is an area of massifs and of plateau country. Lowland Britain, within the margins, is an area of plains, wide vales, low plateaus, and scarplands.

Jurassic Scarplands

Adjoining the Midland Triangle and the vale country between Nottingham and Middlesbrough is the belt of Jurassic scarpland. Its rocks are marine sediments—clays, limestones, and sandstones. The clays are weak, and have been eroded into broad strips of lowland, while the limestones and sandstones are strong, and rise in cuestas[1] with their scarps for the most part facing west or northwest. There is no single line of scarp, for the succession of Jurassic rocks is very varied. Furthermore, the strong formations vary in thickness, so that in some places they form high ground whereas in others the terrain is composed of low, irregular, broken hills. Thick sandstones form a bold cuesta in the North York Moors, rising to more than 300 m. (1,000 ft.) and leading down to the Vale of Pickering by a dissected back-slope.[1] About the head of the Humber the rocks thin out and are concealed by younger sediments; but Jurassic

---

[1] *Cuesta* is the only available term for a belt of hills developed by erosion, on a dipping formation of sedimentary rocks. It includes two elements: (*a*) the scarp, scarp-face, or escarpment—strictly synonymous expressions—and (*b*) the back-slope. If the back-slope coincides with the surface of a strong formation, it can be called the *dip-slope*; but since true dip-slopes are uncommon, the term back-slope is used throughout the following text.

limestones appear in Lincoln Edge, with overlying clays to the east in the Witham valley. In the Leicestershire Wolds and the Northamptonshire Uplands the country is strongly dissected and is largely covered by boulder clay, so that the relief is confused; but strong limestones thicken towards the southeast, giving rise to the dissected plateaus of the North Oxfordshire Hills and of the Cotswolds (Plate 64). Here the scarp-face is high, prominent, and continuous, and the crest of the cuesta rises again to 300 m. The outcrop of Jurassic rocks swings southwards across the Mendips, continues through the irregular hilly country on the eastern border of the Somerset Plain, and reappears on the Dorset coast where it laps round the Hampshire Basin.

In the Fenlands the solid rocks are obscured by peat and silt, but thick Jurassic clays appear again in the Great Ouse Valley, forming a wide vale which extends southwestwards for more than a hundred miles. The Jurassic clays are covered in places by glacial deposits, but these too consist mainly of clay. The whole belt is one of lowland, except where a formation of limestone occurs to form hills running SW–NE across the line of the Cherwell.

Cretaceous Scarplands

East and southeast of the Jurassic belt comes the outcrop of Cretaceous rocks, dominated by the prominent cuesta formed by the Chalk. The Chalk scarpland begins at Flamborough Head, at the extremity of the Yorkshire Wolds. Swinging round to the south, it obscures the thin Jurassic rocks near the head of the Humber, and then swings away again in the Lincolnshire Wolds, a belt of low hills where the Chalk is covered by glacial deposits. Beyond the Wash, again, boulder clay is widespread, and very little Chalk appears at the surface, but the underlying Greensand forms a scarp which overlooks the Fens. Bold, continuous scarps are magnificently developed on the faces of the Chilterns and the Berkshire Downs, which rise to even crests at about 240 m. (800 ft.) and descend in backslopes dissected by numerous dry valleys. From place to place the Greensand protrudes from beneath the Chalk, varying in importance because it varies in thickness, and indeed vanishing altogether in some localities. At the eastern edge of Salisbury Plain, the Chalk outcrop is deeply indented where upfolds have been eroded. In the same area the Greensand becomes really thick, and forms an outfacing scarp as bold as that of the Chalk itself. In the dissected, tabular Blackdown

Hills it is the Greensand which forms the high ground. The Chalk thins out here, but thickens again round the southern rim of the Hampshire Basin.

Salisbury Plain forms a node from which the Chalk outcrops run southwestwards, northeastwards, and eastwards. The Plain itself is an area of gentle uplift. Farther east, in the Weald, the strongly uplifted Chalk has been eroded away (Plate 77), revealing the alternating strong and weak formations in the Wealden series, which have been dissected into infacing cuestas and concentric vales.

Tertiary Basins

To the north of the Weald lies the London Basin; to the south of Salisbury Plain lies the Hampshire Basin. The former is a funnel-shaped structural depression, which received muddy and sandy sediments during Tertiary times. The muds formed the London Clay which is now widely exposed at the surface. Sandy and gravelly sediments appear from beneath the London Clay in North Kent, and relics of quite thick sands above the clay occur in the Bagshot district. The Hampshire Basin is almost encircled by a rim of Chalk. It subsided persistently in Tertiary times, receiving mud, like the London Basin, but subsequently being filled with the widespread sands which today form the geological basis of the New Forest.

ORIGINS OF THE PRESENT LANDSCAPE

Much of the present land-surface has been produced by a sequence of erosion which began when the floor of the Chalk Sea was elevated. Like the Carboniferous Sea, the Chalk Sea was transgressive. Its northern and western limits are uncertain; it may have lapped against the margins of Wales, the Pennines, the Southern Uplands, the Scottish Highlands, and the blocks of Irish hills, or it may have passed right over them. In either case, transgression ended with uplift in the west. This uplift, exposing the Chalk as new land, initiated new rivers which drained across Great Britain from west to east.

The crustal movements which caused the uplift were accompanied by volcanic outbursts. In northeast Ireland floods of basaltic lava poured from fissures, spreading far outwards in thick, gently-sloping sheets. The remains of these sheets, strongly eroded round the edges, now underlie the basalt plateau of Antrim. In the area of the Inner Hebrides were central volcanoes—i.e., volcanoes with localised vents which erupted streams of lava and formed conical mountains. Their ruins now appear in Skye, Mull, and Arran. In southeastern England there was movement of another kind. The subsidence of the London and Hampshire Basins was accompanied by the rise of the Wealden area, and also by compression from the south. Short, offset folds were formed, running in a sheaf from the east of the Weald to the borders of the West Country. Streams ran down the flanks of the rising Weald, and additional streams flowed southwards across the site of the Hampshire Basin.

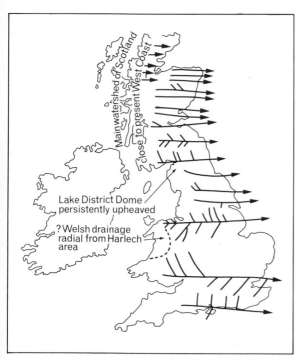

FIG. 2:2. Some early elements in the drainage of Great Britain. Trunk streams flowing from west to east are reconstructed consequents

The consequent streams flowing down the various slopes of the new land (Fig. 2:2) were certain to be dismembered by capture. They flowed across outcrops of contrasted strength, on which they were superimposed—in places at least—from the cover of Chalk. In the Scottish Highlands the drainage has become largely adjusted to the lines of structural weakness in the ancient rocks. On the eastern side of the Pennines, many of the headstreams have been collected by the subsequent Ouse and Trent, which worked along the unresistant outcrop of Permo-Trias. The former Dee-Trent has almost vanished from the Midland Triangle. Its headwaters have been captured to the Irish Sea, its

lower part beheaded; the upper Severn, a former tributary, has been diverted by glaciation to the Bristol Channel, and much of the former Soar reversed to form the Warwickshire Avon. The Kennet-Thames now flows in its lower reaches far south of its old line, having been displaced by lobes of the ice-sheet. In the Wealden area, subsequent streams extending themselves along belts of weak rock have developed at the expense of the original consequents.

Changes of Sea-level

River-development has been influenced not only by the changes of plan which have accompanied capture and glacial diversion, but also by changes of sea-level. For at least a million years, and possibly for very much longer, sea-level has been falling intermittently. The effects of intermittent falls in level are most clearly illustrated by the high ground of the north and west, where, whatever the complications introduced by the cutting of valleys by rivers or by glaciers, the land of the massifs can be seen to ascend in steps. The broad upland surfaces which are so extensive in some districts are erosional in origin. They represent platforms cut across the underlying rocks, either by wave-action on the shore or by running water on land. Dissected plateau country is very widespread indeed. It is moreover not confined to the highlands, for the crests and backslopes of the Jurassic and Chalk cuestas are also remains of erosional platforms related to high base-levels.

Periods of stable base-level enabled the platforms to be cut: periods of falling base-level caused the rivers to be rejuvenated. All the rivers of the British Isles have undergone rejuvenation, so that they are sharply incised into the plateaus and flow in terraced valleys across the low ground.

The Ice Age

The sequence of intermittent rejuvenation goes back far into Tertiary times, long pre-dating the Ice Age. Glaciation, setting in when base-level stood about 100 m. (300 ft.) above its present mark, introduced complications.

Down to about 100 m. the great steps of the erosional platforms are well-marked. Halts in the fall of the sea at this and higher levels were long enough for large areas to be reduced to gently-sloping, continuous plateau surfaces. When the great ice-sheets formed, their waxings and wanings made the level of the sea fall and rise by turns. The lower parts of valleys were deepened when sea-level fell, and infilled when it rose again. But because the movements of glacial times were superimposed on the general tendency for base-level to fall, the net effect has been to produce valleys in which terrace deposits record old flood-plains at successively lower heights. The changes of the Ice Age were too rapid to permit the cutting of platforms across strong rocks, but from the weaker outcrops a great deal of material was removed; in all cases terraces are the rule rather than the exception.

Around the shores of the British Isles, raised beach deposits are widely distributed. In the south they belong to times when sea-level stood higher than it does today; but the last movement has been one of submergence, for the mouths of all valleys have been drowned by the rising sea (Plates 33, 66). In the northwest the land has risen, having been relieved of its former load of ice, and has carried the beaches up with it.

Whatever its ultimate cause, the Ice Age began with a lowering of air temperature and an increase in snowfall. Snow-fields and glaciers established themselves on the high ground of the British Isles; the valley-heads became corries and the valleys glacier troughs. Peaks and ridges rising above the glaciers were shattered by frost. The typical features of glaciated highland are best developed on the highest land of all, which broadly speaking is based on the most resistant rocks (Fig. 2:1). Those parts of the massifs which are underlain by fine-grained sediments or by rocks of Carboniferous age fail to exhibit the full range of glacial features, partly because of the nature of their material and partly because they were entirely covered by the ice-cap. The Southern Uplands, the Pennines, and Central Wales are especially deficient in corries, arêtes, and ribbon lakes, although their principal valleys have been converted into deep grooves.

The ice spread over Lowland Britain as far south as the Cotswolds, crossed the Northampton Uplands and the clay belt to the south, and passed over the Chalk country east of the Chilterns. East Anglia and Lincolnshire were deeply buried by the united fringes of the sheets which spread from northern Britain and from Scandinavia. When the ice finally melted away, the lowland on which it had rested was mantled with sand, gravel, and boulder clay. Parts of this cover have been stripped off, but large spreads still remain in East Anglia, the eastern Midlands, the low ground on the east of the Pennines, and the Lancs.–Cheshire Plain (Fig. 2:1). Most of Ireland is covered by glacial drift, which is also extensive on the flanks of the Lake District and the Southern Uplands, in the Midland Valley of Scotland, and along the eastern margins of the Scottish Highlands. Tongues of drift run up the valleys in these areas between the steep, rocky walls of the glaciated troughs.

A most severe climate of the tundra type affected the lands south of the ice-edge. The ground was deeply frozen. When the topsoil melted in summer, it tended to sludge downslope and to form spreads of the dirty rubble called *head*. Only in the south-east was the climate dry enough for dust-storms to deposit the loess which appears on geological maps as brickearth.

The chief types of post-glacial deposit are alluvium, peat, and the material of present-day beaches. It is impossible to give an account of beaches except at great length, and they will not be treated here. The formation and distribution of peat fall more readily into the following chapter than into this. The alluvium of present flood-plains is restricted to the valley floors, and is more widely developed in the lowlands than in the highlands. In the Fens and in the Somerset Levels, large inlets of the sea have been enclosed by beach-bars and filled with peat and silt, so that sizeable areas have been added to the land; on the eastern side of Romney Marsh shingle ridges are still being added, extending seaward the remarkable cusp of low-lying ground which has been formed during the last two thousand years.

Superficial deposits of glacial débris, head, brick-earth, terrace material, alluvium, and peat are of high geographical importance wherever they occur. Although in places they greatly modify the form of the ground, their significance lies less in this fact than in the profound influence which they have on the quality of the soils which are developed on them.

APPENDIX
The Geological Time-scale

Era	System	Approximate age (in millions of years)
Tertiary	Recent* Pleistocene* Pliocene Miocene Oligocene Eocene	
		60
Secondary	Cretaceous	
		135
	Jurassic (including Rhaetic)	
		180
	Triassic	
		225
Primary	Permian	
		270
	Carboniferous	
		350
	Devonian	
		400
	Silurian	
		440
	Ordovician	
		500
	Cambrian	
		600
	pre-Cambrian extending back to about 4,500 million years ago	

* The Recent and Pleistocene systems are sometimes grouped together under the title *Quaternary*.

Chapter 3

Climate, Vegetation, and Soils

THE British Isles lie between 50° and 61°N, on the western side of a great landmass, and within the belt of prevailing westerlies. Their climate is dominated by marine influences and is rainy and equable. Within the limits of the general climatic type—maritime, temperate, with no dry season and with summers only moderately warm—there is, however, room for considerable variation between one region and another.

Because the British Isles lie so far from the equator, the length of daylight which they experience is much greater in summer than in winter. There is also a marked seasonal range in the height above the horizon of the noonday sun. But although, in these latitudes, temperature must vary from season to season, the seasonal range is far less than latitude alone would suggest. The ocean to the west, and the westerlies which transport its in-

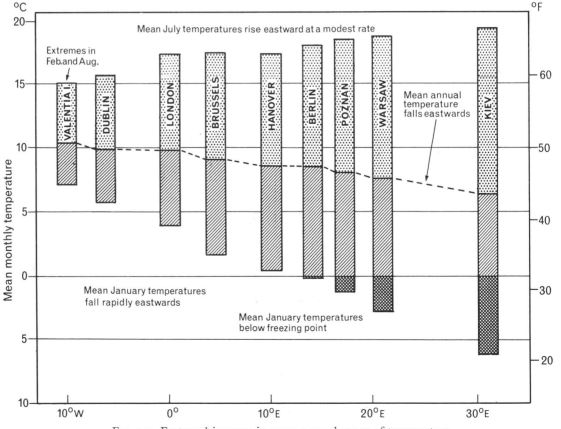

FIG. 3:1. Eastward increase in mean annual range of temperature

fluences over the British land, ensure that seasonal contrasts in temperature are minimised. Fig. 3:1 shows how the annual temperature range—the difference between the mean temperatures of the warmest and of the coldest months—increases from Britain eastwards across the European mainland; it also shows that the increase in range is due mainly to the winter cold, which increases in intensity towards the interior of the landmass. Conversely, the low annual ranges in Britain result mainly from the mildness of British winters. Whereas in summer the air over Britain is no more than 1 °C. (2 °F.) cooler than the average for the latitude, in winter it is some 17 °C. (30 °F.) warmer.

OCEANIC INFLUENCES

The supply of heat to the overlying air in winter is one of the most notable of all the oceanic influences on British climate. The ultimate source of the heat is, of course, the sun. The proximate source is the North Atlantic Drift. This rather shallow skin of surface water, light because it is

west of the British Isles warm in winter. During the winter months water which has been heated in far lower latitudes is arriving in the North Atlantic. Furthermore, the ocean surface becomes warmer or cooler, according to season, far more slowly than does a land surface in similar latitudes. The maximum surface temperature off the British coasts is reached in August, or even as late as September. Thus, when winter comes, there is much heat available to warm the air of the westerlies, and the seasonal fall of air temperature over Britain is slow and slight.

The moderating effect of the ocean on air temperature is stronger in winter than in summer (Fig. 3:2). When the surface water is cooler than the air above it—as frequently happens during the summer months—the air tends to lose its heat to the water. The lowest layers of air are chilled and become denser by contraction, and the chilled air tends to remain at low levels. The surface water expands because it is warmed, and remains on the surface of the ocean. Unless the air is turbulent, little of it can be cooled, for little heat is exchanged. Opposite conditions apply in winter. The air in winter is

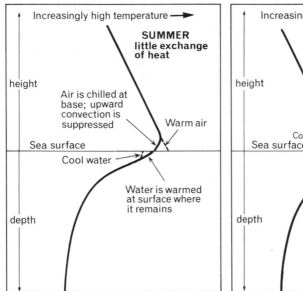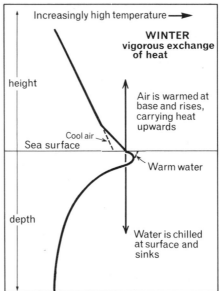

FIG. 3:2. Effect of sea on air temperature, summer and winter

warm, is driven north-eastward across the ocean by the westerly winds. It forms part of the Gulf Stream system, which begins where Florida Current pours vast quantities of remarkably warm water into the circulation of the North Atlantic. In its journey across that ocean the water loses part of its heat, but retains enough to keep the ocean surface

likely to be cooler than the surface water, so that heat passes from water to air. Air at low levels is warmed and expands and rises, carrying oceanic heat with it, while the chilled surface water contracts and sinks, to be replaced by unchilled water from below. This convectional overturning both of water and of air leads to a vigorous exchange of heat.

The westerlies which bring the air over the land exist mainly as a kind of statistical abstraction. There are indeed times when the British Isles are traversed by a powerful westerly airstream, but wind-direction is typically variable at all stations (Fig. 3:3). Only when the resultant wind-direction is determined by cancelling winds from opposite directions against one another does it become clear that the net transport of air is from the west (Fig. 3:4).

The sea-level isotherms for July (Fig. 3:6) run broadly from east to west, the highest mean temperatures occurring in the south and the lowest in the north. But although the effects of location are weaker in this month than in January, they can still be made out. The 16° isotherm closes round southern England, and the 15° line loops northward over the land and southward towards the sea.

Mean annual ranges (Fig. 3:7) also reveal the difference between coastal and inland locations.

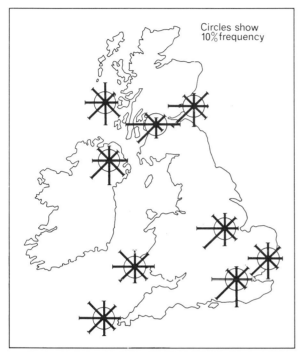

FIG. 3:3. Wind-roses for selected stations

FIG. 3:4. Net transport of air

TEMPERATURE

It is this eastward flow which brings warmth to the western seaboard in winter, and raises temperatures there above the figures recorded inland and to the east (Fig. 3:5). The map of sea-level isotherms for January reveals in striking fashion that mean temperature in mid-winter is a function of location rather than of latitude. The isotherm of 6°C. runs through the western peninsulas of Ireland, and that of 5° crosses the peninsulas of Wales. Even on the east, where the shallow North Sea is cooler in January than is the deep Atlantic, the coastlands are slightly warmer than the inland areas behind them. The course of the 4° isotherm as a whole records the effect of the chilling of air over land in winter.

Ranges, below 9°C. on the western coastlands of Ireland, rise to more than 12° in East Anglia and the London Basin. Both in Ireland and in Great Britain the greatest ranges occur well to the east of centre—another illustration of the effects of the westerlies in moderating climate. Mean *daily* ranges, however, increase generally from the coasts inland, running at some 2°C. or less near the sea and rising to 3° or so in the interior districts.

With the small annual ranges of temperature recorded at all stations in the British Isles goes a slow and smooth change in the mean temperature from month to month. At most places July is the warmest month and January the coldest. A certain time-lag is to be expected between the greatest noonday height of the sun and the peak of the temperature-curve, for incoming solar radiation continues to exceed outgoing radiation for some

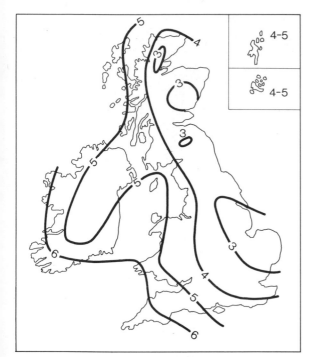

FIG. 3:5. Sea-level isotherms for January, °C

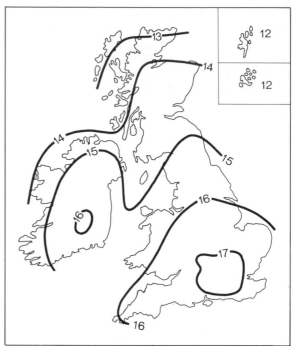

FIG. 3:6. Sea-level isotherms for July, °C

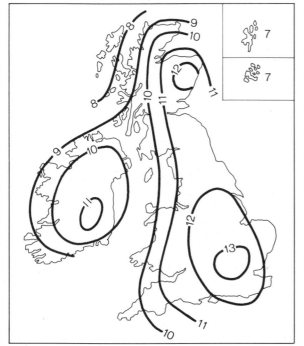

FIG. 3:7. Mean annual range of temperature, °C

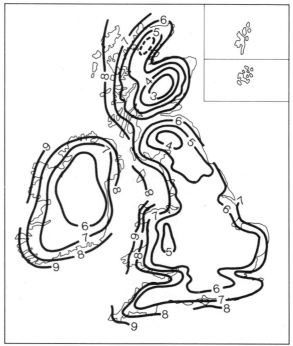

FIG. 3:8. Mean length of frost-free period, months

time after midsummer day. The influence of the ocean so increases the time-lag that, at such stations as Falmouth in Cornwall and Valentia in Kerry, August is slightly warmer than July, and at

many places in the west there is very little difference in the average temperature of the two months. Similarly, maritime stations in the west are very little, if at all, warmer in February than in January.

The delayed rise of the temperature-curve for western stations in the early months of the year makes nonsense of the statement that Cornwall has early springs. Climatically speaking, spring there is late. Winters, however, are very mild, so that plants in low-lying and sheltered localities can grow throughout the winter season, or can start their spring growth very early in the calendar year.

Frost

Situation with respect to the sea has much influence on the likelihood of frost. Coastal districts have the longest frost-free period (Fig. 3:8), which lasts on the average for 9 months in the western extremities of Ireland, Southwest England, Pembrokeshire, Anglesey and the Lleyn Peninsula. Along the Channel coast the duration is reduced to some 7 months, and northwards along the east coast to about 6 months, but places near the shore are everywhere less liable to frost than are near-by places inland. In Wales the effect of high ground reduces the frost-free period to less than five months; in the northern Pennines and the Southern Uplands it falls below 4, and in the Grampians to less than 3.

Actual Temperature

The map in Fig. 3.8 refers to actual frosts—that is, to actual records of temperatures of 0 °C. or below. In this it differs from the isothermal maps already given, which are constructed from temperatures reduced to sea level. Sea-level figures are necessary to reveal the influences of latitude and of inland or coastal location, for isotherms of actual temperatures look very much like maps of relief, whereas sea-level isotherms arrange themselves in simple patterns. But as soon as temperature is considered in relation to wild plant-life, to cultivated crops, or to the keeping of livestock, actual figures are required.

The change of temperature with height is far more rapid than the change with latitude or with distance from the sea. On the Channel coast, for instance, the mean annual *sea-level* temperature is about 10 °C., while in the centre of the Scottish Highlands it is about 8 °C.—that is, a difference of some 600 km (370 mi.) in latitude produces a difference of 2° in mean temperature. But mean temperature falls about 1° for every 180 m. of height, so that a rise of 900 m. (about 2,700 ft., roughly ½ mi.) lowers mean temperature by 5 °C. In other words, from the Channel to the Highlands

FIG. 3:9. Actual isotherms for January: generalised

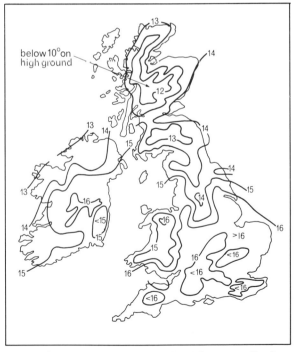

FIG. 3:10. Actual isotherms for July: generalised

the mean temperature falls about 2,500 times faster with height than with distance.

This very rapid fall of temperature with height

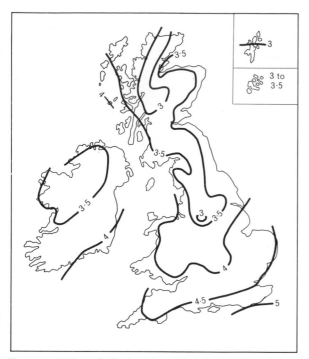

FIG. 3:11. Mean daily duration of bright sunshine, hours

actual temperatures, even though the whole island displays the effect of moderating oceanic influences.

Sunshine

The maps of actual temperature and of the duration of the frost-free period should be read in conjunction with the map (Fig. 3:11) of the duration of sunshine. Naturally enough, the sunniest areas occur in the south—on the coasts of Cornwall, the Channel, and East Anglia—and it is here that many seaside resorts and market-gardens are found. But in Great Britain generally the coasts are everywhere sunnier than neighbouring inland districts, for the amount of cloud is increased by turbulence in the air over land. The frequency of cloud rapidly increases over high ground, and the duration of sunshine as rapidly diminishes. Ireland is subject to frequent cloud, and records little sunshine. Its high western rim, broken though it is, suffices to provoke heavy cloud in the damp winds which blow from the open Atlantic, and the passage of air over the moist Central Plain does little to reduce the cloud cover.

PRECIPITATION

Precipitation is the most important of all climatic elements. Without water there could be no life, and water-supply depends on precipitation. Some large towns in the British Isles suffer a shortage of water in dry years. Agriculture in some areas would benefit from increased rainfall in the summer, when evaporation tends to dry out the soil, although the annual total is everywhere adequate. Precipitation is excessive in most of Scotland, Ireland, and Wales, the wettest areas of all receiving more than 2,500 mm. a year.

The map of mean annual precipitation (Fig. 3:13) shows that the highest falls occur on the high ground of the north and west. The wettest areas lie west of the axis of high ground instead of centrally on its highest parts, as is clearly indicated in Scotland. Over the low ground, too, there is a general fall in the total from west to east: 1,250 mm. in the Clyde Valley becomes 750 mm. on the Firth of Forth, 1,000 mm. on the west of the Central Plain of Ireland falls to 750 mm. on the east, and the 750 mm. recorded at Gloucester is significantly greater than the 625 mm. at London.

This westward displacement of heavy precipitation is due simply to the prevalence of the westerly winds. If rain falls in the west it is not available for the east, and eastern districts lie in rain-shadow (Fig. 3:15). Similarly, the number of

emphasises the contrasts between highland and lowland, especially since the most extensive lowlands of the British Isles lie in the south while the highest ground occurs in the north. There is a very great actual difference between, say, Ipswich, with an annual mean of 10 °C., and the summit of Ben Nevis where the annual mean is slightly below freezing point. The contrast is as great as that between Ipswich and the coast of southern Greenland, about 150 km (100 mi.) from the edge of an ice-cap.

Detailed map of actual temperature are bound to resemble maps of relief. The generalised representations in Figs. 3:9, 3:10 emphasise, in a general way, the manner in which air-temperature is modified by height. In January, mean actual temperatures of less than 0 °C. are recorded for all the highest summits, from the Peak to the north of Scotland. On the high plateaus of Wales, the mean monthly figure is in the neighbourhood of 1°. The eastern part of the English Plain records actual means of some 3°, while patches of the western Plain approach 5°. In July, when actual means on the low ground of central and southern England run above 15°, the figure for much of the Southern Uplands is 12° or below, and means lower than 10° occur widely in the Grampians and north of the Great Glen. The highly-fragmented uplands of Ireland are faithfully reflected in the maps of rain-days is greatest in the west, falling from more than 250 a year on extreme western coasts to below 175 in some parts of the east (Fig. 3:14). Throughout most of the massifs the average is above 200 days a year, and very little of Ireland—which is fully exposed to the westerlies—records fewer than this, even on low ground.

Totals of precipitation are however not due solely to the combined influences of the westerlies and of the height of the land. Orographic precipitation is the type produced by the flow of air over high ground—in the British Isles, mainly by the ascent of the westerlies over the upland areas of the north and west. Air from the Atlantic, rising over the west-facing highlands, ascends into levels of reduced pressure where it expands and cools. Being typically moist, the maritime air frequently reaches condensation-point in cooling, becoming still more cloudy and discharging precipitation. Latent heat released during condensation often makes the rising air unstable; lifting occurs, resulting in further expansion, cooling and precipitation. Indeed, the ascent due to instability of the air itself is more powerful in causing precipitation than is the forced ascent of moving air over relief barriers. The converse of lifting is subsidence, which occurs on the eastern flanks of the highlands. The subsiding air becomes more stable; already carrying the latent heat of condensation, it is further warmed by compression, and tends to be notably warmer, drier, and less rainy than when it rose over the western slopes of the highlands. Here is the explanation of rain-shadow.

Cyclonic precipitation is brought by travelling low-pressure systems (see below). Warm air in travelling lows ascends over cold air instead of over high ground. Ascent is again accompanied by increased instability, lifting and precipitation. In the wettest areas, cyclonic precipitation serves merely to increase the total fall, but in the east and over the low ground generally it is responsible for most of the precipitation which occurs.

Convectional precipitation tends to complicate the distribution map, for thunderstorms are most frequent in inland districts. The lower Trent valley and East Anglia are the most thundery areas, with more than 15 thunderstorms a year; much of the English lowlands records more than ten. These are mainly summer thunderstorms, due to the heating from below of moist air, which becomes markedly unstable and rises in the turbulent columns of thunderclouds. Thunder in the cooler months is almost entirely restricted to western districts.

Most of the precipitation which falls in the

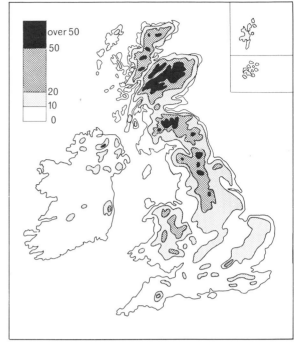

Fig. 3:12. Mean annual number of mornings with lying snow

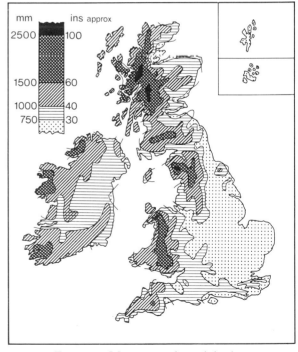

Fig. 3:13. Mean annual precipitation

British Isles comes as rain, but snow is frequent in the north. In a general way the likelihood of

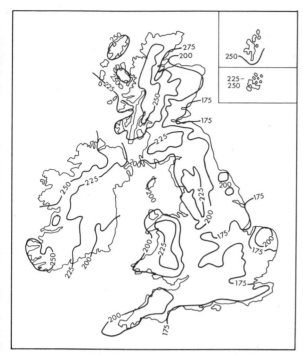

Fig. 3:14. Mean annual number of rain-days

snow increases from southwest to northeast, but snowfall is much affected by the distribution of relief. The map of mornings with snow lying (Fig. 3:12) reveals that the snowiest areas, unlike the wettest areas, lie squarely on the highest ground. In this as in other maps, the influence of the ocean is well displayed, for a low frequency of lying snow characterises most of Ireland and the entire western and southern coastlands of Great Britain.

Régimes of Precipitation

Varying combinations of orographic, cyclonic, and convectional precipitation are seen in the régimes of individual stations. Precipitation in the west is heaviest in the winter half-year, when winds are strongest and travelling lows are most vigorous,

but the summer months there can by no means be called dry. An excellent example of heavy precipitation, both cyclonic and orographic, is given by the record from Loch Quoich, Inverness (Fig. 3:16), where the January total is over 375 mm. and that of July nearly 150 mm., with the yearly average well above 2,500 mm. At Aberdeen the winter half-year is also the wetter, but there is a significantly greater fall in August and September than in October. At Hull August becomes the wettest single month, as it also is in London. Over a considerable part of the eastern Midlands, East Anglia, and the London Basin the summer half-year is wetter than the winter half, because thunderstorms combined with the weak summer lows bring more precipitation than do the vigorous lows which alone occur in winter. There is a faint development of a régime typical of continental rather than of oceanic stations.

August, the main holiday month, is rainy at many stations, even in those parts of the British Isles which receive more than half their total of precipitation in the winter half-year. At Valentia, Co. Kerry—a station fully exposed to the westerlies —August is wetter than September. A secondary maximum of precipitation in August is very common. At some stations where August is the wettest single month, considerable summer thunder is experienced—e.g., at Southport—but at others, such as Dublin, summer thunder is rare. The typical raininess of August cannot be wholly due to thunderstorms, but is to be accounted for in part by the arrival of unstable maritime air.

WEATHER

In direct contrast with climate, in which short-term variations disappear with the calculation of averages, the weather of the British Isles is notoriously variable. Not only is it liable to day-to-day changes—some whole seasons are markedly wet,

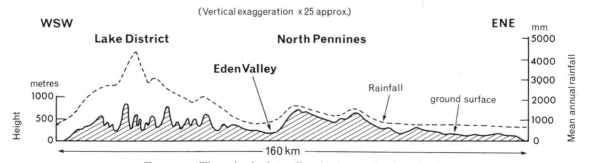

Fig. 3:15. The rain-shadow effect in the north of England

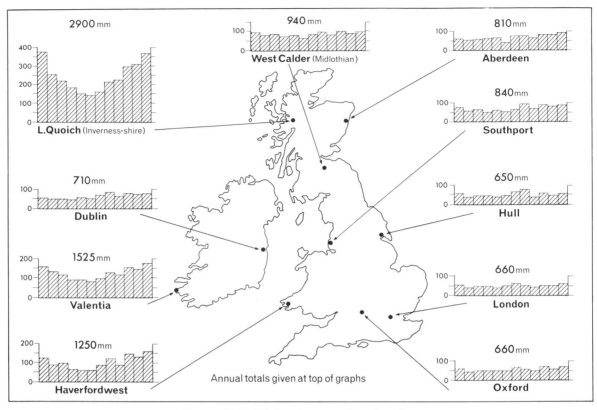

FIG. 3:16. Rainfall régimes at selected stations

markedly dry, unusually cold, or unusually warm. Even though variations from season to season tend to cancel one another in figures for the whole year, the yearly total of precipitation ranges widely (Fig. 3:17). There is no single month which, during the last 80 years, has not been the wettest in some one year and the driest in some other.

Weather is produced in the air which overlies a place at a given time. Three main kinds of air flow over the British Isles—maritime tropical air from the southwest, maritime polar air from the west or northwest, and continental polar air from the European mainland in winter. Each kind arrives as an *airstream*, having acquired its original characteristics in the source region of an *air mass*.

An air mass is a large body of air, perhaps thousands of miles across. Stagnating over an expanse of land or of sea, it is cooled, warmed, dried or moistened according to the character of the underlying surface. In a very few days it can reach equilibrium, in respect of temperature and humidity, with that surface; and when it moves away from the source region as an airstream, it retains its distinctive character for some time.

Maritime air, whether maritime tropical (mT) or maritime polar (mP) air is brought in by the westerlies. Maritime tropical air is supplied to the British Isles by the Azores High; although it is typically moist it is also usually stable, so that it tends to give little precipitation. In summer it can produce warm, settled weather, and in winter it gives unseasonable warmth—as, for instance, during the winter of 1956/57. Maritime polar (mP) air is very variable. Its source regions lie over the North Atlantic and eastern Canada. When it comes from a northerly quarter, and when it arrives during the summer, it is liable to be unstable and to discharge much precipitation, as in the summer of 1958, but it can also come in from the west after a long traverse of the warm ocean, and may then be fairly stable and bring little rain to lowland areas. Continental air sometimes reaches the British Isles in summer as a warm, dry airstream, but it is more frequently experienced in winter when, as icy currents of continental polar (cP) air, it crosses the North Sea and brings bitter weather to eastern and inland districts of Great Britain. In some winters, cP air overspreads the whole of

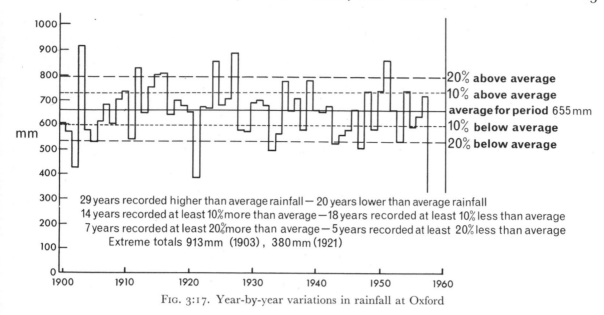

FIG. 3:17. Year-by-year variations in rainfall at Oxford

the British Isles and occasions severe and prolonged frost. Such a winter was that of 1946/47.

Travelling Lows

Airstreams of varying type are drawn, or blown, across the British Isles by temporary pressure-systems, some of which are themselves moving. Low-pressure systems tend to be both vigorous and mobile. Most of the travelling lows which cross the British Isles move from west to east or from southwest to northeast, in accordance with the general flow of the westerlies. Many of them are frontal depressions, in which the individual airstreams are separated from one another by narrow zones of transition known as fronts. Lows commonly originate on the polar front, the boundary between the westerlies on the south and cold air blowing outwards from higher latitudes on the north. A bulge on the polar front becomes enlarged into a deep re-entrant (Fig. 3:18) which encloses a warm sector surrounded by cold air. The whole system travels towards the east; since it can cross the British Isles in the space of one or two days, a given station can experience three distinct kinds of weather in a short time. In the forepart of the low, in advance of the warm front, polar air is drawn northwards; in winter it reaches most of Great Britain from the mainland of Europe, and may well be very cold. Cloud thickens and rain or snow falls as the warm front approaches; but as it passes there is a rise in temperature, for the warm sector is typically occupied by maritime tropical air. Precipitation in the warm sector is not often heavy,

although there is much cloud; precipitation is renewed along the cold front, the passage of which is marked by a drop in temperature. If the maritime polar air behind the cold front is unstable, it is likely to give heavy showers.

Lows are often partly or wholly occluded by the time that they reach the British Isles, the cold front having caught up the warm front, so that the air in the warm sector is raised above the ground. The weather typical of the warm sector is omitted from the sequence, and the two frontal rain-belts merge into one.

In the heart of a travelling low, whether it is occluded or not, general rain often occurs. This means that any low which traverses the British Isles is likely to supply more precipitation in the north than in the south, even when the effect of high ground in the north is left aside. Moreover, highs tend to form over the English lowlands in the latter part of winter, fending off the moving lows, forcing them to take a north-easterly path and to bring precipitation to the northwest rather than to the southeast. In both these ways the contrast between the drier and the wetter parts of Great Britain is increased.

Systems of High Pressure

Systems of high pressure are simpler than those of low pressure. Highs are stagnant systems of stable air which give little precipitation. Some bring overcast skies; if there is little cloud, highs result in warm sunny weather in summer and in sunny but frosty weather in winter. Because they are

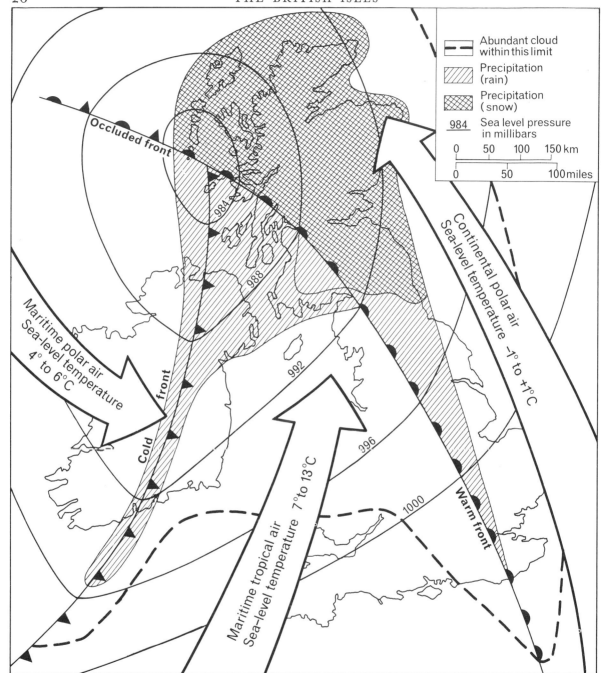

FIG. 3:18. Pressure, fronts, weather, and airstreams in a travelling low, winter

stable and inert, highs may persist for days on end.

Seasonal Weather

British weather is affected by several other types of pressure-systems, in addition to simple travelling lows and more-or-less stationary highs, all of which increase the general variability of British weather. But the number, strength, and frequency of travelling lows and stagnant highs are the chief influences upon the character of seasonal weather.

The contrast between weather dominated by travelling lows and that dominated by persistent highs has rarely been better shown than in the two

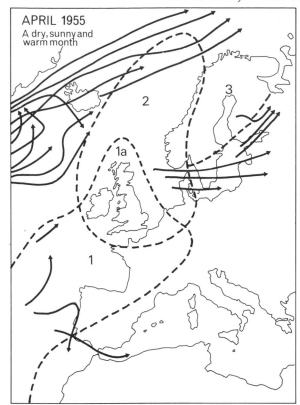

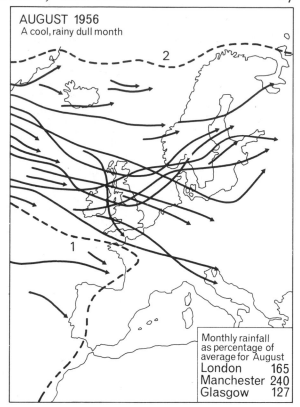

FIG. 3:19. Tracks of travelling lows, April 1955. Dotted lines mark the boundaries of persistent to fairly persistent high-pressure systems

FIG. 3:20. Tracks of travelling lows, August 1956. Dotted lines mark the boundaries of persistent to fairly persistent high-pressure systems

summers of 1955 and 1956. In the first of these two seasons highs were dominant. They blocked the approaching lows, which moved away to the northeast (Fig. 3:19); prolonged droughts occurred, even in the west of Ireland. By contrast, during the summer of 1956 many lows passed across the British Isles (Fig. 3:20). Unusually heavy rain was recorded in all parts, for large quantities of polar maritime air streamed in and frontal rain was common. Many stations recorded more than twice the average rainfall in August, and the difficulties of harvesting will long be remembered. Nevertheless, the total precipitation for the whole year of 1956 differed very little from the average, for the very wet summer was compensated by slight precipitation both in spring and in late autumn and early winter.

LOCAL CLIMATES

Just as weather varies during short periods, so does climate vary over short distances. Local climate in highland areas changes very rapidly from place to place. The contrasts are not merely those of height, although precipitation can increase with height as strikingly as temperature falls. Nor are they to be explained wholly by aspect, although contrasts in aspect are important where—as in the Scottish Highlands—climate is so generally severe that every advantageous circumstance becomes significant. In highland areas especially, and on uneven ground everywhere, cold-air drainage exerts a powerful influence on local climate. Cold air can only drain downhill when the air as a whole is still, or very nearly so, and the air can remain still only during the calm weather brought by high-pressure systems. Although calms in the British Isles are not very common, they occur often enough to encourage the drainage of cold air into certain enclosed valleys, which in consequence experience frequent fog and frost in the colder months. The Lea Valley is perhaps the most notorious example, but there is no doubt that many Welsh, Pennine, and Scottish valleys suffer in a similar way. In coastal districts, air chilled during the night can flow out to sea; sea breezes rise by day if the air is still, giving the coasts their characteristically small daily range of temperature.

A special case of local climate is the urban climate: that is, the climate of an urban area where heat emission, and often also the emission of pollutants, significantly modifies the natural climate. Metropolitan London is a leading case. Industrial and domestic heating raise the mean temperature of the built-up area perceptibly above the temperatures of surrounding districts. For many years, the smoke and gases produced by the burning of coal, especially for domestic heating, seriously reduced the incidence of bright sunshine in the London area, reduced visibility, and poured poison into the fogs held down by natural temperature inversions and by cold-air pooling in the London Basin. Since 1956, however, the successive implementation of the Clean Air Act has reduced the incidence in the London area of smog, fog, and even of cloud.

VEGETATION

There is little in the British Isles that can be called natural vegetation, in the sense of spontaneous vegetation which has been little modified by man and his domestic animals. The 60 per cent of the whole area which is classed as improved farmland can be eliminated at once from a general discussion of wild plant life. Parts of the wooded land and much of the unfenced expanses of rough grazing can be described as clothed in semi-natural vegetation—i.e., in vegetation which is spontaneous in origin but has been much modified in the course of human history.

Vegetation in the natural state is powerfully affected by climate, soils, and animals. The respective groups of influences at work are called the climatic, edaphic, and biotic; of these, the most powerful group is usually the climatic. Wild vegetation left to itself tends to develop the most complex community of plants with the largest dominant members which the climate permits. Such a community is the *climax community*, or more properly the *climatic climax*. Throughout most of England, and in parts of Wales, Scotland, and Ireland, the climatic climax is deciduous summer forest. In many northern and western areas the climatic climax is northern coniferous forest, dominated by the native Scots pine but also including birch. Where drainage is especially poor, the highlands run to blanket bog which is frequently colonised by ling.

Although soils are to be separately treated below, it is impossible to refer to climax communities of plants without mentioning the variations in them which may result from variations in soil. Within the area of lowland which was once covered mainly by deciduous forest were patches of heath; these lay in highly permeable, sandy districts, where percolating water had removed the soluble matter and had produced acid soils. On the mild peat soils of fenland and on the silt of marshes grew reeds and sedges; and even in the lowlands there were some vigorously-growing peat-bogs, for instance in the Somerset Levels and on the Lancashire Plain. In all such places the vegetation tended towards an *edaphic climax*.

Biotic influences came into operation as soon as grazing by domestic animals began. Their effects are seen throughout those parts of the British Isles which are now classed as rough grazing, except on unused blanket bog. With the assistance of felling, grazing has destroyed most of the woodland which used to grow on the hillsides of Wales, the Pennines, the Lake District, the Southern Uplands, and the Scottish Highlands. The hill grassland seen there today represents a *biotic climax* of vegetation.

The somewhat static notion of climax vegetation, as here outlined, can however usefully be modified into the concept of *dynamic climax* and *dysclimax*. In any set of given circumstances, vegetation communities maintain themselves only if they are capable of withstanding invasion along their margins. Thus, if a given community establishes itself and holds its ground, it does so only because it can overcome competition. Communities in dysclimax represent less than what could be called the optimum assemblage for the local conditions, but are able to persist on account of special checks on competitors. The repeated climatic shifts of the last 10,000 years or so, some of which are mentioned in the succeeding section, recommend a dynamic rather than a static point of view.

Climatic Change

Vegetation—whether wild, semi-natural, or cultivated—is never static. It shares a dynamic quality with soils, whether natural or agricultural soils. The story of the existing vegetation of the British Isles begins with the disappearance of the great glaciers of the Ice Age. At the last glacial maximum, ice covered the highlands and spread in lobes on to the fringes of the lowlands. Beyond the ice-edge the land was subject to a very severe climate which kept the subsoil permanently frozen, and on the seasonally melted topsoil grew vegetation of the tundra kind, interspersed in places with hardy trees such as birch. This cover is called *park-tundra*. The birch spread far and wide as temperatures rose and the glaciers melted back, but its dominance did not last. Some 9,000 years ago (Fig. 3:21) there was a rather sudden change in climate. The British area came under continental influences, which caused precipitation to decrease and brought long spells of dry weather. The hazel spread vigorously, and pine also came in. The typical vegetation of the Boreal climatic phase was at first hazel–birch–pine forest, which was later replaced by hazel–pine forest as the birch declined. At this time elm and oak appeared. Pine alone became dominant in many parts of Ireland where it was widespread.

wooded. On the lower slopes and in the English Lowlands, the damp-loving alder suddenly increased in importance in damp places, while mixed-oak-forest established itself elsewhere.

These highly oceanic conditions were modified in the sub-Boreal phase, which lasted from about 2000 to 750 BC. The sub-Boreal was climatically similar to the earlier Boreal, but its continental character was too weakly marked to bring back the forests typical of Boreal times. Oak and alder retained their dominance in the lowlands, but some of the bogs of the uplands dried out enough to allow birch and pine to colonise them. The regrowth of the northern forests was halted by a return to oceanic conditions in the sub-Atlantic phase, which set in about 750 BC. Increased rain again enabled the upland bogs to grow. Surviving

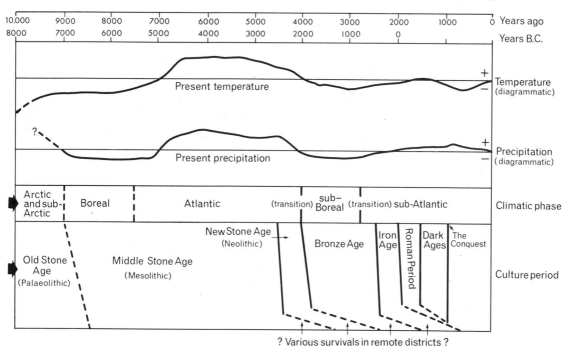

FIG. 3:21. Climatic trends, climate phases, and culture-periods

The next climatic development produced the Atlantic phase, which lasted from about 5500 to 2000 BC and was marked by the powerful streaming of oceanic westerly air over the British Isles. Mean temperatures rose because the prevailing winds blew strongly and often from a warm sea, reaching a maximum which they have never since attained, and probably representing the peak of an interglacial. But the westerly winds brought heavy rainfall to the north and west, where blanket bog spread over much land that had formerly been

forests on the rainy plateaus were rooted in heavily leached soils of the podsol type. Dominated by the Scots pine, they formed an outlier of the great belt of coniferous forest land which stretched across the north of Eurasia. The deciduous woodland which covered very large parts of the lowlands contained a great deal of oak, but with enough alder and birch to justify the name of alder–birch–oak forest. Beech and hornbeam entered the southeast, the former rising to dominance in districts where the soils were developed directly on limestone.

Forests Today

It is very many centuries since climatic conditions suitable to forests were established in the British Isles. The only large areas which would not be naturally forested today are those which are too wet because the soil drainage is very poor, those which are too dry because the soil is highly permeable, and those where there is too little soil for trees. The reduction of woodland to 5 per cent of the total land area is a measure of the changes wrought in the visible scene by man—a conservative measure, for much of the existing woodland is the result of deliberate planting.

If any relic of the former natural forests is to be seen, it probably lies in the shreds of oakwood which survive on the valley-sides of Southwest England, Wales, the Southern Uplands, and the sheltered parts of the Scottish Highlands. There are, too, some stands of Scots pine in the Highlands, and of ash on the limestone soils of the Pennines, which may serve for samples of the once extensive native woodland. Beechwoods on the limestone soils of the Jurassic and Chalk cuestas are growing in their native localities, but are nearly everywhere so subject to management that they can hardly be called even semi-natural. The same may be said of most of the oak-woods of the lowlands, whether they are dominated by the stalked oak (*Quercus robor*), which favours damp situations, or by the durmast oak (*Q. sessiliflora*, also known as the pedunculate or sessile oak)—which is suited to well-drained soils.

The character of British forests is still changing. The Forestry Commission, established in 1919, is carrying out a programme of planting in places which are not now forested, and of improving existing woodland. Although hardwoods are planted in some of the Commission's forests, most of the newly-planted ground carries conifers—mainly spruces and larches (Plate 2). Patches of softwood are spreading across ground which has long been under rough grazing, but which before clearance supported deciduous forest. Similar planting is going on in the Irish Republic. There is no dispute that the gloomy ranks of conifers are scenically less attractive than the native hardwoods, but afforestation is being practised for economic purposes. Over 90 per cent of the main demand from industry is for softwood timber, and over 90 per cent of the timber used in the U.K. is imported. Imports in fact fall short of demand, for the main potential supplier is Canada which lies in the dollar area. There is no prospect that supplies from Europe can be increased, for reserves

PLATE 2. Planted conifers in Thetford Chase.

of timber on the Continental mainland tend to decline and consumption there to increase. The stated aim of the Forestry Commission is to rehabilitate some 800,000 ha. (2M ac.) of existing woodland and to plant an additional 1,250,000 ha. (some 3M ac.), in order to supply a third of the normal need for timber. Up to 1970, 700,000 ha. (1¾M ac.) had been planted in Great Britain and 40,000 ha. (100,000 ac) in Northern Ireland, representing more than half the eventual total. The Irish Republic has an afforestation programme of its own, which by 1970 had involved the planting of 200,000 ha. (500,000 ac.). The oceanic climate of the British Isles ensures rapid maturing, so that thinning can produce timber large enough for pit-props in 15 years after planting, and felling for sawtimber can begin in 20 years. Softwood forests will inevitably spread.

Rough Grazing

The land taken over for planting falls almost entirely into the class of rough grazing. It has already been stated that a great deal of the vegetation of rough hill pasture constitutes a biotic climax, the old forests having been removed by felling and kept down by grazing. Large areas of Wales, the Southern Uplands, and the Scottish Highlands provide instances of the nearly complete destruction of thick forests which formerly occupied all but the broad exposed summits. The attacks were made by charcoal-burners and by sheep-graziers. Fine forests still stood in the Scottish Highlands in the late Middle Ages, on land which is now open treeless moor. They outlived the forests of the Southern Uplands because they were the more remote, but finally vanished in the great expansion of sheep-farming in the late 18th and the 19th centuries. Irish forests had almost vanished by the end of Tudor times.

The existing vegetation of unenclosed hill districts is shown in a generalised and simplified manner in Fig. 3:22. Subdued summits in the north and west are extensively mantled with acid peat, which also occurs at many places in the valleys. Peat—mainly of the acid type—covers a fifth of

Ireland. But some of the bogs, formed under the oceanic conditions of the sub-Atlantic climatic phase, are no longer growing, being unable to expand either vertically or horizontally for lack of moisture.

On the areas shown as *peat moor*, sphagnum is common. It is usually colonised by cotton-grass, another major contributor to the formation of peat. The distribution of peat moor is patchy, for its development depends on very poor site drainage as well as on a moist climate, but large expanses of peat moorland occur in the far north of Scotland, in parts of the Grampians, in the west of the Southern Uplands, and on the north Pennines. Peat moor is common in all the Irish west, and on upland everywhere in Ireland. In the southwest of the Scottish Highlands it is intermingled with Molinia moor, and in the central Pennines with Nardus-Fescue moor (see below).

Heather moor, dominated by Calluna, covers very large areas on the eastern flanks of the Scottish Highlands, fringes the Pennines, characterises the North York Moors, and occurs patchily in Wales. The heathery areas mapped in the Lake District and Southwest England are best called *heather fell*. The heather moors of Scotland are periodically

PLATE 3. Part of the interior plateau of Wales, at about 600 metres. Subdued crests carry moorland vegetation under a cloud-laden sky.

burned over to promote new growth and to give shelter to grouse. Grazing destroys heather; if grazing ceases, heather takes over the mountain grasslands.

Fescue-Agrostis grassland is dominated by species of bent (agrostis) and of fescue. It is well developed in the SW of the Grampians and in parts of the NW Highlands, and fescue grassland forms a fringe all round the edges of the Welsh upland.

Molinia moor, which in Fig. 3:22 includes Molinia-Nardus moor, is dominated by the purple moor-grass. It occurs in small blocks at high elevations in SW England and broadly on the high platforms of Wales (Plate 3), and is intermingled with heather moor in the western half of the Southern Uplands. Molinia grows in wet sites where water does not stagnate in the soil. It thus contrasts with the matgrass, nardus, which does best where the soil is not always wet. *Nardus moor* typifies the eastern, drier, half of the Southern Uplands and fringes the low ground around Moray Firth.

The distributions in much of the Northern Highlands are too complex to record on Fig. 3:22, because the ground is very broken. Molinia moor is typical of the lower ground, Fescue-Agrostis grassland of intermediate levels, and specialised Arctic-Alpine vegetation of the highest summits. This last type is also recorded in the eastern Grampians.

The distribution map does not show the former heaths of the Breckland, where the highly-leached soils developed on glacial outwash are now mainly under planted conifers, nor does it show the small patchy heaths of the East Anglian coastland. Two districts of *Heath of the New Forest Type* are represented. That in the Hampshire Basin includes the New Forest itself; in this locality, acid soils have formed on permeable Tertiary sandstones, and heather (Calluna) and small oaks are the most noticeable plants. The heathland on the Hampshire–Surrey border is far more scattered than the map suggests. It is based on acid soils developed both on Tertiary sandstones in the London Basin and on the Lower Greensand within the Weald. Its plants include oak and birch, along with the pine which was long ago introduced and has now naturalised itself.

SOILS

Soil may be defined as that part of the mantle of weathered rock which has been transformed by the action of organisms and by the re-arrangement of its material. Its character is affected by the nature of the parent material from which it is formed, by the vegetation which grows on it, by climate, and by the length of time during which soil-forming processes have been at work. Many British soils have been greatly changed from the natural state by cultivation, whether by being disturbed, by losing nutrient materials to plants, or by the deliberate addition of fertilisers.

The parent material is provided by weathering, which breaks down the rocks. In the various developments of climate which occur in the British Isles, the end-products of weathering consist mainly of sand and of clay. The calibre of weathered material is controlled partly by the texture of the rocks which provide it; conglomerates, sandstones, gravels, and sands yield gravelly and sandy rock-waste on which coarse-textured soils develop, whereas fine-grained rocks—slates, shales, clays, and mudstones—weather into fine-grained waste and are transformed into clayey soils. The crystalline rocks of the massifs weather very slowly; since they have for the most part been scoured by ice, any soil lying on them is developed mainly on glacial material rather than on the rocks themselves. Large expanses of the highlands are overspread by peat, which forms organic soils and effectively covers both the drift and the solid rocks.

The results of soil-forming processes are as varied as the processes themselves are complex. When the maps of the Soils Surveys of England and Wales and of Scotland have been completed, thousands of different soils will have been located, named, and described. The mapping carried out by the two Surveys undoubtedly represents actual distributions and real differences between adjacent soils (Figs. 3:23, 15:2), but for the present purpose it is sufficient to concentrate mainly on the classification of soils into groups.

Very many of the soils of the British Isles fall into one of seven soil groups, each group being recognised by its profile—i.e., by its arrangement in section. Soils of three groups are especially widely developed, having formed under the influence of climate and of climatic-climax vegetation: the podsols associated with the northern coniferous forest, the brown earths formed under deciduous summer forest, and the blanket bog peats of wet and gently-sloping upland areas. Soil groups developed in special conditions of soil-drainage or of parent material include meadow soils, rendzinas, fen peat, and raised bog. Podsols are developed in moist, cool conditions under the influence of leaching, where water percolates

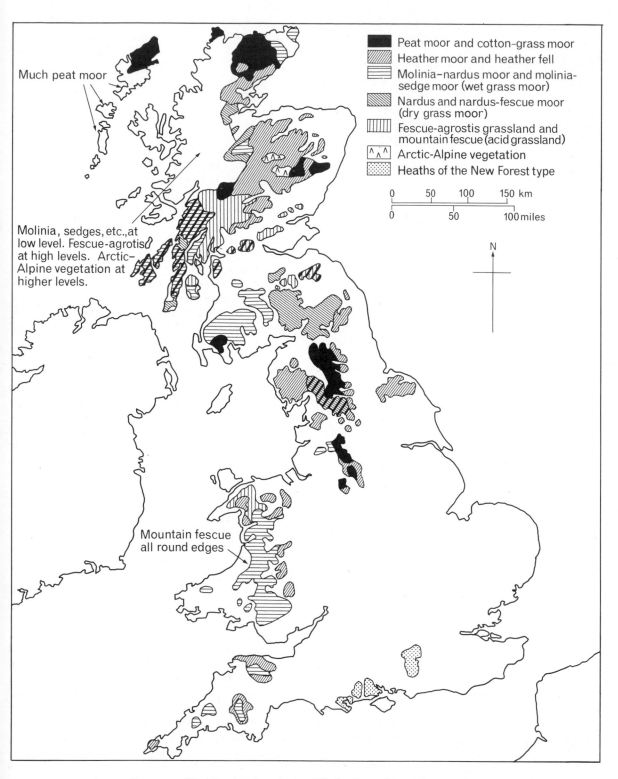

Much peat moor

Molinia, sedges, etc., at
low level. Fescue-agrotis
at high levels. Arctic-
Alpine vegetation at
higher levels.

Mountain fescue
all round edges

■ Peat moor and cotton-grass moor
▨ Heather moor and heather fell
▤ Molinia–nardus moor and molinia-
   sedge moor (wet grass moor)
▧ Nardus and nardus-fescue moor
   (dry grass moor)
▥ Fescue-agrostis grassland and
   mountain fescue (acid grassland)
⌃⌃ Arctic-Alpine vegetation
⋯ Heaths of the New Forest type

0   50   100   150 km

0   50   100 miles

N

FIG. 3:22. Distribution (much simplified) of uncultivated vegetation

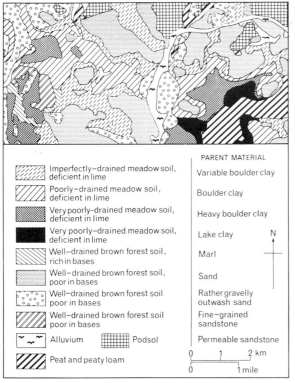

FIG. 3:23. Sample of soil-distribution on the Shropshire Plain. Parent materials are glacial deposits or Triassic rocks

downwards through the soil and raw humus is added by the vegetation. These conditions were most widely realised under the former cover of coniferous forest, but also applied to areas in the southeast where the rock-waste was coarse and highly permeable and leaching was highly effective. Podsols occur in the Weald on part of the Lower Greensand, on the weak sandstones in the southwest of the London Basin, and on the sandy rocks of the central Hampshire Basin. The typical podsol profile shows a clear distinction between the several horizons (layers) of the soil (Fig. 3:24). The topmost horizon is blackened by raw humus; below this comes a layer of coarse grey sand devoid of soluble material, and at the base an iron-stained and often well-cemented layer of *pan* rests on the weathered but otherwise unchanged parent rock.

Brown forest soils formed widely under the deciduous summer forest from which they received an increment of mild humus. They have been very commonly modified by cultivation and their arrangement in horizons has been disturbed. In any event their layers, even in the natural state, are never as strongly distinguished as are those of mature podsols. The humified upper part of the brown forest soil grades downwards into the lighter-toned material beneath, which in turn passes into weathered rock. The brown forest soils of the British Isles suffer leaching and lose their lime, becoming somewhat acid; but water also moves upward through them in dry seasons, so that the very powerful leaching which produces the strongly acid podsols is inhibited.

Blanket bog, an organic soil, is acid and permanently wet. It consists of little but a grossly exaggerated development of the layer of raw humus in the upper part of a podsol.

Meadow soils occur in flood-plains. Although their drainage is typically impeded, they can be rich in lime and humus. The permanently-saturated layer lies well below the surface (Fig. 3:24), so that meadow soils well repay cultivation if flooding can be prevented. Rendzinas form on limestones where the slope is great enough for rock-waste to creep constantly downhill; they are best illustrated from chalk scarps, where they are shallow, blackened with humus, and enriched with lime from beneath. Where the surface is flat, as on parts of the Chalk crests, residual material can accumulate thickly. The soil developed at such sites resembles the terra rossa (red earth) of the Mediterranean lands; the leading example is provided by the soil formed on Clay-with-Flints.

Fen peat is rich in mild humus. As agricultural material fen peat soils are very different from blanket-bog peat, as may be seen from a comparison between the Fenlands and the blanket-bogs of western Ireland. The two localities differ in climate as well as in soil, but the two sets of differences are interrelated. Fen peat forms in waterlogged areas where the stagnant water is rich in lime: in the Fenland region the lime was brought in solution by rivers draining from the Jurassic limestone belt.

Where the climate is moist enough, peat will continue to grow after a basin has already been infilled by fen peat. It has done so in very many places in Ireland, especially on the Central Plain. Sphagnum is the first great contributor to raised bogs, which carry their own water-table up with them as they grow. It is typically followed by cotton-grass and bell heather (Erica), with Calluna spreading as the level of the bog rises and especially when drainage is improved by the cutting of peat. Raised bogs are uncultivated and their soils acid.

Soil groups are subdivided into soil series, according to the parent material on which they are developed. On the maps of the Soil Surveys, soil series are named after places. Soil series will not be discussed here.

Soil series are further subdivided into soil types, on the basis of texture. For the present purpose it is enough to recognise five grades of texture—clay, clay loam, loam, sandy loam, and sand (Appendix 1). Clays and clay loams are heavy soils, tending to be cold in the sense that they warm up slowly

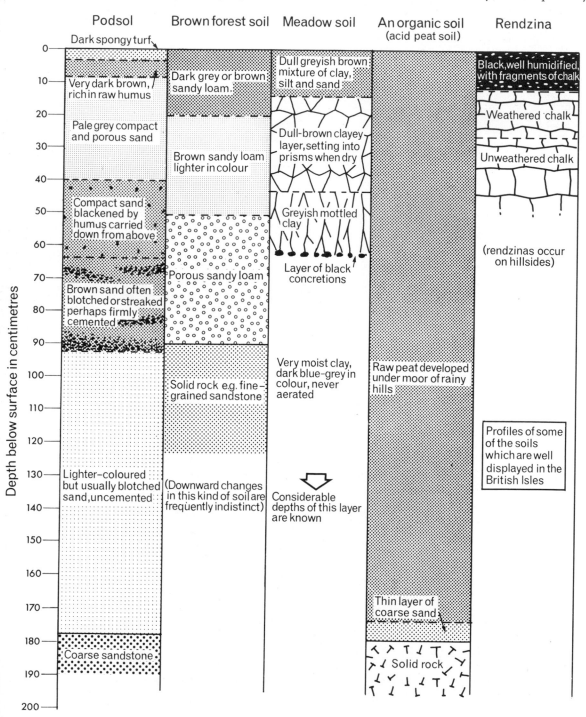

Fig. 3:24. Contrasted profiles of some mature soils

PLATE 4. Part of the Lower Greensand belt in Bedfordshire—planted conifers replacing oak-birch scrub and bracken; contrast Plate 5.

PLATE 5. Part of the Lower Greensand belt in Bedfordshire, adjacent to that shown in Plate 4; market-garden land on light sandy loam.

when the air temperature rises. In addition, they are not readily permeable. Loams possess the texture most generally favourable for cultivation, although sands and sandy loams have advantages in special circumstances. Sands are loose and light, highly permeable, and liable to suffer leaching— hence their tendency to develop podsols—but some sandy loams contain enough fine material to check leaching to some extent, and are remarkably warm: their air-spaces allow warm air to raise the soil temperature. Sandy loams are in many places under the intensive cultivation of market-gardens and orchards, as for instance in the fruit-growing districts of North Kent, the Medway valley, and the southern fringe of the Hampshire Basin. Heavy fertilisation of sandy loams is repaid by early cropping (cf. Plates 4, 5).

APPENDIX

Soil Texture

Soils can be subdivided, according to texture, into more than 20 grades. For many practical purposes, however, it is enough to subdivide them into five grades, as follows:

1. *Sand:* incoherent soil, which feels very gritty when rubbed between finger and thumb.
2. *Sandy loam:* soil which, although it coheres, feels gritty.
3. *Loam:* soil which can be smeared when rubbed between finger and thumb; smooth feel, no grittiness; surface of rubbed sample tears, giving broken surface.
4. *Clay loam:* soil which feels very smooth when rubbed, and can be made to take a dull sheen when buffed with thumb.
5. *Clay:* soil which is very stiff to mould, and can be made to take a high gloss.

Chapter 4

The Pattern of Peopling

THE present distribution of people in the British Isles is the outcome of very lengthy development. The distribution of rural population is still strongly influenced by the original founding of pioneer settlements, by early settlement-patterns, and by modifications of settlement-pattern which occurred in the distant past. Each of these topics is related to some body of knowledge which lies beyond the strict scope of geography. Many of the Dark-Age settlements, for example, were founded by immigrants from Europe, whose arrival was a manifestation of the widespread wandering of peoples. The cause of this wandering is most obscure, and may never be fully understood. The original pattern of Dark-Age settlement on the English Plain depended not only on the quality of the land, but also upon the social structure and the farming customs of the immigrants. Changes in the pattern of settlement and in the distribution of population have been linked with changes in agriculture, in industry, and in social and political habits. At all points, the geographical treatment of peopling becomes entangled with other studies. One theme, however, runs throughout the history of peopling from the earliest days up to the Conquest—the successive arrivals of new groups of settlers or invaders, and the successive defeat, displacement, or absorption of those in possession.

PREHISTORIC IMMIGRATIONS

Immigration into the British area began well before the last[1] glacial maximum of the Ice Age. The first immigrants belonged, culturally speaking, to the Old Stone Age, living as hunters on the river-

terraces and tundra-lands of southern Britain. They have left no enduring mark on the visible landscape. Their successors of the Middle Stone Age are equally unrecorded on the modern map. The change from the one culture to another corresponded quite closely to a drastic change in the natural environment. The hunters of the Old Stone Age disappeared—by migration or by dying off—when the great ice-caps waned, and when improving climate allowed the trees of the Boreal period to colonise large parts of the British Isles. The tundras which had fringed the ice-caps were replaced by forests, and their inhabitants were succeeded by the forest-dwellers of the Middle Stone Age, who used carpenters' tools of stone, and kept dogs to help them in the chase.

The New Stone Age

When the maritime climate of the Atlantic phase set in, the water-table in southern England rose. Its rise made possible the farming of a new group of immigrant peoples—those of the New Stone Age. These newcomers arrived in the British Isles some 4,500 years ago, bringing with them the essential achievement of their culture-period—farming. Whereas their forerunners had depended on hunting and gathering, the peoples of the New Stone Age raised crops and kept flocks and herds. To judge by the burial mounds which they constructed, the familiar long barrows, they lived in well-organised societies and practised a highly-developed religion, for none but the people of a complex society would have been able to build the barrows, and none but those with a strong religious sense would have cared to. Long barrows are especially numerous on the limestone uplands of the Cotswolds and of Salisbury Plain, where the rainy climate of the time supplied plentiful soil-moisture. These areas were the most easily farmed, for the

---

[1] The word *last* is used here for convenience, for we are probably now living in an interglacial, with another glacial phase still to come.

highlands were largely under peat, and the low-lying clay country of the Midlands and the south-east was covered by forest, marsh, or fen. Farming of the New Stone Age seems to have been restricted to those parts of the limestone plateaus where shallow limestone soils occur—avoiding, for instance, the rather heavy soils of the Clay-with-Flints. The shallow soils were the most lightly wooded and the most easily cleared, and their shallowness was no handicap to the use of the scratch plough. The small tilled plots were customarily abandoned after a few seasons' use, tillage in Britain in the New Stone Age taking the form of shifting cultivation.

There was a lag of 3,000 years between the change to a maritime climate and the immigration of farmers. This lag was due partly to the situation of the British Isles, which lay on the unknown fringe of the known world of the time. Cultural advances flowed very slowly across the mainland from the Middle East or from the shores of the Mediterranean, reaching the British Isles tardily and in a thin stream. Within the British area, the currents set weakly towards the north and west, so that technical advances and social changes tended to occur later in the highlands than in the low-lands, if ever they reached the highlands at all.

The Bronze Age

The New Stone Age in Britain lasted for about five centuries—i.e., until about 4,000 years ago. It was brought to an end by a new series of immigrations, which happened to coincide roughly with a further change in climate. The maritime conditions of the Atlantic phase changed to the cooler but drier conditions of the succeeding sub-Boreal. The water-table in the permeable rocks was lowered. The new culture-period was the Bronze Age, in which the inhabitants of the British Isles were introduced to the use of metal. The Bronze Age was a time of prolonged peace, permitting an increase in population and in wealth—an increase recorded in the great numbers of round barrows. Some allowance must be made for the fact that the Bronze Age in the British Isles lasted three times as long as the New Stone Age, but Bronze Age barrows outnumber those of the former period by far more than three to one. Significantly enough, in view of the falling water-table, the round barrows are typically sited on false crests, so that they appear on the skyline when seen from lower levels. Habitations lay below the crests, but the Bronze Age peoples in Britain, being mainly herders, have left little in the way of permanent settlements. The distribution of their burial-mounds, however, is enough to show that the limestone plateaus continued to provide the best land and to support many of the inhabitants of these islands.

All but the hilliest and swampiest districts were however populated to some extent. There was a considerable population on the Atlantic coastlands, which were connected to Brittany and Iberia by long-established sea-routes. Among the trade-goods carried by the little ships were fine gold ornaments made by Irish craftsmen.

The Iron Age

The next culture-period was the Iron Age. Iron-Age culture did not reach the British Isles until about 2,500 years ago, long after the rather difficult technique of smelting iron ore was widely known in many parts of Europe. The nearest parts of the mainland were quite well peopled by this time, and some of the best land was possibly overcrowded. At about the time that iron-users invaded the British Isles, there was a change towards more maritime conditions of climate—the change from the sub-Boreal to the sub-Atlantic. Summers became moist and cool, so that peat once more grew vigorously in the highlands and killed large portions of the forest. Those small groups of people who retained the culture of the Bronze Age, or even of the New Stone Age, were driven into the remote and rainy north and west. Most of the British Isles was in time occupied by the iron-users, who once more put the limestone uplands of the south under the plough, and also farmed parts of the Pennines.

With the aid of a water-table which again stood high, and of limestone soils which were damper than they are today, tillage was practised in these areas. The plough used was still the scratch plough, with which little rectangular fields were worked in two directions. Many groups of such fields have been located on air photographs, mainly on Salisbury Plain and the neighbouring Chalkland districts. Farming was so prosperous that southern England could export surplus grain to Gaul. Minerals were exploited at a number of places—tin and copper in the Southwest, lead in the Mendips and in the Pennines.

Both farming and mining, however, were liable to interruption by war. The Iron-Age inhabitants of the British Isles were organised in shifting alliances of tribal groups, with frequent hostilities occurring between one group and another. Many commanding hilltops in the southeastern lowlands and on the fringes of the highlands were heavily fortified (Fig. 4:1, Plate 6), the strongholds often absorbing the compounds erected during the New Stone Age. But, despite the generally disordered nature of the time, towns arose—Colchester, London, and Canterbury among them—on or very near to sites which are occupied by towns today.

In all the most accessible parts of the British Isles, the languages of the Iron Age were Celtic. An evolved form of Celtic speech still survives in Scotland, Ireland, and Wales, and its Cornish variety has not long been extinct. It is highly probable that Iron-Age culture and Celtic speech spread through the highlands, and especially through Ireland, by diffusion rather than by conquest, and quite likely that the diffusion was still going on long after the British tribal power in the lowlands had been overthrown. It is certain that tribal power and tribal culture survived in Highland Britain for a long time, resisting with varying success the Roman, Saxon, Scandinavian, and Norman invasions.

Roman Times

Caesar's expeditions of 55 and 54 BC involved the destruction of a tribal fortress at Wheathampstead, near St. Albans, and an unsatisfactory treaty with the British. It was left to the emperor Claudius, in AD 43, to establish the new Roman province of Britannia. Forty years were necessary to subjugate the peoples of eastern and southern England and to subdue the few inhabitants of the Pennines. The advancing wave of conquest did not break until it had reached the Welsh Border and washed over the Southern Uplands of Scotland.

Behind the expanding military frontier came order of the Roman kind. The lowlands became a civil province, with a network of planned roads intersecting in planned towns. Lowland Britain was incorporated in the Roman Empire. Portions of the Roman arterial roads survive in the modern network—not all of them, however, represented by main roads today (Fig. 4:2). Most of the minor Roman roads have been lost, and some Roman town-sites have been abandoned. Enough remains to show that the usual routes from the mainland to Britain passed across the eastern Channel; ships made land at Dover, Lympne, Richborough, or Reculver, according to weather; roads from these ports converged on Canterbury, whence Watling Street led to London. London was a Roman metropolis, with a fortified wall enclosing a square mile of ground. Roads radiated from it to such country towns as Bath, Uriconium, York, and Colchester.

The pieces of the Roman pattern which have come down to us are impressive. Arterial roads in the lowlands ran straight for long distances, well adapted to the broad features of relief. On the highland borders, where roads led to fortresses and

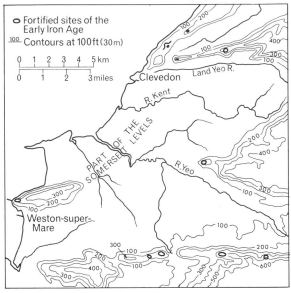

FIG. 4:1. Defended hilltops in part of Somerset; the sites have clear tactical advantages

PLATE 6. Cadbury Camp, Somerset. A defended hilltop, on a prong of high ground overlooking the Somerset Levels.

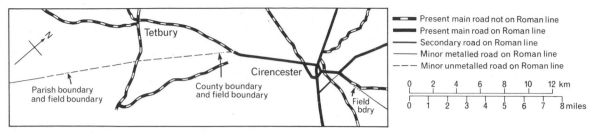

FIG. 4:2. Comparison and contrast between parts of Roman and the present road-systems

to mines, the form of the ground exercised a sterner control. The highlands themselves, difficult to traverse and unpromising to farmers, remained for the most part in native hands.

Wealthy citizens in the province of Britannia enjoyed many of the benefits of a complex civilisation. Although the Roman towns tended to decay after about AD 300, the country villas flourished. Trade with the Continent was considerable: lead, copper, and gold were smelted and worked for export, iron was made in the central Weald, wool was sold abroad, and kilns for the making of bricks, tiles, and pottery were numerous. The mark of Roman life was heavily impressed both on the land and on the life of its half-million inhabitants.

THE DARK AGES

That mark was all but erased by the Saxon invasions of the 5th century. Roman rule in Britain was ended by threats to the Imperial capital (by that time Constantinople). The legions were withdrawn; Britain and its inhabitants lay open to attack by forest-dwellers from the northern mainland of Europe.

Piracy had long troubled the Roman administrators of the southeast coasts. Piracy soon turned to settlement when the armies departed. Saxon ships beached in creeks along the whole range of shore from the Tweed to Southampton Water. The invaders penetrated far inland, sacking settlements, killing or enslaving all those who did not flee, and establishing themselves in farming communities on sites of their own choosing.

The period of history thus begun in about AD 450 is known as the Dark Ages. Its title is justified by the lack of written records; the illiterate invaders, by destroying towns and villages, by overthrowing the Christian Church, and by displacing the Latin language, removed both the art of writing and the men who could practise it. Contrasting strongly with the absence of documents is the mark of the

Dark Ages on the actual land. Many of the rural settlements of today were founded in the Dark Ages. The term *rural settlement*[1] must be used instead of *village*, for by no means all the pioneers were organised in compact village communities. The village was typical in Saxon England, an area comprising most of Lowland England except the southeast (Fig. 4:3). The unit of rural settlement in the southeast was the hamlet, as it remains to this day.

The name *Saxons* was given by the Romans to pirates attacking the southeastern coasts. The same

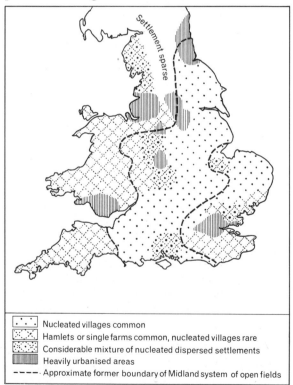

Nucleated villages common
Hamlets or single farms common, nucleated villages rare
Considerable mixture of nucleated dispersed settlements
Heavily urbanised areas
Approximate former boundary of Midland system of open fields

FIG. 4:3. Forms of rural settlement in England and Wales (considerably generalised)

[1] The word *settlement* can mean either an inhabited place, the pattern made by many such places, or the process of settling, according to context.

word forms an element in the county-names Essex, Middlesex, and Sussex, and in the old kingdom-name Wessex. But Saxon settlement spread far to the north of these areas, for by AD 700 writers in Northumbria were describing their peoples as Saxon. Southeastern England was settled by Jutes; but it is not clear whether these were a distinct body of invaders, or whether the Jutish nation arose in the region itself. The third group, the Angles, gave their name to England, to the English language, and to the surviving kingdom-name East Anglia; they came from a single homeland and preserved their traditions in their new country. It is difficult to say how the ambiguous term Anglo-Saxon arose, or what led the Saxon king Alfred to speak of an Angle-race and to call his language English. The Angles, like the Saxons, settled in compact villages; and the word *Saxon* will serve as a generic title for all the Teutonic invaders, to whatever group they belonged.

The general course, and the extent, of Saxon settlement can be traced by means of place-names (cf. Fig. 4:4). The distribution of place-name elements shows that the Saxon settlers gained complete control over most of the lowlands. Few Celtic words survive there, either in place-names or in the English language itself. There were two main phases of pioneering settlement. In the first, the *penetration phase*, the pioneers occupied the eastern parts of the lowlands. Their advance was then checked for a time by the Celts, who, descending from their hills and mountain valleys when the Roman legions withdrew, assumed control of the western plains. Eventually the Celts were driven back, not by small groups of armed settlers, but by armies of the kingdoms which emerged in the east. This was the *expansion phase*, during which the frontier was forced over the Pennines, up to the Welsh Border and well into the West Country.

Behind the moving frontier the numbers of settlements increased, as new immigrants arrived and as secondary settlements were made by already-established communities. Whatever their form or date, Saxon settlements were everywhere carefully related to the form and quality of the ground (cf. Fig. 4:6). Very many of them were set in forest, part of which was cleared to provide arable land. Here was the real beginning of the clearance of the extensive woodlands—a clearance which was to continue for many centuries.

During the 9th and 10th centuries there were further attacks and invasions, those of the Danes and Norsemen. By that time the term *Saxon* had been superseded by *English*, and it was on English kingdoms that the new invaders fell. The Danes established a state which at one time stretched as far southwestwards as Watling Street. Norsemen settled the fringing islands of Scotland, the Isle of Man, and northwestern England (Fig. 4:4). In Ireland and in Wales, where the interior remained in Celtic hands, Norse settlements took the form of coastal towns which were strongholds, ports, and the capitals of little coastal kingdoms. On the pattern of rural settlement, however, the Scandinavian invasions had little effect, except for adding new settlements and changing existing names.

Throughout the whole of the British Isles, the form of rural settlement in the Dark Ages was related to the system of agriculture and of land-tenure. Three main types of combination can be distinguished in the Saxon areas. The simplest of these combinations was associated with the best-known element of rural settlement—the nucleated village, formed in the beginning by a number of dwellings set close together. Nucleated villages were typical of most of England except for the southeast, and remain so to this day (Fig. 4:3). Except in East Anglia and in some parts of the north, the village lands were held in common by the village community, and were worked in large open fields. Very many villages at the outset had two great fields, which lay fallow in alternate years. The ploughed land was worked in strips, each farmer holding a number of strips scattered through the arable (Plate 7).

In much of southeastern England, the unit of settlement was the hamlet—a small group of dwellings associated with a small, compact block of ploughland and occupied by members of a single family. The difference between the Kentish field-system and the open-field system of the Midlands had little to do with the quality of the land. The Midland system was brought from Europe by the settlers; that of Kent was either introduced in the same way, or was adopted from local Romano-British practice. The arable of the southeast came to be subdivided, so that each patch of arable was distributed among a number of farmers. The subdivision was due to the practice of gavelkind—i.e., inheritance by a number of heirs instead of by a single one. In the Midlands, where land was held by the whole village, subdivision of this kind was impossible. If village population increased, the number of strips available for ploughing could be increased either by taking in more land or by converting the existing two fields to three, but the village remained intact and its open fields survived.

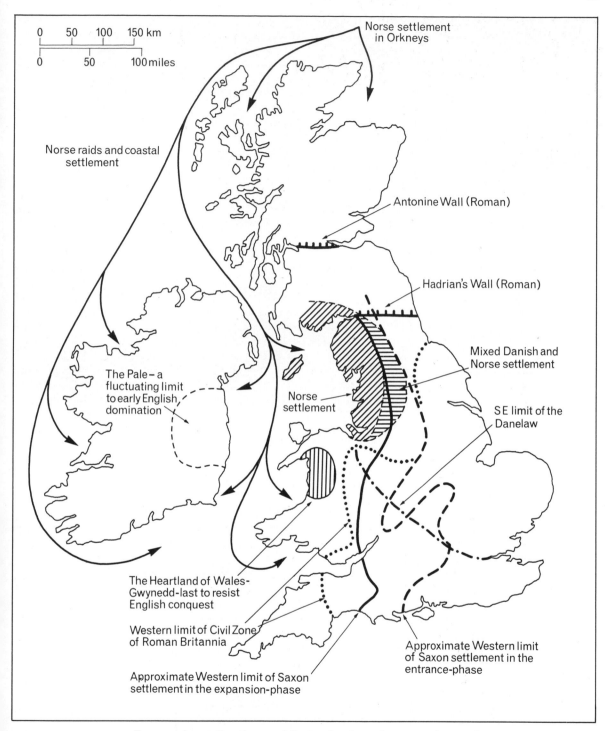

Scale:
0   50   100   150 km

0   50   100 miles

Norse settlement
in Orkneys

Norse raids and coastal
settlement

Antonine Wall (Roman)

Hadrian's Wall (Roman)

The Pale – a
fluctuating limit
to early English
domination

Mixed Danish and
Norse settlement

Norse
settlement

SE limit of the
Danelaw

The Heartland of Wales-
Gwynedd-last to resist
English conquest

Western limit of Civil Zone
of Roman Britannia

Approximate Western limit
of Saxon settlement in the
entrance-phase

Approximate Western limit of Saxon
settlement in the expansion-phase

FIG. 4:4. Some directions and limits of early settlement and control

Although in East Anglia the original settlements were nucleated villages, the land was worked in scattered rectangles instead of in scattered strips. It is thought that there, as in Kent, originally compact blocks were fragmented by the operation of gavelkind; but the subdivision was arrested by

PLATE 7. Strip-pattern of surviving open fields at Laxton, Notts. Contrast the pattern of enclosure-boundaries in the surrounding area.

the Danish invasions, so that East Anglian plough-land was less fragmented than that of the south-east.

Every one of the original settlements which can be identified today has manifest physical advantages of siting. The simplest illustrations are given by nucleated villages in scarpland country. Settlement at the scarp-foot secured a supply of water from springs. The village itself lay on, or immediately next to, the belt of deep mixed soil which characteristically occurs below the scarp. This belt provided the best arable land, while the scarp-slope gave wood, the scarp-top supplied rough grazing, and the lower ground supported damp woodland with meadow alongside the rivers. Scarp-foot settlements had access to land of contrasting quality—a great advantage to self-sufficient communities. The wet meadows were

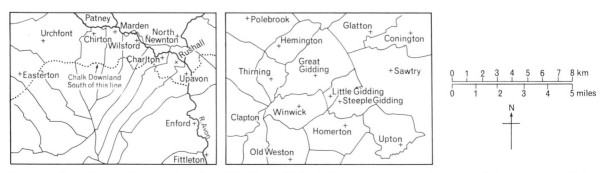

FIG. 4:5. Strip-like parishes on the edge of Salisbury Plain (left), running across the grain of the country; cellular parishes in clayland between Huntingdon and Oundle (right)

cut for hay, the woodland yielded timber for building and gave pasture for pigs, while the rough grazing for sheep and cattle supplemented the fallow arable and the stubble which was left after harvest.

In different terrains, different patterns evolved. On the great spreads of boulder-clay, for instance, settlements were located on patches of glacial gravel or of river terrace. A rough circle was cut out of the surrounding forest, so that when parish boundaries were laid down they formed a cellular pattern (Fig. 4:5). Settlements on the flanks of the Pennines avoided both the plateaus and the wet flood-plains, and typically lay near the edge of the valley-bottom. The heaviest clayland was everywhere avoided, and remained largely under forest. To this day there are large expanses of clay country without nucleated settlement, within the areas where villages are typical (Fig. 4:6). The forests were by no means unused, however, for in large portions of them pigs were grazed. The Wealden forests in particular were much exploited in this way by the people living on their margins.

The first pioneers had been free men; even when kingdoms began to emerge, the structure of society was by no means rigid, but the rise of a nobility and the threats of Scandinavian invasions combined to lower the status of the people who worked the land. The kingdom came to be owned by the king; by a kind of sub-letting, all but the king's personal holdings were administered by tenants, and a fundamental unit of administration evolved which appears in Domesday Book as the manor. Many of the manors were co-extensive with ecclesiastical parishes, for Christianity had been re-introduced and officially adopted well before the coming of the Normans. Thus to nucleated villages were added churches and the houses of local lords. In regions of hamlet settlement, such as the southeast and southwest of England, the small foci selected as centres of parishes often failed to grow as a result of their increased importance, so that very few large villages developed.

The most densely-peopled parts of England at the time of the Domesday survey lay southeast of the Jurassic scarp, with the greatest concentrations

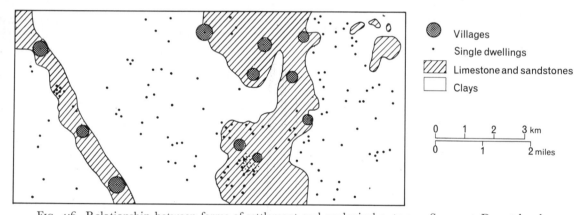

Villages
Single dwellings
Limestone and sandstones
Clays

0   1   2   3 km
0   1   2 miles

FIG. 4:6. Relationship between forms of settlement and geological outcrops, Somerset–Dorset border

NORMAN TIMES AND THE EARLY MIDDLE AGES

Domesday Book records most of what is known about the Dark-Age settlements; but it was compiled in 1086, twenty years after the Norman Conquest, and centuries later than the foundation of many of the settlements. The rural pattern, both of habitation and of administration, had already been modified before the Conquest. The Normans, however, completed the stratification of society and the binding of cultivators to the land. They set a social pattern which was to last throughout the early Middle Ages.

in East Anglia. By the mid-14th century, three hundred years later, a second area of high density had emerged in the eastern Midlands, and it was the speech of this part of the country which prevailed over other dialects to become the direct ancestor of the English language in its present form. A slow increase in population had led to the founding of new settlements, and also to the clearing of more woodland—except where the land lay in the extensive hunting-preserves of the king. Where the land was worked in open fields, many villages had converted from two-field to three-field working, putting one-third instead of one-half of the arable into fallow each year. In general, however, the pattern of rural settlement had changed little in the three hundred years since the Conquest. Agricultural practice was set in the mould of custom, just as the structure of rural society was held rigid by the feudal system.

THE LATER MIDDLE AGES

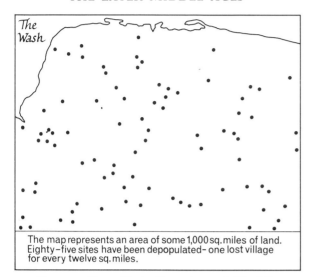

The map represents an area of some 1,000 sq. miles of land. Eighty–five sites have been depopulated– one lost village for every twelve sq. miles.

FIG. 4:7. Sites of lost villages in north Norfolk

These conservative arrangements were seriously disturbed, by a climatic shift in the moderate term and by a biological disaster in the very short term. How the two are related, if at all, is not known: but the general facts are clear. From about 1300 onwards, a progressive increase in the severity of winter weather and the effective duration of the winter season cut back the limits of successful farming. Many late-established daughter settlements failed. Eventually, the vineyards of early medieval times, formerly cultivated on sunny slopes of the English Plain, all failed. More dramatically, the epidemic Black Death, entering the country in 1348, killed at least a third of the people in less than a generation. The whole economy, and in consequence the socio-political structure, was transformed. Labour for the land became scarce, and the scarcity led to the decline of bondage and to the common use of hired labour. It also promoted the letting of land for rent, and the spread of sheep-grazing. These developments favoured commercial farming and commercial landlords as against feudal tenure, barter, and the discharge of customary services. So profitable did sheep-farming prove that, in the two centuries between 1350 and 1550, no fewer than a half-

million ha. were withdrawn from the arable of communal fields. Many settlements were depopulated, their inhabitants being driven out to make way for sheep (Fig. 4:7). Sheep and sheep-farms increased greatly in number, producing large quantities of wool, which were at first sent mainly for export and later used for the manufacture of cloth within the country.

POST-MEDIEVAL TIMES

Although many elements were thus removed from the pattern of rural settlement, that pattern was by no means obliterated. On the other hand, the pattern of fields was changing, even in that wide belt where large open fields were typical and where farming was most conservative. During the 16th and early 17th centuries, a four-field system, involving one year's fallow in four, appeared and spread in the Midlands. Frequently the four fields were created by the subdivision of the two open fields which already existed, but at some places additional land was taken in to make up the number.

Modification of the open fields was accompanied by enclosure of part of the cultivated land, which was removed from common holdings. Enclosure of one kind was already long-established, for the lord's house of the early Middle Ages was surrounded by the lord's estate. During Tudor times, however, there was considerable enclosure of a piecemeal kind, which took in small irregular fields—often called *closes* today—at the edges of a village (Fig. 4:8). Official policy and small farmers were alike hostile to enclosure, the depopulation of villages by grazing magnates having caused much alarm, and penalties were set on enclosure under Elizabeth I, encouragement being given to arable farming. Grain grown on land formerly grazed by sheep yielded heavily—a great benefit at a time of rising population; but the lesson of heavy yields was not understood, any more than the practice of enclosure was abolished or reversed. The pace of enclosure was indeed checked in those districts where the land was worked in open fields, Oxfordshire retaining one-third of its whole extent in common arable as late as 1750; but in the southeast, the southwest, and along the Welsh Border, enclosure of open land or subdivision of already enclosed land continued. Kent, and to a lesser extent East Anglia, were largely enclosed by the mid-18th century, while Herefordshire by that time had but one-fortieth of its area still in open arable fields.

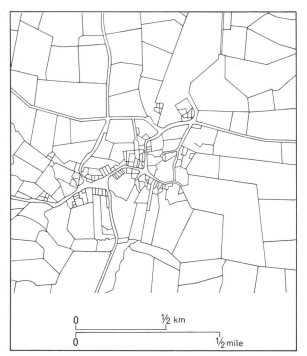

FIG. 4:8. Pattern of enclosure-boundaries at Newnham, Northants (village buildings omitted). The very small regular enclosures are gardens; next outward come the irregular closes of late-medieval times, and then the large regular fields of Parliamentary enclosure

---

THE CELTIC WEST

In most parts of the Celtic west there was never anything like the compact villages of Midland England. Most districts seem to have been characterised by a kind of hamlet settlement. The matter is not easy to investigate, for the small and loosely-grouped units of rural settlement in the Celtic

areas seem to have been less stable than the Midland villages. There seems, however, to have been a marked contrast in size between the typical Midland village and the typical hamlet of the Celtic districts; whereas the Midland villages of the early Middle Ages had up to a hundred tenants holding land, and 500 ha. or so under cultivation, the Celtic units of land ran to about 50 ha. and the number of tenants to about five. That is to say, a representative *clachan* (hamlet) in Scotland and Ireland included some five families.

In Scotland and in Ireland the land held by a community was typically divided into infield and outfield (Fig. 4:9). The infield, perhaps a quarter of the whole, was manured each year and sown with grain. The outfield was divided into ten parts, each of which was cropped with oats for four or five years and then left to fallow for the remainder of the ten-year period. Sowing of part of the outfield was preceded by the folding of stock, so that the ground could be enriched by dung. Variations of practice occurred in a number of districts, but the general scheme of infield-outfield was widespread.

The tilled land was divided into strips, both in the infield and in the outfield, so that each tenant had a share in every kind of soil. The strips were steeply ridged, giving the name of *runrig* or *rundale* to the land so worked. The infield-outfield system, with land cultivated in runrig, lasted best in Scotland, where nearly all of the land was still unenclosed by 1750. It seems likely that from time to time the landlords reconsolidated the land, offsetting the subdivision which resulted from inheritance. A similar process went on in Ireland, where gavelkind was capable of producing a complete fragmentation of holdings in two generations. By means of reconsolidation, the Irish townlands were preserved until the 19th century

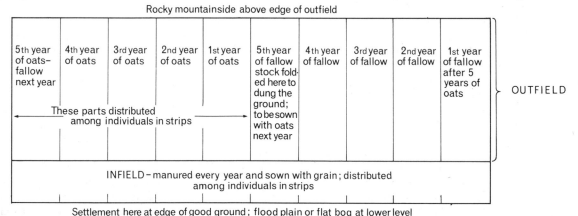

FIG. 4:9. Diagrammatic summary of the infield-outfield system; progression in the outfield is from left to right

(Fig. 4:10). Wales contrasts strongly with Ireland: gavelkind in Wales tended not only to subdivide plots of land but also to disperse settlements, until it was made illegal by Henry VIII. In addition, Wales was influenced by the agricultural practice of the Marchlands, and its land was early enclosed. Southwestern England was conquered by the English before Norman times, but its rural settlements remained dominantly of the hamlet type. Like Wales, it experienced enclosure at an early date.

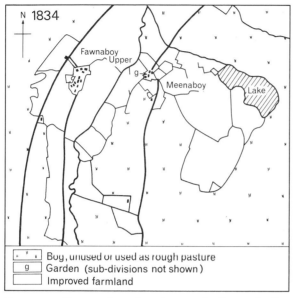

FIG. 4:10a. Two nucleated settlements in Donegal, 1834

TOWNS

A new start had to be made with town life during the Dark Ages, and town growth was slow throughout the Middle Ages. It is difficult to realise today, when four out of every five people in Britain live in towns, how few and how small were the towns of five hundred years ago. Those of a thousand years ago were even smaller and fewer. Their location and origin are important, however, for most of them are towns today, with their centres still on the original sites.

The Roman towns were sacked either by the local inhabitants, by Celts from the west, or by the invading Saxons. Dark-Age settlers tended to avoid the sites both of towns and of villas, possibly for superstitious reasons, just as they made little use of Roman roads. The rural communities of the pioneers were organised as if towns did not exist.

When towns arose once more, their growth was due to several factors which worked in a variable combination—the practice of administration, the influence of the Church, the need for defence, and the need for markets.

Of the origin of some towns very little is known. London, Canterbury, Rochester, and York were already centres of government, religion, and trade at the time of the Scandinavian onslaughts. The danger from Danes and Norsemen provoked the foundation of strongholds—e.g., Oxford—and

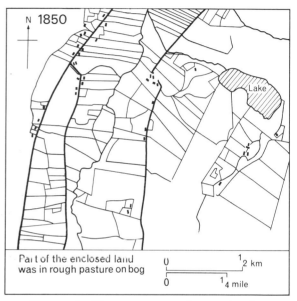

FIG. 4:10b. The same two settlements in 1850

the fortification of existing settlements. In the territory held by Scandinavians, fortresses were also established, as already noted for the Welsh and Irish coastlands.

Places which had already grown to some size with the aid of flourishing markets were naturally selected for fortification, while the defensive works themselves gave protection to merchants and to church buildings. Thus came about, at the very outset, the interplay of more than one factor in town growth. Each town is a special case, but every site offered certain natural advantages to the founders. Durham and Shrewsbury, for example, are almost enclosed by incised meanders and were consequently easy to defend in their early days. Situation, in addition to site, was influential. Fortified towns were established on the Welsh and Scottish Borders to withhold the unruly Celts, Norman strongholds were built in Ireland. During the early Middle Ages, when local magnates became very powerful, private armies were based on walled towns throughout the land.

Because of the effects of walls and castles upon the plans of towns, defensive works and defensive sites attract much attention; but town walls lost most of their usefulness when cannon were introduced, and local strongholds lost much of theirs as the power of the monarchy increased and as feudalism decayed. The powers of central and local government and of the Church were exercised principally from urban centres, but it was the function of marketing which was common to all towns of the Dark Ages and medieval times. That function is still discharged by all towns at the present day. No single feature of a town is more distinctive than the old market-place. In some towns the market-place still lies open, forming a broad stretch of street, a triangle, or a square in or near the main shopping district; in others it has been built over, carrying a guildhall, a corn exchange, and a huddle of shops separated by narrow alleys. Although the medieval fair has degenerated into the modern fun-fair, and cattle-markets have been banished to the outskirts of many English towns, the weekly produce market still flourishes on its traditional site (cf. Plate 68).

Town life in the Middle Ages was almost as strictly regulated as was rural life under the feudal system. Trade and craft-industry were organised and controlled by the town-based gilds, whose rise marks the elaboration of urban functions. The special status of town-dwellers encouraged migration from country to town as soon as the bonds of serfdom were loosened. Even so, nothing occurred to foreshadow the explosive growth of towns which was to accompany industrialisation during the 18th and 19th centuries. In the mid-14th century, when the population of England was perhaps two million in all, London had some 35,000 people, York 11,000, Bristol 10,000, Coventry and Plymouth each 7,000, and Norwich 6,000. In other words, the aggregate population of the six largest towns of the time was but 76,000—less than the present population of Bath. In the late 17th century London had grown to a population of half a million—a huge figure for those days: Bristol and Norwich had perhaps 35,000 each, Birmingham 15,000, and Manchester, 10,000. The rise of Bristol was associated with the town's ocean trade; that of Birmingham and Manchester marks the beginnings of manufacture. But although a quarter of England's population already lived in towns by 1700, the total for the country was no more than 5 or $5\frac{1}{2}$ million, so that the inhabitants of all other towns than London numbered only $1\frac{1}{4}$ million—a figure comparable to the present population of Birmingham. The economy of the British Isles was not yet dominated by manufacture; the countryside supplied a large surplus of grain for export, as it continued to do until well into the 18th century, and the largest social groups were formed by country-dwellers (see Appendix 1).

APPENDIX

Estimated Character of the Population
of England in 1688

Group	Total	Arbitrary allocation to	
		Country	*Town*
cottagers, paupers, vagrants	1,330,000	1,115,000	215,000
labourers, outservants	1,275,000	1,000,000	275,000
freeholders	940,000	840,000	100,000
farmers	750,000	750,000	—
artisans and craftsmen	240,000	40,000	200,000
shopkeepers and tradesmen	225,000	25,000	200,000
esquires, gentlemen, office-holders	196,000	100,000	96,000
law and clergy	122,000	61,000	61,000
liberal arts and sciences	75,000	—	75,000
traders and merchants	64,000	—	64,000
titled aristocracy	27,520	13,760	13,760
armed forces	256,000	56,000	200,000
Totals	5,500,520	4,000,760 (72·5%)	1,499,760 (27·5%)

Source (first column of figures): estimates made by King and
    Davenant, quoted in Ernle: *English Farming, Past and Present.*

Chapter 5

Agriculture from 1700

ALTHOUGH the rigid rules of feudalism in England were relaxed and modified from 1350 onwards, nothing occurred for another four centuries to transform the whole pattern of rural landscape, despite the effects of two centuries of expanding sheep-farming and of Tudor enclosures. The organisation of society which is called feudalism started to break down in the 14th century, but the manorial system—an organisation of land-tenure—persisted. During the 17th century, in which England saw two political revolutions and a civil war, the most noteworthy changes in the English countryside were the enclosure and improvement of parts of the Pennines and the drainage of much of the Fenland; and these extensions of the available farmland, remarkable though they were, are overshadowed by the events of the 18th century.

THE AGRICULTURAL REVOLUTION

It was in the 18th century that the movement began which is called the agricultural revolution. This movement is impossible to explain but was transfiguring in its effects. Much had already been learned by individuals in Tudor and Stuart times about the possible application of new ideas to husbandry, but, in the common fields which included much of the arable land of England, experiment and change were alike impossible. Outside the belt of common fields, and in Wales, Scotland, and Ireland, farming was also notably conservative in its methods. Most farmers and all farm workers were illiterate, and agricultural science as it is now understood had not yet developed. Scientific agriculture had still to be learned by trial and error. Many successful trials were made, and their results disseminated, during the 18th century, when such improvers as Tull, Townshend, Coke, and Bakewell provided farmers

with the drill and horse-hoe, a scheme of crop-rotation which included courses of roots and clover, and livestock improved out of recognition by deliberate and careful breeding.

It is possible to see, in the agricultural experiments of the 18th century, a manifestation of the spirit of improvement which pervaded 18th-century thought. This spirit was responsible for many of the planned estates and reconstructed great houses which still adorn the English countryside. Even more important were its effects on farming in general, and through farming upon the location and structure of rural settlement.

Parliamentary Enclosures

As the new ideas about farming gained support, the enclosure necessary to put them into practice gained momentum. In 1750 the open-field system, in some variety or other, still survived in one out of every two English manors. During the reign of George III (1760–1820), hundreds of enclosure acts were passed, applying to $2\frac{1}{4}$ million ha. of land. First the open fields were enclosed and parcelled into consolidated holdings, then the common grazing-land was taken. The direct results were the redistribution of land in compact farms, a great increase in total yields, the creation of a large class of landless labourers, and a new network of field-boundaries in the districts where open fields had been (cf. Plate 73).

Enclosure undoubtedly involved much injustice and hardship, especially to smallholders, cottagers, and squatters. The main problem was one of expense: not only had legal fees and surveyors' fees to be paid, but the new fields had to be fenced. The poor sold out to the rich. Even many of the more well-to-do could not afford to build on the new farms, and the erection of farmhouses and out-buildings had to wait in many places for a generation. The process of secondary dispersion of settlement—the movement away from an existing nucleus—was deferred. This is why so many existing farmsteads date from the early or middle 19th century rather than from the time of the actual enclosures.

Eighteenth-century enclosures could only affect those parts of the country where open fields still survived. It has already been observed that Southeast England, East Anglia, Southwest England, and much of Wales underwent enclosure in earlier times. Irish land remained liable to repeated subdivision and consolidation until the mid-19th century, and the island has never experienced a swift and drastic alteration of farming practice such as that which took place in England between the mid-18th and the mid-19th centuries. In parts of Scotland, on the other hand, agricultural changes were still more rapid than in England. Many of the small holdings worked on the runrig system were consolidated during the late 18th century, leases were lengthened, crop rotation was introduced, land was enclosed in fields, and lime was applied to the soil. At the same time much land was taken for large sheep-farms, which could be established all the more easily in the Highlands because the clan-structure of society was deliberately broken after the failure of the rebellion of 1745 (Ch. 14). The spread of sheep-farms was accompanied by emigration. Raw wool was sent to the thriving mills of the West Riding, and people moved to the rising factory towns or emigrated overseas.

From a distance of a century-and-a-half, it is possible to regard the parliamentary enclosures and their attendant distress with some detachment —the modern world has problems of its own, which divert attention from past tragedies. In their social aspects, the emergence of a labouring class, the division of rural society into farmers and labourers, and the pauperising of many countryfolk can only be condemned. These accompaniments of enclosure were not wholly compensated by the rise of a class of independent farmers, some of them secure in ownership or in long leases. Technically, however, the agricultural revolution was wholly beneficial. It enabled the country to be fed during the Napoleonic Wars, and to support the rapidly-growing towns of the early years of industrialisation.

CHANGING EXTERNAL RELATIONS

The agricultural revolution brought into existence much of the rural landscape of Great Britain as we know it today. But although it set the pattern of fields and of holdings, it did not immediately transform the aims of farming. Although the new farms were commercial undertakings from the beginning, they were still worked in order to provide basic foodstuffs. The British Isles in 1800 were still approximately self-supporting in essential foods. By 1900 a profound change had occurred, for by that time heavy reliance was being placed on farms abroad. Two main factors account for the change—the increase in population which accompanied industrialisation at home, and the spread of farming in mid-latitudes overseas. A combination of influences strengthened the commercial nature of British farming, promoted the growth of towns, and depressed the status and numbers of rural labourers.

In 1750 the population of Britain was about $5\frac{1}{2}$ million. By 1801 England and Wales alone contained 9 million and by 1851, 18 million. Food shortage was already a possibility by 1800, but the pressures of wartime led both to high prices and to the reclamation and improvement of land. Agriculture flourished, the cultivated area was increased, and the country was fed. After the long war ended in 1815 at the Battle of Waterloo, the strong tariffs of the Corn Laws were imposed by a parliament dominated by landowners, in order to protect the cultivation of cereals. The Corn Laws weighed heavily on a country whose population was increasing faster than the supply of food from its farms, and became unpopular with manufacturers because they kept up the price of food and the level of wages. They survived, however, into the mid-century. The famine in Ireland forced their modification (Ch. 12), and in 1869 duties on imported grain were abolished, in accordance with the prevailing esteem of free trade at that time. While they lasted, the Corn Laws protected British farming from foreign competition and discouraged any tendency to replace cereals as the main kind of tillage crop.

Between 1850 and 1860 the external trade of Britain trebled in volume. In the mid-century Britain enjoyed the position—never before held and never since regained—of workshop of the world. Farm workers were attracted to the growing industrial towns by wages which were one-third or one-half as great again as those offered in the country. At first the new towns killed many of their immigrants, for they provided unbelievably hard conditions of work and of living, and suffered frequent epidemics. As public health improved, the towns were able to grow with increasing speed and to become ever more attractive to the country people.

British agriculture and agricultural workers were especially hard hit by the spread of grainfields in the New World—in the U.S.A., in Canada, and in the Argentine—and by the rapid increase in British imports of grain made possible by railways and steamships. Keepers of livestock also suffered. Competition from Australian wool was already severe by 1850, and in the later half of the 19th century much land in Scotland was withdrawn from sheepwalks and put to use as deer-forest and grouse-moor. The most impressive single event was the disastrous British harvest of 1879, when it became clear—even to those who had hitherto resisted conviction—that Britain had become dependent on foreign suppliers for large imports of food grain. British farming never recovered. Between 1870 and 1890, the area of corn production fell by 40 per cent, and from 1890 onwards oversea farms sent into Britain great quantities of meat, cheese, and butter.

CHANGES IN LAND USE

Contemporary estimates make it possible to compare the land use of England and Wales in the late 17th century with the use in the early 19th century (Fig. 5:1). Records are available from the 1860s; the changes which they indicate (Fig. 5:2) culminate in the distributions mapped below.

well into the years of World War I. Permanent grassland, on the other hand, expanded up to 1890, at the expense both of tillage and of 'other land'—in addition to conversion of arable to grass, there was some improvement of rough grazing. But the expansion of permanent grass ceased after 1890 in the face of competition from meat-producers overseas. Some of the worst grassland was allowed to revert to rough grazing, and reversion continued right up to World War II.

After World War I, the grassland which had been hastily ploughed-up was soon seeded down again. The decline of ploughland went so far that, in the 1930s, under 3 million ha. (7 million ac.) were in tillage—less than half the total for 1870. Farming throughout England and Wales suffered severe depression in the 1930s—depression made still worse by the slump in trade and industry. Every effort had to be made to reduce working costs, and the loss of farm-workers to the towns was accelerated.

The great exception to the story of progressive decline was dairy-farming. During the inter-war period, this branch of farming was favoured by the impossibility of importing fresh milk, by an advertising campaign designed to increase milk-consumption, and by the high prices which dairy-farmers secured by means of collective bargaining. Dairying paid better than beef-production in

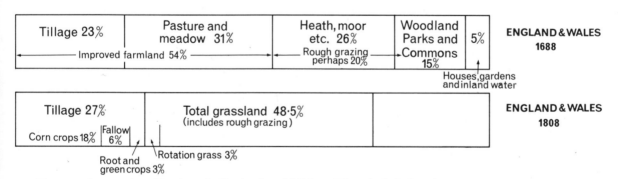

FIG. 5:1. Summaries of land use in England and Wales 1688 and 1808; based on contemporary estimates

Changes in England and Wales

The graph for England and Wales just includes those peak years about 1870 which immediately preceded severe agricultural depression. Nearly a third of the land in 1870 was under tillage crops, and rather more than a third under grass. The marked subsequent decline in the arable area was at the expense of tillage crops and not of rotation grass. As the graph shows, the decline was checked but not arrested in the late 1800s, and continued

England, and numbers of Welsh farms also converted to dairying.

In all this, factors quite unrelated to the physical environment can be seen at work. Direct government action to encourage certain types of farming by subsidies or by guaranteed prices, and discouragement of other types by lack of support, became familiar in the years between the wars. Tariffs, import quotas and marketing boards were freely used to carry agricultural policy into effect.

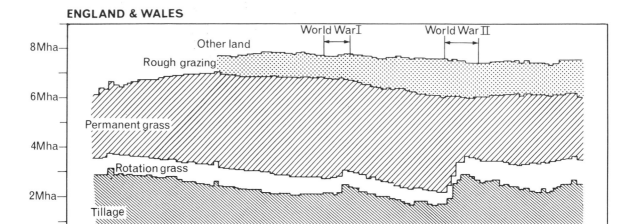

ENGLAND & WALES

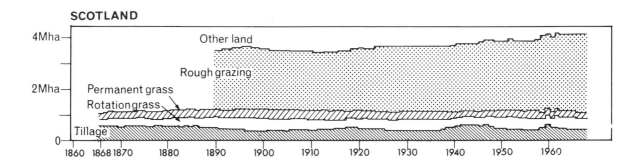

SCOTLAND

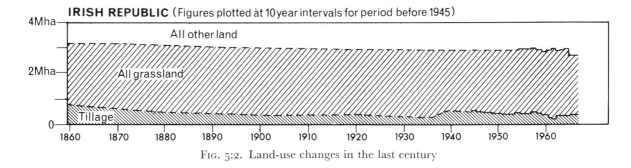

IRISH REPUBLIC (Figures plotted àt 10 year intervals for period before 1945)

FIG. 5:2. Land-use changes in the last century

When World War II broke out, a great campaign was launched to increase the area of tillage, in order to offset as much as possible the effects of the expected blockade, and compulsion as well as persuasion was employed. Some of the results appear strikingly in Fig. 5:2. The total area of tillage increased to a figure unknown for seventy years. The expansion becomes even more impressive when it is recalled that much good farm-land was taken for military use—especially for airfields and training-grounds. But the total area of farmland was not increased, as the graph shows,

and the extension of ploughland was secured at the expense of permanent grass. The reduction of the extent of meadow was accompanied by a marked fall in the number of sheep.

During and after World War II, selected branches of farming were heavily subsidised. This fact goes far to explain the retention of tillage in the post-war period near the level of 1900. The policy of subsidising agriculture has been most beneficial in the short run, since it has meant working capital for farms which needed capital very badly. Farms in the United Kingdom today are in general

PLATE 8. Harrowing by caterpillar tractor, Lincolnshire.

efficient, productive, highly mechanised and with their buildings in good order. Yields per area of the chief crops are up to 50 per cent to 100 per cent above the level of the late 1930s. The number of tractors at work on farms today is more than eleven times as great as in 1938, and there has been a corresponding increase in the use of tractor-drawn implements. Labour for the land was short during wartime, and the deficiency had to be met by machines; but mechanisation has continued in the post-war period, effecting great changes in farming practice (Plate 8). In a sense, continuing pressure for increased productivity is exerted by land-use competition, population growth, and specifically the attrition of farmland. In detail, however, conversion of farmland to town uses is a complex matter (see bibliography: Best and Champion), for population growth and the extension of towns are not everywhere related. The clearest relationship appears in the traditional axial belt running from the industrial northwest and the West Midlands to London, with conversion most evident in the northwest and weakest in the rural midlands.

Another change with clearly visible results is the great increase in the use of chemical fertilisers, weedkillers, and insecticides. All contribute to the increase in yields, and the weedkillers made

standing crops look remarkably clean (their use is not common in the Irish Republic, where in some districts crops are always thick with weeds). A rapid improvement in cattle has been made possible by artificial insemination, by means of which one bull can become the sire of 10,000 calves instead of 500. It is now possible to breed desirable characteristics into large numbers of stock in a short time, and dairy-farming in particular has benefited (cf. Plates 9, 10). A further sign of intensified working is the increase in irrigation, wherein farming enters the competition for water use; southeast of a line from Boston to Weymouth, farming exerts an irrigation demand in eight or more years in ten (cf. bibliography: O'Riordan).

The long-term effects of subsidies or other forms of assistance to agriculture are keenly debated. Successive governments have, however, been determined to keep farms in good order, both for the sake of reducing imports and as a safeguard against food-shortage in case of renewed war. Under the Agriculture Act of 1947 the principal farm products of Great Britain were assured markets at guaranteed prices, and when a change of government brought a change of policy, support continued to be given to products which failed to obtain a minimum or standard price. The current cost of such support is about £250 million a year.

PLATE 9. Free grazing by pedigree Guernsey cows, in parkland with ornamental hardwood trees in the background.

PLATE 10. Grazing of pedigree Friesian cows controlled by electric fencing. The pasture is of ryegrass, sown in April after kale.

It is of course obvious that if agriculture is to be directed or guided to any significant extent, the price of direction or guidance must be paid.

Changes in Scotland and Northern Ireland

Much of what has been said of England and Wales applies also to Scotland. Contrasts arise, however, between England and Wales on the one hand, and Scotland on the other, from the fact that so large a proportion of Scotland's farmland is under the plough. The decline of tillage in Scotland lagged behind that in England, mainly because the great tillage crop of Scottish farms is oats, which is not so susceptible to foreign competition as are wheat and barley. Nevertheless the area under the plough in Scotland began to decrease in the late 1880s, and has remained at a relatively low level ever since, except during the two World Wars. The expansion of Scottish tillage during World War II has been largely offset by reversion to rotation grass since 1945. A slight but steady loss of farmland to rough grazing has been going on since 1900; much of this loss represents the abandonment of small, remote, unprofitable farms in the highland districts.

Figures for Northern Ireland since 1922 show a tendency for tillage to decline, and a reduction in the acreages of the leading crops—oats and potatoes. The trend was reversed during World War II, but has subsequently been resumed. In Northern Ireland, as in Great Britain, agriculture is much influenced by government policy, and at the present time prices are guaranteed and markets assured for some 70 per cent of all farm produce.

A distinctive feature of agriculture in Northern Ireland is the conacre system of letting small parcels of land for short terms—by original custom, eleven months. Something less than one-fifth of the farmland in Northern Ireland is still let in conacre, accounting for instance for a quarter of the total potato crop. The system has its disadvantages; on the other hand, it has, in numerous instances, helped to encourage mechanisation.

Changing Areas, Productions, and Yields in the U.K.

Between the depressed and neglectful 1930s and the far more prosperous but economically trialsome 1960s, farming in the U.K. transformed itself. The observed effects are referable in part, in the immediate sense, to the urgent need for maximum farm outputs during World War II, but in the longer term they belong with the increasing yields characteristic of Western agriculture gener-ally during the mid-century. Outputs of wheat, barley, and potatoes have all risen, and have changed faster than the amount of land devoted to these crops: that is, yields per area have turned markedly upward. The per-area yield of oats has also increased, but falling demand has reduced total production, and has still more reduced total extent.

Livestock, too, in response to improved techniques of management and to improvements of breed, have increased in numbers, although numbers of cattle in particular have been lately held steady by reason of increases in milk yield or in weight of carcass. We are here dealing with an agricultural revolution as effective as that of one to two centuries back.

Item	Relative extent in 1970: late 1930s = 100	Production in 1970: late 1930s = 100	Per-area yield in 1970: late 1930s = 100
Tillage plus temporary grass	150	—	—
Wheat	145	270	180
Barley	720	1,550	195
Oats	32	55	145
Potatoes	85	136	135

Numbers of livestock in 1970: late 1930s = 100

Cattle	137
Sheep	112
Pigs	200
Poultry	165

Changes in the Irish Republic

The graph of land-use changes in the Irish Republic begins with tillage in steep decline (Fig. 5:2). The reduction of tillage began in the mid-19th century, with the famine of 1845 and the mass emigration which resulted. Many holdings were abandoned as they stood, and in some of the western counties a quarter, or even a third, of the farmland fell into disuse. But tillage was also diminished by the changeover from wheat and oats—formerly grown for export to Great Britain—to livestock farming. Some of the main tillage crops display a long-term tendency to decline in importance, their extent rising abruptly during the two periods of world war but rapidly diminishing again and continuing to fall in time of peace. This group includes potatoes, oats, and turnips. Areas under other and much less extensive crops have changed little, except in the cases of wheat and sugar beet, which have been subsidised since the early 1930s and have actually increased in extent.

Up to the partition of 1921, Northern Ireland displayed similar agricultural trends to those in the twenty-six counties of the Republic. The farming of the North since partition has reacted to changing conditions in a similar way to the farming of Great Britain, while, in the Republic, the land ploughed-up during the time of World War II has again gone back to grass. Were it not for the bounties on wheat and sugar beet, the total extent of tillage would be less today even than it was in the late 1930s. Resumption of pre-war trends has been so effective that agriculture in the Irish Republic displays no such contrasts as those observable in the foregoing tables for the U.K.

Changes in Livestock

Variations in land use, themselves constituting changes in the visible landscape, were associated with changes in numbers of livestock. Between the mid-19th century and the 1930s, the number of cattle in the British Isles increased by half. The increase began as a response to the competition of foreign grain. It was least marked in Scotland, where oats, the leading grain, was not primarily a cash crop, but many grain-farmers in eastern England turned to stock-fattening, and many Welsh farmers took to raising store cattle for sale in England. The collapse of grain-farming in Ireland and the turnover to cattle has already been noted. The expansion of dairy-farming in the inter-war period occurred mainly in England and on farms with access to urban markets. Wales took some share in this expansion, but Scotland very little. The Irish Republic has developed a highly success-ful export of fat and store cattle; it also exports butter, but its trade in dairy produce has been damaged by disputes with the U.K. Northern Ireland has developed its farming on different lines, with pigs, milk and dairy produce, and eggs the chief items of agricultural produce in that order.

At the present time there are some 18 million cattle in the British Isles, an increase of about 6 million over the figure for 1938, and the greatest total yet recorded. Between 5 and 6 million are dairy animals. In contrast with cattle farming, which has more than held its own since the mid-19th century, sheep-farming has suffered a number of setbacks. The decline of grain-growing led to a decline in the number of sheep in the arable dis-tricts of England, where they had formerly been

folded on ploughland in large numbers. The total flock numbered about 30 million in 1870, declined to little more than 20 million in the 1920s, and fluctuated considerably up to 1938. There were heavy slaughterings in World War I, and again in World War II when numbers were reduced from 30 million to 22½ million. The present figure is about 32 million, representing a recovery to peak numbers.

AGRICULTURAL DISTRIBUTIONS

The distribution-maps in Figs. 5:3–5:25 are drawn from statistics for whole counties, except for the few instances where a county is subdivided in the official returns.

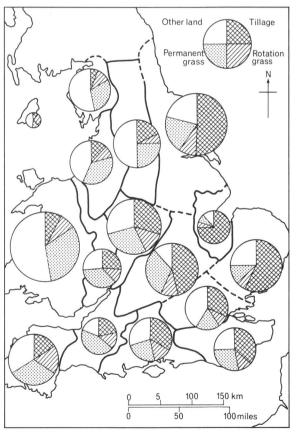

FIG. 5:3. Summary of land use in England and Wales, by regions, 1970. Compare Figs. 5:4, 12:3. Regions are named in Fig. 13:1

Improved Farmland

Fig. 5:5 is generalised from county data, to show improved farmland as a fraction of the total land area. Generalisation in this and similar maps is

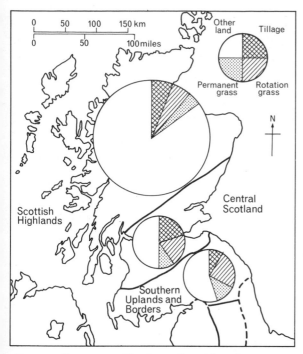

FIG. 5:4. Summary of land use, Scottish regions, 1970

thought to be justified by the awkward relationship of some county boundaries to rapid known changes in agricultural distributions. As the map indicates, a large block of England records more than three-quarters of its area in improved farmland. The concentration lies athwart the Humber and the Wash, extends into East Anglia, and links through the southern Midlands along the Jurassic belt with highly-farmed parts of the West Midlands, the Welsh Border, and the Borders of the West Country. More detailed information would show an extension into the Lancs.–Cheshire Plain. Much of the eastern part of Ireland, except for the Wicklow Mountains, also has at least three-quarters of its area in improved farmland, which extends in force southwestwards into Limerick and parts of near-by counties.

These two patches of the British Isles include the largest and most continuous patches of improved farmland, which, simply because they are large and continuous, are reflected in the figures for whole counties. The relative extent of farmland is reduced in southern England by various means—by woods of the southeast, by heaths, by the un-improved Chalkland of Salisbury Plain, and by the high moors of the Southwest. In parts of Wales the fraction falls below one-tenth. In the northern Midlands, farmland laps round the end of the Pennines and encroaches on their flanks, but much

ground here is used for industrial purposes. In the north of England and in Scotland, the difference between the wet hilly west and the drier east with its more extensive lowland is well brought out. In very large areas of the Scottish Highlands there is no improved farmland at all, by contrast to the west of Ireland, where the highlands are broken and where no whole county records less than a quarter of its area as improved farmland.

Rough Grazing

Rough grazing in Great Britain (Fig. 5:11) is very nearly coincident with the areas of moorland shown on Fig. 3:22 (see also Chap. 3). It accounts for a great deal of the Scottish Highlands, and is also extensive in the Southern Uplands, the North and Central Pennines, the Lake District, and the heart of Wales. It is less widespread in Ireland than might be expected, being most common there on the broken high ground of the northern, western, and southern parts of the island, but limited in extent in the lowland districts. The maps of rough grazing provide negative information, since they represent a great deal of the land which is not in improved farms.

Cropland

The maps of cropland (Figs. 5:5–5:11) show a concentration in the east of England, especially in East Anglia and the Fenland. Tillage amounts to more than a quarter of the land area in most of the English Lowlands, rising to more than half in the east and to more than three-quarters in the heart of the Fens. It is most widespread on the drier side of Great Britain, in areas where good arable soils are most widely developed. In all highland areas tillage is limited; throughout northern England, in Scotland, and in Wales, it is much commoner on the drier eastern side than in the wetter west. The eastern and western flanks of the massifs are separated by the highland of the interior, but in Central Scotland and in Ireland, which are not thus subdivided, tillage is also most extensive in eastern districts.

Grassland

Grassland in the English lowlands is least ex-tensive in the much-tilled regions of East Anglia and the Fens, or near the urban centres of London, the West Midlands, and the industrial districts of the North Midlands (Fig. 5:10). In highland areas it gives way to rough grazing, but is very common indeed in Ireland. There is an obvious correlation

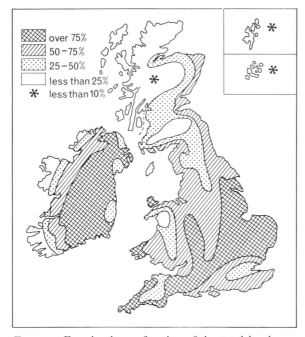

FIG. 5:5. Farmland as a fraction of the total land area, 1970

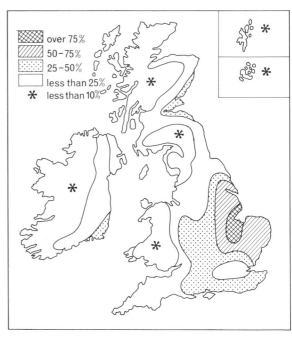

FIG. 5:7. Improved grassland as a fraction of the total land area, 1970

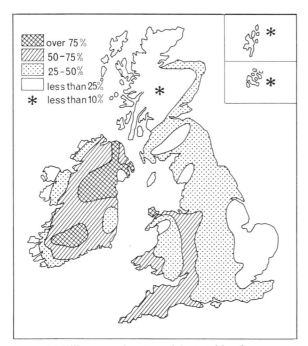

FIG. 5:6. Tillage as a fraction of the total land area, 1970

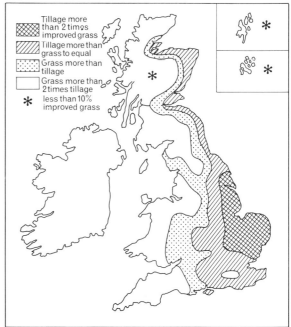

FIG. 5:8. Relative extents of cropland and grassland, 1970

between rainy lowland and land in grass, but some allowance has also to be made for soil-type: heavy clay soils are often put to grass in all parts of England, while much Irish grassland is developed on lime-rich glacial drift and serves the needs of cattle-producers.

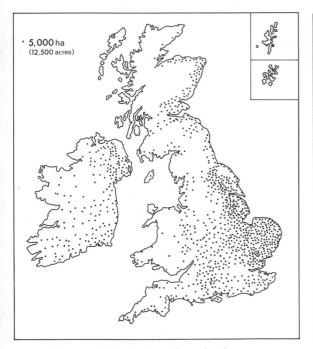

FIG. 5:9. Distribution of cropland, 1970

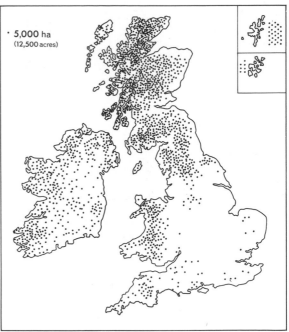

FIG. 5:11. Distribution of rough grazing, 1970

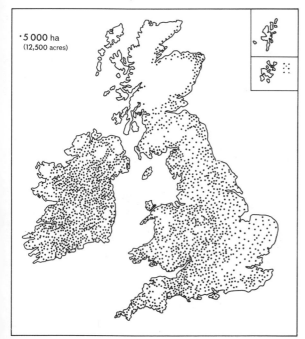

FIG. 5:10. Distribution of improved grassland (all types),
1970

As a feature of the landscape, grass is commonest in the eastern part of the Central Plain of Ireland and in the lowlands of Limerick, where it amounts to more than three-quarters of all land. In Ireland as a whole, only the hilly districts of the west and the Wicklow Mountains have less than half their total area under improved grass. In Great Britain, grass is most widespread in Southwest England, Southwest Wales, the borders of the West Country, and in the Welsh Borderland and its English fringe; there is an outlier of grazing land in the clay belts of Northamptonshire and Leicestershire.

Ratio of Cropland to Grassland

Fig. 5:8 gives a highly generalised comparison of the relative extents of tillage and of improved grassland. In East Anglia and the Fenland, tillage is at least twice as extensive as improved grass. In an adjoining belt, and on the eastern fringe of Scotland, tillage is at least equal in area to improved grass. The relative extent of grassland increases westwards, until it becomes more than twice as common as tillage. This map once more emphasises the contrasts in farming between the drier east and the wetter west.

Leading Crops

Figs. 5:12–5:14 show the distribution of the chief grain crops in 1970, after a fifteen-year period during which barley more than doubled its acreage. This crop now occupies more than half the grainland of the British Isles, except in the Fens where wheat remains dominant. The area

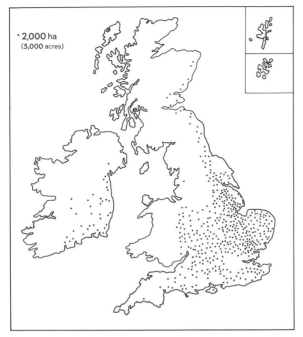

FIG. 5:12. Distribution of wheat, 1970

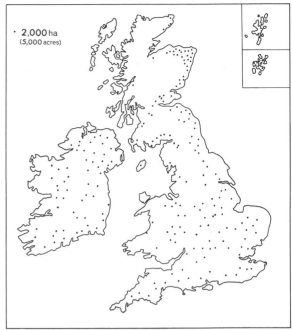

FIG. 5:14. Distribution of oats, 1970

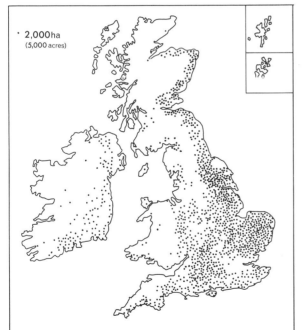

FIG. 5:13. Distribution of barley, 1970

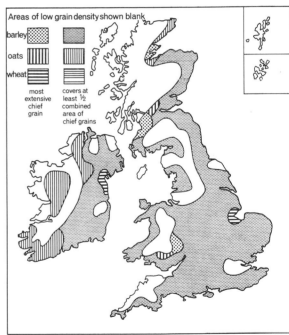

FIG. 5:15. Relative extent of the chief grain crops, 1970

under wheat in England has also increased, although less markedly, while at the same time wheat-growing has tended to become concentrated in East Anglia at the expense of other areas. The extent under oats has fallen by half or more, partly

no doubt in response to the final supplanting, in many districts, of workhorses by machines. Oats remain dominant, however—indeed in some districts practically the only grain—in the west and northwest of Ireland and in the

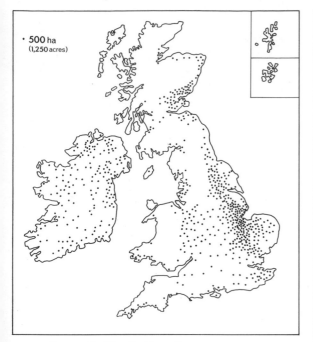

Fig. 5:16. Distribution of potatoes, 1970

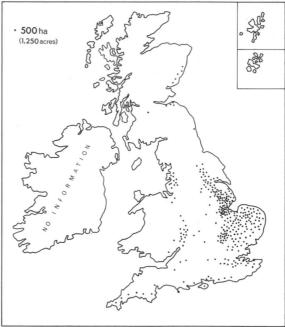

Fig. 5:18. Distribution of commercial vegetable crops, 1970

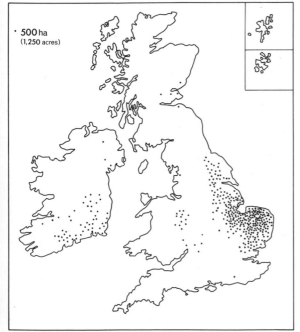

Fig. 5:17. Distribution of sugar beet, 1970

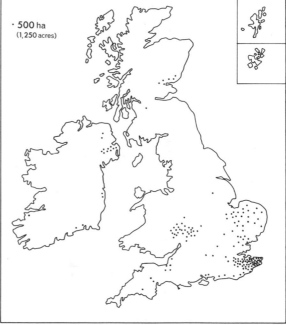

Fig. 5:19. Distribution of commercial fruit crops (tree, bush, soft), 1970

Scottish mountains, where it is a food grain.

Potato farming, widespread but nowhere especially concentrated in Ireland, is located mainly on the drier side of the main island, where in some areas potatoes are the main cash crop. The distri-bution map conceals something of the importance of the production of seed potatoes and first earlies, but does reveal the effective concentration in the eastern part of Central Scotland, and especially in that part of England extending from the Vale of

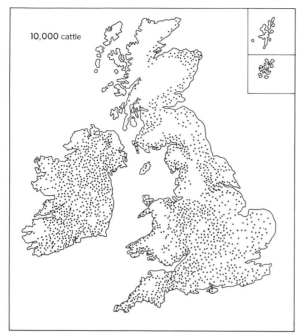

FIG. 5:20. Distribution of cattle, 1970

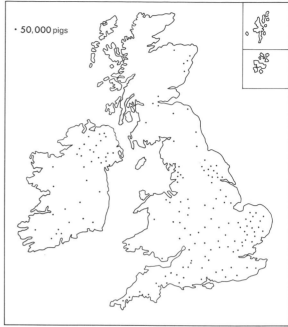

FIG. 5:22. Distribution of pigs, 1970

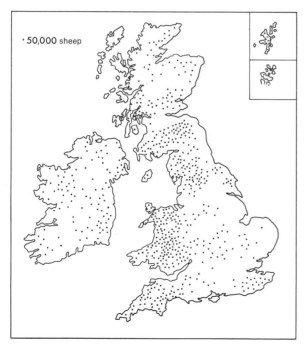

FIG. 5:21. Distribution of sheep, 1970

FIG. 5:23. Distribution of poultry, 1970

York, through the Fenlands, and into the northern portion of the London Basin. Sugar beet and vegetables (with the exception of vegetable production in Ireland, for which there is no information) are grown mainly in the Irish south and the English east, with noteworthy supplements from the western English Midlands (Figs. 5:17, 5:18). Vegetable-growing today, like the production of soft fruit, is strongly linked to the canning industry. Fruit (including orchard fruit)

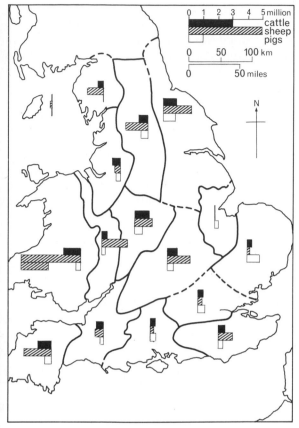

FIG. 5:24. Farm livestock in England and Wales, by regions, 1970

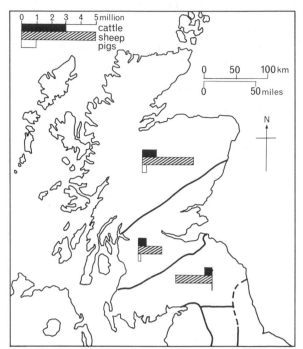

FIG. 5:25. Farm livestock in Scotland, by regions, 1970

is the most highly concentrated of all, mainly in North Kent with lesser producing areas in the southern Welsh border and the Fenland–East Anglia margin. A perceptible tendency revealed by the records is for intensive annual and short-term crops (broadly speaking, new potatoes, vegetables, soft fruit) to become progressively concentrated, especially in the Fenlands, which display the greatest concentration, and in East Anglia, which shows the greatest rate of increase. Among the complex range of interlocking factors at work, improved transport and rising yields of basic farm crops combine to favour specialisation within farms and within regions, and enhanced contrasts among regions (see bibliography: Gasson).

Distributions of Livestock

The distribution of cattle (Figs. 5:20, 5:24, 5:25, 12:4) is, as might be expected, similar in most respects to that of improved grassland. Cattle are widespread throughout Ireland, except on the bleakest uplands and the boggiest lowlands. In

Scotland, they are largely excluded from the remoter parts of the Highlands and from the central portions of the Southern Uplands. In the upland parts of England and Wales they are also scarce to absent, the main concentrations appearing along the drier margins of the high ground, in the Midlands, and in the lower-lying parts of the Southwest and its margins (Fig. 5:20).

In direct contrast, sheep today are concentrated chiefly in certain upland areas—the plateau country of Wales, the Central and North Pennines, the Lake District, and the Southern Uplands. Minor concentrations occur in Southwest England and in Southeast England. The total flock increased considerably in the ten years up to 1965, part of the increase being accounted for by farms in the central and western English Midlands. The present distribution of sheep represents, to some extent, their displacement from the best grassland by cattle, although they are used to keep down the rapidly-growing grass of summer in the cattle-farming districts. In some areas they are pastured on flood-plains in summer, and on many lowland farms are folded on arable in the winter.

Pigs are found mainly in lowland England, with the suggestion of a concentration in East Anglia. In Southwest England they are associated with dairying. In Northeast Ireland, where they are especially numerous in relation to area of farmland, they form part of the system of pigmeat–dairy production.

Poultry meat, once something of a luxury, has been put widely on the retail market with the aid of broiler factories. In addition to the long-established concentration of poultry in Lancashire, fowl farming has spread broadly throughout lowland England and parts of the Southwest, and, concerned largely with egg production, is vigorously established in Northeast Ireland (Fig. 5:23).

Factors Influencing Distribution

It is clear from the distribution-maps that some kind of connection exists between quality of land and of climate on the one hand and type of farming on the other. Farming, however, is carried on for profit, and not merely in order to satisfy the principles of geography. Farmers decide on particular crops and on types of livestock according to their own judgement of what will pay best. Their decisions are affected by government policy, by how well their neighbours do, and by their own ability. Some of the results of official policy have already been mentioned; for comparison, an instance may be given of the effect of example. In the years following World War II, a number of Lincolnshire farmers moved into Kent, taking over land on Romney Marsh; used to arable farming in the Fenland, they put their land to tillage crops in place of the traditional sheep-pasture, and their success did far more than subsidies to establish tillage on the Romney Marsh alluvium.

Because most farming in the British Isles is cash-farming, and because it needs to pay in the face of competition, the distribution-maps may be regarded as showing which kinds of crop and stock pay best in particular areas *in existing circumstances*. These circumstances, as has been stressed, include political as well as geographical facts.

Patterns of Size

In view of the commercial nature of British farming, it is surprising to find that numerous holdings are quite tiny (Fig. 5:26). The comparisons made in the diagram are somewhat obscured by the least orders of holding size reported in returned statistics. Even so, the small farm sizes recorded for Northern Ireland, where many farm units are not viable, are real. As shown, the farms in all five countries tend to arrange themselves in log-normal distributions of size, with Northern Ireland, the Irish Republic, Wales, and England, in that order, recording a range in modal (peak) size from 12 ha. (30 ac.) to 27 ha. (64 ac.). Especially in England, the smaller holdings tend to be horticultural rather than agricultural, compensating by high levels of capital and working investment for restricted area; but in the north and west, small sizes generally go with uneconomic operation. Holdings in Scotland are spread more widely through the size classes than are holdings in the other countries, in response to the combination there of ranch-type operations in the Highlands with intensive market gardening in the east of the centre; obviously, holdings of intermediate type are also reasonably numerous, although far less dominant than in other parts of Britain.

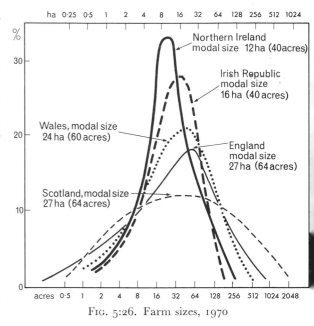

FIG. 5:26. Farm sizes, 1970

Chapter 6

The Rise of Industry

In the foregoing account of agricultural change, a number of references were made to industrialisation. To some extent, agricultural change and industrial change were interdependent; but the revolution in farming had already passed its peak when the first climax of industrial change had still to come. Industry was to expand so fast, and in so many directions, that it was to transform the entire economic, social, and political structure of Great Britain, and to remove agriculture from its former dominant position.

THE INDUSTRIAL REVOLUTION

The term *industrial revolution*, which is often applied to the sum of technical advances in the hundred years from the mid-18th to the mid-19th century, has today fallen out of fashion. Its critics justly draw attention in particular to the flourishing state of the woollen industry in earlier centuries. There can, however, be no dispute that between 1750 and 1850 the rate of industrial development was greater than anything previously known, and that in this period were laid many of the foundations of our present industrial economy. The geography of Great Britain was indeed revolutionised, and the term will therefore be retained.

Iron and Steam

Two great achievements of the industrial revolution were the discovery and development of processes for producing cheaply large quantities of iron, and the application of steam power to machines. In themselves, these achievements were no more than technical advances. Iron-smelting had already been practised for thousands of years before the 18th century; coal-mining had been carried on for hundreds of years, and a coasting trade in coal from the northeast was already well established; mechanical power had been employed for a very long time in the windmills, watermills, and fulling-mills which were scattered up and down the country, and in the water-powered hammers in the more localised forges of ironmakers. Nor was an elaborate organisation of manufacture unknown. Wool and flax were spun and woven mainly in the home, but the supply of raw wool, the distribution of yarn, and the marketing of finished cloth were largely in the hands of powerful clothiers and merchants. There were even a few factories in the present-day sense of the term. All the precedents for industry existed long before rapid growth took place. Two things only were lacking: an abundant supply of power, and adequate engineering materials.

These were provided by the steam-engine and by great improvements in smelting practice. The use of mechanical power and of cheap iron led to the concentration of manufacture in large factories, to the concentration of the factories on the coalfields, to the emergence of new towns, and to the astonishing rise of Great Britain as the first great industrial nation.

Production of iron during the Middle Ages fell short of demand. Armour and cannon, or readysmelted iron for making them, were in part imported from abroad. In Tudor times the matter became very serious, for smelting-furnaces were fired by charcoal, and charcoal-making threatened to destroy much of the country's timber. There was an illustration of competition for the use of land—the small furnaces of the iron-makers competed with one another for supplies of timber, and iron-making as a whole competed with shipbuilding. Under Elizabeth I, the demand by the navy for slow-growing oak timber was so great that cutting was severely restricted by law. Iron-making, already much dispersed because the furnaces tended to follow the receding edges of the woodland, declined steeply. The Weald, which had been the chief region for the production of iron, was particularly hard hit. By the mid-18th century the domestic output of iron in the British Isles fell to the wholly inadequate total of 20,000 tons a year, and iron was regularly imported from Sweden, Russia, and the North American colonies.

Many experiments had been made in smelting with coal instead of with charcoal. All had failed. The main difficulty was due to the sulphur which is often present in coal, combined with iron as iron pyrites—the sulphur entered the iron during smelting and made it brittle. But if coal is baked in closed ovens, many of its impurities are driven off; it is converted to coke, which, being free of sulphur, can be used in smelting iron ore. The earliest authenticated use of coke in smelting is that by the two Darbys (father and son), one of whose first blast-furnaces can still be seen at Coalbrookdale in Shropshire. The Darbys produced coke-smelted iron early in the 18th century, freeing themselves from the need for charcoal and drawing on the accessible local reserves of coal. For a number of years they kept their process secret; but when in the latter part of the 18th century the knowledge escaped, many new ironworks were founded; they stood not in the forests but on the coalfields. The coke-fired furnaces could be larger than those which used charcoal, for the coke could support the weight of large quantities of iron ore. The total output of smelted iron increased rapidly, but smelting with charcoal declined; the last furnace in Sussex went out for the last time in 1827. Thus occurred both a rise in the output of the smelting industry and a change in its location. Only where smelting with charcoal had already been established on or near a coalfield, as in Staffordshire and South Wales, could the industry stay where it was and convert to the use of coke. The ores used in these two districts, as in most of the newly-developed smelting areas, came mainly from the Coal Measures themselves.

Iron run directly from the furnace and allowed to solidify is pig iron. If it is remelted and run into moulds it becomes cast iron. Cast iron, containing from 2 to 5 per cent of carbon, is brittle by comparison with wrought iron or with steel, but is reliable in quality and can be used for many purposes. For many years it was widely used; bridges, rails, and a great range of machine parts were made from it; cast-iron cooking-pots were still common until the 1920s. Wrought iron, on the other hand, can be hammered into shape; it is practically free from carbon and is not brittle. The manufacture of wrought iron in quantity was perfected by Cort, who by 1784 had discovered how to drive off the impurities from molten iron by puddling—that is, by stirring molten pig-iron—and had so improved earlier designs of rollers that he could produce rolled malleable sheets of chosen thickness. Although cast iron and wrought iron are both inferior to steel, they were far better than any engineering material which had previously been produced at a reasonable cost. By the later years of the 18th century, therefore, the rapid growth of civil and mechanical engineering became possible.

The application of steam power to manufacture and to engineering increased the pull exerted by the coalfields on the new industries of Britain. Steam-power was first used in pumping water. Savery invented a steam-pump shortly before 1700, and Newcomen's first patent was taken out soon after. In these early days the obvious use of steam-power was in the pumping of mines, for there was as yet no great engineering industry. Coal-mines at that time were mainly shallow workings on the outcrops of the seams, and the problem of drainage was seldom difficult, but in the deep Cornish tin-mines the inflow of water to deep workings caused endless trouble. It is not surprising that Newcomen engines were known chiefly in the southwest. They used much fuel to produce little power, and were by no means reliable; but they were the best steam-engines available until Smeaton and Watt made their great improvements on existing designs.

Like the development of coke smelting, the manufacture of the new steam engines was at first slow. Although Watt's engines were made by the firm of Boulton and Watt and also by other firms under licence, no more than eighty-four were in use in the British Isles by 1800. It was already clear, however, that they were good for other things than pumping; steam power was made to supply a forced blast in iron-smelting in 1790, and a hot blast was used in 1828. Thus the steam-engine, itself owing much to the improvements in the smelting of iron, contributed to further improvements. As soon as its use became at all general, its manufacture increased the demand for iron.

Textiles: The Background

The way in which the various developments of the industrial revolution reinforced one another is well seen in the changes taking place in textile manufacture. At first these changes were contemporary with, but independent of, the advances in the techniques of smelting and the improvements of the steam-engine. Nevertheless, the final result of changes in textile working was to concentrate much of the textile manufacture of the British Isles on coalfields, and to produce a whole new industry. As in other cases of industrial change, technical, social, and political factors are interwoven.

Textile manufacture in England had been officially encouraged for many years, e.g., by the prohibition in 1660 of the export of raw wool, and by the regulation of 1678 that corpses should be swathed in wool for burial. The Huguenot immigration from France after 1685 greatly stimulated the working of silk, and the linen industry of Scotland was given tariff protection. In the later Middle Ages there was a considerable export trade in woollen cloth, and by the 17th century the total output far exceeded home demand. Much of the spinning and weaving was commercial, and was additional to that needed to supply the needs of a family or even of a whole village. The country-wide manufacture of wool had, however, developed from spinning and weaving for family needs alone, and until the 18th century was widely dispersed in the homes of working people everywhere.

Machines of a kind had been known for centuries, but the traditional spinning-wheel and hand-loom were simple in construction and slow in working. Many experimenters realised that it was possible to make more elaborate devices, but not until the late 18th century did numbers of them succeed. Rather strangely, perhaps, the advances came first in the working of cotton, which suffered from the restrictions and prohibitions imposed by governments which aimed at protecting woollen manufacture. In a sense, however, it was these very limitations which eventually made possible the swift rise of a cotton textile industry. Despite adverse regulations, an export trade in printed cottons had been established with West Africa and the New World. By the late 18th century all restrictions on the use of cotton cloth in the British Isles were abolished, and at about the same time the Southern States of the U.S.A. became great suppliers of raw cotton. There was thus scope for great expansion in a manufacture which had hitherto been deliberately confined, and which, unlike the favoured manufacture of wool, had no extensive, well-organised, and nation-wide organisation already in being.

Mechanisation of Cotton-Manufacture

Inventions of cotton-working machinery came fast in the late 18th century. The first great difficulty of the newly-freed industry was a shortage of yarn—the supply of hand-spun cotton could not meet the demands of the weavers. It was a weaver, Hargreaves, who in the 1760s made the first successful spinning-machine, the jenny. Being hand-driven, it did not affect the location of weaving in the weaver's home. In the same decade Arkwright produced his water-frame, which was power-driven and unsuitable for home use. Like the mule developed by Crompton in the 1770s, the water-frame was a spinning-machine; the mule, at first small and hand-powered, was in time developed into a machine capable of turning hundreds of spindles and requiring a workshop to accommodate it. Here were the beginnings of cotton-making in large factories. By 1800 the cotton-spinning industry was fully mechanised, with much of the total output coming from new mills which depended on water-power.

Of the localising factors which influenced the rising cotton textile industry, two deserve special notice. One was the supply of power, the other the supply of raw material. Since the rise of the industry was closely associated with the development of powered machines, power supply was important in all but the earliest stages of expansion. Since the power first used was water-power, those areas most favoured were those where many streams, nourished by a rainy climate, descended the steep broken flanks of high ground. With the Southern States of the U.S.A. supplying most of the raw cotton, western ports functioned as inlets for raw material; and of these, Liverpool and Glasgow already had close trading connections with the New World. Thus it was that numbers of cotton-mills were established in their hinterlands, on the western slopes of the Pennines and in the Clyde Valley.[1] In both districts, similar in their general setting and in their external relations, the new industry flourished.

Mechanisation of cotton-weaving was slower than that of spinning. In part this circumstance was due to technical obstacles, for the early power-looms were not very successful. The stimulus for invention was there, for output from the new spinning-machines outpaced the total capacity of hand-weavers to deal with the machine-made yarn, and the wages of weavers rose steeply. But when

---

[1] It is true that in the early days of the new factories the humid atmosphere of these two districts was an advantage, for it helped to prevent the cotton threads from snapping; but there are many parts of the British Isles which are at least as humid, and in any case humidity in the cotton-mills is now artificially controlled. The former and incidental advantage of a humid atmosphere has no significance today.

many returning soldiers took to weaving, after the peace of 1815, wages fell as fast as they had formerly risen. Hand-weaving of cotton lasted well into the 1800s. It was destroyed mainly by the application of steam-power to the manufacture of cotton textiles. The change from hand-weaving to the use of power-looms driven by steam, and the conversion from water-powered to steam-powered spindles, was quite slow, and was not sensibly completed until the middle of the 19th century. It eventually fixed the cotton textile industry firmly on or near a single coalfield—that of Lancashire—for, in the Clyde valley, shipbuilding competed successfully with cotton manufacture for the supply both of capital and of labour.

Mechanisation of Woollen-Manufacture

At first there seemed far less scope for mechanisation in the manufacture of wool than in that of cotton. The woollen industry was well organised, despite its wide dispersal; it was also well balanced. The supply of raw wool was roughly equal to the demand exerted by the markets and by the capacity of domestic spinners and weavers. Nevertheless, the hand-driven jenny was used in some places to spin wool before 1800, and the first half of the 19th century saw hand-working in rapid decline. Two fundamental changes occurred; the concentration of most woollen manufacture on a single coalfield, and a great increase in total output.

The rise in output resulted from the use of powered machinery, which was driven first by water and then by steam. It reflected the rise in the population of the British Isles, the increase of national wealth due to the growth of industry, and the expansion of overseas markets. As with cotton, industrial growth was aided by a rapid increase in the supply of raw material. Sheep-farmers in New Zealand and Australia, taking in enormous areas of land in the early 19th century, swiftly increased the numbers of their sheep and the size of their annual clip of wool. Wool produced by sheep-farmers in the British Isles was at first greatly supplemented by imported wool, and in the second half of the 19th century imports were so great that they competed strongly with the home product.

Although the manufacture of wool was in time converted from domestic craft to an industry carried on in factories, it has never become as highly concentrated as has the manufacture of cotton. In terms of output and of numbers employed, the textile-manufacturing districts of Lancashire acquired some 90 per cent of the cotton industry; most of the remainder is located either in the hosiery-making towns of the Midlands (mainly Nottingham and Leicester) or in Paisley. The West Riding of Yorkshire acquired 75 per cent of the woollen industry, rising thereby to undisputed dominance; but other manufacturing centres persisted in Norfolk, the Cotswolds, the Leicester–Nottingham area, the West Country, and the Tweed valley. Factories in these areas succeeded because they specialised. Norwich retained its worsted-making while East Anglia generally lost its production of woollen cloth; some Cotswolds mills concentrated on blankets, others—like those of the West Country—on serge. Woollen manufacture in Nottingham and Leicester continued in association with the working of cotton, both kinds of textile being needed in the production of hosiery. The factories of the Tweed valley became noted for tweeds; in addition, the home craft persisted in the western highlands of Scotland and in Ireland, where it still survives.

The manner in which the West Riding came to dominate the woollen industry shows very clearly the combined influence of a whole group of circumstances. The area was noted for its woollens long before industry was revolutionised by the application of machine-power. Many monastic sheep-farms were to be found on the Pennines in the late Middle Ages, and after the dissolution of the monasteries in the 16th century graziers continued to produce wool which was used in the domestic craft. The villages set in the incised valleys of the Pennine flank benefited from the soft water flowing copiously off the Millstone Grit, for the treatment of wool demands a great deal of water and for some processes the water needs to be soft. Sheep-farms within reach, and water at hand, enabled the settlements of the West Riding to develop a manufacture of woollen cloth which had reached industrial proportions by 1700. The introduction of power-driven machines increased their advantages. Wool-workers in the West Riding were far better able to employ water-power than were, for example, those in Norfolk and the Cotswolds; in Norfolk all streams are modest in power because the relief is subdued, and in both areas streams are small because catchments are restricted and rainfall is not heavy. When in due course steam-power superseded water-power, some of the West Riding mills could obtain their coal almost on the spot. It was a mere accident of history that wool-working should have been firmly established on or near a coalfield before the days of machine-power; this one wool-working district was so favoured that it became pre-eminent in the industry, inevitably damaging others by its competition.

ROADS AND CANALS

The establishment of textile factories and of textile machinery, and the development of iron manufacture in which coke was used for smelting, were two of the three main achievements of British industry between 1750 and 1830. The third was the improvement of roads and the making of canals. The great railway boom did not take place until the mid-19th century, cheap steel was not produced in bulk until the later half of that century, and the remarkable increase in the output of coal from British fields was also achieved mainly after 1870. It is true that the greatest days of the woollen and cotton industries came as late as the early 20th century, but there is nevertheless a great contrast between Great Britain of 1750 and Great Britain of 1850, at the two ends of a century in which the foundations of her industrial greatness were laid. It was during these hundred years that manufacturing became dominant over agriculture in its output and in its demand for workers. The subsequent spread of railways, rise of the steel industry, and expansion of coal-mining continued trends already begun in the first phase of industrial development.

British roads in the Middle Ages were indescribably bad, and remained so until the 18th century. If any two reasons are to be cited, one must be technical and one political. Until the industrial era, the chief commodities moved about the country were wool and grain. Pack-trains sufficed to carry part of the wool; grain was moved by river wherever possible, and went overland by waggon in quantities which seem small by present-day standards. Until machines were used in overland transport, it was possible to make do with poor roads, especially since the country districts were roughly self-sufficient in foodstuffs and many small towns could be fed by their immediate surroundings. There was no irresistible reason to construct roads which would be serviceable in all weathers, and no sound technique of road-making was developed. Again, until the 18th century the maintenance of roads fell upon individuals or upon small groups. This state of affairs was a legacy of the former feudal structure of society; it made for much neglect, and was adverse to the spread of any satisfactory methods of construction which might have been invented.

Turnpike Roads

During the 18th century, however, private enterprise and the prevailing spirit of improvement led to the formation of many Turnpike Trusts, each charging tolls which were supposed to pay for the maintenance of roads in addition to giving a profit. The first Turnpike Act was passed as early as 1663, but the turnpike system was not widely established until the later part of the 18th century. In spite of its many defects, it made possible the coaching services which connected important towns to one another. In the closing years of the 18th century and in the early 19th the technique of road-building was greatly changed. Macadam is the best-known of those who contributed to the new advances, but several other eminent engineers of the time were also concerned with road-building. The significance of improved roads lay in the improved facilities which they afforded to travellers rather than in their direct service to industry. It is impossible to estimate the effect of the increased and swifter travel upon the spread of ideas and the movement of people in this period of industrial and social ferment, but the new roads certainly helped to break down the barriers of remoteness which cut off many country districts from the towns, and thereby to unify the industrial society which was evolving.

The greatest single scheme of road-building was carried out not for civil but for military purposes, when roads were driven into the Scottish Highlands after the failure of the 1745 rebellion. Elsewhere, however, new construction was applied mainly to existing roads, so that the road network of today represents very largely the pattern of pre-industrial days.

Inland Navigation

When the rising industries demanded supplies of heavy goods in bulk, canals and rivers first met the growing need. Canals with locks were known before 1700—e.g., that which connects the Aire with the Calder—and various piecemeal improvements had been made to navigable rivers. But the great period of canal-making came in the late 18th and early 19th centuries. Canal boats were from the outset carriers of goods, and particularly of coal, which went by water as quickly as it could by road. Industrial sites alongside canals were eagerly sought. Now that some canals are derelict and many are little used, it is difficult to realise their former importance to industry; their decline has been due to several factors, chief of which was competition from railways. Canals in country districts were constructed in a spirit of optimism which has not been justified, while canal transport in industrial areas has suffered from the small dimensions of locks and barges and the variation of these dimensions between one canal and another. Like the Turnpike Acts, the Canal Acts were passed in favour of individuals or of small companies; each canal project was designed with little thought to other schemes, and no satisfactory network of canals arose. Those canals which still carry appreciable traffic serve mainly to link industrial areas with navigable natural water; such are the Bridgewater Canal between Manchester and Runcorn, the Aire and Calder Canal, the Gloucester and Berkeley Canal, and the Manchester Ship Canal which was not completed until 1893. There is today nothing that can be called a working system of canals.[1]

The absence of a general plan for canals must be regretted, but can scarcely be condemned. Planning and control by a central authority was not to be expected either in the 18th or in the 19th centuries. The railways of today suffer from the effects of a layout which evolved in a similar way to that of the canals. Obsolete though many canals may now be, they were highly effective in the first century of industrialisation.

RAILWAYS

Although the construction of railways does not belong to the first phase of industrial change, it may fittingly be discussed at this point. The impetus of canal-making had already run down when the great period of railway-building began; this period, lasting roughly from about 1830 to 1860, came after the industrialisation of the manufacture of iron and textiles, but preceded the further changes of the later 19th century, bridging the gap of transition between the first and second phases of industrial development.

Railways of a kind had been in use for more than a century before the first successful steam locomotive was made. The first ways were constructed of plates, which were in time superseded by rails, just as wood was superseded by iron as a structural material. Heavy goods such as coal and corn were carried in trucks hauled by men or horses. Locomotives began running on private mineral lines in the first years of the 19th century, and in 1825

Stephenson supplied a locomotive to the first *public* railway to use one. This was, as is generally known, the Stockton and Darlington line. The Liverpool and Manchester railway, opened in 1830, had immediate success with passenger trains drawn by steam locomotives. By 1840 there were some 3,000 km of railways in the British Isles, and by 1860 over 16,000 km (10,000 mi.). Further expansion was to come, but a country-wide network already existed by 1860. Canals and roads could not compete with railways either in capacity or in speed; passenger travel soon became a leading interest of the railway companies, and the new railways influenced the location of industry and the spread of urban settlement as strongly as canals had formerly influenced the location of factories.

INLAND TRANSPORT AND COMMUNICATIONS IN IRELAND

It may seem surprising that Ireland shared in the movements to improve roads and construct canals and railways, in view of the modest development of industry in the island as a whole. But many of the projects executed in Great Britain were promoted and financed by wealthy landowners, and members of this class were numerous in Ireland in the late 18th and early 19th centuries. So many short roads were made in Ireland during the late 1700s that the best settled and least boggy districts came to be remarkably well served. In Ireland, as in southern England, it was hoped that canals would attract industry and simulate trade, but few enjoyed any marked success. The Grand Canal, which connects Dublin with the Shannon and the Barrow and was completed in 1804, was the most effective, but even its traffic has now fallen below 100,000 tons of goods a year and is still declining. The most optimistic and the least successful scheme of all was that for a canal between Loughs Mask and Corrib, where the canal was made through Carboniferous Limestone and failed to hold water. The Newry Canal was busy at one time, but is little used now that the export trade of Northern Ireland goes mainly through Belfast. Total traffic on the canals of Northern Ireland does not now exceed 20,000 tons of cargo a year; building materials are prominent among the goods carried.

Railway-building in Ireland began with the linking of Dún Laoghaire (Kingstown) to Dublin in 1834—very shortly after the opening of the first passenger line in England. A complete network, with foci in Dublin and Belfast, was completed by

---

[1] See, however, Chap. 9.

1863. Thus Ireland kept pace with Great Britain in the construction of railways, although it never developed such mazes of lines as are to be found in the industrial regions of England, Wales, and Scotland. The hope that the building of railways would be followed by the general rise of industry was false, for, like the canals before them, the railways could not compensate for the lack of industrial minerals.

GREAT BRITAIN IN 1850

Great Britain by 1850 had been transfigured by the growth of industry, and was being further changed by the rapid spread of railways. It dominated the world's export trade in industrial goods. Peace and prosperity at home were reflected in power abroad—for instance in the increase in the number and size of colonies, which provided raw materials and bought manufactures. Those larger and longer-established colonies which later became the first Dominions had increasing populations and carried on ever-growing trade with the homeland.

The distribution of industry and population as we now see them had been broadly sketched, and many of the details of the picture had already been filled in. Attention could be turned to political and social problems. Although such problems are outside the scope of this book, it ought to be observed that during the 19th century those changes were made, or at least begun, which have produced the present political and social structure of the U.K. and of the Irish Republic. The reformers of the 19th century could tackle their high tasks without —as it seemed—much fear of distraction from abroad.

Chapter 7

Coal and Industrial Power

In the preceding discussion of the rapid expansion of industry in the British Isles, stress has been laid on the manufacture of iron, wool, and cotton, rather than on the use of coal for raising steam or in making industrial coke. It is true that, without the aid of coal, industrialisation could not have gone so far, or so fast, as it did go between the mid-18th and mid-19th centuries. It is also true that coal had been worked for many centuries before the 18th. The expansion of the coal-mining industry and of the coal export trade nevertheless occurred mainly in the second half of the 19th century and in the early part of the 20th. It was associated not so much with the establishment of the iron industry as with the rise of steel-making and with the growth of overseas trade.

RISE AND FALL OF THE COAL-EXPORT TRADE

All the coalfields of Great Britain, with the exception of the concealed Kentish field, were being exploited by the late 1500s. Annual output then ran at about 200,000 tons. The Northumberland and Durham field led the list of producers, supplying the 10,000 tons or more which were shipped to London each year as well as sending coal to nearby ports of Europe. A hundred years later—i.e., at about the end of the 17th century—the total output had reached the considerable figure of 3 million tons, of which $1\frac{1}{4}$ million were raised in Northumberland and Durham. A hundred years later still, in the middle of the industrial revolution, the total was more than 10 million tons. The northeastern field was still the greatest single producer, but mining in the Yorkshire, Derby, and Notts. field, in the Black Country, and along the Welsh Border had already been stimulated by newly-founded industries. Demand and output

had quintupled by 1850. Total production ran at about 50 million tons a year; by 1870 it exceeded 100 million (Fig. 7:1).

Up to this time, the demand for coal came mainly from consumers within the country. The rise in production and in sales is therefore a measure of the increase in population and of the expansion of home industry. In the 1870s another factor began to operate—a rapid increase in the demand for coal from abroad. In the earlier part of the 19th century many European countries were politically unsettled—Germany and Italy, for instance, had not yet emerged as nations—and Great Britain had in any case gained a long lead in the development of heavy industry. When European politics became more stable, and industrialisation on the mainland could go forward, British coal found a ready market. An increase in coal exports began suddenly in about 1875 and continued right up to 1913, raising the tonnage annually exported from about 12 million tons to nearly 100. At one time British coalfields supplied no less than 90 per cent of the world's seaborne coal, and over half the coal sent across all national boundaries, whether by sea or by land. One-third of the country's output went for export in 1913.

This spectacular rise in the coal export trade was associated with—and assisted by—an equally impressive fall in the rates charged on seaborne freight. During the period in question these were reduced by two-thirds. The reduction was made possible in part by the use of steel ships. Not only were these lighter than iron ships of comparable capacity, and therefore cheaper to operate, size for size, but the general increase in the size of new ships also meant a fall in operating costs per ton of cargo. Cheap shipment of coal over long distances favoured, and was in turn favoured by, the replacement of sail by steam, the substitution of iron by steel, and the expansion of world trade as a whole.

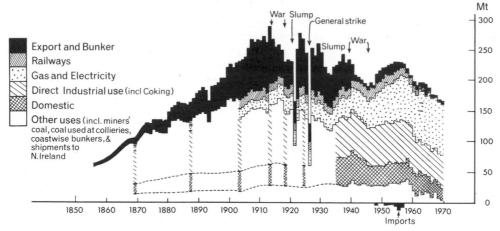

FIG. 7:1. Great Britain: output and disposal of coal, from the mid-19th century onwards

In 1913 it was predicted that by 1951 the population of the British Isles would have risen to 57 millions, and that the domestic consumption of coal would be 265 million tons a year. The predicted population is close to the census total of 54 millions, while the difference between the predicted consumption of coal, and the actual consumption of 220 million tons, is not great: it is readily explicable by improvements in coal-burning equipment, by industrial growth which proved slower than expected, and by competition from oil. But a third prediction, that by 1951 coal exports would be 270 million tons a year, and total output 500 million tons, was grossly falsified by events. The coal export trade had vanished, without prospect of reappearance. In consequence, output at 220 million tons a year was less than half the total forecast. It is still falling.

Political and economic events of World War I, of the inter-war period, of World War II, and of the post-war years have combined to produce a grave depression of the coal-export trade. Not only has this depression damaged the coal-mining industry —it has also had adverse effects on overseas trade generally. The low freight rates made possible by the coal trade were of the greatest help to British exporters, especially in the days when British shipping dominated seaborne commerce. Even during the later part of the inter-war period of 1919–39, when coal exports were but 45 to 50 million tons a year, coal provided 10 per cent of all exports by value and 80 per cent by bulk. As in the prosperous years before 1914, the carriage of a bulky export kept a large volume of shipping at sea and maintained the freight-charges on imports at a low level. Since World War II, coal exports have

amounted, at best, to 15 or 16 million tons a year. In some single years consumption has exceeded production, and the deficiency has had to be met partly by drawing on stocks and partly by importing. Exports today, about 5 million tons a year, are half those of a century ago, and total annual production is about 90 million tons below the peak reached before World War I. The existing 1,500 collieries are less than half the 1900 total of more than 3,000, and the number of men employed in coal-mining has sunk back to less than $\frac{1}{2}$ million, after exceeding 1 million as late as 1925. The decline in the number of collieries is no bad thing, in so far as it reflects the closing of old and small pits; nor is the decline in the industry's labour force to be regretted, in so far as it reflects the increasing use of machines in place of muscles. But the fall in total output cannot be gainsaid; neither can the adverse effect of diminished coal export upon seaborne trade in general. In the present economic circumstances of Great Britain, with external trade more vital than at any other time in the nation's history, the influence of the loss of coal exports upon freight rates is exceptionally serious.

More than four-fifths of the coal exported from Great Britain in 1913 went to ports on the Atlantic coast of Europe, on the Baltic, or on the Mediterranean. There was in addition an appreciable traffic with South American countries, and a demand from coaling stations on the world's great shipping lanes. France, Italy, Germany, Russia, Sweden, the Argentine, Denmark, Egypt, Spain, and Norway were the chief customers, in that order, in 1913, buying between them 57 million tons of British coal in the year. By 1931 their purchases had fallen to $27\frac{1}{2}$ million tons in the year, and by 1955 to little more than 4 million. The loss of their custom accounts for much of the total loss of exports, which in turn is equivalent to the fall in production from 1913 to the present day.

World War I and the Inter-War Period

The first heavy blow to the coal export trade was dealt by World War I. Shipping during that war was needed for other purposes than those of normal trade, and exports had to run the submarine blockade. A new pattern of European economy emerged when the war ended. French mines which had been wrecked by the enemy were re-equipped with up-to-date machinery. In Italy industry grew apace, but with the aid of hydro-electric power developed in the Alps rather than that of imported coal. Exports to Germany were reduced by the competition of German lignite, which not only provided industrial power but also freed German bituminous coal for foreign markets; both in France and in Italy German coal competed successfully with the British product. In Sweden, Norway, Spain, and Egypt, as in Italy, the development of H.E.P. reduced the demand for coal. The Argentine, too, came to rely more and more on hydro-electricity for industrial power; but in that country in particular there was another and still more formidable competitor—oil. During the inter-war period coal was coming into increasing competition throughout the whole world with water-power, oil, and natural gas. Coal no longer possessed its former near-monopoly in the supply of power to industry. Whereas for many years up to 1913 the world consumption of coal had increased by about 4 per cent a year, in the inter-war period the rate was but 0·3 per cent—less than a tenth as great. Great Britain, by far the principal coal-exporting country, was by far the worst hit. In addition to the adversities of falling demand, the British coal export trade with Europe had to bear the effects of the peace treaties. The reparations imposed by these treaties included the delivery of large amounts of coal, and the new boundaries of Poland included rich fields which enabled that country to become a large exporter.

The inter-war period was one of appalling fluctuations in the coal export trade and in the coal-mining industry in general. Nothing like the 1913 level of production and export had been regained before the slump of 1921. In the years immediately after 1921 exports did indeed rise in a remarkable fashion, but the rise was in the main due to the French occupation of the Ruhr coalfield from 1923 to 1925. In 1926, figures of production and of export plunged because of the general strike; the subsequent rise reflects, in part, the fulfilling of arrears of orders. The early 1930s, with their prolonged industrial depression throughout the western world, caused the annual output of coal in Great Britain to fall towards the level of 200 million tons. Neither output nor export were able to complete their slow recovery before World War II broke out in 1939, severely reducing output and almost stopping exports altogether.

World War II and the Post-war Period

Conditions in the post-war period differ in several important ways from those of earlier times. The expansion of industrial production for purposes of war pushed up the nation's consumption of coal during World War I. In the inter-war period, the general tendency was for home consumption to decline until the mid-1930s, as can readily be seen from Fig. 7:1. The rise in consumption which marks recovery from the Great Slump was sharply increased in the early part of World War II, but was followed by another decline as factories were damaged by bombing and as men were drafted into the armed forces. In the post-war period the rise in consumption has almost kept pace with the rise in total output—another reason for the depressed state of the export trade. Very little coal is now available for export; consumption has reached the 1913 level and is still rising.

CHANGES IN CONSUMPTION OF COAL

Over the years, there have been significant changes in the demands made by different classes of consumer. Up to 1913, industry was taking half the coal consumed within the U.K. The years since the Great Slump have witnessed a marked increase in the supply of gas and electricity—especially of the latter—until generating stations buy more coal today than do industrial concerns. They take some 50 per cent of all coal used in the country. In part the change merely reflects the replacement of steam-power in industry and coal fires in the home by power from the mains, but, even so, it indicates a significant alteration both in factory practice and in the habits of living. It is associated with the spread of light industry and the widening use of electrical equipment. The most rapid increase in the supply of electricity has been to homes and farms. In the years 1920–70, their share in the total consumption of electricity rose from 8 to 40 per cent; that of shops and offices rose slightly, from

11 to 15 per cent; and that of industry fell from 69 to 42 per cent. This does not mean that the actual consumption of power by industry declined —it increased nearly thirty times; but consumption by other users rose faster still. The installed capacity of generating plant increased by 19 times and the consumption per head of population by 40 times. Both of these increases were associated with the establishment of the national electricity grid and the extension of supply lines into rural areas.

Of the coal taken directly by industrial users, some 25 million tons a year—the largest single share—are taken by coke oven plants. Of the coke produced, some 12 million tons a year goes for use in blast-furnaces, another $2\frac{1}{2}$ million tons is taken by other metal and engineering works, and more than a million tons by the chemical industry. Direct industrial use is about steady, despite efforts by the metallurgical, chemical, and engineering industries to expand; demand by generating plants is also roughly constant, and it seems unlikely that coal production in the future will much exceed 150M tons a year.

RESERVES AND PROSPECTS

Ninety per cent of the coal got in British coalfields is worked on the advancing longwall system, in which a long working face is driven into the seam. In all but a few pits the longwall is advancing: that is, the working face was first opened near the bottom of the shaft, and as the coal is taken out moves further and further from the pit-bottom. Hence the longer a seam is worked, the greater becomes the distance from the shaft to the face, the more time is lost, and the greater the costs of haulage underground—costs of working inevitably increase with the age of the pit. Rising costs can be held in check by mechanisation. The percentage of coal mechanically cut rose from 1·6 in 1900 to 61·5 in 1939 and 84·4 in 1954, and no less than 90 per cent is now mechanically conveyed underground. But in the 1930s, despite a great deal of mechanisation already effected, the average profit on coal was only 3p a ton, and the mine equipment was largely obsolete.

Reserves of coal in the U.K. are variously estimated at about 200,000 million tons. At the present rate of extraction this is enough for about a thousand years, but the estimated figure includes seams as deep as 1,200 m. and as thin as 30 cm. It is possible that deep and thin seams may be exploited by underground gasification, although increasing use of natural gas makes this unlikely.

Meantime, a realistic estimate of the economic life of the coalfields is two centuries at most. Furthermore, against the existence of reserves has to be set the fact that the seams first worked were the best and most accessible. As time goes on, the proportion of coal coming from thick seams, where working is easy and cheap, tends to decline. Nearly half the coal raised at present time is got from seams between 0·5 and 1·5 m. thick—i.e., less than the most convenient and most economical thickness. It is not surprising that on all coalfields there are abandoned collieries. Every depression in the industry has left its records in forsaken pits. The National Coal Board has been closing numbers of uneconomic pits in the post-war years, the latest list of closures being announced in 1967. Many of the abandoned collieries stand on or near outcrops, where initial working was easiest but reserves were least. The newest, largest, most successful collieries work hidden reserves. With coal, as with many other branches of industry, production has tended to concentrate itself in a limited number of undertakings, each individually of a large size (Plate 14). Four-fifths of the total output came from a quarter of the collieries as early as 1924, and 60 per cent of the output of today is got in mines with between 750 and 2,000 wage-earners on their books.

Trends in Single Coalfields

Individual coalfields have been variously affected. Fig. 7:2 makes a comparison for each field of the outputs of 1870, 1913, 1927–28, and 1969—years which are fairly representative of the end of the industrial revolution, of the peak of success of the coal industry and its export trade, of the inter-war period, and of the present time. The main exporting fields of Northumberland and Durham, South Wales, and Scotland naturally suffered most from the decline in coal exports. They and the Lancashire field show an absolute decline in output from 1913 onwards: their peaks of production were in fact reached in that year. Not all the decline can be referred to the fall in exports—part is also due to increased difficulties and costs of working. By contrast, the fields of Yorkshire, Derby and Notts., of Staffordshire, and the Midlands generally withstood reasonably well the afflictions of the inter-war period, and are now producing more than they did in 1913; in consequence, each accounts for an increased fraction of the national output.

South Wales and the Northumberland and Durham fields were the worst hit by the loss of exports. The former shipped 70 per cent of its production by ocean-going or coasting vessels in 1913, but less than 50 per cent in the inter-war period. Shipments from the Northumberland and Durham field were maintained at the 1913 level of two-thirds of output, but only because a decline in exports abroad was compensated by a rise in coastal traffic; in any case, the industry in that field suffered very severely in times of industrial depression. The Scottish fields, exporting either to Northern Ireland or to Europe, were also involved in the decline of exports. They were moreover affected, and continue to be affected, by the rise in costs of working which results from partial ex-

away beneath younger rocks and extend at workable depths in the concealed coalfield for some distance east of the exposed field. The conditions here contrast strongly with those in Scotland and in South Wales, where there are no hidden reserves, and also with those in Lancashire, where the hidden seams plunge sharply downwards and are much broken by faults. The Midland fields, which are grouped together in Fig. 7:2, display strong contrasts among themselves. As a group they produce more coal than in 1913, although less than in 1927–29, and have retained their full share in national production. Some individual fields within

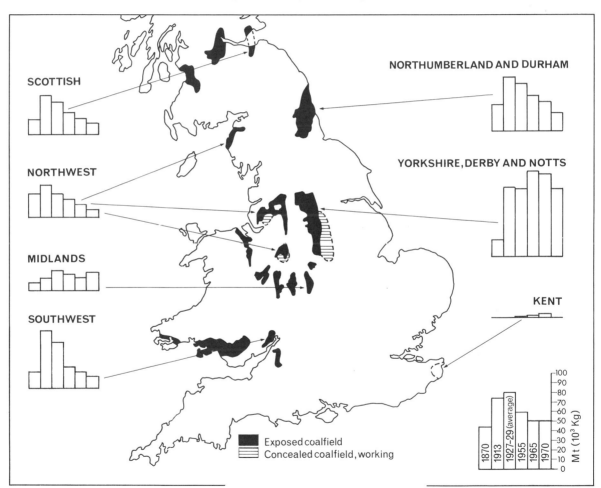

Fig. 7:2. Location and output of coalfields in Great Britain

haustion of their best seams and from the increasing length of travel underground. The Yorkshire, Derby, and Notts. field was able to maintain its output during the inter-war period and to increase it after 1945, chiefly because its seams dip gently

the group produce very little nowadays—the Black Country coal, for instance, is almost worked out—but output from the North Staffs., Cannock Chase, Leicestershire, and Warwickshire field tends to increase.

PLATE 11. Kinneil Colliery, near Bo'ness, West Lothian. This modern, fully electrified colliery can produce 3,000 tons of coal a day, mainly from seams under the sea.

OIL AND NATURAL GAS

Oil has now almost replaced coal as the source of power for railway locomotives: diesel traction is increasingly the rule. Electrification of some lines does not necessarily increase the demand for coal, since generating stations can be powered by water (in some areas), by oil, or by natural gas. As will be stated below, some generating stations can use either coal or oil; and the shift to oil in this connection would have been more rapid than it has been in fact, had not use of coal been kept up for political reasons—the political need to check falling employment on the coalfields. This circumstance is precisely the reverse of what was intended or expected: the generating stations equipped to burn oil were planned at a time when a coal shortage seemed likely. In later years, oil refining capacity increased signally during the 1960s, with major refining concentrations appearing on the Thames estuary—expected to account for about a quarter of total national capacity—on Southampton Water, in South Wales, on Merseyside, on Morecambe Bay, and on Teesside, Humberside, and the Firth of Forth (see bibliography: Luckas). Problems for some importing inlets are foreseeable, connected with the swift increase in the size of the most economical tankers.

After trial shipments had been made in the late 1950s, imports of the natural gas methane began. For long-distance transport, as for instance from the Saharan fields which were the first suppliers, the gas is converted to the liquid state. The receiving terminal at Canvey Island on the Thames estuary distributes gas by pipeline (Fig. 7:5), while gas pipeline systems of associated kinds are also extending steadily. In 1959, a very large reserve of natural gas was located in the Groningen province of the Netherlands. During the mid-1960s, prospecting initially for oil in the North Sea basin proved additional and major gas supplies (see bibliography: Kent). Gas lines run from the offshore fields to the Humber, and therefrom to the West Riding and Southeast Lancashire, and from Canvey Island to the Midlands and the industrial north. The pipeline net promises to become an analogue to the electricity grid. Meantime, additional gas/oil exploration is taking place in the Irish Sea basin.

As with oil, so with natural gas—competition against coal has been kept down by political means for political reasons. On the technical side the main problem with natural gas is that of storage, which is required to supplement direct supply at times of peak demand. The practicable solution is to make use of natural storage reservoirs underground, where permeable rocks can be injected with gas, and where water is present to act as a seal. The most promising of the necessary dome structures, with impermeable covers, occur below ground in the Lower Greensand, between Dorset and the Wash.

ELECTRICITY

The increase in the generation and consumption of electricity during the inter-war period was greatly helped by the establishment of the national electricity grid. The linking of power stations into a single system made it possible to reduce working costs, for power could be transferred from one area to another according to variations in local demand. In addition, the large power stations built during this period were more efficient than the smaller, older stations which they replaced. The rapid extension of supply-lines not only widened the market for power, but also made possible a dispersion of light industry. The national grid, working at 132,000 volts, already promised to become inadequate before World War II. To it has been added the supergrid, transferring baseload current in bulk, at 400,000 volts, from stations on the Trent to southern England and South Lancs., and from the Aire and Calder stations into industrial Lancashire generally. A cross-channel cable, for exchange of electricity between England and France, was completed in 1961.

The cost of electricity has been kept remarkably low in the post-war period by means of continued improvements in the efficiency of generating plant. In comparison with working costs, the cost of coal has risen very high indeed, so that location with respect to sources of fuel is an important factor in the siting of power-stations. Water transport of fuel is cheaper than transport by rail over any considerable distance, but it is also cheaper to transmit power than to haul coal by rail at distances over 80 km or so. The power stations on the Trent, Aire and Calder lack the advantage of water routes, but obtain coal from near-by fields where the costs of mining are low. In other parts of the country the main localising factor is access to tidewater, as for instance in the case of the station at Marchwood on Southampton Water which is equipped to burn oil as well as coal.

The huge thermal stations so prominent in the landscape are most carefully sited. The *situation* of new plant—its location in a particular area—depends primarily on the demand for power, and is primarily determined by the relative costs of transmission and of haulage of fuel; but *sites* of individual stations are so chosen as to provide

reasonably level ground which can withstand heavy loads, access by road and rail during construction, facilities for bulk delivery of fuel, and ample water—either for condensing, or, if cooling towers are used, for compensating for evaporation. Thus the factors governing situation are economic, while siting is a problem of civil engineering (cf. Plate 60).

Hydro-Electric Power

A striking increase in the generation of hydro-electricity has occurred in the Scottish Highlands during the post-war period (cf. Plate 39). Construction of dams and generating stations is going on so quickly that it is impossible to give a general review of progress. A contrast can be drawn, however, with conditions in 1939. In that year, H.E.P. was developed only at Foyers, Kinlochleven, and Lochaber, where the plants are owned by aluminium smelters, and at Rannoch, Tummel, and Loch Luichart, where the stations

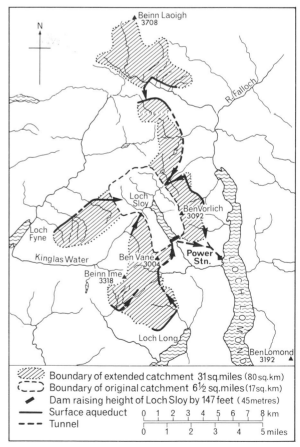

FIG. 7:3. The Loch Sloy H.E.P. Scheme, Scottish Highlands

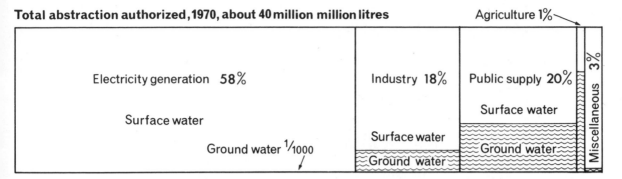

FIG. 7:4. Comparative water use, Great Britain

belonged to electricity supply companies. The North of Scotland Hydro-Electricity Board today operates more than 50 H.E.P. stations. Some 20 per cent of the potential has now been developed, and another 20 per cent is under construction and survey.

It is very doubtful if H.E.P. in the Scottish Highlands would have been so greatly developed if it had not been made a matter of national concern, for the market is very scattered. From the beginning, however, the policy has been to supply power to farms and crofts as well as to make it available to industry, and well over half the 20,000 farms and 20,000 crofts in the area are already connected to the mains. It is highly likely that the development of H.E.P. in the Highlands will bring about an increase in agricultural production, and possible that it will check the chronic loss of rural population (Chap. 14). Industries working with electrical power have been established, half of them however in Aberdeen, Dundee, and Perth; they are concerned mainly with the production of electrical goods.

The great advantage of the Highlands in the development of H.E.P. is their heavy rainfall, which in some catchments averages well over 2,500 mm. a year. Ribbon lakes are selected as reservoirs, having their levels raised by dams. Since the natural catchments are often small, tunnels and aqueducts are used to increase the drainage to the reservoirs (Fig. 7:3). In discussions of the location of H.E.P. stations, much is often made of the suitability of sites for building. To some extent this topic is irrelevant, for every site poses its own engineering problems. A head of water is usually secured in the Highlands by siting the stations at a lower altitude than the reservoirs, leading in the water if necessary by long pipelines or tunnels.

The speed of the rivers themselves also has nothing to do with the siting of stations, since the water is drawn from reservoirs: in any case, the banks of the short swift rivers which are extremely numerous in the Highlands are eminently *unsuitable* as sites for H.E.P. stations, since short rivers are typically irregular in régime.[1] By contrast, the question of the supply of capital for construction is directly relevant. It alone is enough to account for the failure to develop all but a little of the potential H.E.P. of the Highlands until recent years.

Although much of the hydro-electricity generated in the Scottish Highlands is consumed in the Electricity's Board's area, this area includes a number of towns on the southeastern and southern flanks of the Highland region. Some electricity is transferred across the area boundary to the power lines serving the factories of Central Scotland. As more H.E.P. is developed such transfer is certain to increase, so that H.E.P. will join with nuclear power in moderating the increase in the demand for coal made by thermal-electric stations. Meantime, electricity generation takes well over half the water extracted from available sources, almost all of it surface water (Fig. 7:4).

Nuclear Power

When sites are chosen for nuclear power stations, a different set of factors comes into play. The building-sites demand much the same qualities as those for thermal stations, but problems of the

---

[1] It is hard to account for the widespread impression that short swift rivers are advantageous in the development of H.E.P. The reverse is true, as is well shown by the Kitimat scheme in British Columbia, where water is brought through a mountain range because the local short swift rivers are of no use.

PLATE 12. Berkeley Nuclear Power Station—an example of large-scale modern works of civil engineering.

transport of bulky fuels do not arise. The policy has been adopted of locating nuclear power stations as far as possible from built-up areas (Fig. 7:5, Plate 12).

FIG. 7:5. Nuclear power stations: pipelines (diagrammatic)

Ten such stations had come into operation by 1965. Electricity from the Calder Hall station was switched into the national grid in 1956; Chapelcross, Dumfriesshire, followed in 1959. Commercial stations began full operation in 1962. The plant at Dounreay on the north coast of Scotland is a breeder reactor producing fuel. By 1968, a total output capacity of 5,000 megawatts was planned for nuclear stations, at a cost comparable with that of coal-fired plant, saving 18 million tons of coal a year, and generating at least as cheaply as the best coal-fired stations by the mid-1970s.[1]

ENERGY CONSUMPTION IN GENERAL

The proportionate contribution of coal to energy production in the United Kingdom declined at an accelerating rate during the 1960s. Already in about 1960, petroleum accounted for about one-quarter (Fig. 7:6), while the contribution of coal passed below 50 per cent in the late 1960s. Nuclear power, hydro-electricity, and natural gas combined accounted for about 10 per cent by 1970, displaying perhaps the beginning of a sharply-increasing trend.

[1] See also bibliography, at P. R. Mounfield.

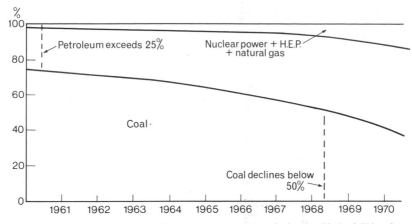

FIG. 7:6. Proportionate contribution to power supply in the United Kingdom

Industrial Power in Ireland

Ireland as a whole is very differently placed from the U.K. with regard to supplies of industrial power. The geological map of Ireland shows extensive outcrops of Coal Measures, but the coal reserves are actually very small and the already almost-negligible output is still declining. The industries of Belfast and the neighbouring much smaller towns rely on thermal power raised by imported coal (mainly from the Ayrshire field). A nuclear power station in Northern Ireland is projected for the 1970s. The Irish Republic, with a dominantly agricultural population, makes a rather small demand for power per head of population, but demand is growing as industrialisation gets under way. The leading single station is the thermal installation at Ringsend (Dublin), generating about one-third of the electricity produced in the Republic, but the Ardnacrusha hydro-station, responsible for about 9 per cent of national electric power output, still stands as a fine example of what can be done where runoff is copious and dependable, and where total downstream gradient is high although no natural waterfall exists. The second ranking power station in the Republic is at Cork; like the Ringsend plant, it is thermal, with about 13 per cent of national power output. In summary, the hydro plants generate some 19 per cent of the country's electricity, thermal plants about 54 per cent, and peat-fired plants about 27 per cent. The apparent success of the peat-fired plants is somewhat qualified by the fact that the governmental peat-working operations work at a persistent deficit. Nevertheless, the scattered location of the generating plants as a group, plus the short transmission distances and the governmental policy of rural electrification, suggest that industrialisation in the Republic is likely to assume the form illustrated by southern Sweden rather than by England.

Chapter 8

The Age of Steel

STEEL is an iron–carbon alloy containing not more than 1·7 per cent of carbon. Mild steel, which is used in very large quantities at the present day, contains from 0·15 to 0·25 per cent of carbon. The main problem of steel-making is one of controlling the carbon content of molten iron.

Various processes of steel-making were known in pre-industrial days. For instance, the material known as *wootz* was being produced in India two thousand years ago. Wootz was made by melting wrought iron in a crucible with carbonaceous matter, and by repeatedly forging the small ingot. The steel thus produced would take a fine cutting edge, and was used for making the famous swords of Damascus and Toledo. It was not until the early 17th century that European inventors developed processes almost identical with those of the Indian smelters, and not until the 18th century that the steel industry, as now understood, was founded.

The first advance was made by the Sheffield clockmaker, Huntsman, who in 1740 produced a crucible which could withstand the very high temperature needed to melt steel. He was able, therefore, to produce homogeneous ingots which could be forged. Several factors, however, combined to prevent the immediate rise of a large steel-making industry. For some time the new technical knowledge was confined to a small group of men in Huntsman's factory. Even when it escaped, and when Cort's invention of the rolling-mill in 1783 enabled large ingots to be treated, steel remained far more expensive than iron. Steel was available to the engineers of the industrial revolution only in limited quantities and at a high price.

PROCESSES OF PRODUCTION IN BULK

It was not until a century after Huntsman that the change came. In 1856 Bessemer perfected his converter, in which carbon was removed from molten iron by the passage of a forced blast of air; the carbon combined with the oxygen of the air and was blown out in the waste gases. So successful was the converter that Bessemer produced steel at £12 a ton, compared with the £60 a ton charged for crucible steel. Other notable discoveries followed in rapid succession. In 1862 Siemens invented the open-hearth process, in which a mixture of pre-heated gas and pre-heated air supplies heat for smelting. The open-hearth furnace takes longer to change iron to steel than does the Bessemer converter, but, on the other hand, permits easy control of the quality of the crude steel and the use of scrap as well as of pig-iron.

Both the Bessemer converter and the open-hearth furnace were originally designed to treat iron smelted from high-grade ores. The impurities to be removed included carbon, silicon, and manganese. Furnace linings were chosen accordingly: they belonged to the acid type. Low-grade ores yield iron which contains the additional impurities of sulphur and phosphorus, which attack the linings of acid furnaces. Before iron from these ores could be used in steel-making, basic furnace-linings had to be perfected. The Gilchrist-Thomas process of smelting was developed by 1878; it is also known as the basic Bessemer process, since it involves the lining of the Bessemer converter with basic material. In Europe it was rapidly and widely adopted; but in Britain open-hearth furnaces were preferred, partly perhaps because of the many difficulties which Bessemer was known to have met in developing his converter. The change in this country, when it came, was from the acid open-hearth furnaces which used hematite iron to basic open-hearth furnaces capable of taking iron made from the low-grade Jurassic ores.

COMPETITION BETWEEN IRON AND STEEL

World output of steel was to rise from $\frac{1}{3}$ m. tons in 1866 to 275 m. a year at the present time. The new steel industry, however, needed time to expand, and also had to overcome the established interests of ironmasters. For some time iron and steel competed seriously in the British Isles.

The early civil engineers achieved much with iron. Four of the best-known bridges in Britain are iron-built—Darby's structure at Ironbridge, which spanned the Severn in 1780, the Menai Suspension Bridge built by Telford in 1826, Stephenson's tubular bridge (also across the Menai Strait) finished in 1850, and the Newcastle high-level railway bridge, erected by Robert Stephenson in 1846–50. The first great bridge of steel, the Forth Bridge, was not built until the latter years of the 19th century, being finished in 1890.

Railway engineers did much to encourage the iron-making industry from the 1830s onwards. When the Bessemer process of steel-making was invented, British iron-works were producing some three-quarters of a million tons of iron rails a year—a figure which reflects not so much the extension of the railway network as the rapid wear of the rails themselves. On some lines the iron rails had to be replaced every four months. Tests begun at Crewe and Chalk Farm in 1861 showed that rails rolled from Bessemer steel lasted more than twenty times as long as iron rails, and steel was rapidly substituted for iron on railway track throughout the country.

At about the same time shipbuilders increased their demands for iron, for in shipbuilding the change from the traditional wood to the new industrial metals was gradual. After slow beginnings, the building of iron ships increased rapidly in the mid-19th century. There was still time for the shipbuilding industry to be transformed by the use of iron, not only because the Bessemer process had yet to be invented, but also because the first ships' plates made from steel were not consistent in quality. Cheap, ductile, reliable steel plates were not produced until 1870, the Admiralty did not begin using steel for warships until 1875, and the use of steel in building merchant ships did not become general until 1877. For twenty years, therefore, the use of iron predominated in the shipbuilding industry; but when the change to steel came, it came rapidly. Ten years proved that steel was reliable and that steel ships could be lighter and stronger than those of iron. By 1890 nine out of every ten ships classed at Lloyd's were made of steel.

THE MODERN STEEL INDUSTRY: CHANGING STRUCTURE

During the period 1870–90, iron-working was largely absorbed into the growing industry of steel manufacture. The production of iron was reduced mainly to a preliminary process. Four-fifths of the pig-iron produced in the British Isles today goes for conversion into steel, and the end-products of the combined iron and steel industry are mainly steel goods. The industry has continued to expand since the late years of the 19th century, undergoing profound internal changes. Not only has its output increased and its fundamental working technique improved—it has overcome, by the development of special processes, some of the competition offered by aluminium and aluminium alloys, in addition to providing a whole range of alloys of steel.

Basic furnaces were not providing much more than half the total output of crude steel as late as 1920s; among the basic furnaces, open-hearth plants predominated greatly over basic Bessemer converters. Acid open-hearth furnaces and acid Bessemer converters, designed to deal with pig made from high-grade ores, were still producing nearly half the total of crude steel despite the ultimate dependence of many of them upon imported ore. By the 1960s, the basic processes had become dominant, accounting for nearly three-quarters of total production by the end of the decade (Fig. 8:1). The output of acid furnaces had become almost negligible; electric furnaces, on the other hand, were claiming an increasing share of the total. These various trends have involved a wholesale reorganisation of the steel industry, related partly to the increased demand for alloy steels and in part to the increased use of domestic iron ore of low grade. Critics of the industry maintain that the reorganisation has not yet gone anywhere like far enough, and that further changes, equally drastic or further-reaching still, are required.

Alloy Steels

Alloy steels are produced in smaller quantities than mild steel and other carbon steels (see Appendix 2), but their share in the total output remains steady. They are of great importance in modern industry because of their distinctive properties—hardness, resistance to corrosion, and high tensile strength. Commercial production of alloy steel began in 1883, when Hadfield first produced manganese steel. The same inventor made silicon steel, which is used both in machine

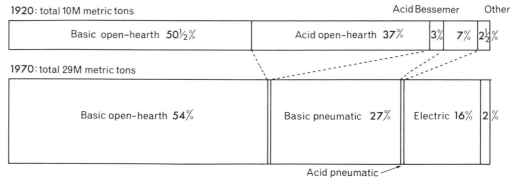

FIG. 8:1. Great Britain: production of crude steel, by percentage and quality

tools for cutting and in electrical engineering, for which its magnetic properties make it especially suitable. Stainless steel, a chrome-steel alloy, was developed by 1913, and in later years alloys of steel with nickel, chromium, and vanadium came into widespread use. Research into the character and properties of alloy steels was to some extent forced on the steel industry by the growing use made of the light metal aluminium, but was also greatly encouraged by the needs of manufacturers of machine tools and of engines. Both steam-engines and internal combustion engines have been improved with the aid of alloy steels. In the early 1900s the standard steam boiler had to withstand pressures of some 125 N/cm.² at 275°C. (180 lb./sq. in. at 500°F.), whereas the modern boiler is designed for 625 N/cm.² at 500°C. (900 lb./sq. in. at 900°F.). Even more rigorous demands are made in jet engines and gas turbines, with complex steel alloys meeting stresses in excess of 25,000 N/cm.² (15 tons/sq. in.) at temperatures higher than 550°C. (1,000°F.).

One result of the demand for alloy steels has been the increased use of electric furnaces, which permit fine control of the quality of the product. At the present day rather more than half the alloy steel made in Britain comes from electric furnaces, the remainder being made by the open-hearth process. Since the 1920s, electric smelting has greatly expanded its relative importance in the steel industry.

Imported Ores

As the steel industry expanded, the failing supplies of high-grade domestic ore could no longer keep pace with the demands for pig-iron suitable for use in steel furnaces of the acid type. Home production was greatly supplemented, and later greatly surpassed, by imports. Domestic out-put of high-grade ore was 2½ million tons in 1913, against the imports of more than 7 million tons which came chiefly from Spain, Spanish North Africa, and French North Africa. Although imports were down to 6½ million tons in 1920, home output had fallen still more greatly—to 1½ million tons. It continued to decline during the inter-war period, whereas imports, recovering from the low levels reached in the Great Slump, ran at some 5 million tons a year just before World War II and have broken all previous records in the post-war period (Fig. 8:2).

Sweden meanwhile has emerged as the chief supplier (Fig. 8:3), followed in order by North Africa, Canada, West Africa, and South America. These suppliers account for nearly 90 per cent of total imports, Sweden alone sending nearly one-third. The U.S.S.R. is a recent addition to the list.

Imported ores are generally far richer than those produced domestically. Home ores average less than 30 per cent iron content, while imported ores average nearly 60 per cent. Nearly two-thirds of the iron content of the ore smelted is supplied by imported ores. Imported ores need to be of high grade, for low-grade ores could not in present circumstances bear the cost of shipping. Overseas orefields which supply Britain all have easy access to tidewater, and the blast-furnaces in which imported ore is consumed are located on or near the coast.

Low-grade Domestic Ores

Some 30 million tons of ore are fed yearly into the blast-furnaces of Britain. Almost 40 per cent of this total comes from domestic orefields, and more than nine-tenths of domestic production (by weight) is of low-grade ore. Over half comes from the Inferior Oolite formation of the Midlands (Figs. 8:4, 8:5), and nearly all of it is extracted from

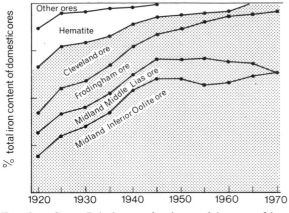

Fig. 8:2. Great Britain: production and import of iron ore, from 1920

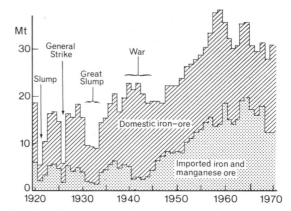

Fig. 8:4. Changing relative importance of domestic iron ores, in terms of iron content

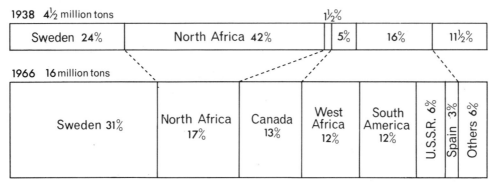

Fig. 8:3. Great Britain: sources of imported iron ore, by weight and percentage, 1938 and 1966

rocks of Jurassic age. In the early days of industrialisation, when the high-grade hematites of Cumberland, Lancashire, and Glamorgan, or the bedded ores which occurred in the Coal Measures, were used, there was no need to exploit the low-grade Jurassic ores. When the steel industry first developed, the technical difficulties of treating phosphoric ores—in which group the Jurassic ores are included—encouraged the smelting of high-grade ores, the use of acid furnace-linings, and the production of acid steel. Thus by a series of historical accidents the iron and steel industry became located mainly on the coalfields, and came to depend largely on imported high-grade ore. The present minor significance of the high-grade domestic ores used by the early ironmasters is obvious from Fig. 8:5, and the decline in their production in recent years is brought out by Fig. 8:4. This diagram shows the rise to dominance of Jurassic ores, in the relative importance of which, however, changes have also occurred. In 1920 the Cleveland district was the main producer. Five

years later it had already been outstripped by the orefields on the Inferior Oolite of the Midlands—mainly in Northamptonshire (Plate 13). While the Cleveland district was suffering from the rising costs due to partial exhaustion of reserves and to increasingly difficult working, the Midlands were profiting from their practical advantages. The essential difference between the two areas lies in the fact that the Cleveland ore passes deeply underground in the cuesta of the North York Moors, while that of the Northamptonshire ironfield is itself a scarp-former which lies either at the surface of the ground or beneath a thin overburden. The Middle Lias ore of the Midlands, much worked in the neighbourhood of Banbury and Melton Mowbray, is also a scarp-former, which over large areas has been cleanly denuded of its former cover of clay. The Frodingham ores similarly appear in small cuestas where they can easily be worked opencast. Total domestic production, severely checked in the slump of the 1930s but much stimulated during World War II and in the post-

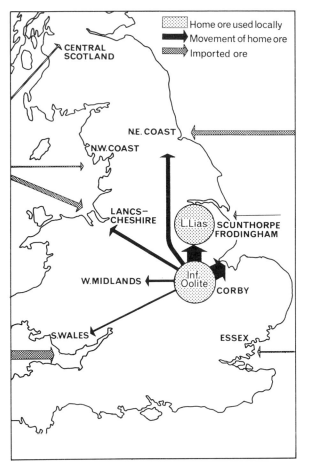

FIG. 8:5. Great Britain: use and movement of iron ore, 1970

After a check, output again rose in the mid-60s and was promising a slight but steady increase by the end of the decade.

As the graph (Fig. 8:6) shows, 8 million tons of pig were made in 1920. This was a boom year,

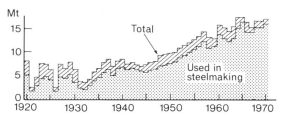

FIG. 8:6. Great Britain: output of pig iron from 1920

followed immediately by a short but severe slump; the subsequent recovery failed to raise production to the 1920 level, and output fell very low during the general strike of 1926. The smelting industry was unable to regain the whole of its lost strength before the Great Depression of the 1930s once more seriously reduced activity, and the slow recovery which followed was interrupted during World War II by a slight but steady decline, which reflected the difficulty in importing foreign ores (cf. Fig. 8:2). Not until the late 1940s did production of pig iron rise, and remain, above the level reached in 1920.

Despite the marked rises and falls in output, the graph shows clearly that during the inter-war period the steel industry was taking an increasing fraction of the total output of pig. More than 90 per cent of that total now goes to steel works and steel foundries. Most blast-furnaces today are owned by steel companies; no less than 85 per cent of the iron is recorded as *used in own works*, and although this percentage includes the material used in making iron goods, most of it is fed into steel furnaces. Furthermore, the greater part of the iron used in steel-making is taken from the blast-furnace in a molten state.

The integration of many blast-furnaces into steelworks means that the two distribution maps, Figs. 8:7, 8:8, should be read together. They have been drawn separately in order to bring out the influence of locating factors on the smelting of iron. The first map, Fig. 8:7, shows that blast-furnaces are located on or near the coalfields, on the orefields, or on tidewater at a distance both from coal and from ore. This last type of location is seen at Dagenham, where iron is smelted and steel is made for use in the motor industry. Location on orefields occurs on the Northamptonshire iron-

war period, seems now to have reached, and passed, its peak. Exploitation of Cleveland ore ceased in 1964, that of the Middle Lias ore in Oxfordshire and Northamptonshire in 1968. The Middle Lias orefields in south Lincolnshire and Leicestershire also recorded a declining output during the late 1960s, leaving the Inferior Oolite and Lower Lias beds, respectively in South Lincs.–Leics.–Northants.–Rutland, and in North Lincolnshire, to account for the main bulk of domestic ore extraction.

Pig-Iron

By 1960, the annual production of pig-iron in Britain rose above 15 million tons. Broadly speaking, the inter-war period (1919–39) was one of rapid changes in annual production, while the period subsequent to World War II saw a marked increase culminate in the record output of 1960.

PLATE 13. Giant dragline excavator at work in Northamptonshire Ironstone Field. Draglines are used for stripping overburden and for spreading soil when quarrying ceases. Spoil (stripped overburden) here lies in ridges in the background.

field and in the Scunthorpe–Frodingham district, where the blast-furnaces are fed with low-grade Jurassic ore worked locally (Plate 14). The smelting industry at Barrow relied originally on local supplies of hematite, and had access to seaborne coal from the Cumberland coalfield. The most advantageous location of all was, for many years, that of the Middlesbrough district, which until about 1960 produced a quarter of all the iron smelted. It has however been overtaken by South Wales, where the extension of smelting has been deliberately promoted by the government. The Middlesbrough district exemplifies geographical inertia: coal continues to be available from the northeastern fields, but ore supply from the adjacent Cleveland district has now ceased: ore now comes from abroad by sea, or by rail (for blending purposes) from the Jurassic orefields to the south.

The existing smelting industry is dominated by South Wales, the Middlesbrough district, and the works located on the Jurassic outcrops (Fig. 8:9). Elsewhere, the exhaustion of Coal Measure ores has eventually been followed by the closing of furnaces. The Black Country, once heavily begrimed by furnace fumes, has lost all furnaces but one. Latest in the list of closures come certain groups of furnaces in the Chesterfield area.

FIG. 8:7. Location of blast furnaces in Great Britain, 1970

Output of Steel

The output of steel fluctuated wildly in the inter-war period, at the same times, in much the same ways, and for the same reasons as that of iron. But the graph (Fig. 8:10) reveals that the high level of steel production reached in 1920 was exceeded by 1935, and that output since that year has remained well above the 1920 figure. A high level of output was possible in the late 1930s because a great deal of scrap was available to the steel industry. Thus the recovery of the steel industry from the Great Depression failed to stimulate a corresponding demand for pig-iron—indeed, the present steel industry absorbs as much scrap as pig-iron (Fig. 8:11). This is why the total output of crude steel, 27 million tons a year, is much greater than the output of pig-iron (cf. Fig. 8:6). Steel-making, like iron-smelting, declined slowly during World War II, but has expanded remarkably in the post-war period.

PLATE 14. Charging a basic oxygen converter, Corby.

FIG. 8:8. Location of steel furnaces in Great Britain, 1970

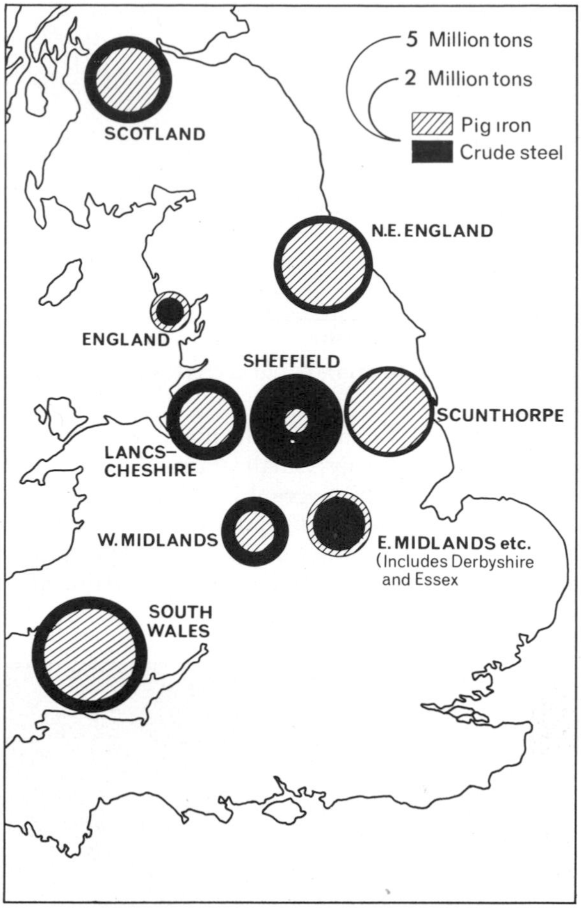

FIG. 8:9. Output of pig iron and crude steel, by districts, 1970

Present Distribution of Steel-making and the Future of the Industry

Thanks mainly to the new plant built during the 1960s, South Wales entered the decade of the 1970s as the leading regional steel producer, followed in order by the Northeast, Sheffield, and Lincolnshire. Heavy goods and fine steel products are typical of the Sheffield district (Plate 15), steel strip and tinplate of South Wales. In times of ship-building prosperity, the steel output of Central Scotland is considerably absorbed by ship construction and marine engineering, while the Middlesbrough district is noted for heavy steel. Midland steelworks are oriented in considerable part to the mechanical engineering industry, while automotive manufacture is a large and growing consumer of steel plate.

The several distributions mapped in this chapter give an interim account of the steel and the associated iron industry at 1970. A signal development during the 1960s was the increase in size and efficiency of blast-furnaces. In addition, the conversion to oxygen steel-making (use of the L.D. process) reduced capital and running costs for new works. Thus, it could happen that by 1980 ten blast-furnaces in full work could make all the iron required for the domestic industry, while large L.D. converters can each do the work of six or seven furnaces of an older type (see bibliography: Warren). It seems likely, therefore, that the existing (1970) considerable dissemination of iron smelting, and the marked dissemination of steel production, will be replaced by concentration in a very few centres with modernised and completely integrated works. At the time of writing, Teesside, Port Talbot, and Ravenscraig in the Midland Valley promise to be among the first of these.

The sizes of individual operations require bulk handling of large quantities of ore, including

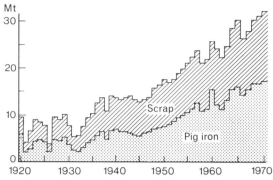

FIG. 8:10. Great Britain: output of crude steel from 1920

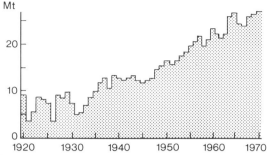

FIG. 8:11. Great Britain: use of pig iron and scrap in steel-making, from 1920

imported ore. Small British ports, capable of accommodating only small carriers, are dis-advantaged (see bibliography: Manners), while the inadequacy of port facilities tends to keep the British steel industry out of the very long-distance ore trade with its bulk carriers, and thus artificially to shape the import system. Deep-water ore terminals at Immingham and Redcar, plus the ore docks at Port Talbot, may however change the picture. They are in any event likely to reverse the locational forces that relate to a strong reliance for a time on home ore.

PLATE 15. Charging an ingot of special steel into a Sheffield furnace, for heat-treatment.

APPENDIX 1
Grades of Carbon Steels

Grade	Percentage carbon content
Low carbon steels	(a) less than 0,07
	(b) 0·07–0·15
Mild steels	0·15–0·25
Medium carbon steels	0·20–0·50
High carbon steels	0·50–1·40

APPENDIX 2
Crude Steel of Alloy Qualities

	Thousand tons, approx.			
	1956	1961	1966	1970
Steel ingots of alloy qualities	1,153	1,428	1,608	1,357
Steel of alloy qualities for castings	136	133	152	15
Total	1,289	1,561	1,760	1,372
Total as % of all crude steel produced	$6\frac{1}{2}$	7	$7\frac{1}{4}$	$5\frac{1}{2}$

Chapter 9

Trade, Transport, and Communication

SOME fundamental contrasts between the respective external trades of the U.K. and of the Irish Republic were noted previously, when certain major differences between the two countries were established (Chap. 1). When trade statistics (Appendices 1, 2) are examined in somewhat greater detail, complex problems at once arise—problems of sources of imports, directions of export, change in progress, and the composition of the major classes of commodity. A complete analysis of external trade, item by item, would be as tedious as it would be unnecessary; the following sections are confined to broad implications, whether of trade in its present state or of the changes which have occurred since the years immediately before World War II.

EXTERNAL TRADE OF THE UNITED KINGDOM

Imports

As Fig. 9:1 shows, the relative proportion of imports (by value) changed greatly in the 30 years from the late 1930s to the end of the 1960s. Whereas the food–beverage–tobacco group ac-counted for nearly half the value of imports in 1938, by the close of the 1960s it had been reduced to about one-quarter. Simultaneously, the fraction of imports accounted for by manufactured goods rose from about one-quarter to about one-half. Part of the proportionate reduction in edible imports results from increased agricultural productivity on the domestic front, amounting to a 30 per cent increase during the 1960s, when population increased only by 4 per cent. The summary statistics from which Fig. 9:1 is drawn are, needless to state, affected by comparative price movements between and within import classes, but the general picture is clear enough.

In the food–beverage–tobacco group, and considering only the most expensive items, butter imports increased slightly by volume during the 1960s; wheat, maize, tea, lamb, and bacon held roughly steady; and beef, canned meat, sugar, and tobacco all recorded absolute decline. No very marked changes in the volume of raw material imports occurred during this decade, except that imports of raw wool and raw cotton fell away. Imports of crude and refined petroleum roughly doubled, their increase being reflected in a distinct expansion of their share in the per-value reckoning.

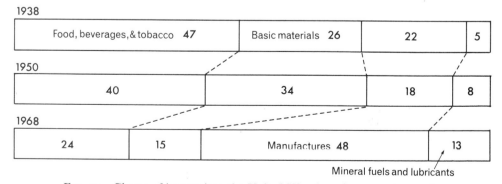

FIG. 9:1. Classes of import into the United Kingdom, by percentage value

The list of manufactured imports is long and complex, but here again the principal items can be singled out. Of these, during the 1960s, imports of cotton fabrics held roughly steady, those of copper declined; but per-volume imports rose in newsprint, finished steel and ferro-alloys, aluminium, silver bullion, aircraft engines and parts, and in office machinery and parts, in this last case by more than 100 per cent.

Increases in the volume (and value) of imports can mean either failure or success, according to the context of the consuming industry. The relative and in part absolute decline of the textile industries dependent on natural fibres is faithfully reflected in the statistics. On the other hand, increases in imports of manufactures can often be read as signs of manufacturing success. The view that trading nations are divided into two groups, one supplying raw materials and one providing manufactures, is not only far too simple but also partly false. The greatest exchanges in actuality take place between nations which are highly industrialised. Politicians and manufacturers alike aspire to combine a large volume of trade with a favourable balance.

Exports

The relative reduction in the export trade in mineral fuels and lubricants between 1938 and 1950 corresponded to the wartime loss of most of the remaining portion of the trade in coal. The decline of the coal trade far more than offset the increase in exports of refined petroleum; indeed, in 1955 the value of coal imports was greater than that of exports. Textile exports, once like coal exports a mainstay of trade, have much declined. The loss of the foreign market for manufactured cottons has been primarily responsible for this development, but the trade in woollens and worsteds is also under threat from the trend towards man-made fibres.

Metals and engineering products form large and complex classes of exports, in which some items have done better than others. There has for instance been a considerable expansion in the export trade in iron, crude steel, and semi-finished steel; but the iron and steel industry is at least as vulnerable, in relation to export trading, as is British industry in general. The most notable developments since 1945 have been in the engineering sector, where powered machinery, vehicles, tractors, and aircraft have all increased their stake in the export list. Transport equipment alone brings in about 15 per cent of all the money raised by exported products. Manufactured chemicals also appear in force in the post-war data (Fig. 9:2).

Textiles and coal, which were fundamentally significant to the export trade of the U.K. in 1913, and were still of great importance in 1938, have lost ground which cannot be regained. The engineering industries, supplying about two-fifths of all exports by value, have come to occupy a truly dominant position. However, the situation today is very different from that obtaining when Britain led the world in the mechanisation of industry. Quite apart from complications resulting from political events, from the formation of trading blocs, and from the condition of trade balances, Britain now has to contend with very powerful foreign competition in respect of some of the main engineering products. In every case competition is savage. With cars especially, but to a lesser extent also with aircraft, design changes can be rapid; and the machines have a limited working life. Thus, although the total market is vast, it is possible for a given competitor suddenly to lose ground.

The simplest, and severest, critics of British industry and of British export policy maintain that production and trade are alike handicapped by too little attention to modernisation, re-equipping, and external market demand.

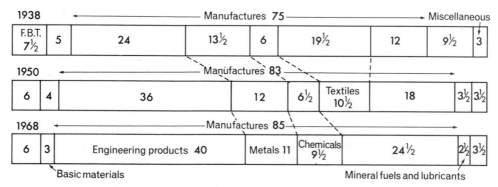

FIG. 9:2. Classes of export from the United Kingdom, by percentage value

Changed Trading Position of the United Kingdom

The volume of trade passing through the ports of the United Kingdom is far greater than in the immediately pre-war period—imports increased by more than half in volume, between 1938 and 1960, and exports by more than one-quarter. During the 1960s, imports and exports alike underwent a further increase, by about 50 per cent in volume in each case. By comparison with the depressed economy and the stagnant trade of the early 1930s, the present picture is bright. On the other hand, the post-war years have brought extraordinary fluctuations in prices, and the great manufacturing nations are competing with one another for raw materials, some of which are not so plentiful as they once were; in the even more highly competitive export market, everything possible must be done to keep selling prices down.

Another weakness in the present trade of the U.K. is that re-exports are running at only about one-third of their pre-war volume. Re-exports of wool, and to a lesser extent those of cotton, have very seriously diminished. Several influences combine to depress the entrepôt trade: home industry tends to absorb more of the imported raw material than it did; because of the decline in coal exports, import freights are far higher than they were; newly-established industries in other countries tend to develop markets of their own and to trade direct; and—perhaps the most important of all—overseas trade in general was severely curtailed during World War II. The entrepôt trade of Great Britain was almost wholly brought to an end, and—once lost—has proved extremely difficult to recover. The U.S.A., by far the leading industrial nation of the western world, enormously increased its merchant marine during the war and maintained it for some time afterwards. But the greatest obstacle to the restoration of the re-export trade is probably the very great expansion of merchant fleets sailing under flags of convenience (notably those of Liberia and Panama) plus technical changes in the construction of ships and the handling of cargo. The multiple handling and the increased number of routings implied in entrepôt business mean diseconomies in ocean transport.

Balance of Trade

Commodities imported and exported constitute visible trade. The end of World War II was followed by a period in which imports cost more than exports brought in, so that the balance of visible trade was adverse. But since services, as well as goods, can be sold abroad, and since money can be invested overseas to bring in profits at home, the total trade balance must allow for invisible trade—paper transactions—as well as for the movement of actual goods. With regard to invisible trade the U.K. is far worse off than in pre-war years, for, during World War II, overseas insurance business was lost, income from shipping almost vanished, and foreign investments were sold under compulsion. In the post-war period, therefore, the balance of invisible trade, which has proved favourable in at least some groups of years, has not compensated for the balance of visible trade, which has been strongly unfavourable in the decade 1957–67 (Fig. 9:3). Rising hopes in the late 1950s were destroyed by a sharp decline in the trading position, which involved a marked fall-off in invisible trade, and the hint of a recovery in the early 1960s has not been confirmed by events. Depletion of reserves, inflation of the currency, and worsening esteem of sterling produced in 1967 another devaluation of the pound.

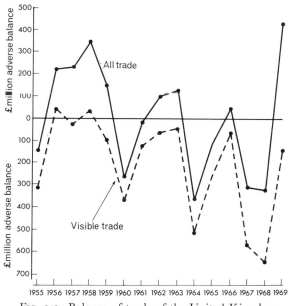

FIG. 9:3. Balance of trade of the United Kingdom

Governmental Action

It would be quite wrong, however, to suppose that the tendencies expressed in these developments are new, or that they were the outcome of World War II alone. On the contrary the conversion of the economy of the U.K. from an uncontrolled to a regulated condition occurred during World War I. Although the control was neither so rigorous nor so direct in the inter-war period as it is today, the change from the free economy of the period before 1914 was as revolutionary as it was abrupt. The various political influences exerted both on production and on trade have naturally been designed in many cases to counteract the effect of geographical and economic factors.

As G. D. H. Cole has written, 'Up to 1914 Great Britain furnished an almost perfect example of . . . the working of an economic system in accordance with the "natural laws" beloved of the classical economists. This freedom could not, of course, survive the experience of war [i.e., World War I] . . . production had to be directed to meeting war needs, and the Government . . . acquired an extensive power over industry and agriculture. . . . Foreign trade necessarily ceased to be free . . . the export of capital ceased abruptly . . . Great Britain, from being the world's greatest lender, became a borrower of capital . . . overseas investments had to be sold.'

In all these ways the experience of World War II was anticipated by that of World War I. After 1918, very many controls were relaxed or abolished, only a few protective duties remaining; but neither the cotton trade nor the coal trade was fully re-established, and markets lost during wartime were generally difficult to regain, not only because of increasing competition from new factories overseas but also because the pound was overvalued in relation to the dollar. The great slump which started in 1929 reduced the prices of imports, so that the U.K., being the world's great free market, maintained for a time a high level of import trade, but exports declined severely, and a large adverse balance of payments was recorded by 1931.

Two political measures were adopted: the gold value of the pound was reduced, in order to bring down the selling price of British goods abroad, and protective tariffs were imposed to check the flow of imports. Free trade was abandoned. The Government was compelled to decide what quantities of imports would be allowed to enter from the main suppliers. Subsidies on the home production of sugar beet and wheat were already in force, and power was taken in 1933 to regulate the import of agricultural produce. Substantial tariff protection was given to the steel industry, and agreements on export shipments of coal were negotiated with customer countries. In Cole's words, 'Great Britain . . . departed a long distance from the almost entirely planless economy of the years before the slump, having . . . a managed currency, a largely managed foreign trade, a considerably managed

system of agricultural production, and a managed system of industrial production extending to coal and steel. . . . All this adds up to a quite formidable total of State intervention in industry.'

Now that Government control of industry, agriculture, and trade is far more extensive and far more direct than it was in the 1930s, it would be nonsensical to speak of the economic activity of the United Kingdom as if it were the outcome of geographical factors alone. Whatever may be the status in later years of industries which are now nationalised, it seems improbable that they will be left in the foreseeable future entirely to their own devices. Control over the volume and nature of trade can be exercised by means of the system of import and export licences, which also affects the direction of trade for political purposes. All the measures referred to are those taken by the home Government; further complications ensue from the political and economic policies of the governments of foreign countries.

Direction of Trade

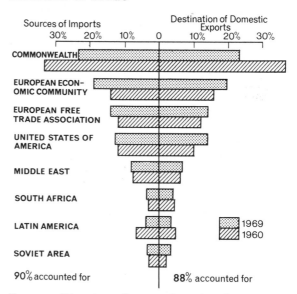

FIG. 9:4. Direction of external trade of the United Kingdom, 1950 and 1969, by value

Figure 9:4 illustrates the chief trading relations of the United Kingdom for the two years 1950 and 1969. The bars are drawn to represent percentages of total export and import trade, by value, and take no account of changed volume of trade. In a diagram of this kind, the impression given is affected by the grouping of countries which is adopted. The graph succeeds in representing about

90 per cent of total external trade, and includes the leading customers and suppliers.

Between the late pre-war years and the mid-1950s, there was no very great change in the direction of trade, except for decreases in trade with the Argentine and Germany, and for increases in trade with Nigeria, East African countries, and oil-exporters in the Middle East. The comparison of 1960 with 1969, however, reveals that trade with Commonwealth countries (mainly Australia) has greatly contracted, while that with European countries and the U.S.A. has been relatively enlarged. Australia, with vast mineral reserves newly proved and in part developed during the 1960s—reserves in particular of iron ore, bauxite, and nickel—is turning progressively towards Japan and the U.S.A. as leading customers, and appears certain in consequence to take greatly increasing supplies of imports from these same two countries.

In the European scene we are dealing with a wholesale regrouping of trading nations. The customs union of Benelux was formed in 1948, with the European Coal and Steel Community, subsequently the European Economic Community (E.E.C.) of Belgium, France, West Germany, Italy, Luxemburg, and the Netherlands following in 1952. The U.K. quite early adopted a policy of acceding to the Common Market, as the E.E.C. is usually called; but political complications during the 1960s held matters up. The dependence of New Zealand on Britain for an export market, and the domestic U.K. practice of agricultural support, were grave obstructions, not lessened by the effects of internal political competition. However, decimalisation of the currency, and metrication of systems of measurement, can be read as indicating a disposition to join the E.E.C., or, at the least, to secure a practical trading advantage. During 1972, the U.K. government succeeded in rousing enough favourable opinion for accession to the Market, and successfully applied to join. From 1973 onwards, then, the U.K. will belong to the world's greatest trading bloc. Probably drastic, but as yet obscure, economic changes can be expected to result.

EXTERNAL TRADE OF THE IRISH REPUBLIC

The external trade of the Irish Republic presents a far simpler picture than does that of the United Kingdom, in accordance with the general simplicity of the Republic's economy and its reliance on a single external market. Manufactures bulk very large in the import trade, foodstuffs and live animals in the export trade. The live animals are mostly cattle; well over half the price realised for exported live animals comes from the sale of beef cattle, with store beasts dominating fatstock.

The United Kingdom supplies about half the imports by value, and takes something like 60 per cent of exports. The sale of beef cattle to the United Kingdom alone accounts for some 10 per cent of all export trade, a most unusual concentration on a single commodity in a single market for a European country.

Foodstuffs of animal origin account for about one-fifth—and in some years more than one-quarter—of the total value of exports. Beef, bacon, butter, and cheese are prominent in this part of the list. Among other exports, beer from the Dublin breweries has long been sent abroad, and the export trade in wool, textiles, and clothing and footwear has traditional bases. More recent additions to the range of prominent single exports are lead–zinc ore, confectionery (especially chocolate), and chemicals (especially pharmaceutical products). These and others, including electronic

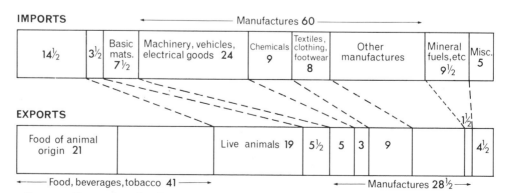

FIG. 9:5. External trade of the Irish Republic, by percentage value, at the end of the 1960s

equipment, can be expected to increase both in volume and in relative value, as the industrialisation of Ireland at last gets vigorously under way. Manufactures as a class are already approaching one-third of total export value (Fig. 9:5).

Among the imports into the Irish Republic, the leading raw materials are textile fibres, wood, and fertilisers in the unprocessed state. The comprehensive class of machinery, vehicles, and electrical goods dominates the import trade in manufactures, costing about a quarter of the total outlay for imports. The relative significance of mineral fuels is increasing, in response to the needs of thermal power stations: in this class, petroleum accounts for a very large fraction of the total.

The heavy dependence of the Republic on trade with the United Kingdom has not prevented efforts to increase trade with the U.S.A. and with the E.E.C. (especially Western Germany). Some limited success can be claimed (Fig. 9:6). However, the whole position is likely to change drastically if Ireland and the U.K. both join the Common Market.

previous trading volumes; some new ports, including specialised centres, rose to prominence; and the combined share in total trade by volume accounted for by London and Liverpool fell from about 50 per cent to about 40 per cent. Nevertheless, at the end of the decade London was still handling a quarter of all shipborne trade by value, Liverpool something under 20 per cent. The five leading ports—London, Liverpool, Hull, Harwich, and Southampton, in that order, accounted for about 60 per cent of shipborne traffic by value, and the leading ten ports for about 70 per cent (Appendix 3; Fig. 9:7). The list of twenty ports in Appendix 3 accounts for about 85 per cent of all traffic by value, while the trade of Belfast and Dublin, respectively, is even more highly dominant in Northern Ireland and the Irish Republic.

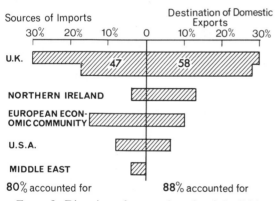

Sources of Imports / Destination of Domestic Exports

FIG. 9:6. Direction of external trade of the Irish Republic, by value

LEADING PORTS

Of the goods exported and imported through the ports of Great Britain, about half by value went through the two ports of London and Liverpool from the mid-1940s, through the 1950s, and into the 1960s, with London alone commanding about one-third of the total. During the decade of the 1960s the general position altered somewhat. Some traditional ports of already modest rank continued to decline in relative standing, being hard pressed to maintain—or at best to increase slightly—their

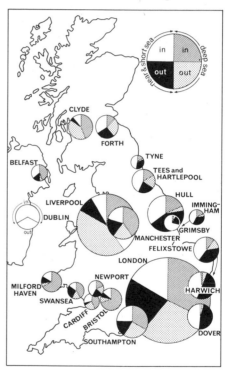

FIG. 9:7. Simple analysis of port trade, by value, at the end of the 1960s. About 85 per cent of total trade, by value, is accounted for

Appendix 4 and Fig. 9:7 show that the per-value balance between imports and exports, and the relative significance of deep-sea trading on the one hand, and near and short-sea trading on the other, vary greatly from port to port. Aside from London, Harwich, and Liverpool the re-export trade is of no great significance; accordingly, the data presented can be read as giving a reasonable general description of the functions of the ports involved. Among the ports of the east and south coasts, near and short-sea imports account for 25 per cent or more of all traffic by value, rising to half at Harwich and Dover; and in this group, only the Forth ports, the Tees–Hartlepool ports, London, and Southampton are very deeply committed to deep-sea trade on a value basis.

In the southwest, Newport and Swansea resemble the east-coast group in being heavily engaged in short-haul traffic, the trade structure of Newport resembling that of the Tees, and the structure of Swansea that of Southampton. Cardiff, Bristol, and Milford Haven display superficial resemblances to one another at first glance; but the dominant deep-sea import function of Milford Haven relates to the petroleum trade, while Cardiff achieves a nearer balance in its general cargo traffic than does Bristol, which for long has been troubled by a shortage of return cargoes.

Manchester and Liverpool in the northwest, like the Clyde in Scotland, reflect their westward outlooks in the dominance of deep-water trade. Belfast and Dublin, for political reasons, and also for reasons of the classification of statistics, constitute somewhat special cases in the present discussion.

Among the five leading ports by value of trade, manufactured goods dominate in cargoes handled, accounting for 65 per cent of traffic at Hull and Liverpool, 75 per cent at Southampton, and 85 per cent or more at Harwich and London.

This fact raises the whole question of economy of transport. For centuries now, the increasing size of ships, and since the mid-19th century the conversion to powered ships, have tended to displace ports activities in the estuaries of Britain ever further towards the mouths to the sea. Additional developments that gathered full force during the 1960s have not only accelerated this general trend, but have also increased the prevailing tendency for traffic by volume to be concentrated on fewer and fewer ports. In point of fact, this tendency is double. On the one hand, facilities for rapid bulk handling, roll-on roll-off transhipment, container traffic, and delivery by bulk transports, must inevitably be provided in selected ports only, to the detriment of competitors. On the other hand, long-distance traffic in oil and ore can dispense with return cargoes, provided that the sea haul is long enough to secure the economies offered by giant vessels—and provided also, of course, that the giants can dock.

The land hinterlands of British ports, even of most of the leading ports, remained quite restricted even as late as 1970, with outward flows being determined mainly by the frequency and type of sailing offered (see bibliography: Bird); but unit transport, especially with the aid of unit trains, can be expected to enlarge the hinterlands of ports that possess the relevant handling facilities. Deep-water anchorages for oil tankers are reflected in the oil import works at Loch Finnart, Bantry Bay, and Milford Haven; but, within no long time after its opening, the Milford Haven port needed to be improved by dredging, when tankers began to surpass 150,000 tons. Now that 1-million-ton tankers are envisaged, the economies of scale in bulk transport of oil promise to centre themselves on fewer and fewer ports than ever; and corresponding difficulties for the bulk carriage of iron ore were already making themselves felt before the 1960s came to an end.

On this count, the distribution of traffic by cargo volume, mapped in Fig. 9:8, must be taken as an interim picture. Already by 1969, however, Milford Haven had become the second port in the British Isles by volume; and fifteen ports in Great

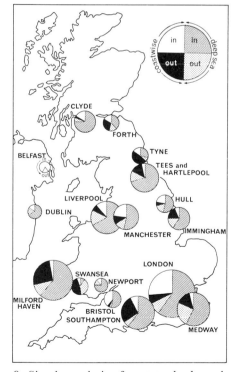

FIG. 9:8. Simple analysis of port trade, by volume, at the end of the 1960s. About 85 per cent of total trade, by volume, is accounted for. Both in this diagram and in Fig. 9:7, ports are omitted if they record less than 1 per cent of the total involved

Britain were handling 85 per cent by volume of all traffic, with more than 50 per cent concentrated on the leaders, London, Milford Haven, Liverpool, Southampton, and the Medway ports. The petroleum traffic dominated all these in terms of cargo volume, ranging from some 50 per cent at London and Liverpool to 95–100 per cent at the others. Equally, traffic volume had become progressively directed to estuarine ports, with the Thames Estuary handling about 25 per cent of the total for Great Britain. Except for the Forth and Tyne (with Belfast and Dublin again providing exceptional cases), all the ports mapped in Fig. 9:8 had half or more of their 1969 volume of traffic accounted for by deep water inward shipments.

Expectable changes in the fairly near future depend in part on the further development of bulk handling and the further increase in size of ships. They appear likely to include the continued rise of Milford Haven in terms of trade volume, a rapid response to the port improvements at Port Talbot, continued response to the extensions at Tilbury, a re-orientation of iron ore import traffic, the successful development of deep-water operations on Moray Firth, and—more speculatively—ambitious harbour works on the lower Thames estuary.

TRANSPORT AND COMMUNICATION

Roads, Railways, and Pipelines

The assembly and collection of goods for export, the distribution of imports, and the internal distribution of domestic products depend on internal transport and communications. The networks of road and rail, supplemented in places by rivers and canals, must obviously meet present-day needs to some extent, for goods and people are in fact moved from place to place and the movement does not clog to a standstill. But, for a number of reasons, the services are defective; their defects appear mainly in the lack of flexibility and interconnections on railways, and in the congestion of certain roads at certain times. The shortcomings of the railways are due largely to the manner of their development; difficulties on the roads are caused mainly by the huge increase of traffic, which was made possible by the petrol engine and was effected on roads of medieval pattern or 18th-century design. It could scarcely have been expected that improvements of roads would keep pace with the growth of traffic; but additional difficulties arise from the daily movement of great numbers of people to and from the centres of large towns, from the tendency of some industrial concerns to establish scattered factories working on a single product, and from the concentration of external trade on a few ports. All these factors affect railways as well as roads, but traffic jams can scarcely occur on railways; part of the congestion of some roads is due precisely to the fact that road transport is flexible where rail transport is not—road vehicles run from door to door and carry individual people and small consignments of goods, whereas railways are at their best with long hauls and bulky loads.

In Great Britain there are some $14\frac{1}{2}$ million road vehicles and 150,000 km (95,000 mi.) of classified roads. The number of vehicles has increased more than fourfold since the late 1930s. Goods vehicles alone now total more than $1\frac{1}{2}$ million, shifting about 16M tons of freight a year, nearly eight times the amount carried by rail. About one-third of the railway traffic, measured in wagon-miles, is coal or coke. Apart from this item, the total long-haul freight carried by road is far greater than that carried by rail. The numbers of road shipments generated by rail transport tends to increase, as rail freight services become concentrated on a decreasing number of stations. Simultaneously, the size and speed of goods vehicles plying on the roads are increasing, in response to road improvement and particularly to the extension of the motorway network.

Despite extensive re-equipment, railways remain handicapped by the loading gauges determined last century and in use ever since; these prevent the carriage of the very large single loads required for modern industry (Plate 16).

Up to 1913 the railways of England, Scotland, and Wales were on the whole highly successful, despite the over-optimism of some early promoters. In the inter-war period began the struggle between road and rail transport which, becoming especially severe in the 1930s, was resumed with added strength in the 1950s. As in a number of other western countries, the railways have lost a great deal of their passenger traffic to road transport and to internal airlines. Unprofitable lines and uneconomic stations have been progressively closed from 1945 onwards. The remaining parts of the network have been considerably modernised, with their tracks improved and in part electrified, and with diesel locomotives replacing those powered by steam. Some stations and marshalling yards have also been added or improved. However, in the ten years 1957–67 there was very little change in

PLATE 16. A cracking tower, 42 metres long, at Manchester, during a journey from Stockton-on-Tees to Birkenhead. Enormous loads of this kind cannot go by rail. The tower was eventually launched at Birkenhead, and drawn by tug to the new oil refinery at Whitegate, Co. Cork.

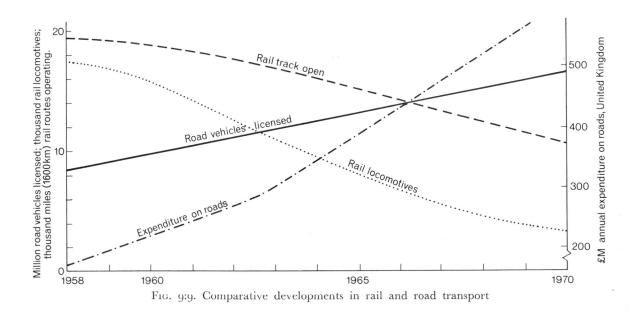

FIG. 9:9. Comparative developments in rail and road transport

PLATE 17. A 45-ton diesel-drawn block train load of tankers.

traffic receipts, while the provision of rail services declined in all main respects. Passenger journeys became steadily fewer, coal and coke traffic fell away, and shipments of iron and steel were reduced, despite a rise in production by the iron and steel industry. The painful rationalisation of the railways calls to mind the fate of the cotton industry: its final outcome remains to be seen.

Fig. 9:9 summarises the reciprocal developments in road and rail transport in the United Kingdom during the 1960s. As shown, expenditure on roads increased sharply during the mid-60s, in considerable part as a consequence of the development of motorways. A linear increase in the number of road vehicles listed was accompanied by a marked decrease in the number of railway locomotives operating, and by a plunge in the total length of operating rail track, which reduced that total by about half during the decade.

The first pipelines of any length to operate in Britain were installed during World War II. The construction and elaboration of whole pipeline networks has been largely a matter of the 1960s,

and is planned to continue into the 1970s (cf. Fig. 7:4). Pipelines carry methane gas, whether imported to the Thames Estuary or raised from the North Sea fields; they transport about as much oil as railways do; and one, 90 km (about 60 mi.) in length, takes chalk slurry from the scarp near Luton to cement works in the Rugby area of the Midland Triangle (see bibliography: Foster, Grimshaw). Their competition can scarcely fail to cut into potential rail traffic, whether by diverting some kinds of bulk carriage before the railways ever become involved, or by capturing existing rail trade.

Branch lines began to fail in Ireland earlier than in Great Britain. During the period 1860–1900, numbers of narrow-gauge railways with 3-ft. track were built in Ireland—mainly in the west—with much financial help from the government. Few of them still operate today, and their numbers are still declining. Their traffic has been taken over, or at least greatly reduced, by road transport. In the absence of other signs of industrialisation, the railways of Ireland could scarcely be expected to flourish. In this connection, as in others, Ireland lies on the very fringes of the industrial world.

The chief items carried on the railways of Northern Ireland are livestock, grain and flour, oilcake, and potatoes. Much of the railway goods traffic in the Irish Republic consists of sugar beet, grain and flour, groceries, coal, and beer.

Transport in some parts of Ireland depends on bicycles and asses rather than on railways and motor vehicles. The internal combustion engine has nevertheless produced its effects, among them a much-needed scheme to modernise main roads. The Republic has about 15,000 km of these, large stretches of which are now being reconstructed; the £10 million being spent each year on the roads of the Republic compares quite creditably with the £175 million in Great Britain, where, however, the total is rising as new works make progress. Since the Republic has only some 275,000 road vehicles of its own, an important function of the reconstructed roads is to encourage tourist traffic.

Canals

Difficulties afflicting canals in Ireland have been described previously (Chap. 6). Canal transport in Great Britain is largely defunct, although such private or corporate undertakings as the Manchester Ship Canal, and the nationally operated Aire and Calder Canal, provide exceptions. The policy adopted in the late 1950s was to improve, restore, and maintain a selected inland waterway net; but of the 2,100 km (1,300 mi.) of waterway then recommended for improvement, only about a quarter carried substantial traffic, and little of this was through traffic. The potential long-haul advantage of waterways was certainly not realised on average hauls of 46 km ($17\frac{1}{2}$ mi.). Policy shifted finally to abandonment during the 1960s, accepting what was in fact practice on large parts of the former canal system, limiting itself to the maintenance of waterways, in part river channels, running from the Severn Estuary to the West Midland industrial area, from Humberhead by radial routes into West Yorkshire, from the Mersey into Cheshire, and along short lines north and west from London (see bibliography: Watts). More than 90 per cent of all inland waterway traffic, two-thirds of the whole consisting of bulk fuels, moves along only 640 km of major waterways, and most is one-way. The use of waterways, including canals, for water supply conflicts in practice with use for navigation. Very little canal-borne cargo is recorded in Scotland, but the Forth and Clyde Canal and the Caledonian Canal are used by fishing vessels and yachts.

Air Transport

Civil aircraft operating from bases in the United Kingdom made about half a million flights in 1970, carrying 15 million fare-paying passengers, and flying something like 300 million aircraft-km. The 1960s witnessed the outpacing of international sea travel by international air travel (Fig. 9:10), sea travel displaying a linear but very slow

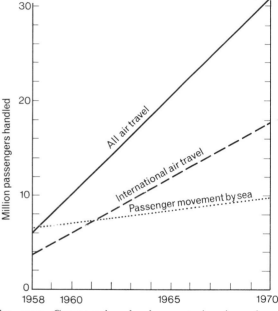

FIG. 9:10. Comparative developments in air and sea travel

increase, and air travel an equally linear but far more rapid increase, which enabled it to overtake sea travel very early in the decade.

Air travel is a great time-saver over long distances. Although internal airlines, and charter lines concentrating mainly on short-distance hauls, are steadily increasing their traffic, it is the external lines which have undergone the most spectacular development. The central problems are those of transit to the airports from city centres, and the increasing task of handling the passengers and baggage discharged by enormous jet-planes. Electric railways, surface and underground, and possibly also over-head monorail, may meet London's particular difficulties; alternatively, helicopter services from airport to city terminal may be brought into wide operation. Meanwhile, the major terminals tend to establish alternate or out stations, satellites, and additional fields. London/ Heathrow has a rail-served twin at Gatwick, relies in some emergency situations on Luton, and is to be complemented by Foulness. Meantime, Glasgow/Prestwick functions on occasions as an alternate.

The turn to air travel, reducing the demand for sea passages, has caused some former liner ships to be diverted to the cruising trade. Since large ships appear unlikely to be built specifically for cruising, passenger ship construction would seem to be facing the kind of competition that canals faced from railways, and that railways have faced from road transport. But the demands made by air transport, like the development of the air transport industry, are not without their critics. The U.K. (mainly England) contains hundreds of World War II airfields, representing about 1 per cent of agricultural land, in various states ranging from adaptation to dereliction (see bibliography: Blake) while the inter-regional connections are generally poor (see bibliography: Sealy).

APPENDIX 1

External Trade by Value, £million approx.

1. United Kingdom

Imports	1960	1963	1965	1969
Total	4,655	4,983	5,764	8,374
Food, beverages, tobacco	1,540	1,676	1,711	1,940
Raw materials and fuels	1,560	1,548	1,727	1,354
Manufactures	1,522	1,702	2,253	4,137

Exports of U.K. produce and manufacture	1960	1963	1965	1969
Total	3,648	4,211	4,724	7,338
Manufactures of which	3,059	3,499	3,993	6,255
Metals and Engineering products	2,042	2,344	2,644	3,931
Textiles (excluding clothing)	258	254	274	470
Re-exports total	141	154	173	254

2. Irish Republic

Imports	1958	1962	1964	1967
Total	198	274	349	390
Food, beverages, tobacco	33	41	47	70
Raw materials and manufactures	144	205	267	28

Exports of domestic produce and manufacture	1958	1962	1964	1967
Total	138	169	217	275
Food, beverages, tobacco	46	63	71	110
Live animals	47	48	67	53

APPENDIX 2

Direction of External Trade, £million approx.

1. Value of imports into the U.K., by source

	1958	1960	1962	1965	1969
Total	3,834	4,655	4,628	5,764	8,324
U.S.A.	353	571	484	627	1,124
Commonwealth of which	1,336	1,510	1,442	1,720	1,993
Canada	311	378	354	459	506
Australia	199	198	186	220	238
New Zealand	161	183	170	208	216
European Economic Community	538	670	724	995	1,611
European Free Trade Association	436	561	554	782	1,248
Middle East (mainly oil)	306	345	371	394	661

2. Destination of exports of U.K. produce and manufacture

	1957	1960	1963	1965	1969
Total	3,374	3,648	4,211	4,724	7,338
North America	268	355	380	494	1,223
Australia and New Zealand	376	381	352	405	445
South Africa	180	161	205	261	293
West Germany	106	165	215	255	416
France	111	111	196	193	313
Sweden	111	31	169	219	302

3. Value of imports into the Irish Republic, by source

	1961	1963	1965	1967
Total	261	307	372	390
Great Britain	119	142	173	178
Northern Ireland	14	14	15	17
U.S.A.	20	18	30	32
West Germany	14	20	24	25
France	6	7	10	9
Netherlands	7	10	10	12

4. Destinations of exports (including re-exports) consigned from the Irish Republic

	1961	1963	1965	1967
Total	180	196	221	284
Great Britain	110	111	127	170
Northern Ireland	23	30	27	35
West Germany	6	6	12	7
U.S.A.	13	14	9	26
Netherlands	2	2	7	5
France	1	3	6	7

APPENDIX 3
Value of Trade at Leading Ports During the 1960s
£million approx.: Exports and Imports Combined

	1960	1964	1969		1960	1964	1969
London	2,793	3,268	3,249	Bristol	213	245	273
Liverpool	1,760	1,917	2,180	Tees & Hartlepool	—	—	268
Hull	444	540	807	Milford Haven	—	—	208
Harwich	—	259	746	Immingham	—	—	201
Southampton	320	336	585	Grimsby	86	125	138
Manchester	414	419	560	Newport	63	69	137
Felixstowe	—	—	433	Swansea	119	138	133
Dover	—	195	351	Cardiff	47	58	115
Clyde	294	320	343	Tyne	112	116	110
Forth	—	—	282				

The above handle some 85 per cent of Great Britain's shipborne traffic, by value

Belfast	70	93	144	Dublin	—	138	

APPENDIX 4

Comparison of Import and Export Trades at Leading Ports During the 1960s, £million approx.

	1960		1964		1969	
	Imports	Exports and Re-exports	Imports	Exports and Re-exports	Imports	Exports and Re-exports
London	1,523	1,270	1,728	1,540	1,974	2,085
Liverpool	810	950	932	985	1,031	1,149
Hull	259	185	315	215	426	381
Harwich	—	—	131	128	328	408
Southampton	192	128	203	133	318	267
Manchester	285	129	286	133	347	213
Felixstowe	—	—	—	—	222	211
Dover	—	—	81	104	175	176
Clyde	137	157	155	165	187	156
Forth	—	—	—	—	130	152
Bristol	180	33	213	32	228	45
Tees & Hartlepool	—	—	—	—	161	107
Milford Haven	—	—	—	—	173	35
Immingham	—	—	—	—	123	78
Grimsby	70	16	94	31	105	33
Newport	28	35	32	37	75	62
Swansea	61	58	69	69	70	63
Cardiff	36	11	47	11	82	33
Tyne	64	48	59	47	68	42
Belfast	61	9	82	11	117	27
Dublin	—	—	80	58		

Chapter 10

Population

It can be urged that the density and distribution of people epitomise much of the geography of the British Isles. During the last hundred-and-fifty years the total population has increased enormously, mainly through increases in England—Scotland, Wales, and Ireland are in some ways special cases; trends in England have had much in common with those of western Europe in general.

CHANGES IN RELATION OF BIRTH-RATE TO DEATH-RATE

Quite simply, the high present total of population in England is due to a great excess of births over deaths in the period from about 1750 to 1880. During this time the population-total trebled. Numbers have continued to increase since the late 1880s, and were increased by half between 1880 and 1930, but a change has occurred in the ratio of births to deaths which has caused the rate of increase to decline.[1]

Until about 1750 the total did not exceed 8 millions. Numbers had risen slowly during the Middle Ages, but times of gradual increase were offset by the sharp declines caused by epidemic diseases. The Black Death of the 14th century was the greatest setback of all, but mortality from plague was frequently severe until (and including) the 17th century. Although the birth-rate was high, it was roughly equalled by the death-rate, and no great rise in total numbers was possible (Figs. 10:1, 10:2).

Improvements in Public Health

This first stage was brought to an end by what

has been called the medical and sanitary revolution The medical discoveries of the 18th century eliminated many diseases and checked others, and the rate of infant mortality was greatly reduced. Improvements in agriculture prevented famine, technical achievements provided means of transport and widened markets. It is quite impossible to judge how strongly these several developments interacted on one another, and to what extent they were all the outcome of the spirit of the age, but numbers certainly grew. In the country as a whole, people had about as good a chance of eating and working as in former times; babies had a far better chance than before of living to be adults, and adults had a better chance of reaching a reasonable age. It was more than a century before a significant fall occurred in the birth-rate, and by that time the population of England stood at some 24 million.

Decline in the Birth-Rate

The second stage—the stage of rapid increase under the influence of a high birth-rate and a low death-rate—came to an end about 1880. At this time the birth-rate began a steep decline, continuing to fall until about 1930. The *rate of increase* was reduced, although actual numbers increased and the total population of course remained high, standing in 1930 at about 37 million. Since 1930 the birth-rate has been similar to the death-rate, but since the rate of births slightly exceeds the rate of deaths there is a tendency for numbers to increase slightly.

During the inter-war period, and especially during the 1930s, there was much speculation about the future population trends in Great Britain. It seemed to some observers that the birth-rate had fallen so low that numbers would scarcely maintain themselves. It seemed also that, in consequence, the proportion of old people to total population

---

[1] The immediately following paragraphs about population trends are based on *World Population and Resources*, a report by P.E.P. (1955).

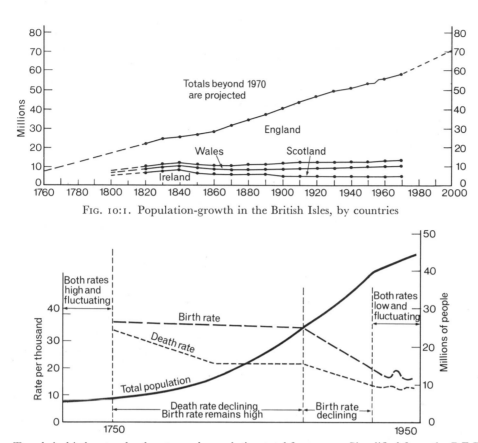

FIG. 10:1. Population-growth in the British Isles, by countries

FIG. 10:2. Trends in birth-rate, death-rate, and population-total from 1750. Simplified from the P.E.P. Report

would rise, and that the death-rate must increase later in the century with a possible decline in total numbers. The rising proportion of old people has in fact become one of the urgent social problems of the day, although it has been partly offset by the lengthening expectation of life and by the sharp increase in the birth-rate at the end of World War II. During the decade of the 1960s the position stabilised itself somewhat, the proportion in the United Kingdom aged 65 and over increasing but slightly, from 12 to $12\frac{1}{2}$ per cent. Meanwhile, estimates of future population up to the year 2000, extrapolated from the existing demographic structure and from observed trends, suggest that the total population for the British Isles, about 57,575,000 in 1970, will increase by the end of the century to slightly above 71,000,000.

EMIGRATION AND INTERNAL MIGRATION

Scotland, Wales, and Northern Ireland have

been affected by trends similar to those operating in England, but have also undergone losses of migrants to England, in addition to experiencing considerable migration within their own borders. The increase in population has been less spectacular than in England, Scotland and Wales having merely trebled their numbers of people in the last hundred-and-thirty years. Many people have deserted the upland districts since industrialisation began, moving into the manufacturing towns of Central Scotland, South Wales, and the English coalfields. The population of Belfast has been increased by the inward movement of people from the surrounding rural areas, and London has attracted many from all parts of the British Isles.

During the 19th century there was much emigration from the British Isles to countries abroad. At first the movement was directed mainly to the U.S.A. Canada took many British immigrants in the late 19th and early 20th centuries. Up to about the mid-20th century, England and Wales combined recorded a net loss by migration of about 1 per cent per decade, reckoned on the starting total at each decade's beginning. The data conceal migration from Wales to England, which is counted as internal migration. Since about 1950, however, the trend has been reversed, largely on account of the immigration of West Indians, Indians, and Pakistanis, to a net gain by migration of about 1 per cent per decade. Scotland and Northern Ireland, throughout the 20th century, have averaged a net loss by migration of about 6 per cent per decade, although a 5 per cent rate might correspond more closely to actual population figures.

The Irish Republic

Ireland is exceptional in western Europe in having far fewer people today than a century ago. In 1840 the total was about 8 million, today it is but 4½ million. The astonishing reduction is due mainly to events in the south, i.e., in that part which now forms the Republic of Ireland. The population of Northern Ireland declined slightly from 1851 to 1891, but a slow recovery has again brought its numbers near the total of 1·7 million reached in the mid-19th century. Matters are very different in the Republic, where the total exceeded 6½ million in 1841 but was slightly below 3 million in 1961. The birth-rate and death-rate in the Republic are both low, but there is an excess of births over deaths which would result in a steady increase in numbers, were it not for emigration on an impressive scale. In some single decades more than half-a-million people have emigrated from Ireland. The movement is so pronounced and so continuous that emigration appears to be a national custom. The intercensal period 1946–51 was the first for more than a century in which a net increase of population was recorded—an increase of 5,500; the period 1961–66 recorded another increase, this time of about 66,000. Rates of emigration from the Republic vary widely; through the 20th century they have averaged about 10 per cent per decade, but their stimulation from time to time by particular events suggests that a kind of base rate probably runs at 7 per cent.

The basic cause of emigration from Ireland is the poverty of much of the land. The small development of industry and the well-established attractions of the New World are complementary and contributing factors. But the first great wave of emigration was a response to a single event—the disastrous famine of 1845.

In the early years of the 19th century potatoes were the staple food of countryfolk in Ireland. In 1845 the crop was ruined by blight. Food grain was kept out by the Corn Laws; there were no reserves of food in the country itself, for much of the cultivated land was worked in small parcels which could provide subsistence only at the lowest level. It has been estimated that during the famine three-quarters of a million Irish people starved to death; among the survivors there was an understandable rush to emigrate.

After the initial disaster, another factor came into operation. The famine showed clearly that the minute subdivision of land had gone too far, and the custom was established of passing an entire holding to a single heir. While the new practice ensured that the chosen heir should receive a farm undiminished in size, the other sons and daughters of the dead farmer inherited no land at all. There were few towns where they could find work in Ireland, and emigration was in consequence further encouraged.

Prospective heirs of Irish farmers today tend to marry late. It is common for them to defer marriage until they inherit their fathers' land, and the Irish birth-rate is thus kept lower than it might otherwise be. With the total of population kept low by emigration and by late marriages, it has been possible for the average standard of living in the Republic to rise significantly during the last few decades, despite the fact that the country has never undergone an industrial revolution.

CONCENTRATION IN TOWNS

The increase in the total population of the British Isles during the last two centuries corresponds to an increase in the numbers and sizes of towns. The combined populations of towns have increased at a greater rate than has the total population, for numbers in many rural areas have been declining for many years. Several factors combine to attract people to towns—prospects of better pay, wider choice of employment, better conditions of living, and more varied social life than farms and villages can offer. Mechanisation of farm work has reduced the demand for rural labour, and the extension of country bus services in the inter-war period has tightened the grip of the towns on the country. Large towns became technically possible only when public sanitation overcame most epidemic disease, and when transport services were capable of bringing in enough food to supply large numbers who lived concentrated in small areas. Whatever the technical and social complexities involved in the growth of towns, the net result is simple—some 80 per cent of the present inhabitants of the United Kingdom are town-dwellers.

A map of towns can thus be used to show some of the leading features in the distribution of people. Fig. 10:3, which represents towns with 50,000 or more inhabitants, locates 30 million people—57 per cent of the inhabitants of the British Isles. In actuality it locates a higher fraction, for many towns have spread beyond the official boundaries to which population statistics are related.

Any town with 50,000 or more people can be taken as successful, in the sense that it is likely to have firmly-established manufacturing or service industries, and that it discharges the full range of urban functions. It can be assumed to provide its inhabitants with work, shops, markets, banks, schools, and places of entertainment, and to make similar provision for people from surrounding districts. The largest towns of all have a national or an international importance; but any successful town, simply because it is successful, is likely to increase in numbers of people, and to expand physically and in the complexity of its activities.

Although all fully-developed towns have certain functions in common, some are characterised by particular kinds of activity which have greatly aided their growth. At the same time, the functions of a town are typically so complex that they cannot adequately be indicated by a one-word label. It is very rare indeed for more than half the workers in a given town to be engaged in a single class of occupation, and any form of employment which takes one worker in every ten is likely to be the leading form.

Location of Towns

Most of the towns mapped in Fig. 10:3 stand on the coast, on or near the coalfields, or in the English Midlands. These types of location are combined in a number of cases, as where the Tyneside Conurbation is both on the coast and on a coalfield, and where the West Midland Conurbation is (in part) on a coalfield and also in the Midlands. The relation between coal, industry, and population is well expressed by the Conurbations of Clydeside, Tyneside, Southeast Lancashire, and West Yorkshire, by the remaining manufacturing towns of Lancashire and the West Riding, by Nottingham and its neighbours, by Stoke and its neighbours, by the West Midland Conurbation, and by the large towns of South Wales. On Clyde-

side and Tyneside, and in South Wales, some of the industrial towns are also ports, but the largest town of South Wales—Cardiff—does not stand on the actual coalfield. It is thus similar to Middlesbrough and its neighbours, which are coastal (or nearly so) and have access to near-by coal. The greatest development of this kind has, however, taken place on the Mersey, where Liverpool and Birkenhead have effectively merged with adjacent settlements in the Merseyside Conurbation.

Hull, Bristol, and Belfast are flourishing coastal towns, Hull with 300,000 people and the other two approaching the half-million mark. They are sufficiently far from large coalfields for emphasis to be laid mainly on their coastal location. Belfast illustrates better than any other town the triumph of locational advantage over lack of local resources for industry, but Dundee and Aberdeen also deserve mention.

The towns of the English Midlands include some where industry has enjoyed remarkable success. The expansion of Coventry has admittedly been associated with the industrial growth of the Black Country, but this town, like Leicester and Nottingham, was already well-established before the industrial revolution. In recent times these three have profited by developments in the engineering industry, as to a lesser extent have Northampton, Oxford, and Luton. Although some of the Midland towns plotted in Fig. 10:3 are famous for specialised industry of one kind or another, engineering is the main single factor in their current expansion.

Significantly enough, the successful Midland towns lie between London and the industrial areas of the coalfields. There is a separation of space and of function between these towns and the large settlements on the south coast, nearly all of which have grown large because they are resorts.

Dublin, Edinburgh, and London are all coastal. They stand on the eastern coasts of their respective countries, two facing continental Europe and one facing Great Britain. Edinburgh has rather fewer than half a million people, and Dublin rather more. Both owe much of their present size to their status as capitals, just as Belfast benefits from being the chief town of Northern Ireland. Cardiff has become the official capital of Wales so recently that the effects of its new status have yet to appear.

Conurbations

The seven conurbations marked in Fig. 10:3 contain some 19 million people, about 1 in 3 of the population. They are composed of agglomerations of towns which are so close-knit that each forms an

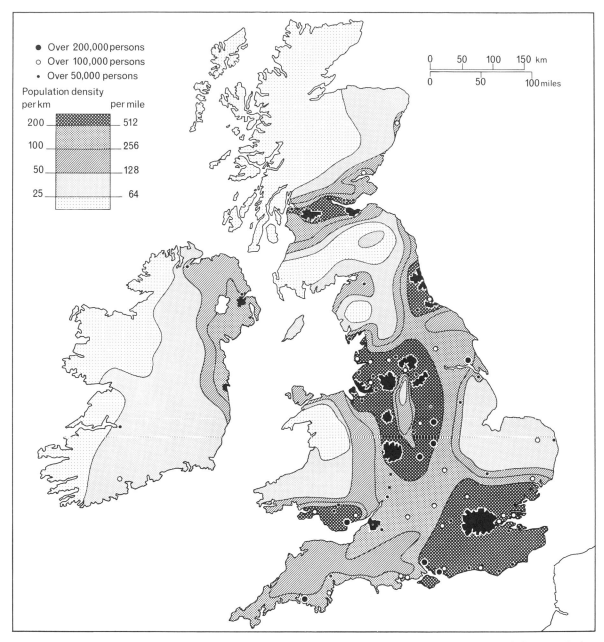

FIG. 10:3. Large urban areas and individual towns. Densities, highly generalised, relate to the remaining population. Data for 1968–70

urbanised region. Building is far more continuous in some than in others—Greater London, containing 8 million people, is very heavily built-up, whereas separate towns can still be distinguished in Southeast Lancashire—but each conurbation is marked by urban sprawl, by a tendency to spread, and by the progressive filling-in of its remaining vacant spaces.

The main development of most of the conurbations took place during the 19th century, although the spread of suburban housing continued up to 1939 and is again in progress today. Already by 1900 the rate of increase in population had fallen below the average for England and Wales in the Conurbations of Greater London, Southeast Lancashire, and West Yorkshire (Appendix 1); the

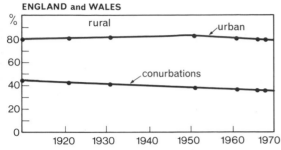

FIG. 10:4. Relative distribution of people, England and Wales, from 1910

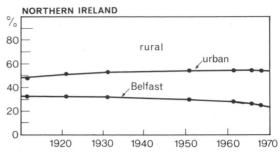

FIG. 10:6. Relative distribution of people, Northern Ireland, from 1910

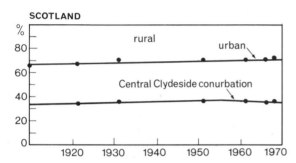

FIG. 10:5. Relative distribution of people, Scotland, from 1910

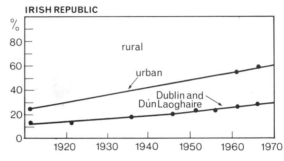

FIG. 10:7. Relative distribution of people in the territory of the Irish Republic, from 1910

rate of increase in the Tyneside Conurbation fell behind the national rate in the 1920s, and that of Merseyside in the 1930s. All these five now record little or no increase. The West Midland Conurbation provides an exception, for up to 1951 its population was still rising at a rate well above the national average. The difference between the trend and that in the other conurbations is to be associated with the change in West Midland industry from heavy metallurgy to highly successful specialised engineering.

Rates of increase in the conurbations would be lower still if people did not move in from other towns, from the country, or from abroad. Four million people—one in four of their inhabitants—were born outside the limits of the English conurbations: internal migration is still a powerful influence on the distribution of people in the British Isles. It has been supplemented since 1945 by immigration, which, made politically possible at a time of labour shortage, has resulted in the establishment in most big towns of groups of West Indians, Indians, and Pakistanis. In addition, in times of high employment Britain attracts many workers from Ireland.

The significance of conurbations, and of major concentrations of population generally, is illustrated in Figs. 10:4 to 10:7. Conurbations have been taking a progressively smaller proportionate share in the combined population of England and Wales throughout the present century (Fig. 10:4); and, since about 1950, the percentage classed as urban has actually been falling. Although in Scotland the urban percentage has persisted in a slight rise (Fig. 10:5), the proportionate share of the Clydeside conurbation has lately declined somewhat, also since about 1950. The urban percentage in Northern Ireland seems at present to be stabilised at about 50, but possible signs of the beginning of a decline have recently set in; Belfast has been taking a progressively smaller fraction of the total population since as early as 1930 (Fig. 10:6). Some allowance must be made in interpreting the highly generalised data for the influence of administrative boundaries, and especially for the lag between suburban expansion and extension of urban limits. Nevertheless, it appears conceivable that the concentrated town growth so typical of the 19th century may at last be coming to a halt in many parts of the United Kingdom. The Irish Republic, as in numerous other respects, provides a contrast (Fig. 10:7). The proportionate concentration of people in Dublin–Dún Laoghaire has accelerated during the 1950s and 1960s, with the total urban fraction now running above 50 per cent for the country and showing no sign of a slackening rate of increase.

Morphology of Towns

Large towns can usually be subdivided into parts which differ in function—shopping districts, residential districts, manufacturing districts, and business districts. The discharge of particular functions in particular areas of a town is strictly comparable with the concentration of certain industries in certain industrial regions, and secures the same kinds of advantage. The study of functional subdivision in towns usually reveals that the various parts recognised differ in age. In very many towns, the shopping and business districts occupy the medieval site. Together, they are known as the Central Business District, customarily abbreviated to C.B.D. or CBD. Towns with a far briefer than medieval and later history, such as those of North America, also generate their own CBDs; in a town of more than threshold size, a CBD is evidently part of the organic structure. In numbers of large British towns, the CBD is typically surrounded in whole or in part by 19th-century housing, often terraced. That, in its turn, is frequently enclosed by a broad belt of 20th-century dwellings in which the semi-detached house is the commonest feature. If industrial districts occur, they are likely to occupy extensive flat ground—if it is available—and in consequence to lie adjacent to a river. All kinds of variations occur in particular cases, and each town is unique, just as a geographical region is unique; but the concept of functional subdivision is a most useful one, aiding the study of an individual town and helping to reveal the changes which are going on. Further modifications apply to towns which in the later years of the 20th century have embarked on extensive rebuilding, whether or not their centres and/or industrial areas were devastated by bombing during World War II. Roughly speaking, the tendency seems to be for the CBD to be reconstructed first, under the strong pressure of commercial demand and congestion, and for the rundown inner residential areas to be tackled next—or, alternatively, to be tackled piecemeal at the same time.

If a town succeeds in its discharge of a particular function, it does more than merely grow in size. Buildings are converted from one use to another,

often being altered, later entirely reconstructed, and eventually replaced. For example, when the number of shops increases in an old-established town, some houses are converted to shops merely by construction of a counter in a room opening on to the street. The next step is the making of a shop-front which is built on to the house and provides a window for display (Plate 19). If business continues to be good, this alteration is likely to be followed by the reconstruction of the whole face of the lower floor, and that in turn by modernisation of the interior of the shop and by the conversion of the upper floor to offices or flats. The extreme case is entire rebuilding, during which the number of storeys is likely to be increased (cf. Plates 18–20).

Any of these stages may be omitted, and change may stop short of the last of them. In very many towns, however, examples of each stage are numerous, and it is easy to see how fast and in which directions the shopping districts are spreading.

The growth and reconstruction of a shopping district represents one kind of urban success, which can be compared to the establishment of climax vegetation (Chap. 3). Examples of urban failure, which are also numerous, have an equal value in showing change of function. In every large town there is at least one district which is degraded, having lost the esteem which it once held. London has many quarters where terraced streets of large 19th-century houses have become unfashionable and are no longer occupied by wealthy families; instead, the houses are let as single rooms or as flats, often without any reconstruction. In some such districts the houses are fast decaying, and decay of this kind is a cumulative process which, if unchecked, will inevitably produce slums. The change of status involves a change of inhabitants, so that urban failure as well as urban success means a shifting of people.

Both kinds of development are linked to the outward spread of all large towns (Plate 58). This spread is a result not only of increasing numbers, but also of the demands on the central districts made by commerce and business, and of the wish of many people to live near the country. The rapid spread of suburbs is a feature of our time, made possible by modern transport and in part enforced by competition for space. It is, however, merely one of the expressions of urban change; large towns are not static, but dynamic.

Except for towns dependent on unsuccessful industries, all the large towns of the British Isles

PLATE 18. Buildings, mainly 18th century, in the main market-place at King's Lynn. The spacious square is used as a car-park, except on market-days, but lies mainly empty on Sundays (as here).

PLATE 19. Transformation of a town street; late 19th-century terraced houses at Enfield, Middx., with shop-fronts.

PLATE 20. Modern building-part of Crawley New Town, with flats above shops.

must continue to grow. It seems likely that towns with populations between $\frac{1}{4}$ million and $\frac{1}{2}$ million will grow the fastest, so that the distribution of people roughed out by Fig. 10:3 will be modified in the future, but there is no reason to look for a reversal of the movement from country to town, or for any lessening in the strength and populations of towns in general.

APPENDIX

Comparative Percentage Increase in Population Since 1871: England and Wales, and Six Conurbations

Period	England & Wales	Greater London	S.E. Lancashire	West Midlands	West Yorks.	Merseyside	Tyneside
1871–1881	14·4	22·6	21·6	17·1	19·2	19·4	23·1
1881–1891	11·7	18·2	12·3	11·8	11·1	10·2	29·4
1891–1901	12·2	16·8	11·8	16·9	8·1	13·4	23·1
1901–1911	10·9	10·2	10·0	10·2	4·3	12·3	12·3
1911–1921	5·0	3·2	1·4	8·5	1·5	9·2	7·1
1921–1931	5·5	9·7	2·8	9·0	2·6	6·6	1·4
1931–1951	9·5	1·6	0·2	15·7	2·3	2·7	1·0
1951–1961	0·51	—0·21	0·02	0·46	0·06	0·00	0·20
1961–1966	—	—5·0	—2·0	1·0	0·0	—3·0	—3·0
1961–1971	5·2	—	—	—	—	—	—

PART TWO

Chapter II

Introduction to Part Two

In the eyes of many geographers, regional geography is geography at its best. It is also geography at its most complex, requiring the synthesis instead of the analysis of information. It requires the setting of limits to the regions which are distinguished, the identification of regional unity, and the description of regional character.

The word *region* originally meant an area subject to a single governing authority. Its meaning, that is to say, was wholly political. In the course of the natural evolution of language the original meaning has been greatly modified—indeed, it has been almost lost, for *region* in everyday speech has no precise significance. A geographical region may be described as a part of the earth's surface with recognisable geographical qualities which distinguish it from adjacent regions; but this description, attractive though it may at first appear, makes no contribution to the problem of selecting, estimating, or measuring the qualities on which identification depends.

So long as the distinctive qualities of a region, whatever they may be, are recognisable in the central parts, the region can be given a regional name and accorded separate treatment. But those vaguely-apprehended properties which are held to amount, in combination, to regional character are extremely difficult to define. Personal impressions are as limited in value as they are subjective in nature. If relief, geology, soils, climate, weather, population, land use, livestock, agricultural and industrial production, and employment were analysed parish by parish, some kind of precision might be imparted both to regional character and to regional limits. The task of analysis would be enormous; even so, it would be insufficient, for regional boundaries cut across many parishes—particularly in those areas where strip-like parishes run across the grain of the country.

For all these reasons, the fixing of regional boundaries can amount at best but to an approximation. It is partly a matter of choice. No two textbooks on the British Isles agree completely on a scheme of regions and of regional boundaries. In practice, varying criteria are used both in identifying a region and in fixing its limits.

Physical (or physiographic) regions, defined by reference to geological structure and surface form, differ from one to another because they have had contrasted histories of physical evolution. The simplest contrasts consist in the difference between high ground based on strong rocks and low ground based on weak rocks. The rise from low ground to high, coinciding with a geological boundary, is invariably accompanied by a change in climate, and usually by a change in soil. Physical boundaries in some parts of the British Isles coincide so closely with rapid spatial changes in land quality, land use, and the form and pattern of rural settlement that they fix the limits of geographical regions—as where the Scottish Highlands, ending at the Highland Boundary Fault, descend sharply to the well-populated farmland of Central Scotland. Elsewhere, however, physical boundaries and boundaries of other kinds are ill-marked, one region being separated from another by a fairly wide band of transition. The narrower the band, and the sharper the transition, the more satisfactory is the regional boundary which appears on a small-scale map as a solid line.

Except in the case of industrial regions, most regional boundaries are defined mainly with reference to physical and agricultural distributions; that is, the typical quality of the region as a whole, and its differences from adjacent regions, are determined largely by means of physique, climate, and agriculture. Industrial regions, however, are delimited by reference to economy and population. They transgress the boundaries which separate low ground from high, which distinguish contrasting climatic environments, and which mark changes in soils and agriculture. Deriving their unity neither from physique nor from land-use, industrial regions in the following text—as in reality—are superimposed on regions bounded by physical and agricultural limits (Fig. 13:1).

The term *industrial region* illustrates the way in which regional character may, on occasion, be indicated by a single word. Generally speaking, it is neither possible nor desirable to attach simple labels to regions, any more than to towns. Moreover, even the term *industrial region* tends to lose much of its apparent precision when it is closely examined. If an industrial region be defined as one dominated by industry, the problem at once arises of how to judge whether industry is dominant or not—by no means an easy problem to solve.

Even when they have been recognised and given boundaries of some kind, industrial regions raise further problems—those of accounting for the origin and growth of manufacture. Since heavy industry in the British Isles is based chiefly on or near coalfields, it is natural that the presence of workable coal should be recorded when any attempt is made to explain the distribution of heavy industry today. On the other hand, iron-working originally depended not on coal but on charcoal (Chap. 6). The well-known tendency for manufacturing industry to become concentrated on the coalfields was largely an expression of technical change—change in type of fuel and in source of power. While such a tendency is easy to understand, it is very difficult to describe in explanatory terms.

In one sense the matter is a philosophical one, for if the rise of industry is regarded as an effect it is proper to look for causes. As soon as the acts of men are admitted into the list of causes, the whole question at once becomes incredibly complex. It is so difficult to explain the activities of human beings in terms of causes that the classical economists invented the abstraction called *economic man*, to whom was imputed an intelligent self-interest which would ensure economic activity. The concept of economic man has lost favour, and the expression itself is no longer thought useful, but their one-time vogue illustrates an attempt to reduce the problem of explaining economic activity from a philosophical to a linguistic level—an attempt which succeeded merely in providing an additional way of stating that economic activity is carried on. In other words, description was achieved but explanation was not. In geography, as in economics, it is extremely difficult to arrive at satisfactory causal explanations.

Since people take the active part in establishing and developing industry, it is not permissible to speak of industry as *caused by* the presence of raw materials. The alternative statement, that the presence of raw materials led to the rise of industry, means something quite different—it embodies much more than a change of wording. It still, however, seems to imply too high a degree of inevitability and of direct causation. If it is said that the presence of raw materials made industrial growth possible, the statement becomes both reasonable and correct, but also so weak and obvious that it loses nearly all its force.

There is no reason to believe that any complete solution of the linguistic problem must exist. There may be no acceptable way of summarising the origins of industry in a brief phrase, especially since so much caution is required in implying causes. On the other hand, the concentrations of industry which we know today are the outcome of technical, economic and social developments which were typically localised in their effects and fairly rapid in their progress. The establishment of a single concern in a particular place is often to be ascribed to an individual, and it is far too much to expect that all industry will display geographical advantages of location; but in the case of an industrial region it is right to look for manifest physical advantages, and at the same time to appeal to history in order to show how industry developed along certain lines rather than along others. Industrial development in South Wales (Chap. 13) provides an excellent case in point.

In the following regional chapters, Ireland, Wales, and Scotland are taken first, in that order. Later chapters lead, in a general way, across England from north to south, ending with the London Basin and the metropolis. Some of the outstanding qualities of each region are named, and reasons are given for the choice of regional boundaries. The term *sub-region* is not used, because of its implication that there can be an orderly sequence of regional subdivision, and because it would involve cumbersome names; at the same time, quite strong internal contrasts are described for a number of whole regions. Statistical summaries for each region include area, data of land use and livestock, total population, and individual populations of leading towns. The town lists—some of them lengthy—are intended for purposes of reference, and to show where many of the people live and work.

Place-names have been kept to a minimum. Most of the places mentioned in the text are marked on the accompanying maps, but a large-scale atlas is an indispensable adjunct to reading, and the $\frac{1}{4}$-inch/mile and 10 miles/inch official maps are also strongly recommended. Selected maps of various scales, chosen as particularly relevant to the topics discussed, are specified in the bibliography for each chapter.

Wherever field-work can be carried out, it cannot fail to illuminate regional study. While a rapid traverse across a region cannot contribute to exact understanding, it is nevertheless capable of revealing that regional differences do occur. Detailed field-work can always be relied on to give significance to, and to amplify, the general statements of which regional accounts unavoidably consist.

Chapter 12

The Regions of Ireland

THE small degree of industrial development in Ireland means that the regional geography of that island is simpler than that of Great Britain, and especially than the regional geography of England. Regional boundaries in Ireland, drawn mainly with reference to physical and agricultural distributions, offer the simplest examples of how such boundaries are defined. On the other hand, Ireland includes a political boundary—the sole instance of an international boundary (Plate 21) in the British Isles.[1]

Before too much stress comes to be laid on physical and rural-demographic considerations, however, a precautionary word is in order. The Irish Republic, coping until the late 1950s chiefly with its farming problems, then switched policy, offering direct encouragement to foreign industrialists (see bibliography: Tarrant). Although it still counts only about a quarter of a million industrial workers, not so many more than Northeast Ireland with half as many people, industrialisation is at last under way. Local and regional effects will be noticed below; the general effect is to encourage investment by firms based especially in the U.K. (where Irish manufactured goods enter duty-free), Germany, and the U.S.A.

With increasing industrialisation goes increase in power supply. The Irish Republic has developed hydro-electric power, and has done even better (in terms of power production) with peat-firing. Well over half the total output of electricity in the country, however, comes from thermal stations, the three greatest plants being the thermal installations at Ringsend (near Dublin), Marina (Cork), and the Tarbert station in Kerry.

The scheme of regional division adopted for Ireland is illustrated in Fig. 12:1. The regions fall into four groups. Group 1, consisting entirely of lowland, coincides with the Central Plain; Group 2 includes all the hill country and the wide but enclosed valleys between the Central Plain and the south coast, with the quite extensive lowlands flanking the Shannon estuary; Group 3 is formed by the mountainous northwestern fringe of Ireland from Galway to Donegal, while Group 4 is almost identical with the political unit of Northern Ireland. Groups 2, 3, and 4 include all the high ground of the island.

Limits of areas differing strongly in soil, climate, and agriculture correspond closely to the boundaries which separate the regional groups. Each group is subdivided in accordance with rapid spatial changes in physique, in the character and aim of farming, or in both. Agricultural distributions are highly significant in the regional geography of Ireland, not only because of the great importance of farming in the economy, but also because they display contrasts of the kind which might be expected in the climax communities of wild vegetation. Irish agriculture, like climax vegetation, displays complex adaptations which result from complex and long-operating causes, with few effects of political direction or influence. Thus, while some regions such as the Wicklow Mountains(2c) have well-defined physical limits, the single physical unit of the Central Plain is divided into two geographical regions (1a, 1b) in accordance with the use made of the land.

A number of general statements apply to most or all of the island. The differences between one region and another are superimposed on certain common characteristics—form of rural settlement, status of towns, and supply of labour for farm work.

In most districts rural settlement is typically dispersed (Fig. 12:5). It is by no means evenly spread, for the worst land has no inhabitants, while the

---

[1] The Channel Islands (Chap. 26), which have never formed part of a kingdom ruled from London, are conventionally excluded from the British Isles.

PLATE 21. Border station at Newton Butler, on the border of Northern Ireland with the Irish Republic.

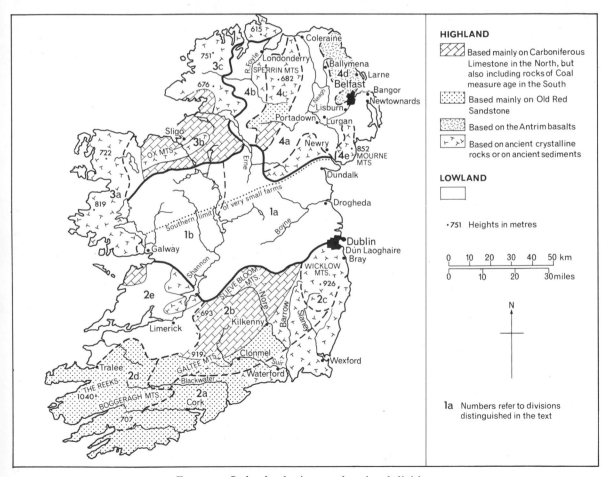

FIG. 12:1. Ireland: physique and regional division

peopled areas record densities of farm population which is high by English standards. Where houses occur, they are scattered singly or in tiny groups throughout the farmland. Dispersion of settlement in some areas is known to have occurred as late as the 19th century (cf. Fig. 4:10), when land tenure and the arrangement of holdings were reorganised and many nucleated settlements disintegrated. Late as it was, dispersion has been remarkably complete, and the main unit of rural settlement is the single farm. The architectural style of small country dwellings is far less varied than in England, and its variety is reduced to a minimum in the west of the country where single-storeyed, stone-built, thatched, and whitewashed cottages are everywhere to be seen.

Most Irish country towns are small, depressing in appearance, and unlikely to expand at any great rate (Plate 22). To some extent Irish rural life is carried on as if towns did not exist, or as if they existed merely to discharge the functions of periodic markets. However, signs of selective urbanisation are making themselves evident in recent times (Fig. 12:2). Dublin, Cork, Dún Laoghaire, Limerick, Waterford, Galway, Dundalk, Drogheda, and (marginally) Bray, in that

PLATE 22. The centre of Armagh, a small Irish town.

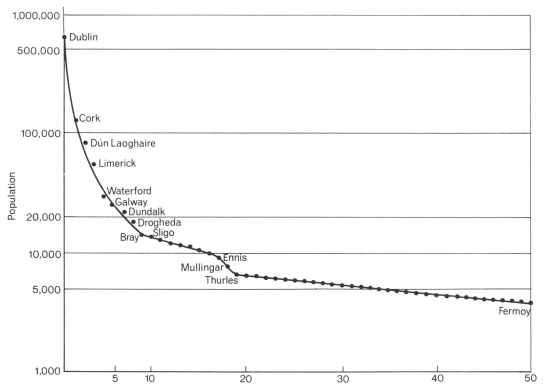

FIG. 12:2. Size-rank ordering of towns in the Irish Republic: vertical scale is logarithmic

order of rank-size, can be regarded as having accomplished an urban take-off that lesser Irish towns have yet to achieve. The next-ranking series, ranging from Sligo (about 13,500) to Carlow (fewer than 10,000) conceivably represents the tail of the distribution of the more successful. Then comes a sudden drop, through Ennis (about 9,000) to Mullingar (about 8,000), after which the rank-size distribution declines in exponential fashion. We can infer that the approximate 10,000 mark is critical. Above this, urban strengthening feeds itself. Below this, town size and town activity depend strictly on the demands of the immediate hinterland.

product of farms in the Republic, a third is consumed on the farms themselves. Thus farming involves the Irish country-dwellers directly, to a degree unknown in England for the last two centuries, and farming for subsistence is an important element in Irish agriculture, even though few farms sell no part of their produce.

The distinctive characteristics of Irish farming and of Irish rural life are most pronounced in the west, where remoteness weakens and retards influences from outside, where the Irish language is still used in daily speech, and where endemic rural poverty is still to be observed in places. Conversely, the eastern parts of the island contain the highest

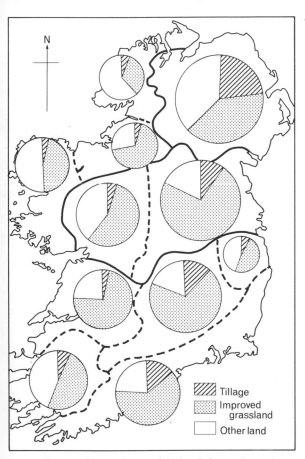

FIG. 12:3. Land use of Ireland, by regions

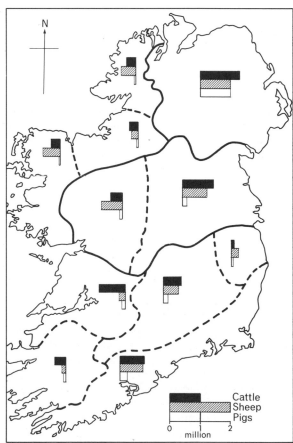

FIG. 12:4. Farm livestock in Ireland, by regions

Farming in Ireland is typically a family affair, four-fifths of the labour being supplied by farmers and their relatives. Paid labourers are scarcely known in the less prosperous areas, where the emphasis is on production for use on the farm rather than on production for sale. Of the total

proportion of town-dwellers to total population, are the most deeply committed to farming for sale, and most readily employ paid labour on the land. They are also the best favoured agriculturally, as may readily be seen from Figs. 12:3 and 12:4.

1a THE EASTERN CENTRAL PLAIN

Area: about 12,750 km² (4,900 sq. mi.).
Population: about 1,250,000.
Largest towns: Dublin (655,000 with suburbs).
           Dún Laoghaire (100,000 with
                suburbs).
           Dundalk (22,000).
           Drogheda (18,500).

Seven additional towns have more than 5,000 inhabitants each.
Density of population: about 30/km² (85/sq. mi.) outside the eleven towns.

Ninety per cent of this region is in improved farmland, and nearly three-quarters of the region is in improved grass.
Numbers of livestock: cattle, 1,125,000;
                    sheep, 835,000;
                    pigs, 200,000;
                    poultry, 1,865,000.

One out of every three people in the Irish Republic lives in the Eastern Central Plain, and one out of every five lives in Dublin. Dublin dominates the Republic even more strongly than London dominates England, for it is ten times as populous as the next largest towns of Cork and Dún Laoghaire, accounts for nearly half the industrial output of the whole country, and employs more than two-fifths of the industrial labour force. As the capital of the Republic, the one large industrial town, and by far the greatest port, Dublin has a status far higher than that of the capital of its region; but the region under discussion is effectively that part of the Central Plain which sends a large part of its agricultural produce to the port of Dublin for export.

The Eastern Central Plain is a region of lowland, lying for the most part below 100 m. (300 ft.) and containing extensive bogs. Its foundation, chiefly of Carboniferous Limestone, is almost everywhere concealed by glacial drift or by peat. Bog is limited in extent within some 40 km (25 mi.) of Dublin, but becomes more common on the low divide which separates the Boyne and Liffey from Shannon. The extent of bog increases still further on the far side of the watershed towards the Shannon river, which roughly marks the regional boundary. The region as a whole, and the boggy districts in particular, are diversified by eskers— long winding ridges of glacial outwash which stand above the peat and give access from east to west.

This is the least rainy part of Ireland, with between 200 and 225 rain-days a year and an annual precipitation averaging between 750 and 1,000 mm. The 1,000 mm. isohyet runs approximately around the regional boundary. Climatically the region is comparable to the Lancs.–Cheshire Plain (Chap. 18), and like it, is intensively farmed.

Farming is dominated by the keeping of livestock, among which cattle are rather more numerous than sheep (Fig. 12:4). It is for the sake of cattle that so large a fraction of the farmland is kept in improved grass. The winter season is long for Ireland, but the frost-free period is no shorter than that experienced in the agricultural heart of Cheshire, and the generally humid atmosphere encourages a thick growth of grass to which the soils developed on limy glacial drift are well suited. In the immediate neighbourhood of Dublin, dairy-farming and market-gardening are carried on, supplying the large urban market on the coast, but throughout most of the region the production of beef cattle is the main interest (Plate 23). The live cattle sent for export from this region are noted in England for their good condition, but more store cattle than fatstock are exported. The Eastern Central Plain contributes largely to the live-cattle export which is so prominent in the external trade of the Republic (Fig. 9:5). Only in the southwest of the region does cattle-grazing lose its dominance, where a transition occurs through mixed farming towards the dairy-farming of Clare and Limerick. The racehorses for which Irish breeders are famous come from the eastern part of the region. Sheep-farming is scattered around its margins and on the acid peat of raised bogs. Tillage crops in-

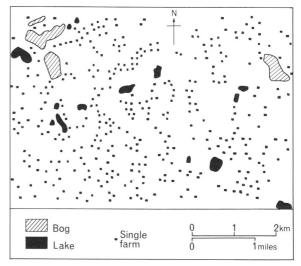

FIG. 12:5. Sample of dispersed settlement in Ireland: part of the main drumlin-belt in County Monaghan

Bog
Lake
Single farm
0   1   2km
0   1miles

PLATE 23. Bullocks on permanent grassland, Irish Central Plain.

clude oats, potatoes, and wheat, but—as throughout Ireland generally—the principal cut crop is hay.

The raised bogs began with the formation of mild fen peat in hollows of the lime-rich drift, but as the peat grew thicker, and rose above the level of its surroundings, its character changed. Proposals have been made to strip off the acid peat, in order to reveal the underlying fen peat which could be usefully cultivated if it were drained.

Settlement is widely scattered. In addition to the coastal towns listed above, there are small market centres inland, some loose-knit villages, hamlets, and many single houses. Dispersal is most marked in the north of the region, where holdings of land are small and rural dwellings closely-spaced (Fig. 12:5). The region here overlaps on to a belt of drumlins which extends broadly across the width of Ireland; dairying and mixed farming, with arable land intensively worked, become prominent in this part.

Dublin and Dún Laoghaire

The four largest towns stand on the coast. Dublin, as an old Gaelic name[1] shows, first developed as a small settlement associated with a ford across the Liffey, becoming a fortified estuary-head town under the Norsemen. The Norse stronghold stood on patches of river-terrace and raised beach alongside the creek where the ships lay. The Normans added a castle during the 13th century, when a cathedral was also founded, and in later times Dublin became the chief port of entry to Ireland and the centre of the fluctuating English power. A great deal of rebuilding occurred during the late 18th and early 19th centuries, its main legacy being the elegant Georgian architecture for which Dublin is justly famed (Plate 24). It was also in the 18th century that reclamation began in Dublin Bay, where the dock and industrial districts

---

[1] Baile Atha Cliath, now the official name of Dublin.

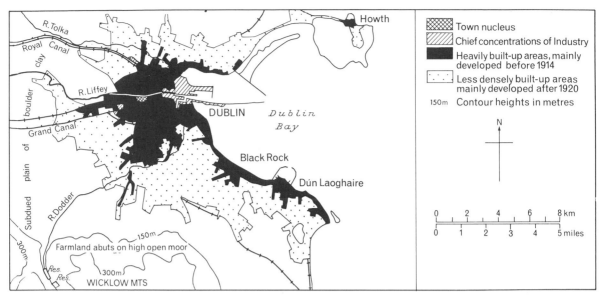

FIG. 12:6. Dublin and its local setting

PLATE 24. Severe but elegant Georgian houses, Dublin.

are located on reclaimed land (Fig. 12:6). The functional growth of Dublin has outpaced its rate of expansion in size, and some of the poorer residential districts are severely overcrowded.

The Liffey constitutes the long axis of an ellipse which, including the inner part of Dublin, is enclosed by the arcs formed by a ring-road and by the eastern ends of the Royal and Grand Canals. Growth of the town has been most vigorous towards the northeast and the southeast, where settlements in the coastal belt have been engulfed. The urban stimulus of Dublin is felt beyond the resort of Bray, twelve miles away to the south, and is responsible for part of the scatter of dwelling on the extreme northeast flank of the Wicklow Mountains.

The industries of Dublin include metal-working and engineering, the manufacture of wool, cotton, clothing and footwear, meat-canning and bacon-processing, brewing, distilling, and the making of biscuits, chocolate, jam, cigarettes, tobacco, and fertilisers. Dublin absorbs much of the raw material imported into the Republic for industrial use, takes a large share in the processing of foodstuffs imported from abroad and produced at home, and commands the manufacturing industries which produce for export. The city is among the principal beneficiaries from the revised policy of encouraging industrial investment from abroad; in consequence, its industrial base is being diversified.

Dublin, with its ample bay sheltered on the north by Howth Head, is by far the best gateway into the Central Plain and into the whole of Ireland. Immediately to the south, the Wicklow Mountains rise almost directly from the coast, while north of Dublin the shore is low and sandy. It is natural that Dublin should have come to dominate the external trade of the Republic, but Dún Laoghaire is the main passenger port. Although the two towns are still administratively separate, the former gap of five miles between them has now been closed by building. Dún Laoghaire stands where firm rock reaches the shore at the southern extremity of the sand-fringed bay, its two breakwaters enclosing the artificial harbour which shelters packets from Holyhead, $3\frac{1}{4}$ hours away by sea. Dublin has direct passenger services of its own to Liverpool and Glasgow.

Smaller Coastal Towns

Small coastal resorts have developed on the low shoreline north of Dublin. The two main breaks through the beaches occur at the mouths of the Boyne and Castletown rivers, on which stand Drogheda and Dundalk. These two towns resemble Dublin in being estuary-head settlements, each standing at the inner end of a drowned valley-mouth and being the lowest bridging-point of its river. With their small and shallow harbours, their more difficult access to the interior, and their inferior administrative status, they have grown but to modest size; they are, however, considerable towns for Ireland. Each has a small port trade, and manufactures tobacco, cotton, linen, and beer. Fertilisers are made in Drogheda, cement and leather in Dundalk.

1b THE WESTERN CENTRAL PLAIN

Area: about 6,750 km² (2,600 sq. mi.).
Population: about 167,500.
Largest town: Galway (30,000).
The second largest town, Ballinasloe, has 6,000 people.
Density of population outside these two towns: about 20/km² (50/sq. mi.).
About two-thirds of this region is farmland, almost all of it improved grass. Non-agricultural land is extensive.
Numbers of livestock: cattle, 450,000;
     sheep, 750,000;
     pigs, 55,000;
     poultry, 825,000.

The Central Plain is as low-lying to the west of the Shannon as it is to the east. It is much more boggy, for rainfall in this region rises above 1,000 mm. a year and the number of rain-days increases correspondingly. A good deal of the unimproved land consists of bog, which is commoner here than in the adjacent region to the east, because the air is usually damp and because many enclosed hollows occur in the glacial drift. Among the lakes which occupy the largest hollows of all are Lough Ree, 27 km long, and Lough Derg, 40 km long. Their irregular shallow basins are probably due, in the main, to glacial scouring, but are thought to have been enlarged by solution of the underlying Carboniferous Limestone. The solid rock is rarely exposed, being masked by glacial deposits which in the north are moulded into drumlins. Eskers are numerous.

In this rainy and maritime region, sheep are as common as cattle are in the Eastern Central Plain. The contrast between the two regions in numbers of livestock is well brought out by the bargraphs of Fig. 12:4, just as the general contrast in the use of land is shown by the wheels in Fig. 12:3. The region relies almost wholly on farming. There are very few towns of any size, and rural settlement is highly dispersed, being denser in the better-drained north than in the waterlogged and boggy south. The boundary of the belt of small farms marked in Fig. 12:1 coincides roughly with a transition from dominant sheep-farming in the south of the region to dominant mixed farming with production of store cattle in the north.

The regional capital, Galway, stands on the Atlantic coast where the Central Plain breaks through its rim of upland. Routes are focused on Galway by the deep bite of Galway Bay into the land, and by the long stretch of Lough Corrib and its surrounding blanket-bogs, but the western districts are poor, and demands for urban services are limited throughout the area served. Galway is hampered as a port by a submerged dyke offshore, and nothing has come of the optimistic proposal that a terminal for transatlantic services should be established. The industries of the town include the milling of flour and timber, the making of furniture, and small-scale iron-founding, but Galway can scarcely be said to have taken a full share in the industrial development of the Irish Republic, limited though that development has been.

2a THE SOUTH IRISH COASTLANDS

Area: about 8,250 km² (3,200 sq. mi.).
Population: about 425,000.
Largest towns: Cork (135,000 with suburbs).
　　　　　　　　Waterford (13,000).
　　　　　　　　Wexford (13,000).
Four additional towns have more than 5,000 inhabitants each.
Density of population: about 27/km² (70/sq. mi.) outside the seven towns.

Nearly 80 per cent of this region is in improved farmland, with grass four times as extensive as tillage.
Numbers of livestock: cattle, 850,000;
　　　　　　　　　　　sheep, 550,000;
　　　　　　　　　　　pigs, 200,000;
　　　　　　　　　　　poultry, 1,500,000.

The South Irish Coastlands stretch from the Wicklow Mountains to the head of Bantry Bay, including the lower valleys of the Slaney, Barrow, and Suir, and most of the basins of the Blackwater and Lee. The eastern part of the region is based chiefly on Cambrian and Ordovician sediments,

metamorphosed in places and heavily intruded by igneous rocks, while the west is underlain mainly by Old Red Sandstone. Structurally the region belongs to the belt of Altaid folding, and the east–west grain is well marked. It is reflected in the arrangement of numerous valleys excavated by subsequents along weak outcrops, but traces of an earlier drainage-pattern survive in reaches where streams break through the belts of strong rock towards the south. The terrain rises in a staircase of erosional platforms, which continues upwards beyond the inner limit of the region at about 200 m. (600 ft.) O.D. The rivers have cut deeply below the general level of the broad, subdued divides, but there is little ground at very low levels except near the estuaries. All of these have been drowned, and resemble the rias of Southwest England with which they are identical in origin. Wexford, Waterford, and Cork are located on the three largest rias, and the banks of some of the smaller inlets provide sites for lesser towns.

The region benefits climatically from its southerly position and maritime exposure. Although rainfall is quite heavy, ranging between 1,000 and 1,250 mm. a year, the frost-free period is from 7 months long at the inland boundary to more than 9 months on the coast in the west. The coastland around Waterford and Wexford is the sunniest part of Ireland.

There is some bog which can be used only for turf-cutting or as rough pasture for sheep, but most of the land is in improved farms. Farming is dominantly mixed, and it is this characteristic which separates the region from the adjacent inland region (2c) on the north, for in the latter dairying is the leading interest. The proportion of tillage in the South Coastland Region is high for Ireland. In addition to oats, tillage crops include potatoes, wheat, barley, and sugar beet. These last three do best in the comparatively sunny eastern half of the region (Figs. 5:12–5:17), barley being in demand by breweries and wheat and sugar beet being fostered by subsidy.

Cork, Waterford, and Wexford

Cork (Fig. 12:7), the second largest town of the Republic, is the regional capital, although in practice Wexford and Waterford act as urban foci for their own surroundings. Cork has about 7 per cent of the country's workers in manufacturing industry. Its engineering includes vehicle-building and the making of agricultural machinery; rubber, wool, and leather are manufactured, and clothing and footwear produced for the wholesale trade.

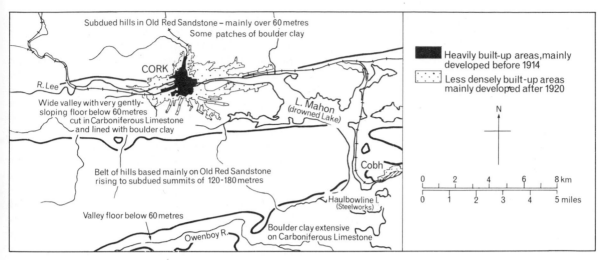

Heavily built-up areas, mainly developed before 1914

Less densely built-up areas mainly developed after 1920

FIG. 12:7. Cork and its local setting

Steel-making was established near Cobh in 1938, alongside the deepwater harbour of the former naval base. Cork holds a leading position in the butter trade, and has jam factories, breweries, distilleries, and flour mills. Like Dublin and Shannon, the Cork area is a principal focus for foreign industrial investment, possessing manufactures of new and varied kind, and of a footloose character whereby advantages of location, labour supply, and state aid are interchangeable.

When the whole of Ireland was politically united to the U.K., Cork's outport of Queenstown was a port of call on a number of transatlantic lines. The ria at the mouth of the Lee is the largest and most sheltered harbour on the south coast of Ireland, and has access to the interior of the country by gaps less than 175 m. high. The rail link with Dublin made possible the growth of a passenger traffic geographically comparable with that of Plymouth. Under its present name Cobh, the terminal is busy enough to make it the second port in the Republic (i.e., second to Dublin) in tonnage of shipping. Dún Laoghaire takes third place, and Cork, dealing in freight rather than in passengers, fourth. Cork receives raw materials, including coal for its thermal-electric station, and exports agricultural produce and processed foodstuffs.

Waterford and Wexford resemble Cork as Dundalk and Drogheda resemble Dublin—that is, they are comparably sited, but are much smaller. Waterford commands the lowest bridge on the Suir, 13 km from the head of Waterford Harbour and 25 km from the open sea. Wexford possesses the lowest bridge over the Slaney ria, but Wexford Harbour is a lagoon cut off from the sea by long, arcuate spits. The entrance is shallow, and passenger services which require frequent and regular sailings are concentrated on Rosslare, 13 km away to the southeast. The location of Rosslare resembles that of Dún Laoghaire, for the place stands on the open coast where firm ground appears at the side of South Bay. A breakwater protects the harbour from which packets sail to Fishguard.

Waterford and Wexford are shopping and market centres, with industries which are directly linked to farming. Both manufacture agricultural machinery—now under tariff protection—and Waterford has a bacon factory, breweries, and flour mills. It seems likely that industries of a more general character might have developed quite early in each of these towns, had it not been for the official policy of industrial dispersal; however, the operation of changed policy during the 1960s has given Waterford an industrial estate.

2b HILLS AND VALLEYS OF THE INLAND SOUTH

Area: about 7,000 km² (2,700 sq. mi.).
Population: about 205,500.
Largest towns: Kilkenny (12,000).
   Clonmel (11,500).
   Carlow (10,000).
   Mallow (6,000).
Density of population: about 25/km² (65/sq. mi.) outside the towns named.

About 80 per cent of this region is in improved farmland, with grassland six times as extensive as tillage.

Numbers of livestock: cattle, 625,000;
sheep, 455,000;
pigs, 150,000;
poultry, 885,000.

The Inland South is roughly separated from the Southern Coastlands by the 200-m. contour on the main divides, and by the change from dominantly mixed farming to dominant dairying. Any climatic significance which the boundary may possess lies in the moderation of maritime influences as the coast is left behind. The frost-free period in the Inland South falls below 7 months, the amount of sunshine decreases, and the annual and daily ranges of temperature rise a little. Precipitation increases to more than 1,250 mm. a year on the outer flanks of the high ground, and, when it falls towards 1,000 mm. on the inland side of the crests, the decrease is accompanied by cooler and longer winters. The contrast in actual temperatures between the coastlands and the interior is greater than that recorded in sea-level figures, for the ground rises generally from the coast inland, reaching more than 1,000 m. in height in the Galtee Mountains. But the hills of the Inland South are interpenetrated by broad corridors of low ground, which blur the regional boundary drawn diagrammatically in Figs. 12:1 and 12:3–12:4; the Barrow is already less than 65 m. above sea-level when it enters the region from the north, and the divide between the Suir and the Shannon lies little above 80 m. at the highest, so that maritime influences are not blocked by a continuous barrier.

The really high ground is generally under rough pasture, with blanket bog on flat sites. The extensive lower slopes are developed on rocks mainly of Carboniferous age, with limestones prominent among them, although the Old Red Sandstone appears in the south. Glacial drift is patchy, and the soils into which it weathers tend to be limy or warm, like those formed on the solid rocks which constitute the parent materials of the drift. Although rainfall is more than adequate, the lower plateau steps are extensively farmed. The proportion of improved land to total area is high for Ireland, and the good land is well worked. Sugar beet is significantly important among tillage crops, although oats, potatoes, and wheat cover larger acreages. The high ratio of cattle to sheep indicates a high agricultural status for the region. Dairying is dominant but not exclusive, for fat and store cattle are also produced.

Much of the milk produced on the dairy-farms goes to one or other of the scattered creameries. The size and shape of the area from which a creamery draws its supplies depends on accessibility. Butter is likely to be made on the farm if the nearest creamery lies at an inconvenient distance, while fresh milk can be sold if a town is near-by. Towns are characteristically small, however, and population is essentially agricultural, rural, and dispersed. The usual minor market centres occur at intervals. Kilkenny on the Nore and Clonmel on the Suir rank as major centres in this region, the one making clothing, footwear, and beer, and the other motor-bodies and cider.

More than any other region, the Inland South has profited from the subsidised growing of sugar beet. It possesses two of the nation's four sugar-beet factories, which have a total capacity roughly equal to the total demand for sugar in the Republic. Neither the processing of sugar-beet nor the making of creamery butter, however, encourages the growth of towns, and Kilkenny and Clonmel show little sign of expanding.

North of Kilkenny, between the Nore and the Barrow, occurs the only Irish coalfield with a noticeable output. In times other than those of war, annual production runs at about 200,000 tons. The seams are thin, but the coals are anthracitic—a fact which is a handicap rather than a help, since ordinary household coal of the bituminous kind would be more readily sold. Coal-mining has stimulated no industry to develop, and, except when imports are restricted by wartime conditions, this Irish coal cannot meet the competition of seaborne coal along the east and south-east coasts. On the other hand, it encounters no insuperable competition from peat fuel: the Bord na Móna (Turf Board), producing some $3\frac{1}{2}$ million tons of mainly milled peat a year, operates at a persistent loss.

2c THE WICKLOW MOUNTAINS
2d THE PENINSULAR SOUTHWEST

These small regions differ from their neighbours by their generally high relief, their high proportion of non-agricultural land, and their low densities of population. The contrasts between them and the adjoining regions are apparent in Figs. 12:3 and 12:4, and in the following summaries:

THE WICKLOW MOUNTAINS
Area: about 2,100 km² (800 sq. mi.).
Population: about 61,500.

Largest town: Bray (14,500).

The only other town with more than 5,000 people is Arklow (6,500).

Density of population outside Bray and Arklow: about 20/km² (50/sq. mi.).

Only about half this region is in improved farmland. Grass is about five times as extensive as tillage.

Numbers of livestock: cattle, 105,000;
         sheep, 250,000;
         pigs, 15,000;
         poultry, 400,000.

THE PENINSULAR SOUTHWEST

Area: about 5,500 km² (2,100 sq. mi.).

Population: about 125,000.

Largest town: Tralee (12,500: on the regional boundary).

Only Killarney (7,000) also has more than 5,000 inhabitants.

Density of population outside Tralee and Killarney: about 20/km² (50/sq. mi.).

Something more than half this region is in improved farmland, with grass seven times as extensive as tillage.

Numbers of livestock: cattle, 425,000;
         sheep, 200,000;
         pigs, 105,000;
         poultry, 525,000.

The Wicklow Mountains are based on a large granitic mass and on the cover of indurated sediments which surrounds the exposed granite. The Wicklows form the most compact block of high ground in Ireland, their broad spurs rising between glacially deepened valleys to heights of 800 m. and more; the highest summit exceeds 1,000 m. This is a rainy region, with annual falls of 1,500 mm. on the highest ground; the number of rain-days is little above that recorded in the near-by lowlands, but lifting of damp air over the mountains promotes instability, and individual falls are apt to be heavy. Dublin's problem of water supply has been solved, for the time being at least, by the raising of the level of Lake Poulaphouca, where H.E.P. is generated.

Cotton-grass moor occurs on the peat of the gently-sloping upland summits, with sedge moor in the shallow valley-heads. At lower levels come heather moor and gorse moor, while strips of woodland line the flanks of the trough-like valleys. Very few people live in the heart of the region, where the land is used as rough pasturage for sheep. Cultivation and cattle are confined to the deep valley-floors and to the low outer slopes. Stock-farming is

practised on the western side, dairying for the Dublin market on the east, and the coastal strip between Bray and Wicklow is intensively farmed. Bray—previously noted as a resort for Dubliners—has doubled in numbers of people in the last seventy years, and is the chief centre for tourism in the Wicklows. The county town of Wicklow has fewer than 3,500 people and is not expanding.

The Peninsular Southwest is based on strongly folded sediments in which the Armorican trend is displayed with exceptional clarity. The east–west grain of structures is even better seen here than in the hinterland of Cork, for the upfolded outcrops of Old Red Sandstone form long spines of high ground, while the Carboniferous Limestone depressed in the intervening downfolds has been deeply eroded to form great longitudinal valleys. Between the drowned extremities of the valleys the highland projects in long promontories. In this western part of the region the land has undergone severe erosion, not only by rivers, but also by the ice which was nourished by snowy winds at glacial maximum. Corries bite savagely into the flanks of the mountains, but there are few cross-gaps, and travel across the trend of relief is difficult.

The whole region receives more than 1,500 mm. of rain a year, and some central parts have more than 2,000 mm. The high totals are explained partly by exposure to winds off the Atlantic, and partly by altitude—there is much land above 500 m., and Macgillicuddy's Reeks surpass 1,100 m. A general decline in height towards the east is offset by a greater development of gentle slopes of high levels, which favours the growth of blanket bog.

Population is confined to low levels and to sloping ground. Losses by emigration have been very heavy and numbers are still declining, although farming is fairly successful. Cattle outnumber sheep, and milk is sent to creameries, but sheep are numerous enough to suggest that much of the land is of poor quality. A distinctive feature of the western coastlands is cottage farming,[1] a form of agriculture which represents an incomplete transition from crofting to commercial farming. The cottage farmer counts on selling some of his produce off the farm, thus differing from the crofter whose aim is self-sufficiency, but he is not sufficiently committed to producing for sale to be called a commercial farmer.

Like the Wicklow Mountains, this region is noteworthy for its tourist trade. The leading inland

---

[1] The term is due to T. W. Freeman.

centre of tourism is Killarney, but the small towns at the heads of the western bays also take a share. Tralee, the largest town of the region, acts as an urban centre for the northern districts and also for part of the lowlands alongside the Shannon in Region 2e. The most notable industry of Tralee was formerly the manufacture of enamelware, which had no possibly explicable geographical basis, but which enjoyed (as it continues to enjoy) a national market. More lately, ball-bearing manufacture has been added, in consequence of the encouragement of entry into the Republic of foreign-based manufacturing firms. Simultaneously, the increasing size of oil tankers has promoted the opening of a deep-water terminal in Bantry Bay, where 25 m. (75 ft.) of draught is available close inshore, and where vessels up to 300,000 tons can enter.

2e THE CLARE–LIMERICK LOWLAND

Area: about 9,000 km² (3,500 sq. mi.).
Population: about 400,000.
Largest town: Limerick (65,000).

The only other towns with more than 5,000 people are Ennis (9,500) and Thurles (7,000).
Density of population: about 35/km² (90/sq. mi.) outside the three towns named.

About three-quarters of this region is in improved farmland, almost the whole of it grass.
Numbers of livestock: cattle, 205,000;
  sheep, 210,000;
  pigs, 110,000;
  poultry, 1,250,000.

Most of the Clare–Limerick Lowland stands less than 80 m. above sea-level, where lowland extends broadly on either side of the upper estuary of the Shannon. Nevertheless, its affinities are with the hill country of the south of Ireland rather than with the central plain. It is partly enclosed by hills on the northeast, where Silurian, Devonian, and Carboniferous strata rise to the surface and project in blocks of hills reaching 700 m. in places. Upland occurs also in the west of the region, where bare Carboniferous Limestone is exposed in wide, barren erosional platforms ranging up to 270 m. in height.

Rainfall varies from 1,000 mm. on the low ground to more than 1,250 mm. on the hills. Raindays exceed 250 a year in some districts, and the mild winters do not compensate for the prevalent high humidity. Numerous patches of blanket bog variegate the clayey blanket of glacial deposits which borders the alluvial flats of the drowned inlets. Arable farming is very restricted, with oats and potatoes the chief crops, but improved grass used for cattle-pasture and hay is very common.

The southern part of the region—in effect, the hinterland of Limerick—is noted for its dairying. Rural creameries are numerous and well-established, but farm butter is a typical product of the less accessible north, where breeding and rearing of cattle for sale become common in addition to dairying. The limited number of sheep in this region corresponds to the rather limited extent of upland pasture, and to the very poor quality of the limestone plateaus in the west.

The terrain is more varied than altitude might suggest, for small hills break the profile of the plains, and soils of differing quality are very patchily distributed. The variety of detail emphasises rather than diminishes dispersion of rural settlement, and rural habitations are widely scattered. The figure given for mean density of population is, however, at least as misleading as comparable figures for other regions, for the best land in Clare–Limerick Lowland is about as well peopled as are the best parts of the Inland South. These two regions are linked by the broad strip of particularly productive land called the Golden Vein (or Golden Vale) which runs from Limerick past Tipperary into the valley of the Suir.

Limerick

Limerick (Fig. 12:8) is the undisputed regional capital. Founded as a coastal stronghold of the Norsemen, it was for a long time constricted by its medieval walls. With a population of some 60,000, it is today the fourth largest town of the Republic and the third most important industrial centre after Dublin and Cork. It shows a slight but persistent tendency to increase in population and to expand in area. Growth has been chiefly directed towards the southwest, along the left bank of the Shannon downstream of the medieval site, and suburbs have been stimulated into development on the far side of the river. But Limerick lags behind Cork in the speed of its growth and in its urban strength. It accounts for some 3 per cent of the country's industrial production and 2 per cent of the industrial labour force. The leading industries include flour-milling, tanning, clothing manufacture, the processing and canning of bacon and milk, and butter-making. Its port trade is not great, consisting of coastal traffic in imported grain and fuel and in exports of dairy produce. In terms of

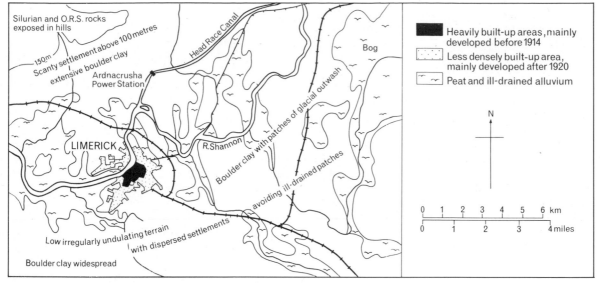

Fig. 12:8. Limerick and its local setting

shipping movement, Limerick ranks well below the packet-station Rosslare and has traffic only half as heavy as that of Waterford.

The near-by Shannon Airport was established in 1945 as a staging-point and a point of entry for tourists, most from the U.S.A.; but the increasing range of transatlantic aircraft led to considerable by-passing of Shannon during the 1960s, except by strictly Irish-routed traffic plus such general tourist traffic as Ireland could divert. As a counter-measure, the Shannon Free Airport scheme was instituted, offering on certain terms highly advantageous customs concessions to manufacturers; and in consequence, Shannon is emerging as a noteworthy growth area for Irish manufacture, especially in electronics and intricate engineering goods.

Electric Power

In much of the Irish west, the people talk of 'having the Shannon Scheme'—the Shannon Scheme being popularly synonymous with electric power supply. The ambitious and successful Shannon project met with all the more approval because it was the first great public work in the Free State established in 1922. Work began on the installations in 1925 and was completed in 1929. A dam on the river below Lough Derg raises the lake-level above 30 m. O.D., and a wide canal 12 km long carries water to the power-station at Ardnacrusha. The remarkably high natural gradient of 2·5 m./km on the lower Shannon is perhaps

due to incomplete rejuvenation controlled by a low sea-level in glacial times. The Shannon Scheme relies on the generally copious rainfall of its large catchment. Discharge falls off rapidly in time of drought—probably because water soaks into the highly permeable Carboniferous Limestone. Even with this limitation, the station at Ardnacrusha remained for a considerable time the greatest single producer of electricity in the Republic; but it is now surpassed by the largest thermal stations, including the Tarbert plant, completed in 1969 on the Shannon in County Kerry. Nevertheless, the success of Ardnacrusha can be assumed to have encouraged the construction of hydro stations on the Erne and in western Donegal.

3a HILL COUNTRY OF MAYO AND GALWAY; 3b HILL COUNTRY OF SLIGO AND LEITRIM; 3c HILL COUNTRY OF DONEGAL

These three regions have much in common (Figs. 12:1, 12:2). They contain much hill or mountain land, have extensive blanket-bogs, are on the average sparsely peopled, and are agriculturally poor. They suffer from an extreme development of maritime climate. Like peninsular Kerry, they have lost very many people by emigration and are typified by cottage farming in their remoter parts. Sligo alone among the towns has more than

PLATE 25. Shannon Airport. Terminal buildings on the left, the industrial estate foreground and right.

10,000 inhabitants. Nevertheless, contrasts are strong enough to justify their separation from one another. The Hill Country of Sligo and Leitrim (3b) is much the most productive of the three, differing unmistakably from its neighbours on either side.

3a. HILL COUNTRY OF MAYO AND GALWAY

Area: about 7,000 km² (2,700 sq. mi.).
Population: about 150,000.

There are no large towns. Ballina and Castlebar each has about 6,000 people.

Density of population outside these two towns: about 20/km² (50/sq. mi.).

Only half this region is in improved farmland, almost all of it grass.

Numbers of livestock: cattle, 360,000;
       sheep, 520,000;
       pigs, 42,500;
       poultry, 800,000.

The two broad peninsulas in western Mayo and western Galway, lying between Galway Bay and Donegal Bay, are separated from one another by Clew Bay on which Westport stands. At the landward ends of the peninsulas occur huge lakes— Conn, Mask, and Corrib. The centre of each peninsula consists of a knot of dissected mountain. The Mountains of Mayo are eroded in Carboniferous sediments and underlying metamorphic rocks, while metamorphic rocks alone predominate in the Connemara Mountains, which reach the west coast at some points. Both groups rise above 800 m., and the mountain country is almost unpeopled. It has been heavily scoured by ice, its summits receive more than 1,250 mm. of rain a year, and blanket bog is widely developed. Habitations are concentrated round the margins of both blocks of country, in districts where rural poverty on the small farms is a chronic problem, and would be still more severe without the money sent home by emigrants in America. The inhabited parts of the region combine a very low standard of living with a surprisingly high density of population.

3b. HILL COUNTRY OF SLIGO AND LEITRIM

Area: about 4,500 km² (1,750 sq. mi.).
Population: about 110,000.
Largest town: Sligo (13,500).
Density of population: about 22/km² (55/sq. mi.) outside Sligo.

About three-quarters of this region is in improved farmland, almost all of it grass.
Numbers of livestock: cattle, 335,000;
sheep, 225,000;
pigs, 35,000;
poultry, 525,000.

The Hill Country of Sligo and Leitrim is distinguished from the hillier regions on either side by its fairly extensive patches of lowland, which are underlain by Carboniferous rocks and covered by glacial drift. The Ox Mountains in the west of the region are developed on a strip of resistant metamorphic rocks, but the tabular hill-masses between Sligo Bay and the Erne are composed of gently-inclined Carboniferous sediments, in which limestone forms bold outfacing scarps. The subdued summits between 425 and 650 m. in height are in rough pasture, which also occurs at lower levels and amounts to a third of the total area, but many parts of the lowland are well farmed. The drift is lime-rich and drumlins are quite numerous —this region contains the westernmost extensions of the drumlin-belt mentioned above. Rainfall of below 1,250 mm. a year is significantly less than that recorded in western Donegal, western Mayo, and western Galway. The proportion of land improved is roughly twice as great in the Sligo–Leitrim country as in those regions, and cattle are more numerous than sheep. Dairying is dominant on the whole, with milk sent to creameries, but stock-rearing is also carried on.

H.E.P. is developed on the Erne at Ballyshannon,[1] where the output promises to exceed that of Ardnacrusha. Storage is provided by Lower and Upper Loughs Erne, where drumlins rise from the water and from the marginal bogs; drainage-works now in progress are likely to improve some of the land near the river.

Sligo town stands where the low coastal platform is constricted between steep-faced hills on the in-

land side and drowned sandy inlets on the seaward. It is a shopping and market centre, with a bacon factory, flour mills, and a flourishing wholesale trade. Its population tends to increase slowly. As a port it has had little success, and is still declining. A recent development in the neighbourhood is the working of lead ore for export to Belgium.

3c. HILL COUNTRY OF DONEGAL

Area: about 4,700 km² (1,800 sq. mi.).
Population: about 105,000.

There are no considerable towns in this region. Donegal town has about 1,500 people.
Density of population: about 23/km² (60/sq. mi.).

Only about 40 per cent of the region is in improved farmland, with grass nearly six times as extensive as tillage.
Numbers of livestock: cattle, 170,000;
sheep, 250,000;
pigs, 18,500;
poultry, 500,000.

A description generally similar to that given for the Hill Country of Mayo and Galway may be applied to the Hill Country of Donegal, where mountains rise to more than 650 m. in the midst of compact blocks of upland. The geological basis of this region comprises granitic masses and slowly-weathering metamorphic rocks, truncated by erosional platforms, ice-scoured, and peat-covered. The Caledonian trend is highly developed, with some of the larger structures continuing those known in the Scottish Highlands. Rainfall varies from 1,250 to 1,500 mm. a year, and at heights greater than 200 m. the land is fit merely for rough grazing or peat-cutting. Population is again peripheral, cottage farming is dominant, and emigration has been going on for at least a century (Plates 26, 27). Sheep, which are more numerous than cattle, are light in weight and not very suitable for meat-production. Their wool is the basis of a scattered manufacture of homespun cloth, with which knitwear and embroidery are associated, and of the industrialised making of the well-known Donegal tweed.

The lack of urban development in this region is well illustrated by the condition of Donegal town, which exemplifies the effects of the checks on urban growth typical of Ireland. Donegal town has fewer than 1,500 people, despite its status of county town, its position as the focus of a well-farmed drumlin-swarm at the head of Donegal Bay (cf. Fig. 12:9), its location on tidewater, and its narrow-gauge railway. In spite of all these apparent

---

[1] Ballyshannon is located in Co. Donegal, just over the county boundary.

PLATE 26. Turf-cutting in Connemara. Bare rock protrudes through the peat, which contains roots of old forest.

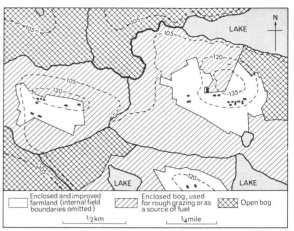

FIG. 12:9. Farming settlement and farmland on two drumlins, Co. Donegal: contours are in feet

advantages, it has failed to grow. The demands for urban services in its hinterland are slight, and can be met by visits to the town on market-days and the distribution of groceries by vans light enough to run on mountain roads. Donegal town has spread little beyond the edges of the open

PLATE 27. Cottages in Donegal. One lies in ruins, but the other is newly lime-washed and thatched with flax straw. Reedy pasture occurs in the foreground, ice-scoured hills in the distance.

space at its centre. Such a space is very common in Ireland, where it is usually called the diamond, even where (as at Donegal) it is triangular.

H.E.P. is being developed in the west of the region, where glacial lake-basins provide the main storage but water is also being collected from several small rivers (Fig. 12:10). The aqueduct runs across the ice-scoured granite of The Rosses, an erosional platform laid bare by the cutting of peat, to a power-station near the shore where there is a sharp drop of more than 30 m.

Killybegs, on the south coast, is a fishing port, with a fish-meal factory and a tweed mill.

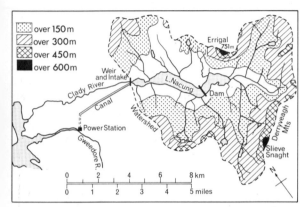
FIG. 12:10. The Clady power scheme, Donegal

The Gaelic Language in the West of Ireland

Gaelic (Irish) has for centuries been yielding to English; but a determined official campaign, which includes the use of Irish in schools, appears now to be meeting some success. About a quarter of the country's population is recorded as able to speak Irish. Only in the far west, however, has it survived continuously as the language of everyday speech, still used by 80 or 90 per cent of the people of the westermost coastlands (Fig. 12:11).

The main Irish-speaking districts coincide roughly with areas of cottage farming and of rural poverty. They rely on turf for domestic fuel: bog-moss grows rapidly in the humid western air, trees in the west are scarce, and the people of the west have poor access to coal and little if any money to spare to buy it. Western poverty is however a complicated matter, as is to some extent suggested by the Figure: the southward increase in size of holdings cuts boldly across the westward increase of dependence on turf as fuel, and also across the westward increase in the everyday use of Irish.

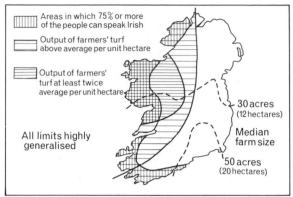
FIG. 12:11. Concentration of the Irish language, and of private turf-cutting, in the west of Ireland

NORTHEAST IRELAND

Area: about 14,750 km² (5,700 sq. mi.).
Population: about 1,550,000.
Largest towns: Belfast (395,000).
        Londonderry (58,000).
        Newtownabbey (55,000).
        Craigavon (31,000)*
        Bangor (30,000).
        Lisburn (25,000).
        Portadown (22,000).
        Lurgan (21,500).

               * 1967 estimate

In addition, the towns of Larne, Ballymena, Coleraine, Newtownards, Newry, Armagh, Carrickfergus, Omagh, and Strabane, in that order, have populations ranging below 20,000 to 10,000 people; and Dungannon, Holywood, Enniskillen, Banbridge, Cookstown, and Limavady, in that order, have populations ranging from 7,500 to 5,000 people.

Density of population outside the towns named: 55/km² (140/sq. mi.).

About two-thirds of this region is in improved farmland, about one-quarter of the total area in tillage.

Numbers of livestock: cattle, 1,355,000;
               sheep, 1,020,000;
               pigs, 1,030,000;
               poultry, 16,500,000.

Much of what will be said under this head applies to the political unit of Northern Ireland, although, for purposes of regional description, most of County Fermanagh has been detached from the Northeast, and County Monaghan and some of eastern County Donegal have been added from the Republic. A careful comparison of the regional boundary marked on Fig. 12:1 with a map of Irish counties will show the difference between political and geographical divisions. Where the two kinds of boundary do not coincide, the regional division adopted here can be justified by reference to land quality, as well as by the fact that the areas served by certain market towns transgress the political boundary.

Some 45 per cent of the inhabitants of Northeast Ireland live in one or other of the towns listed. A higher proportion of town-dwellers than this is recorded in the Eastern Central Plain, but the Northeast, area for area, has a higher proportion of sizeable towns than any other part of Ireland. The density of rural population is also higher than usual. The physique and quality of the land, the nature of the climate, and the political status of Northern Ireland combine to favour this region. Although the Northeast includes four blocks of upland, it also possesses lowland which can be intensively farmed, and enjoys the climatic advantages of the eastern side of Ireland. Its farm products find a market in Great Britain, and its principal towns are engaged in a successful textile industry. Belfast has overcome the lack of local coal and iron-ore in becoming a major centre of shipbuilding and heavy engineering.

Subdivision of the Region

Statistics for the regional groups distinguished in the Irish Republic can be derived, with fair accuracy, from data for whole counties. Figures quoted for single units (e.g., 3a, 3b, 3c) have been obtained from county figures by a process of somewhat arbitrary adjustment, but the tables and the diagrams (Figs. 12:3, 12:4) alike show that real differences distinguish one unit from another. No adjustment of county figures is possible within Northeast Ireland, for no grouping of counties can be made to correspond to the division into upland and lowland shown in Fig. 12:1. Consequently, the contrasts between lowland and highland and the internal variation of both cannot be defined statistically, but must be described in general terms.

The Lowland Districts

Fig. 12:1, representing in diagrammatic fashion the distribution and geological basis of relief, shows that the heart of the region consists of the Bann valley, in which Lough Neagh is centrally placed. Tongues of lowland radiate from the plain around Lough Neagh. One tongue extends down the valley of the lower Bann; one passes along the Lagan valley to Belfast; a narrow corridor forms the gap commanded by Newry, and a broad strip of low ground passes southwestwards towards the valley of the upper Erne; the Erne valley is linked by a broad low saddle with the valley of the Foyle.

All the lowlands in Northeast Ireland show signs of glaciation, in the form of outwash deposits and boulder clay. Drumlins are characteristic from the coastlands southeast of Belfast to the middle Erne, and lesser swarms occur in the Bann valley north of Lough Neagh. Although the quality of the soils developed on the drumlins varies with the parent material of the glacial drift, their slopes are everywhere free of bog. Some of the intervening hollows are quite well-drained in the natural state, and artificial drainage of others has extended the total area of improved farmland. It is no accident that plantations carried out under the Tudors and Stuarts spread along the wide belt of drumlins far into the northern Central Plain.

There are variations in farming within each lowland subdivision. Dairying predominates on the middle Erne, where much of the milk produced is taken by creameries, but grades into mixed farming in the lower Foyle basin where many fields are under the plough. Mixed farming is also typical of about half the branching lowland of the Bann Valley and its extensions. It is displaced by dairying around Ballymena and in the Lagan Valley, where the demands of Belfast are strongly felt, while the Bann Valley upstream of Lough Neagh and the drumlin country southeast of Belfast are characterised by the raising and fattening of beefstock. Market-gardens occur patchily from Bangor to beyond Portadown, with a concentration of fruit-growing around the southern end of Lough Neagh.

The character of lowland farming accounts for the fact that, in Northeast Ireland, cattle outnumber sheep. Sheep, typical of the uplands rather than of the lowlands, outnumber pigs, but pigs are proportionately more numerous here than in any other region of Ireland. Pigs take a shorter time to become ready for market than do fat beef cattle, and they pay better than fat sheep. In consequence, they head the list of farm produce, in order of gross product by value. Next come milk and dairy produce, eggs, and cattle.

Agricultural exports from the northeast include beefstock, dairy cows, eggs, and pigmeat. The success of pig-farming in this region is due partly to the deliberate processing of bacon to suit the

PLATE 28. Lifting potatoes, County Antrim, in sight of Slemish Mt.

southern English market. Numbers of livestock in the region tend to increase, while the total extent of tillage crops is roughly steady. Oats and potatoes (Plate 28) were for many years the most extensive tillage crops, but the extent of barley passed that of potatoes in 1961, that of oats in 1963, and both combined in 1965. Flax, once widely cultivated, now occupies less than 200 ha. (500 ac.), and can be taken as effectively eliminated from the list of commercial crops. For many years it has contributed little to industrial supply.

The Upland Districts

The four upland blocks of the northeast are varied in origin and in landform, but the highest ground is everywhere open, windswept, and peaty. Most of it is given over to rough grazing for sheep. Whereas the lowland receives about 1,000 mm. of rain a year, totals in the upland districts generally rise above 1,250 mm. and surpass 1,500 mm. in the central Mournes.

The Antrim Plateau is based on basalt sheets of Tertiary age, rising to more than 400 m. over wide areas and presenting scarped edges to the east and north. Despite its compactness and its tabular, moor-covered top, the Plateau is less of a barrier than might be expected, for a raised beach at about 8 m. O.D. allows an easy coast road to run far northwards from Belfast and to give access to the farmland of the glens which gash the coastal edge. The basalts are downwarped beneath Lough Neagh and the Bann Valley, reappearing on the western side, where they form scarps facing westwards on the flanks of the Sperrin Uplands in the second upland block. The Sperrin Mountains proper are formed of ancient metamorphic rocks, with rounded summits rising to more than 650 m. between wide valleys. The road from Belfast to Londonderry climbs to 300 m. in Glenshane Pass, descending on the western side between open hillsides and coniferous plantations. The uplands fall away towards the south, where farmland laps on to the drift-plastered slopes eroded in Old Red Sandstone and Carboniferous rocks.

PLATE 29. Horned blackface sheep in the Mourne Mountains. Small fields of low-grade pasture are enclosed by stone walls, while rough grazing covers part of the mountain slopes.

The rainy Mourne Mountains, the third hill-mass, have a granitic core like that of the Wicklow Mountains, and, also like the Wicklows, make step-like descents between deeply-cut valleys. There is rough grazing on the heather moors of the higher slopes (Plate 29), some coniferous plantation at lower levels, and farmland in the valleys. Just as the Wicklows supply water to Dublin, so do the Mournes supply Belfast from the Silent Valley reservoir.

The fourth upland subdivision of the Northeast lies in Armagh and Monaghan, athwart the boundary between Northern Ireland and the Republic. At few points does it exceed 300 m. in height, but it effectively divides the hinterland of Dundalk Bay from the lowland corridor between the Bann and Erne valleys. The bedrock in this subdivision consists of fine-grained Cambrian and Silurian sediments, so that the glacial drift is generally clayey, but a rainfall less than 1,000 mm. a year makes cultivation possible on the numerous drumlins. Rough grazing occurs at heights greater than some 275 m. O.D., and there are patches of bog in some of the enclosed hollows.

Industrial Structure

Figures in brackets show the percentage contribution to total net output made by the principal groups of industries in Northeast Ireland: engineering and metal industry (29); textile manufacture (21); manufacture and processing of food, drink, and tobacco (18). There are some 200,000 manufacturing workers: among the industrial groups of employment, engineering, textiles, clothing, the food–beverage–tobacco group, and construction are dominant. More than half the workers in manufacture are in Belfast, and only 1 in 20 in the second greatest town, Londonderry. The industrial dominance of Belfast is much greater in engineering and metal-working than in the other two groups, which are considerably dispersed through the region. Textile-working was established before Belfast grew large, partly in the form of a domestic craft, while the processing of food-stuffs is apt to be located in the producing areas; engineering works on the other hand were located in Belfast at the outset, depending (as they still do) on the port for their raw materials.

Textiles and Clothing

Linen manufacture had early beginnings as a domestic craft, which developed rapidly during the 18th century and was slowly superseded by factory-working during the 19th. Local flax was undoubtedly the basis of the industry, but it is seldom realised that the home supply was insufficient as early as the late 1700s, when imports had already become necessary. Like the wool-manufacturing of England, the linen-working of Northeast Ireland was well and widely established and resisted centralising tendencies. Of the towns indicated in Fig. 12:1, Londonderry, Coleraine, Lurgan, and Portadown in addition to Belfast have large linen mills. The industry as a whole employs some 35,000 people.

The clothing industry is centred in Londonderry, which has about half the region's total of clothing workers. Shirts are the chief product. Since workers in clothing factories are mainly women, Londonderry suffers a chronic surplus of employable males, whereas Belfast provides employment for men in engineering. An important fraction of the output of linen and clothing, of the cordage produced in Belfast, and of the recently-added products of hosiery and synthetic textiles, goes for export.

Shipbuilding and Marine Engineering

Work on the port of Belfast began in 1840, and the shipyard was founded in 1853. With 20,000 workers and a huge output of ships, this is one of the great yards in the world. It is particularly noted for large vessels, and in sharing in the construction of giant modern tankers: in 1967 it launched the tanker *Myrenan*, of 190,000 gross tons. This size was already obsolete for large carriers by 1970, but Belfast now has a building dock in which ships up to 1 million tons deadweight (total carrying capacity, including fuel) can be built. Relatively speaking, the Belfast yards are more than holding their own, having risen to third place in the U.K. by 1970, after the Tyne and the Clyde, as opposed to fifth place in the mid-1950s, and having in the same period increased their production in absolute terms. Associated with shipbuilding is marine engineering. Other engineering activities include the construction of aircraft, textile machinery, electrical and electronic goods, and agricultural machinery.

Towns

Londonderry (Fig. 12:12) possesses the lowest bridge across the navigable Foyle. It owes something (including the first element of its name) to its mercantile connection with London—a connection dating from the 17th century, when London Companies were given land and rights here. Although it is somewhat hampered today by lying close to the political border, it is still the chief urban focus of well-cultivated land of the lower Foyle valley,

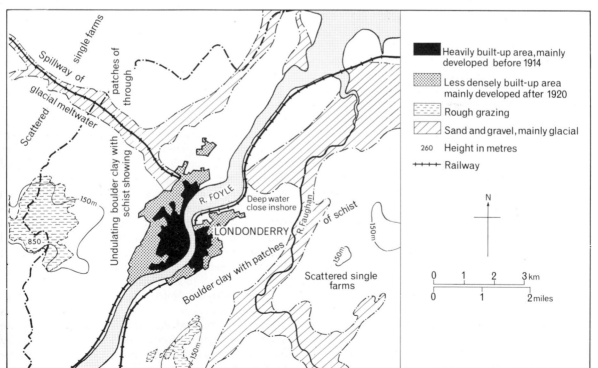

FIG. 12:12. Londonderry and its local setting: contours in feet

profiting by the harbour works carried out during
World War II and by the overland distance of
Belfast. Freight routes connect it with Glasgow and
Liverpool. Its clothing and linen industries have
been referred to above; there are also flour-milling,
distilling, tanning, and bacon-curing. The numbers
of population tend to rise slowly, as Londonderry
tightens its economic grip on the surrounding
farmland.

Coleraine also lies at the head of an estuary and
commands the lowest bridge. This former Norman
stronghold and present centre of linen-manufacture has a small port trade on the routes which
serve Londonderry. It is the principal town of the
lower Bann valley.

Ballymena has a tradition of linen manufacture,
and a noteworthy history as the market centre of a
dairying district. However, in common with Antrim
at the northeast corner of Lough Neagh, and
Craigavon at the southern entrance to the Lough,
it has been designated a new town. The respective
total populations expected for these three centres
(? by AD 2000) are 70,000, 30,000, and 150,000.
The central dominance of Belfast, in numbers of
people, in industrial location, and particularly in
industrial structure appears likely to be modified.
Portadown, Lurgan, and Lisburn are the largest
of a group of towns southwest of Belfast, in a lowland district where the industrial power of the
capital makes itself felt. Portadown is the largest,
with jam-making and fruit-canning related to the
market-gardening of its surroundings, and carpet-
making, bacon-processing, and linen-working.
Lurgan and Lisburn, smaller than Portadown, are
still dependent principally on linen-manufacture,
but are likely to attract subsidiary manufactures
from Belfast—e.g., of light engineering products.

Newry commands an ice-deepened corridor
which penetrates the upland rim of Ireland and
reaches the sea, to which the town is connected by
a ship canal. Its port trade was once flourishing but
is now very small, Newry having been superseded
as a port by Belfast, and the town is no longer
growing in population. It too manufactures linen,
and is the market of an agricultural countryside.
In the intensively-farmed hinterland of Newtownards, early potatoes are a well-known crop;
the town itself is fast becoming an industrial outpost of Belfast. Bangor, at the mouth of Belfast
Lough and with a frequent train service to the
capital, is a residential town and seaside resort.
Larne exercises a number of functions. It is at the
same time a local centre for marketing and shopping, a seaside resort, a port, and an industrial

town with manufactures which include aluminium
products for the industries of Belfast. A cargo
link to Preston has been added to the packet service
to Stranraer, enabling Larne to supersede Londonderry as the second port of Northern Ireland.

Belfast stands at the head of its wide Lough
where the Lagan reaches the shore (Fig. 12:13). Its

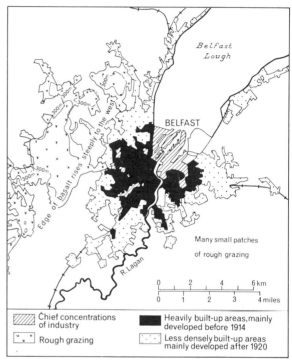

FIG. 12:13. Belfast and its local setting

physical advantages in shipbuilding are confined
to the depth of water in the Lough, which in the
early days was generous, and to the sheltered
anchorage. These alone cannot account for the
development of shipbuilding and of the dependent
or ancillary engineering industries, and any
attempt to explain the industrial success of Belfast
in physical terms is bound to fail. Heavy industries
can obtain coal from Ayrshire and Cumberland,
and steel can be shipped in from Clydeside. Nevertheless, the persistence and growth of shipbuilding
and engineering in such a location are the result of
far more complex factors than access to seaborne
raw materials.

The fundamental factor in location was the
original decision to found the industry at Belfast.
Once that decision had been taken, the local
reserve of labour was a distinct advantage, for
wages remained for a long time below those paid

PLATE 30. Limited-access motorway in Northern Ireland.

for comparable work in Great Britain. The low level of wages enabled shipbuilders in Belfast to offset the cost of importing coal and metal. Once the industry was well established, industrial inertia enabled it to withstand the serious fluctuations to which shipbuilding was subject from time to time. The original advantage of low labour-cost no longer obtains, for wages in the shipbuilding and engineer-industries are uniform throughout the U.K. It is partly for this reason that the purchase of industrial coal is subsidised in Northern Ireland at the present day.

Official support is also given to industrial expansion and to new industrial development. This support, responsible for a certain dispersal of light industry in Northern Ireland in the post-war period, is to be compared with the similar but longer-standing measures taken in the Republic, but it seems unlikely that any serious challenge can come to the prime industrial position of Belfast. Whereas distilling and the manufacture of farm products are quite widely dispersed, Belfast is pre-eminent in the manufacture of food, drink, and tobacco. It is the main focus of the linen industry, possesses the usual flour-milling and furniture-making of large towns, and has a wide range of miscellaneous industry. Wholesale and retail trade are naturally considerable.

External Trade

Through the port of Belfast goes three-quarters of the external trade of Northern Ireland, trade which is dominantly with Great Britain. Manufactures amount to nearly 60 per cent of imports, the chief imported items being cotton and woollen goods and yarns, machinery and vehicles, petroleum, paper, iron and steel plates and sheets, coal, flax, timber, and wool. Leading exports are textiles, ships, aircraft, tobacco, eggs, and pigmeat. The nature of trade is clearly related to the agricultural and industrial status of Northern Ireland. In volume, trade is half as great again as that of the Republic, and nearly $3\frac{1}{2}$ times as great per head of population.

Chapter 13

Wales and the Welsh Borderland

THE combined extent of Wales and the Welsh Borderland is about 27,000 km² (10,250 sq. mi.), and their total population is about 3,100,000. The significance of total figures is, however, more than usually weakened by geographical variation, which requires a subdivision of the area into three regions —the Welsh Massif, Industrial South Wales, and the Welsh Borderland (Figs. 13:1, 13:2).

The Welsh Massif is mainly plateau country, high, bleak, rainy, and open, with much land in moor and with settlement and improved farmland concentrated in the valleys and along the coast. A fundamental contrast divides the broad upland from the limited and scattered lowland. Industrial South Wales, based upon the coalfield and its coastal fringe, is superimposed on the division between central moor and peripheral farms. The Welsh Borderland is hilly and irregular in relief, but most of it stands much lower than the interior plateaus. It benefits from rain-shadow and is well farmed, but differs strongly from the highly urbanised West Midlands in being poor in towns.

Boundaries of geographical regions coincide neither with geological boundaries nor with the political limit of Wales. A well-defined geological boundary, at the western limit of Permo-Trias, separates the Welsh area from the marl-filled Midland basins and their extensions towards the estuaries of the Dee and the Severn. In places— but only in places—this boundary coincides with the break of slope where the plains end and the hills of the Borderland begin. Elsewhere, the geological junction is obscured by glacial deposits. Elsewhere again, the ancient rocks of the Welsh block have been much denuded—as in the neighbourhood of Shrewsbury, where a structurally complex prong running towards the northeast is reflected merely in isolated hills which rise from English plainlands. In addition, small coalfields occur on the very margins of the plains, modifying or blurring the regional boundary.

The regional boundary between the Borderland and the Massif is fixed where the irregular terrain of the former passes into the largely intact plateaus of the latter. The change does not agree with geological divisions, but is defined by a marked change of relief and landscape-texture and by the associated change in climate—the change from the rain-shadow of the Borderland to the severe climate of the interior uplands. In places—but again only

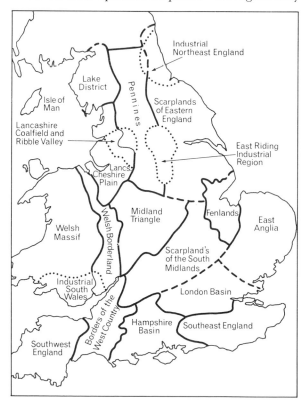

FIG. 13:1. Regional division of England and Wales: compare Fig. 2:1

in places—the political limit of Wales runs along the margin of the interior plateaus, having been driven right across the Borderland by successive conquests and encroachments.

THE WELSH MASSIF

Area: about 19,500 km² (7,500 sq. mi.).

Population: about 2,775,000; some 1,650,000 of these live in Industrial South Wales, leaving 1,125,000 for the rest of the area.

Largest towns (apart from those of the Industrial South):

Colwyn Bay (23,000).
Rhyl (20,000).
Llandudno (18,000).
Bangor (14,000).
Carmarthen (13,250).
Pembroke (12,750).
Conway (11,500).
Aberystwyth (10,500).

About half the extent of the Massif is in improved farmland; permanent grass takes about one-third of the whole, and total grassland is seven times as extensive as tillage. Rough grazing amounts to rather less than one-third of the whole.

Numbers of livestock: cattle, 1,155,000;
sheep, 5,750,000;
pigs, 205,000;
poultry, 3,650,000.

One impressive fact about Wales is that the Welsh language has maintained itself as successfully as any other native language of the west. Cornish has vanished entirely, Scots Gaelic has almost gone, Manx survives only in ceremonial use, and the Norman-French patois of the Channel Islands are steadily fading out. Both Welsh and Irish have a long history of decline, although (as stated on another page) that of Irish now seems to have been checked. Some 600,000 people can still speak Welsh—about the same total, and the same proportion, as those who can speak Irish. No deliberate assaults were made on Welsh, comparable to those on the use of Irish; nevertheless, it still seems remarkable that the Welsh language should have resisted, for so many centuries, the effects of a more-or-less accepted political union with England. The inherent strength of the Welsh

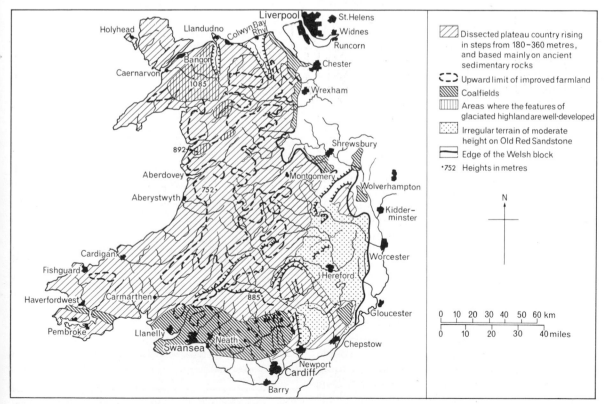

FIG. 13:2. Wales: physique and main settlements

tongue is associated with strong cultural heritage and traditions.

If there is a geographical basis for the survival of Welsh language and Welsh culture, it lies in the great physical differences between the terrain of Wales and the terrain of the English Plain. That difference has its foundation in geology, and its superstructure in erosional history and in climate. On the other hand, the facts of physical geography obstructed the unification of an independent Wales, and assisted penetration of its margins. It was in the valleys that the independent Welsh of the Middle Ages lived, and in the valleys that their food was produced. The valleys radiate outwards, offering no natural focus to the plateau country—all physical guidance is centrifugal. Wales became politically united only under recurrent attacks from Romans, English, Danes, Scandinavians, and Normans. Significantly enough, the English counties of the Borderland were established and extended precisely where wide valleys and well-drained ridges struck far to the west, but the routes of much of the Borderland led merely to the high plateaus of the interior. Lines of fortresses were extended along the northern and southern coastlands, in a kind of pincer movement; as the jaws of the pincer closed, the still-independent Welsh were driven into the Welsh heartland of Gwynedd in the northwest. It is here that the Welsh language and the distinctive qualities of Welsh life are most prominent today, having endured the subjugation and political union of the 13th century, and having been least affected by industrialisation.

The Plateaus

The rigid crustal block which constitutes the Welsh Massif is based mainly upon fine-grained sediments of Ordovician and Silurian age. The pronounced SW–NE structural trends of the stumps of the Caledonides are well displayed by these rocks in the centre and north, but the ancient folds have been broadly truncated by erosion, and plateaus are very extensive (Plate 3). Under the influence of a falling base-level, very subdued land-surfaces developed between 500 and 600 m., between 360 and 480 m., and between 240 and 300 m. At lower altitudes, old wave-cut benches run along the coastlands. Up-domed Cambrian rocks appear in the Harlech Dome, forming concentric infacing scarps. Sandstones and conglomerates of the Old Red Sandstone lap on to the flanks of the older rocks from the southeast, rising above 750 m. in the Black Mountains and closely approaching 1,000 m. in the corrie-scalloped

Brecon Beacons. For the most part, however, heights in the region of 1,000 m. are confined to volcanic rocks, which rise dramatically from the monotonous platforms in the Snowdon District, in the Arenigs, and in Cader Idris. Craggy land-forms and the features of highland glaciation—peaks, corries, tarns, ribbon lakes, and fretted ridges—are well developed on the volcanic rocks (Plate 31), as on some of the coarser sediments, but in much of the region the main effect of glaciation has been to deepen the larger valleys into grooves, to scour rock-waste from the high ground, and to line the valley-floors and lower hillsides with boulder clay.

Actual mean temperatures on the highest ground are in the neighbourhood of 2 °C. in January and 12 °C. in July. Precipitation is frequent, coming on two days out of three. Although actual temperatures increase, and precipitation decreases, with decrease of height, the climate remains cloudy, cool, and rainy at least as far down as the 250 m. contour, with annual totals of precipitation exceeding 1,250 mm. Peat tends to accumulate on all gently-sloping summits; blanket-bog is less typical in Wales than in the soaking air of western Ireland, but the plateau soils all have a high content of raw humus.

Whatever the effects of felling and of centuries of sheep-grazing, the windy high plateaus can scarcely be regarded as natural woodland. The area at present in rough grazing—approximately enclosed by the 1,500 mm. isohyet—includes

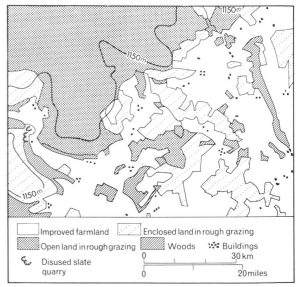

FIG. 13:3. Sample of land use and dispersed rural settlement, central Wales

PLATE 31. Snowdon (1,085 metres) from the northeast, showing features of highland glaciation. Contrast Plate 3.

varieties of molinia moor, with a continuous fringe of mountain fescue round its lower edge. Patches of heather moor occur in the east, where precipitation decreases, while heather fell is found on the rainy flanks of the Snowdon group (Fig. 3:22).

The moorland of the central plateaus has little use except as rough pasture for sheep, which are very numerous indeed on the uplands (Fig. 5:21, Plate 32). Sheep can survive severe weather better than cattle can. They do not require the daily attention which is given to dairy animals; they graze closer than do cattle, and are adapted to living on poor or coarse pasture.[1] For all these reasons they have been largely displaced from the improved farmland to the districts of rough grazing (cf. Chap. 5). Sheep-grazing on moorlands employs few men in comparison with the size of the area grazed, and in any case many of the shepherds live in the valleys. The high plateaus of Wales are very scantily peopled; the average of less than 20 per km[2] for the rough-grazing districts, which is in any case low, includes the populations of the higher valleys.

Settlements in the interior of Wales are typically small (Fig. 13:3). There are scattered single farmsteads as well as small groups of grey stone cottages.

---

[1] In some inexplicable fashion, the legend has arisen that sheep cannot be kept in rainy areas because of footrot. This erroneous belief is completely refuted by the actual distribution of sheep in the British Isles, as mapped in Fig. 5:21, which shows clearly that sheep today are numerous in the very rainy uplands but scarcely anywhere else. Footrot is due not directly to dampness underfoot but to a micro-organism, which is favoured by dirt as well as by wetness. Thus the danger of footrot is absent from dry pastures, but present in overstocked folds on arable land. Stagnant conditions are far more likely to encourage the disease than are the moorland pastures, where water runs freely down the steep slopes or soaks into the peaty soil. Moreover, the hooves of hill sheep are continually abraded by the bare rocks underfoot.

PLATE 32. Dipping sheep in the interior of Wales, near Cader Idris.

The small irregular fields characteristic of early and piecemeal enclosure contain the farmland in a net of stone walls. Woodland is sparse, the merest remnants of hardwood forest having survived the axes of charcoal-burners and the teeth of sheep. One ubiquitous feature is the stone-built set of pens, where sheep are brought to be washed in the waters of a mountain stream.

The Valleys and the Coastlands

The valleys are an altogether different proposition from the divides. They possess soils other than the peaty soils of the uplands, they are largely in improved farmland, and many parts of them are sheltered from the raw winds which sweep across the plateaus (cf. Fig. 13:4, Plate 33).

The present valley-system has evolved from one initiated by uplift in the west. The original consequent rivers ran northeast, east, and southeast from a watershed some 30 km (20 mi.) inland of Cardigan Bay. Capture has modified the original pattern, especially in the upper basins of the Dee,

Severn, Wye, Towy, and Teifi, where subsequent streams have extended themselves along northeast–southwest or southwest–northeast lines of weakness, but the radial tendency is still apparent. The short rivers draining directly into Cardigan Bay show very clearly the effects of repeated rejuvenation. Glacial grooving has converted many of the larger valleys into steep-sided troughs, and ice was responsible for diverting a number of streams in the Welsh Borderland.

As the head-valleys are left behind, and the middle and lower reaches approached, settlement becomes progressively denser, individual settlements larger, and farmland richer and more extensive. Sheep-farming is still the main interest at the higher levels, but in the lower valleys, and on the broad coastal benches of Anglesey and the south, the emphasis changes from sheep to cattle. Soils generally have undergone heavy leaching and are poor in lime—in the natural state, they tend to be podsolised. Climate, however, improves greatly with decreasing height and with increasing nearness to the sea; the frost-free season lengthens to 7, 8, or even 9 months, the yearly total of precipitation falls towards 1,000 mm., cloudiness decreases, mean temperatures rise. The annual range of temperature decreases very rapidly—a sign of greatly improved winter weather. Thus it becomes possible and profitable for farmers to take advantage of the long growing-season and to concentrate on cattle.

Tillage is subordinate to grassland, not only in extent but also in the character of its crops. About a quarter of all tillage is under oats, a crop intended for animal feed as opposed to food for human beings; mixed corn and fodder crops are also widely grown. Dairying is more common than the rearing and fattening of beef-stock, as it is in Southwest England; and, again as in Southwest England, the rise of dairying has been a response to the growth of industrial towns and to the spread of railways. The difficult gradients of much of Wales limited the possible choice of routes for railways; the only two through-routes run along the coastlands in the north and south to the packet-stations of Holyhead and Fishguard, providing rapid services for the dairying districts of Anglesey and Pembrokeshire. These lines follow the early routes of armed conquest, which were also guided by the terrain. They tap country where the climatic advantages of a western location and of fairly low ground are particularly great in dairy-farming.

The Welsh Black breed of beef cattle, well known for being extremely hardy, is most common today in northwest Wales. Welsh Black cattle from the massif, and Herefords from the Border country, used to be driven in herds along the drove roads which in the 18th and early 19th centuries led from Wales to London. Welsh Roads are still so called in the Midlands, but the droving trade has been superseded by rail transport. Store cattle are still sent for fattening to the Midlands, where some Welsh graziers followed them to take over Midland farms.

The markets for Welsh dairy produce are not all in England. Anglesey and the narrow coastal plain of North Wales—with its extensions up the rifted valleys of the Conway and the Clwyd—naturally contribute mainly to the supply of the Lancs.–Cheshire region, but the farms of Pembrokeshire, south Carmarthenshire, and south Glamorganshire can depend on a heavy demand from Industrial South Wales. Agriculture in the Plain of Gwent has been particularly stimulated by the near-by industrial towns, and includes considerable market-gardening. It is favoured by the equable

climate which results from location near the coast, and also by soils which, developed on Permo-Triassic and Jurassic sediments, are deeper and warmer than the soils of almost every other part of

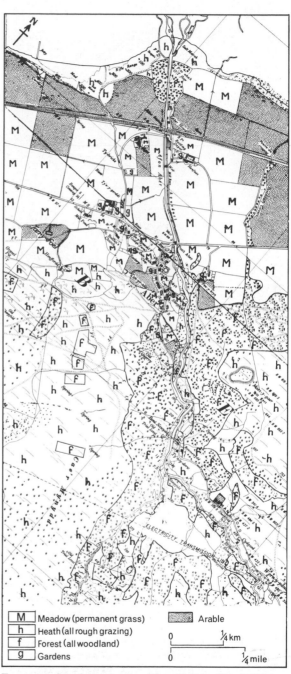

M	Meadow (permanent grass)
h	Heath (all rough grazing)
f	Forest (all woodland)
g	Gardens

Arable

0   ¼ km

0   ¼ mile

FIG. 13:4. Land use in the Aber Valley, North Wales. The low coastal platform (raised beach) is in improved farmland; rough grazing appears at 70 to 100 m.; and woodland occurs on the valley-sides

PLATE 33. Great Orme's Head, North Wales. Old cliffs cut in flexured Carboniferous Limestone overtop a raised beach.

Wales. Geologically speaking, the Plain of Gwent belongs to Lowland Britain.

Intensive dairy-farming in Europe is often associated with small farms, so that a district dominated by dairying is liable to have a quite high density of rural population. There are however at least two ways in which these conditions may arise. In Denmark and Holland they have been deliberately brought about. In more broken terrain they can result from the conversion to dairying of existing farms, which were already small because the limited good land available had been repeatedly subdivided. Such is the case in parts of southern Sweden and of Ireland, and also in the dairying districts of Wales; in Anglesey, for instance, more than a quarter of the farms are between 2 and 6 ha. (5 and 15 ac.) in size, and farms in the same group are also numerous in Pembrokeshire.

The early subdivision of farmland in Wales was accompanied by a dispersion of the rural settlement which, in some districts at least, had been originally nucleated. All the valley lands were affected by the process of redistribution, and their settlements are mostly small today. As in Ireland, there is little demand for urban services, especially since sheep-markets are far less frequent than cattle-markets. As the tentacles of the very large towns outside rural Wales reached into the interior, they drew country-folk away instead of touching off town growth. Rural Wales, like the rural parts of Ireland and Scotland, has lost many of its people by emigration, which did more than keep numbers down. Industrial South Wales, the great and growing towns of England, and the New World all received their groups of Welsh migrants. Local industries of the plateau and its margins could support few people.

Town Population and Industry

Montgomery, although a county town and a

PLATE 34. The tanker *British Explorer* (215,000 tons) at a Milford Haven oil terminal.

centre of woollen manufacture, with a site on the upper Severn, has few more than 900 people. The neighbouring town of Welshpool, lower down the river, has about 6,500. Both are roughly static in population. A modest start with industrial and commercial invasion was made in 1967, when Newtown, up-river from Montgomery, was designated a new town in the planning sense, being expected to increase its population from 5,000 at the time of designation to an ultimate 13,000. The largest towns of North Wales are the most successful resorts, but none exceeds a modest size, and the tourist trade is widely dispersed. Colwyn Bay, Bangor, Llandudno, and Conway are strung along the coast, while very small but well-known settlements in the mountains cater for visitors to the Snowdon group. Aberystwyth is the leading resort on Cardigan Bay, located at the centre of a crescentic low-lying platform. Carmarthen and Pembroke are collecting and distributing centres for the farmlands of the southwest.

No large settlements have grown at the ends of the passenger routes to Ireland, for the rail and shipping services are designed to move travellers through Holyhead and Fishguard as rapidly as possible. The water-supply undertakings which serve Liverpool and Birmingham and which include the Vyrnwy and Elan Valley schemes, employ small numbers on maintenance, and cannot be expected to affect local towns. H.E.P. is as yet developed only on a minor scale. Manufacturing industry is limited in scope and extent throughout the central and northern massif, and the slate-quarrying of the north has seen its best days. The great quarries on the flanks of the Snowdon group, where the shales have been metamorphosed into slate, are working at about a third of their capacity. The demand for slate is much less than it was in the 19th century, when other roofing materials were less common and less cheap than they now are, and when the rapid growth of English towns produced terraced rows of brick-built and slated houses. Anglesey is acquiring new light industries, but its mines in Parys Mountain are derelict today. They once led the world in the production of copper ore, but the reserves now available are complex lead–zinc ores which could not be treated by the smelting techniques of former days. The most recent and most promising industrial development is the construction of a terminal port for oil-tankers in the huge ria of Milford Haven, which in sundry respects belongs with Industrial South Wales rather than the Massif. Formerly a naval base, and in peacetime a leading Welsh fishing port, Milford Haven is now primarily an oil terminal. However, its automated refineries and lack of ancillary industry prevent it from generating much employment (see bibliography: Watts); and although its shipping traffic increased 15-fold during the 1960s, the increase in tanker size past the 150,000-ton limit has already involved dredging. Allied to the import of oil is an oil-fired power station near Pembroke, an additional sign perhaps that, despite the present isolation of the area, industrialisation will spread westward along the south Welsh coast.

INDUSTRIAL SOUTH WALES

Population: about 1,650,000.
Largest towns: Cardiff (290,000).*
            Swansea (172,500).*
            Newport (112,500).*
            Rhondda (92,500).*
            Merthyr Tydfil (55,000).*
            Port Talbot (50,250).
            Barry (42,000).
            Pontypool (40,000).
            Aberdare (39,000).
            Caerphilly (36,000).
            Pontypridd (35,500).
            Gelligaer (34,500).
            Neath (31,000).
            Llanelli (30,000).
            Mountain Ash (29,500).
                              * 1969 estimates

This region is usually called South Wales for short. Its area is of the order of 2,500 km², so that something approaching two-thirds of the people of Wales inhabit one-eighth of the total area. The people are most unevenly distributed, for densely-settled industrial valleys are divided from one another by unpeopled belts of moorland, and stretches of open country intervene between the large coastal towns. Interpenetration of urban and rural landscapes is more pronounced than any-where else in the British Isles, except perhaps along the fringes of the industrial region of the West Riding (Fig. 13:5, Plate 35).

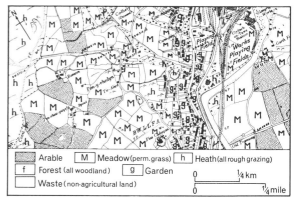

Fig. 13:5. Land-use sample for the Tawe valley, upstream from Swansea

The close-packed inhabitants of the towns are supported either directly or indirectly by industry—industry dominated by the manufacturing of ferrous metals, and drawing on local coal for its power. The coal seams are contained in a basin produced by Altaid folding; the outcrop of the Coal Measures narrows westwards, and in the same direction the rank of coal rises, until anthracite occurs in the western part of the field. Although coal-mining is so prominent in the industrial geography of South Wales today that the region is often called the South Wales Coalfield, industrialisation began before coal-mining. Metal-working in this region has developed along highly distinctive lines, and the whole industrial life of South Wales has undergone violent fluctuations in output in addition to marked shifts of location. The region provides outstanding examples of changes in geographical values.

Rise and Fall of the Iron Industry

The first establishment of an iron-smelting industry in South Wales constituted a response to the national demand for iron goods, at a time when the Wealden forests had long been inadequate and the timber of Staffordshire was already seriously depleted. Iron-manufacture in the early 18th century was located with reference to supplies of timber and of iron-ore; South Wales was well supplied with both.

The ores used in smelting with charcoal included those occurring in the Coal Measures. In South Wales, as on certain English coalfields, the rather limited local reserves of ironstone were ample in the early days. They were exploited mainly along the northeastern rim of the coalfield, where the Carboniferous strata dip quite gently and where the land is dissected by a series of deep

PLATE 35. A Welsh mining valley, at Ferndale, Glamorganshire.

young valleys. On both these counts the ores were accessible. Accessibility was important at a time when mining technique was crude and the thin beds of ore were taken from shallow pits or short drifts. The change from charcoal to coke fixed the iron-works firmly upon the outcrop of the coal-bearing rocks, and a vigorous iron-smelting industry developed. Most of the blast-furnaces and foundries were built in the district where charcoal-smelting was already established—i.e., in the north-east of the coalfield—where the gently-dipping rocks and deep valleys constituted great practical advantages in coal-working. In this development

can be seen the joint effects of physical environment and of inertia. There was no reason why the smelting industry should be displaced from its home district when the new fuel, coal, could be locally worked in drifts along the northern outcrop or in adits in the valleys.

The ironworks which depended on coke were accordingly concentrated in and near Aber-gavenny, Brynmawr, Ebbw Vale, Tredegar, Rhymney, Merthyr Tydfil, and Aberdare (Figs. 13:2, 13:3). These towns lie in, or at gateways to, a long depression excavated in the gently-dipping Lower Coal Measures, stretching in a line from the

Usk to the Taff. On the north, the Carboniferous Limestone rises in a north-facing cuesta to 600 m. To the south, the productive Lower Coal Measures disappear beneath the barren Pennant Sandstone, which forms flat-topped hills rising many places to more than 450 m. The early coke-using iron-works arose in the strike vale and in the heads of valleys leading southeastwards from it.

The gentle dips of the northeastern rim of the coalfield belong to the northern flank of the coal-field syncline. The thick, coarse, well-cemented Pennant Sandstone separates the northeastern outcrop of productive Coal Measures from the downbent, coal-bearing Upper Coal Measures of the axial part of the field, and from the reappearing Lower Coal Measures of the southern flank. The 30 km journey between the iron-making towns and the coast was eventually to prove a grave handicap. The first severe blows came in the latter half of the 19th century, when steel was replacing iron as an industrial material, and when the Coal-Measure ores were running out. Steel-working was estab-lished on or near the coast. The towns in the north-east failed to secure many steelworks, and their metallurgical industry fell on hard times.

Rise of the Coal Export Trade

Meanwhile, the coal-export trade was flourish-ing. Coal had been worked in South Wales at least as early as the 13th century, and a small export trade came into being long before industrialisation began. Cardiff, however, was still *importing* coal at the beginning of the 18th century, and did not share the export trade until the 19th. In the vast increase in British coal exports during the second half of the 19th century and in the early years of the 20th, however, the eastern part of the South Wales Coalfield, and particularly the northeastern part, became heavily involved.

In addition to the change of rank from bitu-minous coal in the east to anthracite in the west, changes occur within the bituminous series. There are large deposits of coal highly suitable for coking, for firing large boilers, and for household use. The demand for coking coal rose with the growth of smelting; the demand for household coal kept pace with increase in population and with rising living-standards; sales of steam coal were promoted by the vigorous expansion of world trade and of steam-powered merchant navies. Bunker coal from South Wales was distributed along the sea-lanes of the world.

Cardiff, Newport, and somewhat later Swansea, became very great exporters of coal. Each lies at the focus of valley-routes. The western part of the dissected coalfield plateaus is drained by the southwestward-flowing Loughor, Tawe, and Neath, which are partly adjusted to lines of faulting and shattering. In the east, the Taff, Rhymney, Ebbw, and Usk form, with their tributaries, a group of sub-parallel consequents, superimposed on the structures of the coalfield and draining towards the southeast. Roads, railways, and canals in the incised valleys connected the mines to the ports, bringing coal from the northern outcrop, from the Upper Coal Measures in the centre of the field, and from the flexured and more steeply-dipping seams of the Lower Coal Measures in the south. Mines were able to absorb some of the men no longer wanted by the ironworks. Some of the iron-works were abandoned, others continued to produce, partly because they had plant in running order. But the facts of location were as adverse to the iron industry as rising demand was favourable to mining. The emphasis of industry changed, accordingly, from manufacture to primary pro-duction. In the circumstances this retrograde step was only to be expected, but the mining industry and the coal trade were to prove at least as vul-nerable to changing demand as iron-manufacturing had already been. While the export trade con-tinued to flourish, the port facilities were extended and the port towns grew. Mining centres in the narrow valleys expanded into elongated towns, their brick-built terraces of 19th-century houses crowded on the lower slopes.

Rise of the Steel and Tinplate Industries

The steel-working which developed on and near the coast of South Wales derived great benefits from its location. High-grade ore could be brought in by sea, coal came by short hauls down the valleys, and metal manufacture of various kinds was already in being. Here also, however, industry became concentrated on a limited range of activities which were from time to time much hampered by changes outside the region.

One notable early development was the refining and smelting of the ores of non-ferrous metals. The bases of this industry were coal from South Wales itself, and ores of copper and tin from Southwest England. The furnaces and mills were established mainly in the valleys of the Loughor, Tawe, and Neath. Competition tended in time to concentrate them near the coast, for works inland had to pay for the haulage of ores and concentrates without saving much on the transport of coal. There is still a copper industry, but it has been little concerned

PLATE 36. Five-stand-cold reduction mill, Port Talbot; part of the strip milling sequence.

with initial processes since the U.S.A. became dominant in the production and control of copper ores. By contrast, the processing of tin has been retained and successfully developed. The U.S.A. has no domestic supplies of tin ore, while South Wales was able to draw on Malayan supplies when the mines of Southwest England began to fail. Of the three great producers of tin ore— Malaya, Nigeria, and Bolivia—two were under British control at a critical period, and tin-manufacture in South Wales was able to persist and to expand, even though it lost its near-by reserves of raw material.

Tin was required, as it still is, for use in plating. The plating industry uses zinc as well as tin in the production of a wide range of materials, which consist of sheet steel with a thin protective covering of some base metal. The ultimate uses of the products are manifold, but two main types are of particular importance. Tin-plate is widely employed in the making of rust-resistant metal con-tainers, especially containers for foodstuffs. Output of this kind of product increased with the development of canning, particularly the canning of the fruit shipped in increasing quantities from the tropics and the southern hemisphere to northwest Europe. Demand for tin-plate is still expanding, for sales of canned and standardised fruit and vegetables continue to rise, and the manufacture of containers absorbs four-fifths of the output of tin-plate. Canning has the great practical advantages that canned goods can enter distant markets and seasonal gluts of perishable foodstuffs can be held over. One factor contributing to the demand for canned goods is the post-war labour shortage in the British Isles, which has encouraged women to work in factories and has reduced the time available for home cooking.

The second leading type of product is galvanised sheeting, either flat or corrugated. When parts of the tropical lands were developed economically during the later 19th century, the materials known rather loosely as corrugated or galvanised iron proved of great value. In countries where local timber was either too soft or too hard to be usable, and where imported softwood was liable to be devoured by termites, rustproofed steel was imported as building material. It also found a wide market in Great Britain, first in industry and later in agriculture. Plated steel sheet is used in great quantities today in the manufacture of car-bodies.

The steel industry of South Wales, then, developed largely as one of the processes in the manufacture of tin-plate. This manufacture absorbed a great deal of the steel made in South Wales. Although tin-plating and galvanising spread to all parts of the coalfield, it remained typical chiefly of the western part, and especially of Swansea, Llanelli, and their smaller neighbours. Few of the towns concerned with plating grew to a large size, and the industry is still quite well dispersed. Some of the older works, however, are poorly designed and inefficient by modern standards, and a number have already been closed down in the course of industrial reorganisation.

Industrial Vulnerability and Recent Change

While the eastern part of the coalfield relied very heavily first on iron-working, and then on coal export, the western part, having lost much of its copper manufacture, depended on coal export, and on tin-plating and galvanising with their associated production of steel sheet and strip. Because of their lack of variety, the industries of South Wales were dangerously exposed to change. Destructive change came in the inter-war period, in the forms of falling demand for coal and of industrial slump.

The origin and character of the difficulties which beset the coal trade (Chap. 7) included the alternation of boom and slump in the inter-war period, the disturbance of European coal traffic, and the progressive replacement of coal by oil as a fuel for ships. Difficulties reinforced one another, for, with the whole mining industry severely depressed, it was impossible to modernise pits or to repair dilapidations. Mining in some districts became more and more expensive and risky because of the sporadic and unrecorded working of the early industrial days. Unemployment reached appalling levels in the early 1930s; nearly 90 per cent of the men in Rhondda then depended on coal for employment, and more than half of them lost their jobs. At Brynmawr 75 per cent were unemployed; in the region as a whole there was no work for one man in three, and in the steel industry none for two

in every three. Nearly half a million left for London and the industrial Midlands.

The worst-hit towns were those depending most directly on mining. Cardiff, Newport, and Barry increased in population between the censuses of 1931 and 1951, and have continued to increase subsequently. Swansea and Neath, losing numbers during the slump, have not yet fully recovered, while Llanelli, its population reduced by 10 per cent in the period 1931–51, has not reversed the falling trend. Far higher losses, however, were recorded in the mining towns, rising to more than 20 per cent in Ebbw Vale and Rhondda. At very few places on the coalfield is population tending to increase at the present time.

Nevertheless, the industrial scene has changed profoundly. The threat of large-scale unemployment seems far more remote than at any time in the inter-war period. Industrial recovery and industrial change, greatly stimulated by the demands of World War II and by deliberate encouragement in the post-war years, were actually under way before 1939. Government aid was given to a mixed range of light industry, producing such goods as clothing and foodstuffs. The war gave new life to old industries, produced new industrial premises, and introduced a new variety into manufacturing. Whereas coal-mining, steel-making, and plating employ 175,000 people, other industries now take nearly 200,000.

With 400 new factories established by Government action alone, it is impossible to specify all the kinds of development. The Treforest Estate outside Cardiff exemplifies the success of official schemes. Independent firms have established, at Pontypool, manufactures of plate glass and of nylon; the production of nylon yarn in the Pontypool works is largely responsible for Britain's rank as the second greatest producer of this commodity in the world.

The new town of Cwmbran, 8 km from Newport on the Abergavenny road, with a planned population of 35,000, is being built to solve problems of travel to work rather than those of unvaried industry.

Reorganisation and expansion of the steel-making and tin-plating industries has been accompanied by the reorganisation of coal-mining; but this reorganisation has meant contraction. The projected output for South Wales of 32 million tons a year by 1965 turned out, in practice, to be an actual output of less than 20 million tons, at the end of a decade when the trend of production was steadily downward. Modernisation and increased mechanisation of some collieries has been accompanied by the closure of others which are obsolete, unprofitable, or limited as to reserves. Prospects are best in the anthracite field of the west, and on the southern rim of the main part of the field where much coking coal is still available. It seems most unlikely that a significant export trade in coal can ever be re-established; meanwhile, about half the coal raised in South Wales is used locally, with another quarter going to thermal power stations in Wales, on the Channel coast, and on the Thames.

Present Status of the Iron and Steel Industry

Little iron is now smelted on the northeastern rim of the coalfield. The combined output of blast-furnaces here, at Cardiff, and in the Port Talbot–Briton Ferry area amounts to some 25 per cent of the total for Great Britain. The hematite worked near the southern margin of the coalfield in Glamorganshire is far too limited to meet the local demand for ore, which is imported from Sweden, Spain, French Africa, Newfoundland, and France. Similarly, the blast-furnaces of South Wales produce too little pig-iron for the local steel-making industry, and pig-iron is brought in, mainly from the Northamptonshire ironstone field, but local output is steadily expanding. Imported scrap metal is used in great quantities.

Steel furnaces occur on the northeast margin of the coalfield, but the main concentration is in the coastal belt, where Newport, Cardiff, Briton Ferry, Port Talbot, Neath, Swansea, and Llanelli are all great steel-producers. South Wales produces about a quarter of Britain's total output of crude steel, almost the whole of the tin-plate, and nearly two-thirds of the hot mill make of steel sheets. Great changes have occurred in the steel and plating industries since the depressed years of the early 1930s, for industrial recovery has been accompanied and much assisted by modernisation. Many of the older plants were ill-organised, poorly sited, and working with outworn machinery. In 1936 a new integrated iron and steel works, built on a coastal site at Cardiff, was opened. In 1938 an integrated works was completed at Ebbw Vale, including coke ovens, rebuilt blast-furnaces, a basic Bessemer converter, a continuous strip mill, and plating works. An electrolytic tinning plant has been added here since the end of World War II. Four great companies combined to form the Steel Company of Wales, which is responsible for the Margam complex of factories. The Abbey works at Margam itself, built on an area of marshland and sandhills adjoining Port Talbot, begin with blast-furnaces and end with the continuous strip mill and rolling mills, where the strip can be rolled into light and medium steel plates. Plant for the cold reduction of Margam strip into tin-plate has been built at Trostre, near Llanelli, and at Velindre, near Swansea. A hot strip mill at Llanevern, near Newport, has a planned eventual capacity of 12 million tons of ingot steel a year. Gas from the new coke ovens at Margam and Cardiff is fed into the system of pipelines which now serves South Wales. A railway marshalling yard was opened at Margam in 1960, and an iron ore terminal at Port Talbot, with a tidal basin, dredged channel, and breakwater was opened at Port Talbot in 1969.

Towns and Industrial Employment

The towns of Industrial South Wales fall into two groups, one located on or very near the coalfield, the other along the coast. Although the coast and the southern edge of the coalfield converge towards the west, there is in practice no significant overlap between the two groups of towns, for the coastal centres offer very little employment to miners. This circumstance is partly illustrated in Fig. 13:6, which, drawn from the preliminary employment data for the 1966 Census, does not include towns of less than 50,000 in total population.

The group of coalfield towns can, in turn, be subdivided. Along the northeastern rim of the field stand Aberdare, Merthyr Tydfil, Tredegar, Ebbw Vale, and Abergavenny. Mining is prominent among the categories of production employment, as is indicated for Merthyr Tydfil, although the metal trades are tending to outstrip mining in this part of the region as a whole. Abergavenny differs from other towns of this part in functioning as a distributive centre, with many of its total working population in commercial and financial work.

The second set of coalfield towns, scattered across the centre of the field or located near its southern edge, includes Pontypool, Caerphilly, Pontypridd, Gelligaer, Mountain Ash, and Rhondda; the last of these appears in Fig. 13:6, with more than half its production workers in coal mining and more than three-quarters in mining and the metal trades combined. In most of the remainder, mining is also prominent. It is in these two districts, and especially in their smaller towns, that mine closures are most severely felt.

Mining employment in the coastal towns takes no more than 2, 3, or 4 per cent of production workers. By contrast, all towns in this group are

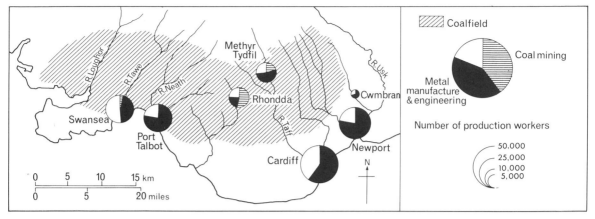

Fig. 13:6. Production workers in Industrial South Wales, 1966

heavily committed to the metal industries, which take two-thirds or more of all production workers; indeed, these industries in Port Talbot take more than half of all those in paid employment. Local variations, such as the prominence of transport workers in Barry, do not obscure the general state of affairs; these variations include considerable employment in commercial and financial work in Penarth and Bridgend. Cardiff also provides a notable range of occupations, as would be expected from its geographical attributes: half its paid work-foce is in service and professional occupations. The town had already developed the characteristics of a regional—if not of a national—capital, before it gained official status as capital of Wales.

All the towns in the coastal group have access to some part of the coalfield. All but Neath and Bridgend are on the coast itself, and all but Barry are on the main coast road. Both Neath and Bridgend are served by main-line railway; the former is connected by the Neath valley with the northeastern coalfield, and the latter is without a near-by rival of equal size. But Cardiff, Newport, and Swansea are outstandingly large among the towns of Industrial South Wales. They include about a third of all the people in the region. Except for Newport, which is surpassed in numbers by Rhondda, they are more populous than any of the remaining towns.

Their success has, no doubt, been promoted in part by their focal positions, although it is hard to say exactly how location has produced its effects. Like Llanelli, Briton Ferry, Port Talbot, and Barry—all of them industrial ports—Cardiff, Newport, and Swansea are set at the junction of firm rising ground with flat, low-lying coastal and riverine alluvium. Much of this part of the shore is

fringed with marine mud, and the lower ends of the valleys are filled with river-laid sediments. Dock-making began in the mid-19th century, in response to the increasing demands of the coal-export trade and of metal-works. At all seven ports, the docks were dug in the weak sediments fringing the coast.

At the beginning of the 19th century, Swansea already had 6,000 inhabitants. With an interest in copper-smelting dating back nearly a hundred years, it was significantly larger than Cardiff (less than 2,000 people) and Newport (just over 1,000). Although copper-smelting has been lost, Swansea retains the making of copper goods. Zinc concentrates are smelted, yielding zinc for galvanising and sulphuric acid for use in making tin-plate. Swansea is a great centre of steel-making, most of the steel going to tin-plate mills. The export trade in anthracite is only half what it was in the 1930s, but oil refining flourishes.

Swansea's growth occurred mainly during the 19th century. Its present population is just over the figure for 1931, and the steelworks and plating mills built in the vicinity since 1945 are expected to encourage new expansion. The town has spread in two main directions—along the coast on both sides of the Tawe, and up the valley alongside the canal, railway and main road. Suburbs have appeared on the hilly ground west of the river-mouth (Fig. 13:7).

Cardiff (Fig. 13:8) experienced phenomenal expansion during the 19th century. In the first fifty years its numbers increased 15-fold, and a further 7-fold increase converted a population of some 30,000 at mid-century to one of 200,000 in 1900. In later years the rate of growth declined, for no more than 50,000 inhabitants were added in the first half of the 20th century.

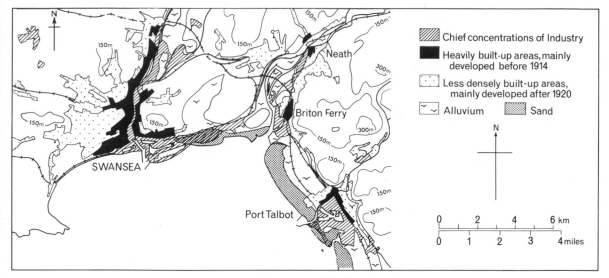

Fig. 13:7. Swansea and its local setting

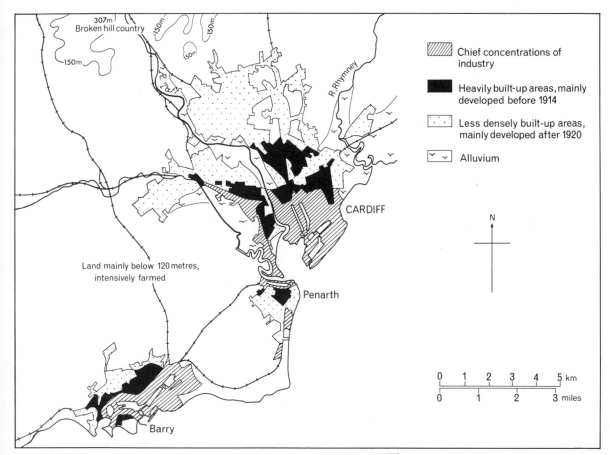

Fig. 13:8. Cardiff and its local setting

Among the measures taken in response to industrial growth were the construction of the Taff Vale Railway in 1840–41, and the making of the first dock, in 1839. Given docks, and a railway link with its mining hinterland, Cardiff was very well placed to develop a most vigorous export trade in coal, at a time when the demand for bunker coal was rising fast. Its metal industries date from the latter part of the 19th century, although it served as the outlet for the Merthyr Tydfil works from the time of their foundation in 1759. Engineering in Cardiff includes ship-repairing and the making of railway wagons, oil engines, vehicles, and electrical gear. As would be expected from a regional capital, there is a great range of light industry.

The heart of the town is located on a patch of river-terrace, between the valleys of the Taff and the Rhymney, above the level of the coastal alluvium where the docks and many of the factories are found. The immediate surroundings are much less industrialised than are those of Swansea.

Newport, on the tidal Usk (Fig. 13:9), commands routes along the valleys of the Usk itself, of the Ebbw, and of the Lywd. Two miles upstream lies the Roman stronghold Isca Silurum (Caerleon), where, as at Newport, firm ground closely approaches the river on both sides. In many respects the industrial history of Newport resembles that of Cardiff, and, like Cardiff, Newport owes its present size mainly to 19th-century growth. But Newport, unlike its larger neighbour, has not developed that complex range of employment which typifies a highly successful town. It has ship-repairing facilities and a modest shipbuilding industry.

Cardiff, Newport, and Swansea have much in common in their port trade. Leading imports include crude petroleum, pig-iron, steel bars, ores and concentrates of non-ferrous metals, grain, and timber. Among the chief exports are refined oil, iron and steel manufactures, tinplate, coal, coke, and patent fuel. Large amounts of general merchandise are handled. The relative status of these three ports is liable to quite rapid change, in response to industrial developments in their near hinterlands. At the beginning of the 1970s they were sub-equal in respect of cargo value, ranking in their combined traffic roughly with the Clyde and Dover. However, Milford Haven had already far surpassed them in terms of tonnage, and was also ahead in terms of value. It can be expected that, during the 1970s, the improved port works at Port Talbot will introduce a fourth main inlet/outlet to this part of the South Wales coast.

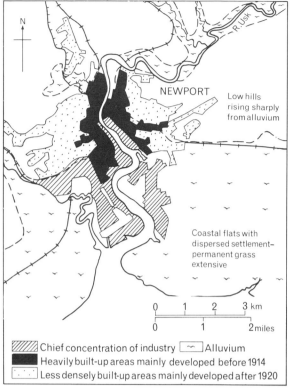

FIG. 13:9. Newport and its local setting

THE WELSH BORDER

Area: about 7,300 km² (2,800 sq. mi.).
Population: about 500,000.
Largest towns: Shrewsbury (49,750).
  Hereford (40,500).
  Wrexham (35,500).
  Malvern (24,500).
  Oswestry (11,250).
  Ludlow (6,750).
  Leominster (6,500).
  Monmouth (5,500).

About three-quarters of this region is in improved farmland, with half the farmland in permanent grass and total grass twice as extensive as tillage.

Numbers of livestock: cattle, 645,000;
  sheep, 1,655,000;
  pigs, 250,000;
  poultry, 5,500,000.

Physique

The structure, pattern of geological outcrops, and relief-pattern of this region are, in detail, very complicated indeed. Rocks exposed at the surface vary greatly in their resistance to erosion. Quite severe dissection has left the stronger rocks rising abruptly above the deep valleys cut in weak outcrops. Carboniferous rocks dip off the Welsh block in the north, the Carboniferous Limestone forming impressive west-facing scarps, and the Coal Measures constituting the Flint and Denbigh coalfields. Hills project northeastwards in south Shropshire, where a fine belt of scarpland is developed on Primary sediments in the Wenlock country. The pattern is confused by the appearance of pre-Cambrian rocks, including the metamorphics of The Wrekin and The Lawley, and also by considerable faulting; Carboniferous sediments, including Coal Measures, occur patchily and disappear beneath the Permo-Trias of the adjacent plains. The immediate environs of Shrewsbury belong to the Midland Triangle, but there is no powerful objection to linking the town itself to the Welsh Borderland.

North of the defile cut by the Severn at Ironbridge through the prong of Primary rocks, drainage of the Border country is collected either by the Dee or by the upper Severn. Below the defile, the Severn receives the Teme and Lead as principal left-bank tributaries, with the Wye and Usk entering its estuary. These rivers drain various parts of the highly-dissected Old Red Sandstone country which is somewhat loosely known as the Herefordshire Plain. A better although more cumbersome term would be the Plains of Herefordshire and Monmouthshire, for maps on a scale of about 1:2,000,000 show quite clearly that part of the basin of the lower Usk is quite as deeply dissected and as widely opened as is the middle basin of the Wye. In these two areas the country is by no means flat; the lower ground is based generally upon marls, while strong sandstones and conglomerates interbedded with the marls stand up as hills. Folding, faulting, and lateral variations of rock strength combine with dissection to produce alternating broken hills and stretches of wide valley. This irregular terrain is partly enclosed on the east by elongated compact blocks of resistant rock which separate it from the Midland Triangle, but, even when no such blocks intervene, there is an immediate change in the texture of relief as one passes from the subdued Permo-Trias country to the hill districts of the Old Red Sandstone. The two principal barriers are formed by the Malverns and the Forest of Dean. The Malverns are composed of an upthrust slice of highly metamorphosed pre-Cambrian rocks, which rises as a long ridge to summits exceeding 300 m. in height. The Forest of

Dean is synclinal in structure, with Coal Measures preserved in the centre and with the top planed off by erosion at about 250–275 m. As is well known, the Wye has been superimposed obliquely across it and exposes the Carboniferous Limestone in sheer cliffs in its valley meanders.

Climate and Soils

There is a very rapid climatic transition across the Welsh Borderland from the Welsh Massif to the Midland Triangle. In the Borderland itself the effect of rain-shadow is strongly felt, and annual totals of precipitation fall sharply from about 1,250 mm. along the edges of the plateaus to some 850 mm. along the eastern boundary. The number of rain-days falls below 200 a year, the number of mornings with snow lying falls to about 10, and the average length of the frost-free season rises above 5 months (Figs. 3:5–3:14). In all these ways the Borderland is far better favoured than is the heart of Wales, but ranges of temperature increase with distance from the sea, mainly because of increasing winter cold. The most valuable improvement of all is one not usually recorded in atlas maps, namely, a rise in actual temperatures during the warmer months. This rise is due partly to the release of latent heat to the air over the Welsh plateau, and partly to the decrease in altitude in the Border country.

Parts of the Border are well favoured in their soils. In the natural state, many of the soils of this region belonged to the group of Brown Forest Soils formed under deciduous woodland. As agricultural material they are mainly warm, having developed on glacial drift derived from the Permo-Trias in the north, and on Old Red Sandstone or drift derived from it in the south. In many places they are of the sandy loam grade, stiff enough to support plants but coarse enough to respond rapidly to rising air-temperature. With such soils, and in the climate of a rain-shadow area, the Welsh Borderland has become a notable farming region. The generally prosperous look of its fields owes something to the high standards maintained on the best farms, and something also to the vigorous growth of hardwood timber in hedgerows and small woods (cf. Plate 37). Trees are especially numerous because parts of this region underwent enclosure at an early date (cf. Chap. 4), with the result that fields tend to be on the small side and hedges a prominent feature of the scene. The southern part of the region is perhaps best seen in spring, when the soil of newly-ploughed fields shows reddish-pink and combines in a

PLATE 37. Half-timbered buildings at Weobley, Herefordshire, in the Welsh Borderland. Medieval timber frames indicate a former abundance of deciduous woodland.

patchwork with the solid green of pasture and the delicate tints of sprouting crops.

Land Use

On the general maps of agricultural distributions (Figs. 5:6–5:23) the Welsh Borderland shows up reasonably well, partly because of the contrast with the Welsh Massif, and partly because it is very roughly comparable to the three counties of Shropshire, Herefordshire, and Monmouthshire. It differs from the Midland Triangle not so much in its proportion of land in farms as in the aims of its farming. Its improved grassland is used chiefly for cattle-grazing. Dairy cattle far outnumber beef-stock in the northern part of the region, where many of the industrial towns of the Midlands, Lancashire, and Cheshire lie within a radius of 75 km. In all parts, dairy cattle have increased in numbers and fodder crops have increased in extent since the beginning of World War II. Dairy cattle outnumber beefstock by two to one in the Hereford-shire Plain, but the rearing and fattening of the native Herefordshire breed still flourishes.

The most extensive single crops are grains—wheat, barley, oats, and mixed corn. Roots and green crops for stockfeeding are widely grown, as also are potatoes and sugar beet. The northern part of the region has particularly large numbers of poultry, which produce eggs for the great urban markets. The large numbers of sheep recorded for the region represent an extension into the bordering hills of the sheep-farming typical of the Welsh interior, and to some extent correspond to the presence of rather poor pasture in some hilly areas.

One highly distinctive feature of the farming of this region is the fruit-production of Herefordshire. The dairying and poultry-farming of the north is to be compared with the town-controlled economy of the farms of the Lancs.–Cheshire Plain, and the fruit-growing in the south should be likened to that of the Avon valley about Evesham. Orchard fruit is more typical than small fruit, and the chief product is cider apples. The Herefordshire Plain is rather too liable to late frosts to become an out-standing producer of soft fruit, and it is in any case traditionally committed to the cider industry which absorbs a large part of its apple crop. Some of the firms which produce cider for the national market have their own orchards in Herefordshire. The great physical advantages of orchard cultivation include warm soils, shelter supplied by hills, and cold-air drainage across sloping ground (cf. Fig. 13:10). Hop-growing, also extensively practised, benefits in the same ways.

the region. The Norman Earl Roger of Montgomery made Shrewsbury his principal stronghold, and it was involved in the Border disputes of the Middle Ages. Prosperity under the Tudors and in the 18th century is recorded by Tudor and 18th-century architecture in the central parts. Later expansion has, perforce, occurred outside the loop of the encircling river, residential suburbs and new factories arising on the north bank. Shrewsbury

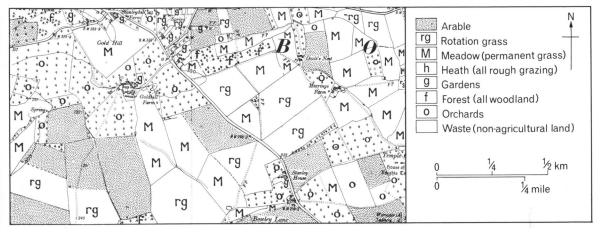

FIG. 13:10. Land-use for the Herefordshire Plain

Towns and Industries

Wrexham stands on the Flint and Denbigh Coal-field, where coal-mining was known as early as the 14th century. During the early 17th century coal was shipped out via the Dee; the field played a part in the industrialisation of the 18th century, but the exposed part of the field is now largely worked out, and future prospects are doubtful. The best that can be hoped for is some 2 million tons a year, partly from the one colliery in Flintshire which works coal under the Dee estuary. Some coal is sent to the industrial towns of Lancashire and Cheshire, but most is used locally. Iron ore is smelted at Mostyn, smelting and steel-making are carried on at Brymbo, and Shotton has a fully-integrated works, where the processes begin with smelting and end with the production of continuous steel strip. Wrexham's main industries are metal-manufacture and mining; industrial chemicals are also produced.

The site of Shrewsbury on a meander-core of the incised Severn has been described above. For centuries its defensive properties were of much importance. The original British settlement was taken by Offa during the Dark Ages, when he pushed the boundary of Mercia westward across

today is the urban focus of a large area, with flourishing cattle- and produce-markets. Its manufactures include safes, vehicles, and machine tools, modern industry being strongly influenced by the spread of engineering in large towns generally. A more direct influence is observable in the designation during the 1960s of the near-by Telford site for a new town, with an ultimate population of 90,000. Here is represented the invasion of the Welsh Borderland by West Midland industry.

Hereford is approached by ridge-routes and valley-routes from all parts of the surrounding Plain. This cathedral centre is, like Shrewsbury, notable for its markets. Its most distinctive industries, depending on local agriculture, include brewing, cider-manufacture, the canning of fruit and vegetables, and the milling of flour.

Oswestry is less centrally placed than is Shrewsbury, and Leominster and Ludlow compare similarly with Hereford. There was no call for more than one large town in either part of the region, and none has developed. Monmouth during the Middle Ages was a heavily-fortified Border stronghold, but has remained small in subsequent times. Its defensive site at the junction of the Wye and Monnow has lost its value, as has the site of

Chepstow, whose castle guarded a more southerly crossing of the Wye.

Malvern includes part of a group of resorts, originally dependent on the fame of the local springs but now expanding steadily under their own impetus. These settlements, finely placed along the lower flanks of the hills and overlooking rural countryside, differ in every possible way from the settlements of the Forest of Dean coalfield. The Forest itself is well-managed, although patches of young conifers are inevitably supplanting some of the older hardwood forest; against the background of trees the mining settlements look incongruous, for small pieces of early 19th-century town seem to have been scattered at random through the countryside. There are signs of former iron-working in abandoned tips and foundries, and of former coal-working in abandoned drifts. Future prospects for coal-mining are poor to nil, the last mines operated by the Coal Board having closed during the 1960s. Light manufacturing industry has supplanted mining as the chief employer (see bibliography: Beard), invading the Forest proper from marginal footholds established prior to the 1960s.

Chapter 14

The Scottish Highlands

Area: about 50,000 km² (20,000 sq. mi.).

Population: about 850,000.

Largest towns: Aberdeen (182,000).*

Inverness (28,600).

Peterhead (12,900).

Elgin (11,700).

Fraserburgh (10,400).

Wick (7,900).

Oban (6,000).

Lerwick (Shetlands) (5,600).

Stornoway (Hebrides) (5,300).

Kirkwall (Orkneys) (4,200).

* 1967 estimate

Outside these towns the average density of population is about 12/km² (30/sq. mi.); large areas are uninhabited.

About 15 per cent of the region is in improved farmland, most of the remainder being classed as rough grazing (including deer forests).

Grassland is more extensive than tillage in the farmland as a whole.

Numbers of livestock: cattle, 915,000

(of which 125,000 dairy cattle);

sheep, 3,750,000;

pigs, 300,000;

poultry, 3,655,000.

In several ways the Scottish Highlands resemble the upland block of Wales. Each of the two forms a massif, each has been denuded under the control of a falling base-level, and both have been glaciated. In both, the northeast–southwest Caledonian trends of geological structure are reflected in the grain of the relief. In the Scottish Highlands, as in Wales, the resistant rocks of the higher plateaus sink eastwards under a cover of Old Red Sandstone on which is based a distinctive eastern border (Fig. 2:1). But of these two massifs the Scottish Highlands possess the more resistant rocks, rise the

higher, and have been much the more heavily glaciated. Correspondingly, the Scottish Highlands are scenically more attractive than Wales, but far more severe climatically and far poorer agriculturally (cf. also Figs. 5:4, 5:25).

Physique

Most of the region is based on ancient metamorphosed rocks which have been invaded in places by large bodies of granite. Parts of two distinct structural belts are present (Chap. 2). The Hebrides and the extreme northwestern coastland, a rigid crustal block composed of Torridonian Sandstone and Lewisian gneiss, represent the foreland of the Caledonides. The main mass of the Highlands is based on the highly altered and much deformed rocks of the Moine and Dalradian Series, which were incorporated in the northwest flank of the Caledonian mountain system. The block is transected by Glen More, a hundred-mile-long trench which, eroded along the line of a fault, separates the Northern Highlands from the Grampians. These latter are notable for the huge outcrops of granite which deep denudation has revealed. On their southeastern side the Grampians overlook the lower ground of Central Scotland on the line of the Highland Boundary Fault.

One result of the intense glaciation of the Scottish Highlands is the presence of deep fiords all along the west coast. These flooded ends of glacier troughs cut deep into the land, leading towards the great fault-guided glens in many of which occur ribbon lakes—the freshwater lochs. The rugged and irregular west coast is still further diversified by the impressive ruins of Tertiary volcanoes in Skye, Mull, and Arran; typical features of highland glaciation are particularly well developed in the Cuillin Hills of Skye.

Severe and general glaciation of the interior

included the scouring of plateau-surfaces, the cutting of corries in peaks rising above the ice-cap, the deepening of main valleys—including Glen More—and the excavation of numerous lake-basins. North of Glen More the land has been greatly impoverished by the general removal of weathered rock. Here, in the Northern Highlands, passes were cut through the main watershed by tongues of ice streaming westward. South of the Great Glen, compact blocks of high ground in the Cairngorms and in the Ben Nevis District, rising above 1,200 m., were scalloped and fretted by ice and frost. Great lake-basins are typical of the southwestern part of the Grampians, while the deep but wide valleys of the Spey, Don and Dee lead down to the sea in the east (Fig. 14:1).

The east coast is less lofty and more regular than the west coast. Around Moray Firth the meta-morphic rocks disappear beneath the sediments of the Old Red Sandstone, just as the massif of South-west England vanishes eastward beneath the Permo-Trias. Even on the Aberdeenshire coast,

where crystalline rocks reach the shore, there is no deep inlet of the fiord type.

Climate

In Scotland, as in Wales, climate deteriorates rapidly from the west coast inland, and the high ground of the interior divides the climate of the western coastlands from the contrasted climate of the lowland on the eastern fringes. The frost-free period in the west is about a month longer than that in the east (7 months against 6), and the west has the slightly smaller mean annual range of temperature. The west, however, is fully exposed to strong winds from the Atlantic, and is cloudy and rainy, with more than 1,250 mm. of precipitation a year. The extreme east is remarkably dry, with as little as 625 mm. on the coast itself.

In the interior is developed the worst climate in the whole of the British Isles. Latitude and height combine to bring the annual total of precipitation to well above 2,500 mm. in the wettest districts, which include Ben Nevis and the summits im-

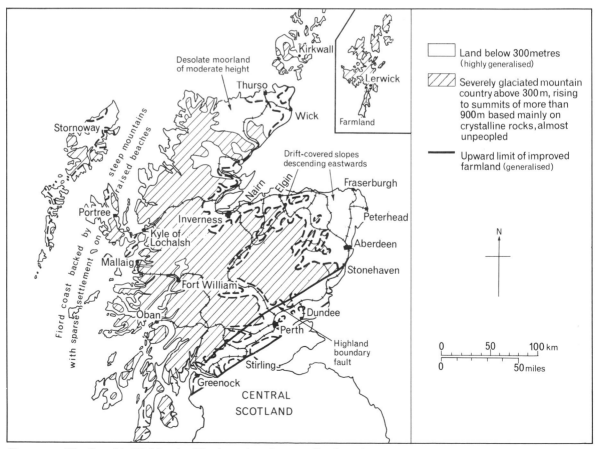

FIG. 14:1. The Scottish Highlands: Physique (much generalised) and main settlements. Compare Figs. 2:1, 3:22

mediately beyond the Great Glen. Further eastwards, although the highest ground still lies high,
precipitation diminishes. It has been lost on the
western flanks of the highlands, where the ascend-
ing air of the westerlies becomes unstable and
releases most of its moisture. The wettest areas of
all, therefore, lie somewhat to the west of the main
axis of high ground; they are the areas of most
frequent cloud, with the sun obscured for three-
quarters of the time, and of the most frequent
precipitation, with rain or snow on two days out of
three.

Very many places in the interior record lying
snow on at least 20 mornings in the year, and in
about half the region the number rises above 40
(Fig. 3:12). Even if the snow-cover were concentrated in a single, unbroken spell, it would last
for six weeks in many places. Frost is very frequent,
the frost-free period diminishing to 90 days in the
high eastern parts of the Grampians (Fig. 3:8).
Ben Nevis just fails to rise high enough to have a
permanent snow-cap, and snow lies throughout
the summer, in some years, in high sheltered gullies
which face north. Throughout this whole region,
deeply grooved as it is by glacier troughs or by
large stream-valleys, local variations in climate,
altitude, slope, and soil count for much.

THE WEST

In the west, where high ground rises abruptly
from the sea, the only possible sites for cultivation
are raised beaches and valley-flats; the latter result
from the redistribution of rock-waste in glacier
troughs, the former from the intermittent recovery
of the crust from its heavy load of ice. Settlement
in the west is concentrated near the shore. A
typical location for a loose group of dwellings is at
the inner edge of a patch of raised beach, with little
tilled fields on the seaward side and rough grazing
on the hills behind (Fig. 14:2). The main tillage
crops are oats and potatoes, which may be combined with hay in some kind of rotation; most of
the hay crop, however, is taken from permanent
grass. Cattle are confined to low levels, while sheep
graze on the hillsides.

Part-time and spare-time farms account for more
than three-quarters of all holdings. Family labour
is widely employed, being most common in the
northwest of the Highland region.

Crofting

The present farming practices in the western

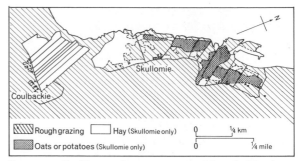

Fig. 14:2. Crofting settlements on raised beach, Northern
Highlands of Scotland

coastlands owe much to crofting, which developed
not only a system of land-management but also a
style of domestic architecture. Crofting in its pure
form is a kind of subsistence farming. It is well
suited to unproductive land remote from large
towns, being designed for self-sufficiency and not
relying on cash transactions. The arable land of a
croft can produce a vegetable crop comparable to
that taken from an English allotment, although
less varied. The oat and hay crops provide oatmeal
and winter feed. Cattle supply milk, with meat
from time to time, and the sheep yield meat in
addition to the wool used for hand-made clothing.
Dwelling-house and cowshed were traditionally
combined in the stone-built *black house*, which
externally was quite similar to the typical country
cottage of Ireland. Despite the name, the black
house was often whitewashed on the outside. It was
the inside which was blackened by the smoke
from peat fires. The dividing wall between the two
parts—one occupied by humans and one by
animals—rose but to the level of the eaves. Today,
many black houses are used only to shelter cattle,
and cottages of a more modern type have been
built by the crofters for their own use.

To people living in English towns, the idea of
self-sufficient agriculture often seems romantic and
attractive, but a visit to the poorer rural areas of
Ireland or of the Scottish Highlands would soon
make it clear that the actual inhabitants have no
illusions. Many are bound to their birthplaces by
ties of affection or of habit, but many others leave.
Crofting represents a close adaptation to a highly
characterised environment, and in consequence is
greatly interesting to the geographer, but to the
people of the crofts it offers very little. The poor
land and the harsh climate lay a heavy burden of
work on crofters, who cannot hope to share the
material wealth of better-favoured regions.

Improvements in communications have been

PLATE 38. A crofter weaving Harris Tweed at his own home.

followed by emigration. Roads and railways have not brought wealth in—they have led many of the people away. The number of crofters in the region today is less than 6,500, while the number of crofters' sons and daughters at work on the crofts is but 500. Scottish crofts are fast losing both their labour-supply and their potential inheritors.

The crofting system has been modified considerably during the last two centuries. Some holdings have been converted to commercial farming, where produce can be sold off the farm in a near-by town, but the scope for commercial farming is limited, since there are few towns on the west coast. The rise of Oban and Mallaig as commercial fishing ports has tended to reduce the number of fishermen-crofters, for fishing has become a full-time occupation—whether in in-shore fishing, in deep-sea fishing, or in Antarctic whaling. The number of fishermen-crofters in the whole Highland region is less than 250. Fish caught for home consumption remain, however, an important item of diet in the coastal settlements. Spinning and weaving for domestic use is dying out, but hand-made goods are produced for the luxury markets of the great British towns (Plate 38).

In these various ways, the principle of self-sufficiency has been losing force. Hill sheep, largely kept on common grazing, are the main interest of the Highland croft today. Even where it is best represented—in the Hebrides, the Orkneys, and the Shetlands—crofting is something of a survival from a past age; and even in the islands, it is disappearing under the influence of commercial fishing, tourism, and hydro-electricity. The Hebrides and the west coast of the Scottish mainland are freely accessible in summer to pleasure cruisers, which ply from Glasgow and Fort William. Skye and the Ben Nevis group are much favoured by climbers. The roads of the mainland are frequented by tourists, whether in private cars

PLATE 39. View from the southwest across Quoich Dam, part of the Garry H.E.P. scheme. Glaciated mountains rise above cloudbase, with boulder clay swathing their lower slopes.

or in coaches. Coach touring in the Highlands has boomed in the post-war period, and many hotels are wholly given over to feeding and lodging coach-parties. The tourist trade, however, is strictly seasonal, and commercial fishing is concentrated in a few ports. Agriculture in some form or other is still the greatest employer.

Hydro-Electric Power

Factory industry has been slow and limited in its development on the west coast. It is represented mainly by the aluminium works at Kinlochleven and Fort William. The use of hydro-electric power in the processing of aluminium at these two places suggests a comparison with Norway, which the west Scottish coast generally resembles. The factories, H.E.P. stations, dams, and aqueducts, constructed in the inter-war period, rely on the heavy precipitation on the high ground behind the coast, and on water-storage in ribbon lakes. The lake-levels are raised and controlled by dams, water being led to the Fort William plant by a tunnel round the flank of Ben Nevis. Aluminium ore (bauxite) comes by sea to the factory piers. The two sets of works are excellent examples of industrial location, for the long inlets on which they stand penetrate the land deeply and reach to the very feet of the rainy mountains. These company installations pre-date the Governmental projects. A more recent addition to Highland industry is the pulp and paper mill at Corpach, overlooking Loch Linnhe.

THE INTERIOR

If the west coastlands are unrewarding, the interior of the Scottish Highlands is still more so. Considerable parts have no inhabitants at all. The Northern Highlands have been heavily dissected, and glaciers have cut deep trenches through the axis of high ground which runs from the head of Loch Linnhe in the south towards Loch Erribol in the north. Widely-spaced main roads run through some of these passes, linking the east coastal route with the tortuous west-coast road. Without the ice-deepened gaps, the west coast of the Northern Highlands would be remote indeed. As it is, the district is accessible to tourists. Its agricultural resources are low. Several of its corrie-bitten peaks rise above 1,000 m. and carry arctic-alpine vegetation, while at medium levels, where the rocks have been heavily scoured by ice, fescue-agrostis grassland is common; at lower levels, molinia and sedge moorland come in (Fig. 3:22). There is little low ground in the interior of the Northern Highlands, and no cultivable flat ground except on the floors of the glacier troughs. The severe climate all but forbids tillage (cf. Plate 1).

The Grampians are higher and more compact than the Northern Highlands. Extensive remnants of old plateaus between the incised valleys record the erosional history of the Grampians; there is a wide distribution of bleak, exposed upland surfaces at about 950 m., overlooked by the even bleaker and more exposed hill-masses of the Ben Nevis group and the Cairngorms which surpass 1,200 m. Here, as in the Northern Highlands, peat soils are widely developed, and nearly all the land is classed as rough grazing. Fescue-agrostis and mountain fescue are typical of the west, while a decrease of rainfall towards the east brings in heather moor. Very little remains of the native forests of Scots pine. The stools of trees are often to be seen where peat has been cut or eroded away, showing how a centuries-old increase in rainfall diminished the extent of woodland; the trees which survived this change in the natural environment have been nearly all destroyed by felling or grazing in historical times. Coniferous forests have been planted on some hillsides, and oakwoods occur in some of the valleys in the east; Strathspey is quite well wooded, but a very great deal of the whole Highland region is bare of trees.

Where farmlands exist, half the farms are run as part-time or spare-time undertakings. Family labour is slightly less usual than in the west, but is still common.

Forests and Deer Forests

There are fewer sheep than could be expected from the huge extent of rough grazing, even though the total number is large. One-fifth or more of the entire Highlands is in deer forest, which takes about 1¼M ha. Deer forests are hunting preserves, typically poor in trees. About half the area could be used for grazing livestock; but the sheep and cattle populations of the deer forests are only about 150,000 and 1,500 respectively. Reforestation in some areas however is producing stands of commercial softwood. The Caledonian Canal has been improved to facilitate the import of wood chips from Canada, which supplement the wood cut from local forests in the supply of a new integrated pulp and paper mill.

Loss of Population

As has been explained in Chapter 7, the post-war period has been marked by rapid progress in the development of H.E.P. in the Scottish Highlands (Plate 39). It is hoped that the spread of power lines and the distribution of current will help to check the movement of people from the region. With very few localised exceptions, the Highlands in general have been losing people by persistent emigration for well over a century. It remains to be seen whether the development of H.E.P. can reverse or even arrest the decline in numbers, for the factors which encourage emigration are as complex as they are powerful. Far more is involved than a shift from Highland country to Lowland town; the movement had its origins in the deliberate abolition of the structure of Highland society. This socially and economically disastrous abolition was the culminating act of centuries of hostility between Scotland and England. In a sense, therefore, it had its origins in the emergence of independent and hostile kingdoms. Little is known of events in Scotland during the Dark Ages, but the Picts and Scots united in about 850 in the Kingdom of Alban. In the course of complex medieval changes this became the Kingdom of Scotland, which was extended westwards when the Hebrides were ceded by Norway in the 13th century. On the south there was repeated war with the English until 1603, when the two kingdoms were joined under a single king. But peace had not yet come—risings took place in 1689, 1715, and 1745. After 1715 forts were built in the Highlands—e.g., at Fort William, Fort Augustus, and Inverness—and military roads began to open up the region. After 1745 punitive measures of the harshest kind were enforced. Some chiefs had been killed at Culloden, others were banished and their lands confiscated; laws were passed to forbid the carrying of arms and the wearing of the tartan, and to abolish the powers of clan chiefs. It was perhaps inevitable that the clan system should be modified as the Highlands were brought into contact with the Scottish Lowlands and with England, but there can be no doubt that the aftermath of rebellion was a great increase in the rate of social change. The arrival of new land-owners and the conversion of much land to sheep-pasture may well have been less influential than the suppression of the clan system. The Highlands illustrate the familiar process of a breakdown of economy associated with a breakdown of social order. One of the obvious responses was emigration, and in twenty years 20,000 people had left. With the disruption of society and with long-continued emigration has gone a decline in the Gaelic language. Only about 75,000 Gaelic-speakers exist today, and of these very few speak Gaelic alone.

The clan system was well adapted to the Highland terrain. The territorial unit was the Highland glen, occupied by a unit of society. Not every group living in its glen had full clan status, but all were integrated into the system, chiefs exercising patriarchal authority over their clansmen. Order within the clan was remarkably stable, even though feuds between clans seriously reduced the united social strength of the region as a whole, and the clan system prevailed for five hundred years. When it was destroyed, the Highlands were left as low in social strength as they are poor in natural resources. The greatest damage was done in the interior, where neither fishing nor cash-cropping could provide the basis for a new social and economic organisation.

THE EAST

The eastern side of the Highland region is better placed, both physically and economically, than the west coast, and is far better placed than the mountainous interior. Most of the inhabitants of the region live on the eastern side, which contains all the towns with more than 10,000 inhabitants, the only large town, nearly all the arable land, and nearly all the farm livestock.

The essential contrasts between west and east are apparent in the land-use figures for the counties of Argyll and Aberdeen. The former has 5 per cent of its area in improved farmland, the latter 50 per cent. In Buchan—the northeastern projection of the Grampians towards Buchan Ness—most of the land is farmed. Farmland stretches through the coastal belt towards Moray Firth, around which it spreads over the low ground. It becomes sparse and patchy further to the north, but

reappears in the northeastern tip of the Northern Highlands and in the Orkneys. On the farms of all these localities, permanent grass is uncommon. Rotation grass and tillage each take about half the improved land, the leading tillage crops being oats, fodder roots (mainly turnips and swedes), potatoes, and barley.

The physical and agricultural contrasts between the western and eastern sides of the Scottish Highlands resemble the differences between the south of Norway and the lowlands of southern Sweden. In Scotland, as in Scandinavia, the eastern side has more extensive low ground, the lower total of precipitation, the less humid air, and the better soils. But the comparison should not be pushed too far—the eastern side of the Scottish Highlands is subjected to very little of the continental influence which so strongly affects the Swedish climate. Its mean annual range of temperature varies between 8° and 10°C.—little higher than ranges on the west coast; mean January temperature runs at about 3°; the average frost-free season is six months long at places near the sea; precipitation is frequent, coming on some 200 days a year. All these are characteristics of a maritime climate. On the other hand, the annual total of precipitation is low; in the immediate neighbourhood of the coast, it ranges from 625 mm. at Buchan Ness and at the head of Moray Firth to 750 mm. at Wick, and remains below 900 mm. throughout the farming areas. The low totals express the powerful effect of rain-shadow produced by the interior highlands. Since most of the farmland lies below 125 m., it is not very greatly affected by lifting, condensation, and precipitation occurring when air comes in from the North Sea.

Soils and Farming

The low precipitation makes tillage possible, the quality of the soils encourages it. Around the head of Moray Firth, and in the hinterland of Wick, the land is based on Old Red Sandstone, and local glacial deposits include a high proportion of rock-waste derived from that formation. Further east, the drifts are derived from metamorphic rocks and from granites. Throughout the coastal belt of the eastern Highlands, therefore, the parent materials of the soils developed on glacial drift are generally coarse. In the natural state the soils belonged to the podsol group, and were strongly acid in reaction. They have been much improved by heavy fertilisation and wise management during the last hundred or hundred-and-fifty years, but although they have been enriched, little can be done about

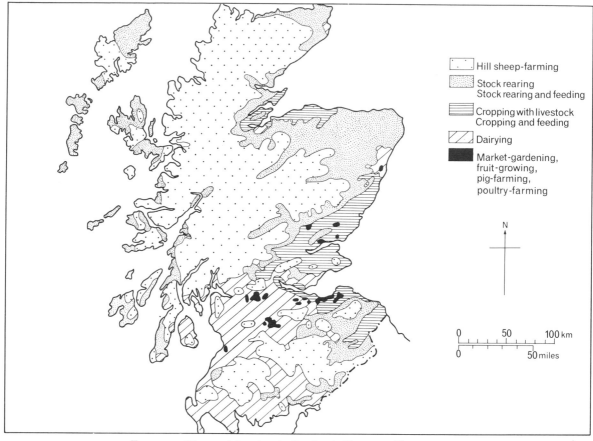

FIG. 14:3. Types of farming in Scotland. Compare Figs. 5:4, 5:25

their texture. They will warm up quite readily, but remain too permeable and therefore too acid to be well suited to permanent grass. Tillage and ley-grass between them take nearly all the farmed acreage. Long leys are unusual, since the quality of their grass deteriorates.

Many of the farms are too far from urban markets to rely on dairying, but some kind of stock-farming is dominant in most of the district as it is throughout Scotland generally (Fig. 14:3). Many farms produce winter feed for sheep, but cattle are more numerous than sheep except in the hills. The main beef breed is the well-known Aberdeen-Angus. There is a rough gradation from stock-rearing on the landward side, through a broad central belt of rearing and feeding, to coastal patches where cash-cropping is combined with fattening. Tillage is best favoured around the head of Moray Firth, where the soils are developed on débris of Old Red Sandstone, and where daytime temperatures of summer, rising higher than elsewhere in the district, enable the long days to compensate somewhat for the typical coolness of the season. Part of the oat crop is sold for milling into oatmeal.

Part-time and spare-time farms are far less common in the east than in the west and the interior. Family labour is also less usual, although it is still used—half the farms in the entire Highland region are worked by family labour.

Settlements

Settlements in the eastern part of the Highland region are generally small and well scattered. Every town is the urban focus of some piece of lowland, but in few cases do urban influences reach far afield. Coastal settlement is inhibited by long, smooth stretches of sandy shore, and the growth of coastal towns is restricted by the lack of demand for ports. Wick is scarcely holding its own in numbers of inhabitants. Peterhead and Fraserburgh record but slight increases in the last twenty-five years, despite the share they take in the herring fishery. Elgin, with woollen manufacture and tanning, has outgrown Fraserburgh, where pneumatic tools are made. Inverness profits both from its industries and from tourist traffic. It stands at the northeastern end of the Great Glen, which provides by far the easiest routeway from the western to the eastern side of the Highland region, and carries pleasure-steamers in summer on the Caledonian Canal. Manufactured products of Inverness include whisky, woollens, and welded metal goods.

Aberdeen

Aberdeen is growing only half as fast as Inverness, but has a long start. Until 1350 it was the most populous town in the whole of Scotland, and still ranks third after Glasgow and Edinburgh. It is the northernmost large town of the British Isles (Fig. 10:3), and is alone among the towns of the Highlands in providing a full range of urban services. Not least, it is a university town.

As its name shows, Aberdeen stands at the mouth of the Dee (Fig. 14:4). There was formerly a corresponding settlement, Aberdon, at the mouth of the river Don, but this has been absorbed by the larger town and now goes under the name of Old Aberdeen. Aberdeen has access to the wide lower reaches of the Dee and Don valleys, commands

routes along the coastland, and is the main urban focus of the farmlands from Stonehaven to Elgin. In medieval times, Aberdeen merchants and Aberdeen ships were busy in the Baltic trade. The local shipbuilding and ancillary occupations achieved their greatest success with the construction of clippers. The change from wooden to metal ships depressed the Aberdeen yards, of which the three remaining today employ some 2,000 people. Timber-mills and paper-mills take the wood which is imported nowadays. Textile industry is represented by the working of linen and wool, hosiery and overcoating being leading products. But the textile and garment trades employ only 18 per cent of the manufacturing workers of Aberdeen, and the timber trades only 14 per cent, while metal manufacture and engineering employ 40 per cent. No more than a few hundreds are directly employed in working the granites of Aberdeen and Peterhead.

Of the workers in metal in Aberdeen, about a quarter are employed in the shipyards. Three times as many are needed by the varied engineering industry, which produces oil engines, agricultural machinery, and mechanical handling appliances. Light electrical engineering is tending to expand under the influence of H.E.P. generated in the Highlands. The dominance of engineering among

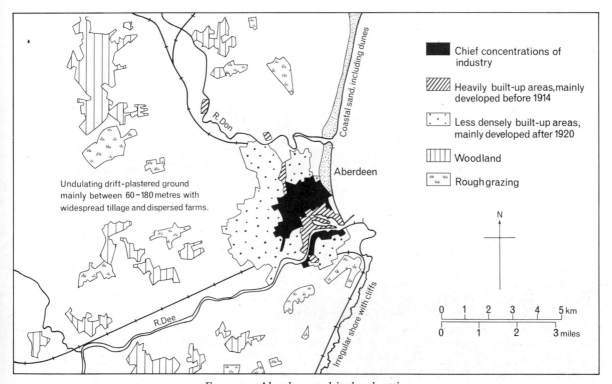

FIG. 14:4. Aberdeen and its local setting

PLATE 40. The fishing fleet in Aberdeen harbour.

the industries of Aberdeen brings the town into line with numerous other manufacturing centres in the British Isles, but Aberdeen is not primarily an industrial town. Dundee has nearly twice as many workers in manufacture, and Aberdeen is no more highly industrialised than is Edinburgh. Distributive trades and transport services employ twice as many people in Aberdeen as does manufacture; retail trade is vigorous, and in its functions of resort and tourist centre the town employs many people in personal service.

FISHING IN THE HIGHLAND REGION

Aberdeen is the greatest base of fishing vessels, not only in the Highlands, but also in the whole of Scotland. Nine out of every ten Scottish fishermen have their homes in the Highland region; one in every four lives in the county of Aberdeen, and one in seven in Aberdeen itself (Plate 40).

Aberdeen is the chief Scottish port for landings of white fish—cod, haddock, hake, and plaice. Its trawlers go to the fishing-grounds off Iceland, the

Faroes, Northwest Scotland, the Orkneys, and the Shetlands, plus the West Greenland and Labrador grounds which have been assuming increasing importance, perhaps because other grounds are being fished out. Aberdeen is among the list of four ports in the British Isles (Hull, Grimsby, and Fleetwood being the other three) that account for three-quarters of the landings of demersal fish; but the town suffers chronically from the tendency of demand to concentrate on the cheaper grades of fish.

The Scottish herring fishery, handicapped by being organised in small units, has also suffered a serious decline. Landings are shared by several little ports, among which are Stornoway, Ullapool, Mallaig, Oban, Inverness, and Fraserburgh (see bibliography, Ch. 24: Day). Inshore fishing is still more widely dispersed; landings are made at very many places, mainly on the east coast of Scotland from Wick to Arbroath.

In explaining the decline of Highland sea-fishery, some allowance must be made for the effects of World War II and its aftermath. Many vessels were lost in the war years, when replacement was impossible, and post-war inflation greatly hampered recovery. The net results of the various difficulties are seen in the steep decline in numbers of fishermen—a decline amounting to 40 per cent in the inter-censal period 1931–51.

FUTURE PROSPECTS OF THE REGION

Government support for the crofting population began as early as the 1880s, but seems in the event to have proved ineffective. It appears likely that agriculture will recede from the Highlands as it has long been receding from the western Islands. By the 1961 census, the total population of the crofting counties (Argyll, Caithness, Inverness, Ross and Cromarty, and the small archipelagoes of Orkney and Shetland) had fallen close to the mark of 250,000 (see bibliography: Turnock). Agricultural resources are limited, mineral resources except for road-metal are few. But hydro-electric power is considerably developed, more than fifty stations now operating. A change of policy in the mid-1960s involves attempts to attract manufacturing industry. It is having a marked impact on the area at the head of the Moray Firth, where Inverness is emerging as the centre of a complex that includes aluminium and petrochemical processing. Invergordon, a naval base in World Wars I and II, on Cromarty Firth, uses its deepwater harbour to serve the smelting and refining plants (see bibliography: Mather and Smith). The Loch Awe power scheme, with its station at Cruachan, uses excess electricity generated by night at the Hunsterston nuclear station to pump water back into storage (see bibliography: Lea). Industrialisation about the head of the Moray Firth is probably a response to publicity and to inducements, rather than to advantages of location and access from the sea; but its rise must be welcome to the economy of the region in general, even though it must tend to depeople still more rapidly than ever the disadvantaged areas in the west.

Chapter 15

Central Scotland

Area: about 11,000 km² (4,000 sq. mi.).
Population: about 4,000,000.
Largest towns: (*a*) The Central Clydeside Conur-
bation (1,760,000), of which the
leading members are:
Glasgow (960,000).*
Paisley (95,500).*
Motherwell (75,500).*
Coatbridge (53,250).*
Clydebank (50,500).*
(*b*) Other industrial towns located
on or very near to the coalfields:
Greenock (71,750).*
Kirkcaldy (52,000).*
Dunfermline (51,750).*
Kilmarnock (47,750).*
Ayr (46,750).*
Hamilton (46,000).*
Falkirk (37,750).*
Dumbarton (27,000).
(*c*) Remaining towns:
Edinburgh (467,500).*
Dundee (182,250).*
Perth (41,250).*
Stirling (27,100).
* 1967 estimates

The average density of population outside these
towns is about 90/km² (225/sq. mi.).

Rather more than half this region is in improved
farmland, with 40 per cent of the farmland in
tillage.

Numbers of livestock: cattle, 575,000 (of which about
half dairy cattle);
sheep, 1,675,000;
pigs, 175,000;
poultry, 3,750,000.

This region, located between the Scottish Highlands and the Southern Uplands, has several

names. It has been variously called the Midland
Valley, the Central Valley, the Central Lowland,
the Mid-Lowland, the Scottish Midlands, and
Central Scotland. None of these possible titles has
yet been generally accepted. The names *Lowlands
of Scotland* or *Scottish Lowlands* are not applied to this
region except by the misguided, for the Lowlands
include the whole of Scotland south of the Highland Line. Two of the possible names have been
selected for use in this book. The first of these is *The
Midland Valley*, a term in general use by geologists
to connote a well-defined crustal belt underlain
and bounded by distinctive structures, which has
already appeared in a geological context in
Chapter 2. The name *Central Scotland* will be used
for the geographical region.

Central Scotland accounts for about one-seventh
of the total land area of Scotland, and contains
some three-quarters of the total population. In
many ways it compares favourably with the adjoining regions on the north and the south. Little
of its land stands really high above sea-level, and
the bleak mountain climates typical of the Highlands and of parts of the Southern Uplands are not
widely represented. Although many of the soils
were naturally poor in the uncultivated state,
they do at least exist. There are large coalfields
which provided one of the original bases of heavy
industry, and long inlets which give access to
busy sea-lanes. Central Scotland is the only one
of the three Scottish regions where large numbers of
people can make a living. In this region alone
have numerous industrial towns arisen.

The present high total of population in Central
Scotland is due mainly to natural increase within
the region itself. If ever there was a time when the
industrial towns owed their growth chiefly to
migration from the two upland regions, that time
has long since passed. During the seventy years
from 1861 to 1931, for instance, the combined loss

by migration from the Highlands and the Southern Uplands was about 850,000; during the same period, the population of Central Scotland rose by nearly 1,850,000. Thus, even if all the migrants from the upland regions had settled in Central Scotland, they would not have accounted for half the actual increase in population. But not all of them went to Central Scotland, and of those who did so, not all settled in the region. Central Scotland also lost people by migration, either to England or to places overseas. Perhaps a quarter of its net increase in population during the last century is to be ascribed to migration within Scotland, the remaining three-quarters being due to the regional excess of births over the combined loss by death and migration.

During periods of industrial depression in the inter-war period, standards of diet in the towns of Central Scotland were commonly lower than those on the coastal crofts of the Highlands. But there was no migration from Central Scotland to the crofting districts—rather did people leave the region for towns in England or for places overseas. The drift from the land and into towns involved far more than a change of work, a choice of occupation, and—in times of prosperity—a better standard of living than the countryside could provide. Living in towns is today a firmly-rooted social habit. Consequently people will move from one town to another, but will rarely go from the town to the country. Very many, of course, never consider the possibility of moving far from the places where they were born, but, when movement occurs, the highly urbanised region of Central Scotland is able to retain many of its own natives and to attract Scots from elsewhere. Even if they were fully understood, the possible disadvantages of life in an industrial town would be unlikely to outweigh the attractions.

The greatest social and industrial resources of Central Scotland today consist in towns and industries already in being. Both the manufacturing and the farming of this region represent the results of generations of effort, during which natural advantages have been realised, and difficulties of various kinds have been overcome. Here, as in other industrialised parts of the British Isles, profound changes have occurred in the nature, aims, and economic relations of the regional industry. The story of industrial growth has been far more complex than the mere rise of manufacturing on coalfields or on tidewater. The present status of farming has been attained by adaptation to the regional climate and by deliberate improvements of the soils. Nevertheless, it was the presence of coal and iron-ore which made possible the first growth of modern industry, just as the nature of the climate and of the soil made it possible for farming to become profitable.

Physique

The Midland Valley is a structural depression, bounded on the northwest by the Highland Boundary Fault and on the southeast by the Southern Uplands Fault. The line of the Highland Boundary Fault corresponds to the Highland Edge, where a sharp descent of 300 metres or more marks the dissected margin of the Grampian block. The Southern Uplands Fault, separating the Midland Valley from the intensely-crumpled Ordovician and Silurian rocks of the Southern Uplands, is more clearly marked on the geological map than on the ground, for the physical boundary on this side of Central Scotland is obscured by hill-masses within the region.

Between the two faulted boundaries, a strip of crust some 50–80 km. wide has been depressed. Sediments laid down in the sagging trough belong chiefly to the Old Red Sandstone and Carboniferous systems. Subsidence was greatest in the centre, so that Old Red Sandstone appears at the surface along either margin and Carboniferous rocks are exposed in a broad central belt. Volcanic eruptions accompanied crustal movement, with the result that lavas and tuffs (solidified volcanic dust) are interbedded with the sediments in many places; the outbreaks continued well into Permian times. Generally speaking, the volcanic rocks are more resistant than the sedimentaries, and underlie the groups of hills which diversify the relief of the region. The Sidlaw Hills and the Ochils are based on volcanic rocks of Old Red Sandstone age, while the Campsie Fells, the Kilpatrick Hills, and the Renfrew Hills are underlain by Carboniferous volcanics. These five hill-groups are aligned from southwest to northeast across the northern part of the region, separated from the margin of the Grampians by a long vale eroded in Old Red Sandstone (Fig. 15:1). Their sides rise abruptly from the surrounding lower ground, and tabular summits exceed 600 m. in the Ochils.

The patterns of geology and relief along the southeastern border of the Midland Valley are complex. Here too occur outcrops of sedimentary Old Red Sandstone and of volcanic rocks, but there is no strip of lowland to define the regional boundary. The Pentland Hills rise above 550 m. on lavas and tuffs, Tinto Hill reaches a summit

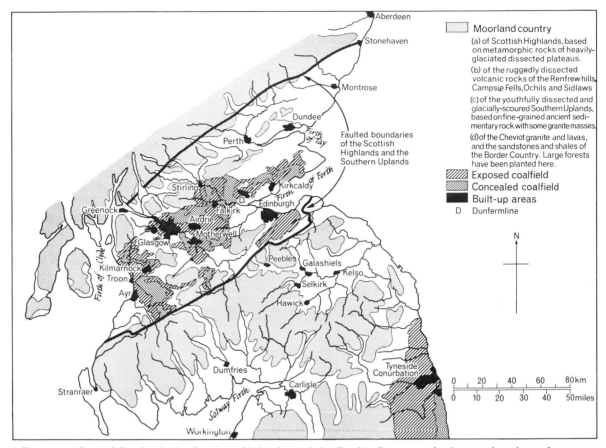

FIG. 15:1. Central Scotland, the Southern Uplands, and the Border Country: physique and main settlements

more than 600 m. high on intrusive igneous rock, and Cairn Table approaches 600 m. on resistant Old Red Sandstone sediments. A dissected belt of hilly country runs northwestwards from Cairn Table between the Ayr and Lanark coalfields, crossing upfaulted Silurian rocks on to volcanics of Carboniferous age.

Between the two flanking belts lie the coalfields. Each field is a structural basin, bounded by tracts where coal-bearing rocks thin out and disappear. The older rocks surrounding the coalfields offer no prospects of concealed reserves. The structural pattern of each coalfield is complicated by minor folding and faulting, and the Fife and Midlothian field is broken across by the wide estuary of the Forth.

Little is directly known of the geological history of the region after Permian times. It seems highly likely that the Highlands and the Southern Uplands were uplifted during the Tertiary period, when volcanoes broke out in the Hebrides and basalt flows occurred in Antrim. Presumably the

Midland Valley was also uplifted, but, if so, its fill of weak sediments has long been denuded away. Differential erosion during the Tertiary period produced a pattern of relief generally similar to that of the present day.

Many of the hilltops are gently-sloping and display accordant summits—signs of partial planation in previous cycles of erosion, whether the platforms represent old wave-cut benches, or whether they are the remains of old land-surfaces. Most of the ground is between 550 and 50 m. above sea-level, although patches lower than 50 m. occur near the shore and in the bottoms of large valleys. Many of the details of surface form are due to glacial and fluvio-glacial deposits, but the erosional platforms are well in evidence in a general view of the landscape, their gentle slopes impeding soil-drainage in many places.

Just as the erosional platforms truncate rocks and structures in profile, so do the main lines of drainage cut across the grain of relief in plan. The North and South Esk, the Tay and the Earn, the

Teith and the Forth all emerge from the Highlands to run across the fringing belt of lowland. The Tay and the Earn empty through the Perth Gap into the Firth of Tay, where tidewater runs up between the Sidlaws and the Ochils. The Teith joins the Forth before the combined stream flows through the Stirling Gap, between the Ochils and the Campsie Fells, into the Firth of Forth. A neck of land less than 50 km. across separates the Firth of Forth from the head of the Firth of Clyde, into which the Clyde flows from the southeast. Lesser streams—the Irvine and the Ayr—drain the Ayrshire Plain, and the Almond, Esk and Tyne flow across the Lothian coastlands.

Apart from subsequent streams aligned on weak outcrops, the drainage-pattern of Central Scotland is difficult to explain. The main streams show signs of having been superimposed—hence the gaps which they cut through belts of high ground. The Perth and Stirling gaps had very great strategic importance in past times, but the gap occupied by the Clyde estuary between the Renfrew and the Kilpatrick Hills led northward routes only to the wild country of the southwest Highlands.

Glaciation and Its Effects

Ice and meltwater deposited a great bulk of rock-waste in Central Scotland. Stiff boulder-clay, up to 30 metres or more in thickness, is widely distributed; drumlins occur on the Ayrshire Plain, on the coalfield country of the centre of the region, and north of the Tweed. Deposits of sand and gravel are well known from the eastern side of the region, where they are diversified by kettle-holes and old lake basins.

In immediate pre-glacial times the Scottish land stood higher than it does today, and rivers were cutting deep valleys in their lower reaches. The great weight of the ice-sheets depressed the land during glacial maximum; after deglaciation the land began to rise again, carrying the late-glacial beach up to 30 m. above the present shore. Post-glacial uplift, however, has not yet compensated fully for glacial depression, and in any case the general level of the sea has fallen. Thus raised beaches and river-terraces, indicating emergence of the land and rejuvenation of the streams, adjoin the drowned valleys of the Firths.

Soils

The soils developed on the various types of superficial deposit—boulder clay, sand and gravel, terrace material, and raised beach—are very

varied (Fig. 15:2). On the stiffer of the boulder clays, soils are usually cold, and in the natural state poorly drained, while the sands and gravels develop coarse-textured soils which are readily leached and tend to be podsolised. Leaching is most severe in western districts. The raised beaches—particularly well-developed on the eastern side—provide some of the most useful soils of all under heavy fertilisation.

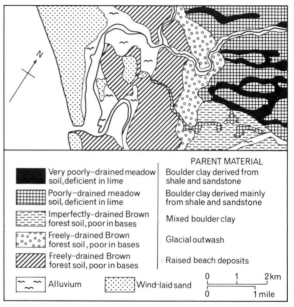

Fig. 15:2. Sample of soil-distribution in the Ayrshire coastland

Climatic and Agricultural Contrasts

Climatically and agriculturally the two sides of the region differ strongly from one another. Contrasts in agriculture represent adaptations to, and not the direct effects of, contrasts in climate. They are well illustrated by a comparison between Ayrshire in the west and Fife in the east. In Ayrshire less than one-fifth of the farmland is under tillage crops, in Fifeshire more than one-half; the most extensive tillage crops in Ayrshire are oats, potatoes, fodder roots, and green fodder crops, in that order; oats and potatoes also lead in Fifeshire, but are followed by barley, fodder roots, wheat, and sugar beet. Permanent grass is twice as extensive as rotation grass in Ayrshire, but rotation grass occupies slightly the larger acreage in Fifeshire. The ratio of beefstock to dairy cattle is far higher in Fifeshire than in Ayrshire.

Such differences are associated with a rainier climate in the western than in the eastern parts of

Central Scotland. There is little contrast between the west and the east in annual range of temperature, incidence of snowfall, or length of frost-free period, although the west is slightly more maritime and thus slightly more equable than the east. The east receives rather more frost but also rather more sun than the west. The most significant contrasts are in rainfall. Little of the west receives less than 1,000 mm. a year, and the total rises above 1,250 mm. on the hills west of the middle Clyde. All the lowland of the east records an average below 1,000 mm., the total falling to 650 mm. on the coast between Edinburgh and the Tweed. Correspondingly, the number of rain-days falls from well over 200 a year in the west to 175 days on the east coast.

Types of Farming

The net results of agricultural response to these spatial variations in climate are clearly revealed in Fig. 14:3. Cropping with stock-farming is dominant north of the Forth, while dairying is the main interest to the west and south of that river. Hill sheep are kept on the Pentlands and other masses of high ground in the south of the region, as well as on the hills of volcanic rock in the north, as far northeastwards as the Ochils.

Grain-growing was dominant in the east until the late 1800s, when increasing imports of cheap North American grain brought about a general change. Very few farms carry no livestock at the present day, but a considerable number north of the Tay, on the peninsula between the Tay and the Forth, and along the southern coastland of the Forth estuary concentrate on a combination of cropping and fattening. Many Irish store cattle are bought for fattening, except in the northern part of the district where homebred stores are typical. The cropping-and-fattening farms are surrounded by more numerous, but similarly distributed, farms where cropping is combined with rearing as well as with fattening.

The farms of the eastern side of Central Scotland have produced several notable pioneers of agriculture, and the area has been well in the van of agricultural advance for more than two centuries. Among the local developments were four-course and six-course rotations, which are still widely practised. In general, farming in this part of the region is notable for its high yields, which result more from good management than from any naturally favourable circumstance. The impression of prosperity and of a high standard of cultivation is enhanced rather than weakened by a scarcity of hedgerow timber and by large fields. On the wide raised beaches the land is flat, and tillage is particularly extensive.

Intensive farming of a specialised kind is localised. Pig-farms and poultry-farms occur north of Glasgow and west of Edinburgh, while market gardens are concentrated east of Edinburgh, in the Clyde valley upstream of Glasgow, and around the town of Ayr. The greatest single concentration is located on the Lothian coastlands, which contain half the market-gardening area of Scotland and yield two-thirds of the country's production of market-garden crops. Musselburgh is the centre of a district where, on the shore of the Forth estuary, a raised beach provides a foot of very light soil overlying shelly gravel; the topsoil has been transformed and made highly productive by heavy dunging. Deliberate improvement has also been highly effective in Strathmore and in the Carse of Gowrie. Strathmore, between the Sidlaw Hills and the Highlands, is floored by alluvium and glacial drift. The local soils are, in the main, loamy, and have well repaid the draining and fertilisation which began in the 18th century; at that time, shell-marl from the bottoms of lochs was widely applied to the lime-poor soils, and many years of wise management have converted Strathmore to a highly arable district noted for potatoes in the western part and for fodder crops in the east. The Carse of Gowrie is based on estuarine clays exposed by the post-glacial rise of the land. Until the 18th century this district was very marshy. Drainage, ploughing, and fertilisation have enabled it to gain a high reputation for small fruit, orchard fruit, and dairy produce. Cattle-fattening in the Carse of Gowrie is associated with rich grassland, but dairying, market-gardening, and fruit-growing are closely linked to the demands of Dundee. Other specialisms include the production of high-grade potatoes on the red soils around Dunbar and the growing of early potatoes on the coastal sands of Ayrshire. A different kind of specialism is exemplified by the development of the Ayrshire breed of dairy cattle, now represented in many parts of Great Britain as well as in its home area.

Industry

Although well over half the area of Central Scotland is in improved farmland, and although the average standard of farming is high, agriculture takes but 3 per cent of the workers in the region. A high degree of mechanisation—which is particularly characteristic of eastern districts—helps to explain the fact that farm workers number no more than 55,000; but the contrast between this low figure and the total of 1¾ million at work in Central Scotland is almost entirely due to the fact that most of the inhabitants live and work in towns. Three quarters of the people live in one or other of the towns listed at the head of this chapter, and nearly half live in the Central Clydeside Conurbation. About half the people at work in Central Scotland are absorbed by commerce, finance, insurance, clerical work, metal-manufacture and engineering, transport and communication, or mining—typical occupations of an industrial society.

That industrial society, however, is in process of change. During the intercensal period 1931–51, the numbers employed in metal manufacture and engineering rose by one-fifth. At the same time the numbers engaged in mining and quarrying diminished by one-third. The trends expressed by these figures are due principally to the progress made by the steel industry and to the contrasted decline of coal-mining.

Coal, Iron Ore, and Oil-Shale

Apart from small and isolated outcrops of coal-bearing rocks, the coalfields of Central Scotland include the Ayrshire field, which adjoins a low, sandy shore with few inlets; the Lanarkshire or Central field, which straddles the middle Clyde and extends northeastwards towards the Forth at Grangemouth; the Fife and Clackmannan field, where seams in the Limestone Coal Group are exploited in the central part of the field west of Kirkcaldy; and the Midlothian field southeast of Edinburgh.

The location and extent of the working coalfields are not accurately shown by small-scale geological maps. Coal seams are not confined, in Central Scotland, to the Coal Measures. Indeed, hydrocarbons of organic origin are found low down in the local Carboniferous succession, in the Calciferous Sandstone (App. 1) which contains oil-shales. Next above this formation comes the Carboniferous Limestone Series, including the Limestone Coal Group with productive coal-seams which are much exploited. Also in the Limestone Coal Group are the clayband and blackband iron-stones. Next comes the Millstone Grit, which is worked for ganister in places, and above that the Coal Measures. These are divided into a productive Lower group and a barren Upper group of beds.

Coal is known to have been worked in Scotland in the 12th century, and the export trade dates at least from the 16th century, when many shipments went to London from ports on the Forth. There was little metal-working until 1759, when the Carron Ironworks began to use clayband ore. This type of ironstone occurs as concretions in the Limestone Coal Group, and could be worked by means of colliery shafts. Blackband ironstone, a variety of clayband ore, contains enough carbonaceous matter to make it self-calcining. It came into use from 1828 onwards, with the application of the hot-blast process to smelting. These two kinds of ore supplied a vigorous metallurgical industry. The peak of extraction was recorded in 1880, when more than 2½ million tons of ore were raised, but there was a rapid decline in later years as the richest deposits were exhausted and costs of working rose sharply. The present output is very small, and the manufacture of iron and steel in Central Scotland now relies on imports of ore and on supplies of scrap.

Reserves of coal, like those of iron ore, have been seriously depleted. The annual output of coal from the combined fields of Central Scotland reached its peak of 42 million tons before World War I. Present output runs at about 23 million tons a year, and the most to be hoped from planned developments is an increase to 30 million tons. The Lanarkshire field has undergone the worst decline. Its production fell from 24 million tons in 1910 to 9 million tons in 1950, accounting for most of the total fall in regional output. Mining in the Lanarkshire field is handicapped by thin seams, water in old workings, falling productivity and rising costs. The variety of coal known as *splint*, which was suitable for charging raw into the early hot-blast furnaces, has been superseded by metallurgical coke, and Scottish supplies of high-grade coking coal are limited.

Reserves in the Ayrshire field are scattered, but new drift mines are planned to increase the output of 4½ million tons a year by more than 50 per cent. Prospects are best in the eastern fields, where Fife and Clackmannan possess 4,000 million tons of workable reserves. The Fife and Clackmannan field produced 10 million tons of coal in 1913; the present output from its 40 working collieries is between 7 and 7½ million tons a year, and an increase to 11 million tons is projected. Since the richest reserves lie deep, large new collieries are required to work them. The most promising part of the coalfield is near the coast, with extensions of the seams under the sea, for the western part is heavily faulted and its seams dip steeply underground. Little is hoped from the 12 collieries in West Lothian, but the output from East Lothian and Midlothian, where there are 20 collieries, is planned to increase from less than 4 million to nearly 6 million tons a year. Reserves here total 1,200 million tons; however, the present state of the coal industry does not suggest a hopeful future, except in relation to the generation of thermal power. The Longannet power station on the Firth of Forth southeast of Alloa, the largest conventional coal-fired station in the U.K., joins the big Kincardine and Cockenzie (east of Edinburgh) stations on the same inlet; in full production, Longannet will consume 6 million tons of coal a year, about half from seams in the Upper Limestone Coal. The ash content is high, but constitutes no grave obstacle to use in power generation (see bibliography: Jones and Marshall).

In drift mining, a sloping gallery instead of a vertical shaft is driven into the ground. Drift mining has long been common in parts of the Scottish coalfields, especially where the seams are repeated by faulting—a circumstance which also favours opencast working—but opencast workings and drift mines alike have a short working life, most drifts operating for 6 to 10 years only. As deep mining in large collieries becomes concentrated in the eastern part of the region, there must be a redistribution of miners. These now number some 80,000—far fewer than in 1913; the decline in numbers has naturally been greatest in the Lanarkshire field.

The export trade in Scottish coal has suffered severely from declining output, rising home demand for certain types of coal, and a shrinking foreign market for general-purpose coals. Of the coals suited to industrial uses, a high proportion is taken by industry in Central Scotland, but power stations at maximum demand will take about half the total output.

The working of oil-shale, like that of coal, reached its peak in 1913. It persisted into the mid-twentieth century, when it employed some 4,000 workers, supplying the Pumpherston refinery with its output of 100,000 tons of oil a year. Subsequently, however, oil-shale extraction has ceased entirely.

The almost complete exhaustion of economically workable iron ore, the serious decline in coal production, and the greatly reduced output of shale-oil contrast sharply with the progress made by the iron and steel industry. The present-day manufacturing of Central Scotland well illustrates the power of industrial momentum, for the depletion of local reserves of ore and fuel have been more than offset. Nowhere in the British Isles is the result of industrial momentum better displayed than in Central Clydeside, where industry has perforce had to adapt itself to the decline of the Lanarkshire coalfield.

The Rise of Glasgow: Industrialisation of the Clyde Valley

The rise of Glasgow to the rank of great port and manufacturing town began early in the 18th century, when trading links were forged between the Clyde and the American colonies. The political union of England and Scotland, in 1603, barely preceded successful colonisation on the mid-Atlantic coast of North America; but the English Parliament favoured English merchants to the extent of imposing restrictions on colonial trade with Glasgow, and the town did not become heavily engaged in transatlantic traffic for another century. When the restrictions were removed and Glasgow secured its commercial freedom, its merchants could freely import Virginian tobacco and West Indian sugar. Workshops in and near Glasgow produced leather goods, textiles, and furniture for export to the expanding colonies.

The War of American Independence and the Napoleonic Wars hit Glasgow hard, but the bankrupted traders were soon succeeded by prosperous manufacturers of cotton textiles. Technical developments and new building provided the Glasgow area with more than a hundred cotton-factories by the early 1800s. The population of the town rose from 43,000 in 1780 to 77,000 in 1800, and by 1840 it was more than 250,000. Then came a pause in the growth of the cotton textile industry, followed by the American Civil War and by the loss of textile-manufacturing to Lancashire. Industrialists on Clydeside forsook textiles for metals, investments went into engineering and shipbuilding, textile-making machines were allowed to wear out without replacement, and the cotton mills closed one by one. Paisley alone retained the manufacture of cotton textiles as a main interest, being very well-known today for its production of cotton thread. Glasgow produces cotton shirtings and muslins, but employs more people in making woollens than in making cottons; carpets, hosiery, and knitting wools come from the town's mills.

Textile manufacture today employs but $2\frac{1}{2}$ per cent—1 in 40—of the workers in the Central Clydeside Conurbation. Metal-manufacture and engineering are outstandingly dominant. These two industries, in their modern form, were first established in Scotland in 1760, when James Watt joined forces with Roebuck at the Carron Works near Falkirk. The rise of metal-manufacture on Clydeside began in the early 1800s, and during the 19th century a number of shipyards were established—all the largest by manufacturers of marine engines. Heavy industry was favoured by local supplies of coal and of the economical blackband ore. It developed on Clydeside step by step with the replacement of sail by steam, the accompanying replacement of wood by iron, and the supersession of iron by steel. The Clyde was deeply dredged to make possible the launching of larger and larger ships, and the Clydeside shipyards gained a great reputation for building enormous vessels.

The Clyde, long ranking an easy first in the shipbuilding districts of the British Isles, had fallen to second place by 1970. Like British yards in general, it has been gravely affected by foreign competition; and, probably more than most, it has been troubled by internal labour disputes.

British launchings amounted to between one-third and one-half of the world total during the 1930s, and production increased after World War II into the 1950s. By 1960, however, Japan was producing one-quarter of the known world total (this excludes launchings by Mainland China, likely to be small, and those by the U.S.S.R., certain to be great), and by 1970 had increased its share to about half. Simultaneously, West Germany, Sweden, France, and other West European shipbuilding countries cut deeply into the remaining share. During much of the 1960s, the U.K. was a net *importer* of shipping. Its sharp relative decline in the shipbuilding industry has been accompanied by a less marked, but still pronounced, absolute decline, which brought launchings down from about $1\frac{1}{4}$ million tons a year in the late 1950s to about 1 million tons at the end of the 1960s, the latter figure representing only about 5 per cent of known world production. The Clyde yards, with the most at stake, have been the most severely affected, especially those on the Upper Clyde. In an attempt to achieve economies of operation, these undertook a merger during the late 1960s, when they employed some 14,000 workers. By mid-1971 the level of employment was down to 8,500, but economic success appeared as distant as ever; part of the combined operation had failed, and one-third of its remaining labour force seemed to have no further prospects in the shipbuilding industry.

The present concentration of Scottish steelmaking in the Clyde valley is shown in Figs. 8:8 and 8:9. Outliers of the industry occur at Glengarnock in the west and at Armadale in the east. Annual output is between $2\frac{1}{2}$ and 3 million tons, of which

open-hearth basic furnaces supply some two-thirds; but the use of electric furnaces, and still more of converters, is increasing. Heavy steel products are typical of this region's works, with considerable demands coming from shipbuilding, marine engineering, constructional engineering, railway engineering, and boiler-making. Between one-fifth and one-third of total output of finished and semi-finished steel is exported each year, with tubes, plates, and other heavy products providing more than half the total export tonnage. It is the persistence of Clydeside steelmaking which, more than anything else, exemplifies the result of industrial momentum in Central Scotland.

Among the adaptations to changing circumstances has been a great reduction in the number of blast-furnaces. A peak annual production of $1\frac{1}{2}$ million tons of pig-iron was reached in the early 1900s. At that time there were more than 100 blast-furnaces in Central Scotland, concentrated on the Lanarkshire (Central) coalfield. The local output of iron ore, however, was already well past its peak, and the home product was fast being replaced by imported ore. The old-fashioned, small, hand-charged furnaces went out of use. Today there are 6 large mechanically-charged furnaces, one at Coatbridge (Gartsherrie), three at Motherwell (Ravenscraig), and two on the upstream side of Glasgow. Their combined annual output is about 2 million tons, greater than the peak of the early 1900s; much of it goes molten to the steelworks. Steelworks and blast furnaces alike depend heavily on scrap, but variations in comparative costs justified the installation of an ore-handling plant at Glasgow Harbour to permit the blast-furnaces to receive some half-million tons of imported ore a year. The iron industry of Central Scotland is now closely integrated with steel production.

Industrial Population

Figure 15:3 shows the relative sizes of the Central Scottish towns in terms of people actually at work (1961 Industrial Census). The circles are proportional in area to the number of people employed in each place, while the segments marked in solid black indicate the proportions directly engaged in production work. Only in Port Glasgow and Clydebank do production workers amount to more than half of the total workforce; in most of the towns which are easily recognised as industrial, production workers take between a third and half of the employed workforce, a range which seems to correspond to deep involvement with industry. Edinburgh, large and varied in its employment

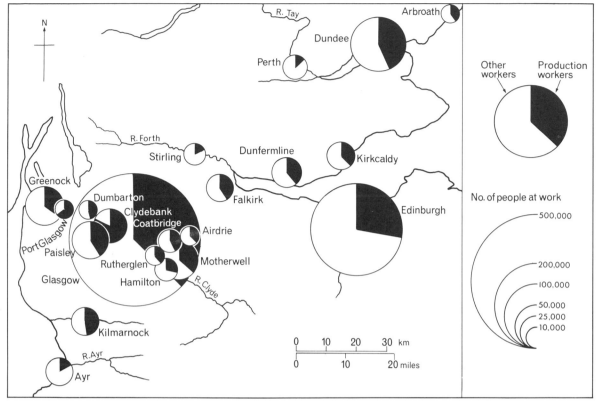

FIG. 15:3. Central Scotland: numbers at work, 1961. Compare the next Fig.

structure, has about 25 per cent of its workers in production industry, while Ayr, Stirling, and Perth have smaller proportions still.

Figure 15:4 makes a simple analysis of production employment. The circles in this map represent the black segments in Fig. 15:3. Coal-mining is not shown: by contrast with the 1951 situation, it nowhere makes any considerable demand on the workforce. Except for Rutherglen, the Clyde valley towns are all heavily committed to metal manufacture and engineering, with the somewhat out-lying Paisley absorbing nearly half its production workers in the textile and allied trades. Among the remaining towns, the metal industries are prominent also at Ayr and Dunfermline. Textile and garment making are fairly widespread, occurring chiefly in towns where industrial variety provides also for the processing of food, drink, and tobacco. The chemical industry is more restricted, being prominent mainly at Rutherglen and Ayr, while leather manufacture is practically limited to Kilmarnock. Another special item is the strength of the papermaking, printing, and publishing industries in Edinburgh, where they take nearly a fifth of production workers.

TOWNS

Glasgow, Edinburgh, and Dundee, in that order, have the largest industrial populations. They are also the only towns of Central Scotland with more than 100,000 inhabitants, despite the facts that the region as a whole is well urbanised and that some 2 million people live outside these three towns. It is characteristic of Central Scotland that most of its towns are of moderate size. Glasgow, for instance, is overwhelmingly the dominant member of the Central Clydeside Conurbation, being more than ten times as populous as Paisley, the next largest.

Towns of the Clyde Valley

Glasgow, like Liverpool, is a major west-coast port, deeply committed to transatlantic trade. But, unlike Liverpool, Glasgow lies well inland. In this respect it resembles Bristol, but has been more successful than Bristol in developing outports—Greenock and Port Glasgow, 15 km down the river, which are very closely linked to Glasgow by road, rail, and trading arrangements (Figs. 15:5–15:7). The central part of Glasgow is based on

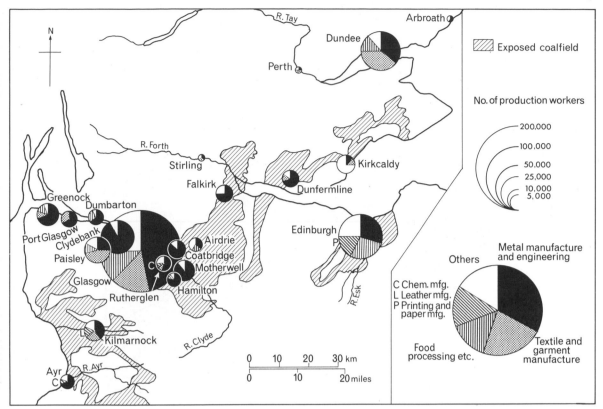

FIG. 15:4. Central Scotland: Manufacturing employment, 1961

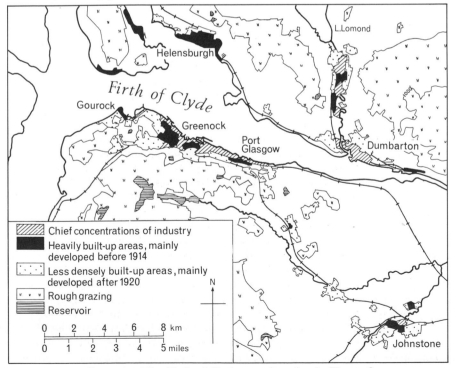

FIG. 15:5. The Firth of Clyde; continuation in Fig. 15:6

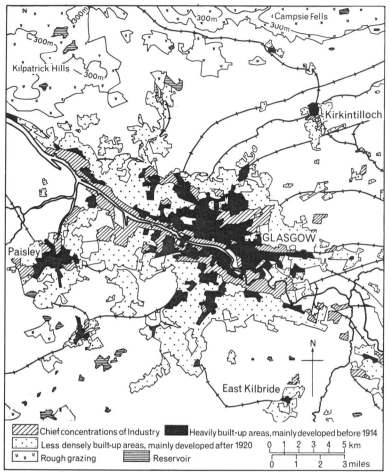

Fig. 15:6. Glasgow and its local setting; continuations in Figs. 15:5 and 15:7; contours in feet

raised beach, terrace, and drumlins. Here the silty Clyde is crossed by the lowest bridges, towards which routes converge along the valley and, crossing broad saddles between obstructive groups of hills, from the east and the west.

Although the town has spread on to both flanks of the Clyde valley, its expansion has been too slow to prevent serious overcrowding in its older residential parts. During the depression years of the inter-war period there was little chance of rebuilding or even of repairs, and urban blight settled heavily on some portions of the town. The standard tenements, four-storey terraced flats of the 19th-century model, and many of them constructed in the boom years of the 19th century, persisted into the middle 1900s, accommodating more than 80 per cent of the total population. At the 1961 cen-

sus, one-third of this population was classed as living in overcrowded conditions (see bibliography: Miller). Few would have claimed that Glasgow in the early half of the present century was a handsome town, even though its central squares and shopping streets were spacious. Furthermore, its peripheral housing built between the two World Wars was in the main part just that—housing, lacking services and social amenities. During the 1960s there began a drastic scheme of modernisation. The last tramcar went off the then stone-sett streets in 1962. Tunnels under the Clyde opened in 1964; the inner part of the old port began to be closed, inner residential suburbs were penetrated by new motorways, and high-rise flats appeared, including some in the outer suburbs. The municipal airport rose to a

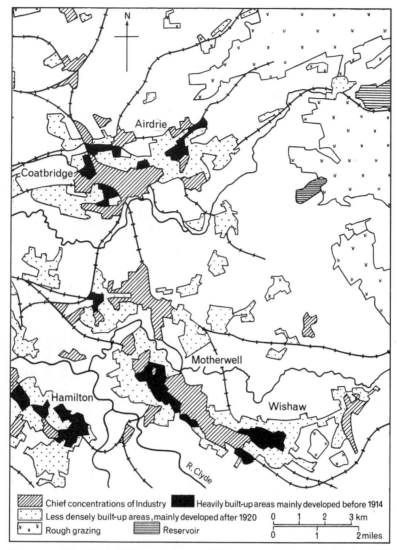

FIG. 15:7. The Clyde Valley upstream of Glasgow; čóntinuation in Fig. 15:6

prominent position in European traffic, and rail improvements, including electrification, benefited commuter services.

Glasgow today has more than half-a-million people at work, of whom nearly 90,000 are employed in metal-manufacture and engineering. This is the leading industrial group, taking nearly 20 per cent of the town's workforce and nearly 50 per cent of production workers. Iron, steel, ships, marine engines, aero-engines, road vehicles, and machine tools are among the many metal products. The textile and garment trades are also well established here, in addition to the varied food-processing industries typical of large towns.

Motherwell, Coatbridge, Airdrie, and Hamilton are satellites of Glasgow. As a group they concentrate on metal-manufacture, Coatbridge and Motherwell being great producers of steel. Coatbridge takes a minor part in coal-mining, and Motherwell has the smallest proportionate share in the making of textiles and clothing.

On the west and northwest, the tentacles of Glasgow are entangled with those of Paisley and Clydebank. Clydebank records a higher proportion of workers in the metal trades than does any other Scottish town, concentrating on ship-building and marine engineering. Ships and engines are also produced further down the river at Dumbarton on the north bank, where non-ferrous metals are worked, and at Greenock on the south

PLATE 41. A 32,000-ton oil-tanker being launched on the Clyde.

PLATE 42. Urban redevelopment in Glasgow. New housing, including high-rise blocks, and new factories are replacing tenements of the kind still present on the right.

bank, where there are sugar refineries. Greenock and Port Glasgow benefit from deep water close inshore; Greenock possesses a huge dry dock and a container terminal, with accommodation for ships of 14 m. draught. As in the Thames estuary, so on the Clyde, the ancient pattern of downstream displacement of port activity is being repeated.

Towns in Ayrshire

The Ayrshire coalfield has not experienced industrialisation comparable with that of the Clyde Valley. The sand-fringed Ayrshire coast provides no deep and sheltered inlets. Ardrossan and Troon, sharing with Ayr the export of coal to Ireland, have not grown large; Ayr remains a centre of coal-mining, but the export trade has declined with the decline of coal production. The industries of Kilmarnock include, in addition to leather-working, engineering, and the making of carpets and blankets.

Towns East of the Clyde

Falkirk, although located on the Central Coal-field, has little importance as a mining centre. Its engineering industries take a large fraction of the industrial labour force, the Carron Ironworks having migrated to the Clyde Valley. Leading products are light castings and rolled aluminium. The ancient, strategically-placed towns of Stirling and Perth have lost all their former defensive functions and part of their practical nodality. Perth, at the head of the Tay estuary, has been deprived of traffic in turn by the Tay rail bridge, by ferries from Dundee, and then by the Tay road bridge which supersedes the ferries. Similarly, Stirling at the head of the Forth estuary has been by-passed. The Forth road bridge, completed in 1964, and the Tay road bridge, slightly later in date, are two of the almost obligatory responses to the increase in motor transport and motor travel. Mining, still significant at Stirling, exploits the Limestone Coals.

Kirkcaldy and Dunfermline are the chief towns of the Fife and Clackmannan coalfield. In addition to their engineering, Kirkcaldy is concerned with the making of linoleum and Dunfermline with the production of linens. Burntisland and Grange-mouth are among the small ports handling coal and suffering from the loss of export trade. Alloa and Bo'ness are closed. Iron ore goes directly to the Clyde rather than through ports on the Forth, especially now that very large ore-carriers are coming into use, and the import of pit-props has declined both with the depletion of the Lanark-shire coalfield and with the progressive replacement of wooden props by steel. Thus in various ways the demand for port facilities on the Forth is weakened. Grangemouth, exceptionally, is expanding fast. It has acquired chemical engineering, light manu-facturing, and a refinery to which oil is piped 100 km from the west coast (Plate 43). The oil is landed at Finnart, on Loch Long, where the harbour has been extended in order to accommodate tankers of up to 100,000 tons.

Arbroath may be regarded as an industrial out-post of Dundee, sharing with that town ship-building, ship-repairing, and engineering of various kinds, but Dundee is best known for its manu-

PLATE 43. Refinery plant for the production of high-grade motor spirit at Grangemouth.

factures of jute, which account for the very high proportion of workers employed in its textile industry. During the late 1700s the manufacture of linen spread widely through Angus and Fife, Dundee specialising in heavy linen goods such as canvas. The problems of spinning and weaving jute were first solved at Dundee, and in the second quarter of the 18th century the working of jute largely supplanted that of linen in the town's mills. The manufacture of jute bags and jute cordage was soon followed by the production of jute-backed linoleum. Although Dundee has had to face severe competition from the mills of Calcutta, jute goods still constitute the town's leading products.

Upstream of Dundee lies the Carse of Gowrie, a low-lying belt of coastland which includes broad raised beaches and is sheltered from the north by the compact Sidlaw Hills. Fruit-farms from this district supplied the first jam factories of Dundee, and the preserving industry was vastly extended during the later 19th century when the import of great quantities of foreign fruit began. Dundee jams and marmalades are sold throughout

PLATE 44. View across Edinburgh to the outcrops of volcanic rocks on Arthur's seat.

the U.K., and Dundee cakes are widely distributed in Scotland. The town maintains a paper industry which serves its publishing houses and package-making works, and light industries established in the post-war period include the making of cash registers.

Edinburgh

Edinburgh (Plate 44) had emerged as the accepted capital of Scotland by 1500. Its castle on Castle Rock had great tactical importance in war between Scots and English, just as the town had great strategic value in commanding the east-coast route. The union of Scotland with England in 1603, and the union of Parliaments in 1707, lessened the political significance of Edinburgh, but came too late to arrest the growth of the town, which was unsurpassed in Scotland until the early 19th century, when it was outstripped by Glasgow.

A contrast is often drawn between Glasgow and Edinburgh, the one being dominated by heavy industry and the other regarded as a centre of service and administration. Although, as Fig. 15:3 shows, Edinburgh employs a far smaller proportion of its workers in manufacture than does Glasgow, its total population of nearly half a million includes some 60,000 workers in manufacture, so that Edinburgh ranks next to Glasgow and above Dundee and Aberdeen as an industrial town. Four-milling, brewing, distilling, textile-working, rubber manufacture, and the processing of foodstuffs are among its wide range of industrial activities. For paper-making, printing, and publishing, Edinburgh is noted throughout the world. Their growth has been associated in a number of ways with the educational, administrative, and financial functions of the town. Edinburgh is expectedly a great centre of retail trade.

Leith, the port of Edinburgh, is the third port of Scotland. Like near-by Granton, formerly a ferry terminal, it is a trawling base. From 1329 to 1833 Leith was administratively united to Edinburgh, and the two were reunited in 1920, the present population of Leith being included in the total given for Edinburgh. The two towns are firmly welded together by buildings and roads (Fig. 15:8).

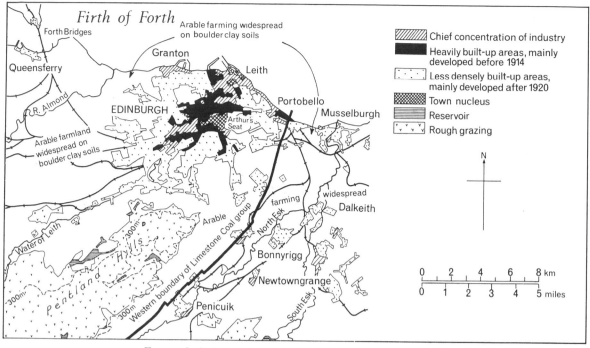

FIG. 15:8. Edinburgh and its local setting: contour in feet

Leith processes an extremely varied range of imported materials, producing flour, fertilisers, sugar, tobacco, leather, paints, and chemicals.

THE FUTURE OF THE REGION

An earlier edition of this text, under this sub-head, suggested that a probable eastward shift of mining might well be followed by industrial expansion in the east, but not by the migration of heavy industry from the Clyde valley; it also suggested that the industries of Central Scotland as a whole would probably be diversified. The predictions have been borne out by the events of the 1960s. A Clyde Port Authority was established in 1966, following the opening of new graving docks in 1964 and 1965, but appears regrettably to have to cope with plans that, by the end of the 1960s, already seemed outmoded. The location of iron and steel manufacture is discussed on other pages. It was during the 1960s that the inflow of immigrant manufacturing industry gathered full force (see bibliography: Welch), encouraged by government aid, with about one-quarter coming from North America. The incoming firms have located chiefly on the southern side of the central hill belt in the region, from Dundee–Kirkcaldy to Ardrossan. Although a general emphasis on chemical, engineering, electrical, vehicle, and plastic manufacture can be made out, the revised industrial structure is in actuality highly diversified. Science-based electronic manufacture is especially prominent and promising.

New towns, industrial estates attached to older towns, and government aid have all taken large parts in the swift and hopeful change; and the Forth and Tay road bridges have also helped (Plates 45 and 46). The switch of policy from sustaining areas of economic decline, to promoting the increase of activity in areas of potential growth, has proved wise and effective. Among the new towns, East Kilbride lies south of Glasgow, taking Glasgow overspill population with an eventual target of 100,000 people. Cumbernauld is east of Glasgow, between this city and Falkirk, with a target population of 75,000 and a well-developed manufacture of office machinery. Livingston, west of Edinburgh, looks towards a population of 70,000; it too takes Glasgow outspill; and, some-what exceptionally among new towns in Britain generally, is developing heavy engineering. Glenrothes, north of Kirkcaldy, is also active in heavy engineering, but is engaged also in electronic manufacture. Ironically, this new town was first projected as a mining centre; but the science-based electronics industry in Scotland is now a greater employer than either coal-mining or shipbuilding (see bibliography: McGovern, Pocock, Robertson).

PLATE 45. The Forth Road Bridge, looking north.

PLATE 46. The Tay Road Bridge, looking north; Dundee on the far side.

APPENDIX 1
The Carboniferous Succession in Central Scotland

4	COAL MEASURES	Barren Red Measures
		Productive Coal Measures
3		MILLSTONE GRIT
2	CARBONIFEROUS LIMESTONE SERIES	Upper Limestone Group
		Limestone Coal Group
		Lower Limestone Group
1		CALCIFEROUS SANDSTONE SERIES (includes oil-shales in upper part)

APPENDIX 2
Shipbuilding Districts of the United Kingdom

District	Annual launchings, gross, 000 tons		
	1954-6	1959-60	1972
Tyne	234	260	264
Clyde	450	340	224
Belfast	123	153	189
Wear	190	228	274
Tees	128	128	132
Mersey	78	58	91
Forth	36	23	3
Others	183	162	67
Total	1,422	1,352	1,244

Chapter 16

The Southern Uplands and the Border Country

Area: about 13,000 km² (5,000 sq. m.).
Population: about 500,000.
Largest towns: Dumfries (27,800).

                Hawick (16,600).

                Berwick upon Tweed (12,250)

                  (on the English side of the border).

                Galashiels (12,200).

                Stranraer (9,100).

Outside these towns the average density of population is about 30/km² (80/sq. mi.), but the central parts of the region have few inhabitants.

Less than half the region is in improved farmland; grass is about five times as extensive as tillage.
Numbers of livestock: cattle, 600,000 (of which about half dairy cattle);

                sheep, 2,450,000;

                pigs, 70,000;

                poultry, 1,350,000.

This region is far less extensive than the Scottish Highlands, and far less populous than Central Scotland. Much of it consists of high ground, and the region as a whole contrasts strongly with adjacent regions, even though linear boundaries are not easy to fix. On the northern side, hill-masses project across the geological boundary of the Southern Uplands into Central Scotland (Fig. 15:1), where the Pentland Hills form a true outpost of upland country. On the southwest, estuarine flats and coastal lowland begin on the west of the Nith, sweeping eastwards round the head of Solway Firth and linking the region with the margins of the Lake District. The political boundary between England and Scotland runs northeastwards from the Solway, placing in Cumberland and Northumberland a tract of hill country which lies north of the Tyne Gap; this tract, with the Cheviot and the Southern Uplands proper, will be described in the present chapter.

Physique

The Southern Uplands, underlain by hardened sedimentary rocks of Ordovician and Silurian age, rise well above the limit of cultivation, reaching heights of more than 750 m. in places. The country is much dissected and has been heavily glaciated, but, because the rocks are dominantly fine in grain and uniform in texture, the signs of highland glaciation are not everywhere obvious. A noteworthy exception occurs west of the Nith, where a group of granitic hills culminating in Merrick (about 830 m.) is rugged, indented with corries, and dotted with tarns. Elsewhere the main effects of ice seem to have been the enlargement and deepening of valleys, the scouring of summits, and the deposition of drift on low ground.

Much of this upland country, like the uplands of central Wales, consists of broad, subdued divides separated by steep-sided, narrow valleys—the plateau-remnants of former landscapes, dissected by young rivers. The Upper Clyde, the Doon, and smaller streams escape to the north-west. The Cree, Ken, Nith, Annan, and Liddel discharge to the south coast. The Tweed drains a wide valley-basin between the Lammermuir Hills and the Cheviot, receiving the Yarrow and Ettrick as major tributaries. The Nith and some feeders of the Tweed flow right through the upland region, having risen north-west of the crestal belt of summits.

The Cheviot Hills are based mainly on volcanic rocks and granite. They are completely dissected by radial streams, two of which—the Aln and the Coquet—break through an infacing scarp of sandstone to reach the Northumberland coast. The Rede and the North Tyne collect most of the drainage of the Border hills north of the Tyne Gap, flowing in glacially-deepened valleys between sandstone-capped hills.

Climate and Vegetation

The scenery of the large dales is enriched by woods, and the basin of the lower Tweed is much diversified by widely-distributed patches of ornamental timber. The Forestry Commission has planted large blocks of conifers—for instance, in Glentress Forest, Peeblesshire, and Kielder Forest, Northumberland. The upland platforms, however, carry very few trees, and well over half the region is classed as rough pasture. The existing vegetation represents a biotic rather than a climatic climax, for it results from centuries of grazing. Sheep prevent the growth of trees, as they do in Wales and the Pennines.

There is, nevertheless, a change in the character of the open grazing-land from west to east (Fig. 3:22). West of Nith, where precipitation exceeds 1,500 mm. a year on the higher ground, a patchy combination of heather, molinia, and nardus is characteristic, with peat moor on the low, ill-drained hills north of Luce Bay. Precipitation decreases to 650 mm. a year at the mouth of the Tweed, and the eastern parts of the upland carry a great deal of nardus moor. Fescue becomes dominant on the Moorfoot and Lammermuir Hills, and heather on the sandstone cuesta of Rothbury Forest on either side of the Coquet.

The wind-scoured uplands are subject to frequent rain or snow, frosts in 7 or even 8 months of the year, much cloud, and mean actual temperatures which descend in January to freezing-point or below. Improved farmland is confined to the valleys and the coastal lowlands, being roughly limited by the 150 m. contour on the west, but rising to 300 m. in the rain-shadowed east. The farms near the Solway are linked with those of the Ayrshire Plain through the valley of the Nith, and tongues of improved land project into the enclosing hills from the basin of the middle Tweed.

Hill-grazing

Grazing has been practised in this region for at least six hundred years, medieval religious houses having done much to foster a pastoral economy. The presence of nearly 3 million sheep in the region shows the importance of grazing today. Blackface sheep, raised for their mutton, typical of the moorland grazings, can endure the frequent snow of the high plateaus. Cheviot sheep can be kept on the best of the hill lands, and are particularly numerous in their home area of the Cheviot and in adjacent districts. One example of the elaborate systems of cross-breeding practised in the region is the crossing of Border Leicesters with Cheviots, in order to improve the quality of wool. Border Leicester rams appear at the Kelso sales as crossing sires, while large numbers of Cheviot and Blackface lambs are bought and sold at Hawick.

A variation in the quality of hill grazing occurs in the east Cheviot, where soils deficient in the

PLATE 47. Summer sheep fair at Rothbury, Northumberland.

trace-element cobalt have developed on andesite lava, and the pastures have to be sprayed or the flocks dosed. The standard of pasturage can vary in time as well as in space; if heather is left a long time before being burnt-over it is slow to regenerate itself, and the grazings are liable to be invaded by bracken.

The Scottish portion of this region contains one-third of the full-time shepherds in the whole of Scotland. One in every ten of those at work on the farms is a shepherd.

Lowland Farming

Farming in general takes a quarter of all workers. The heaviest demands on labour are made by the lowland farms, with their arable fields and improved grassland. In this group a marked contrast appears between the east and the west. To the west of Nithsdale dairying is dominant, some 90 per cent of the farmland in the rainy country of Wigtown being in grass. In the Tweed basin, the hill-grazings overlook a belt of stock-rearing and feeding farms, and these in turn give way to farms where cropping is the main and stock-fattening the secondary interest (Fig. 16:1). Grassland is reduced in Berwickshire to 60 per cent of the farmland; barley, oats, fodder crops, and potatoes take most of the land in tillage. The difference between Wigtown and Berwick repeats the difference noted in the previous chapter for Ayr and Fife.

of the high ground or penetrating it by way of deep valleys cut in from either side. Today, however, the main lines are reduced to two—the west-coast route to Glasgow and the east-coast route to Edinburgh. Although through traffic does little or nothing to affect the economy of a region such as this, the reduction in rail linkages must inevitably serve to increase its remoteness.

Routes between east and west are confined to the Tweed valley, the coastal belt in the southwest, and the Tyne Gap, the last-named running along the regional boundary and linking Newcastle with Carlisle. The line across the southwest coastland terminates at Stranraer, a packet station for services to Larne. Stranraer occupies a very sheltered position on Loch Ryan, behind the hammerhead of the Galloway Peninsula. Its rail-served pier overcomes the obstacle of a shelving, sandy shore.

The West

The coastal lowland between Stranraer and the head of the Solway is highly indented by wide, sandy estuaries, which are surrounded on the landward side by patches of low ground. Drift is widespread—boulder clay, glacial outwash, river terraces, coastal deposits, and peat all contribute to the form and quality of the ground. Whitewashed stone farms dot the undulating, grass-clad countryside. The native Galloway cattle are kept as beef-stock, particularly in exposed situations, but dairy

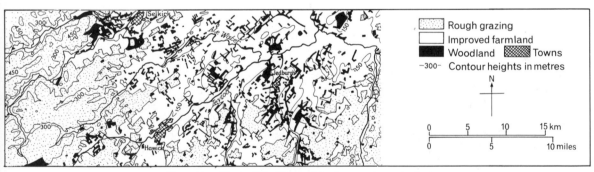

FIG. 16:1. Part of the Tweed basin: contours in feet

Routes

There is very little settlement in the heart of the uplands, where high continuous divides limit the number of practicable routes through the region, and easy passages between industrial Central Scotland and industrial England are few. Before the drastic reorganisation of the rail services and the railway nets, there were no fewer than six routes across this region, running either around the flanks

herds of Ayrshires and dual-purpose Galloway-Shorthorn crosses are the most common.

Market towns are located at river-crossings, in central positions in small lowland basins, and at the heads of estuaries. They range in population from about 1,250 to 5,000. Some have small industries connected with the agriculture of their surrounding districts, and large seasonal sales of livestock are held at Castle Douglas and Lockerbie. Dumfries has lost its former port trade, and the lead ore of the Leadhills district of the Lowther Hills has been largely worked out, but Dumfries serves the biggest patch of lowland along this coast, and with the aid of its retail trade and industries has become the largest town in the region. A quarter of its workers are in manufacture. The largest share of industrial labour is taken by engineering, but textile-making is also prominent, hosiery for the home market being the chief type of textile product. Chemicals— including synthetic fibres—and rubber are also made here.

The Tweed Valley

Textiles for the export market are produced in the Tweed valley, where the woollen industry was established in the late 18th century. At that time the farming of the Tweed basin was entering a period of drastic change, which produced consolidated, well-managed farms and large scattered farmsteads, but reduced the rural population. The wool-working towns grew faster than the villages, until in the late 1900s the textile industry passed its peak of success. There has been very little net change in town population during the last 25 years, except at Jedburgh, which had added rayon-making to the manufacture of wool. Among the other towns there is much specialisation. Hawick concentrates on hosiery[1] for the home market, Galashiels on woollen cloth—including cloth for naval uniforms—and Peebles on tweed. Selkirk also has woollen mills, but Kelso functions mainly as a market town and a centre of livestock sales. Berwick-upon-Tweed may have suffered in the long run from the neutrality granted to it in the 16th century, for it failed to grow large either as an English outpost against the Scots or as a Scottish focus for the Tweed basin.

The prosperity of the woollen industry in general, and of the making of tweeds in particular, varies rapidly with the state of the market. There is a domestic market for tweeds which can be relied on for a minimum demand. Exports to Central Europe have fluctuated widely for many years, under the impact of economic and political changes, and the U.S.A. offers the best prospects of sales abroad at the present time. Sellers of Scottish tweeds must overcome, if they can, the effects of changing fashions, and have to meet the competition of tweed made in Ireland. The two types are now competing strongly, especially in the great fashion-houses of Europe and North America.

The Country South of the Cheviot

The area between the Cheviot, the Tyne Gap, and the Industrial Northeast of England is, as a whole, thinly peopled. In all respects it is transitional. Although it is based on rocks of Carboniferous age, it resembles neither the limestone country of the North and South Pennines nor the shale-based farmland and industrialised districts of the coalfields. Historically it was frontier land for many centuries, doubtfully held by Romans, penetrated in places by small groups of Scandinavians and Danes, and disputed by English and Scots.

The western portion, between the South Tyne and the Rede, is underlain by a shaly and sandy development of the Carboniferous Limestone Series. The broad hilltops are covered in nardus moor, interspersed with peat-bog in the hollows. There is scarcely any settlement, and the deposits of lead ore, zinc ore, and barytes characteristic of the North Pennines are absent. Rough pasture used for the grazing of sheep is extensive (cf. Plate 47). Otterburn, on the Rede, produces tweeds which are well known in the fashion-trade. A recent development is the planting of Kielder Forest, where the dispersed houses first built for the foresters have been replaced by nucleated settlements.

Northeast of the Rede the rivers have cut well down, excavating a strike vale in the limestone-shale beds known as Cementstones. This vale, drained to the Coquet, the Aln, and the subsequent Till, separates the Cheviot block from the broken cuesta of Rothbury Forest. It carries scattered rural settlement and small mixed farms. The enclosing sandstone hills with their cover of moorland form the structural and physical boundary of a narrow strip of coastal lowland which, broadening southwards, merges into the coal-mining country of the Wansbeck and Blyth valleys.

---

[1] The term *hosiery* means knitwear of all kinds.

Chapter 17

The Lake District, the Isle of Man, and the Pennines

THESE upland blocks do not constitute a single region. The Isle of Man stands physically apart from the others, while the Lake District and the Pennines, although linked by the hilly tract of the Howgill Fells, differ strongly from one another in landscape-texture. Pronounced internal variation is typical of each division: the Central Lake District differs from the margins, the Isle of Man contains northern lowland in addition to central and south-ern upland, while the Pennines are subdivisible into contrasting northern, central, and southern parts. Nevertheless, certain characteristics are com-mon to most parts of the entire area. Much of the

land is high, rainy, sparsely inhabited, and used chiefly as rough pasture for sheep. Settlement is mainly peripheral. Resources are developed partly in response to the demands of lowland regions, whose inhabitants come as tourists or utilise the abundant surface water.

The internal differences within the area are closely associated with variations in rock-type and geological structure (Fig. 17:1). The Isle of Man is a fault-block, while the Lake District is a structural dome, deeply gouged by radiating glacial troughs. The North Pennines are based on gently-tilted Carboniferous Limestone, on which the

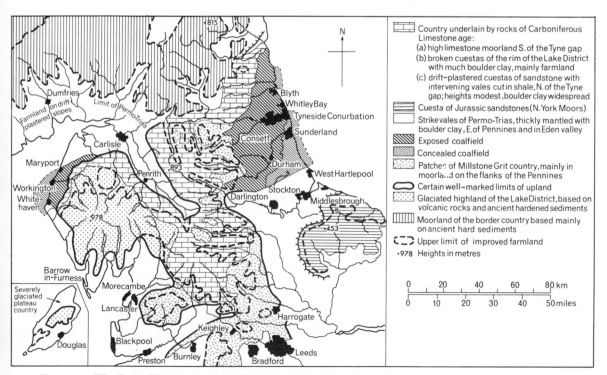

FIG. 17:1. The Lake District, the Isle of Man, and the North Pennines: physique and main settlements

distinctive landforms of limestone country are well developed; the lower and narrower Central Pennines are underlain mainly by Millstone Grit, while Carboniferous Limestone is again revealed in the scarp-rimmed Derbyshire Dome of the South Pennines. Climate becomes more extreme across the area from west to east, and less severe from north to south, underlining the physical contrasts between the Lake District and the Pennines and among the several subdivisions of the Pennine Upland.

THE LAKE DISTRICT AND ITS BORDERS

Area: about 6,000 km² (2,250 sq. mi.).
Population: about 350,000.
Largest towns: Carlisle (71,000).*
           Barrow-in-Furness (63,500).*
           Workington (29,500).
           Whitehaven (27,500).
           Kendal (18,500).
           Maryport (12,250).
           Penrith (11,000).
                        * 1969 estimates.

More of this region is in improved farmland than might be expected—namely, about 45 per cent— but only 6 per cent is in tillage. About 40 per cent is classed as rough grazing.
Numbers of livestock: cattle, 470,000;
                    sheep, 1,180,000;
                    pigs, 40,000;
                    poultry, 1,275,000.

Physique

Ordovician and Silurian rocks are uplifted in the Lake District dome. They consist partly of tough shales produced by the hardening of fine-grained rocks, but in the high central part of the area occurs a great thickness of volcanic rocks. These, the Borrowdale Volcanics, include solidified dusts in addition to lavas, but it is particularly on the lavas that the most spectacular Lakeland scenery is developed. At one time the whole area was mantled with sedimentary rocks of Carboniferous age, and probably also with Permo-Trias, but upheaval of the dome initiated consequent rivers which flowed radially outwards and in due course stripped away a great deal of the cover. So far has denudation gone that the Carboniferous Limestone survives only in low, broken cuestas on the outer flanks of the dome, where scarps face inwards. The Permo-Trias is preserved mainly in the fault-angle valley

drained by the Eden, between the Lake District and the northern end of the Pennines.

The radial consequents, cutting sharply into the dome, were incised into the older rocks of the core. Their valleys were deepened and still more firmly impressed with a radial pattern by glaciers, which hollowed out the lake-basins from which the district takes its name. Windermere, Coniston Water, Ennerdale Water, Thirlmere, Ullswater, and Hawes Water are all ribbon lakes. Two former single lakes have been divided into two by lateral deltas, Buttermere being separated from Crummock Water and Derwentwater from Bassenthwaite (cf. Plate 48).

Climate

Corrie-scalloped mountains rise high between the main valleys, exceeding 1,000 m. on Scafell, Helvellyn, and Skiddaw. The high ground is fully exposed to maritime winds from the west, and the degree of exposure is increased by the presence of wide, subdued summits, which are remnants of old erosional platforms now high above sea-level. Precipitation is heavy, annual totals exceeding 2,000 mm. in the central parts and rising well above 2,500 mm. at some places. The westerly location of the Lake District makes for a low annual range of temperature and for a moderation of winter cold, but these effects are offset by the height of the ground, which brings actual January means on the mountains into the region of freezing-point and at times promotes heavy falls of snow. Above the limit of cultivation, the vegetation consists principally of heather fell, grading eastwards into mountain grassland which typifies the Howgill Fells. Trees are limited to low levels, except where plantations extend up hillsides, or between Windermere and Coniston Water where deciduous and coniferous woodland are alike abundant.

The Central Districts

The open land of the Lake District is useful only for sheep-farming, tourism, water-supply, and afforestation. Rough grazing on the mountains supports large numbers of sheep (Fig. 5:21). Stone-built sheep-pens and washbrooks occur high up in the valleys, but the extreme valley-heads, like the mountains, are uninhabited even by shepherds.

Private motoring in the inter-war and post-war periods has done much for tourism, although most of the Lakeland settlements famous in the tourist trade are places of very modest size. Industrial growth in other regions has led to heavy demands

PLATE 48. View to the west across the head of Hawes Water, up the open trough of Riggindale. The tarn in the middle distances is Blea Water: High Street, immediately beyond, rises above 750 metres.

on Lakeland water, Hawes Water and Thirlmere both supplying Manchester, 120 km distant.

Afforestation is changing the scenery of some central parts of the Lake District. It used to be maintained that planting in catchment areas secures an increase in the supply of water, but it is now held that a forest cover tends in fact to reduce surface runoff. The degree of reduction is, however, too small to affect the Lake District at all seriously, and it seems likely that planting as well as the impounding of reservoirs will continue—particularly since forests reduce the risk of pollution.

Agriculture and Rural Settlement of the Margins

Improved farmland runs up the valley-bottoms, with hay almost the only cut crop at the higher levels. The inner fringe of settlement consists of single farmsteads, each surrounded by little fields enclosed by stone walls. Farmsteads become steadily more numerous down-valley, where tillage crops begin to appear, and are well distributed over the margins of the Lake District region where they are interspersed with villages. Many of the village names are of Scandinavian origin, for the whole northeast of England was subject to Scandinavian penetration and settlement during the Dark Ages.

The climate improves as the mountains are left behind, but most of the farmland on the low ground is under grass—conditions are far too wet to favour tillage crops. Oats, the main cereal, is cultivated in the south, where an extension of the Lancastrian Plain lies between Kendal and the sea, and also in the Eden valley where the slopes of drumlins promote surface drainage (Fig. 17:2). In these two

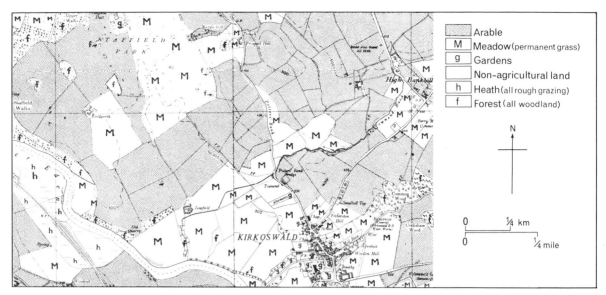

Fig. 17:2. Land-use sample for the Eden Valley. Boulder clay, partly moulded into drumlins, is extensive in this area

localities are also found most of the cattle of the area.

Industrial Economy: Minerals other than Coal

The Lake District proper has few mineral resources of economic quality. Copper ores were worked under Elizabeth I, but ores of other non-ferrous metals have usually proved too poor or too limited to be worth mining. The Borrowdale graphite mine, formerly the basis of pencil-manufacture at Keswick, has been worked out. Roadstone is quarried at a number of places, and Shap granite is used as a monumental stone. The Permo-Triassic rocks of the Eden valley yield gypsum—used in plaster-making—and the handsome red Penrith Sandstone, which is widely used for building. Evaporites from the Permo-Trias are also extracted near Workington (see below).

The weakness of local industry, other than that at Barrow, Carlisle, and the coalfield towns, corresponds to the scarcity of minerals in most of the region. Penrith, the chief centre of the Eden valley, has but 11,000 people, while Kendal, with woollen manufactures and a large share in the tourist trade, has not yet reached the 20,000 mark.

Industrial Economy: The Cumberland Coalfield

The Cumberland coalfield lies on the north-western seaboard of the region. Most of the seams on the inland portion of this coalfield have been worked out, and galleries run for as much as three miles beneath the sea-bed. The seams are heavily faulted, difficult to work, and gassy—natural methane fires the boilers at one colliery. In the 18th century there was a flourishing export of coal to Ireland, Scotland, and the Isle of Man, and iron-working was established early in the 19th century, in time absorbing one-third of the coal raised. Smelting and steel-making are still carried on, with coke ovens near Workington taking one-third of the present-day output of coal, but the prospects of mining on this coalfield are poor. The planned annual output of coal is but 1 million tons, and there is no reasonable hope that the lengthy decline in production will be reversed.

Although their mining and engineering were very severely depressed during the Great Slump, and continue to be handicapped by the exhaustion of the most accessible coals, the small towns of Workington, Whitehaven, and Maryport increased their populations by 25 per cent between 1930 and 1955. In the years of depression some 20,000 people left the district, leaving behind them 15,000 at work and 18,000 unemployed, but industrial estates founded in the late 1930s flourished during World War II, and in the post-war period have continued to prosper so greatly that industrial and social decline have been reversed. A new manufacture is that of chemicals—including detergents—for which anhydrite ($CaSO_4$) is extracted from local deposits in the Permo-Trias.

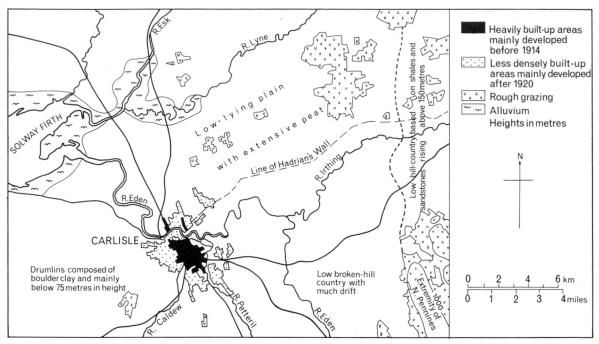

FIG. 17:3. Carlisle and its local setting

The selection of Calder Hall as the site of Britain's first atomic power station emphasises the remoteness of the Lake District region, not the expected local demand for electric power. Calder Hall may well benefit the Lake District generally, and the coalfield in particular, by reducing the cost of electricity, but it is to be compared with the use of Hawes Water and Thirlmere as reservoirs, rather than with the H.E.P. stations of the Scottish Highlands.

Industrial Economy: Barrow and Carlisle

Barrow has done less well than the coalfield towns, its population remaining stationary. As a manufacturing centre it developed late, its main period of growth coming in the second half of the 19th century. The high-grade hematitic iron ore then discovered in pockets in the Carboniferous Limestone, and the development of the Bessemer process, made possible the rise of a steel-making industry. The paper-mills and railway workshops of Barrow are less well known than the shipyards and engineering works, where naval craft and marine engines of various specialised types are constructed. Some 11,000 people are employed at Barrow in shipbuilding and heavy engineering. Up to about 1960 the shipbuilding industry appeared to hold considerable promise, with launching including passenger liners and oil tankers which were

large for the time: the average size of vessel launched at Barrow was greater than the average for shipbuilding districts in the U.K. in general, and not uncommonly led the list. However, the relative decline and roughly stagnant prospects of passenger travel by sea (the tourist trade always excepted), plus the decline of naval construction, plus also the competition of super-tankers built abroad, have gravely damaged Barrow's prospects as a shipbuilding centre. It no longer figures in the main list of U.K. builders.

Carlisle (Fig. 17:3), the largest town of the region, has changed hands many times. Its troubled history is a measure of the tactical advantages of its site and of the strategic importance of its situation. A Roman fort was located on the north bank of the Eden, on the line of Hadrian's Wall, but the medieval castle stood on the narrow neck of land between a meander of the Eden and the tributary Caldew, with some additional protection given by the Petteril a mile to the east. Strategically, Carlisle lay between the estuarine marshes of the Solway and the steep western edge of the North Pennines. Routes converged on it from the north, an easy passage led towards it from Newcastle on the east, and it commanded the approaches to Shap and to the west coastal route on the south. For 650 years Carlisle was involved in successive Border troubles, being last captured in 1745.

Its industrial development dates from the late 18th century, when manufactures of woollen, linen, and cotton textiles were established. Demolition of the old walls in the early 1800s reflected the end of raids and the expansion of the town. In the mid-19th century began the mechanised production of the biscuits for which Carlisle is nationally famous, while a focal position on routes between England and Scotland made the town a great railway junction. Vehicles, cranes, and metal boxes are among its modern engineering products, but manufacture takes only one-third of its workers; nearly two-thirds are employed in the service industries appropriate to a flourishing centre of shopping and marketing.

THE ISLE OF MAN

Area: 570 km² (222 sq. mi.).
Population: about 48,000.
Largest towns: Douglas (20,250).
Ramsey (4,750).
Some 50 per cent of the Isle of Man is in improved farmland, with grass five times as extensive as tillage. Most of the remainder is in rough grazing.
Numbers of livestock: cattle, 30,000;
sheep, 125,000;
pigs, 4,000;
poultry, 125,000.

Most of the Isle of Man (Fig. 17:1) is based on the tough, fine-grained rocks of the Manx Slates, which underlie the well-dissected highland exceeding 600 m. in Snaefell. Severe glaciation has deepened the valleys and scoured the mountains, without destroying the plateau-steps on the divides. Running northwestwards from Douglas, the Central Valley divides the highland into two and leads to Peel on the west coast. Coastal platforms end in cliffs at their seaward edge, and there is little low ground except in the north, where glacial drift conceals Carboniferous and Permo-Triassic rocks and ends in a gently-shelving, sandy shore.

The Isle of Man has its own legislature, the Tynwald. Its administration has evolved from that established by Scandinavian conquerors, to whom the obsolescent Manx language owes part of its vocabulary. In this the Isle of Man resembles the Channel Islands, which also have considerable independence of government and retain Norman–French *patois*. Again like the Channel Islands, the Isle of Man receives large numbers of visitors each year—more than half a million.

Economy

The tourist trade is the main basis of the island's economy. Few people are occupied in mining ores of lead and zinc, and the thousand or more farms send their summer produce to the resorts. Farming is generally mixed, although there is a complete range from very small market-gardens to the very large hill-farms where sheep are grazed. The main tillage crops are oats, mixed corn, and fodder roots.

The chief port, Douglas, is located on a sheltered bay at the eastern end of the transverse Central Valley. Ramsey is also on the eastern side of the island, at the junction of the main block of highland with the patch of northern lowland. The somewhat indented coastline of the central and southern parts is dotted with smaller settlements, all taking a share of summer visitors. Climatically speaking, the coastlands are better favoured than the high ground of the interior, experiencing far less rain and cloud and much more warmth and sun.

THE PENNINES

Area: about 10,500 km² (4,000 sq. mi).
Population: about 1,000,000 (this total does not include inhabitants of industrial regions on the flanks of the Pennine Upland).
Largest towns: (*a*) in the North Pennines:
Harrogate (56,250).
Skipton (13,000).
(*b*) The small towns of the Central Pennines belong to the woollen-making district of the West Riding.
(*c*) in the South Pennines:
Buxton (19,250).
Leek (19,000).
Matlock (18,500).
About half the Pennine area is in improved farmland, with grass about twice as extensive as tillage. Much of the remainder is in rough grazing.
Numbers of livestock: cattle, 700,000;
sheep, 1,550,000;
pigs, 375,000;
poultry, 7,350,000.

Climate and Vegetation

Although precipitation tends to decrease eastwards across the Pennines, it remains high in all parts. Cloudy skies and rainy days are not much less frequent than in the Lake District. Winters become increasingly severe towards the east, where continental influences begin to make themselves felt, with the result that the average number of mornings with lying snow rises above 40 in much of the North Pennines. A similar total is reached in the Peak District (Fig. 3:12). Improved farmland is confined to the valleys in the north and centre, but spreads on to the lower plateau-tops in the south. Peat moor is common on the upland north of Stainmore Pass, where crevices in the underlying limestone are caulked with boulder clay, but on the southern side of the Pass bare limestone emerges, carrying nardus moor, which is intermixed with peat moor on outcrops of shale and on patches of glacial drift. Peat moor regains its dominance on the Millstone Grit country of the Central Pennines, where water cannot easily soak into the coarse, well-cemented sandstones. The Millstone Grit rim of the Derbyshire Dome is partly covered by peat moor and heather moor, but the limestones exposed over the centre of the Dome carry much improved grassland of reasonable quality. All the open moorland is classed as rough grazing. It carries large numbers of sheep, particularly in the north (Figs. 5:3, 5:21). Thus in land quality and land use the heart of the Pennine Upland broadly resembles the heart of the Lake District.

Contrasts with the Lake District

Both in detail and in general appearance, however, the Pennine and Lakeland scenes are dissimilar. The Pennines were heavily glaciated, snow collecting on their high parts, becoming transformed to ice and moving downhill. Valleys as far south as those of the Aire and Ribble were somewhat widened and greatly deepened by the moving ice, but, as in parts of Wales, there was little development of corries or of sharp peaks. Thus the full range of landforms typical of glaciated highland country is not widely represented in the Pennines, and much of the Upland consists of plateaus standing at various levels and dissected to a varying extent by streams (Figs. 17:1, 18:1).

The North Pennines

The North Tyne drains a moorland plateau of moderate height, where extensive rough grazing links the Pennine Upland with the Cheviot. This plateau descends gradually towards the Tyne Gap —drained by the South Tyne and aligned on the Tyne Faults—where road and rail link Newcastle and Carlisle across a sill less than 200 m. above sea-level. The remains of Hadrian's Wall and the accompanying forts show how the Romans protected this easy and strategically important cross-route against attacks from the north.

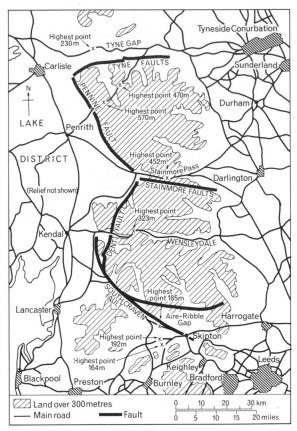

FIG. 17:4. Faults and passes in the North Pennines

On the south side of the Tyne Gap, the North Pennines rise in high plateaus which slope upwards to the west and approach 600 m. in height (Fig. 17:4). This division is based on a rigid crustal block, the Alston Block, which terminates on the west in the fault-line scarp of Cross Fell. Cross Fell, over-topping the drumlin-strewn Eden Valley by 350 to 450 m., is gashed by short streams flowing in narrow, precipitous valleys, between which the strong limestones form steep edges. Highly permeable limestones are marked by lines of swallow-holes at the top and by lines of springs at the base. Many disused shafts and galleries record the former mining of lead.

Eastwards from the scarp, the Carboniferous Limestone dips gently away and the height of the ground decreases, but moorland lying above 300 m. extends far into the basins of the incised Wear and Tees. Settlement in this division of the Pennine Upland is restricted wholly to the main valleys or to the lower ends of tributary valleys. The upper valleys and the divides are without permanent

PLATE 49. Detail of limestone surface in the North Pennines.

settlement, despite the former widespread working of lead ore and the present extraction of fluorspar.

The Alston Block ends on the south at the line of the Stainmore Faults, where Stainmore Pass leads a road from the Eden valley into the upper valley of the eastward-flowing Greta across a sill some 425 m. high. South of Stainmore Pass, the surface features typical of the Alston Block are reproduced in the Askrigg Block, which extends from the Stainmore Faults in the north to the Craven fault-belt in the south, and which ends westwards in the Dent Faults separating the Carboniferous Limestone from the older, highly-dissected, and generally impermeable rocks of Howgill Fells. Like the Alston Block, the Askrigg Block has been highly mineralised, and lead-mining was once common in its eastern part. Fluorspar and barytes are the chief mineral products at the present day.

On the western side, tabular beds of Carboniferous Limestone lie bare in places (Plate 49). Highly distinctive landforms appear—limestone pavements, dry valleys, swallow-holes, powerful springs, and systems of underground caverns. Such features are well displayed on the shoulders of Ingleborough, where Gaping Gill is 100 m. deep. Ingleborough itself, like its neighbours Whernside and Penyghent, rises well above 600 m. and over-tops the surrounding broad shelves of limestone by some 300 m. As the main valleys deepen eastwards, their trough-like sides become ribbed by strong out-cropping limestones. This is part of the Yorkshire Dale country, drained by the Swale, Ure, Nidd, and Wharfe. Further eastwards still, the Carboniferous Limestone disappears under a thickening cover of Millstone Grit (Plate 50).

South of the complex faults of the Craven district lies the flexured belt of the Central Pennines. The Aire-Ribble Gap, guided by the South Craven Fault, sets a recognisable boundary between the north and the central divisions of the Pennine Upland.

Skipton stands in the Gap itself, commanding the approaches to the three broad sills over which main roads run into the valleys of the Ribble and the (Lancashire) Calder. For all its focal position, it is no more than a small route-centre and market town. Harrogate, on the very edge of the Pennines 35 km to the east, gained a great reputation as a

PLATE 50. Pennine farm, Swaledale. Walls are of limestone, with cornerstones of grit; roofs are of slate.

spa with the aid of the mineralised waters which there issue from the Millstone Grit. It is still a watering-place, but also carries on a general resort trade and functions as a conference centre. Among the attractions of its neighbourhood are the ruins of the 12th-century Fountains Abbey.

The Central Pennines

The Central Pennines are traversed by flexures running from northeast to southwest, some of them responsible for the uplift of the Millstone Grit in Bowland Fells and Rossendale Forest. Both of these uplands and the main mass of the Central Pennines have been cut across by erosion in previous cycles, so that the details of the fold-structures are concealed on the ground, and the terrain consists of dissected plateaus. Because the rocks stand lower, formation for formation, than in the Northern Pennines, most of the Central Pennine division is based on Millstone Grit, which reaches great thicknesses.

River erosion, aided in the later stages of glaciation by meltwater, has made much progress in the Central Pennines, which are quite highly dissected. Roads and railways passing along their valleys link the industrial districts of Yorkshire on the one side and Lancashire on the other, while small industrial towns, large industrial villages, and textile mills penetrate far into the upland. In many places there is a most abrupt transition from the industrial scenery of the valleys to the moorland of the divides (Fig. 17:5).

In addition to rough grazing, the Central Pennines provide gathering-grounds for numerous reservoirs. The Pennines as a whole are of very great importance to the water-supply of the densely-peopled districts on their margins, carrying some 400 reservoirs, but it is on the Central Pennines and the extension of the Millstone Grit belt to Harrogate that the greatest demands are made. Water from the surface of the Millstone Grit is typically soft, and in consequence is highly suitable

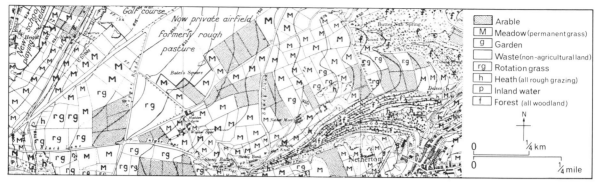

FIG. 17:5. Land-use sample for the Pennines, on the outskirts of Huddersfield

for use in the textile industries—especially in washing and dyeing. It is also abundant, since precipitation is heavy and the rocks of the Grit allow little percolation. The peat of the Grit-based moors acts as a natural regulator of runoff. About half the total area of the Central Pennines drains to one reservoir or another; Manchester draws on the Longdendale valley, while the Derwent Valley Scheme west of Sheffield supplies water to Sheffield, Derby, Nottingham, and Leicester. Three dams impound the headwaters of the river, the water passing for delivery through a filtration plant with a daily capacity of 40,000 m³.

The South Pennines

Unlike the block-faulted North Pennines, the Central Pennines form an unsymmetrical structural arch, the western limb broken by step-faulting at the margin of the Lancashire coalfield. Arching of structures becomes more pronounced in the South Pennines, where Carboniferous Limestone is elevated in the centre of the Derbyshire Dome and the cover of Millstone Grit has been partly removed. Whereas in the Lake District Dome the rocks of the core are stronger than those of the cover, in the Derbyshire Dome the rocks of the core are the weaker; the plateaus cut in the Limestone of the centre are enclosed on three sides by infacing scarps etched in the Grit. The doming is possibly due to the intrusion at depth of a large body of igneous rock, with which the many mineral veins in the limestone are associated.

The higher parts of the Grit cuestas are under rough grazing, which is however less common than in other parts of the Pennines. Grazing and rearing of sheep are the main farming activities of the Millstone Grit country, although some of the enclosed land has been ploughed, re-seeded, limed, and fertilised to provide pasture for cattle, among

which the hardy Galloway breed is prominent. Most of the Carboniferous Limestone country is in farms, on which sheep and cattle are reared and dairy herds are kept. These farms profited by the agricultural stimulus of World War II, but are handicapped by lack of surface water, the main rivers being deeply incised into the tabular limestone plateaus, and the water table lying well below the surface. Much of the rain which falls percolates rapidly into the permeable rock, in which underground features of limestone country are well developed.

Mineral vains include deposits of lead ore, which, like the ores of the North Pennines, have been worked for centuries. In both areas, however, the period of the most intensive mining was the 18th century. Many of the workings have since been abandoned, whether because of exhaustion, because of uncontrollable flooding, or because of too great depth. Lead ore is now a secondary product, fluor spar being of greater importance. About nine-tenths of the output of fluor-spar goes for use as a flux in basic open-hearth and electric furnaces. Barytes, used in paint and as a filler, is taken from the old workings in times of need—e.g., during wartime. The limestone itself is extensively quarried; some $5\frac{1}{2}$ million tons a year are taken for use as roadstone, ballast, and aggregate, or as raw material for the manufacture of lime and cement. The metallurgical, chemical, and textile industries of near-by regions all need great quantities of lime.

The three towns in this division are very similar in size. Buxton near the head of the Wye, and Matlock on the Derwent, are watering-places and health resorts, the former possessing hot springs. Leek is a Pennine outpost of the manufacturing district of Lancs.–Cheshire, for more than one-third of its workers are employed in the textile industry; it is a noted producer of silks.

Chapter 18

The Lancs.–Cheshire Plain and its Industrial Borders

Area: about 7,750 km² (3,000 sq. mi.).
Population: about 6,500,000.
Largest towns: (a) The Southeast Lancashire Conurbation (2,500,000) of which the leading members are:
    Manchester (590,000)*
    Bolton (152,000).*
    Stockport (140,000).*
    Salford (135,000).*
    Oldham (107,500).*
    Rochdale (86,500).*
    Stretford (60,250).
    Bury (67,000).*
    Middleton (56,750).
    Sale (51,250).
    Ashton-under-Lyne (50,250).
    Cheadle & Gatley (45,500).
    Eccles (43,250).
    Altrincham (41,000).
    Swinton & Pendlebury (40,500).
    Prestwich (34,000).
    Chadderton (32,500).
    Hyde (31,750).

(b) Towns of the Ribble Valley:
    Preston (100,000).*
    Blackburn (100,000).*
    Burnley (76,750).*
    Accrington (41,000).
    Nelson (32,000).

(c) The Merseyside Conurbation (1,400,000), of which the leading members are:
    Liverpool (675,000).*
    Birkenhead (142,000).*
    Wallasey (100,000).*
    Bootle (80,000).*
    Huyton with Roby (63,000).
    Crosby (59,750).

    Bebington (52,250).
    Ellesmore Port (44,750).
(d) Towns located between the three groups named above:
    St. Helens (100,000).*
    Wigan (80,000).*
    Warrington (70,000).*
    Widnes (52,250).
    Leigh (46,250).
    Chorley (31,250).
    Darwen (29,500).
    Runcorn (26,000).
(e) Remaining towns:
    Blackpool (146,750).*
    Southport (79,000).*
    Chester (61,000).*
    Crewe (53,500).
    Lancaster (49,000).
    Morecambe & Heysham (41,000).
    Macclesfield (37,500).
    Fleetwood (27,750).
            *1969 estimates.

Well over half this region is in improved farmland, with grassland more than three times as extensive as tillage.
Numbers of livestock: cattle, 605,000;
        sheep, 550,000;
        pigs, 410,000;
        poultry, 12,000,000.

The subject of this chapter is double-tiered. The plainlands of Lancashire and Cheshire constitute an agricultural region, with well-characterised landforms, climate, and land use. Superimposed on their rural pattern is highly-developed and widespread industry, with a wide scatter of towns, not all easy to separate from their rural surroundings. Both in the industrial and in the rural aspects there are contrasts between different parts of the region. Just as the several groups of towns differ among themselves, so does the countryside vary, both in its physical qualities and in its response to the demands which the towns make upon it. Population is notably concentrated in the towns, some $5\frac{1}{2}$ million out of $6\frac{1}{2}$ million inhabitants of the region inhabiting one or other of the towns named above. More than half the people live in one of the two conurbations.

Contrasts in Rural Areas

The region extends for about a hundred miles from north to south. Shrewsbury stands near the margin of the region, Carboniferous strata rise in the Pennines and project westwards in Bowland and Rossendale Forests. All but the lower flanks of the upland belongs agriculturally to the Pennine region, but the industrial districts overlap the physical boundary which separates high ground from low.

Large areas of the lowland are covered with glacial deposits or other superficial material. In the south there is much boulder clay, laid down by a broad tongue of ice entering from the Irish Sea, with small lakes contained in many shallow de-

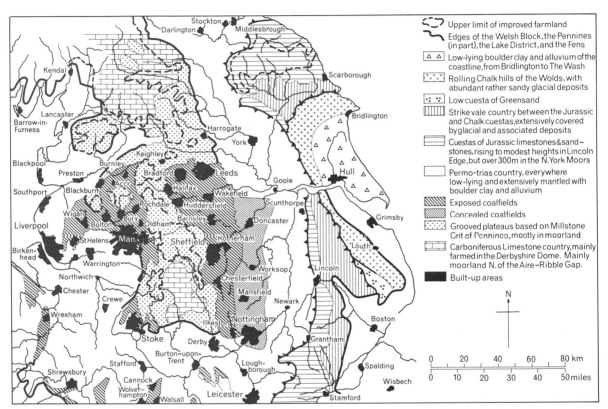

Fig. 18:1. The Lancs.–Cheshire Plain and its borders, the Central and South Pennines, Scarplands of Eastern England: physique and main settlements

southern limit, and Lancaster near the northern (Fig. 18:1). Most of the land is below 75 m. O.D., for it is based mainly on weak rocks. The large southern portion is underlain by Permo-Trias, which reaches great thickness in the elliptical basin between the Pennines and northeast Wales (Chap. 2). The extension of Permo-Trias across the lower Ribble probably represents the flank of another such basin lying between north Wales, the Isle of Man, and the Lake District. Along the eastern

pressions which pock its surface. On the northern side of the Mersey, sandy deposits are widespread and patches of peat occur where bogs formerly grew. The soils of the lowland districts are very diverse in quality, but most of them are under improved farmland. In many places cultivation is specialised and intensive, for enormous markets exist within the region, and the local climate ensures a long growing season.

The low ground receives less than 1,000 mm. of

precipitation a year, the 1,000 mm. isohyet running precisely along the inland border of the plains. Rain is fairly frequent, coming on some 200 days a year, but the coastland is no less sunny than the tip of Holderness (Fig. 3:11). Mild air moves freely in from the sea, giving 6 months free of frost in all but the extreme south, and 7 months in the Wirral and between the Mersey and Ribble estuaries. Lying snow is infrequent on the low ground. The mean annual range of temperature is about 10°C.

Although the whole of the plains experiences an equable climate, their central parts are better favoured than the north and south. The broad peninsula between the Ribble and the Mersey contains the largest block of land with 7 months free of frost, has less than 200 rain-days a year, and experiences particularly mild winters which bring down its annual range of temperature (Figs. 3:5-3:8). On all these counts it is the district best suited to tillage. Further north the climate becomes wetter and cooler, while towards Shrewsbury winters become significantly cooler and more liable to frost. The climatic differences are reinforced by differences of soil, for whereas the northern and southern parts of the region have much stiff and heavy soil developed on boulder clay, the centre contains much post-glacial sand and peat. Tillage is very common upon the sandy and peaty soils between Southport and the Mersey, and also south of the Mersey, where it thins out across the patchy mosses towards Macclesfield.

Cash crops dominate the farming of this highly-tilled central district. Early potatoes on the lighter soils, and maincrop potatoes on the heavier soils, are grown in variable rotation with such crops as oats, wheat, and hay sold off the farm. Were it not for eelworm, potatoes could be grown even more widely than they are, but where eelworm damage is severe they tend to be replaced by peas. Cabbages enter some rotations, while a number of mosses support market-gardens. Farm animals are few, but poultry are extremely numerous (Figs. 5:20–5:23). Towns, roads, railways, and waterways interpenetrate this part of the region.

North of the Ribble estuary, the emphasis of farming changes to dairying. There is some arable, mostly under fodder crops, but grass is far more extensive than tillage. Settlement is sparse in the subdued terrain running towards the sandy estuary of the Lune.

South of the Mersey valley, dairying is again the main interest, having increased considerably since 1939 at the expense of fattening. In the triangle roughly marked by Shrewsbury, Crewe, and

Chester the country is unmistakably rural. Hamlets, small villages, and single farms contain much of the population, but little market towns occur at intervals (Fig. 18:2). This piece of country is very varied in detail, for its soils display abrupt contrasts in quality. Settlements are located with reference to the minor irregularities in relief and in rock type. Seen as a whole, the area is low-lying and subdued, the most prominent set of physical features being the low sandstone hills rising above 150 m. in Delamere Forest, between the Dee and the Weaver, where tillage is widespread around a core of woodland and patches of heath.

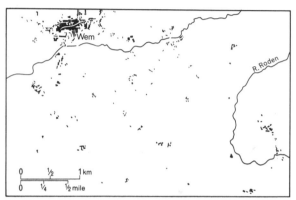

FIG. 18:2. Settlement on the extension of the Lancs.–Cheshire Plain into Shropshire: a small market town, with surrounding hamlets and single farms

INDUSTRIAL CONCENTRATIONS AND INDUSTRIAL POPULATION

Urban Groups of the Ribble Valley and the Southeast Lancashire Conurbation

Two groups of manufacturing towns lie on, or near the edges of, the Lancashire coalfield. In the north, in the Ribble valley, are Preston, Blackburn, Accrington, Burnley, Nelson, and their neighbours. The denuded sandstone hills of Rossendale Forest separate this group from the towns of the Southeast Lancashire Conurbation in the upper Mersey Basin—Bolton, Bury, Rochdale, Oldham, Stockport, and their neighbours, all forming an arc with Manchester and Salford at the focus.

Manchester is located on the Irwell, a tributary of the Mersey. Although an early foundation, the town declined in status in medieval times, beginning its effective growth during the 16th century when it was a market for wool and flax. Its industrial development came with the establishment of cotton-manufacture in 18th century Lancashire, and progressive concentration of the cotton industry benefited the town greatly. It lies on the edge of the exposed coalfield, and was well equipped to share in the conversion to power-milling, but, as its central position in relation to other textile towns became steadily more influential, its land-values rose and industry was partly displaced in favour of commerce. In round numbers, its population rose from 36,250 in 1773, to 72,250 in 1801, to 303,500 in 1851, and to 607,000 in 1901. In 1830 it was linked to Liverpool by railway, and in 1893 became a seaport with the completion of the Ship Canal.

The spread and functional change of building converted the angle between the Irwell and its tributary Medlock to the heart of a great town, with railway premises near the two rivers, and canal wharves and heavy industry near their confluence. Numerous bridges bound Manchester ever more closely to Salford, on the other side of the Irwell. Although both towns have declined in numbers of resident population since the 1931 census, the decline reflects conversion of residential property to the uses of commerce and business, rather than a weakening of urban functions.

Spreading across the rising ground to the east and north, Manchester has established physical connections with the other towns of the Conurbation. It is not, however, the only focus of the Conurbation, and the other large members still appear as thick knots in the tangled map of manmade features.

Nearly all the increase in the population of the Southeast Lancashire Conurbation took place be-

PLATE 51. Urban redevelopment in central Manchester; high rectangular blocks belong to the latest phase of building.

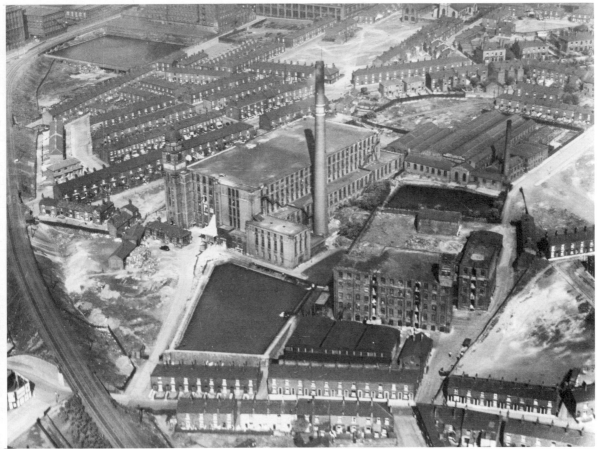

PLATE 52. Cotton mills, Oldham. The pools (lodges) receive water from the mills, which are surrounded by brick-built, terraced houses.

fore 1911, since when there has been very little change. The rate of increase in the last half-century has been well below that for England and Wales as a whole and more. Without inward migration there might well have been a decline in numbers, for some 750,000 of the present inhabitants were born outside the Conurbation; but the large towns of Southeast Lancashire are not alone in failing to maintain their numbers without the aid of immigration, and it would be a mistake to relate their population-trends solely to the difficulties of the cotton-textile industry (see below).

Many of the buildings in Southeast Lancashire were erected in the late 19th century, when little planning was practised, although Manchester—usually well to the fore of national thought—built large numbers of municipal houses in the inter-war period. The towns merge into surroundings which can scarcely be called rural, even when buildings are few, and throughout the Conurbation there is much intermixture of old factories, new factories, and blocks of houses of varying date (cf. Plate 52). Only on the north and east is town fairly sharply separated from countryside.

Cotton Manufacture

The present cotton-textile industry of the British Isles is very strongly localised in the Southeast Lancashire Conurbation and the Ribble Valley. The general history of its localisation is well known, even though the power of some of the localising factors is often misjudged. At the end of the 18th century, cloth-making was widely diffused throughout the populated areas of the British Isles, and cotton manufacture promised to become as widespread as the spinning and weaving of wool. When powered machines capable of working cotton were invented, many small mills were established in the uplands between the Midland Triangle in the south

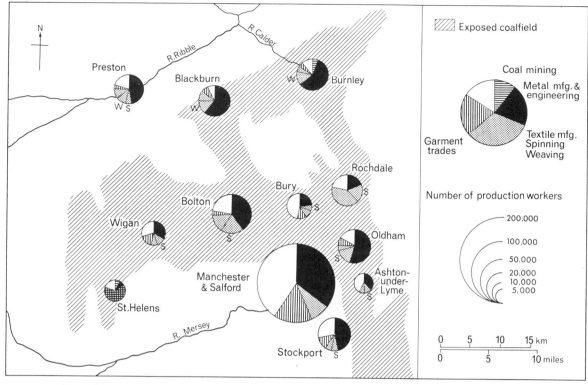

FIG. 18:3. Production employment in large towns on or near the Lancashire coalfield, 1966

and the Scottish Highlands in the north. Natural humidity of the atmosphere was an advantage common to all parts of a very large area, and cannot possibly be regarded as having favoured Lancashire in particular. Soft water is available in Lancashire from the surface drainage of Millstone Grit and Coal Measures, but the same formations also supply the West Riding, and soft water is also to be had in the west of the Central Lowlands of Scotland; in any event the degree of softness is relevant only to dyeing, bleaching, and printing. Lancashire had no monopoly of the physical conditions which suited the early cotton industry.

When water-power was superseded by steam-power, access to coal became a locating factor. As the output of raw cotton from the U.S.A. increased, two parts of the British Isles were well placed to develop and concentrate the manufacture of cotton textiles—Lancashire and the Clyde Valley. Both had coalfields, both had west-facing ports already engaged in transatlantic trade. Lancashire achieved unrivalled supremacy for two main reasons: the export market of the 19th century demanded coarse goods, whereas fine goods were the chief products of the Scottish mills; the cotton famine of the 1860s additionally weakened the Scottish industry, and

diverted the attention of manufacturers in the Clyde valley to metals.

The Lancashire cotton industry reached its peak of success in 1913, having in a hundred years secured nearly all the cotton manufacturing of the British Isles, developing a huge output and a correspondingly great export trade. Exports were severely and progressively reduced during the inter-war period, partly by two slumps and partly by competition from foreign producers. India, China, and Japan developed large cotton manufactures of their own, Japan forcibly entering the export market. Some two-thirds of the lost exports were due to production in consumer countries, the remaining one-third to Japanese competition. The export of cotton piece goods had sunk, by 1939, to the level of 1850. The number of looms and spindles was back at the level of 1880, and would have been still smaller had it not been for the custom of short-time working adopted in the face of reduced export demand.

The chronic difficulties of the cotton industry during the last fifty years have been reflected in unemployment, which was very severe during the 1930s and still tends to remain above the national average. Conversion to other forms of manufacture has, however, been slow. It was not fully realised during the inter-war period that the cotton industry had seen its best days, partly because some sections of the industry, concentrating on fine counts of yarn and on piece goods of high quality, escaped the worst of the depression. The lost markets were those which had taken the coarser and cheaper grades of cloth. It is ironical that the least vulnerable forms of manufacture should have been those which had earlier proved a handicap in Scotland, and that one of the obvious alternatives to cotton-manufacture—metal-making and engineering—should be precisely the one chosen in the Clyde valley.

Textile manufacture today (mid-1963 estimates) employs but 8 per cent of the workforce of the region—less than the 12 per cent working in the engineering trades and in the production of electrical and metal goods. Although the clothing industry employs about another 3 per cent, the total employment of about 420,000 in the textile and garment industries is only about 30 per cent of all manufacturing employment, and is distinctly less than the 625,000 in professional and scientific occupations. Those directly concerned with the spinning and weaving of cotton are now reduced to about 150,000, although some of the workforce lost to the cotton industry has been absorbed in the making of artificial fibres. As with the coal export trade, adjustment to changing conditions has been painful; and, as with railways, it has been promoted by government action—in this instance, measures adopted in 1959 onwards to eliminate surplus capacity in the cotton industry, amounting to about half the then-existing plant.

Future prospects are of a continuing decrease in demand for labour, although output appears likely to stabilise itself at the new, lower, level. Like coal-mining, and in contrast to vehicle building, chemical manufacture, food processing, paper-making, and rubber manufacture, the cotton industry of this region is coming to assume a minor part in the economy, just as it has done in the comparable, and competing, New England region of the U.S.A. Its record remains, however, of intense interest for historical geography.

Distribution of Processes in Cotton Manufacture

It was during the period when Lancashire was successfully overcoming Scottish competition that the contrast developed between textile-working towns in the Southeast Lancashire Conurbation and those of the Ribble Valley. The former carry out most of the spinning and the latter most of the weaving. Bleaching, dyeing, and printing are also located mainly on the south of Rossendale Forest, where they are supplied with soft surface water and are close to Manchester, but the works where finishing processes are carried on are mostly outside the large towns.

The concentration of spinning and weaving in two separate districts was due to technical factors operating in the third quarter of the 19th century. By 1850 or thereabouts, spinning was firmly established in the south. Powered weaving lagged behind powered spinning in its development, and, when the delay was made up, the Ribble Valley had a large number of hand-loom weavers who could be recruited for the new weaving mills. It also possessed coal to drive the machines. Thus the cotton industry in its mechanised form invaded the Ribble Valley, and a localisation of processes appeared which has been accentuated in later times.

The contrast between the two groups is partly illustrated in Fig. 18:3, which is drawn from the preliminary data of the 1966 Sample Census, the latest available at the time of writing.

The pie-graphs in this Figure relate only to employment in coal mining and in manufacturing industry. The proportion of textile employment within this range is shown by stipple, with segments separately indicated, and marked by s or w, where spinners or weavers are numerous in relation to total textile employment. It seems highly probable that information for smaller towns would point up the observed contrast, on the general ground that large centres tend to be industrially diverse. However, the preponderance of weavers among the textile workers of Blackburn and Burnley is as clear as that of spinners among the textile workers of Bolton, Bury, Rochdale, Oldham, Ashton, and Wigan.

The garment trades are present in all towns, but are best developed in Wigan, Stockport, and Manchester–Salford. In the latter, they employ nearly three times as many workers as does textile manufacture, and about half as many as the metal-and-engineering group which is prominent throughout. The concentration of garment making in Manchester–Salford, both in the relative and in the absolute sense, reflects Manchester's position as the great marketing centre of the cotton industry in its best days. Bolton and Rochdale each has more textile workers than Manchester–Salford, while Oldham and Preston are also prominent in this respect, despite their much smaller sizes, but in the garment industry the largest town is easily supreme. It also has a large stake in textile finishing.

In all the cases illustrated in Fig. 18:3, comparison of the 1951 map shows a reduction of emphasis on the textile–garment range of employment. Although the textile industry was much reduced in the 1960s, the garment industry could well survive, if it switched its dependence to man-made fibres.

Metal Manufacture, Mining, and Other Industries of Southeast Lancashire and the Ribble Valley

The metal industries are well developed throughout the cotton-manufacturing districts, tending on the whole to be more prominent in the larger towns than in the smaller. To some extent they are associated with the manufacture of cotton, producing textile machinery for export as well as for home use, but they also turn out an enormous variety of products unconnected with textiles, with machinery more prominent than heavy steel goods.

Except for the shipbuilding industry of Merseyside (see below), the metal industries of the Lancs.–Cheshire region have been affected similarly to those of the Black Country; that is, by partial exhaustion of workable coals, by vanishing reserves of local ores, and by changes in metallurgical techniques. Smelting in the southeast is now confined to four blast-furnaces at Irlam, on the Manchester Ship Canal. These use Jurassic ore and scrap to produce a very small fraction of the national output. There are some thirty-five steel furnaces, again with the main concentration at Irlam, about half electric and the other half basic open-hearth. Lying close to the southern edge of the Lancashire coalfield, these works correspond in their geological setting to the steelworks and blast-furnaces on the Flint and Denbigh coalfield on the far side of the Cheshire Plain.

The industries of Lancashire consume more coal than is produced from the Lancashire coalfield, where accessible reserves are limited and working costs are high. Good coking coal occurs in the neighbourhood of Burnley, but the Coal Measures there have been thinned by erosion and the output is small. Most of the present output comes from pits in the south, but little mining is done within the Southeast Lancashire Conurbation, which does not include St. Helens or Wigan. Among the large towns for which information is available, only Burnley and St. Helens recorded at the 1966 census a perceptible fraction of their production workers in coal-mining, but the proportion is likely to be higher in some smaller towns. The largest and most productive collieries are concentrated along the southern edge of the exposed field and on a quite narrow strip of the concealed field, where however the seams are heavily faulted and dip sharply down below the Permo-Trias. Working seems unlikely to spread far to the south.

Nearly all the coal raised is used in the Lancs.–Cheshire region. Industry takes half the output, domestic fires and thermal-electric stations nearly all the remainder, while small quantities are exported to Northern Ireland. No increase in output is expected, even with the addition of 5 new drift mines, and the projected figure of 12 million tons a year in the optimistic early 1950s was even then below the 1949 total. Subsequently, output has fallen to about 7 million tons (Fig. 7:2). Costs are likely to be reduced by the use of road transport over short distances, but the prospects for the field are poor. Coal is already brought in by the electrified Sheffield–Manchester railway, the trains being assembled in Wath marshalling-yard between Barnsley and Doncaster; the expected future deficiency is to be met by coal from North Staffs. and Nottinghamshire.

As in other highly industrialised regions, so in this one, certain towns have developed specialisms which differ from the specialisms of the region as a whole. The most outstanding case here is that of St. Helens, where well above half of all production workers are engaged in the glass industry. In this respect the town belongs with the chemical-making centres of the Middle Mersey District. Food processing is well represented in most of the larger towns, while Manchester–Salford has a stake in printing.

The Middle Mersey District

Among the competitors for the declining output of coal from the Lancashire field are the towns of the Middle Mersey district (Fig. 18:4). Warrington, the largest, employs more than half of its workers in the metal and engineering trades, constituting the chief link between the metal manufacturing of Southeast Lancashire and that of Merseyside. Warrington controls a crossing of the Mersey, approached by easy but well-drained routes from the south, and was a vigorous town in medieval times. The industrial revolution stimulated industries which had long been carried on there, and during the 19th century the town grew steadily in size. It is well served by waterways, railways, and roads. Its activities include the making of steel sheets, wire, and nails, the milling of aluminium, brewing, and tanning.

Widnes and Runcorn on the Mersey, and Northwich (19,500) and Winsford (13,000) in the Weaver valley have between 40 and 50 per cent of their workers in the chemical industry. Salt, coal, and limestone are basic raw materials of chemical manufacture, and salt is at hand in the Cheshire saltfield where it occurs as lenses in the Triassic rocks (Plate 53). Salt was obtained by evaporating the waters of brine springs in pre-Roman days, rock-salt was proved in the 17th century, and during the 18th century great quantities of salt were shipped from Liverpool, particularly to Ireland. At the present day, salt is extracted mainly with the aid of brine-pumps; one mine, at Winsford, alone remains in work. Technical developments during the 19th century made possible the rise of a great and varied chemical industry, the innumerable products of which include soaps, detergents, industrial alkalis, sulphuric acid, and explosives. The connection of St. Helens with the chemical industry in respect of its glass-making has already been noticed. The geological basis of this industry is the wind-laid Shirdley Hill Sand.

The Merseyside Conurbation

The Merseyside Conurbation (Fig. 18:4), with a present population of more than $1\frac{1}{3}$ million people, has come into being through the radial growth of Liverpool and Birkenhead round their nuclei on the waterfront. The urban sprawl has involved and incorporated neighbouring settlements, which retain their municipal independence. Unlike the Southeast Lancashire Conurbation, the Merseyside Conurbation ends fairly sharply against the surrounding agricultural land. Its size and its industrial and commercial vigour well exemplify the influences of a coastal location.

Liverpool had a considerable trade with Ireland during the early Middle Ages, but later fell into decline. Revival under the Tudors left it still subsidiary as a port to Chester, and many of its inhabitants had interests in farming as well as in trade, but the Irish rising of 1641 revealed its strategic importance, and after the Restoration its prosperity increased. Tobacco from the North American colonies and sugar from the West Indies supplied raw material for industry; the import of raw cotton began, salt shipped down the Weaver was bought by Liverpool refineries, and the salt export trade was extended to the Baltic and to America, where salt was needed by the cod-fishers of Newfoundland. Liverpool shared in the carriage of salt cod to the West Indies and the Mediter-

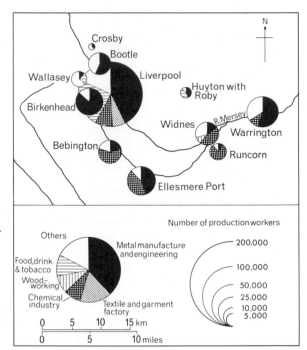

FIG. 18:4. Production employment in Merseyside and the Middle Mersey District, 1966

ranean, and secured imports of coffee, wine, and fruit. During the 18th century, too, the port was engaged in the slave trade. In 1715 was opened the first dock—a most useful addition to the original Pool, which was the small estuary of the right-bank tributary of the tidal Mersey.

As the fortunes of Chester declined with the silting-up of the Dee, and as transatlantic trade increased, so did the prosperity of Liverpool grow. From 5,000 in the year 1700, its population rose to some 75,000 in 1800. A hundred years later it was almost ten times as large again, totalling more than 700,000. The nucleus of the Conurbation had already appeared on either side of the Mersey by the mid-19th century, and subsequent developments have included the replacement of houses by commercial and business premises in the central area. Liverpool, like Birmingham, turned to the Welsh massif for water. Lake Vyrnwy, in the Vyrnwy valley, was impounded in the late 19th century. Additional reservoirs in Wales have been completed since World War II, including the pumped storage works at Blaenau Ffestiniog, Merionethshire.

The physical expansion of Liverpool was associated chiefly with the growth of overseas trade. By the early 19th century the town was a main im-

PLATE 53. A Cheshire salt-works, with evaporating-tanks.

porter for South Lancashire, the West Riding, and the Midlands, and by the mid-century was handling nearly half by value of goods exported from the U.K., against the quarter which went through London. The great oriental and transatlantic services of passenger liners were products of the 19th century, when the increase in the size of big ships steadily reinforced Liverpool's advantages over possible rivals. But the estuary of the Mersey is by no means without its disadvantages. It is commodious, it provides shelter from storms, and strikes far inland; but the great tidal range of 10 m. at springs demanded docks, and docks with unusually deep entrances. The sea-bed offshore is covered with loose sand, which tends to obstruct the ap-

proaches. Work began in 1890 on the harbour bar, where the low-water depth at ordinary spring tides has been increased from 3 to $7\frac{1}{2}$ m. Training walls help to maintain the approach channel, but some 10 million tons of sediment have still to be removed each year. Thus, although the port has manifest natural advantages, the facilities which it offers to modern shipping are to a large extent man-made.

At the present day Liverpool functions as a general cargo port, with world-wide external connections and an enormous hinterland. The main destinations of its imports are Southeast Lancashire, the Nottingham area and the West Riding, and the West Midlands, which also supply much of the produce which it exports, but the Merseyside

PLATE 54. Urban redevelopment in central Liverpool; Lime Street Station and St. George's Hall, bulky structures of an earlier period in the centre.

Conurbation also makes a significant contribution to export trade from its own factories.

The leading early industries of Liverpool dealt with raw materials from the hinterland of the port and with imported colonial produce. Other industries were added in the late 18th and 19th centuries, among them the manufacture of glass, pottery, and metal goods. Industrial and commercial progress were aided by the connection of the Bridgewater Canal to the Mersey (1773), and by the opening of the Leeds and Liverpool Canal (1774). In later years, when the railways came, Merseyside emerged as a considerable employer of manufacturing labour. This it still remains, with an emphasis on metal manufacture and engineering which, in combination, take about a third of its workers in productive industry, with shipbuilding and marine engineering accompanied by a wide range of mechanical engineering and light metal trades. However, the usual elaboration of employment has placed three-quarters of the Conurbation's workers in service occupations and administration, as against one-quarter only in direct production.

Although a simple pattern of distribution is not to be expected from the industries of Merseyside, certain facts of location can be perceived. Heavy industry is concentrated in the port area, where goods can be delivered from ship to mill, flour milling is now located mainly on the Cheshire side, oil is refined near the seaward end of the Manchester Ship Canal, while tanning, sugar refining, the milling of oilseeds, and the manufacture of newsprint are also concentrated near the waterfront.

Shipbuilding is located at the water's edge, on the Birkenhead side of the estuary. Launchings from the Birkenhead yard ran, in the mid-1950s, at ten ships a year, the total launched (in tons gross) representing about 4 per cent of U.K. launchings in 1960. The proportion had about doubled by 1970, but mainly because the total of U.K. production was declining. On the other hand, Birkenhead at least has a fair prospect of a continued share in the construction of tankers and bulk carriers of modest size.

Industries which have been displaced from the dockside area include the manufactures of paint, tobacco, soap, bread, and biscuits, which now depend on direct access to railways as opposed to direct ship-to-shore offloading. Industrial estates and new towns are the least closely linked to the docks. Among their multifarious products are rubber, light metal goods, chemicals, packages, electronic equipment, and plastics. The latest added centres rely on roads for transport, on electricity for power, and on the large labour reserve of Merseyside for workers. The industrial estates at Speke, Aintree, and Kirkby were founded by the Liverpool Corporation, two in the inter-war period and one in 1946, in order to increase the range of industry and to raise the level of employment, which displays a strong tendency to run below the national average. One of the contributing factors is a high local birth-rate, another is immigration from Ireland, especially Belfast. For these and other reasons, the rate of population increase in the Merseyside Conurbation continued at a noticeable level, well after some other conurbations had become static in population total or even begun to decline.

During the 1960s, Skelmersdale, Runcorn, and Warrington were designated for new town growth; they are expected to reach a combined population of some 300,000 by the end of the century. With planned expansion also in progress at Winsford, it may well happen that the distinction which has been drawn above, between the Merseyside Conurbation and the Middle Mersey district, will become blurred, even if it does not vanish altogether. A noteworthy countervailing factor is the motor industry, established on Merseyside during the 1960s under government direction. Concentrated mainly on assembly work, and centred on Halewood (southeast of Liverpool), Hooton (near Ellesmere Port), and Speke, this industry takes about 4 per cent of the Merseyside workforce (see bibliography: Salt), offsetting much of the chronic under-employment indicated above.

Industrialisation in general, and the growth of population in general, along the Mersey have been accompanied by fearsome pollution of the river and some of its tributaries. The Mersey is already badly polluted at the head of tidewater: at Widnes it is black. Untreated sewage and industrial effluents alike contribute to the noisome condition of the river and the inner estuary, both of which are effectively dead. Although pollution is no new condition in the industrial northwest, it is undoubtedly worse than it has ever been. The example of the Thames shows what could be done by way of correction.

Coastal Towns and Isolated Inland Towns

Blackpool, the largest coastal town, receives more than 8 million visitors a year—more than fifty for every one of its permanent inhabitants. Situated on the sandy shore north of the Ribble (Fig. 18:5), Blackpool has long sandy beaches lined with hotels, cafés, and places of entertainment. Its resort trade is the most highly developed in the British Isles; beginning as a seaside town frequented by visitors from industrial Lancashire, Blackpool now serves the whole country. Its success may be gauged from an increase of 50 per cent in the resident population in twenty-five years. More than one-fifth of the working people of Blackpool are engaged in personal service. A similar fraction is recorded at Morecambe, another seaside resort close to Lancaster, and a rather smaller fraction at the third resort of Southport. All three towns are located on stretches of open shore on a low, drowned coast where inlets are lined by salt-marsh.

The population returned for Morecambe includes the inhabitants of Heysham, the two places having been merged in a single borough in 1928. Heysham proper is a terminus of shipping services to Northern Ireland and the Isle of Man, and a centre of oil-refining. It is accessible at all tidal stages, for an extension of the Lune Deep runs close to its shore. Fleetwood also maintains Irish and Manx services, operates coasting services, and engages in fishing. Its older rail-served quays and the layout of its central part were built to a plan of 1836, but the docks subsequently have been greatly extended.

The situation of Lancaster on the Lune is similar to that of Preston on the Ribble. Each stands at the head of tidewater, at the inner edge of the coastal plain, and at a point where main north–south road and railway cross. Until the late 18th century Lancaster remained a market centre, assize town, and seaport. A limited port trade is still maintained, but the former shipbuilding for the West Indian

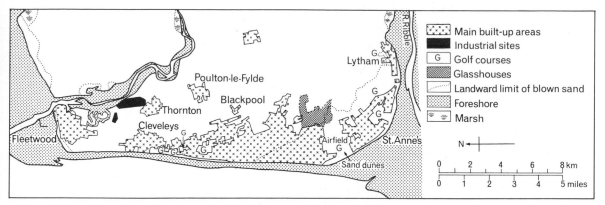

FIG. 18:5. Form and setting of Blackpool

trade has gone, and the leading single industry is now the manufacture of linoleum, which has succeeded the making of sailcloth. Other occupations are ship-repairing and the production of rayon, plastics, and chemicals. Lancaster remains a county town—a fact which recalls its former strategic importance on the west-coast route; it is comparable with Durham on the east-coast route.

Lancaster was once a bastion against the Scots, Chester against the Welsh. The core of Chester occupies a sandstone hill above the incised Dee—a tactically advantageous site which commanded routes into North Wales. The same routes contribute to the town's present importance as a tourist centre. Chester's port trade was destroyed by the silting-up of the Dee estuary—where additional large-scale reclamation is projected—but it has become a centre of inland transport both by road and by rail. Personal service, retail distribution, and local government employ many people in Chester, where manufacturing industry includes light metal and engineering work, as well as the processing of lead which depended originally on lead ore from North Wales.

Chester and Lancaster were Roman foundations; Crewe is a product of the 19th and 20th centuries.

Its central position in relation to the lines of amalgamating railway companies led to the establishment of railway works, on which the town is still partly dependent. For a period it was almost exclusively a railway town, but has been adding to its range of occupations for some time. Its direct links with the industrial districts of Lancs.–Cheshire and the Midlands enable raw materials and semi-finished products to be brought together, and Crewe has been able to attract light industry and rolling-mills.

Macclesfield stands at the very edge of the Pennines, south of Manchester and on the eastern edge of the Cheshire Plain. Long reputed as a centre of silk manufacture, it has been changed technically by the 20th-century growth of the synthetic textile industry, although silk goods are still produced there. More than a quarter of the town's workers are employed in making textiles or clothing. Similar conditions obtain in Congleton (16,750). Leek, which is located in the Pennine Upland (Chap. 17), belongs industrially to the same group as Macclesfield and Congleton—all three towns are specialised outposts of the textile industry of Lancashire.

Chapter 19

Industrial Northeast England

Population: about 1,500,000.

Largest towns: (a) The Tyneside Conurbation (850,000) of which the leading members are:

Newcastle upon Tyne (240,000).*
South Shields (105,000).*
Gateshead (100,000).*
Tynemouth (73,000).*
Wallsend (49,750).
Longbenton (44,750).
Whitley Bay (36,500).
Jarrow (28,750).

(b) Large industrial towns on the estuaries of the Wear and Tees:

Teeside (394,000),* includes Middlesbrough, Stockton-on-Tees, Billingham, Thornaby-on-Tees, Redcar, and Eston.
Sunderland (220,000).*
West Hartlepool (100,000).*

(c) Remaining towns:

Darlington (85,000).*
Consett (39,000).
Blyth (36,000).
Bishop Auckland (35,000).
* 1969 estimates.

Much of this industrial region lies within that part of England described under the title *Scarplands of Eastern England*, in Chap. 21. Details of land use are therefore not required. The population given here for the Industrial Northeast is additional to that quoted elsewhere for the Scarpland region.

Physically, most of the Industrial Northeast belongs to the drift-plastered lowlands of the eastern side of England. Even in the west, where it overlaps the flank of the Pennines, it consists of scarpland country. Sandstones of Carboniferous age form scarps which face towards the Cheviot or merge irregularly into the moors north of the Tyne Gap. Thick boulder clay obscures the solid rocks which underlie the low ground, extending across the eroded Coal Measures and the Magnesian Limestone on to the Trias near the mouth of the Tees (Figs. 17:1, 18:1).

Beyond the inland limits of mining, nucleated and dispersed rural settlements are intermingled, with market towns occurring at intervals. Signs of industry appear towards the east, in the form of collieries, mining settlements of varying size, and manufacturing towns, becoming more and more noticeable with the approach to the great industrial and commercial centres on the coast.

THE COALFIELD

The Northumberland and Durham coalfield, which was the original basis of heavy industry in Northeast England, is the counterpart of the Cumberland coalfield on the west coast and the complement of the Yorkshire, Derby, and Notts. coalfield, further south. Its seams dip eastwards off the flank of the massif, being worked beneath the sea, as in Cumberland, and beneath a cover of Permo-Trias, as in the Trent valley (cf. Plate 55). Coal was taken from the exposed field as early as the 13th century, and coastal shipments to London reached $\frac{1}{4}$ million tons a year by 1600; a hundred years later the figure had been doubled, and collieries large by the standards of the time were at work along the Tyne. Wooden rails came into use in the 17th century for bringing coal from mines a few miles inland to the staithes (jetties) on the incised Tyne. The seam chiefly exploited was the High Main, trucks running downhill from the collieries to the river.

Water became troublesome as the mines went

PLATE 55. Boldon Colliery, Co. Durham. Contrast the design with that of Kinneil Colliery (Plate 11).

deeper, and steam pumps were installed in the 18th century. Development on modern lines began in the period 1820–50, when locomotive transport was introduced to the railways, deeper shafts were sunk, and the demand for industrial coals increased. Blast-furnaces were working at Consett by 1840 and at Bishop Auckland by 1846; smelting in the Middlesbrough district increased rapidly from about 1850. Ten million tons of coal were raised in 1860, but the greatest expansion of mining still awaited the rise of the steel industry and of the coal export trade. Shafts were sunk into the concealed coalfield through the cover of Permo-Trias, and concentrations of heavy industry appeared about the mouths of the Tyne, Wear, and Tees.

The present output of coal is well below the peak reached in 1913 (Fig. 7:2). In south Northumberland and in the exposed field in County Durham the deposits of coal have been much depleted, but large reserves of general-purpose coals exist north of Blyth, where planned improvements include a new colliery and a number of drift mines. Transport from pit to port is cheap in this area, and nearly three-quarters of the coal raised goes coastwise to London and other parts of southern England, where it can compete with railborne coal from the Midlands. The bulk of the shipments goes from ports on the Tyne and from Blyth, power stations taking two-fifths of the shipments to places in the U.K. Further south, in County Durham, occur high-grade gas and coking coals. Some two-thirds of the coal raised in Durham is used in the production of gas and coke, but reserves are limited, and some of the most useful lie beneath the sea. The modest increase in output planned in the 1950s for Durham, in the eastern portion of the field where working costs are lower than in the west, has not come about. On the coalfield as a whole, working is concentrated mainly in a coastal belt about 10 km wide, stretching from the mouth of the Wansbeck in the north to beyond Seaham Harbour in the south, the largest collieries occurring near Blyth and on the concealed coalfield south of the Wear. Annual output from the whole field was about 35 million tons in the mid-1960s, not much more than half the 1913 peak; and future prospects seem to be of further decline.

Blyth at the mouth of the river Blyth, and Longbenton just outside Newcastle, employ more than half their industrial workers in coal-mining, which also takes more than a third of the industrial workers at Consett, near the western edge of the exposed coalfield, and at Bishop Auckland, on the Wear. At Consett, which is a centre of steel-making, the metal trades employ almost as many as mining does, but the other three are dominantly mining towns, with only a quarter of their industrial workers in metal manufacture and engineering.

METAL MANUFACTURE AND OTHER HEAVY INDUSTRIES

The five basic industries of the region are the manufacture of iron and steel, shipbuilding and ship-repairing, engineering, chemical manufacture, and coal-mining. In combination, they employ more than two-fifths of the regional labour force. They are somewhat localised within the region, as is partly shown by Fig. 19:1.

The Chemical Industry

The chemical industry is concentrated on Teesside (Plate 56), where it employs considerable numbers at Stockton and Billingham. It was first established on the Tyne, however, where the LeBlanc process was introduced early in the 19th century. Chemical works were set up at Jarrow after the salt duty had been removed in 1823, and by 1870 or thereabouts the Tyneside works were producing half the national output of industrial alkali. So long as the works prospered they were not modernised, remaining rather small, rather crude, and inefficient, discharging harmful fumes over their surroundings. They began to fail in the face of

competition from other producers and other processes—in particular, the chemical works of the Middle Mersey and the Solvay process. Tyneside factories today make fertilisers, especially sulphate of ammonia and superphosphate, the demand for which rose very sharply during World War II. Paint, soap, and detergents are manufactured at Newcastle, and heat-resisting glass at Sunderland.

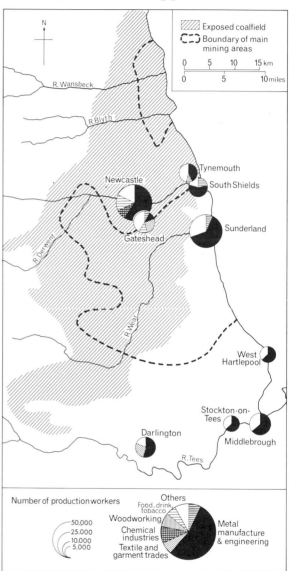

Fig. 19:1. Production employment in Industrial Northeast England, 1966

The chemical works at Billingham are ultimately a product of World War I. The blockade imposed on Britain in 1917 stopped the importing of organic nitrate from Chile, and the Billingham works were

PLATE 56. Chemical works at Billingham-on-Tees.

hastily developed to use the underlying deposits of anhydrite and the near-by rock-salt which occur as lenses in the Permo-Trias. Atmospheric nitrogen and hydrogen separated from steam combine to form ammonia, which can be processed with anhydrite $(CaSO_4)$ to produce sulphate of ammonia, while a different process yields the basic industrial chemical sulphuric acid. The chemical industry of Billingham has become extremely varied since 1918, including at one time the hydrogenation of by-product creosote to make petrol. There is a wide overlap between the chemical and metallurgical industries through coke-making, and between the chemical and textile industries through synthetic textiles.

Non-ferrous Metals

Despite the vigour of the chemical industry, the industrial treatment of non-ferrous metals is not strongly represented in this region. Lead-smelting continued in and near Newcastle for some time after most of the Pennine mines had fallen derelict, but has now almost died out. Magnesia is extracted from sea-water at Hartlepool, but the processing of barytes, copper, and zinc has been wholly annexed

to the chemical industry. Against the decline of smelting, however, must be set the increasing use of non-ferrous metals and their compounds in the varied light industries located on the industrial estates.

Heavy Metal Manufacture on Teesside and at Consett

No distinction is made in Fig. 19:1 among the production of unfinished metal products, engineering, and shipbuilding. In combination with other forms of metal-working, these occupations employ between half and two-thirds of all industrial workers, except in the chief mining towns.

Finished metal products on Teesside, as in Northeast England generally, consist principally of steel. The chief customers of the ironworks and steelworks are shipbuilders, marine engineers, mechanical engineers, and civil engineers. Constructional engineering, shipbuilding, and ship-repairing are especially prominent among the consuming industries, sharing nearly one-third of the total output of steel.

The Middlesbrough district contains the largest single group of blast-furnaces in the British Isles, producing about one-quarter of the pig iron made annually in the U.K. Works line the south bank of the Tees and the Tees estuary, with outposts on the coast at Skinningrove (near Saltburn) and at Redcar. The West Hartlepool works may be re-garded as another outpost of the Teesside group, but the furnaces at Consett stand apart. It is characteristic of the Middlesbrough district that most of the pig is made in large furnaces which form part of integrated steelworks, but steel furn-aces are more widely scattered than are blast-furnaces, occurring at Consett, Bishop Auckland, Jarrow, and Newcastle as well as on or near the mouth of the Tees. The Middlesbrough district, however, has a commanding lead in the regional production of steel, and some of its works have been extended in the post-war period by the addition of blast furnaces and melting-shops.

The Teesside steel industry was effectively founded and vigorously developed during the second half of the 19th century. After the main ironstone seam in the Cleveland Hills was located in 1850, the number of blast furnaces increased rapidly, and the annual production of pig iron reached 2 million tons in the mid-1870s. The grow-ing demand for coking coal was satisfied by the collieries of west Durham. The replacement of iron by steel as a structural material might have been a grave matter for the Teesside works, for, although the Gilchrist–Thomas process made it possible to use the phosphoric Cleveland ore in making basic steel, local shipbuilders and constructional en-gineers preferred acid steel, and ore from Spain had to be imported. The steelworks were converted one by one to the use of the basic open-hearth furnaces which are typical today. Expansion continued, and the population of Middlesbrough increased by more than ten times in 50 years. In 1913 the blast furnaces of Northeast England made nearly 4 million tons of pig, the steelworks produced 2 million tons of crude steel, and the industry consumed 6 million tons of Cleveland ore.

The inter-war period brought a steep decline in the working of Cleveland ore, which by that time was failing. Steel-making maintained itself over the period, but smelting suffered heavily. During times of industrial depression the iron and steel industry, like the mines and the shipyards, lost its markets, and only in the post-war period has new investment raised the output of pig above the 1913 level. The present annual production of some 5 million tons of steel, however, is nearly twice as high as the best figures of the 1930s, and well over twice as great as the figure for 1913.

Expansion has been possible only with the aid of high-grade imported ore and various technical im-provements. In terms of iron content, more than 80 per cent of the ore smelted in Northeast England is now imported, some of the Teesside works having stockyards on the waterside, and the Consett works relying on rapid transport by special trains from the Tyne. The average size of furnaces tends to increase, ore is more and more commonly prepared and sintered before being charged, high top pressure gear has been introduced at Consett, and fuel oil and coke-oven gas are increasingly used to fire steel furnaces. By these and other means work-ing costs are kept down—as they must be, for the main products of the regional iron and steel indus-try are iron, mild steel, and plain steels. Heavy rolled goods—especially plates, sections, bars, and rails—account for three-quarters of the deliveries of finished steel. Unlike the Sheffield district Northeast England makes very little alloy steel.

On Teesside as a whole, constructional engineer-ing and the chemical industry are very highly developed indeed. Shipbuilding, ship-repairing, general engineering, and the manufacture of tex-tiles and garments are also prominent. Darlington —exceptional among the large towns of the region in lying inland—has close industrial associations with Teesside. It shares in the general engineering and the manufacture of textile and clothing which are, indeed, well dispersed throughout the region, but is known mainly for its production of loco-motives and railway equipment. It was chosen as a site for railway workshops because of its strategic position with relation to the 19th-century railway system. Even in heavy engineering, however, it is by no means wholly a railway town, for it produces heavy marine castings and heavy forgings of many kinds.

Industry on Tyneside

Tyneside shared in the industrial developments of the late 18th century, and had more than 100,000 inhabitants by 1800, but the swift rise of industry in its modern form was impossible until the coming of the railways. The existing Conurbation is largely the product of the half-century between 1850 and 1900. Although this is the smallest of the conurba-tions recognised for census purposes, having fewer than a million people, it is truly an agglomeration of towns, which have spread eastwards and west-wards along the steep banks of the incised Tyne. There has been little room for expansion in the inner valley and population-densities remain high in some central parts (Fig. 19:2). Similarly, there has been little scope for the displacement of industry to large vacant sites on the edges of towns, particularly since many works serve shipyards.

Basic heavy industries dominate the economy of Tyneside (cf. Fig. 19:1), although the manufacture of food, clothing, drink, and tobacco, timber-milling, and furniture-making are all well established. Workers employed in shipbuilding, ship-repairing, and marine engineering are mainly men. Large numbers of women find work in light industry.

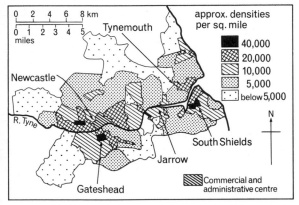

FIG. 19:2. Structure and population-densities of the Tyneside Conurbation

Shipbuilding

Yards on the northeast coast, on the Tyne, Wear,[1] and Tees, produced about half the shipping tonnage launched from British yards in 1970. During the inter-war period there was intense rivalry between the Tyne and the Clyde for contracts for giant passenger liners; but these are now products of bygone days. The yards of the Northeast converted early to tanker production. Despite the huge increase in the size of long-distance carriers, the Northeast has done well with construction in general, outpacing the troubled Clyde as the U.K.'s chief shipbuilding district. Future prospects must obviously depend on the demand for short-haul traffic.

INDUSTRIAL ESTATES AND LIGHT INDUSTRY

A prominent feature of the geography of this region is the number and wide distribution of industrial estates. These contrast in many ways

with older centres—not only in their industrial character, but also in the rate of their development. The Tyneside Conurbation, for example, recorded a rate of population-growth well above the national average for the period 1870–1900, averaging an increase of about 25 per cent per decade, but the impetus was already weakening by the turn of the century, and in the thirty years 1921–51 the *total* increase was but $2\frac{1}{2}$ per cent. The trading estates, with their associated houses, have come into being since 1930.

In Northeast England, as in other industrial regions of Great Britain, the trading estates represent a response to the Great Slump. Unemployment in the Northeast reached in the 1930s levels which seem incredible today—in Jarrow, for instance, 70 per cent of the shipbuilders had no work. This region was one of the worst distressed of the Distressed Areas. After prolonged debate, the Team Valley Estate near Gateshead was founded as a pilot scheme in accordance with the Special Areas Act of 1934; the policy adopted was to build factories to let, and thus to influence the location of industry. The new factories depended on road transport rather than on rail, and the firms likely to be attracted were those making light products. By 1939 there were already 5,000 new jobs in Northeast England, and clothing, tools, foodstuffs, plastics, safety glass, and radio components were coming from the new works. During World War II it became obvious that much existing industry could readily be dispersed, and the new industrial estates in various parts of the country developed fast.

Development has continued in the post-war period. More than thirty industrial estates are scattered through Northeast England today, in a broad crescent running from the Blyth on the north across the Tees in the south. They provide 50,000 jobs where none existed in 1930; their economic and social repercussions cannot be measured. The products of the new factories are extremely diverse, but the clothing industry, light engineering, and the making of electrical and radio equipment are especially prominent.

At Newton Aycliffe, six miles north of Darlington, at Peterlee, ten miles from Durham, and at Washington, between Newcastle and Peterlee, whole new towns have come into being. They are expected to hold a combined total of more than

---

[1] The Wear builds tankers of 80,000 tons; Belfast has launched one of 190,000 tons. The new liner, *Queen Elizabeth II*, of 58,000 tons, was built on Clydeside.

150,000 people by the end of the century, and had already attained 60,000 by the beginning of the 1970s Newton Aycliffe was initially built to house workers on the Aycliffe Trading Estate, converted to peacetime use from a World War II ordnance factory. Further expansion is in progress north of Newcastle, at Killingworth and Cramlington.

The development of trading estates and the growth of new towns amounts to industrial location of a new kind. Social need, labour supply, and political decisions are the locating factors, rather than lines of transport, coalfields, and access to raw materials. Nevertheless, the defects which the industrial estates are meant to remedy arise directly from the particular modes of geographical development in the past.

PORTS AND PORT TRADE

Newcastle began its rise to greatness in 1080, when the New Castle was built where firm ground closes in towards the river on the downstream side of low-lying, floodable valley flats. The full strategic value of the castle was realised when the Normans secured control of Cumberland, and when Carlisle Castle was built. Medieval Newcastle had close links with Scandinavia and the Baltic, and regular passenger and freight services are maintained today with Bergen, Oslo, Gdynia, and Danish ports; other connections include those with Canada, the U.S.A., and the Mediterranean. The chief cargoes handled at the Tyne Dock at Newcastle are coal, timber (including pit-props), and iron ore destined for Consett. Coastwise trade to and from the Tyne is large.

The harbour at the mouth of the Tyne is almost as artificial as the adjoining urban settlement. Although the Tyne, Wear, and Tees all enter the sea by drowned mouths, so that their entrances are landlocked, a great deal of improvement has been necessary. At the beginning of the 19th century, the low-water depth on the bar at the mouth of the Tyne was only 2 m.; by the end of the 19th century massive protecting piers had been built on all three estuaries and channels had been dredged to low-water depths of 8 or 10 m. Docks were constructed at Hartlepool, Middlesbrough, Sunderland, and South Shields in the mid-century, either by private dock companies or by railway companies; docks on the north bank of the Tyne came rather later. In all cases, the new facilities were designed chiefly to assist the coal-export trade. As industry developed, so the docks were improved and extended, and their handling-equipment was modified and replaced.

Sunderland's docks on the Wear are equipped for handling coal, bulk cargoes, and oil. Sweden, Rotterdam, and Antwerp are the main termini of services from Sunderland, while North African ports supply a considerable fraction of total imports. Overseas trade from the Tees goes mainly to and from the Baltic and near-by Continental ports, the Mediterranean, the Far East, and Australasia. Changes in the plans for, and location of, the domestic steel industry promise to bring about considerable changes in the port geography of the Northeast during the 1970s, with a deep-water ore terminal at Redcar. The effects of ever-increasing size of carriers, however, remains to be seen.

Chapter 20

The Industrial Region of the West Riding

Population: about 2,750,000.

Largest towns: (*a*) The West Yorkshire Conurbation (1,700,000) of which the leading members are:

    Leeds (500,000).*
    Bradford (293,250).*
    Huddersfield (130,500).*
    Halifax (93,500).*
    Wakefield (59,000).*
    Keighley (56,000).
    Dewsbury (51,500).*
    Morley (40,250).
    Batley (39,500).
    Spenborough (36,500).
    Pudsey (34,750).
    Brighouse (30,750).
    Shipley (29,750).

(*b*) Large towns between the Conurbation and the south end of the Pennines:

    Sheffield (530,000).*
    Rotherham (86,500).*
    Doncaster (84,000).*
    Barnsley (76,000).*
    Chesterfield (67,750)
    (Derbyshire).

*1969 estimates.

Within this region are two dense concentrations of industry. Manufacturing in the West Yorkshire Conurbation is dominated by the production of textiles and clothing, while steel-making, engineering, and mining are the leading interests of the towns in south Yorkshire and in adjacent parts of Derbyshire and Nottinghamshire. Thus this industrial region is subdivided into two parts, each containing a town with more than half-a-million inhabitants—Leeds in the north and Sheffield in the south. The concealed coalfield in Nottinghamshire is discussed separately at the end of the chapter.

The Setting

Lying on the flanks of the Pennines, the region includes land which is described either in Chapter 21 (Scarplands of Eastern England) or in Chapter 17 (the South and Central Pennine divisions). Industry runs westward up the Pennine valleys between the tongues of moorland which cap divides; industrial outposts on the east are set amid the farmland of the Trent vale. Agriculturally as well as physically, the region overlies the passage from upland to lowland, the agricultural transition being well expressed by an eastward increase in the proportion of tillage to grass.

This transition corresponds to an eastward decline in height, a reduction in rainfall, and an improvement in soil quality. It is complicated, however, and to some extent blurred, by the effects of the large towns on their surroundings. The land use and farming practice of the region have been modified in four main ways by urban influences. First, much land has been lost to non-agricultural use, in addition to the land occupied by the towns themselves, for collieries and tip-heaps are numerous, both along the outcrop of the Coal Measures and on the concealed coalfield to the east, while open-cast working of coal removes large areas from agriculture for a period of years. Secondly, pollution of the atmosphere by industrial smoke and fumes reduces the amount of sunlight, and some of the falling dust is capable of damaging crops and harming livestock. Thirdly, damage by trespass occurs frequently, as it usually does on the outskirts of large towns; it includes trespass by dogs, which strongly discourages the keeping of sheep. On the other hand, the large towns provide enormous markets for farm produce, and their proximity stimulates intensive cultivation, especially in the forms of market-gardening and dairying. Although the modern practice of transporting fresh milk over long distances has reduced the advantages of local dairy-farmers, dairying is still dominant on the flanks of the high ground in a belt which runs northwards by Chesterfield, Sheffield, and Barnsley, and on past Wakefield between Leeds and Bradford. Towards the east of the exposed coalfield, mixed farming becomes common, with its emphasis on tillage crops and beef and store cattle. Still further eastward comes the Magnesian Limestone belt, which is mainly arable (Chap 21). In the northeast of the region the eastward changes are obscured by the presence of Leeds, by the development of low ground about the Aire and the Calder, and also by the intensification of market-gardening. Market-garden produce from the area south of Leeds includes half the rhubarb grown in England.

The transition across this region from Highland to Lowland Britain is well shown by the location of its towns. The westernmost of these lie well within the margin of the Pennines, while those in the southeast are equally clearly in the Trent lowland. Halifax is set some 15 km inside the limit of the uplands, about an equal distance from both Burnley and Rochdale, and Sheffield is notoriously compressed in the valleys of the Don and its tributaries. At the other extreme, Doncaster lies east of the Magnesian Limestone belt. The wideness of the urbanised belt is associated with the gentle dips of the Coal Measures which, exposed in a broad strip of country running from Leeds and Bradford southwards past Chesterfield, sink slowly eastwards beneath younger rocks, where they can be reached by colliery shafts. The passage from upland to lowland occurs mainly on the exposed coalfield, but the boundary of the industrial region does not coincide with the physical boundary between plateau in the west and scarpland in the east.

The Pennine flank is deeply cut by eastward-flowing streams running in incised valleys. The intervening divides typically have the subdued tops which result from planation in previous cycles of erosion, but complications are produced by the etching into relief of west-facing scarps. The Wharfe, Aire, and Calder in the north retain some parts of their west–east consequent lines, trenching the high ground in markedly incised valleys which provide routes through the upland block. Many small dip-streams come off the upland further south, but the Dearne alone maintains its easterly direction across the exposed coalfield. Much of the surface water is collected by the Don, which is fault-guided across the coalfield below Sheffield and receives the upper Don and the Rother as sub-

sequent tributaries. In the south of the region there are no deep valleys leading towards the west; the upland rises above 600 m in the Peak District and broadens in the Derbyshire Dome. Sheffield is isolated in comparison with Leeds; Leeds, moreover, had ready access to the sea—by way of the Humber —when need arose, whereas Sheffield was partly enclosed on the east by the little-inhabited Sherwood Forest and by the ill-drained lowland of the Trent valley. Although the two towns are very similar in population at the present day, the industrial neighbours of Sheffield are fewer and smaller than those of Leeds. Doncaster, Rotherham, and Chesterfield have a total population of some 239,500, whereas Bradford, Huddersfield, and Halifax together contain more than 520,000. But the relative degree of isolation cannot by itself explain the contrast in respect of population and number of towns between the north and south of the region. The essential reason for that contrast is to be sought in different modes of industrial development.

THE WOOLLEN TEXTILE INDUSTRY

Origins and Growth

The ultimate origins of woollen manufacturing in the West Yorkshire Conurbation are hard to define. Sheep-farming and the making of woollen cloth were largely controlled by monks during the Middle Ages, many monastic flocks being kept on the Pennine uplands. Sheep-farming and the crafts of spinning and weaving survived the 16th-century dissolution of the monasteries, but subsequent development of the local textile industry involved far more than the taking-over of land and craft by laymen. The industry was certainly encouraged by the strength previously attained; it had already been able to attract refugee textile-workers from Europe in the late 1400s, but still in 1500 Yorkshire ranked a rather poor third among the woollen-producing areas of England, coming after the West Country and East Anglia. The great advantages of West Yorkshire, in the days before the industrial revolution, lay far less in local supplies of wool than in water-supply.

In early modern times, textile working in west Yorkshire was mainly a family concern, combined with rather unproductive small-scale farming. Family labour was cheap, and production costs were further kept down by the making of coarse cloths, but the local wool was adequate neither in amount nor in quality. It was too coarse even for

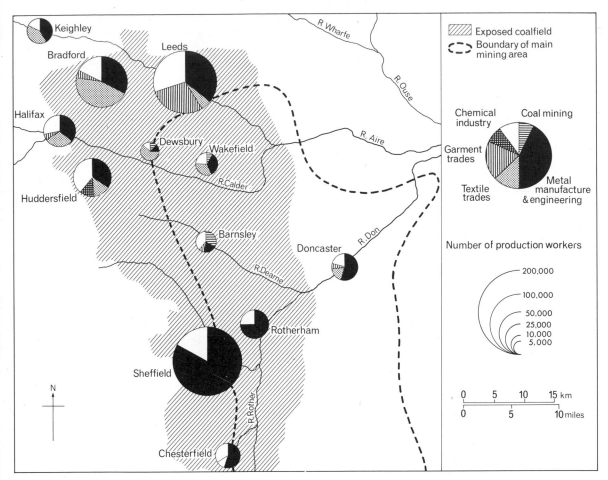

FIG. 20:1. Production employment in the Industrial West Riding, 1966

many of the locally-produced cloths, and during the 16th and 17th centuries, raw wool was brought in from the Midlands and Lancashire. Worsted manufacture, introduced by powerful clothiers towards the end of the 17th century, brought changes into the industrial structure, but much domestic craft persisted for many years afterwards. Defoe in the early 18th century named Leeds, Bradford, Wakefield, Huddersfield, and Halifax as the chief centres of the clothing trade, but also made clear the importance in the neighbouring valleys of small and thickly-scattered manufactories, each with its own water-supply from stream, gutter, or pipe. In the days of hand-craft and small machines, very many single sources of water were needed for washing, fulling, and dyeing. West Yorkshire had the benefit of multitudinous streams of soft water, either from the Millstone Grit or from the Coal Measures,

and of an annual rainfall in the headwater basins ranging up to some 1,500 mm.

As the use of machinery became steadily more extensive, the area profited at the expense of its rivals who were less well supplied with sources of power. Spinning was mechanised first, and west Yorkshire supplied much yarn to East Anglia and the West Country during the 18th century. When steam-power was applied to textile manufacture, the advantages of West Yorkshire over the two other areas became overwhelming. Mechanisation of the woollen industry was slow, however (Chap. 6), and the benefit of local coal produced only a gradual and incomplete concentration of that industry in West Yorkshire. Within West Yorkshire, complete concentration on the coalfield did not take place. Numbers of the worst-placed water-driven mills were abandoned; others, nearer to the mines, were converted to the use of steam, and new steam-driven mills appeared throughout the district, but even today the textile-manufacturing towns do not all stand on the Coal Measures (Fig. 20:1).

Although the total number of sheep in the British Isles is not by any means negligible, the domestic clip could not supply the present Yorkshire mills with wool, even if there were no mills in other parts of these islands Similarly, the output of cloth and clothing far outstrips the needs of the home market. Importing raw wool from abroad—especially from Australia, South Africa, and New Zealand—and exporting part of the output of its textile and clothing industries, West Yorkshire provides an excellent example of the results of industrial momentum. Textile manufacture gives employment to no less than 15 per cent—nearly one in seven—of *all* employed workers in the large wool-manufacturing towns of the West Riding, while the garment trades take about another 7 per cent. In combination, these two industrial groups make a far heavier demand on labour than do the metal and engineering trades: but this demand may be declining.

Localisation within the Industry

Within West Yorkshire, there is much localisation of certain types of textile manufacture. It takes a different form from the spatial separation of spinning and weaving which typifies Lancashire, for the main distinction in Yorkshire is between the making of worsteds and the making of woollens. Worsted manufacture is concentrated in the north and west of the textile district, in and beyond Huddersfield, Halifax, and Bradford. Within the worsted industry there is much specialisation by single mills either in spinning or in weaving, particularly in the larger towns. Woollen manufacture, located chiefly in the south and east of the district, is characterised by integrated mills where both spinning and weaving are carried on (cf. Plate 57).

Some of the reasons for the distinction in practice between worsted spinning and worsted weaving are historical. The worsted industry did not evolve directly from local woollen manufacture, but was superimposed on it Worsted manufacture was, from the outset, in the hands of concerns or individual mill-owners who specialised in a single process—or, at most, in a limited range of processes. In addition, there are technical reasons to encourage the separation of worsted spinning from worsted weaving—for example, the fact that a large

variety of yarns is used in weaving, and that yarn is produced for use outside West Yorkshire.[1]

A number of successive processes were performed in the original small woollen manufactories, in many of which the raw wool was received and finished cloth produced. The industrial structure typical of craft industry was retained in the early days of powered machinery, and has persisted subsequently. Firms producing woollens tend to be smaller than those producing worsteds, even though spinning and weaving are both performed in many single woollen-mills.

The partial separation of worsted making from the making of woollens reduces the significance of separation between spinning and weaving. Some small centres do, however, specialise either in spinning or in weaving, and weavers are at least twice as numerous as spinners in Huddersfield and Dewsbury, and five times as numerous in Batley, while spinners outnumber weavers in Bradford, Shipley, Keighley, and Halifax. The finishing trades are well represented in all the large towns, and especially so in Bradford, Batley, and Halifax.

Garment workers are highly concentrated in Leeds. Despite its huge size, this town has but one-third as many textile operatives as Bradford, half as many as Huddersfield, and fewer even than Halifax, which is but one-fifth as populous as Leeds. Leeds, on the other hand, employs more than 80 per cent of the clothing workers of the whole Conurbation—a figure representing a far higher concentration than is found in Lancashire, where the corresponding figure (for Manchester and Salford combined) is 66 per cent.

THE WEST YORKSHIRE CONURBATION

Industrial Employment

Since the woollen textile industry (including the making of worsteds) is so prominent in the West Yorkshire Conurbation, part of what follows refers directly to the previous section. The proportion of industrial workers taken by the textile and garment industries runs at about 40% in Halifax, Keighley, Leeds, and Wakefield, rising above 50% in Bradford and Huddersfield and above 60% in Dewsbury. Leeds has nearly a third of its industrial workers in the garment trades alone; but, as would be expected from a town of its size, it has a high rate of employment in tertiary occupations.

---

[1] This matter is discussed in Wilfred Smith: *An Economic Geography of Great Britain* (Methuen, London).

PLATE 57. Interior of a woollen mill, West Riding, showing hopper feed of carding machines.

Coal-mining appears in the diagrams for Dewsbury and Wakefield, but is in general not prominent among the activities of the Conurbation. Huddersfield has developed chemical manufacture, initially in relation to the needs of wool-processing (Fig. 20:1). Metal manufacture and engineering are, in the usual way, well distributed, taking between a quarter and a third of industrial workers. Smelting is not practised, the steel furnaces depending on local scrap and on pig-iron and crude steel from elsewhere. Although engineering products include machines for the textile and clothing factories, the metal industry is only partly dependent on the regional production of textiles and garments. Leeds especially has acquired a very large range of engineering, producing aero-engines, aircraft, motor vehicles, and foundry products.

Character and Connections

Many of the great towns of the Conurbation are cramped in smallish tributary valleys. Whereas Leeds and Wakefield stand respectively on the Aire and the Calder, where these rivers emerge from their Pennine trenches, Bradford is crowded into the narrow valley of a tributary of the Aire, Halifax into that of an equally small feeder of the Calder, and Huddersfield is located on the Colne three miles above its confluence with the Calder. Belts of building run up and down the valleys, and the largest towns have spread up the valley-sides to develop suburbs on the hilltops. Large towns, small towns, and swollen industrial villages are all bound together by strings of houses and factories and by a tangle of roads, railways, and canals.

Between a quarter and a third of all the people in the Conurbation live in Leeds, which is the greatest centre of wholesale trade, shopping, and finance It is not however the only centre, Bradford being a vigorous and neighbouring rival. The West Yorkshire Conurbation resembles the Southeast Lancashire and West Midland Conurbations in lacking a single focus.

The West Yorkshire Conurbation developed mainly during the 19th century. In 1801, Leeds had but 53,000 people; like its neighbours, it expanded rapidly with the growth of the wool textile industry, but already by 1900 the rate of growth in this area had fallen below the average for England and Wales. Little increase has taken place in the last twenty-five years. A great many of the buildings in the Conurbation are constructed in the styles of a hundred years ago; the town centres have been progressively transformed by reconstruction, but the old residential parts still include back-to-back houses. The tasks of replanning and rebuilding are made difficult by the intermingling of settlements, and also by the problems of maintaining the basic industry. The manufacture of woollen textiles has held its own longer than has the manufacture of cottons, but may now itself be experiencing a frontal challenge from man-made fibres. Although wool has no great tropical and oriental markets to lose, it can scarcely become progressively cheaper, in the way that synthetics presumably can—quite apart from any comparison of physical qualities.

The overseas connections of the Conurbation in general, and of the woollen textile industry in particular, are provided mainly by Liverpool and Hull. Connections with Liverpool are but slightly handicapped by the Central Pennines, which are crossed not only by a generous number of roads and by several railways but also by three canals. The Leeds and Liverpool Canal, bending far to the north through the Aire-Ribble Gap, still carries some traffic (see Chap. 9), but the canals running up the Calder and Colne towards Southeast Lancashire were from the outset encumbered by too many locks. All the same, it is significant that canals across the Pennines should have been built at all. They show an appreciation of Liverpool as an inlet and outlet for West Yorkshire, and emphasise the fact that land routes can cross the Central Pennines without undue difficulty. The Aire and Calder Navigation remains successful, with single trains of compartment boats carrying up to 700 tons.

COAL-MINING

Local coal greatly aided the textile manufacturers of West Yorkshire in the early days of industrialisation. No large mines operate today in the textile-making district, where the total output of coal is small, and where Wakefield and Dewsbury alone have a significant proportion of their production workers in coal-mining. Barnsley records a fraction of about a third, but is outside the West Yorkshire Conurbation. This means that the principal mining areas do not overlap the main con-

centration of towns engaged in the manufacture of woollens (cf. Plate 58): they approach and penetrate the West Yorkshire Conurbation only in the southeast. The large collieries occur in a belt stretching from the Aire valley below Leeds on the north to beyond Nottingham on the south (cf. Fig. 20:3). The western limit of this belt runs through Wakefield, a little to the west of Barnsley, through the eastern fringes of Sheffield, and past Chesterfield to Nottingham. Its eastern limit projects down the Don valley below Doncaster, and, further south, runs well to the east of Mansfield.

The great and absolute importance of the Yorkshire, Derby, and Notts. coalfield to the English economy has been made clear in Chapter 7. That part which is defined by the National Coal Board as the Yorkshire Coalfield has a very long history of coal-working. Digging was recorded as early as the 14th century, and by the 16th century many collieries were in work. At that time Wakefield was the chief mining centre, but coal was already cheaper than local wood in Sheffield. There are forty coal seams, of which thirty-two are at present worked. Outcrop mining along the western fringe has largely ceased, except for opencast working, and in this field, as in Northumberland and Durham, there has been a shift of mining down the dip of the Coal Measures. At one time about half the coal raised came from the Barnsley (or Top Hard) Seam, which, providing a workable thickness of some 2 m. of coal, is the seam chiefly worked in the concealed coalfield, where two in every five of the large collieries are located. But although the easterly dip of the concealed measures is generally slight, workings tapping the Barnsley Seam have reached depths of 1,000 m. where roof pressures are severe and the dangers of fire and gas are great. The Parkgate Seam some 250 m. deeper still sets great problems of mining.

Reserves are great, being estimated some 10,000 million tons of workable coal in the whole Yorkshire, Derby, and Notts. coalfield. This total, however, is less than previous estimates, for the concealed seams are now known to thin eastwards, and some to have been eroded away before the Permo-Trias was deposited. Prospects are best in the north of the concealed field.

A wide range of coals is produced—household and industrial coal, locomotive coal from the Barnsley and Parkgate seams, and gas and coking coals which are extracted mainly from the northern part of the coalfield. Large reserves of coking coal justify a planned increase in output for the steel industry. Since many working pits are fairly

PLATE 58. Suburban expansion of Barnsley. The pattern of streets and the design of houses are among those typical of the 20th century.

modern, less reconstruction of collieries is necessary than in some other coalfields.

THE SHEFFIELD DISTRICT

The presence of gas and coking coals in South Yorkshire is an obvious benefit to the industries of the Sheffield district, but, as in the West Midlands, the local industries were founded centuries before the industrial revolution. The early iron-workers used Coal Measure ores and smelted by charcoal, combining farming with metal-work during the Middle Ages. Many small smithies operated in the 16th century, when local water-power and local millstones were being used in the making of cutlery.

The effects of industrial momentum were already evident, for steel was then imported from Sweden, Russia, and Spain. The two outstanding early advantages of the industry were the local iron ore which gave iron-working its start, and the supply of power from the Pennine streams: significantly enough, the last water-driven forge ceased work as late as 1955.

Huntsman laid one foundation-stone of Sheffield's present greatness when, in the 18th century, he produced crucible steel which could be cast. Bessemer opened his own very successful works in Sheffield in 1858. During the late 1800s the town's steel-making industry profited from changes in the construction of warships and from the development of alloy steels.

From a total of some 2,000 in 1600, the population of Sheffield grew to 3,500 in 1700, to 35,000 in 1800, and to 400,000 in 1900. In each of the 18th and 19th centuries, that is to say, its numbers increased tenfold, but it was during the 19th century that Sheffield became a huge industrial town. Since 1900 its numbers have continued to increase, but less rapidly than before; indeed, there has been a slight tendency to decline during the last forty years, which is concealed in the census figures by the effects of boundary changes. The built-up area, however, is still expanding, for, like many other great towns, Sheffield is experiencing the so-called flight from the centre.

For all its numbers, Sheffield is not the overwhelmingly dominant town that might be expected from its size. Wedged uncomfortably in the narrow valleys of the Don, the Sheaf, and their tributaries, its central part is not very easily accessible from surrounding areas (Fig. 20:2). Rotherham and Doncaster grip their environs as tightly as Sheffield grips its own surroundings. As an industrial town, however, Sheffield deeply overshadows its neighbours. Some two-fifths of its employed population works in steel-making or in engineering, and 3 out of every 4 industrial workers are in some metal-manufacturing trade (Fig. 20:1). In the Sheffield district is found the greatest concentration of steel furnaces in the British Isles (Fig. 8:8). Acid open-hearth furnaces produce steel which is particularly suitable for large forgings, while electric furnaces make highly alloyed steels. The local blast-furnaces cannot supply all the needs of the steelworks, for which high-grade pig-iron, scrap, and alloying metals are brought in. Most of the steelworks are independent of the blast-furnaces—i.e., there is little integration of the iron and steel industry. Lack of integration would be a handicap in producing large amounts of the standard steels, but the Sheffield district concentrates on special orders and on short runs (Plate 18). It makes much alloy steel for use outside the district, in addition to precision tools and a very wide variety of highly specialised machinery. The centuries-old lighter trades of Sheffield are still pursued. Their main products are metal tableware, cutting tools, and hand tools, in the making of which Sheffield is the leading centre of the British Isles.

Sheffield is one of the main producers of refractories in the British Isles. Local fireclays and ganister were originally used, but nowadays Magnesian Limestone is worked into linings for basic steel furnaces, and ganister for making silica bricks comes from South Wales and Durham.

Rotherham, at the confluence of the Rother with the Don, has some two-thirds of its production workers in the metal trades, its chief manufactured products being machinery and heavy iron and

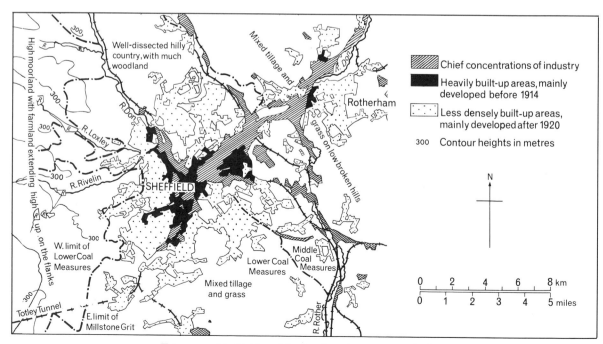

FIG. 20:2. Sheffield and its local setting, contour in feet

steel. More than half the industrial workers of Mexborough (17,000) are employed in collieries, but Doncaster, which has replaced Barnsley as the principal mining centre of the Yorkshire coalfield, still has more than half its industrial workers in the metal trades. Doncaster possesses large railway workshops, makes mining and agricultural machinery, and is a producer of nylon. Industrial estates on the outskirts of Sheffield, Rotherham, and Doncaster include light-engineering works.

Chesterfield, although in Derbyshire, has close affinities with the Sheffield district. Rapid industrial growth began when the railway, by-passing Sheffield, gave access to the local coals, and Chesterfield today makes mining machinery, furnaces, and tubes.

THE CONCEALED COALFIELD IN NOTTINGHAMSHIRE

Towns and industry on the southern concealed portion of the Yorks., Derby, and Notts. coalfield show well the difficulties of regional subdivision. The area belongs physically to the Scarplands of Eastern England (see following chapter); its mining links it with the exposed coalfield, while textile and leather industries associate it with Nottingham. Mansfield (53,250) makes hosiery, footwear, and metal goods; Sutton-in-Ashfield (40,500) has textile works and produces steel alloy castings; Worksop (34,250) has interests in engineering, brewing, and furniture-making. All these towns, like Hucknall (23,250) and Kirkby-in-Ashfield (21,750) include large numbers of miners. Mansfield in particular is surrounded by distended settlements, including mining villages, and by collieries where huge tips rise above the discontinuous remnants of Sherwood Forest (Fig. 20:3). Mining has indeed reached, and passed, the eastern limit of the Forest; the newest colliery hereabouts is but 13 km west of the river Trent. Further south, another new colliery lies on the far side of the river, 8 km southeast of the centre of Nottingham. Mining thus invades not only the eastern Scarplands but also the Midland Triangle.

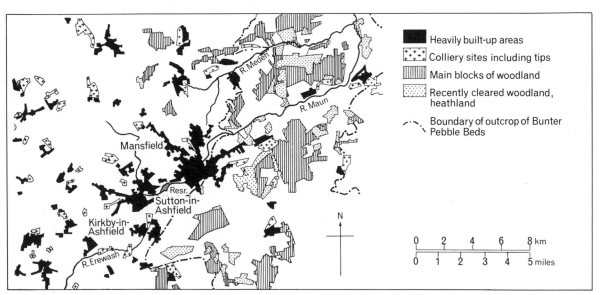

FIG. 20:3. Industrial and mining settlements in part of Nottinghamshire, on the concealed coalfield. The former limits of Sherwood Forest closely resembled the outcrop-boundaries of the Bunter Pebble Beds

Chapter 21

Scarplands of Eastern England

Area: about 15,500 km² (6,000 sq. mi.).
Population: about 1,000,000: but see note below
Largest towns: Hull (290,000).*
          York (110,000).*
          Grimsby (96,500).*
          Lincoln (75,500).*
          Scunthorpe (67,250).
          Scarborough (42,500).
          Cleethorpes (32,750).
          Bridlington (26,000).
          Goole (18,750).
                  *1969 estimates.

This list excludes (i) members of the Tyneside Conurbation, (ii) large industrial towns on or near the Wear and Tees, (iii) members of the West Yorkshire Conurbation, (iv) large industrial towns on the Pennine flanks south of that Conurbation. The population for the region is obtained by subtracting the combined population of these four groups from the total numbers of inhabitants, and rounding-off the resulting figure.

About 75 per cent of this region is in improved farmland, with tillage nearly twice as extensive as grass.

Numbers of livestock: cattle, 820,000;
                sheep, 1,850,000;
                pigs, 765,000;
                poultry, 15,350,000.

The regional unity of this region is imposed by the scarpland character of the terrain, and by contrasts with adjacent regions. Regional boundaries, however, are largely transitional. In the south, the boundary runs along the margin of the Fenland, crosses the Jurassic cuesta where this widens into the Leicestershire Wolds, and crosses the Trent valley at the exit from the Midland Triangle. In the west, hills increase rather slowly with height as the Pennines are approached; the Magnesian Limestone, with a west-facing scarp at the boundary of the exposed coalfield, blurs the passage from vale country to hill country, and a concentration of mining and manufacture tends to obscure the physical boundary. There is, nevertheless, a fundamental difference between the Pennine plateaus and the lower valley of the Trent. In the north, again, the scarpland country reaches into the Industrial Northeast of England, but beyond the industrial region the terrain belongs to the Border country (Figs. 17:1, 18:1).

Climate

Although the North York Moors receive up to 1,000 mm. of precipitation a year, and suffer heavy falls of snow in some winters, most of the scarpland region lies in the strong rain-shadow cast by the Pennines. Annual precipitation declines from 750 mm. on the west to less than 650 mm. on the lower Tees, at the mouth of the Humber, at the head of the Humber and on the lower Trent. Mean annual range of temperature is lower, at about 11 °C, than in the fruit-growing districts of Kent; the frost-free period exceeds 5 months in all lowland parts and rises to 6 or 7 months in Holderness and along the Lincolnshire coast. Actual January mean temperature is below 3 °C. in all parts, but winter cold of this order is in no way a handicap to arable farming—indeed, the most highly-tilled parts of England are roughly enclosed by the 3 °C. sea-level isotherm for January. The practical benefit of moderate frost, capable of breaking up the soil but not of killing autumn-sown crops, is an important one.

Physique and Agriculture: The Western Districts

The Magnesian Limestone belt is dominantly arable. Its sheep-farming has declined somewhat in recent years, partly because of sheep-worrying by dogs from the industrial towns, and cash cropping of potatoes, sugar beet, and grain is on the increase. Cash-cropping has also been established on the lime-poor soils of the adjacent Sherwood Forest district, which is based on permeable sandstones and conglomerates. The stronger of these rocks rise in a low, broken scarp along the west of Sherwood Forest; the eastern side is bordered by a second line of equally low, equally broken scarps where weak sandstones come to the surface. Between the eastern side of the Sherwood belt and the terraces which border the Trent comes a broad strip of low hills, where mixed farming is widely developed on loamy soils. Fruit-farms occur in patches round the small market-towns.

From the mouth of the Tees to the Trent below Nottingham—a distance of more than a hundred miles—stretches a strike vale, eroded in weak marls in the upper Permo-Trias (Fig. 18:1). The vale lies almost everywhere less than 60 m. above sea-level. Its drainage is dominated by strike streams—the lower Tees, the middle Swale, the Ouse, and the lower Trent. These rivers collect the waters of the upper Tees, the upper Swale, the Ure, Nidd, Wharfe, Aire, and Calder, which in their Pennine reaches retain elements of a former west–east consequent system. The competing rivers were dismembered by successive captures, and the number of outlets to the sea reduced to two—one at the mouth of the Tees, where the weak rocks reach the coast, and the other at the Humber, where scarp-forming Jurassic rocks are at their thinnest and weakest. Glacial deposits in the Vale of York—including end-moraines—obliterate the details of the immediately pre-glacial surface.

There is much arable land, for tillage is encouraged by near-by concentrations of industrial population and by the rain-shadow of the Pennines, with the result that parts of the vale were able to resist the reversion to grass which typified the inter-war period. The same factors which favour tillage also favour dairying and market-gardening. In detail, however, land-use distributions are very variable, partly because of variations in soil, and are liable to change from year to year on a single farm (Fig. 21:1). Flood-plains are mainly in permanent grass, which is extensive on the wide alluvial flats of the Humberhead levels.

Physique and Agriculture: The Eastern Districts

East of the Trent lie four cuestas, two north of the Humber and two south of it. The North York Moors and Lincoln Edge are based on Jurassic limestones and sandstones, while the Yorkshire Wolds and the Lincolnshire Wolds are cut in Chalk.

The North York Moors rise well above 300 m. in tabular, windswept crests, their backslope deeply gashed by young valleys. Large areas are in rough pasture, with heather moor extensive at the highest levels. The Vale of Pickering, the strike vale between the Jurassic and Chalk cuestas north of the Humber, was the site of an ice-dammed lake during the Ice Age, when the Derwent was diverted westwards from its original direct course to the sea. Its floor is covered by glacial deposits, lake-sediments, and peaty alluvium. The Vale is enclosed at the eastern end by a terminal moraine, and at the western by the low Howardian Hills, where the Jurassic rocks are thin. Uplift caused the Jurassic sediments to be eroded, and allowed the succeeding Chalk to overstep them to the west, so that the Chalk downs of the Yorkshire Wolds, swinging round to the south, pass across the Jurassic scarp-formers and conceal them.[1] Tillage and grassland are patchily distributed on the floor of the Vale of

---

[1] Compare the way in which the Greensand oversteps underlying formations in the Blackdown Hills (Fig. 26:2).

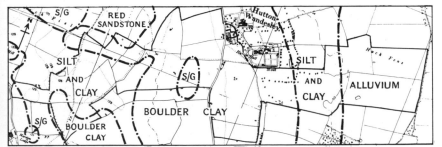

Key to soil plan

Parent material	Soil
Alluvium	Clay
Silt and Clay	Grey-brown clay with stones
Boulder Clay	Brown loam with stones
Glacial sand and gravel S/G	Brown sandy loam with stones
Red Sandstone	Red and brown sand

FIG. 21:1a. Soil map of the Home Farm, Hutton Wandesley Estate, Vale of York

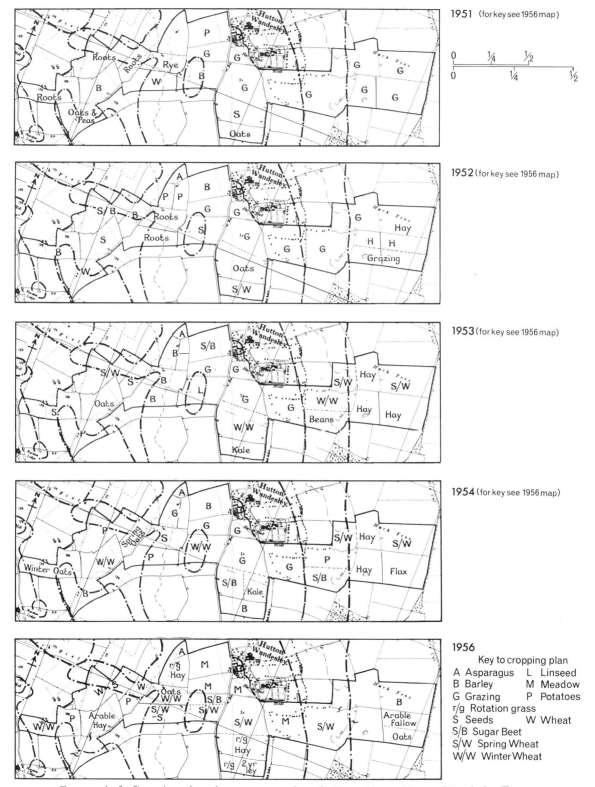

FIG. 21:1b–f. Cropping plans for 1951–54 and 1956, Home Farm, Hutton Wandesley Estate

Pickering, in accordance with the poor drainage of some valley-bottom sites.

The Yorkshire Wolds, rising little above 250 m., are extensively in tillage. Farms here profited from their generally light soils when the sheep-barley combination paid, and even today, with dairying handicapped by the same light soils and by a rainfall little greater than 750 mm. a year, sheep are still quite numerous and barley is still the main tillage crop. To the south, in Holderness, tenacious soils developed on thick boulder clay are widely planted to wheat, and market-gardens take advantage of the long growing-season to produce vegetables in large quantity.

South of the Humber, Jurassic rocks form a low but well-marked cuesta in Lincoln Edge, the crest remaining below 125 m. as far as the neighbourhood of Grantham (cf. Fig. 21:2). The strike vale east of Lincoln Edge, the diverging Lincolnshire Wolds, and the coastal lowland, are all thickly overspread with boulder clay. Broad alluvial flats occur in the Louth and Grimsby marshes, and in the valley of the Ancholme between the two cuestas. Agricultural statistics for Lindsey give a fair summary for this portion of the region. In Lindsey, as a whole, barley and wheat in combination take about two-thirds of the area under tillage crops.

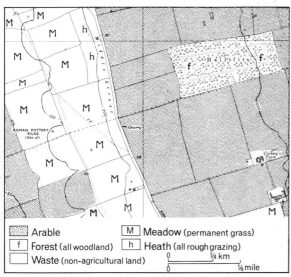

Arable — Meadow (permanent grass)
f Forest (all woodland) — h Heath (all rough grazing)
Waste (non-agricultural land) — 0 ¼ km — 0 ¼ mile

FIG. 21:2. Land-use sample for Lincoln Edge. The top of the low cuesta is almost wholly in tillage, the scarp-face in permanent grass

Potatoes are next most extensive, followed by sugar beet. Vegetables (other than potatoes) and forage crops are also widely grown. Lincoln sheep in considerable numbers are folded on arable land. Beefstock—purebred Lincoln Reds or Lincoln Red crosses—are fattened. A recent increase in numbers of cattle has renewed the demand for summer pasture on the coastal marshes. Dairying is well established.

Settlement

With the vigorous farming of this region goes a considerable rural population. Scarp-foot and dip-foot villages line the margins of the North York Moors, the Yorkshire Wolds, the Lincolnshire Wolds, and Lincoln Edge, many place-names bespeaking a Danish origin (Fig. 21:3). In parts of the vale country, rural settlements are irregularly distributed in accordance with variety in minor detail of terrain, but a distinct group of villages appears along the western boundary of the region between Doncaster and Harrogate. Beyond these towns the rural pattern has been overlaid by industry.

Country towns are few, considering the size of the region. They are more widely spaced than in East Anglia, and far more widely so than in the Borders of the West Country (Chap. 26), their sparsity contributing to the strong social isolation typical of villages in East Lincolnshire. Scarborough, Bridlington, and Cleethorpes are the leading seaside resorts in the region. Goole, Grimsby, and Hull are contrasted ports, and York, Lincoln, and Scunthorpe rank as industrial towns. No one town acts as the regional capital, for the region has too little coherence to possess a single urban focus. Hull, York, and Lincoln have close trading connections with their surroundings, but each has interests extending far beyond its immediate service area.

Towns and Industry

Hull (Fig. 21:4) in 1970 ranked third among ports in the United Kingdom in terms of value of trade, coming however well behind London and Liverpool and not far outpacing its next nearest rival, Harwich. It seems especially well placed to serve the Industrial West Riding, but in fact the hinterlands of Liverpool and Manchester extend on to the eastern side of the Pennines. In terms of tonnage, Hull is deeply involved with external traffic, imports rather than exports; but its trade by value is dominated by short-haul exporting.

Textiles amount but to 0·1 per cent of Hull's exports by weight. Coal, coke, and patent fuels provide three-fifths of total exports by weight, while coal, machinery, and miscellaneous manufactured goods are the chief exports by value. Incoming

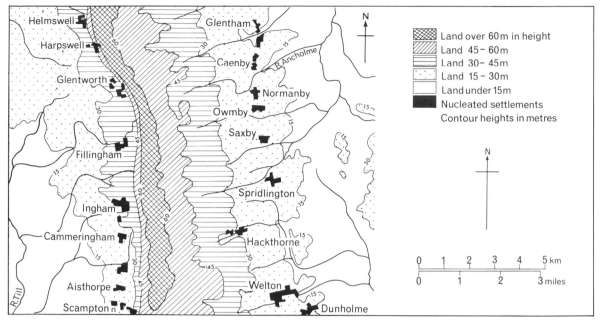

FIG. 21:3. Nucleated scarp-foot and dip-foot villages, Lincoln Edge

produce, destined mainly for use in the industries of Hull itself, includes grain, oilseeds, timber, fruit, wool, foodstuffs, fish, and mineral oils. About three-quarters of Hull's exports go to the Continent, which supplies one-third of the imports.

Hull, in the 12th century, was a trading settlement located on a creek. Profiting by the destruction of Ravenscar, which was destroyed by wave-erosion on the Holderness coast, Hull flourished in

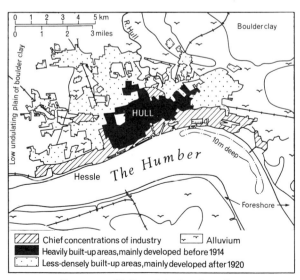

FIG. 21:4. Hull and its local setting

the 14th century, establishing trade links with the Continent. It shared in the Greenland whale fishery of the 17th and 18th centuries, extending its interest in organic oils with the 18th-century import and milling of rape oil—the foundation of the processing of oils and the manufacture of paint which are prominent today. Before docks were made, deep water was ensured by the swing of the Humber against its north bank; the first dock of the present nine was excavated in the 1770s, the alluvium of the Humber offering no obstacle. In the mid-19th century began the smoking of fish, and the discovery of the highly productive Silver Pits of the Dogger Bank in 1850 greatly benefited the Hull fleet. Increasing knowledge of the North Sea fishing-grounds, the construction of docks, and the increase in the size of fishing vessels with resulting concentration on a few ports, all proved to the profit of Hull. However, the progressive shift towards newer and more distant grounds, the increasing size of modern vessels, and the growing practice of freezing the distant-water catch on board, have all militated against the fortune of east-coast fishing ports (see bibliography: Day). But Hull, Grimsby, Aberdeen, and Fleetwood continue to account for some three-quarters of the British take of demersal fish, mainly cod and haddock. The former distinct prosperity of Hull's fishing was accompanied by the rise of shipbuilding in the yards at Beverley, where coasting vessels and power trawlers are constructed.

PLATE 59. Docks and marshalling-yards at Grimsby.

Hull has developed manufactures of chemicals in association with its older production of paints; saw-milling and woodworking reflect its long connection with Baltic ports, as also does flour-milling, although Russian exports of food grain ceased in 1914. The industry of mechanical engineering is partly associated with shipbuilding through marine engineering and ship repairing, but there are in addition manufactures of aircraft and excavating plant. Cement is also produced.

Hull suffered much bomb-damage during World War II, but has subsequently restored its industries and recovered its port trade. Port improvements are in hand, and much new light industry has been acquired since 1945.

Goole, more than 30 km inland of Hull and still on tidewater, is in some ways a rival port. Whereas the port trade of Hull has developed mainly under the influence of the town's own industries, however, Goole has succeeded in establishing close con-

nections with the West Riding. By value of trade, Goole is about the fifteenth port of the U.K., having a trade a sixth as large as that of Hull, and recording an excess of exports over imports.

Grimsby (Plate 59) could at one time claim to be the world's greatest fishing port. Silting destroyed a port trade which had flourished in the Middle Ages, increasing the social isolation of the villages of the hinterland, but the town was reinvigorated when the railway entered in 1848 and when the first dock was finished in 1854. The docks were developed by the railway companies, who provided fast trains to distribute fish. More than one hundred trawlers still remain based on Grimsby, although some difficulty occurs in accommodating large modern vessels; and the increasing trend towards distribution of fish by road has already mitigated the significance of the rail connections. Commercial docks handle timber, wood-pulp, grain, and coal; the shipbuilding industry is connected mainly with fishing, and a number of ancillary industries are carried on. Reclaimed land accommodates most of the factories including those producing chemicals. Ships too big to enter Grimsby go to the docks at Immingham, 10 km away to the northwest, where, as at Hull, there is natural deep water close inshore. The chief incoming cargoes at Immingham are grain, timber, and iron ore; coal is exported.

Lincoln was a Roman town, sited on the Jurassic cuesta above the Witham gap, and on the Roman Ermine Street which ran north and south along the dry ground of the cuesta, avoiding the forests and marshes on either side. Lincoln had considerable strategic importance, for land routes from the east were directed to it by the projecting fenland in the lower Witham valley; it was one of the five Danish boroughs, and acquired a Norman castle and cathedral. During the Middle Ages it was a great centre of the wool trade, with manufactures of woollen cloth, flour, and stained glass, but the decay of the trade in wool—well in evidence by 1500—depressed the town and recovery did not set in until the 18th century Engineering developed during the 19th century, with agricultural machinery a leading product, but the loss of export markets in 1914 led to diversification of the industry. Diesel engines, mining gear, excavators, and gas turbines are among the items produced today. Agricultural chemicals are manufactured, vegetables are canned, and grain and timber brought by barge from Hull are milled at Lincoln.

York also underwent depression in Tudor times, after having been a Roman fortress, the scene of the coronation of the Emperor Constantine the Great in 306, the capital of Northumbria, and a very great medieval market for wool. Its revival began during the 18th century, when York became a fashionable resort, and was accelerated when railways came in the 19th century. In its early days York possessed great strategic advantages, lying on the east coast route to the north, commanding the gate between the Pennines and the Yorkshire Wolds, and serving at one time as a base in wars against the Scots. Tactically, also, the site is advantageous. York stands on one of the two moraines which, curving across the Vale of York, are bordered by marsh—marsh which, north of York, included the flood-plain of the lower Nidd, and which on the south was enclosed between the York moraine and the Escrick moraine 8 km away (Fig. 21:5). With the effective width of the lowland gateway thus reduced, York had some natural protection both on the north and on the south, and was best approached along the hummocky moraine either from east or west.

The present nodality of York is expressed by converging roads and railways. The town has railway workshops, light engineering of various kinds, and flourishing manufactures of cocoa, chocolate, and confectionery. There is a considerable tourist traffic, which the dignified ecclesiastical history of York encourages, and a large retail trade.

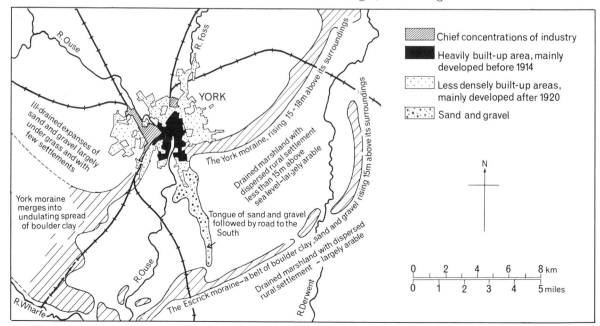

Fig. 21:5. York and its local setting

Both at York and at Lincoln the existence of an old-established town was a factor in attracting railways and modern industry. Scunthorpe is also an old foundation, but, lacking a high ecclesiastical status, became no more than a modest market town until the late 19th century. Industrial development began when the Frodingham ores were drawn upon in the late 1800s. Scunthorpe today ranks third, after the Middlesbrough district and South Wales, as a producer of pig-iron, with $17\frac{1}{2}$ per cent of the national output. Its blast-furnaces are integrated in steelworks, where the molten pig is passed directly to the open-hearth furnaces (Plate 14).

The Frodingham ores belong to the Lower Lias formation. Although their average content of metallic iron is low—20 per cent—they are calcareous and thus self-fluxing. Most of the extraction is open-cast. Coal and coke are brought by rail from the Yorks., Derby, and Notts. coalfield, and additional ore comes from the Northamptonshire Ironfield.

Unlike the Frodingham ores, the petroleum of the Trent valley has given rise to no local manufacturing industry. The output of petroleum makes a very small contribution to national supply, but has understandably aroused much interest. The main producing wells are located either in the neighbourhood of Eakring, 12 km east of Mansfield, or near Plungar, 20 km east-southeast of Nottingham.

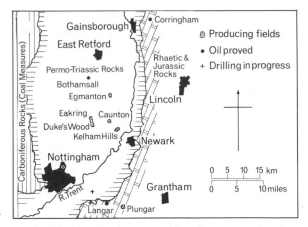

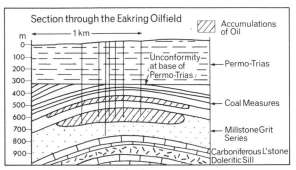

FIG. 21:6. Nottinghamshire oilfields

PLATE 60. Staythorpe Power Station, on the Trent near Newark. The outfall appears on the left (downstream), the intake is just outside the right of the picture (upstream).

The Eakring and Dukes Wood oilfields are adjacent to one another, with the Kelham Hills, Caunton, and Egmanton fields lying to the east (Fig 21:6). The oil is preserved in anticlines in the Millstone Grit, which is up-arched beneath its cover of Permo-Trias.

Drilling in the period 1918–22 gave disappointing results, but oil was proved in a test well in 1939, and the Eakring field was rapidly developed under pressure of war, peak output of 110,000 tons being reached in 1943. A rapid decline in output was checked in 1948 by the injection of water into the oil-bearing strata on the flanks of the fold, and output has subsequently been maintained. Total production from English onshore oilfields—82,000 tons in 1965—comes mainly from the Trent valley.

During the post-war period, large power-stations have been built on the middle Trent. The stations, which are not located with reference to the needs of the region, are fairly centrally placed in the grid system. They use huge quantities of river-water in cooling, and obtain their coal from the southern part of the Yorks., Derby, and Notts. field or from Leicestershire (Plate 60).

Chapter 22

The Midland Triangle and its Northern Borders

IT is far from easy to define the Midlands with any precision. They merge from the Welsh Borderland with the plateau country of Wales; the southern apex of the Midland Triangle projects far down the lower Severn towards Bristol; and while the vales containing Oxford, Aylesbury, and Bedford belong indisputably to the Midlands, the neighbouring Chilterns may be regarded either as the most south-

easterly Midland cuesta or as the northwestern flank of the London Basin. East of the Hitchin Gap, at the extremity of the Chilterns, it is especially difficult to discern a rapid change of regional character amid the low, irregular, drift-covered hills, where the Midlands, the London Basin, and East Anglia fade into one another. The boundary of the Fenlands is, indeed, clearly marked by the

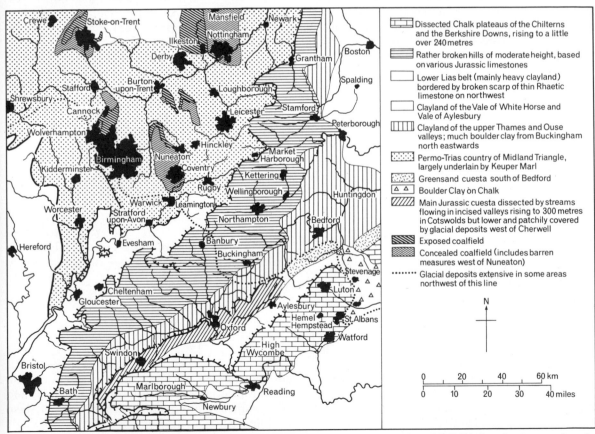

Dissected Chalk plateaus of the Chilterns and the Berkshire Downs, rising to a little over 240 metres

Rather broken hills of moderate height, based on various Jurassic limestones

Lower Lias belt (mainly heavy clayland) bordered by broken scarp of thin Rhaetic limestone on northwest

Clayland of the Vale of White Horse and Vale of Aylesbury

Clayland of the upper Thames and Ouse valleys; much boulder clay from Buckingham north eastwards

Permo-Trias country of Midland Triangle, largely underlain by Keuper Marl

Greensand cuesta south of Bedford

Boulder Clay on Chalk

Main Jurassic cuesta dissected by streams flowing in incised valleys rising to 300 metres in Cotswolds but lower and patchily covered by glacial deposits west of Cherwell

Exposed coalfield

Concealed coalfield (includes barren measures west of Nuneaton)

Glacial deposits extensive in some areas northwest of this line

FIG. 22:1. The Midland Triangle and its northern borders; Scarplands of the South Midlands: physique and main settlements break of slope at the landward edge of the peaty levels, but further north the low ground of the Trent valley continues unbroken towards the head of the Humber. The southern end of the Pennines and the towns which have arisen there lie too far south to be placed in northern England, although two hundred years ago it was the Trent above Nottingham which divided the north from the south. Between the Pennines and the Welsh Border, the Midland Gate links the Midland Triangle with lowland south of the Mersey (Figs. 13:1, 22:1).

Doubtful though their boundaries may be, the Midlands are separable from surrounding regions. They are also themselves divisible into two distinct regions—the Midland Triangle and the Scarplands of the South Midlands; the former will be described in the present chapter, the latter in the next.

The Midland Triangle and the Scarplands of the South Midlands resemble one another only in extent. They differ especially in their richness in large towns. Some 4,000,000 people living in the Midland Triangle inhabit one or other of the largest towns; if the Potteries are taken into account, the figure rises well above 4,000,000 and relates to 80 per cent of the total population. The local accents in nearly all these towns are of the northern kind; accents differ from town to town, but in the southern ear all vowels are unmistakably northern. In the Scarplands of the South Midlands no more than two-thirds of a million—less than a third of the population—live in towns with 30,000 or more people. The largest town in this region is but a tenth of the size of Birmingham. Only in quite recent years have towns large by modern standards developed in the Scarpland region, and even in these, the local speech has a strong rustic flavour—if it has escaped the influence of London.

THE MIDLAND TRIANGLE AND ITS NORTHERN BORDERS

Area: about 11,000 km² (4,250 sq. mi.).
Population: about 5,500,000.
Largest towns: (*a*) The West Midland Conurbation (2,350,000) of which the leading members are:
    Birmingham (1,086,500).*
    Wolverhampton (265,000).*
    Walsall (190,000).*
    Dudley (181,500).*
    West Bromwich (172,500).*
    Warley (168,000).*

    Solihull (100,500).*
    Sutton Coldfield (82,500).*
    Smethwick (68,250).
    Aldridge-Brownhills (86,500)*
    Rowley Regis (48,250).
    Halesowen (44,250).
    Stourbridge (44,000).
    Wednesbury (34,500).
(*b*) Towns with close links to the Conurbation:
    Coventry (335,750).*
    Nuneaton (56,500).
    Cannock (42,250).
    Kidderminster (40,750).
    Bromsgrove (34,500).
    Redditch (34,000).
(*c*) Towns of the Potteries:
    Stoke-on-Trent (273,000).*
    Newcastle-under-Lyme (76,500).
(*d*) Towns of the Middle Trent Basin:
    Nottingham (300,000).*
    Leicester (278,500).*
    Derby (221,250).*
    Beeston (56,750).
    Burton-upon-Trent (51,000).*
    Hinckley (41,500).
    Loughborough (38,500).
    Ilkeston (34,750).
    Coalville (26,250).
(*e*) Remaining towns:
    Gloucester (90,500).*
    Cheltenham (76,000).*
    Worcester (72,500).*
    Rugby (51,750).
    Stafford (47,750).
    Leamington (43,250).
             * 1969 estimates.

About 70 per cent of this region is in improved farmland, grass being half as extensive again as tillage.
Numbers of livestock: cattle, 825,000;
                sheep, 1,075,000;
                pigs, 375,000;
                poultry, 7,300,000.

The large towns of the Midland Triangle and its northern borders are highly industrialised, contain one out of every ten inhabitants of England, and are completely interrelated. While some of them fall into well-defined groups, dominated by a single class of industry, others stand apart, displaying in many cases industrial affinities with more than one neighbour. They are widely distributed—although not evenly distributed—throughout the region.

Around them, and in places merging with their patchy outskirts, stretches extensive farmland. Although the character of farming is affected to some extent by the demands of the great urban markets, well-defined agricultural contrasts still separate one part of the region from another.

Physique and Soils

The Midland Triangle is largely underlain by rocks of Permo-Triassic Age, which abut against the Pennines on the north and the Primary rocks of the Welsh Border on the west (Fig. 22:1). Coal Measures rise from beneath the Permo-Trias on the western boundary and on the extremities of the Pennines, and have been revealed by erosion in the uplifted Black Country, Warwickshire, and Leicestershire coalfields. Extremely ancient volcanic rocks protrude through the Permo-Trias in Charnwood Forest. Along the southeastern margin of the Midland Triangle, the weak Triassic marls vanish beneath the thin Rhaetic limestone, which is followed by the thick clays and clayey limestones of the Lower Lias—the lowest part of the Jurassic system. Being for the most part clayey, the Lower Lias has been deeply eroded, and its claylands are included in the Midland Triangle.

Large parts of the region have been reduced below 125 m., falling to 60 m. or less in the wide, gently-sloping valleys of large streams. Post-glacial erosion has been severe throughout, but has not succeeded in removing all the thick and extensive deposits of boulder clay, which covers much ground in the basins of the Avon and the Soar.

Drainage in the north is to the Trent, which is fed by the Dove, Derwent, and Erewash from the Pennines and by the Penk, Tame, and Soar from the south. In pre-glacial times the Soar used to rise somewhere near Evesham, but a lake impounded the ice-front and the Jurassic scarp first found an outlet to the southwest, and the Warwickshire Avon came into being. The Severn was lengthened during the Ice Age by the diversion of its upper reaches through the Ironbridge gorge; the large and ramifying Severn–Avon system which now drains so much of the Triangle is thus mainly a product of glaciation.

Soils in the Midland Triangle are very varied, as would be expected of a region where patches of glacial drift occur on a varied array of solid rocks. Many belong to the group of Brown Forest Soils, but soils developed on certain permeable rocks of the Permo-Trias are liable to be podsolised. A noticeable feature is the reddish or reddish-purple colour of fresh ploughing both on the Permo-Trias and on the drifts derived from it, but soils become darker and duller along the eastern margin, where they are formed on the Lower Lias or on heavy boulder clay. All the rivers have been intermittently rejuvenated, and on the light well-drained soils of their terraces market-gardens are numerous near the towns, but the highest development of intensive cultivation is found in the south-west of the region, where the orchards of the Evesham district are planted mainly on patches of sludge-gravel. All the flood-plains have developed meadow soils.

Climate and Agriculture

In climate and in farming, as in the pattern of rural settlement, the Midland Triangle is transitional, in the sense that its western parts belong to western England, while the northeast is allied to eastern England, and the southern extremity has strong affinities with the Borders of the West Country.

Annual precipitation ranges from about 850 mm. in the northwest of the region to little more than 60 mm. in the northeast. Liability to thunder, and the proportion of total precipitation coming in summer, both increase from west to east across the region. There is a very slow eastward increase in annual range of temperature which varies about 11 °C., and the frost-free season is below 6 months except in the lower Severn and Avon valleys. Climatically, this southern part is the best-favoured part. Warm air can come in from the Bristol Channel, not bringing heavy rain, but noticeably moderating winter cold, reducing the frequency of snow, extending the frost-free season to more than 6 months, and raising the January mean temperature to 4° or above—a high figure for this inland region where winter chilling of the land-surface is pronounced.

The southern extremity of the region contains part of the second greatest concentration of orchard fruit in the country (cf. Fig. 5:19); the fruit-growing district overlaps into Herefordshire (Chap. 13), but the production of small fruit and especially of vegetables is located mainly within the Midland Triangle. Brussels sprouts, cabbages, cauliflower, onions, peas, beans, and asparagus figure in the long list of market-garden produce, and currants are the most extensive kind of small fruit. Orchards are most continuous in the Vale of Evesham, which is famous for its eating and cooking apples, but are also to be found scattered throughout the country-side.

Rather less than half the farmland of Worcester-shire is in grass. The leading crops, in order of extent, are barley, wheat, vegetables (excluding potatoes), and orchard fruit. Potatoes and sugar beet are also extensive. Stock-farming is varied, but dairying receives increasing attention. The wide extent of tillage, the colourful soils, the many orchards, and the abundant hardwood trees combine with rather scattered settlement to make the countryside look rich and attractive.

In the northeast of the Midland Triangle there is more grass than in the south—grass still takes two-thirds of all farmland in Leicestershire, despite the recent extension of tillage. Permanent grassland becomes particularly common in the east of the county, where heavy boulder clay spread over the subdued Wolds gives rise to heavy soils, and where the boundary between the Midland Triangle and the adjacent scarplands is masked by drift. Fields are divided by sturdy well-kept hedges which contain the numerous livestock. For centuries this area has been noted for its sheep, and it was among those parts of England where villages were depopulated to make way for medieval sheep-farms, but sheep today are no more numerous than cattle, and require far less land than cattle do. Dairy cattle and followers outnumber beefstock, but fattening is still widely practised. The most extensive tillage crops are barley and wheat, which together take about half the total of ploughland. Oats, potatoes, and forage crops are also widespread.

Leicestershire lies well within the belt of originally nucleated villages (Fig 4:3), and the Saxon pattern of settlement was little disturbed by Danish occupation. Nucleated villages are still typical today, although outlying farms have been added, and some villages have swollen greatly as a result of sharing the hosiery industry of Leicester.

The character of agriculture in the northwestern part of the Midland Triangle is roughly indicated by Staffordshire where 75 per cent of the farmland grows grass, cattle somewhat outnumber sheep, and most of the cattle are dairy animals. Grassland farming generally, and dairying in particular, are favoured by rain entering through the Midland Gate. Tillage crops are prominent mainly on the gently-undulating land south of the Pennines, where they include barley, wheat, potatoes, forage crops, and sugar beet. Staffordshire is not a wholly satisfactory sample of this part of the region, as can be seen from a comparison of county with regional boundaries; its differences from Worcestershire and Leicestershire are, therefore, all the more impressive.

TOWNS AND INDUSTRIES

There is a most remarkable industrial contrast between the eastern and western sides of the region. Manufacturing industry in the west is dominated either by the metal trades, which take more than 40 per cent of all the people working in the West Midland Conurbation, or by pottery, which takes more than 25 per cent of the workers in Stoke-on-Trent. In Nottingham the leading occupational group is the textile and garment trades, with nearly 20 per cent of all workers, followed by the metal industries with between 10 and 15 per cent. The textile and garment trades lead in Leicester, with 20 per cent of the workforce, followed by the metal industries (something less than 20 per cent) and by leather-working and footwear production (less than 10 per cent). Such smaller centres as Hinckley concentrate more highly on textiles and leather. Both the metal trades and the pottery-making of the west were founded in pre-industrial days, but have become concentrated on coalfields. The textile and leather industries of the east, developing from medieval crafts, have been industrialised without transference to coalfields.[1]

Industrialisation of the Black Country

The Black Country forms a low plateau, where productive Coal Measures are exposed. Industrialisation has produced an agglomeration of manufacturing towns, which have merged with Birmingham in the West Midland Conurbation.

Coal in the Black Country was worked for use in local smithies as early as the 13th century, and the production of bar-iron—accompanied by the clearance of woodland by charcoal-burners—is attested by documents of the 14th century. Iron-working in South Staffordshire thus long pre-dates 18th-century industrialisation, and its strong medieval development is, in fact, one of the leading objections to the term *industrial revolution*. The best ores, found in the neighbourhood of Walsall, were much worked. Forges, requiring water-power, were sited on streams, but the charcoal-using blast-furnaces introduced in the 16th century were located with reference to fuel-supply. Production of

---

[1] The leather industry is dominant in and near Northampton: see Chap. 23.

iron goods—edge tools, cutlery, and nails—was typically scattered.

In the 18th century came the conversion from smelting with charcoal to smelting with coke, and the thick coal of the Black Country, with its underlying ironstone, was widely mined. Local fireclay served the Stourbridge glassworks, and was distributed to the new blast-furnaces. Reserves of iron ore were still less adequate than they had already proved, and by 1788, when the last charcoal furnace was finally extinguished, pig-iron was being brought from the Forest of Dean up the Severn and along the new canals. Towns and villages were expanding fast by 1800, when the industrial pattern of the Black Country was already evident. Between 1800 and 1860 there was a great increase in coal-mining and in smelting, large quantities of ore and pig being brought in as soon as railways were built. By 1865 there were 172 blast-furnaces in the Black Country, concentrated mainly in a belt from Wolverhampton to Oldbury, and in and near Dudley and Brierley Hill. The two concentrations were separated by an upfaulted strip from which Coal Measures are missing.

Industrial devastation of the Black Country was severe during the first half of the 19th century, and continued into the later 1800s, combining with the intense activity of heavy industry to give the district its traditional name. Pronounced changes were, however, already in progress by the mid-19th century, and the stereotyped concept of the Black Country is a century out-of-date. Some of the best workable coals were exhausted by 1860, when the peak of iron-smelting had already been passed. The numbers of active mines, blast-furnaces, and coke-ovens had fallen greatly by 1900 and continued subsequently to fall. The demand for wrought iron lessened as steel—produced elsewhere—came in quantity upon the industrial market; iron making, tin-plating, galvanising, and the light metal trades were all involved in a progressive decline. Two active blast-furnaces survive today on the western edge of the coalfield, but most of the pig for the steel furnaces now comes from the Jurassic ironfields.

By contrast with its heavy industry and primary processing of the 19th century, the Black Country's later-developed finishing trades prosper (Plate 61). Bicycles, cars, arms, machine tools, and aero-engines are prominent in the list of products, but

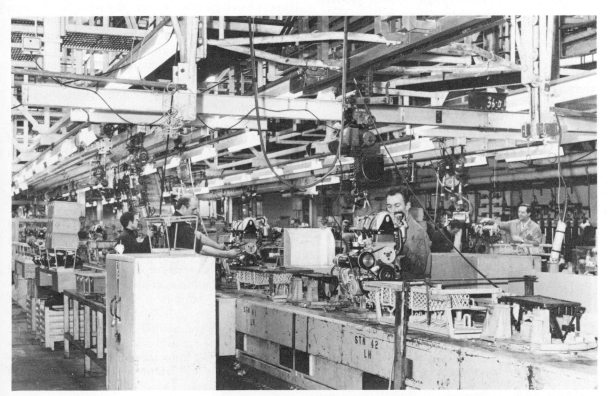

PLATE 61. Automated engine assembly factory at Compton Hackett, Birmingham. The factory, which cost £16 million, is one of the most up-to-date engine assembly factories in the world.

no short list can give any idea of the enormous range of modern products.

In turning to the complex processes of the finishing trades, which absorb much non-ferrous metal, the Black Country has successfully overcome the difficulties of industrial setbacks, scarcity of raw material, and exhaustion of local fuel. Its factories, moreover, lie far inland, away from the ports through which raw materials come and produce goes. It is impossible to judge the extent to which the conversion of industry was enforced by the failure of local mines, by the declining demand for iron, or by the need for goods which could bear cost of transport. The maintenance and expansion of metal-manufacturing supply an outstanding example of the results of industrial momentum.[1]

Industrial Employment in the West Midland Conurbation

In the West Midland Conurbation there are more than a million people at work, and more than a quarter of these are employed in some type of metal manufacture and engineering (Fig. 22:2). The relevant trades are prominent in very many towns throughout Great Britain, but in the West Midland Conurbation they employ twice as many people as in Southeast Lancashire, two-and-a-half times as many as in Central Clydeside, three times as many as in West Yorkshire, four-and-a-half times as many as on Merseyside, and five times as many as on Tyneside. Only the Greater London Conurbation, with its enormously greater total population, has more workers in metal and engineering than has the West Midland Conurbation.

Birmingham

Within the West Midland Conurbation, an important distinction must be made between the Black Country on one hand and Birmingham on the other. Birmingham is a manufacturing town in its own right, but, although it has merged with the Black Country towns, it does not stand on the coalfield. It did not take part in the earliest iron-working of the West Midlands, and its accession to the rank of regional capital is as difficult to explain as is the medieval success of Coventry.

The rise of Birmingham as a market centre, and later as a centre of industry, was at first slow but persistent. The place was recorded as a tiny settlement in Domesday Book, but in the 12th century the de Bermingham family secured a market charter for it. Market rights and freedom from gild regulations seem to have been beneficial, for '. . . in the thirteenth century a man was more likely to be attracted to Birmingham . . . by the prospect of a burgage tenure for which he could pay rent in cash rather than in labour services, or the privilege of setting up as a free and independent craftsman . . . than by any consideration of a good water supply, a sandstone ridge or a bridge over a local brook'.[2] By whatever means, Birmingham secured expanding control over local trade. Its anti-Royalist sympathies and its production of sword-blades for the Parliamentary forces provoked an attack by Prince Rupert in 1643, but by 1650 the recovering town had between 1,500 and 2,000 inhabitants. Birmingham tightened its grip on the developing industries of the Black Country, and also established manufactures of its own. Manufactures of guns, buttons, toys, trinkets, and small brassware were set up in Birmingham during the 17th century, with jewellery and precious-metal working following in the 18th. Boulton's engineering works were founded in 1761, and the new canals of the late 18th century encouraged great progress in brassworking and mechanical engineering generally. As the town expanded, the functions of its inner districts were modified, and its industry also changed, for Birmingham tended to lead the advances forced upon the Black Country by changing circumstance. Its mechanical engineering is extremely varied; the town is one of the greatest centres of retail trade in the British Isles, and employs many workers in woodworking, building, contracting, and transport as well as in commerce, finance, and clerical occupations.

Birmingham's municipal history illustrates a number of the social and administrative problems which pressed hard upon the rising industrial towns of 18th-century and 19th-century England. Although its population exceeded 100,000 in the early

---

[1] The expression *inherited skill* is often used when *industrial momentum* is intended. Industrial skill cannot possibly be transmitted by inheritance. How the social and psychological pressures of industry can be measured is not clear, but children often tend to follow occupations which their parents have found rewarding. Before 1939, and still more before 1914, social mobility was but slightly developed in the British Isles; members of a given generation had little prospect of rising above their parents in the social scale. Similarly, there was not a great deal of interchange of people among manufacturing industries. This state of affairs can aptly be called *social inertia*. Its influence reinforced the economic influences of industrial inertia, which resisted tendencies to transfer established industry.

[2] R. A. Pelham.

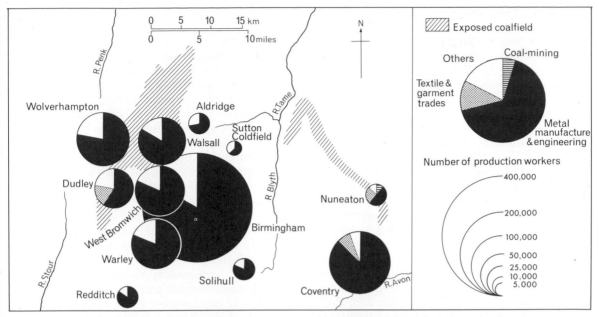

FIG. 22:2. Production employment in the West Midlands, 1966

PLATE 62. Urban redevelopment in Birmingham, northeast of the old centre. Contrast the modern with the older form of layout.

1800s, Birmingham was not directly represented in Parliament until the Reform Act of 1832 came into force, it was not incorporated as a borough until 1838, and responsibility for civic affairs was still divided until 1851. Unified control was urgently needed, for polluted wells and lack of drainage promoted much disease. In the mid-19th century the town suffered from 'unpaved streets, confined courts, open middens and cesspools and stagnant ditches, and crowded lodging-houses'.

Reorganisations of local government made possible a number of far-reaching schemes of public work. Extensive slum clearance and improvements to roads began in 1875, the first of the drastic changes in the face of Birmingham. Enlargement of boundaries first occurred in 1891, city status was conferred in 1899, and the university received its charter in 1900. Partly because of its growing involvement with commerce and administration, Birmingham has chronically suffered from the congestion which typifies the Conurbation as a whole, and which has led to proposals for new towns near Wellington and Ludlow, plus projects for overspill, for instance into the East Midlands where the Birmingham overspill encounters that of London. It faces problems of coloured immigration second only to those of London, with a dispiriting prospect of selective concentration of immigrants in the inner, running-down, residential ring. On the other hand, since the mid-1950s the CBD has been largely reconstructed, being separated into market quarter, shopping centre, a banking-and-office quarter, and a quarter of public administration and cultural activity; the Inner Ring Road keeps much traffic out of the centre; and the inner residential ring has been considerably changed by slum clearance (see bibliography: Jones; Stedman and Wood).

Externally, a persistent concern is that of water supply. Modern Birmingham obtains much of its water from Wales. The watershed of the Black Country Plateau discharges modest streams which, even with the aid of wells and reservoirs, were clearly inadequate by the end of the 19th century. Three reservoirs were impounded in the Elan valley by 1906, and further capacity has been added since the end of World War II by the Clacrwen Dam.

Coventry and other close neighbours of the West Midland Conurbation

Coventry was the fourth largest town in England at the end of the 14th century—only London, York, and Bristol had more people than Coventry's 7,000. Coventry's medieval greatness cannot be explained by any physical advantages of site or situation. The foundation of a well-endowed priory in 1043, followed by the building of a Norman castle, undoubtedly contributed to its urban importance. During the 12th, 13th, and 14th centuries the town secured various rights, among them freedom from toll for Coventry merchants in all parts of the kingdom. Coventry was able to become a very great merchant town, illustrating the principle that '. . . a site which may not be richly endowed by nature may nevertheless be made an important focus of human activity under the guidance and stimulus of able men during the critical early stages of its development'.[1] Fourteenth-century products included wool, soap, needles, and leather. The manufactures of woollens and leather link medieval Coventry to medieval Northampton, Leicester, and Nottingham.

There is some reason to infer that Coventry suffered from the rigid control imposed on craft and trade by its highly-develped gilds, for by 1650 it was little, if any, more populous than it had been in 1500, although it remained a great producer of woollen cloth into the 1700s. Weaving cellars in the surrounding settlements testify to the former presence of the old domestic craft. The emergence of Coventry as a modern industrial town was associated with the technical developments of the late 18th century and later times.

Purely by an accident of siting, Coventry found itself with local supplies of coal. The manufacture of watches and sewing-machines was followed and eclipsed by the production of cycles, motor-cycles, cars, car and aero engines, electrical apparatus, tractors, machine tools, and viscose yarn. Population rose from 70,000 in 1901 to 167,000 in 1931, increasing by 140 per cent in thirty years, and has further increased by over 80 per cent since the 1931 census. The great industrial growth of modern Coventry was made possible by the development of the internal combustion engine and applications of electricity. Thus Coventry as an industrial centre belongs to the late 19th and the 20th centuries. With nearly one in three of its workers engaged in metalwork and engineering, Coventry today has little interest in textiles, clothing or leather. Its old manufactures of wool and silk have either been replaced by mechanical engineering, or superseded by the production of viscose yarn—a type of manufacture which belongs to industrial chemistry and the plastics industry.

Coventry suffered very heavily from bombing

---

[1] R. A. Pelham.

during World War II. Extensive rebuilding in the heart of the town has made it even more attractive than formerly as a centre of shopping and entertainment, but its urban strength was already strongly felt before 1939 in the districts to the south.

Nuneaton is a far smaller town which stands on the exposed Warwickshire coalfield. Nineteenth-century industrial growth is recorded here in terraced houses of brick. Tamworth (13,500), smaller still, was once the capital of Mercia. To the south-west of the West Midland Conurbation, Kidderminster has nearly one-fifth of its workers in textile manufacture and is well known for its carpets; Bromsgrove and Redditch are dominated by engineering. Cannock in the north has more miners than metalworkers, for the Cannock coalfield still produces well from concealed seams. Stafford, a county town far surpassed in size by other towns within its county boundaries, commands the route between Cannock Chase and the Pennines; it is a railway centre, with well-developed electrical engineering and leather industries.

The Potteries

In the Potteries of North Staffordshire occurs a unique concentration of British manufacture. No other industry of comparable size is so strongly localised—the Pottery towns contain four-fifths of all pottery workers in Great Britain. Local potting began at least as early as the 14th century, in the then hamlet of Burslem, where it supplemented farming. It spread slowly through neighbouring settlements, until the 18th century brought tea- and coffee-drinking into fashion; the demand for elegant tableware then made it profitable to bring in clay from Devon and flints from Dorset, in the small quantities which pack-trains could carry, and lead from the Derbyshire Pennines was available for use in glazing. The leading improver was Josiah Wedgwood, who was born at Burslem in 1730 and opened his own works in 1769. His overwhelming success with fine china and new designs was a powerful factor in stimulating the industry, and one of the justifications for the Trent and Mersey Canal which, finished in 1777, enabled raw materials to be imported cheaply and in quantity. But even before the canal was made, the use of materials produced outside the region had reduced locating factors to two: the momentum of success, and the presence of long-flaming coal particularly suitable for firing the kilns.

The factories and the houses of the workpeople were built on the coalfield itself (Plate 63). All the older parts of the Pottery towns were in time under-

mined, and subsidence became serious, while large open pits bit deeply into the marls used in the making of bricks, tiles, and saggars (containers for pottery in the kilns). The towns are congested, for they had little room to spread in the narrow valleys of the Trent headstreams or on the narrow divides. Many of their streets have steep gradients, and collieries, marl-pits, derelict land, terraced houses, canals, railways, and pottery works are knotted in a confused tangle.[1] Only in the inter-war period did road transport begin to encourage much house-building at a distance from the works.

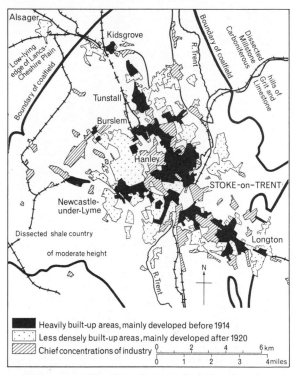

FIG. 22:3. The Potteries and their local setting

The county borough of Stoke-on-Trent, including the formerly separate units of Stoke, Burslem, Hanley, Longton, Fenton, and Tunstall (Fig. 22:3), employs more than a quarter of all its workers in the pottery industry, with another 20 per cent in metal manufacture or mining. In Newcastle-under-Lyme, the three types of work employ roughly equal numbers.

In its widest sense, the pottery industry includes not only the making of household china, ornamental china, and earthenware, but also the production of goods made from the local marl—

---

[1] For census purposes, however, the Potteries do not rank as a conurbation.

PLATE 63. Part of Burslem, in the Potteries—factories, houses, kilns. The Potteries have been declared a smokeless zone.

bricks, roofing tiles, and drainpipes. Most of the work in potting, however, is light, and some two-thirds of those employed in the pottery works are women.

Mining and the metal trades take, between them, far more men than does the pottery industry. Heavy metal manufacture is represented by smelting and steel-making, and engineering is firmly established. There are still useful reserves in the North Staffs. Coalfield, particularly in the centre and south, even though parts of the field have been extensively worked.

The Trent and Soar Valleys

Although Nottingham and Leicester have highly-developed textile and garment industries, they resemble a number of other large Midland towns in combining industrial activity with cattle-marketing, produce-marketing, and a retail trade which serves an area varying with the size of the town. The leading group of industries benefited greatly from the local invention or improvement of machinery—particularly the stocking-frame; it is difficult to judge, however, how much the industry owed to invention and how much invention owed to industry which already existed. The stocking-frame was invented in the 16th century, other textile inventions came early into favour in this district, and by the end of the 19th century a third of the knitting-frames in use in England were to be found in Nottinghamshire alone. The chief group of products today is knitwear of all kinds.

Nottingham and Leicester, the main centres of the industry and the largest towns in their part of the Midland Triangle, display many similarities to one another. Both county towns, both university towns, they were both (with Derby, Lincoln, and Stamford) Danish boroughs. Each lies in a valley, overlooking a broad flood-plain from a patch of terrace, and each commands a crossing.

Leicester was a Roman town on the Fosse Way, and retained a rectangular plan within its square medieval walls. An outbreak of plague caused the gates to be shut, and traffic to pass round the outside of the walls on the eastern side; on this diverted line the main modern shopping street now lies. The town has spread far beyond its medieval limits, losing its walls but retaining a produce market in its centre. Outlying settlements, such as those on the Soar terraces to the north, grew into compact and remarkably large villages during the late 19th century, when hosiery factories and terraced houses were built. Modern industries of Leicester, additional to the making of hosiery and footwear, include engineering, mainly of a specialised kind—the production of hosiery machinery, typewriters,

and instruments. The hosiery industry merges into industrial chemistry through the production of nylon stockings. Leicester's industries offer a wide range of employment to women, and in some households all but the children and the very old are in work.

Nottingham's rock-based Castle, founded in Norman times, dominates the valley-bottom of the Trent, where a long causeway and a bridge provided a crossing in pre-Conquest days. A mile of flood-plain separates the channel of the river from the firm ground on the north bank where the town centre is located (Fig. 22:4). Under the protection of the castle, Nottingham during the Middle Ages acquired a manufacture of cloth, dyeing, tanning, brewing, and iron-working. It was of considerable importance as a market centre, being on or near the limits of contrasting pieces of country—the hills of the southern Pennines, the partly-wooded lowland of the Trent valley, and the dense woodland of Sherwood Forest based on the permeable outcrop of Bunter Pebble Beds. The Trent was navigable for the craft of the time.

Lace-making, for which Nottingham is famous, was originally a domestic craft, widely practised throughout a large area—indeed, hand-made lace was still being made in the villages of the eastern Midlands in the inter-war period. Machine-working became possible in the late 18th century, was greatly developed during the 19th, and now accounts for the total output of Nottingham lace.

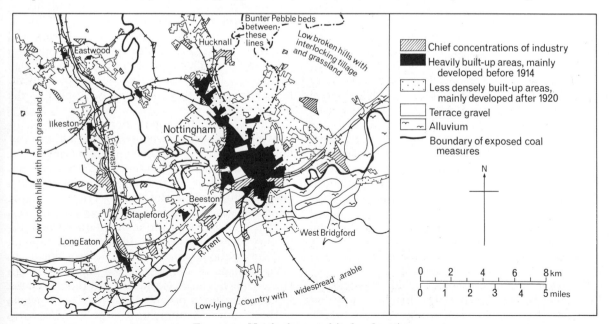

Fig. 22:4. Nottingham and its local setting

Nottingham's engineering industries are partly associated with the manufacture of hosiery, for machines for spinning, weaving, and knitting are made here, as at Leicester. Typewriters are also made at Nottingham, and marine engines and a wide range of other machinery are produced. The manufacture of cycles began in the late 19th century and is still expanding—Nottingham has recently taken over part of the cycle-manufacture hitherto located in Birmingham. The making of pharmaceutical products, again established in Nottingham during the late 19th century, is flourishing, the factory being associated with a nation-wide chain of chemists' shops. The cigarette and tobacco industry, of earlier standing, greatly expanded in the late 19th century and subsequently.

In their modern industrial development, Leicester and Nottingham have been assisted by coal mined near by. In the Leicestershire Coalfield the seams lie close to the surface in a double syncline. Coal is of medium or indifferent quality, but mining costs per ton are lower than anywhere else in Britain. With two new surface mines and reconstruction of old pits, the field is expected to increase its output to 7 million tons a year; at the present time most of the product goes to the Midlands and the south of England, some 30 per cent being sold as domestic fuel and a similar amount going to power stations. The mining towns are Coalville (26,250), which looks industrial, and Ashby-de-la-Zouch (7,500), which does not.

Nottingham is readily supplied from the southern end of the Yorks., Derby and Notts. coalfield, which is separately distinguished by the National Coal Board as the North Derby and Notts. field. There was much early working in the western part, where the seams are exposed, but coal was kept out of the southern English markets by high cost of transport. The proved reserves are large, even though the seams thin underground towards the east as they do in Yorkshire, and the largest mines occur in the east and southeast. Working costs are already low, and may be further reduced by reconstruction, new pits and new surface mines intended to raise output to 40 million tons a year. Over one-third of the coal raised is at present consumed in the Midlands, and another quarter goes by rail to London; increasing output will serve not only London and power stations in the East Midlands, but also the industries of Lancashire.

Beeston, southwest of Nottingham, has recently expanded in engineering rather than in hosiery, but hosiery is still prominent, as at Ilkeston. Ilkeston, on the incised Erewash, is the largest of the industrial settlements strung along valleys cut through the Coal Measures and linking Nottingham and Derby with Chesterfield and Sheffield.

Derby is less than half as populous as Nottingham. Its more modest prospects were foreshadowed when, in Norman times, it was not heavily fortified —perhaps because its routes to the north led but to the Pennine upland. Derby secured borough status during the Middle Ages, however, and became famous for malting as least as early as the 17th century, when coke instead of the customary straw was used in the kilns. By 1693 there were no fewer than seventy-six malthouses in a town of 4,000 people. Hosiery-making was established during the 18th century, and silk-weaving was added when designs for silk-making machinery were stolen from the Italian Piedmont. Pottery, begun in 1750, flourished with the later transfer of the famous Chelsea works. Until the 19th century, however, Derby spread little beyond the medieval site between the incised Derwent and a small right-bank tributary.

The first of its chief present industries was established in the mid-19th century, when the town was linked by railway to Leeds and London, and locomotive workshops were built. At a later date, one man selected Derby for the site of a car-factory because the town offered cheaper electric power than did Leicester. The making of rayon and plastics began with the production of cellulose acetate (used on aircraft fabric) during World War I. Thus the three leading industries of modern Derby— manufacture of locomotives and rolling stock, manufacture of engines for cars and aircraft, and production of rayon and other plastics—result from deliberate acts of location on the part of the railway companies, a single individual, or the government. In combination, they take nearly a third of the town's workers.

Burton-on-Trent is internationally famous for its brewing. Monastic brewhouses gained a high reputation through the use of gypsum-bearing water from local wells; the gypsum (hydrated calcium sulphate, $CaO_4.2SH_2O$), occurring as lenses in the desert sediments of the Permo-Trias, is highly soluble in water, and improves the quality of beer. Burton used much of the malt produced in 17th-century Derby, but was unable to serve a national and international market until improvements to navigation on the Trent enabled exports through Hull to reach Russia, Germany, and India, and the spreading railways provided easy links to the whole of the country. A number of large brewing firms have works at Burton, buying much barley from

East Anglia, and hops from Kent. Local engineering industries are partly allied to brewing, but constructional steelwork is also produced.

The Severn and Avon Valleys

Cheltenham, Gloucester, and Worcester, in the south of the Midland Triangle, are much of a size. Cheltenham, which found favour as a spa in the 18th century, expanded rapidly under the Regency and acquired large, well-designed public buildings. On the map, it seems an obvious urban addition to the area formerly served by Gloucester alone; it shares with Gloucester industries introduced, or greatly stimulated, in time of war—especially the aircraft and aero-engine industry. Clock- and instrument making were assisted by a Government grant-in-aid in 1945. The handsome town-centre, however, looks anything but industrial, and is an asset to Cheltenham's functions as a centre of social and cultural activities.

Gloucester was a flourishing civil town under the Romans, had recovered its urban importance by the Conquest, and developed ironworking during the Middle Ages. Adjoining the Severn flood-plain, on to which its factories have spread (Fig. 22:5), it possesses the lowest bridge across the river. Although it acquired a port charter under Elizabeth I, its rôle as a port began principally with the opening of the Gloucester and Berkeley Canal in 1827. The largest ships unload at the seaward end, where Sharpness receives oil, timber, and grain. Although there is some barge traffic from Gloucester to the Black Country, Gloucester's communications are provided chiefly by busy trunk roads, and by railways with which carriage and wagon works are associated.

The remains of a once great woollen industry survive in the scarp-valleys behind Gloucester and Cheltenham, but numbers of the old mills have been taken over by decentralised modern industry —the making of furniture, plastics, and instruments —which is concentrated in and near Stroud.

Worcester, like Gloucester and Hereford (Chap. 13), is a county town. Like Hereford, it is the centre of a topographic basin and stands on the main river, but like Gloucester it has expanding engineering industries. Its wire-making, brass-founding, and iron-founding associate it with the West Midland Conurbation, but its glove-making is of local origin.

Leamington resembles Cheltenham in having become famous as a spa, but here again, metal manufacture is vigorously developed, taking one in five of the town's workers; domestic heating appliances and automobile parts are among the products.

Warwick is related to Leamington as Gloucester is to Cheltenham, but has been far outdistanced. With only 16,000 people, it has lost much of the regional significance which it once possessed as the home and headquarters of the powerful Earl called *King-maker*. Its bridge and castle are less well known than the bridge and memorial theatre lower down the Avon at Stratford (16,750) where prosperity, founded on the name of Shakespeare, is supported by a cattle-market and a famous brewery.

Rugby, rather oddly located on a flat-topped hill, has grown rapidly in the last hundred years. Alongside its converging railways have developed electrical engineering works, similar to—and in part branches of—those at Stafford. On the outskirts of Rugby and in the area to the southwest, Portland cement is manufactured from the alternating clayey limestones and shales of the Lower Lias.

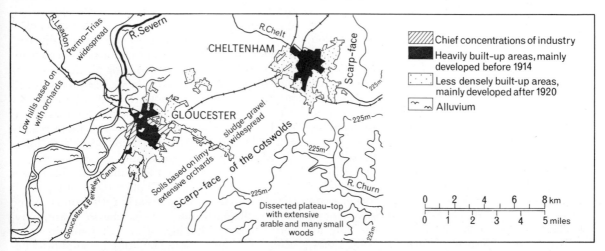

FIG. 22:5. Gloucester and Cheltenham, and their local setting: contours in metres

Chapter 23

Scarplands of the South Midlands

Area: about 10,500 km² (4,000 sq. mi.).
Population: about 2,500,000.
Largest towns: Luton (157,000).*
           Northampton (124,000).*
           Oxford (110,000).*
           Cambridge (100,250).*
           Swindon (100,000).*
           Bedford (63,250).
           Peterborough (62,000).
           Kettering (38,750).
           Corby (36,500).
           Wellingborough (30,000).
           Aylesbury (28,000).
           Banbury (21,000).
                        * 1969 estimate.

This region is largely in farmland, with about 85 per cent improved. Tillage is somewhat more extensive than grass.
Numbers of livestock: cattle, 575,000;
                       sheep, 1,425,000;
                       pigs, 305,000;
                       poultry, 5,745,000.

The grain of structure and relief in this region runs from southwest to northeast (Fig. 22:1). Until the present century the region was too distant, both from London and from the industrial districts of the Midland Triangle, for its towns to be stimulated into rapid growth, and even at the present time nearly all parts of it retain strong rural characteristics.

These scarplands possess no exposed coalfields, and if hidden seams are present they have still to be proved. The coasts are distant and not particularly accessible by the routes which have developed. In most parts of the region the open-field system of agriculture persisted for a long time—as long as anywhere in England—enclosure not being completed until the early 19th century, and compact villages and well-knit village communities remained typical. Secondary dispersion of settlement—recorded by isolated farms, many of them built in the mid-19th century—weakened but did not break the ties of village life. In the early years of the present century it was still usual for people to find wives or husbands either in their own village or in the next village; travel was slow, and carriers' carts were not replaced by motor-coaches until the 1920s. Small village shops and small market towns met the commercial needs of the region.

Rural Depopulation

The drift from the land began in the 19th century, but it was not until the 1930s that disintegration of village communities became really severe. At that time a great deal of ploughland was put to grass, in response to agricultural depression, when farmers decided to reduce costs and the demand for labour fell. Rural bus services increased contacts between town and countryside, making obvious the difference between rural and urban standards of living. The limited number of scholarships and free places in grammar schools diverted some of the most intelligent children from agriculture into work in the towns. For all these reasons the village populations declined. The largest towns profited the most from townward migration, for small towns tended to lose their cattle-markets as road transport became cheaper and more readily available, and also to lose their industries as factories closed during the Great Slump.

Except for council houses, villages in this region contain few dwellings built after 1900, and many of the cottages date from the early 17th century. Some of the villages display all the charm of antiquity, combining it with a high degree of domestic inconvenience. Council-house building began shortly before 1939, but dates mainly from 1945 or later. It represents an attempt to arrest the decay of village life, as do rural electrification—already well under way in 1939—and the post-war supply of piped water. It remains to be seen what the result of these attempts will be.

THE MAIN JURASSIC CUESTA

Southwestern Part

Although rural character and scarpland terrain give the region a certain homogeneity, internal contrasts are easily perceptible. They are associated with differences in altitude and texture of relief, which depend in turn upon geological structure and the history of dissection. The region can be subdivided into belts running from southwest to northeast, some of which change in character from one end to the other.

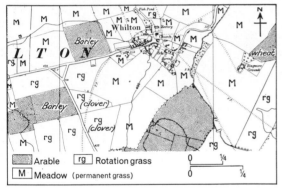

Arable   rg Rotation grass

M Meadow (permanent grass)

FIG. 23:1. Land-use for west Northamptonshire, on a drift-encumbered part of the Main Jurassic Cuesta: mixed farmland on soils developed mainly on boulder clay or glacial sand and gravel

The Cotswold Hills begin south of Bath and extend to the Vale of Moreton at the head of the Evenlode, penetrating the Borders of the West Country beyond a line from Gloucester to Swindon (Fig. 22:1). Northeast of this line, in the South Midlands, the Cotswold backslope is smooth, with broad and remarkably flat interfluves sloping gently to the southeast between the incised valleys draining to the Thames. Limestones of the Inferior and Great Oolite formations are thick and well-cemented in the Cotswolds, forming a steep and continuous scarp which, rising to 300 m., overlooks the lower valleys of the Severn and Avon. Between the North Cotswolds and the head of the Cherwell lie the hills of North Oxfordshire, which are rather more dissected than the Cotswolds. The whole belt of hills west of the Cherwell has been little affected

by glaciation, and carries very little glacial drift.

Before the industrialisation of the 18th and early 19th centuries, this division was noted for its sheep-grazing and its manufacture of woollens. Rich cloth-merchants have left mansions and ornate tombs as signs of their former prosperity. The woollen industry survives today only in the specialised manufacture of blankets at Witney, and in the production of serges in Stroud and its neighbours in the Frome valley.

The villages, large country houses, and small towns of the Cotswolds and North Oxfordshire are exceptionally beautiful, being very largely built of natural stone. Rich brown building-stone from the Middle Lias, which thickens and becomes the main scarp-former north of Banbury, has been much used in the Banbury district, where thatched roofs are common. Further south, towards Oxford, the Inferior and Great Oolite formations appear, extending broadly westwards in the Cotswold Hills. Their oolitic limestones, which are often yellowish in the quarry, become creamy on exposure to the air; they have been very widely employed, and some Cotswold villages are entirely stone-built. The local roofing material is the fissile oolite of Stonesfield, which, as long as the quarries continued to produce, could be worked in large slabs. In the Marlstone country, hedgerows are typical of the countryside and stone walls of the villages, but long stone walls enclose many fields in parts of the Cotswolds, where the limestone lies very close to the surface and has been taken from long shallow pits. The pattern of large rectangular fields typical of late and wholesale enclosure is diversified by numerous plantations, small woods, and belts of ornamental timber (Plate 64).

More powerfully than any other district of comparable size, this has attracted the 20th-century equivalent of the 18th-century and 19th-century country squire—significantly enough, it repeatedly provides illustrations for *Country Life*. Its isolated farmsteads are large and substantial and its fields well managed. Although grassland is more extensive than tillage, there is a great deal of plough-land, especially on the flat interfluves; wheat is the most extensive of the grain crops, although barley also does well and oats is widely grown for stock-feeding. Potatoes and fodder crops are also grown. In many fields the plough throws up fragments of weathered limestone, for the soils are mainly shallow, but their clay content is enough to make them retain some of the water which comes from an annual precipitation of more than 750 mm. Winter temperatures go too low, and the open

PLATE 64. The Cotswold backslope, with farmland—arable, rotation grass, and managed plantations—enclosing the incised Dikler Valley.

plateaus are too exposed, for this to become a district of fruit-growing and market-gardening, but autumn-sown and spring-sown field crops flourish. Both fodder crops and cash crops are much more widely grown nowadays than in the late pre-war years.

The numbers of sheep in the Cotswolds and North Oxfordshire are far lower than in the great days of grazing—past now for some centuries—and also lower than in the pre-war years. Considerable numbers are still kept, however, especially on the flood-plains and walls of the incised valleys. Cattle are numerous, and the totals both of beefstock and of dairy animals have risen since 1939.

Northeastern Part

Northeast of the Cherwell, between Banbury and Grantham, the main Jurassic cuesta forms a belt of rather low hills, rising above 200 m. in a few places and much dissected in the crestal area. Here in the Northamptonshire Uplands and the Leicestershire Wolds the limestones and sandstones are in general both thinner and weaker than those of the Cotswolds while the clays are thick. The feeders of the Ouse Nene, and Welland have excavated wide valleys between which rise irregular hills of varying height. Extensive remnants of the once-continuous mantle of Chalky boulder clay occur in this district, tending to mask the northwest-facing scarps. Large intact patches of boulder clay were at one time heavily wooded with deciduous trees; many small woods still testify to Rockingham Forest, on the broad low divide between the Welland and the Nene and to Whittlewood Forest, Salcey Forest, and Yardley Chase, which lay between the Nene and the Ouse.

Where the Jurassic limestones and sandstones come to the surface their soils are for the most part under the plough. Both on the solid clays and on the boulder clay there is much permanent grassland which is noted for its production of fat cattle—particularly Herefords (cf. Fig. 23:1). The influences of wartime and post-war years have however reduced the extent of permanent grass in favour of tillage, reversing the trend of the 1930s; numbers of beefstock tend to decline slightly, and those of dairy cattle—Ayrshires, Shorthorns, and Friesians—to rise. The increase in tillage is accounted for partly by fodder crops, but cash cropping has increased greatly in the northeast, on the margins of the great arable districts of eastern England, where mean annual rainfall declines towards 650 mm.

The soils on the limestones and sandstones are warm, while those on the clays are both cold and difficult to till, being sticky when wet and hard when dry. The localised influence of soil-type disappears in agricultural statistics for whole counties, but county figures can be used to give a generalised sample of farming. In Northamptonshire as a whole, barley is the most extensive grain—as it is throughout the division—and grain takes over three-quarters of the cropland. Other leading crops include roots, green crops, and pulses grown for forage, maincrop potatoes, sugar beet, and green vegetables. Flax-growing for fibre was encouraged during World War II and has continued subsequently.

This division is well timbered, not only with woods but also with hedgerow trees. Many of the hedges are regularly cut and laid to form stout barriers capable of containing bullocks, and the standard of hedgecutting is maintained by competitions organised by the hunts. As in other farming country which is prospering, however, the electric fence is becoming widely used, and the need for well-kept hedges is diminishing.

Stone and thatch are the traditional materials for building and roofing, one very widely-used type of stone being the iron-bearing Northampton Sand, which has a delicate apricot tint. Very little stone, however, has been used in new building for many years, and quarrying today is almost entirely confined to the extraction of iron ore (Plate 13). The craft of thatching is vanishing; even on the farms, the use of Dutch barns and hay-balers is making it unnecessary to thatch ricks.

THE STRIKE VALES

Southwestern Part

The Strike Vales of the South Midlands lie between the main Jurassic Cuesta and the scarp of the Chilterns. They are subdivided by a discontinuous axial belt of hills running from southwest to northeast, and, like the main Cuesta, can be separated into a southwestern part, which is unglaciated or which retains very little glacial drift, and a northeastern part, where boulder clay is thick and extensive. The boundary between the two parts coincides roughly with the watershed between the Thames and the Ouse (Fig. 22:1).

The Thames above Oxford flows in a broad strike vale—the Vale of Oxford—cut in Oxford Clay. The lowest ground consists of broad flood-plains, which are bordered by gently-undulating clayland drained by numerous small streams. Permanent pasture is extensive, and cattle-farming the dominant type of agriculture, although wartime and post-war pressures have increased tillage. Numbers of cattle of all types have increased in recent years. Villages, located on sites which are naturally well-drained, avoid the flood-plains, but many occur on the adjacent patches of terrace-gravel (Fig. 23:2).

The Vale of Oxford ends on the southeast against a belt of hills—the axial belt mentioned above—which crosses the Thames at the town of Oxford. The much-denuded hills are based on the Corallian beds—a formation of limestone strata composed largely of Jurassic corals. Their uneven landscape resembles that of the country around Banbury, for such flat hilltops as do occur are commonly under the plough. The coral limestones thin away to the northeast, where they are replaced by clays.

Between the Corallian hills and the scarp of the Chalk lies a strike vale, known as the Vale of White Horse on the west of the Thames, and as the Vale of Aylesbury on the east. Its geological basis is the Kimmeridge Clay, a thick formation of weak rock which resembles the Oxford Clay, and this belt of vale country resembles the Vale of Oxford. It carries many surface streams, but little of it is really flat, and its scenery is varied in detail. As in the Vale of Oxford, villages avoid badly-drained sites, and those which border the Thames are located on broad patches of terrace. A high proportion of the land is in permanent pasture, and dairying and poultry-farming are particularly well developed around Aylesbury.

Along the southern edge of the Vale of White Horse and the Vale of Aylesbury, Chalk scarps rise abruptly, with spring-line settlements at their feet. On the face of the Berkshire Downs the scarp is bold and continuous, and is equally well-defined in the southwestern Chilterns, where hanging beechwoods are common on its steep slope, but in the

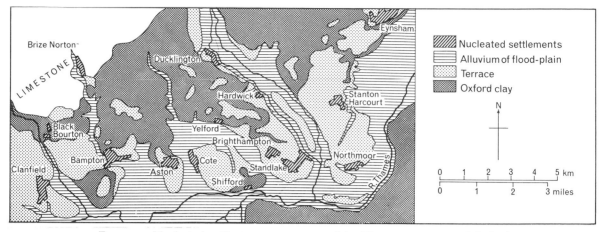

Fig. 23:2. Nucleated settlements on terraces of the Thames, upstream of Oxford

northeastern Chilterns the scarp rises in steps and is penetrated by deep gaps.

Northeastern Part

Beyond the Hitchin Gap—i.e., beyond the end of the Chilterns—the Chalk outcrop continues towards the northeast, but the main Jurassic cuesta swings round to the north in the Northamptonshire Ironstone Field, so that the belt of vale country widens towards the edge of the Fens. The main rivers are all sunk below the general level of the country, the ground is extensively covered by thick spreads of Chalky boulder clay, and relief is subdued. Most settlements are small. The villages include much lath-and-plaster work, as befits a district of clayland which was once heavily wooded, and a few mud walls can still be found. With the three exceptions of Bedford, Cambridge, and Peterborough, the towns of this division display little urban strength. Buckingham, a former county town at the western extremity, has but 4,500 inhabitants, and Huntingdon, a county town centrally placed in the east of the division, has but 8,750.

Livestock farming is far less common than might be expected of clay country. Many of the soils resemble those of East Anglia, for they are developed on identical parent material of Chalky boulder clay. Although they are somewhat heavier than the East Anglian soils, containing a higher clay fraction, they nevertheless provide a satisfactory basis for tillage.

The ratio of tillage to grassland varies. Where mean annual rainfall is above 650 mm., grass is the more extensive, but where precipitation slightly decreases, sunshine slightly increases, and slightly cooler winters reduce the growing season—i.e., towards the Fenland boundary—tillage takes the lead. It is more extensive than grassland in Bedfordshire, and more than twice as extensive at the borders of the Fens. The balance between climatic and economic influences is a delicate one, however. When farming is depressed and costs must be reduced, grassland increases; when farming prospers, tillage increases. The most marked increases of recent years have been in cash-crops, which represent an extension of the cash-cropping in solidly arable areas to the east. There are now very few sheep in this division; numbers of fat cattle are roughly stable, and dairy herds have risen in numbers.

Barley is the most extensive tillage crop in Bedfordshire, next followed by wheat. Oats, mixed corn, and fodder crops are restricted in extent in accordance with the limited numbers of cattle. Potatoes (early as well as maincrop) and sugar beet are grown throughout the division, the extent of sugar beet increasing, like that of barley, into the drier eastern parts.

Vegetables other than potatoes are more extensive than oats in Bedfordshire, which contains much market-garden land. Some of the market-gardens are located on the light, lime-poor, but loose and warm soils of the Lower Greensand,[1] which appears as a scarp-former south of Bedford and rises in a steep, well-wooded edge above the valley of the Ouse (Plates 4, 5). Market-gardens and fruit-farms stretch northeastwards from the Lower Greensand country towards the Fenland boundary, following a belt of generally light soils which repay heavy fertilisation; leading crops include brussels sprouts, parsnips, cabbages, and onions.

---

[1] At Leighton Buzzard, where the sand is particularly pure, it is worked for use in glass-making.

TOWNS AND INDUSTRIES

Luton, Bedford, and Oxford

At the census of 1931, Luton had fewer people than either Northampton or Oxford, and was little more populous than Cambridge. In thirty years its population increased by 100 per cent.[1] The rapid and continuing growth of Luton is largely the effect of the location there of the motor-manufacturing industry, and engineering and metal-manufacture take 22 per cent of the total employed. The next largest group of manufacturing workers is found in the garment industry, which employs large numbers of women, and takes about 10 per cent of the labour force. Among the old-established industries is brewing. The only geographical advantages for the motor industry in Luton were, at the outset, of the most general character—room for building alongside a main railway, freedom from the congestion of districts already industrialised, and the possibility of recruiting labour in the existing town. It is to be assumed that, before the industry was founded, the economic questions of costs (including the costs of transport) were examined. The industry has certainly succeeded, stimulating the town to vigorous growth and thereby increasing the fund of labour on which it can draw.

Luton is actually located in the Chilterns, high up towards the head of the Lea. It is however better regarded as belonging to the South Midlands than to the London Basin, not only because it is close to the Chiltern crest, but also because, as an industrial town, it has strong similarities to Bedford and Oxford. The central parts of these two county towns occupy terraces below which their rivers have cut, and both towns command crossings. Each provides shops and markets for a large rural area, and Oxford retains from the Middle Ages a very well-known fair. In addition to being an ancient university centre, however, Oxford (Fig. 23:3) is an industrial town, for the suburb of Cowley is one of the main single producers of motor-cars in the British Isles. Bedford also takes a share in the motor industry and produces agricultural machinery. Engineering, electrical production, and vehicle manufacture take 13 per cent of the people employed in Bedford, which has an equal fraction in distributive trades and 16 per cent in professional occupations; and they take also 13 per cent of those employed in Oxford. There is a contrast with the high degree of manufacturing orientation to the engineering and metal trades in Luton; nevertheless, mainly on

account of the motor industry, the populations of Oxford and Bedford increased by a third or more in thirty years.

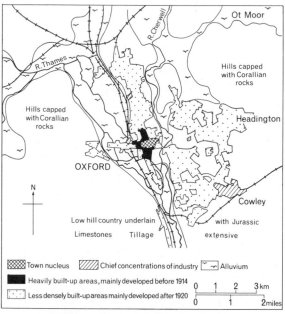

FIG. 23:3. Oxford and its local setting

Cambridge and Swindon

At the extremities of the region lie two towns with markedly different character and history—Cambridge and Swindon. Swindon is to a great extent a product of the railway. Its great workshops produce locomotives and rolling stock, and it is a junction for lines converging from the west. Cambridge is a town whose ancient university maintains a keen rivalry with Oxford's. Like Swindon, aided by light industry, it is growing fast, having added more than a third to its numbers since 1931; it has acquired industries mainly concerned with electrical goods, including radio and television sets and components. It stands on the Cam, acting as the urban focus for a rich agricultural hinterland, with a position on the boundary between the Fens and the Scarplands of the South Midlands which gives it particular advantage as a market centre.

Peterborough: The Brick-Making Industry

Peterborough occupies a position on the Nene like that of Cambridge on the Cam—namely, at the edge of the Fens. In its early days the main factor of growth was the cathedral, but a comparison with Ely shows that more than a cathedral is required

---

[1] 1931–1961; affected by change of boundaries.

PLATE 65. Brickworks near Bedford.

for continued expansion. Peterborough has bene-fited as a market from its location on a regional boundary. About 25 per cent of its workers are employed in engineering and metal manufacture, particularly in producing agricultural machinery for use on the highly-tilled surrounding farmland, and rolling stock for the main railway which passes through the town.

Peterborough is prominent in the brick-making industry, producing 15 million bricks a week. The raw material of brick-making is Oxford Clay, which is well suited to the economical semi-dry process of manufacture. Other large brickworks occur on the Oxford Clay belt near Bedford (Plate 65), where the output is roughly equal to that of Peterborough;

near Bletchley (4 million bricks a week); and at Calvert, near Aylesbury (5 million). The combined production of the various works amounts at least to one-third of the total output of bricks in the U.K. The works are located where railways cross the Oxford Clay belt, but large numbers of bricks are now distributed by road, the markets being in the London area and in the industrial Midlands. Among the brick-making centres named, Bletchley up to the mid-1960s was heavily dependent on the one industry, with a quarter of all its workers taken by the brick manufacturing industry, but has subsequently changed its industrial structure with the arrival of new concerns and additional population.

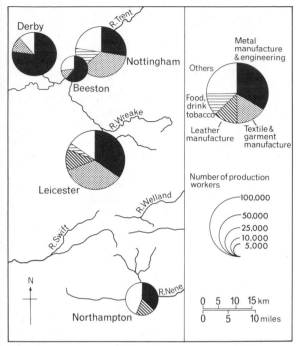

FIG. 23:4. Production workers in Northampton, Leicester, Nottingham, Beeston, and Derby, 1966

Northampton and the Leather Industry

Northampton grows steadily but rather slowly. It has probably suffered industrially from the lack of a trunk railway, which the town authorities rejected. The traditional leather-working long predates the railway age, and, when railways were being built, the Northamptonshire iron ores had still to be developed; thus Northampton's refusal of a main line can be partly understood. The town retains its markets of produce and stock, and has profited greatly as a shopping centre by the inter-war extension of rural bus services. It is well situated at the focus of converging routes along the inter-fluves and along the valleys; when castles had more than a decorative function, Northampton Castle guarded a crossing of the Nene, which below the town has swept out a wide meander-trough in weak clays.

The manufacture of leather, mainly in the foot-wear industry, with a minor supplement from clothing manufacture, remains a principal employer of labour in Northampton, the two classes taking about 15 per cent of all workers but tending to decrease their proportionate demand. The equally ancient brewing industry makes a smaller demand. Both brewing and leather-manufacture were originally dependent on local agriculture, which provided the barley and the hides and skins, while local oakwoods supplied bark for use in tanning. But barley is nowadays brought from far afield, and the boot and shoe industry supplies an international as well as a domestic market, obtaining its raw materials from abroad as well as from the home country. Numbers of smaller towns around Northampton are heavily dependent on boot and shoe manufacture; at Kettering one in every four workers is employed in the industry, and at Wellingborough one in five. Northampton, like Leicester, is surrounded by industrial satellites. Leicester, although with somewhat more leather-workers than Northampton, is a much larger town, and the footwear industry employs only about 7 per cent of its labour force (Fig. 23:4 and Chap. 22).

Something approaching 20 per cent of North-ampton's workers are employed in making electrical and engineering products, or vehicles and parts. This combined class of employment has out-paced the traditional leather-plus-clothing class. However, there is as yet nothing to compare with the prominence of the motor industry in Luton and Oxford, but engineering works in Northampton are expanding both in numbers and in size. Roller and other bearings are among the goods produced.

Iron-ore, Smelting, and Steel-making

The Middle Lias Marlstone was worked in the Banbury district, much of the product being taken by rail to South Wales, while the ore of the Northampton Sand—part of the Inferior Oolite formation—is extracted from the Northamptonshire Iron-stone Field to the northeast of Northampton (Chap. 8). The ore-beds are usually worked opencast, mainly where there is a thin overburden and the ore has not suffered much erosion. Huge mechanical diggers strip off the overburden; the ore is loosened by blasting, and other diggers load it into railborne hoppers. In some quarries the spoil remains in long curving ridges, some of which have been afforested; there is no prospect that the ridges can be made suitable for cultivation, but in other quarries the spoil has been spread evenly and put to tillage or grass (Plate 13).

Part of the Northampton Sand ore is smelted at the expanding town of Corby, and at Wellingborough. The economic reason for smelting on the orefield is the low grade of the ore, which is costly to transport. The same reason encouraged the development of smelting at Melton Mowbray, in Leicestershire, where Marlstone ore was used. Pig-iron is still produced for the West Midlands and South Wales, but the tendency is for local consumption to rise. Corby, increasing in importance as a centre of smelting, also has steelworks which include basic Bessemer converters. A rapidly-growing new town is being added to the older Corby, not without difficulties of retail marketing like those which trouble Oxford and Cowley.

Banbury, Abingdon, and Aylesbury

Abingdon (14,250) has acquired an outpost of the motor-works at Oxford. Banbury acquired an aluminium mill during the 1930s, the principal locating factors apparently being a position roughly midway between Birmingham and London, and the potential labour supply from depressed farmlands where arable had been extensively switched to permanent grass. During the 1960s, Banbury has also gained foodstuff processing, the manufacture of auto products, and metal manufactures. The principal entry of industry has been hitherto from the West Midlands, but overspill population from London contributes largely to the increase in the size of the town, which may reach a total of 70,000 inhabitants by 1981 (see bibliography: Scargill). The stock-markets of Banbury continue to operate, at an increasing level of turnover. Aylesbury, in the process of taking in an overspill of 10,500 people from the metropolis, has received light engineering industry, food manufacturing, and printing from the metropolitan area. Among the smaller centres of the region, Bicester, Witney, and Thame promise to be strongly affected by the out-movement of industry and people from the London region.

THE FUTURE OF THE REGION

During the 1960s, the South Midland Scarplands first began to experience heavy industrial and demographic pressure, in the form of large-scale immigration of manufacturing firms, workers, and families. For about a century before, the region had remained traversed by trunk railways and main roads, connecting the industrialised northwest and the West Midlands with the London metropolis; but its towns had remained generally modest and in many cases distinctly small in size, developing little in the way of new industry except for steel-making at Corby, engineering at Northampton, and auto production on the outskirts of Oxford. Rapid changes, some of which have been noticed, are now however under way: many more are in prospect. By the end of the century, the population of the region is expected to double, the increase being concentrated in Northamptonshire, Wellingborough, Corby, Daventry, Bedford, Peterborough, and the new city of Milton Keynes in Buckinghamshire.

Canals in the earlier 1800s, railways in the later 1800s and earlier 1900s, produced no great impact on the region. Motorways however promise to be another proposition altogether in the later 1900s (Fig. 23:5).

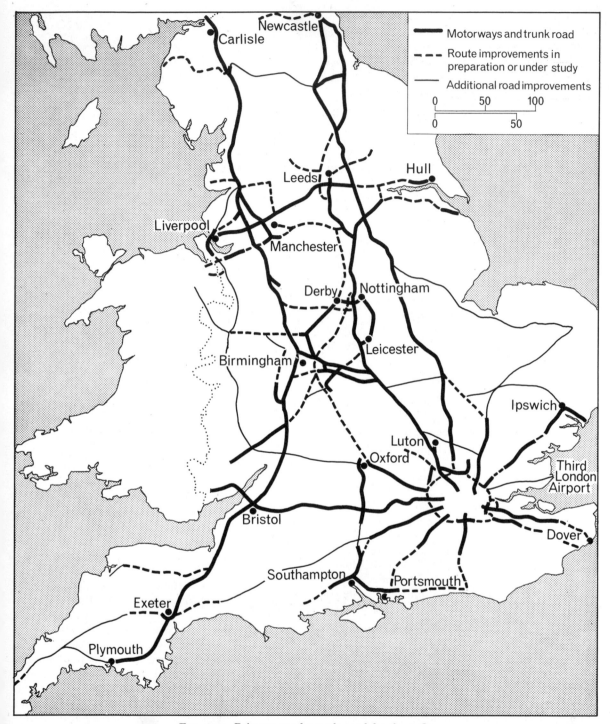

FIG. 23:5. Primary road net planned for the 1980s

Chapter 24

East Anglia and the Fenlands

EAST ANGLIA

Area: about 10,500 km² (4,000 sq. mi.).
Population: about 2,000,000.
Largest towns: Norwich (119,000).*
Ipswich (112,500).*
Colchester (65,000).
Harlow (53,500).
Yarmouth (50,750).*
Chelmsford (49,750).
Lowestoft (45,750).
Clacton (27,500).
Bury St. Edmunds (21,250).
                              * 1969 estimates
About 75 per cent of this region is in improved
farmland, with tillage about four times as extensive
as grassland.
Numbers of livestock: cattle, 335,000;
sheep, 160,000;
pigs, 885,000;
poultry, 14,850,000.

East Anglia consists largely of low plateau
country. It is dominantly rural and dominantly
arable, with less than half the population living in
towns, and more than half the total area under the
plough.

Regional boundaries

Along the edge of the Fens the land rises in a low,
dissected, but noticeable scarp based on Greensand.
The break of slope, separating the flat alluvial
ground to the west from the subdued sandy hills to
the east, fixes the regional boundary. Further south,
East Anglia merges into Midland England along
the belt of low Chalk hills which leads southwestwards past Newmarket. There is no physical feature
on which to locate the boundary between East
Anglia and the London Basin; a gradual transition

occurs from the one region to the other, but a
boundary can probably be drawn at the outer limit
of the transport services which are used by numerous commuters. In Fig. 13:1 it has been traced
between Chelmsford, which is included in East
Anglia, and Southend, which is allocated to the
London Basin. Thus East Anglia is made to com-
prise all but the westernmost part of Norfolk, the
whole of Suffolk, a small part of Cambridgeshire,
and about two-thirds of Essex.

Regional Unity

The physical unity of this region is due to the
wide spread of glacial drift. A very broad strip,
amounting to about half the total area, is mantled
with chalky boulder clay (Fig. 24:1), the product of
successive advances and meltings of Pleistocene ice-
sheets. It is likely that the original surfaces of the
sheets of boulder clay were irregular in detail, but
there has been time since the last deglaciation for
running water to model the terrain into a continuous system of gentle slopes. Most of the streams
drain eastwards to the North Sea—the Bure,
Wensum, Waveney, Orwell, Stour, Colne, and
Chelmer—but the Little Ouse takes the drainage of
the sandy Breckland westwards into the Fens. The
interfluves are low and the valleys shallow, for the
land rises generally to little more than 100 m.

Where the boulder clay has been eroded away, in
the northeast and southeast, the divides between
the valleys are capped by glacial sand and gravel
which, in the centre of the region, still lie hidden
beneath the boulder clay. Where the sand and
gravel has also gone, rocks of Pliocene and Pleistocene age are revealed. These, the Crags, are for the
most part shelly limestones.

The regional unity of East Anglia has roots in
history as well as in physique. A large part of it
formed, during part of the Dark Ages, the kingdom

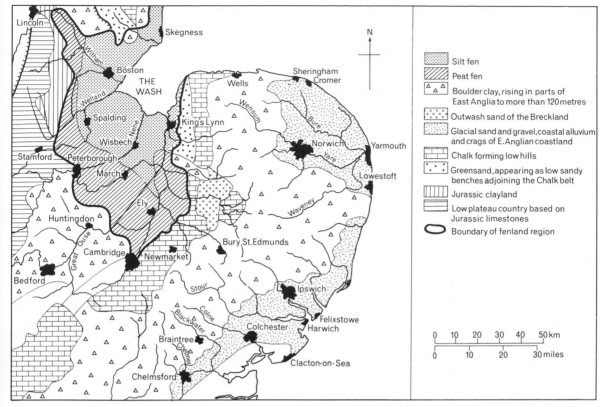

FIG. 24:1. East Anglia and the Fenlands: physique and main settlements. The Fenland boundary is marked by a heavy line

from which the regional name is taken. The contrast between this and adjacent regions was recognised in practice; before the damp forests of the clay lowlands were cleared, East Anglia was hemmed in by thick, tangled wood on the west and south, and fringed by the undrained Fens on the northwest. Within these limits lay a reasonably homogenous piece of country, where gentle slopes led down into shallow valleys, and where marshes were uncommon except along the coast; the coastal marshes, fringing the very inlets which gave the Saxon and Scandinavian settlers access to the land, did not obstruct penetration (cf. Fig. 24:2, Plate 66).

Soils and Climate

Being rich in fragments of Chalk, the boulder clay tends to give rise to a lime-rich soil. Although part of the Chalk content has been leached out during the development of soil on the surface, much is still retained at shallow depth, well within the reach of the roots of plants. In the northeast and the southeast of the region, the pattern of soils is broken and complex; generally speaking, the sands and gravels provide rather light but warm soils,

while the soils developed on the Crags are light and rich in lime.

Precipitation is low for Britain—about 625 mm. a year. The slight approach to a continental régime in East Anglia (Chap. 3) brings the total for the summer half-year up to, or even above, that for the winter half. The summer fall is beneficial in a region where evaporation is quite powerful in the warmer months, when the water need of the soil tends to exceed the supply. Convectional showers in the early summer aid the growing crops; if they come late, when the ears are heavy and the straw is drying out, they are capable of lodging the grain, but the risk is far less than in the wheatlands of Canada. Mean July temperatures rise above 15 °C. The January mean falls below 3°, for this is the most extreme part of the British Isles, with annual ranges generally above 11°. The frost-free period, however, is well over 5 months in length, and rises to 7 months along the coast; and in any case winter frosts are an advantage, for they break up the soil and help to prepare it either for ploughing or for rolling. The low rainfall is associated with frequent and prolonged sunshine. The eastern fringe of coast

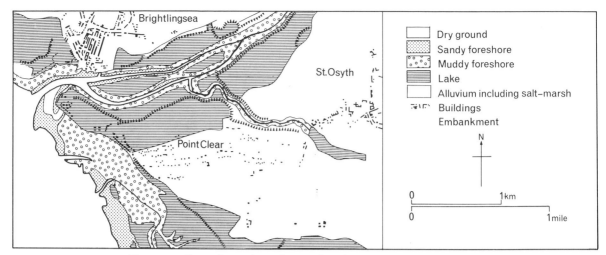

FIG. 24:2. Coastal terrain and coastal settlement: sample from Essex

PLATE 66. Coastal marshes of the Blackwater Estuary, Essex. Reclaimed land, in pasture, lies behind a low sea-wall.

is especially sunny in summer, and the whole region averages more than 4 hours of bright sunshine a day throughout the year.

Agriculture

Tillage is extensive, both the low plateau and its eastern borders being very widely under the plough. The general maps (Figs. 5:3, 5:5–5:8) indicate that in much of the region more than three-quarters of the countryside is in improved farmland. More than half is in tillage crops, which are more than three times as extensive as improved grass-land. Next to the Fenland, indeed, this is the most highly tilled region in the British Isles. Tillage in all but the extreme south of the region was strong enough to resist that conversion to grass which, in the inter-war period, seriously reduced the extent of cropland in Britain, and remained so markedly dominant that there has been little scope for its expansion in wartime or in post-war years.

Internal and marginal contrasts in land use are in consequence all the more remarkable, especially since some of them are very sharp. For instance, the valley-bottoms of the Broadland district in the Bure valley are very largely in permanent pasture, which occupies the flat alluvium and ends abruptly against the tillage of the low divides. Drainage of the flood-plains of Norfolk and Suffolk is hampered by the effects of longshore drift, which has extended bars across the drowned inlets and has bent some river-mouths southwards, lengthening the stream-courses and reducing the gradient. Flood-plains also run inland from the still open estuaries of the Essex coast, and here too are commonly under permanent grass. It is on the flood-plains that cattle are chiefly pastured. Sheep are also kept on the flood-plains in the summer, when the water-table is low, but are frequently folded on arable land at other times.

The patchy distribution of sandy soils in the northeast and southeast of the region is underlined by the alternation between highly intensive cultivation and low-grade grass. In the southwest the Chalk rises to the surface, but the extensive permanent grassland of the Newmarket district is very largely fictitious. Tillage, especially for cash crops, is now the leading interest of many farms around Newmarket, where Scots pine planted in numerous hedges and belts gives the countryside an oddly alien appearance. The lime-poor soils of the Breck-land, further north, carry 12,500 ha. of the Forestry Commission's conifers (Plate 2). On the margins of the Breckland appear patches of the native birch, amid which are specialised farms of various kinds, including duck-farms. Northward again, the soils of the Lower Greensand belt are partly under cultivation, but patchy woodland and heath are quite extensive.

Barley and wheat are the most extensive tillage crops of Norfolk and Suffolk. About half the total cropland is under barley, and about another fifth is wheat. These two crops combined take some two-fifths of the area of the two counties. Potatoes, forage crops, and sugar beet are also common. Some districts have developed specialised market-gardening, particularly in the margins of the region where soils are warm and crops mature early. Vegetables, small fruit, and orchard fruit are grown for sale, especially near the edges of the Fenland, on the loams of North Norfolk, and in the south and southeast of the region where highly intensive cultivation is encouraged by the nearness of London. Some farms in the south concentrate on producing flower seeds.

Poultry are numerous throughout the region, and poultry-farmers raise table birds in addition to addition to keeping laying stock, Norfolk turkeys having a high reputation in the Christmas market. East Anglia, however, displays no such concentration of poultry-farming as is to be found on the Lancs.–Cheshire Plain (Fig. 5:23). Pigs are very numerous, but the number of cattle is low, and that of sheep very low indeed.

Agricultural Change

The present scarcity of sheep represents a very great change from the farming of the Middle Ages, when East Anglia was famous first for its raw wool and later for its woollen manufacture. When the great agricultural improvements took place in the 18th century, experimenters in East Anglia were well to the fore. They succeeded brilliantly in producing a beneficial scheme of crop-rotation—the Norfolk four-course rotation of seeds, wheat, roots, barley. The folding of sheep on arable land ensured that the soil would be well dunged and trodden. But the folding of sheep has very little significance to-day, since there are so few sheep in the region, and the four-course rotation is practised on scarcely any farms.

The four-course rotation was common right up to the early 1920s, when it lost favour during a time of agricultural depression. With this rotation, only half the land is under cash crops. Sugar beet was already being grown in East Anglia before World War I; the seeds (hay) course has been largely replaced by vegetables, including peas; the powerful demand for barley has led to the introduction of a second barley course at some point, and sugar beet is often followed by winter wheat on the best soils. Sugar beet itself has displaced the turnips and swedes which were formerly grown as food for sheep, and in terms of gross yield is the leading crop of Norfolk. During the last twenty or thirty years East Anglian farms have become more highly arable than ever, the large grain-growing farms changing faster and more markedly than smaller farms. The area of barley has doubled in twenty years; the per-area yield of barley, sugar beet and oats has increased by a quarter or more, and the yields of potatoes and wheat by a third. Grassland has been driven into the valley-bottoms, some of which have been improved by drainage works and by reseeding with grasses and clovers produced at the grassland research station at Aberystwyth. Consequently, more stock per area can now be kept than was formerly possible. Red Poll beefstock are less common than dairy herds of Friesians and Ayrshires, but dairying in East Anglia has not advanced so rapidly as that of some other regions —always excepting the southern districts close to London.

The modern arable farming of East Anglia is as much a response to demand as it is to environment. Given the demand for grain, East Anglia is the region best suited to barley-growing, and one of the best suited to wheat. British wheat grown for sale, however, is generally unsuitable for the making of bread-flour, unless it is blended. It yields excellent soft flour for biscuit-making, but bread made from it alone would not sell in the peace-time market, where the demand for white bread made chiefly from hard-wheat flour is very strong. The traditional esteem of wheat-growing is firmly rooted in human history, and its emotional associations are powerful; but bread is no longer a staple food in Great Britain, any more than potatoes are in Ireland. Barley is the great East Anglian crop. Except in the south of the region it takes more land than the other grains combined, and even in the south it is the most extensive grain. The principal buyers of barley are the large breweries. Both barley and wheat are grown mainly for sale off the farm, while oats is meant for the livestock kept in the region.

East Anglia's high success with arable farming has been achieved, despite the fact that many of its soils are no more than moderately fertile in the natural state. Farming in this region has been deliberately designed, ever since the 18th century, to keep the land in good heart; and this it has done, and done well, in addition to responding readily to changing circumstance (Plate 67). Increases of yields, improvements in the scheme of cropping, and more effective selection of strains, are recorded

PLATE 67. Arable farmland in Norfolk—low rolling countryside, fields of cut barley, and tower of an abandoned church.

on farms of all kinds—on fruit- and vegetable-farms no less than on those producing grains, sugar beet, and potatoes.

Settlement

Apart from the increase in arable, and the changes in type of crop, the texture of the essentially rural scene of East Anglia is slow to alter. The region remains one of nucleated villages, isolated farmsteads, and small market towns. At one time the villages were more numerous than they are to-day, for parts of East Anglia suffered very severely from the depopulation which made room for sheep-farms (Fig. 4:7); from place to place a ruined church tower rises amid the ploughland, marking the former site of a vanished village. In the present-day villages can be seen attractive examples of half-timber, lath-and-plaster, and brick building; Finchingfield in Essex is commonly reputed to be one of the finest villages of all, and has attracted a number of artists, but it is difficult to judge the claim that this is the most beautiful village in England. The rural character of the regional land-scape is enhanced by the rather open spacing of main roads and the irregular courses of minor roads; East Anglia stands largely apart from the skein of busy routes which connects London to the industrial North, and some of its railways became butts for humour.

Most of the small towns have little tendency to grow, partly because they are small, but also partly because they are no longer required for stock-marketing. The buying and selling of sheep has almost disappeared with the animals themselves, while cattle-marketing has, in the usual way, become concentrated in a few large centres. The former network of market centres, each serving a limited area, is now too fine. Things are likely to change to some extent, however, as overspill from the metropolis affects the region. New town development will be concentrated in Peterborough (on the regional boundary) and in Ipswich, each of which is expected to achieve a population of about a quarter-million; but some smaller East Anglian towns will be affected by expansion. On the other hand, no major industrial development or motorway system is at present envisaged.

Norwich

The largest town in the region is Norwich, the regional capital (Fig. 24:3). Standing on the Wensum a little way above its confluence with the Yare, this town acts as the principal shopping centre of an area with 250,000 inhabitants (Plate 68). Its medieval history was distinguished; a cathedral was founded shortly after the Conquest, a Norman castle was also built, and the medieval trade fair was famous throughout the country. The huge and numerous flocks of sheep grazed in East Anglia enabled Norwich to be the greatest weaving town in Britain from the early 14th to the late 18th centuries, and it has been estimated that in the early 18th century there were more than 100,000 spinners and weavers in Norfolk and North Suffolk. Weaving survives in Norwich today only in the form of specialised silk-working, the manufacture of wool having been lost to the West Riding during the 19th century. At the same time that woollen manufacture was lost, the manufacture of footwear was established, and thirty footwear factories in Norwich now employ 10,000 people. The great expansion of this industry occurred after World War I. To the mustard-milling started early in the 19th century has been added the production of flour and

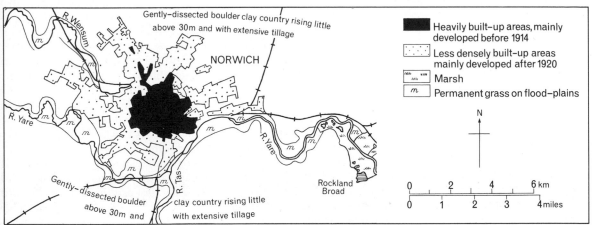

FIG. 24:3. Norwich and its local setting

PLATE 68. Stall-market and medieval buildings, Norwich.

starch. Agricultural and structural engineering have developed from local ironmongery and from the employment of out-of-work weavers in the making of wire netting. Chemical manufacture is a recent development, printing and the making of foodstuffs and confectionery are older-established. Norwich retains its status as a centre of cattle-marketing, and has a large banking and insurance business.

Colchester, Ipswich, and Chelmsford

Colchester commands a crossing of the Colne, inland of a muddy estuary which is noted for its oysters. The place was a major British centre under Cunobelinus, one of the few large pre-Roman settlements built on low ground, and became a colony for retired Roman veterans. The Normans built a castle to defend the town, which at that time had not spread beyond the patch of terrace gravel where the core of Colchester still lies. Craft drawing 3 m. navigate the Colne to Colchester, which formerly had a noticeable port trade. There is no

sizeable town within at least 25 km which can compete with Colchester as an urban centre, and its markets handle large quantities of cattle, eggs, poultry, and market-garden produce.

Colchester is too small for its industries to range widely, and some of them consequently appear distinctive. The same could be said of many moderate-sized towns, numbers of which are engaged in manufacturing of some unusual kind. This matter needs to be seen in proper perspective, however; an unusual but long-established industry, such as the making of mustard at Norwich, is likely to be accepted without question simply because it is well known, whereas the production of photographic equipment at Colchester is less familiar merely because it has developed more recently. Other industrial activities, also without an obvious geographical basis, are the manufacture of diesel engines and electric motors, and the printing of books and periodicals.

Ipswich stands at the estuary-head of the Orwell, Chelmsford on the diminutive Chelmer is some way inland. Both have a general resemblance to Colchester in their location on the route between London and Norwich, in their functions as urban centres for their surroundings, and in their industrial structure. They are concerned in the processing of the agricultural produce of their hinterlands, in the engineering which is common to very many towns, and in some distinctive kind of production. Ipswich, with access to tidewater, is a minor port, produces farm machinery, and processes sugar beet. Chelmsford's large cattle-market handles many dairy animals; its industries include flour-milling, brewing, and malting, the making of electrical equipment of various kinds, and the production of soft drinks.

Other Inland Towns

Of the East Anglian towns which lie well inland, Bury St. Edmunds is the third largest. It occupies a situation in West Suffolk comparable to that of Norwich in Norfolk, but is much the smaller. Once the capital of the kingdom of East Anglia, it is now a small administrative, shopping, and market centre compactly built alongside the few remains of its former huge abbey. The second largest inland town is Harlow, one of the new towns built to drain off people from London. Braintree (20,500), 18 km north-northeast of Chelmsford, deserves special mention for its steel furnaces which are most unexpected in the East Anglian countryside. The locating factor is the successful conversion of 18th-century ironmongery to 20th-century manufacture of metal windows. The ancient textile industry of East Anglia has been succeeded at Braintree by the working of synthetic fibres.

Lowestoft, Yarmouth, and the Herring Fishery

Lowestoft and Yarmouth, located on the sandy east coast of the region, are both resorts, Yarmouth receiving half a million visitors a year. Other and smaller resorts dotted along the coast from Hunstanton to Felixstowe share the seasonal trade, which depends on the frequency of summer sun rather than on sandy beaches—certain flourishing resorts on both sides of the Thames estuary show that sand is not an indispensable asset. A specialised form of the resort trade appears in the sailing and cruising of the Broadland.

Yarmouth and Lowestoft have long histories as fishing ports, connected chiefly with the fishery of the North Sea, where herrings were traditionally caught mainly by drifters. The shoals appeared off the Shetlands and Orkneys in early spring, with successive shoals of different kinds of herring being fished off the Scottish and English coasts during the summer, and with the season reaching its climax off the East Anglian coast in autumn. In 1951, however, the fish failed to appear in the numbers forecast. Subsequent catches continued to run low, 1959 being a particularly bad year at the time. Whether the shortage resulted from a change in natural conditions, or from the increased take made possible by echo-sounders, it has persisted and increased in severity. By the end of the 1960s, the herring landings at Yarmouth and Lowestoft were down to about 3 per cent of the level recorded in 1950. There has accordingly been a marked reduction in the drifter fleets based on East Anglia.

Lowestoft has shipbuilding yards which have been extended in recent years, and canning factories supplied by East Anglian orchards and market-gardens.

Harwich and Clacton

Harwich and Clacton in their present form are the products of modern transport. Harwich, on a promontory at the seaward end of the Stour estuary, has a long-standing connection with the Continental mainland, having been active in the French trade in times of peace and in naval matters in times of war. Its packet services began in the 17th century; today, with an 8 m. anchorage, it is the English terminus of the train-ferry to Zeebrugge, of passenger lines to The Hook, Esbjerg, and Zeebrugge, and of cargo lines to Rotterdam. It makes clothing (especially naval uniforms) and light engineering products, including caravans. Clacton, on the open coast, is almost entirely dependent on its resort trade, and in consequence upon prosperity-levels.

THE FENLANDS

Area: about 4,500 km² (1,750 sq. mi.).
Population: about 475,000.
Largest towns: King's Lynn (27,500).
            Boston (25,000).
            Wisbech (17,500).
            Spalding (14,750).
            March (13,250).
            Ely (9,750).
Much larger towns—Peterborough and Cambridge—stand on the regional boundary.

About 90 per cent of this region is in improved

farmland, with tillage four times as extensive as grassland.

Numbers of livestock: cattle, 65,000;
      sheep, 55,000;
      pigs, 220,000;
      poultry, 2,800,000.

The Fenlands constitute the most distinctive region in the whole of the British Isles, if only because they have been most deliberately and most profoundly transformed by man. The region contains the largest expanses of continuous flat land to be found anywhere in the British Isles, the most continuous tillage, the richest agricultural soils, and the most remarkable development of rectangular patterns in the texture of its landscape.

Except in its very high proportion of cropland, in its climate, and in its generally rural character, the Fenland region contrasts very strongly indeed with the adjoining region of East Anglia. The differences can be traced to, or associated with, differences of physique, for, whereas the central districts of East Anglia are underlain by broad spreads of boulder clay, the Fenlands consist principally of reclaimed swamp (Fig. 24:1).

Origin and Reclamation of the Fens

Along the shallow and muddy shores of the Wash lies a wide strip of silt, much of it deposited by the sea. The fine-grained sediment was very wet in its original state, and had a low angle of rest, so that its slopes today are extremely gentle. The silt fen is too wide to be properly described as a beach bar, but its deposits nevertheless served to shut off a great lagoon from the rising sea of post-glacial times. More silt was laid down alongside the channels of the Witham, Welland, Nene, and Ouse, which maintained courses across the shallow basin to the shore. Behind the widening strip of coastal silt, and between the mud-fringed rivers, reed-swamp flourished in lime-rich waters, its débris accumulating thickly as mild peat, forming peat fen on the inland side of the silt fen. The permanently-flooded area became subdivided in the course of time, and the individual shallow but originally extensive meres were reduced in size. Settlement pushed inwards from the silt fen and from the landward margins, but for many centuries it was confined, in the peat fen, almost entirely to the low islands of gravel and boulder clays which projected through the swamps.

Piecemeal drainage of the Fenland and reclamation of salt-marsh along the borders of the Wash began at least as early as Roman times. The start made on Ely Cathedral in 1083 shows that the Fenlands had no little economic importance in early Norman days, and numbers of Fenland place-names date from the Dark Ages or from the early Middle Ages. Among the chief products of the undrained fens were fish and wildfowl, which for a long time were commercially important; trade in this produce was to a great extent in the hands of the monasteries up to the time of the dissolution, and monastic control over the drainage-system was at one time widespread. It was not until the first half of the 17th century, however, that a well-organised project of artificial drainage was carried out, when the Bedford Level was made available for improvement by the Dutch engineer Vermuyden. More works followed, particularly under the 18th-century improvers, and the last considerable mere (at Whittlesea) was drained more than a hundred years ago. Wicken Fen, near Cambridge, is preserved as a nature reserve.

Very little remains in the peat fen of the natural courses of the Fenland rivers, which have been diverted, regularised, and duplicated. The general problems of drainage are two—that of controlling the water-table for the benefit of agriculture, and that of preventing floods. The second is the more difficult; as long as it can be solved, the first is simple enough.

As soon as the meres were drained and the soil-water table was lowered far enough for cultivation to begin, the fen peat began to shrink. If the peat was well dried out, it became liable to wind erosion, which still occurs in some windy springs before the crops have had time to bind the soil. In places the land-surface has sunk by ten feet or more, but the rivers remained at the old levels in their silt-lined channels, and the danger of widespread floods from burst banks or from overspilling floodwater greatly increased as the peat shrank or blew away. Similarly, the cost of pumping from farm drains into the trunk channels also rose. In some parts of the Fenland, the rivers and man-made watercourses are highly embanked; their water-level at all but the lowest stages is well above the general level of the surrounding countryside, roads run along the outer foot of an embankment, and cropland occupies the lowest level of all (Plate 69).

Limits of embanking and on the cutting of large drains are set by cost and by the calculation of risk. It is simply impracticable to safeguard against great but very infrequent floods—for instance, the floods which can be expected on an average of once in a thousand years. Floods with a far lower frequency than this can be very troublesome, especially since

PLATE 69. Artificial river in the Fenland; view from embankment across pasture, to chimneys of brickworks near Peterborough.

many embankments are already as high as they can be made: added weight in some places would merely make them liable to rotational slipping, such as occurs on the sides of railway cuttings. Dredging of channels, regulation of drainage, and construction and maintenance of drainage works generally are in the hands of River Boards (formerly Catchment Boards) who are also responsible for the operation of sluices at the outfalls to the sea. Pumping is carried out by power-driven machines.

The Landscape-pattern

Straight lines dominate the map of the peat fen. Straightened rivers, artificial cuts, roads, and the field boundaries formed by minor drains, all combine in a system of elongated rectangles (Fig. 24:4). Nucleated settlements are rare. Where they occur, they are typically compressed into long lines of houses, by a watercourse on one side and peat fen on the other—as at Upwell, Outwell, and The Deepings. From place to place a small group of houses clusters about a bridge, but the commonest unit of settlement in the peat fen is the isolated farmstead standing back from the through road. The pale yellow brick of the farmhouses is partly hidden by the trees planted to give some shelter

from otherwise unobstructed winds, and Dutch barns are usually walled-in with corrugated iron. On many farms, Nissen huts sold as war surplus in the late 1940s are used as barns.

The character of the scenery changes immediately the peat fen is left for one of the so-called fen islands. Some tendency to nucleation of settlement is to be noted on many of these, but the most striking difference from the peat fen is the appearance of sloping ground, dry permanent pasture in some of the small fields, and hedgerow timber. The fen-girt hills look like scraps of the English Midlands set down in Holland. Similar but more general differences separate the peat fen from the silt fen, with its most irregular pattern of minor roads, its belt of nucleated villages running from King's Lynn to Boston, and reddish clayey soils developed on the silt which contrast with the deep, black, rather friable soils of the peat fen.

Agriculture

The climate of the Fenlands closely resembles that of East Anglia, being only a little drier and a little less extreme. It would suit barley as well as the East Anglian climate does, but wheat is the great grain crop in the Fenlands. Barley produced in this

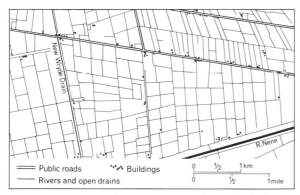

FIG. 24:4. Pattern of settlement, roads, and drains on part of the peat Fen

region often falls below malting standard, and wheat takes half or more of the area given to grain, which covers some two-fifths of all farmland; potatoes, vegetables, and sugar beet are next in order of extent.

Cash-cropping is to be expected in a region which has borne the high costs of reclamation and must still pay heavily for the operations of day-to-day drainage. Livestock, with the exception of poultry, are few in number, and consist chiefly of cattle which are grazed on the permanent pasture of the worst-drained fen or on the low hills. Within the limits of cash-cropping there is much specialisation, which in a rough kind of way amounts to a difference between the peat fen on the one hand, and the silt fen and the fen-islands on the other. Grain, potatoes, and sugar beet are characteristic of the peat fen. Fruit-farming and market-gardening are concentrated on the silts, where some of the soils can be worked into an excellent tilth, and where sloping land provides the cold-air drainage necessary for orchards. The general maps (Figs. 5:5–5:19) record unrivalled concentrations of potato- and vegetable-growing in the Fenlands, a production of small fruit which is second only to that of north Kent, and a minor concentration of orchards. Wisbech is the centre of a compact block of fruit-farms where the most extensive crops are strawberries and gooseberries; a list of all small

fruit and other market-garden produce grown here would, however, be very long indeed. Fruit- and vegetable-farms are also numerous around King's Lynn, while the Spalding district is noted for bulbs, flowers, peas, and beans. Potatoes are as common on the silt fen as on the peat fen, their high yields and ready sales in most years enabling the growers to bear the damage done by eelworm in some districts. The leading area for first early potatoes lies in the coastal strip near Boston, where the tubers ripen a week before those in other parts of the region.

Towns and Town Sites

Urban development in the Fenland is very limited indeed. The towns already named as centres of specialised farming districts are closely dependent on the agriculture of their surroundings. They possess shops, markets, cinemas, and banks; they sell, maintain and repair agricultural machinery; and they offer some industrial employment in canning plants and sugar-beet factories. It is significant that the two largest stand on navigable water in the seaward projections of the region. King's Lynn (Plate 18), once the greatest port of England, is now reduced to a limited coasting trade in grain and sugar, but its fine guildhall and its two market-places testify to the bustling activity of former days, while 18th-century buildings record its last days of wide-reaching importance. Boston takes a small share in the North Sea fishery, and has industries of brewing, malting, and canning. After prolonged stagnation, the Fenland towns are growing anew, recording the following increases in 1951–61: Boston, 18 per cent; Spalding, 20 per cent; March, 14 per cent; Wisbech, 13 per cent; and King's Lynn, 21 per cent.

All these towns occupy sites which, in their natural state, were better-drained than the bulk of the fen. If towns were to develop at all, it was certain that advantage would be taken of rising ground—however slightly rising—and of outcrops of gravel. Only in such places was there ground dry and firm enough for building, and room for a settlement larger than a village to develop.

Chapter 25

Southwest England

Area: about 10,500 km² (4,000 sq. mi.).
Population: about 1,150,000.
Largest towns: Plymouth (250,000).*
              Torbay (100,000).*
              Exeter (93,000).*
              Camborne ⎱ (36,000 together).
              Redruth ⎰
              Paignton (30,250).
              St. Austell (25,000).
              Penzance (19,500).
                       * 1969 estimates.

About 70 per cent of this region is in improved farmland, with grass three times as extensive as tillage.

Numbers of livestock: cattle, 920,000.
                    sheep, 1,855,000;
                    pigs, 425,000;
                    poultry, 5,850,000.

Southwest England contains an upland block of Primary rocks, which, exceptionally in the British Isles, escaped glaciation. Erosional platforms are broadly developed across the whole rigid massif west of the Exe, and in places are largely intact. Rivers are deeply incised into the lower platforms, which fall sharply to the sea in a cliffed shoreline indented by drowned inlets. Agriculture and tourism, the mainstays of the regional economy, are favoured by a climate which at low levels is remarkably mild in winter and sunny in summer. About half the people of the region live in towns, but most of the towns are small; rural settlement is typified by hamlets and isolated farms rather than by compact villages. Regional distinctiveness is as highly developed as in any region of the British Isles, and it can be suspected that the unmeasured quality of regional consciousness is also strong.

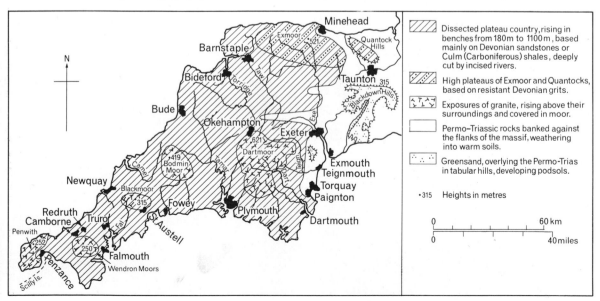

Fig. 25:1. Southwest England: physique and main settlements

Physique

The Carboniferous, Devonian, and older rocks of Southwest England were incorporated in the belt of Altaid folding (Chap. 2). The existing peninsula is broadly synclinal in structure, with Devonian rocks exposed in the north and south, and Carboniferous rocks in the centre. The northern flank of the syncline, represented by Exmoor and the Quantocks, is formed by resistant sandstones and flags which reach heights of 420 to 480 m. The downbent central part is occupied by the shaly Culm Measures, of Carboniferous age. Devonian rocks reappear on the southern flank as the sandstones and limestones of south Devon, extending westwards into Cornwall, which belongs entirely to the southern limb of the fold. The structural pattern is somewhat obscured by the trend of shorelines cutting diagonally across the lines of folding, and is complicated by the six granitic masses of Dartmoor, Bodmin Moor, Hensbarrow, Carn Menellis, Land's End, and the Scilly Islands (Fig. 25:1). The granitic outcrops stand higher than their surroundings, but their altitude decreases westwards, so that whereas Dartmoor rises to 615 m. on High Willhays, the Scillies merely project above sea-level in low, ragged islands (cf. Plates 70, 71).

PLATE 70. Haytor, one of the granite tors of Dartmoor.

PLATE 71. China-clay workings, Cornwall. The generally subdued terrain belongs to erosional platforms.

Although the upland block has been severely de-nuded in places, it clearly forms a single massif, probably being fault-bounded and probably also having been subject to faulting during Tertiary times. On the eastern flank the older rocks are de-pressed, and Permo-Triassic sediments lap on to the flanks of the massif. The sandstones, marls, and pebble beds of the Permo-Trias are in general much weaker than the rocks of the massif, and have been severely eroded, mainly by feeders of the Exe. The regional boundary, running through the wide vales which border Exmoor and stretch through the Exe basin to the Channel coast, includes the plateau country of West Somerset in Southwest England, but excludes the broken hills of easternmost Devon.

The simple erosional history of the massif has produced landforms as significant to the farming community as they are obvious to the eye. Denuda-tion is thought to have been controlled by inter-mittent falls in the relative level of land and sea, broad erosional platforms being cut across the strong rocks of the massif whenever that level re-mained stable for a long period. The platforms, whether cut by waves on the shore or reduced by rain and rivers, extend through the whole range of height from the loftiest plateaus to the tops of the cliffs, so that most of the land in the region is gently-sloping and exposed. All the rivers have been strongly rejuvenated in their lower reaches, flowing in narrow, steep-sided young valleys cut in slowly-weathering resistant rocks. The deeply-dissected coastland obstructs travel between east and west, and roads keep to the divides wherever possible. In the upper reaches, which have so far escaped most rejuvenation, the rivers occupy wide, shallow valleys merging gently into the broad plateaus.

Origins of the drainage-system are still in part obscure. The Exe, obviously superimposed across

PLATE 72. A Devon ria-drowned mouth of the incised Dart, at Dartmouth.

geological structures and geological outcrops, appears to represent original consequent drainage to the south, as also do the Dart, the Fowey, and the Falmouth ria. The upper courses of the Camel and Torridge may have been captured from south-flowing rivers, but their lower courses and the whole trunk of the Taw are superimposed, and the three systems are not due simply to the headward extension of rivers draining to the north coast. Whatever their mode of origin, all the main rivers are small in volume because their catchments are limited. They are useless for navigation except in their drowned lower reaches, both because they are small and also because their long-profiles are broken by knickpoints.

During glacial maximum in the Ice Age, when the sea stood lower than it does today, the rivers of the Southwest cut deeply down near their mouths. With the waning of the ice-caps and the release of meltwater, the sea rose, flooding the lower ends of all the valleys and converting them into the branching inlets known as *rias*. In the old days of sailing-craft, the sheltered harbours of the rias were much used by fishermen (Plate 72).

Agriculture

On the level platforms and flat-topped divides there is no physical obstacle to farming. No ice-caps came to scrape off the wastemantle and to remove the soil. The land of the high moorlands is admittedly poor in quality, and its climate is rainy and bleak at high levels, where actual means range from about 2 °C. in January to 13 ° in July, where rainfall rises above 1,500 mm. a year in places, and where 200 or more rain-days may be expected each year. The rest of the region, however, is almost everywhere in farms; more than half the total area is in improved grass. The region lies too far west, and is too high, open, windy, and wet for its farms to be committed mainly to tillage. Except on the coast, annual rainfall averages more than 1,000 mm. The coastlands fare better than the interior, being sunnier and drier, and sharing the regional advantage of a mean range of temperature generally below 10 °C. (Figs. 3:5–3:14), but they are restricted in extent, and most of the region experiences a distinctly damp climate in which rainfall is well-distributed through the year.

A survey of land use made in a particular year— e.g., the maps of the Land Utilisation Survey—can be guaranteed to show a high fraction of arable land, but much of this arable represents the breaking of grassland. The widespread practice in the Southwest of ploughing-up and re-seeding grassland has a double origin; in part it is a sign of good farming, for the quality of ley grass is more easily controlled and improved than that of permanent pasture, but, in addition to this, ploughing-up is especially suitable to the inland farms of this region, where the gentle slopes tend to impede the natural drainage of the soil and to make any grassland sour in the course of time. Thus the pattern of land use is a patchwork of permanent grass, tillage, and ley-grass of varying age.

The relatively small part played by tillage crops in the farming of this region is clear from the general maps of agricultural distributions (Figs. 5:3, 5:5–5:19). Rotation grass is as extensive as tillage crops in Cornwall, and two-thirds as extensive in Devon. Some 60 per cent of the farmland is under grass of one kind or another; the main interest lies in livestock, and especially in dairying, for some 200,000 of the 700,000 cattle in the region are cows actually in milk. Dairying is practised throughout the region, partly for the supply of local markets— including the few sizeable towns—but also for London. There is some rearing and fattening of beef cattle, but fattening tends to be concentrated in the east of the region, on the red soils of the vales cut in Permo-Trias. The Permo-Trias belt is truly Red Devon, justly noted for its native breed of beef cattle.

Sheep are fairly numerous in the Southwest, being set to graze not only on the enclosed farmland but also on the open granite moorlands and on the higher parts of Exmoor. In the hill districts the soils are much poorer than those developed on the sedimentary rocks of the centre and south. Exmoor stands high, and its rather shallow sandy soils have been made acid by leaching in a damp climate, while the slowly-weathering granites give rise to coarse, shallow, acid soils, which are made still more acid by the raw humus supplied by heather, bracken, and peat-moss. Peat-bogs occur in the shallow valley-heads high on Dartmoor, where the weather is often wet, misty, and cool, and where drainage is particularly bad. Large areas on all the moors are unenclosed. Little fields nip the edges of the unfenced country, but some have reverted to rough grazing (Fig. 25:2). At the present time there is little pressure of enclosure, and the boundary of the improved farmland is stable.

Agriculture in Southwest England has been revolutionised in the last hundred years. In the 17th and 18th centuries its emphasis was on the growing of food grain for local use and the production of wool for manufacture within the region; Exeter at one time had a noted serge-market. Even when the domestic craft of weaving vanished with the industrial revolution, raw wool was still needed for the new mills of Yorkshire. The local demand for locally-produced subsistence foodstuffs persisted until the railway age, with the regional output rising slowly as new ideas about farming seeped in from the east. With the entry of railways, two profound changes became possible: the region was freed from dependence on its own grainfields, and had access to an enormous urban market. Cash-farming in the Southwest, with dairying dominant, is the outcome

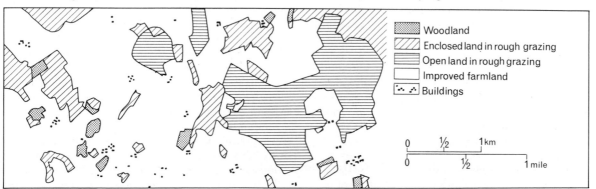

FIG. 25:2. Sample of land use and dispersed settlement, central Devon

of the rise of industry and the provision of rapid transport.

Given the means of transport, the farmers of Devon and Cornwall were able to realise the potential benefits of the regional climate. Although these benefits apply most strongly to cultivation of a specialised kind, they are also advantageous to farming in general. The mild winters (Chap. 3) combine with the inflow of moist air from the Atlantic to promote a rich growth of grass and to extend the growing-season, and the problem of winter feeding of livestock is less severe in the Southwest than in any other part of Great Britain. The smallness of farms is no obstacle to dairying, while the little fields with earthen banks around them are well suited to controlled grazing by small herds, and to giving shelter from the powerful winds. Although most of Cornwall and some parts of Devon are too remote from a railway or too far from London to specialise in the production of fresh milk, they can supply butter and cheese, which are prepared either on the farms themselves or in central creameries.

Along the south coast, bordering sheltered bays and lining the edges of the larger inlets, are found patches of market-gardens. The body of the peninsula gives shelter from the north, various pieces of high ground protect the market-gardens from strong winds from the west, and raised beaches provide warm soils on flat sites. Market-gardening is helped by the generally mild winters of the region, and also by the mild spring nights when temperatures are kept up by the warm near-by sea. Among the crops are green vegetables, early potatoes, and soft fruit. The densest concentrations of market-gardens occur at the head of Mount's and St. Ives Bays, on the western sides of the rias leading inland from Falmouth and Plymouth, and around Exeter. The Scilly Islands, with a climate slightly more oceanic than that of the mainland, specialise in cut flowers, which come into bloom there in the first weeks of the calendar year. As the main markets are London and the industrial towns of the Midlands, the prosperity of flower-growing and market-gardening in Southwest England depend on the power of distant townspeople to buy early and at a high price. In recent years the growers of Southwest England have been meeting severe competition in the London market from producers in Mediterranean countries.

Farms, Field Patterns, and Rural Settlement

The layout of farms and the distribution of farmsteads in Southwest England has been scarcely affected by the conversion of regional agriculture. Farms remain small; half of those in Cornwall are no larger than 8 ha., but there is also a significant group in the range 20–40 ha. Holdings run larger in Devon, the most typical farm being in the 20–40 ha. range, but more than half are still below 20 ha.

Within single farms, fields are also tiny. Their smallness results partly from piecemeal enclosure, partly from social usage, and partly from the original practice of the first settlers. In previous centuries, land has been enclosed and improved at the edges of existing holdings; fields have been subdivided between heirs at the death of the owner, as in Normandy and the Channel Islands; in the remoter parts of the region, it is possible that the present pattern of dispersed farms and hamlets is directly inherited from the pattern established by Celtic people. It used to be thought that the scattered rural dwellings of this region were all the result of primary dispersion of settlement. But though dispersion is generally characteristic of the Celtic West of the British Isles, it is known that, in some areas at least, present dispersion has replaced originally nucleated settlements (cf. Chap. 4). Admittedly, Celtic speech survived in the Southwest up to the 18th century, and Celtic customs presumably survived along with it, but Celtic survivals can throw little light on the obscurity of early settlement. Nucleated villages of the Midland sort are known to have existed in parts of Devon, surrounded by their open fields. Whatever their origins, however, hamlets and isolated farms are typical of the region today (Fig. 25:2), sheltering from the frequent strong winds of the interior plateaus in small folds of the ground, and lodging on the flanks of small valley-heads. Dispersed settlements are well adapted to an environment which includes few nucleating factors, and to a region where piecemeal enclosure and improvement of the formerly extensive open land was the obvious response to any increase in population.

The Resort Trade and Resort Towns

For purposes of publicity, the south coast of Cornwall is often described as the Cornish Riviera. The title is as pretentious as the claim that the coastlands of Southwest England experience a Mediterranean climate. By British standards, however, the climate on the coasts is mild and genial throughout the year, for the peninsula projects far into the warm Atlantic. Sea surfaces temperatures continue to rise after midsummer, prolonging the effective summer season, while frost and snow are rare at low levels in the winter season. Were it not for the national habit of making August the main holiday month, the resorts of the Southwest would in all probability be still more popular than they are; even now, the number of winter visitors is not inconsiderable.

The resorts themselves are mainly small. Many began as fishing villages on little inlets, and some have scarcely expanded in the last two centuries. Their smallness, their irregular houses, their air of sleepy antiquity and their little harbours contribute to the pervasive but indefinable charm of the region. Place-names of a distinctive kind, particularly common in Cornwall, are apt to impress the visitor as romantic, and romantic qualities have a cash value in the tourist trade.

As the tourist industry has grown, so fishing has declined. The coastal settlements survive and prosper, with changed functions. Tiny coves are more typical than large sweeping bays, and some of the coastal villages are huddled in the mouths of incised valleys, with little room to grow. Many, moreover, have little tendency to grow, for tourism in the Southwest is largely decentralised, most of the well-known resort towns ranging between 2,500 and 10,000 in numbers of resident population. Barnstaple on the north coast has 16,000 permanent inhabitants, Bideford 10,250 and Newquay 11,750, Bude 5,000, and Tintagel no more than 1,500. Totals on the south coast may be illustrated by Penzance (19,500) and Teignmouth (11,500); near the other extreme come Babbacombe, with 5,000, and Mevagissey, with 2,200.

The greatest exception to the small or moderate size of resort towns in the Southwest is Torquay, which is estimated to receive a million visitors a year. Its winter trade is important, but summer is by far the main season. Visitors to Torquay come mainly from the great concentrations of towns in England—London, the industrial Midlands, the Bristol area, Lancashire, Yorkshire, and the Northeast. Significantly, Torquay is located on the south coast of the peninsula, near the eastern margin of the region. It stands at one end of Tor Bay, sharing a three-mile stretch of sandy beach with the smaller but rapidly-expanding resort of Paignton.

Plymouth, Exeter, and Falmouth

Plymouth has a strong interest in the resort trade, but is far too complex to be classed merely as a resort town. It is the regional capital of the Southwest, even though Exeter possesses both the cathedral and the university. Plymouth, the more centrally placed, has an excellent deep-water habour,

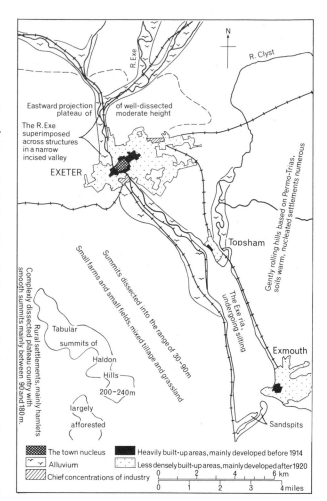

FIG. 25:3. Exeter and its local setting

with Saltash Bridge and the ferries increasing the nodal quality of its position. The town flourished greatly under Elizabeth I, when the Southwest supplied astonishing numbers of fighting ships, seamen, explorers, and pirates. Plymouth's lengthy association with naval affairs relates to a situation near the western end of the Channel; like Brest, on the French side, Plymouth is a port of call, but just as Brest has suffered from the competition of Cherbourg, so has Plymouth suffered from that of Southampton. Both Brest and Plymouth are somewhat remote from the national capitals of their respective countries, and are handicapped as general ports by hinterlands which are little industrialised and none too well peopled.

Exeter, commanding the southern approaches to the region, lies inland of the silty ria-head into which the Exe discharges. The heart of the town occupies a patch of terrace alongside the incised Exe, and adjoining a hill cut in tough igneous rock where the Norman motte-and-bailey castle was built. Exeter is approached from the north along a valley cut through fairly resistant rocks by the superimposed Exe; hills on the north, and the floodable, broadening valley to the south, helped to direct routes to the town (Fig. 25:3).

Although the Exe is small, it was navigable up to Exeter until the 13th century, when the Countess Isabella had the river obstructed by a weir below the town. A canal which by-passes the weir has not enabled Exeter to develop much port trade. Commercially, however, medieval Exeter enjoyed much prosperity as a great centre of the wool trade, and serge-making and tanning were established in the 17th–18th centuries. Manufacturing activities—brewing, printing, paper-making, garment-making, and engineering—are subordinate to clerical and service occupations and distributive trade. Exeter's retailing may well expand in the future, for the shopping district has been reconstructed on the site cleared by concentrated bombing in World War II.

Falmouth (15,500) is located similarly to Plymouth, on the edge of a large ria. Standing nearer to the open sea than does Plymouth, and with less of the available land built over, Falmouth has recently acquired a dry-dock capable of accommodating oil-tankers—great vessels ranging up to 255 m. in length, and some exceeding 65,000 tons deadweight. The repair-yards at Falmouth are already well reputed for work on tankers, and the dry-dock is expected to ensure additional employment, despite competition from Milford Haven.

Inland Towns

The inland centres of Southwest England are mostly market towns. Many of them have developed industry of some kind—in connection with local farming, in response to the trend of industrial dispersal, or as the result of local enterprise—but there is no single industrial pattern. A common type of siting is exemplified by Newton Abbot (18,000), Totnes, and Truro (13,500), which command relatively easy crossings of incised valleys. Camborne, Redruth, and St. Austell are special cases; the first two formerly prospered as centres of ore-mining, while the latter is now the chief centre of kaolin-working.

Mining, Quarrying, and Fishing

Metal ores in Southwest England include ores of tin, copper, lead, zinc, and iron. They are concentrated in a belt about ten miles wide, which runs across the northern part of the Land's End and Carn Menellis granites, cuts squarely across Hensbarrow, and tips the southern extremity of Bodmin Moor. The ores were emplaced when the granites were intruded and volatile gases cooled in fissures, depositing metal compounds. Stream tin was probably exploited as long as 4,000 years ago, and the mining of tin ore was probably carried on in Roman times. Mining was deliberately fostered by Elizabeth I, and output was high during the 18th and the 19th centuries, the chief products being ores of tin and copper sent to smelting-works in South Wales. Some 250 mines were active in the mid-19th century. However, production declined as known reserves were depleted, mines became flooded, and oversea producers came to the fore. Copper ores from the U.S.A. undercut the Cornish product, and Cornish tin was unable to meet the competition of stream-tin from Malaya. Flooding of abandoned mines made recovery less and less profitable or possible; one area that absorbed emigrating Cornish miners was the lead–zinc district of southwest Wisconsin in the U.S.A. The economic fluctuations of the inter-war period almost extinguished mining at times, the maximum output of tin ore between 1919 and 1939 being but 5,500 tons. World War II brought the hasty re-opening of some mines and the expansion of output from others, but the annual output up to the early 1960s amounted to little more than 1,000 tons of pure tin per year, corresponding to about 5 per cent of national consumption. Camborne and Redruth persisted as centres of mining technology and of the manufacture of mining machinery.

During the decade of the 1960s, however, signs of renewed change began to appear (see bibliography: Blunden). The decline in known world reserves of tin, especially of alluvial tin, stimulated exploratory drilling in Cornwall; new reserves were located, distinct from, although not greatly far below, the lodes that had originally been worked. By about 1970, Cornish tin production had risen to about 7 per cent of national consumption, at a level of some 2,000 tons a year, twice as high as the level of ten years earlier. Future prospects, in the light of projected world trends, are by no means unpromising.

The kaolin (china clay) of Southwest England is the result of the metamorphism of granite. The alteration took place at the same time that the mineral lodes were formed, and was due to the same kind of agency—hot volatile gases emanating from the cooling granites. The potash-felspar of the affected granite was changed into kaolin.[1] Kaolin-isation was most pronounced in the St. Austell district, where china-clay workings are mainly concentrated. Par is the chief exporting port. Hydraulic working is practised in the opencast pits. Jets of water are directed against the working face, breaking up the altered material and roughly separating the kaolin from the mica and quartz which are also present. Final separation takes place in tanks, where part of the mica is recovered, the rest going to waste with the quartz grains. Quartz and waste mica are dumped in conical heaps which glitter white in the sunshine.

The rise of kaolin-working in Southwest England was intimately associated with the growth of the pottery industry of North Staffordshire (Chap. 22), and the Potteries take part of the present output, but much kaolin is used as filler for paper and cloth. Output of kaolin from Southwest England has increased since the inter-war period, running at about 1,500,000 tons a year at the present time, against some 600,000 tons a year in the 1930s; part of the increase corresponds to the increased consumption of high-grade glazed paper in North America.

At Bovey Tracey, on the flank of Dartmoor, kaolin is worked in conditions which contrast with those of the St. Austell district. The kaolin of Bovey Tracey was brought down by streams from Dartmoor and deposited in the Tertiary lake which occupied a rift-valley. Lignite in the lake-deposits is of great geological interest, but of no commercial value except in times of extreme need—as, for example, the immediate post-war period, when it was sold in the Channel Islands for heating glasshouse boilers. Part of the output of kaolin from the Bovey Tracey basin is locally manufactured into chinaware, glazed pipes, and tiled fireplaces.

Other extractive industries of Southwest England include the quarrying of slate and of granite. The chief producer of slates is the locality of Delabole, while granite is taken from a number of accessible places on the blocks of moorland. Demand for slates has been seriously reduced by competition of asbestos and earthenware tiles, while granite has been largely replaced, for some purposes, by concrete and by tarmacadam in which stone of other kinds is used. Employment in granite-quarrying has been reduced by the introduction of machines—as, for example, at Newlyn, where granite from the Land's End mass is loaded into coasters by conveyor-belt.

In the whole region, no more than 5,750 people are employed in mining and quarrying. Fishing takes even fewer, with 1,750. Mining, quarrying, and fishing together employ fewer than one in sixty of the regional working population. They have suffered not only an absolute decline, but also a far greater relative decline, particularly by comparison with the tourist industry. The reduction of fishery has occurred despite access to contrasted bodies of water which used to supply a varied range of fish including mackerel from the western Channel; the Southwest, handicapped by small harbours, lack of capital, inflexible customs, and railway connections inferior to those of the great centralised fishing-ports, has abandoned part of its maritime tradition.

---

[1] For example, the felspar $K_2O.Al_2O_3.6SiO_2$ became $Al_2O_3.2SiO_2.2H_2O$.

Chapter 26

The Borders of the West Country: The Hampshire Basin and its Borders: The Channel Islands

THE Borders of the West Country consist partly of scarplands which prolong the Scarplands of the South Midlands (Chap. 23); they also include the Plain of Somerset, the Mendips, and the environs of Bristol—three districts which are structurally allied to the Midland Triangle. The Hampshire Basin constitutes a structural as well as a topographic depression. Each region contains a great port, but the links of each regional hinterland with its port are far weaker than the corresponding links in the London Basin. Consequently, the geographical unity displayed by each of the two regions is not fundamentally due to the presence and size of Bristol and Southampton, and the regional economies are in some measure detached from the trade and manufacture of ports.

Physique

In the Hampshire Basin the Chalk has sagged deeply downwards, the resulting hollow receiving the sediments which now form Tertiary strata.

Along the southern edge of the Basin the almost vertical rim of Chalk has been disrupted by erosion, and the Isle of Wight detached from the mainland. On the north, the Chalk rises in the broad structural arch of Salisbury Plain and the Hampshire Downs (Fig. 26:1), where the crestal belt, planed off by erosion in a previous cycle, rises flatly to 210–240 m., a very few small hills alone protruding and rising above 270 m. Further north still, the Chalk is downfolded under the western tip of the London Basin, rising again in the cuesta of the Berkshire Downs to above 240 m. and forming a north-facing scarp.

The whole belt of Chalkland surrounding the Hampshire Basin is traversed by Tertiary folds which run east–west and die away at their ends. Most of the folds are quite modest in size, and have little effect on relief, but anticlines on the western margin have been eroded to form the Vales of Pewsey, Warminster, and Wardour. The Chalk has been stripped back, forming infacing scarps above the older rocks in the floors of the Vales.

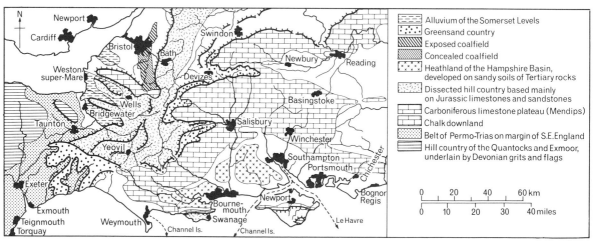

FIG. 26:1. Borders of the West Country; the Hampshire Basin and its borders: physique and main settlements

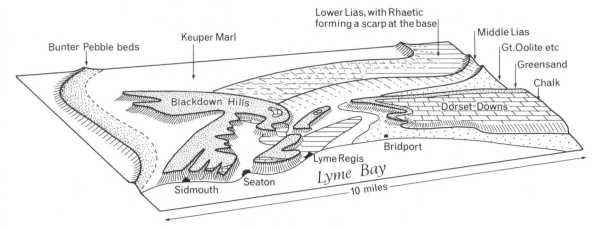

FIG. 26:2. Block-diagram to show westward overstep of Cretaceous rocks in Dorset

Southwards from the Vale of Wardour, the edge of the Chalk becomes less and less marked, for the Chalk formation has been thinned by erosion; Chalk hills reappear northwest of Weymouth, and continue into the Isle of Purbeck, ending in a cliffed coast embellished by buttresses and stacks.

Part of the Borders of the West Country is composed of cuestas facing some westerly direction, with backslopes descending towards the east, southeast, and south. The scarp-forming rocks are limestones and sandstones of Jurassic age, and the Greensand which belongs to the Cretaceous system. Clays tend to be rather thin, so that the strike vales developed on them are narrower than those of the South Midlands or Southeast England, and in any case the structural pattern is confused by faulting and minor folding.

On parts of the boundary between the rim of the Hampshire Basin and the Borders of the West Country, the thickening Greensand forms a steep, tree-clad, west-facing scarp which is even more prominent than the edge of the Chalk. Thickening still further, the Greensand protrudes far to the west in the Blackdown Hills, a well-dissected tabular block with summits rising very gently to more than 300 m. The Greensand oversteps the roded edges of underlying formations, passing in turn across the Jurassic and Permo-Trias towards its outpost in the Haldon Hills beyond the Exe (Fig. 26:2).

The narrowing Cotswolds enter the Borders of the West Country from the north, declining in height towards the incised valley of the superimposed Avon at Bath, and breaking down into irregular hills between the Avon and the Mendips. South of the Mendips comes more broken hilly country, which continues beyond Yeovil to where the Jurassic rocks pass beneath the Greensand.

The Mendips rise above 300 m. in a steep-sided, flat-topped and compact line of hills in which Carboniferous Limestone is brought up by sharp folds. In the south they overlook the Somerset Plain, where eroded folds in Jurassic rocks form little lines of hills projecting into the peaty and alluvial flats of the Somerset Levels. North of the Mendips, the Avon has been superimposed across a district where folded and faulted rocks form hills of no great size, and where Carboniferous rocks, including productive Coal Measures, project through the Permo-Trias.

THE BORDERS OF THE WEST COUNTRY

Area: about 5,250 km² (2,000 sq. mi.).
Population: about 750,000.
Largest towns: Bristol (427,500).*
               Bath (84,750).*
               Weston-super-Mare (44,000).
               Taunton (32,250).
               Bridgwater (25,500).
               Yeovil (24,500).
                       * 1969 estimates.
About 80 per cent of this region is in improved farmland, with grass nearly three times as extensive as tillage.
Numbers of livestock: cattle, 555,000;
                    sheep, 575,000;
                    pigs, 250,000;
                    poultry, 4,700,000.

Climate and Agriculture

The Borders of the West Country receive some 850 to 1,000 mm. of rain a year—about 250 m.

more than the South Midland Scarplands. The former region is slightly more sunny if slightly more equable, and quite noticeably warmer in winter than the South Midlands, with mean January temperatures about 4 °C. Lying snow is infrequent, and the frost-free season exceeds six months. All these conditions promote the growth of grass, and the grazing of stock is so firmly established that tillage has not been much extended since 1939. Such extra tillage as exists grows mainly fodder crops.

This region is not especially well suited to grain in respect of climate, but the prevailing economic conditions have brought about two-thirds of Somerset into grain cropping, with barley leading as it does so commonly elsewhere. Wheat is less than half as extensive as barley. Fodder roots and green fodder crops take in combination about 10 per cent of tilled land. Numerous orchards, individually small but large as a group, mainly produce cider apples.

Some parts of the region are more heavily tilled than others. The Somerset Levels and other alluvial flats, very largely in permanent grass, resemble the Fenlands in being based on the silt and peat which fills a former lagoon; but although their drainage has been improved, the water-table has not been brought under complete control, and the land remains liable to flood. On the exposed top of the Mendips there is much sheep-pasture, some of it in poor condition. The broken hilly country of the central and eastern parts of the region contains clayland in the upper valleys of the Stour and Avon, where permanent pasture is extensive (Plate 73), but there are also warm sandy loams—e.g., around Yeovil—where tillage is common and includes market-gardening.

Dairy-farming is prominent throughout this region; more than a third of the cattle are dairy animals actually in milk, and few of the remainder are beefstock. Butter, cream, and cheese are the leading products of processing plants, and large numbers of eggs are prepared for market in packing-stations. Pigs are numerous, especially in the eastern part of the region, where they are closely dependent on dairying; a large farm which produces its own butter and cheese may keep as many as a thousand pigs. There is a long-established production of bacon and other pigmeat, including the pork sausages for which the small town of Calne is famous.

Settlement and Industry

Most settlements in the region are small. Villages tend to be loose-knit, and hamlets are numerous. The western part of the region lies beyond the main belt of village settlement, but well-nucleated villages become common in the east, where many of them are located at some scarp-foot.

Bristol is the great exception among the towns of the region. At the other extreme come little market towns, which are closely-spaced in all parts except the alluvial flats. Some are closely associated with a particular district—Devizes with the Vale of Pewsey, Gillingham with the Vale of Wardour, and Sturminster Newton with the basin of the upper Stour. Many have long held official town status, without displaying much tendency to expand, and with their irregular, small, colourwashed buildings lining the incoming roads, represent the little English country town in all its architectural attractiveness.

Miscellaneous light industry has been added in places to the widespread processing of dairy produce, particularly during World War II. Woollen-manufacture and flax-milling developed in the region itself. Frome on the river Frome, and Bradford-on-Avon near the Frome confluence, retain elements of the Cotswold woollen industry, having specialised in serges. Flax-milling is not concentrated in towns,[1] the mills occupying riverside sites although they are now worked by steam or electricity; the limited and scattered flax industry, long in grave decline, was revived during World War II.

Yeovil, Bridgwater, Taunton, and Bath have had more success than most other towns of the region—Bristol always excepted. Yeovil has a prosperous manufacture of leather, particularly of gloves. Skins (including furs) are mainly imported. Some of the manufacturing processes cannot easily be mechanised, and a great deal of hand-work is still carried on. The other leading industry of Yeovil is mechanical engineering, of which the best-known products are helicopters and small power plant.

Bridgwater has a minor port trade. Ships pass up and down the tidal Parret, and there is a canal connection to Taunton, but navigation is hampered by silting, and the canal basin needs frequent clearance. Bridgwater stands where the Parret swings against firm ground on its left bank (Fig. 26:3). The town has no near rival, and has secured a firm grip on the retail trade of its surroundings. Some of its activities are closely linked to local farming—e.g., brewing, malting, and agricultural engineering; clay is worked for the making of bricks, pottery, and drainpipes. Signs of elaboration of industry appear

----

[1] Flax in the retting-pit emits a powerful stench.

PLATE 73. Bradford-on-Avon, Wiltshire. Parkland occurs on the near side of the town, with fields established by parliamentary enclosure on the far side.

in garment-making and contracting, both of which are well developed.

Taunton has obvious natural nodality,[1] being in some sense the gateway to the Southwest. It stands on the Tone, between the Quantocks and a north-

east-facing scarp (Fig. 26:1). As a market town it is the focus of the rich farmland in the Vale of Taunton Deane, where high-grade soils are developed on the Permo-Trias, but also serves the country to the south.

Bath owes its location, and directly or indirectly its growth, to its warm springs, which led the Romans to construct their baths and associated buildings where the Fosse Way crossed the incised

[1] Natural nodality due to the convergence of natural route-ways should be distinguished from the man-made nodality which all successful towns possess.

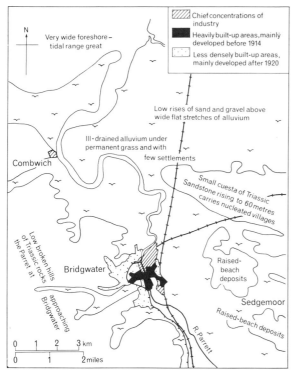

FIG. 26:3. Bridgwater and its local setting

Avon. Bath shared the redevelopment of town life in England during the later Dark Ages and the Middle Ages, becoming a cathedral centre under the Normans, but much of the existing town dates from the 18th century; Bath's high reputation as a spa and a fashionable resort was acquired in the early 1700s, when extensive rebuilding took place. Sheltered by the steep walls of the valley, and spreading up their lower slopes, Bath at this time acquired some of the finest examples of 18th-century architecture; the stone used was the local Cotswold oolite, Bath freestone. A resort and tourist trade is still carried on, but the chief employer of male labour in Bath today is the ubiquitous metalworking and engineering. The functions of Bath have developed similarly to those of its imitators and rivals, Cheltenham and Leamington.

The custom of resorting to English spas belonged essentially to the 18th and early 19th centuries, to the days of coach travel, and to the fashionable world which lived by its landed estates. During the 19th century seaside resorts developed, first under the influence of fashion, later with the aid of railways and rising real incomes. Seaside towns involved in the resort trade are busier today than they have ever been, for coaches bring huge numbers of daily visitors, and there has been a marked redistri-

bution of the national income since 1945. More people than ever before can afford to go to the seaside. The effects of the modern resort trade are well seen in the contrast between Bath and Weston-super-Mare; the former has increased its population by 2 per cent since 1951, the latter by 9 per cent. Weston has the great advantage of a sandy beach on an estuary which is mostly very muddy, and the monotonous alluvial flats which adjoin the coast are out of sight behind detached hills of Carboniferous limestone. Inland lie the Mendips, with their commercialised caves at Cheddar and Wookey, and the old ecclesiastical towns of Glastonbury and Wells. Weston is easily accessible from a large area of the Midlands, and has no near rivals of its own size.

Bristol

Bristol (Fig. 26:4) is to be contrasted with Bridgwater. Each stands on a navigable river and maintains a port trade, both are handicapped as ports by their location. The days when Bristol's trade rivalled or surpassed that of London and Liverpool have long gone: the port now handles only about 2 per cent of Great Britain's shipborne traffic (see Chap. 9). The disparity between imports and exports, common to all large west-coast general ports, has afflicted Bristol at least as heavily as any of the others. It derives in part from the town's commercial history, in part from the port's failure to become an outlet (and inlet) for the industrial West Midlands. The local coalfield is modest in size and output, and Bristol and its immediate hinterland have no great heavy industries; indeed, they have little exporting industry at all, their manufactured products being sold mainly in Great Britain.

Bristol's medieval trade was principally with Ireland, Gascony, and Iberia. Fish and hides from Ireland were imported in exchange for cloth, manufactured leather, salt, and iron; from the 12th to the 15th century, cloth was exported to Gascony and wine brought back, and the Gascon routes were in time extended to Spain and Portugal. Bristol by 1400 was the second greatest seaport of England, soon taking part in the Iceland fisheries, and being selected as the base for Cabot's voyages in the last years of the 15th century. Cloth exported from Bristol was made in the Cotswolds, where the water-powered fulling-mill invented before 1200 was in use at many places.

In 1552 the Merchant Venturers of Bristol received their charter, but the activities of the port were unfortunately reduced by war with Spain and revolts in Ireland. It was during the 17th century,

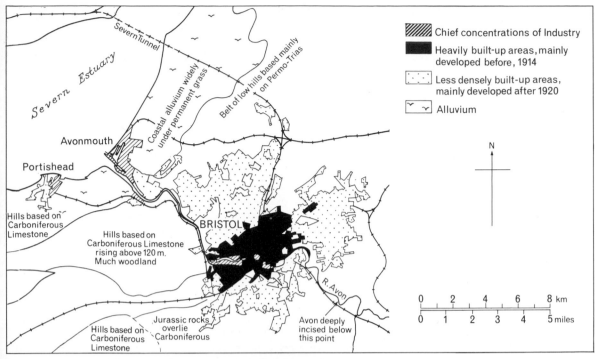

FIG. 26:4. Bristol and its local setting

PLATE 74. The Severn Bridge, carrying a motorway across the estuary-head. View to the northwest.

a time of great prosperity in Bristol, that sugar-refining and tobacco-manufacturing were established, and trade with the Americans increased swiftly after 1650. Bristol's transatlantic connections were with the Caribbean and the Virginia coast rather than with New England; sugar, rum, and tobacco were among its leading imports, and it was involved in the carriage of slaves to America, even though the slave trade had been declared illegal for British merchants. The manufacture of chocolate began in Bristol during the 18th century, when the port's activities continued to increase and a large entrepôt trade developed.

By 1800, however, Bristol had been surpassed in size by Manchester and Birmingham and by their chief port Liverpool. Bristol was handicapped by high dock charges which drove away even its own ships, and its harbour was proving inconvenient. It lost its export of Welsh produce to Cardiff, and the woollen industry of its own hinterland was on the decline; its shipyards pioneered the development of power-driven craft, but they too declined in relative importance during the 19th century. When the docks at Bristol's outport of Avonmouth were opened in 1908, it was too late for Bristol to capture much of the export trade in metal goods.

The town remains a leading centre of sugar-refining and of the manufacture of chocolate and tobacco, with manufactures of leather, clothing, furniture, and paper, besides printing and contracting industries. The engineering industry has a wide range, but is especially well known for its production of aircraft which began in the early 1900s. Bristol today is firmly established as a regional capital. More than five times as large as the next town in the region, it has no rival in the wholesale and retail trades of the area which it serves, and its pre-eminent status is underlined by the presence of a university.

A new industrial complex is expanding on Severnside northeast of Avonmouth (see bibliography: Walker). Land available for industry has been seized by metallurgical and chemical industry, two nuclear power stations, and petrochemical industry; the requisite land linkages are provided by the motorway system. Here, as in the western parts of South Wales, manufacturing is invading a countryside which lay formerly almost untouched.

THE HAMPSHIRE BASIN AND ITS BORDERS

Area: 7,150 km² (2,750 sq. mi.).
Population: about 2,000,000.

Largest towns: Portsmouth (213,000).*
Southampton (212,500).*
Bournemouth (150,000).*
Havant and Waterloo (107,000).*
Poole (102,000).*
Worthing (83,000).*
Gosport (62,500).
Fareham (58,250).
Weymouth (41,000).
Salisbury (35,500).
Winchester (28,750).
Christchurch (26,500).
Chichester (20,250).
*1969 estimates

About 70 per cent of this region is in improved farmland, with grass rather more extensive than tillage.

Numbers of livestock: cattle, 300,000;
sheep, 265,00;
pigs, 300,000;
poultry, 6,650,000.

Southampton, like Bristol, is a university town, a great port, and a regional capital. There the similarities end. Southampton is not the largest town of its region. It is a deep-water port with a very large passenger trade and growing connections with Midland industries. It is far more closely linked than Bristol to metropolitan England, and its immediate hinterland differs in many respects from the hinterland of Bristol. Not only are there physical contrasts —whereas towns in the Borders of the West Country are very numerous but rather small, towns in the Hampshire Basin and its borders are fewer, area for area, but some have grown very big. Despite their presence, however, the country districts of the Hampshire Basin and its borders are more markedly rural than the country districts of the Borders of the West Country (Plate 75), being less widely and less densely peopled. The difference corresponds, in part, to contrasts in geology and in soils.

The Chalklands

The Chalklands, based on a thick and permeable formation, yield water only in the valleys, and it was to the valleys that Dark-Age settlement was largely confined. Here the villages stand today, strung out along the little clear-flowing rivers. Such a distribution is better represented in the Berkshire Downs and on Salisbury Plain, where soils are developed on bare Chalk, than on the Hampshire Downs, the strip of country south of the Wylye, or the Dorset Downs, where Clay-with-Flints occurs as an extensive capping. Oakwood was formerly

PLATE 75. Cottages at Wareham, Dorset, with stone footings, pug walls, and low thatched roofs.

widespread on the Clay-with-Flints, and piecemeal clearance and the presence of groundwater have encouraged denser but more scattered settlement than on the Chalk soils proper.

The compact area of Chalkland in Salisbury Plain was, in prehistoric times, the most heavily-peopled part of the country. The two great religious centres of Avebury and Stonehenge are located centrally in two districts of Chalk soils, respectively north and south of the Vale of Pewsey, and earthworks in great number stud the undulating downlands, round barrows being especially prominent on many skylines. The British and Roman centre of Old Sarum is an obvious focus of Roman roads. Three km. to the south lies its successor Salisbury, a market centre with a famous cathedral; thirty km. to the east is Winchester, also a cathedral town, once the capital of Wessex and at times of England.

The decline in the political status of Wessex and Winchester was accompanied by a decline in the agricultural status of their land. Tilling by means of the scratch-plough may well have continued on the shallow Chalk soils well into the Middle Ages, but eventually the downland became grassed over and put to use as sheep-pasture. The sequence of prehistoric clearance and possible over-cultivation in addition, infestation by rabbits, intensive grazing and cultivation in medieval times, seasonal burning, the spread of sheep, the failure of many farms in the depression years of the turn of the nineteenth century, plus the progressive acquisition of land by the military, have probably combined to effect a prejudiced view of land potential, as opposed to land status. Most commentators tend to rank Salisbury Plain as naturally unpromising, whereas (as will shortly be indicated) it does well for dairy uses. During much of the 19th century, however, it was used largely for open grazing of sheep, in conjunction with irrigation on the floodplains. There, the channels of water-meadows kept the water-

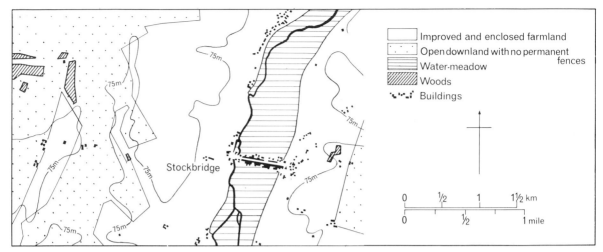

FIG. 26:5. Stockbridge, Hampshire; a small market-town at a river-crossing, surrounded by Chalk downland which is partly open: 75 m. contour is approximate

table high and promoted a lush growth of grass for hay (cf. Fig. 26:5). The 18th-century advances in agriculture introduced barley as a main arable crop on the lower slopes, and the sheep–barley combination prevailed throughout the 19th century and into the 20th.

This combination no longer obtains today. As Figs. 5:21 and 5:24 show, there are now few sheep. Sheep-farming was affected by the violent fluctuations in profits typical of the present century, and farming practice was modified to introduce dairying, grass and clover leys, and a variety of cash crops. Barley is still the chief grain crop, but is nowadays grown in a complex rotation. Changes in agriculture have been going on steadily since about 1900, but have been most rapid since 1939; during World War II a great deal of grassland was ploughed up, and the remaining flocks of sheep were much reduced. Tillage continues to be extensive in the post-war period, both for cash crops and for fodder crops; many of the farms are well adapted to the use of machinery, with their fields typically large and many single farms exceeding 200 ha. (500 acres) in size, and agriculture today is highly mechanised. Where land has been returned to grass, and on the unbroken permanent pasture, dairy-farming and not sheep-grazing is the main interest. Thus, in half a century, the farming of this block of Chalkland country has been completely transformed.

The Centre of the Basin

In the centre of the Hampshire Basin, loose sandy soils of coarse texture are extensively developed on poorly-cemented Tertiary sediments. They provide the edaphic basis of the New Forest, preserved as a royal hunting-ground for a long period and still continuous enough to be represented in Fig. 3:22. Neither the severely-leached podsolic soils of the sandy areas nor the use to which the Forest was put encouraged settlement, which remains sparse and irregular to this day, but on the inland side, where the sandy rocks of the centre are surrounded by a belt of London Clay, dip-foot villages mark the geological junction where springs put out at the edge of the Chalk, and mixed farmland encircles the scrub and heath of the Forest. Ribbons of cultivation extend along the wide terraces of the rejuvenated rivers.

Although most of the Forest is unpromising as agricultural land, some of the sandy soils well repay intensive cultivation; highly specialised market-gardening has developed in the coastal belt, with an extension along the raised beach of the Sussex Coastal Plain as far as Worthing. The coastlands of the Hampshire Basin are sunny, receiving their 750 mm. of rainfall in no more than 175 rain-days; they profit from a frost-free season 7 months in length and a January mean temperature of about 4 °C. Crops include green vegetables, peas, and beans, but market-gardens in Hampshire are particularly noted for their production of strawberries, while glasshouse crops and flowers grown in the open are increasingly produced near Worthing.

Towns of the Coastal Belt

Weymouth, Poole, Bournemouth, and Worthing are eminently successful resorts, linked through the last-named to the chain of seaside towns in South-east England. The Hampshire Basin and the Isle of Wight contain many other smaller resorts, all benefiting from sunny weather, sandy beaches, and attractive inland scenery. Portsmouth, Gosport, Havant, and Fareham form a distinctive group of their own, while Southampton stands apart, except for the share taken by Weymouth in port and passenger trade.

Bournemouth has merged with Boscombe along the cliffs which overlook a long, curving sweep of shore. As at Brighton, Worthing, and Weston-super-Mare—to name but three similarly-located towns—the beach is the nucleating factor. The largest and most expensive hotels, and the public buildings constructed to serve the resort trade, stand on or near the front; the size of buildings decreases inland, numerous boarding-houses marking the transition to the spreading suburban fringe. Bournemouth first became highly popular as a resort about a hundred years ago, and is still growing steadily, with $2\frac{1}{2}$ million visitors a year. Poole sprang into prominence rather later; its shallow but protected harbour favours yachting, which is much practised on this coast and became a sport for the many in the inter-war period. The population of Poole has increased by 60 per cent since 1931.

As a naval base, Portsmouth is related to Southampton and Southampton Water as Chatham and Gillingham are to London and the Thames. Its landlocked harbour, like that of Poole, is the result of the drowning of shallow valleys by a rise of sea-level; but Portsmouth's harbour is the deeper as well as the more easterly, and Portsmouth was selected as a naval centre. Naval activity in general, and the maintenance and repair of warships, were the main factors in the town's growth. Gosport on the far side of the inlet is linked by ferry and floating bridge to Portsmouth, of which it is effectively a partner and suburb. Portsmouth is congested on Portsea Island, and both Fareham and Havant, which lie further inland at the heads of inlets, have become to some extent suburbs and dormitories of Portsmouth. The population of Portsmouth is actually less today than it was in 1931, while the combined population of Gosport, Fareham, and Havant has more than trebled.

Strictly speaking, Weymouth lies outside the Hampshire Basin, but its resort trade is very similar in character to that of Bournemouth and its port activities resemble some of those of Southampton. The ships which ply between Weymouth and the Channel Islands enter a harbour protected by large breakwaters, one of which springs from Portland Islands, where stone for Wren's London buildings was quarried.

Southampton

As a port, Southampton (Fig. 26:6) enjoys the advantages of a peculiar tidal régime which pro-

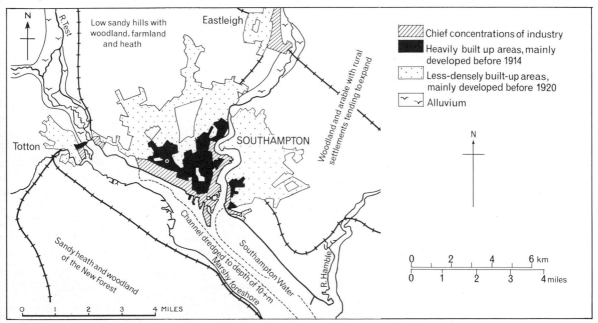

FIG. 26:6. Southampton and its local setting

longs high water; tidal waves produced in the Solent and Southampton Water are considered to be responsible. Southampton developed into a great terminal port for the transatlantic passenger run, maintaining its hold on the seaborne passenger trade when liner services began their conversion to pleasure cruising. It has in addition acquired considerable industrial activity, and ranks among the first six of the ports of Great Britain (see Chap. 9).

Its history as a port goes back long before the days of the railways which, during the early half of the 20th century, contributed so much to found its present-day activity. The original settlement, between the drowned mouths of the Test and Itchen, was founded early in the Dark Ages. Under the Normans the town was important enough to be walled, and during the Middle Ages it shared in the importing of French wine and the exporting of English cloth, but Southampton did not develop trading connections comparable to those of Bristol, and was even less well placed to serve the developing industries of the 17th and 18th centuries. Its modern development did not begin until 1836, when the Southampton Dock Company was founded. The railway which entered in that year took over the docks themselves in 1872. The prolonged high water—maintained for 2 hours twice daily—the railway access to the waterfront, and the room available for making and extending docks in the alluvium, all favoured the growth of a deep-water port standing in the same kind of relation to London as Cherbourg has to Paris.

The rise of passenger traffic has been due fundamentally to demand for services. Once they were provided, the services in turn encouraged the development of travel, justifying considerable improvements to the harbour works and their approaches. A channel with a minimum width of 200 m. and a depth of 12 m. at low water is now maintained by dredging. The New Docks were completed in 1934, and the Ocean Terminal in 1950; there are now $2\frac{1}{2}$ km of deep-water quay, large transit sheds, 9 liner berths and 7 drydocks. Half the ocean travellers to and from Great Britain, and 80 per cent of those going to or coming from South Africa and the U.S.A., pass through Southampton.

In its passenger trade Southampton profits from its nearness to London, which is 125 km away and reached by train in $1\frac{1}{2}$ hours. The cargo trade is in part somewhat specialised, although, with 16 million people living within a radius of 150 km, the port is busy with trade of a general nature. Perishable imports handled at Southampton include food-stuffs and fruit, which are received in increasing quantities. South Africa sends fruit, eggs, wool, hides, and skins; among other leading suppliers of cargo are the West Indies, the Canary Islands, the Channel Islands, France, and West Africa.

The shipbuilding industry of Southampton produces small and moderate-sized craft, and is overshadowed by the maintenance, repair, and refitting of ships of all sizes. Industries encouraged to develop around the New Docks include flour-milling, timber-milling, and the manufacture of radio equipment and rubber. The railway works at Eastleigh and the local aircraft industry represent 19th-century and 20th-century engineering, while the great oil refinery at Fawley has an output of some 7 million tons a year, supplying about a quarter of the country's need of motor spirit and sending large quantities for export. A pipeline from Fawley to a depot near London Airport has been built.

THE CHANNEL ISLANDS

Area: 195 km² (75 sq. mi.).
Population: about 104,250.
Largest towns: St. Helier (Jersey) (about 22,500 in built-up area).
　　　　　　　St. Peter Port (Guernsey) (about 14,000 in built-up area).

Some 53 per cent of the total land area is in farms and market-gardens. Tillage is one-and-a-third times as extensive as grassland.
Numbers of livestock: cattle, 14,000;
　　　　　　　　　　　 pigs, 5,000.

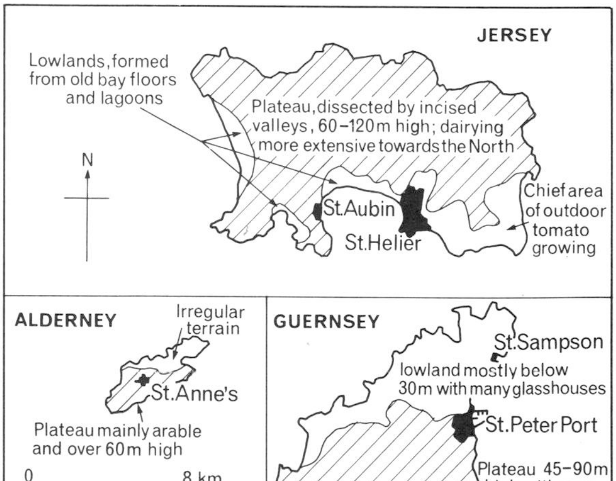

FIG. 26:7. The Channel Islands: physique and main settlements

About 180 km² of the combined extent of the Channel Islands, and nearly all the inhabitants, are accounted for by Jersey and Guernsey. Other islands are Alderney, Sark, Herm, Jethou, and Lihou.

Lying off the Cotentin Peninsula, well within sight of the French coast on clear days, the Channel Islands have been attached to the English Crown since 1066. They rank politically as Crown Dependencies. They are outside the limits of the regulations on customs and excise which apply in the United Kingdom, and, unless they are specified in Acts of Parliament, are unaffected by British law. Feudal powers are enforced in Sark; government in the remaining islands, although revised to some extent in recent years, is distinctly late-medieval in structure.

Physique, Climate, and Agriculture

Physically, the Islands (Fig. 26:7) constitute detached fragments of the Armorican massif of France. They are based mainly upon ancient metamorphic, plutonic, and extrusive rocks, rising abruptly from the sea in lines of indented cliffs. Sweeping bays and numerous small inlets variegate their shores (Plate 76). Only in the north of Guernsey is there any considerable extent of low ground; elsewhere the terrain is of the plateau type, composed of old beach-platforms which approach 135 m. in Jersey and 100 m. in Guernsey. These two islands are considerably dissected by young valleys. The plateau-tops are widely mantled with loess, while raised-beach deposits occur up to heights of a hundred feet above present sea-level.

PLATE 76. Part of north Guernsey, with extensive glasshouses.

Climate is markedly maritime, with very mild winters—mean temperatures for February, the coldest month, are above 3 °C.; frost and snow are infrequent, and the growing season is very long. Mean annual rainfall varies from 1,000 mm. on the highest ground to below 750 mm. in the drier parts, and sunshine is more abundant than it is anywhere in the British Isles proper.

Except in Alderney, where the field-pattern has been influenced by the holding of land in common, farmland on the Islands is minutely subdivided—partly because of the operation of complex laws of inheritance. Fragmentation is emphasised by the stout earthen banks, some of them topped by hedges, which divide the tiny fields from one another. Dairy-farming, stock-breeding, and market-gardening are well established. The native breeds of Jersey and Guernsey cattle are famous for high-grade milk, and breeding-stock is exported. Farming and market-gardening combined take one-fifth of the labour force; in Guernsey, more than four-fifths of the workers on the land are employed in market-gardening, and fewer than one-fifth in farming; the proportions are exactly reversed in Jersey.

This striking contrast is due mainly to the great development in Guernsey of cultivation under glass. With rather poor light land in the north, and with a slightly unfavourable aspect, Guernsey has concentrated on glasshouse working, with an area of glass among the greatest in the world. Most of the glasshouses are heated by anthracite-fired boilers, the leading crop being early tomatoes. Jersey, with its plateau sloping towards the south, is noted mainly for early potatoes and for tomatoes grown in the open. Market-garden produce, including cut flowers, is shipped to England from the Channel Islands, competing in London and the West Midlands with the produce of Southwest England, the Netherlands, and Italy.

Economic Change

Market-gardening and farming, although both need much labour, cannot possibly support the dense populations of the Channel Islands, where overcrowding and underemployment have formed a constant threat for some centuries past. The 17th-century production of hand-knitted clothes failed with the industrial revolution. During the 18th century, about a third of the cropped area was under orchards of cider-apple trees, a large surplus of cider being exported to France. Numbers of Channel Islanders were employed at this time in home fisheries, the Newfoundland fisheries, and in the carrying trade, but there was still persistent emigration. Both Jersey and Guernsey did well for a time in shipbuilding during the 19th century, and in its later part profited by stone-quarrying—some London streets are still paved with Channel Island stone. But technical developments elsewhere ruined the local shipyards, just as changes in the techniques of road-making and building caused most quarries to be abandoned, and highly intensive cultivation for export developed in the late 19th century, with the aid of increasingly fast sea-transport.

A vigorous tourist trade has grown up during the 20th century; some half-a-million visitors from Britain go to the Channel Islands each year. The air journey from London to the Islands takes less time than the rail journey from London to the resorts of Southwest England, while sea passages from Southampton or Weymouth take half a day. The Channel Islands have climatic attractions fully equal to those of the Southwest, possess the same kind of indefinable charm, and are sufficiently distant from England to give the illusion of foreign travel. This illusion is heightened by the distinctive style of native domestic architecture, by the abundance of local surnames on shop-fronts, by the use of patois by some islanders, and by the freedom from British customs and excise. Economic depression apart, the tourist trade promises to continue to flourish, in common with the specialised cultivation of these heavily-settled and intensively-worked islands.

Settlement

The largest nucleated settlements are St. Helier, St. Peter Port, St. Sampson's—Guernsey's second port—and St. Anne's on Alderney. Houses on the two largest islands are scattered in little groups throughout the interior. With increase in population the best sites are becoming well built-up, and small concentrations of dwellings are newly emerging. Broadly speaking, however, the Islands succeed in retaining their rural character, even though the extent of cultivated land has been declining for more than fifty years. The Channel Islands are notably free from that peculiar brashness which typifies some of the resort towns of England.

Chapter 27

Southeast England

Area: about 7,800 km² (3,000 sq. mi.).
Population: about 2,250,000.
Largest towns: Brighton (163,750).*
            Gillingham (91,000).*
            Hove (72,750).
            Hastings (70,000).*
            Eastbourne (69,250).*
            Maidstone (59,750).
            Guildford (54,000).
            Reigate (53,750) (includes Redhill).
            Rochester (50, 250).
            Chatham (49,000).
            Margate (45,750).
            Folkestone (44,000).
            Tunbridge Wells (39,750).
            Ramsgate (37,000).
            Dover (35,250).
            Canterbury (33,250).*
            Ashford (28,000).

* 1969 estimates.

About 75 per cent of this region is in improved farmland, with tillage roughly equal in extent to grass.

Numbers of livestock: cattle, 415,000;
            sheep, 975,000;
            pigs, 325,000;
            poultry, 6,750,000.

About half of Surrey and most of Kent and Sussex are included in Southeast England. The regional boundary, drawn from the estuary of the Thames near Gravesend, along the crest of the Chalk hills which face into the Weald, and thence to the Channel coast near Shoreham, separates it from the London and Hampshire Basins. The whole coastal belt of North Kent is included in Southeast England, but the Coastal Plain of Sussex is excluded (Figs. 13:1, 27:1).

On a small-scale map such a boundary is clear and well-defined, but when the scale is large enough to give the appreciable width to the Chalk cuestas a problem immediately arises. A cuesta is a distinctive physical unit, which a boundary fixed on the scarp-crest divides artificially into two parts. For many purposes it is convenient to refer to the whole of the North and South Downs in describing

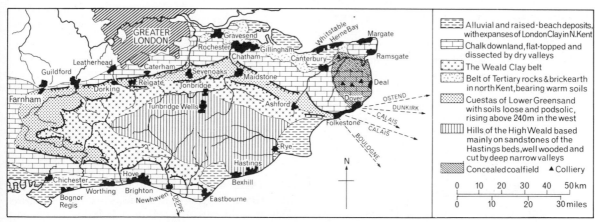

FIG. 27:1. Southeast England: physique and main settlements

Southeast England, just as the backslopes of the North Downs and of the Chilterns may suitably be included in an account of the London Basin.

Structure and Drainage

Southeast England contrasts very strongly indeed with the regions which adjoin it. Structurally it is an area of uplift, while the London and Hampshire Basins are areas of structural depression. Whereas the land of these two basins slopes down towards large inlets on which the two regional capitals are located, Southeast England is a region of infacing scarps and concentric vales which encircle a hilly core. Most of the Southeast is taken up by the Weald, where the pattern of relief delicately reflects the strength and attitude of the underlying rocks. The Weald was not glaciated, its rocks vary greatly in resistance to erosion, and its trunk rivers have cut deeply into weak strata. The Wealden landforms are therefore boldly carved. As the structural pattern is fairly simple, the groups of relief-elements are few in number.

Many fine examples of two classes of stream are to be found in Southeast England. The vales eroded along the strike of weak outcrops have been excavated, in the main, by subsequent streams, but the rock-waste has been, and is still being, carried away by streams which flow on consequent lines and break through the encircling hills in deep gaps. They cross the broken belt of Lower Greensand and the more continuous Chalk downland because they have been superimposed across the geological grain. The gaps of the Stour, Medway, Darent, Mole, and Wey on the north, and those of the Arun, Adur, Ouse, and Cuckmere on the south bear witness to a former pattern of consequents draining more-or-less directly outwards from the central part of the Weald. The consequents were initiated by up-warping during Tertiary times; as they have cut down they have thrown out subsequents along the clay-belts, and these subsequents have taken over most of the drainage-system. The longest subsequents naturally belong to the most powerful streams—the Medway, the Wey, and the Arun. Some of the wind-gaps in the Chalk mark the lines of former streams which have been dismembered; the latest known capture is that of the Blackwater, which used to flow through the Farnham Gap but has lost its headwaters to the piratical Wey.

The Forest Ridges

The centrally hilly portion of this region goes under various names—the High Weald, the Forest Ridges, and Ashdown Forest. It is based on the Hastings Beds, which were laid down in a subsiding basin where continuous sedimentation bridged the gap of time between the Jurassic and Cretaceous periods. The Hastings Beds consist mostly of sandstones spearated by thin formations of clay; being rather poorly cemented, they weather freely into a deep soil, and being permeable, they are little affected by surface wash. The Forest Ridges rise to more than 180 m. between sharply-cut young valleys, many of which run east–west along the lines of the folds and faults produced by Tertiary earth-movement. In the natural state the Forest Ridges were covered in woodland dominated by durmast oak, for their soils are not coarse and permeable enough to be podsolised.

Large numbers of pigs were pastured in the forests of the Central Weald during the Dark Ages and the early Middle Ages, each manor on the outskirts of the region having customary rights over a certain portion of the woodland. The area became slowly more accessible as small settlements were established in clearings, and place-names significantly ending in *hurst* and *den* were widely applied, but the main attack on the trees came from the iron-workers who exploited the ore of the Hastings Beds and used the local trees in making charcoal; abandoned hammer-ponds which supplied water-power to the medieval and post-medieval forges can still be seen. Oak timber was also cut for ship-building, particularly during the 18th century. Despite the concern already felt during Tudor times over the depletion of the Wealden forests, the Forest Ridges are quite heavily wooded at the present day—indeed, this area and the vale which surrounds it are richer in hardwood trees than any other part of the British Isles. Individual woods are small and well-managed, the post-war shortage of timber having made them attractive prospects for investment. Oak-hazel and chestnut coppices yield small timber, including hop-poles.

The Low Weald

Surrounding the Forest Ridges is a great horse-shoe-shaped belt of vale country, eroded in the thick and weak Weald Clay which dips off the Hastings Beds on all sides. This is the Low Weald, where the ground stands well below the levels of the Forest Ridges and where the surface is gently undulating. The Weald Clay cannot sustain steep slopes such as occur on the Hastings Beds. As it is impermeable, there are many surface streams. Where gradients are gentle it is liable to develop meadow soils, and the broad flood-plains along the larger rivers were formerly very ill-drained indeed. The Weald Clay is siliceous, so that it becomes very sticky in wet weather, and travel in the vale was difficult before the days of well-surfaced roads. The forests, dominated by the stalked oak, long resisted clearing.

Inner Cuestas

The belt of lowland is overlooked on the north and west by scarps based on the Lower Greensand, a generally sandy formation which varies in strength and in thickness from place to place. At the eastern end it is much eroded and the scarp is discontinuous, but the ground rises in a ridge west of the Medway and exceeds 290 m. on Leith Hill between the Mole and the Wey. At the western end of the Weald comes a whole block of high ground, culminating in Blackdown (about 280 m.), but, as the outcrop swings round towards the southeast, the formation thins out and the line of hills tails away. The Lower Greensand is typically very permeable, and the soils formed on its coarse sandstones have been heavily leached, tending strongly to form podsols. Left to themselves, they would probably carry heather, bracken, bramble, birch and occasional oaks, and heathland and scrubby woods do indeed occur in places, but conifers which may originally have been introduced by man have spread far and wide.

Along the northern rim of the Weald, the hills eroded in the Lower Greensand are separated from the Chalk downs by a narrow but continuous vale eroded in the Gault. The largest development of this vale occurs in the basins of the Medway and the Darent, where it is called the Vale of Holmesdale. On its northern side there may be a minor scarp formed on the Upper Greensand, but the Gault vale is everywhere overlooked by the infacing Chalk scarps which enclose the Weald.

The Chalk Rim

Seen from a distance, the Chalk scarps appear to rise in continuous walls, and they are in actuality continuous for long distances, having retreated as a whole instead of being dissected into fragments. The Chalk forms high ground because it is thick, permeable, and much stronger than the Gault beneath it or the Tertiary rocks above. Water easily passes through its many joints, so that the valleys of the backslopes are streamless (Plate 77).

The width of the Chalk downland varies according to the dip. In the South Downs the dip changes little, but in the North Downs it ranges from very

FIG. 27:2. Land-use sample for the northern rim of the Weald, in Kent. The rough grazing occurs on the scarp of the North Downs: contours in feet

steep in the Hog's Back to very gentle in the area south of Canterbury. Consequently the Hog's Back is narrow and slopes steeply down on either side, whereas in East Kent the block of Chalkland is wide. In the Isle of Thanet the Chalk rises in a small anticline beyond the floodplain of the Stour.

The soils of the Chalk scarps are of the shallow, humified, and lime-rich group called rendzina. Soil-creep on the steep scarps keeps the rendzinas shallow, but thickens and enriches the soils of the scarp-foot belt. Soils on the crests of the Downs are quite varied, the reddish, stony soils of the Clay-with-Flints attaining considerable depth on the highest summits, bare Chalk soils occurring on old marine benches at about 180 m., and sandy patches complicating the pattern in places. Bare Chalk soils

PLATE 77. Scarp-face of the South Downs. Most of the visible part of the backslope is in permanent grass, the scarp is in rough grazing, and the vale country below is in mixed farmland and wood.

are most widespread on the South Downs, where in the natural state they would probably be covered by scrub and coarse grass; soils of the Clay-with-Flints can support thick woodland, while the loose sands, restricted in extent, tend to be under heath. If short grassland exists on the Downs, it is the product of centuries of burning, clearing, and grazing (cf. Fig. 27:2).

North Kent

The backslope of the Chalk in North Kent passes under a broad strip of Tertiary rocks, where warm sandy loams have developed on friable parent materials, and where soils formed on patches of loess (brickearth) are also loamy and warm. These warm soils are the physical basis of the market-gardening and fruit-growing of North Kent. Cultivation of the same kind is carried on within the Weald near Maidstone, where warm soils occur on

brickearth, river terraces, and a lime-rich development of the Lower Greensand.

The Seaward End

The several belts of contrasted terrain in Southeast England are all truncated by the sea in the east. The tip of the Weald lies beyond the Channel in the Boulonnais. Resistant formations project in headlands: the North Foreland is the cliffed extremity of the Chalk in Thanet, the South Foreland, and the cliffs of Dover mark the end of the North Downs, the sandy Hastings Beds reach the sea in cliffs at the town of Hastings, and the South Downs terminate in the Seven Sisters and Beachy Head. But the greatest projection of the land occurs in Romney Marsh, a depositional feature, with its tip at Dungeness. Constructive waves have been adding shingle ridges on the eastern side for at least two thousand years, and floodwater has covered the shingle with alluvium. The fact that Romney Marsh abuts directly on to the Weald Clay belt is accidental, for old cliffs cut in the Weald Clay rise sharply from the levels of the Marsh (Plate 78). The Pevensey Levels at the other end of the Weald Clay outcrop have a different origin, being due to the impounding of a lagoon by a bar and to subsequent infilling by sediment.

January temperature of about 2 °C. is adequately compensated by warm summers in which the July mean rises to 16° or more. Summers are very sunny for the British Isles, and the countryside wears a genial aspect in all but the worst years. Standing crops in the rather small fields are set off by their background of woods and flourishing hedgerow trees.

PLATE 78. View across the northern tip of Romney Marsh, to the Chalk cliffs beyond Folkestone.

Climate and Agriculture

The rural aspect of the Wealden scene is enhanced by the effects of climate on growing plants. By comparison with, say, the Midland Triangle, the Weald looks lush. Rainfall is not heavy—from about 600 mm. in the northeast to something more than 750 in the west—and the rather low mean

Tillage is widespread in Southeast England, especially since it has greatly increased in extent since 1939 in response to wartime and post-war conditions. This region was certain to share in the conversion of permanent grass to rotation grass or tillage, for it lies on the drier side of England and is well suited climatically to arable farming. Its farmers, however, are less heavily committed to arable working than are those of Holderness, Lincolnshire, the Fenlands, and East Anglia, so that much land was put to grass in the depressed 1930s and land was available for ploughing-up when conditions changed.

There are differences between the northeast and the southwest parts of the region. The former is drier, sunnier, more highly tilled, and more involved in cash-cropping than is the latter, which has the higher proportion of grassland, fodder crops, and cattle. It contains much bare Chalkland in the South Downs, and has the heavier rainfall. The several terrains of the region also differ from one to another, quite apart from the general transition across the region. The sandy soils of the Forest Ridges are much tilled, while the heavy clays of the Low Weald are largely in permanent grass. Parts of the Lower Greensand belt and of the Gault vale are under the plough today, and cropland, extending on to the flanks of the North Downs, is also well in evidence on the summits wherever the Chalk is mantled by some other deposit.

Grain crops take about two-thirds of the tillage in the region, with barley the main crop throughout, although there is also a considerable wheat acreage. Potatoes are grown the more widely in the northeast and fodder crops in the southwest, but in general the internal differences in the agriculture of this region are chiefly matters of transition rather than of contrast.

Dairy cattle everywhere outnumber beefstock, for farms are well within reach either of London or of the coastal towns. The large number of pigs corresponds to the high development of dairy-farming. There are nearly three times as many sheep as cattle in this region, which records one of the three concentrations of sheep outside Highland Britain (Fig. 5:21). The main areas of sheep pasture lie on the North Downs and on Romney Marsh, but the sheep do not live always on permanent grassland—they are not very numerous on the South Downs, having been displaced by dairy cattle, and have been partly displaced from Romney Marsh by arable farming.

The second most extensive crop in Kent is orchard fruit, which takes nearly a quarter of all cropland. The combined acreage of orchard fruit, small fruits, hops, flowers, and vegetables other than potatoes amounts in Kent to more than a third of the land in crops. Much of the fruit-growing and market-gardening is concentrated in the two belts of warm soils in the Medway valley and in North Kent, but specialised cultivation is well represented in most parts of the county. The orchard lands of Kent are unrivalled in the British Isles (Fig. 5:19), and Kentish hopfields produce more than half the British crop of hops.

The highly specialised production of fruit and vegetables, depending largely on London for its market and for its enormous force of seasonal labour, has been greatly helped by the development of road transport. London itself consumes much of the produce, but some is sold in London for redistribution.

Fruit-farming is a highly competitive undertaking, with very highly-developed techniques. The orchards are planted on ground where slopes ensure that cold air will drain away during still nights in spring; in the Medway valley they line the face and crest of the Lower Greensand scarp, in North Kent they lie on the slopes of the gently-dissected belt of Tertiary rocks. Apples and cherries are the most common orchard fruits; on the best farms, the varieties of a single fruit are planted in accordance with subtle differences in the properties of the soils.

The production of soft fruits and of market-garden vegetables relies still more heavily upon rapid transport than does the growing of hard fruit. Kent is particularly successful with strawberries, raspberries, currants, gooseberries, cabbages, beans, and peas. Market-gardens are, however, to be found throughout the region, and hopfields are common in all eastern parts. Hop-growing is carried on under contract for the large breweries—including those of Burton-upon-Trent—which also take much of the barley crop for malting.

Distribution of People

Very intensive cultivation helps to account for the quite dense population of the region, which averages 900/km² outside the towns listed above. Although the true figure of rural population is somewhat lower than this, the largest towns contain under half the total population.

A wide scatter of small rural settlements is one of the outstanding characteristics of Southeast England, where a dispersed pattern has been inherited from the array of settlement established by the Jutes (Chap. 4). Some of the Wealden settlements have inevitably become larger in the course of the centuries, emerging as compact villages or growing into small towns, but nucleation is not typical of the region as a whole. Strings of spring-line villages are absent from the feet of some scarps.

Good building-stone is rare in most of the region, and the traditional building-materials are lath-and-plaster or brick, except in Northeast Kent where ragstone from the Lower Greensand is used. Half-timbered or palely coloured houses, set among abundant trees, contrast strongly with the suburban dwellings on the southern outskirts of the metropolis, and farmland interlocks with woodland in a countryside where large settlements are rare (Fig. 27:3).

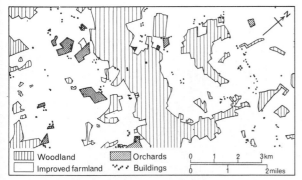

		0	1	2	3km
Woodland	Orchards				
Improved farmland	Buildings	0	1		2 miles

FIG. 27:3. Farmland, woodland, orchards, and scattered settlement in the central Weald

The deep gaps through the Chalk make Southeast England accessible from the London Basin, roads and railways leading to the interior and to the Channel coast. Parts of the northern Weald are well within the limits of daily commuting to London, and some towns have been stimulated into expansion by functioning as dormitories. Only two of the seventeen largest towns are located in the interior of the region, however, while nearly a quarter of the regional population lives in one of the seven largest coastal towns, and one in nine lives either in Brighton or in Hove. Coastal situation obviously favours town growth. Only along the shore is the effect of the metropolis fully expressed, in a chain of resorts and cross-Channel termini.

Resorts and Packet-Stations

Hove, Brighton, Eastbourne, Hastings, Ramsgate, and Margate, located in that order along the coast, function chiefly as resorts. Among them, they receive anything up to 12 million visitors a year. Their resort trade relied originally on the fashion for sea-bathing which developed in the late 18th and early 19th centuries, on their shelving beaches, and on their sunny climate. Brighton enjoyed royal favour in the late 1700s, but it was the railways which made all the resorts accessible to large numbers of visitors. Transport by road and rail, the impetus of success, the custom of taking holidays by the seaside, and vigorous publicity lend power-ful support to the modern resort trade (Plate 79).

The large resorts of Southeast England, located on continuous beaches, are ill-equipped to take part in seafaring, except for the inshore fishing which they practised when they were still no more than villages. Seaborne traffic has, indeed, been handicapped in some way along the whole coast throughout historical times. Rye and Winchelsea are among the ancient ports which have had their harbours blocked by marine deposition; Folkestone suffers from erosion, which has removed the original harbour and part of the early site of the town, and which continues to endanger the railway to Dover.

London is able to receive shipping in the broad Thames, and Southeast England gets its imported produce by way of London Docks; passenger services, however, demand speed, and great numbers of travellers to and from the Continent pass through the packet stations of Dover, Folkestone, and Newhaven (8,000), with their chief respective links to Calais, Boulogne, and Dieppe. All these have long histories as ports engaged in coasting trade, Continental trade, and fishing; their harbours are all served by railway, and are protected by breakwaters. Folkestone has a share in the resort trade, and both it and Dover have engineering industries.

To the sea routes across the Channel with termini in Southeast England has been added the post-war air ferry which operates from Lydd, on Romney Marsh. The airfield first used was at Lympne, at the top of the old cliffs which fringe the lowlying Marsh, but low cloud coming in from the sea frequently interrupted services and led to the transfer to Lydd. The ferry service, which has greatly increased in frequency with booming demand, takes cars and their passengers to Le Touquet in twenty minutes.

Dormitory Towns and Metropolitan Invasion

Guildford, Reigate, Tunbridge Wells, Dorking (22,500), and Sevenoaks (17,500) are members of the group of dormitory towns which lie on routes radiating from London. Tunbridge Wells, located —exceptionally for a large town—in the heart of the region, gained fame as a watering-place in the 18th century. Numbers of the most-used dormitories, however, are situated at one end of the gaps through the North Downs.

Where the Downs are wide, towns occur in pairs —for instance, Dorking and Leatherhead on the Mole Gap. Guildford, at the eastern end of the Hog's Back, occupies a very short gap and spreads up the slopes on to the adjacent hilltops; but even Guildford incorporates the sites of two early

PLATE 79. Brighton beach in summer.

settlements, and belongs both to the scarp-foot and to the dip-foot lines. In former times, Guildford controlled routes running not through but across the gap; for many centuries travel along the valley-bottom was difficult because of poor drainage, and Guildford arose where the dry route coming in from the west diverged to pass along the dip-foot to London and beneath the scarp to Canterbury. Dorking, Reigate and Redhill, Sevenoaks, and Maidstone are all on the Canterbury road.

London's grip on the northern and central parts of Southeast England is tightening. The airport at Gatwick (p. 327) and the new town at Crawley (Plate 20, Chap. 28) lie well within the Weald.

Maidstone and the North Coastal Belt

At Maidstone (Fig. 27:1), the navigable Medway is approached from the west by a road on the flank of the Lower Greensand cuesta. Maidstone, the county town of Kent, is the urban focus of an intensively-cultivated district. Its industries include the making of agricultural machinery, paper, beer, and cement, but cement-manufacture is concentrated chiefly in the Medway Gap through the North Downs.

At the other end of the Medway Gap, the Medway towns of Gillingham, Chatham, and Rochester stand on the tidal estuary where it is crossed by Watling Street. Rochester is well known for its manufacture of agricultural implements and road-rollers; it formerly made flying-boats and other aircraft, but its aircraft industry has been transferred to Belfast. Cement is manufactured here from chalk and estuarine mud. Chatham, the site of a naval dockyard which was founded by Elizabeth I, has a long record of naval construction. Its growth has stimulated the growth of Gillingham, which is also heavily dependent on naval orders, and, with more room to expand, has become larger than Chatham. The occupational census of 1951 recorded one in six of the working inhabitants of the two towns as members of the armed forces.

Sittingbourne (23,500) and Faversham (13,000) are at the heads of creeks, where tongues of firm rock exposed by river-erosion project towards the muddy shores of the estuary. Around them extend the orchards and market-gardens of North Kent, through them passes Watling Street on its way to Canterbury. Herne Bay and Whitstable on the coast demonstrate that a muddy sea-bed can favour an oyster fishery, without preventing a resort trade so long as there is a rapid rail connection with London.

Canterbury and Ashford

Canterbury and Ashford are at opposite ends of the long gap made by the Stour through the widening Downs. It would be difficult to find a more strongly-contrasting pair of towns. Canterbury, successively a British, Roman, and Jutish town, had its cathedral founded by St. Augustine in AD 597, and the city became a centre of pilgrimage after the murder of Thomas à Becket. It did not grow very large, however, and had spread very little beyond its stout walls by the end of the 18th century. The system of roads converging on Canterbury has evolved in part from the Roman ways leading inland from Lympne, Dover, Richborough, and Reculver.

Whereas Canterbury is exceptionally well nucleated, Ashford (Fig. 27:4) is tripartite. The old centre of the town is cramped by the buildings which occupy part of the former market-square, and displays many of the typical alterations of the form and function of buildings which accompany the town growth. The railway town with its locomotive shops lies apart, beyond the flood-plain of the Stour. It offers a striking example of 19th-century town-planning, with its houses arranged in a triangle and built in accordance with the rank in the railway service of their intended occupants. The third element of Ashford consists of the suburbs growing haphazardly along the roads to the south. A fourth element consists of a second new town.

The Kent Coalfield

Like the railway works at Ashford, the coal-mines of Kent needed workers brought from out-

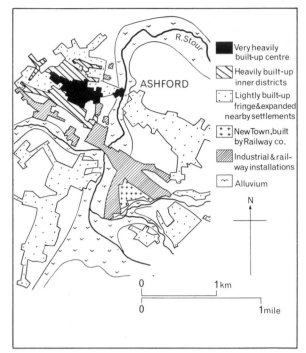

FIG. 27:4. Ashford, Kent: internal structure and near-by surroundings

side the region. The exploration of the coalfield was intertwined with the extension of railways in east Kent, both developments showing private enterprise at its least effective. Coal was proved in 1886 in a boring near Dover; the borehole was made, when work on the Channel Tunnel project was halted by Government order, in the bottom of the shaft. After a long, involved, and deplorable series of technical and financial failures, coal-mining started in 1918. Annual production reached 2 million tons in 1935, and future production was forecast at $2\frac{1}{2}$ million tons a year in the initial development plan. However, by 1970 the actual output was only about 1 million tons a year and showed no signs of increasing. Four collieries exist, at Chislet, Snowdon, Betteshanger, and Tilmanstone (Fig. 27:1). The seams are preserved in an eroded syncline in the Palaeozoic block which underlies the Cretaceous and Jurassic strata of the region, and shafts are deep. The friable coal, suited to the domestic rather than to the industrial market, can be sold over a wide area in competition with seaborne coal from the Northeast and rail-borne coal from the Midlands.

Chapter 28

The London Basin

Area: about 7,750 km² (3,000 sq. mi.).

Population: about 10,750,000.

Largest towns (*a*) The Greater London Conurbation (8,172,000).

(*b*) Towns near the Conurbation but not included in it:

    Thurrock (125,000).*

    Woking (67,500).

    Gravesend (51,500).

    Dartford (45,750).

    Leatherhead (35,500).

(*c*) Outlying towns:

    Southend (165,000).*

    Reading (130,000).*

    Slough (93,000).*

    Watford (75,750).

    High Wycombe (50,250).

    St. Albans (50,250).

    Staines (49,250).

    Aldershot (31,250).

The following are new towns; the figures given in brackets are those of planned totals of population:

    Basildon (106,000) (but cf. 122,750*).

    Bracknell (60,000).

    Crawley (75,000).

    Harlow (80,000).

    Hatfield (28,000).

    Hemel Hempstead (80,000).

    Stevenage (80,000).

    Welwyn Garden City (50,000).

Rather less than 60 per cent of this region is in improved farmland; a considerable fraction of the remainder is taken by urban and associated uses. Within the farmland, tillage is rather more extensive than grass.

Numbers of livestock: cattle, 325,000; sheep, 275,000; pigs, 430,000; poultry, 7,000,000.

The London Basin is broadly synclinal in structure. The Chalk which forms the upstanding Chilterns sinks gently underground towards the south-east, passing beneath the younger rocks which occupy the central parts of the Basin and reappearing in the North Downs. The syncline widens and deepens eastward, so that the Chalk outcrops diverge in this direction; it becomes narrower and shallower towards the west, so that the topographical basin narrows westward and the two belts of Chalkland finally unite beyond Newbury (Fig. 28:1).

Physical Evolution

The whole area has been affected by alternating submergence and emergence. At times of submergence the sea invaded the basin from the east, and marine and estuarine deposits accumulated above the downwarped Chalk. Such deposits are represented by the Thanet Beds, Woolwich Beds, and Blackheath Beds, all of which are mainly sandy or pebbly. Fairly deep submergence in a muddy sea is recorded in the overlying London Clay, which is widely preserved throughout the Basin. Upstream of London are found extensive remains of the Bagshot Beds, a sandy and permeable deposit which rests on the London Clay and forms blocks of low plateau.

A great deal is known of the erosional history of the London Basin. At heights above 240 m. are preserved remnants of a peneplain, in the form of subdued Chalk summits capped with Clay-with-Flints. Between 165 and 195 m. come the remains of a marine bench, appearing as broad flat-topped spurs on the backslope of the Chilterns and in places cutting right across the North Downs. At a little

---

* 1969 estimates.

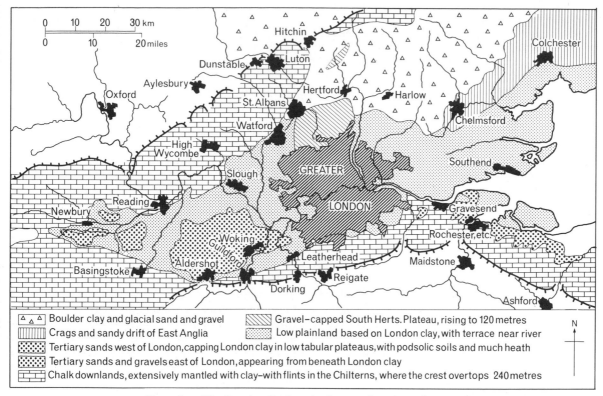

Boulder clay and glacial sand and gravel
Crags and sandy drift of East Anglia
Tertiary sands west of London, capping London clay in low tabular plateaus, with podsolic soils and much heath
Tertiary sands and gravels east of London, appearing from beneath London clay
Chalk downlands, extensively mantled with clay–with flints in the Chilterns, where the crest overtops 240 metres

Gravel–capped South Herts. Plateau, rising to 120 metres
Low plainland based on London clay, with terrace near river

FIG. 28:1. The London Basin: physique and main settlements

over 120 m. are the relics of a gravel spread laid down by the ancestral Thames when sea-level stood at about the 120 m. mark; these gravels are well in evidence on the South Herts. Plateau, a dissected block based on London Clay but much obscured by younger material.

The ancestral Thames flowed from west-south-west to east-northeast, well to the north of the present line. Part of the old track is indicated by the reach between Henley and Marlow, where the Thames is incised into the Chiltern Chalk. The river was diverted to the south by ice, which over-rode the Chalkland as far west as the Hitchin gap and sent prongs up the river-valleys which it invaded. The full story of the diversion is long and complex, but the net effect is that the Thames now flows round the south of the South Herts. Plateau. Thick deposits of sand and gravel washed out from the melting ice lined the bottom of the Vale of St. Albans, where they are partly covered by boulder clay, and boulder clay becomes thick and wide-spread east of the river Lea.

Intermittent falls of sea-level caused the Thames and its tributaries to be rejuvenated and to cut down anew. The deposits of their old valley-floors remain as terraces, covered in places by brickearth, which line the inner valley of the main river throughout the whole length of the Basin, but are most widely developed in the reach from Slough downstream, where they form wide, gravel-strewn flats above the level of the flood-plain.

The last recorded movement was one of sub-mergence, which flooded the river-mouths at the eastern end of the Basin and converted them into wide, shallow estuaries. This submergence was due in part to the post-glacial rise in sea-level which has affected all the coasts of the British Isles, but in the very east of the London Basin the crust itself sagged gently downwards, increasing the extent of sub-mergence and encouraging the development of muddy creeks and coastal marshes.

THE REGION OUTSIDE THE METROPOLIS

The West

Much of the London Basin beyond the bounds of Greater London is still rural. Slough is the last big metropolitan outpost on the upstream side, although Maidenhead (35,000) functions as a dormitory for London as well as a riverside resort. The western part of the London Basin has an urban focus of its own in Reading, with Newbury (20,500) and Hungerford (3,000) as lesser centres.

Newbury is located on the Kennet, in the middle of a valley-basin four or five miles in radius, while Reading has spread on both sides of the Kennet just above the confluence with the Thames, and lies near the edge of a piece of vale country some twenty miles across. Thus the immediate hinterland of Reading is about five times as large as that of Newbury. Here is one reason for the difference in the sizes of the two towns; another lies in the situation of Reading on the route through Goring Gap and close to the navigable Thames.

The industrial history of Newbury illustrates the detachment of manufacture from its original dependence on farming. The story includes the decline of the weaving for which Newbury was famous in the late 15th and early 16th centuries, when Jack of Newbury set up the first real factory in England; but if weaving went, brewing and flour-milling were retained. The town mills date from Saxon times. Engineering began with a local millwright in the late 1700s, who became an agricultural engineer and produced a plough of improved design, and the firm which he founded now makes marine engines. The making of oak furniture—an industry rooted in the local countryside—has been succeeded by the production of light aircraft and gliders. Newbury remains a small town, however, with all the charm of a southern English market centre. Even the Kennet–Avon Canal, from which so much was hoped in the way of trade and industry, is now obsolete after less than 150 years of use, and ranks as an antiquity of civil engineering.

Similar trends to those epitomised in Newbury are traceable in the more complex case of Reading. Successively a British, Romano-British, and Saxon settlement, the centre of Reading is based on a patch of terrace above the fordable Kennet (Fig. 28:2). Reading as a royal burgh was second in Berkshire only to Wallingford at the time of the Domesday Survey, and became, like Newbury, a medieval centre of textile-making. The cloth trade was destroyed by the Civil War, but the corn and cattle markets continued to operate, as they still do. Reading became a considerable centre of commerce, but its industrial days did not reopen until the late 18th century. Brewing, the manufacture of farm equipment and horticultural machinery, seed-growing, and biscuit-making were all more or less closely related, at the outset, to the activities of the neighbouring farms and gardens, but the last two activities in particular have far outgrown their origins. The largest single manufacturing concern in Reading today is a biscuit factory, the largest single industry is engineering. Weighing machines, pumps, electrical equipment, metal boxes, and windows are among the engineering products; for none of the relevant trades can any obvious locating factor be given. Industrial Reading was greatly stimulated by the railway, which reached the town in 1840. In these present days of heavy road traffic, Reading is a centre of bus routes—a sign of its importance in retail trade, which amounts to £30 million a year.

The rural environs of Newbury and Reading are largely in farmland. The general character of local farming is indicated by figures for Berkshire, even though the county—extending over the Chalk belt into the Vale of White Horse—does not give a wholly satisfactory sample. Eighty per cent of Berkshire is in farmland, with half the farmland in grass

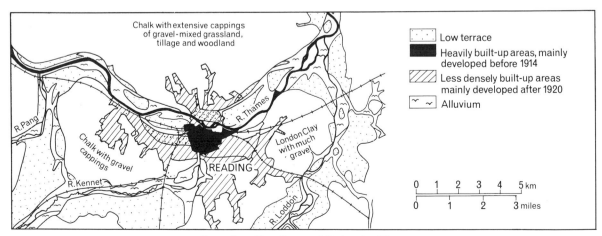

FIG. 28:2. Reading and its local setting

and half in tillage. The main tillage crops are cereals, with barley leading; permanent grass is more extensive than rotation grass, and dairying and the growing of cereals for sale are the principal farming interests. Since 1939 there has been a marked increase in tillage, both for cash and for fodder crops, in the whole western part of the London Basin, but at the same time the number of cattle—both beef and dairy—has risen.

The Bagshot Plateau and its Surroundings

Rural settlement is quite thickly scattered throughout the upper part of the London Basin, avoiding the broad flood-plains but being well represented on the adjoining river-terraces. Villages are more typical of the lower levels than of the modest hills, where signs of piecemeal reclamation appear in scattered dwellings. There is still woodland and near-heath on the podsols developed on the Bagshot sand on either side of the Kennet, and country of the same kind extends across the Blackwater in the southeast.

Here, however, the countryside begins to appear either military or residential. Part of the former block of dry heathland between the Blackwater and the Wey has been taken for training-grounds, on which lie Aldershot, Farnborough, Camberley, and Bisley. A criss-cross of electrified suburban railways denotes the nearness of London, with Virginia Water, the climax of dormitory settlement, still building detached houses amid mature coniferous trees. Between the steep-sided Bagshot Plateau and the southward extension of London on to the North Downs lie the broad lower valleys of the Wey and Mole, containing Guildford and Leatherhead at the mouths of gaps through the Chalk, and the dormitory town of Woking between Guildford and the congested Thames crossing at Staines.

The Chilterns

Northeast of Reading the Thames enters the Chilterns, which are highly dissected by systems of dry valleys running between tabular divides. The water-table lies far beneath most of the surface, and rural settlement is rather sparse. Elongated towns are wedged into the valleys, most of them on roads leading to gaps in the crest of the cuesta—High Wycombe on the Wye, Amersham on the Misbourne, Chesham on the Chess, Hemel Hempstead on the Gade, and Berkhampstead on the tributary Bulbourne, Harpenden in a dry valley. Stevenage lies in the broad, drift-encumbered corridor at the northeast end of the Chiltern plateau, Dunstable on Watling Street.

The past fortunes of Chiltern towns have been as varied as their predictable futures are dissimilar. Most of them serve to some extent as dormitories for London. High Wycombe, possessing a manufacture of furniture, was able to attract engineering; Dunstable, engaged like its larger neighbour Luton (Chap. 23) in the motor industry, has more than trebled its population since the 1931 census, while Hemel Hempstead and Stevenage have expanded with the addition of new towns, their modern factories and houses spreading rapidly across country. Much of Hemel Hempstead New Town stands on the top of the Chiltern Plateau, but the older towns are mainly confined in their narrow valleys, out of sight from the flat summits. The typical Chiltern scene consists of farmland diversified by woods and belts of ornamental timber.

Most of the Chiltern timber is deciduous. Beech—the original basis of furniture-making at High Wycombe—is quite prominent still, although oak-woods are the most characteristic. In some places the woods deteriorate into tangled hawthorn scrub, which can grow thickly on the widely-developed soils of the Clay-with-Flints; these explain the one-time presence of almost continuous forest on the Chiltern Plateau, and favour tillage where the land is farmed.

At the present time there is far more tillage on the Chilterns than there was in 1939. The Chilterns lie in that belt which, stretching from Kent to Nottinghamshire, has experienced a marked war-time and post-war extension of tillage, especially for cash crops. The figures for Hertfordshire give a very rough guide to the land-use of the district; about 70 per cent of the county is in farmland, with 60 per cent of the farmland in tillage, and 40 per cent in grass. Cereals are by far the most extensive tillage crops, occupying nearly four-fifths of the cropland, with barley leading.

The perceptible difference between the farming of the Chiltern Plateau and that of the environs of Newbury and Reading corresponds to difference of soils and of climate. The second of the two areas includes quite extensive soils developed on the London Clay, while the soils of the Chiltern Plateau are, in general, of lighter kinds. Hertfordshire is slightly less rainy than Berkshire, with some 550 mm. of rain a year against 700, and is slightly the more extreme in range of temperature. Thus the northeastern part of the London Basin falls within the area where the growing of cereals and potatoes is apt to increase in times of increasing demand for these crops, whereas Berkshire has some affinities with the grazing-lands of the Midlands and the Borders of the West Country.

The Vale of St. Albans, the Lea Valley, the South Herts. Plateau, the Thames Valley above and below London

South of the Chilterns comes the drift-filled Vale of St. Albans, with Hertford and Ware, two small country towns of great antiquity, at the eastern end. These two towns have not developed industry on the scale displayed by Hatfield, St. Albans, and Watford, which lies on routes between London and the industrial Midlands, and where engineering is well established with products including aircraft, aircraft components, and tractors.

Many gravel pits in the glacial outwash of the Vale of St. Albans supply building-sand and aggregate to the metropolis, and other pits are at work in the river-laid gravels west of London, in the valleys of the Thames and the Colne. Here, on the upstream side of the capital, is a stretch of low-lying vale, where flood-plains and wide, flat terraces line gently-sloping valleys cut in London Clay. For a very long time the clayland was thickly wooded, and even after it had been cleared it carried little settlement. Drainage works begun in the 19th century, however, have enabled building to spread far beyond the limits of the well-drained terraces, and the outlying settlements of former times have been joined to London. Mechanical engineering is well developed in this part of the region, and there are many factories producing foodstuffs, clothing, light electrical goods, and plastics. Slough lies at the western end of the industrial ribbon, on the opposite side of the river to the royal seat of Windsor.

Parts of the floodplains above London have been taken for use as reservoirs. Parts of the terraces are under market-gardens, which have been pushed westwards and have expanded as London grew. In places the terrace gravels are covered by loess (brickearth), and on the brickearth soils market-gardening is especially prominent. In the natural state the brickearth soils were infertile, being seriously deficient in humus and potash, liable to dry out in summer, and becoming soggy in winter; they were avoided by early settlement, which was generally located on the water-bearing terrace gravels. As raw material for intensive cultivation, however, the brickearth soils are good. The demands of the London market made it profitable to fertilise them heavily, and their warmth promotes rapid growth of vegetable crops.

Similar developments have occurred in the Lea Valley downstream of Ware (Fig. 28:3). The Lea flows southwards, on the western side of the South Herts. Plateau, in a broad trench floored with alluvium, below terraces widely mantled with loess. As in the Thames valley above London, Dark-Age settlement avoided the brickearth, which came under intensive cultivation only as metropolitan demands enforced themselves. Here too the market-gardens were pushed further and further up the valley as London spread. During the 19th century and in the early part of the 20th century, many glasshouses were built in the Lea Valley, despite the drainage of cold air into the valley on still nights, and despite the increasing pollution of the atmosphere by London smoke. The greatest single concentration of glasshouses in the world is located in the Lea Valley, but growing under glass in this locality has passed its peak. Market-gardens are disappearing under buildings. Where the brickearth has been used in brickworks, the shallow worked-out pits are commonly occupied by factories. Light industry—especially electrical industry—lines the main roads to the north, but heavy metalwork is confined to the floodplain. Gravel-pits and reservoirs recur in the valley-bottom (Plate 80).

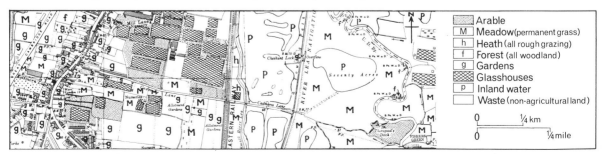

FIG. 28:3. Land-use for the Lea Valley. The railway in the centre follows the boundary between the flood-plain on the east and terrace on the west. The terrace is widely covered with brickearth, the flood-plain has been exploited for gravel

PLATE 80. Wet gravel-workings in the Lea Valley where the water-table is always high.

West of the Lea Valley, north of London, and south of the Vale of St. Albans lies the South Herts. Plateau, still in part well wooded, with sparse hamlets and single settlements. Its southern flank, however, is within the suburban limits of London, and land which produced hay and milk fifty or a hundred years ago is now heavily built-up.

North London has spread more widely on the western side of the Lea Valley than on the eastern. On the east the metropolis ends rather abruptly against the farmland of Essex. Epping Forest has been in part saved from destruction, and remains a bastion of country against spreading town. Further east still, Romford has not yet lost its character of market town, although it is growing fast by virtue of its tightening links with London. Southend is a resort whose nearness to London offsets the disadvantage of a muddy foreshore.

On the Thames itself, Tilbury is an outport of London. Thurrock, Gravesend, and Dartford have been reduced almost to annexes of the metropolis, and Dartford is not far from being physically incorporated in the sprawl of London building. The segment of country between Dartford and Croydon resembles the triangle defined by Staines, Guildford, and Kingston in being bound to London by electrified suburban railways.

THE METROPOLIS

So huge has London become that it inevitably overshadows every other town of the British Isles. Its size becomes still more impressive in a comparison with other towns of its region. Reading is the only town very largely independent of London which has reached a total of 100,000 inhabitants, and few of the other independent towns exceed 50,000. London apart, the London Basin has not done a great deal to encourage urban growth. Some allowance must be made for the centripetal pull of the capital, but a comparison of the London Basin with, say, East Anglia or the South Midlands, suggests that the other towns are normal and London the phenomenal exception.

No single factor or small group of factors can be held to account for the remarkable growth of the town, either in medieval or in modern times. Even when every possible allowance has been made for a location on an estuary facing the mouths of the Rhine delta, it is still clear that the urban strength of London has diverse and ancient origins. Its size and urban force made it the object of jealousy and mistrust in medieval days, when the citizens of other towns regarded London much as some inhabitants of northern England are apt to regard it today.

The difficulties of explaining—or even of describing—the growth of London may be illustrated by a few statements of fact. Unlike Liverpool, Hull, and Glasgow, it serves no near coalfield. It has an enormous hinterland today, serving as an inlet and outlet for much of the country's external trade, but the chief hinterland of the Port of London is Greater London itself, and in earlier times the London Basin was much more rural than most of it is now. As an ecclesiastical centre London ranks below Canterbury and York. It became a university town only in the 19th century, and even then its university was partly a paper organisation. Admittedly it is the centre of national and Commonwealth government; but it was already the greatest town in England before a powerful Parliament was seated at Westminster, and long before colonies were founded overseas.

Complex though its origins have been, London is a geographical reality. The expanding town has survived repeated epidemics—including epidemics of plague and cholera—and has recovered from the devastating fires of 1666 and 1940. The Greater London Conurbation holds nearly one in five of the total population of England and Wales, and one in six of the total of industrial workers. More people live in Greater London than in Austria, Ceylon, Chile, Peru, Sweden, or Venezuela, and almost as many as in Australia, Belgium, or Portugal. The Conurbation sprawls across the London Basin, reaching from the North Downs to the South Herts. Plateau, laying a tight grip on settlements upstream in the Thames valley and downstream on the estuary.

Setting and Early Growth

The distribution of rock-types illuminates the study of the setting and early growth of London. Thick forests and unproductive heaths survived in this region well into the Middle Ages, and have not yet entirely vanished. Their general effect was to isolate London from remote parts of the Basin and, even more strongly, from places outside the region. Extensive woods covered much of Essex during Roman times and the Dark Ages, the trees growing thickly on the soils developed on bare London Clay or glacial deposits, while the bottom of the Lea Valley was under a mile-wide strip of marsh, and forest came in again on the clay and gravel soils of the South Herts. Plateau. The notoriously sticky soils of lowlands based on London Clay also supported trees, while the podsols developed on the Blackheath and Bagshot Beds were under oak-birch heath, gorse, and broom. Even on parts of the Chilterns there was much natural wood, for the soils of the Clay-with-Flints could retain ample moisture to sustain trees. The environs of early London, therefore, consisted of lightly-vegetated spreads of terrace, encircled on three sides by abundant forest. The fourth side, however, lay open to the sea. There was a land-route leading eastwards along the flank of the North Downs, across the belt of light soils which lies between the tabular crest of the Chalk and the indented, muddy shore of Kent (Chap. 4). It was when Roman invaders approached by this route that certain advantages of the site of London were made clear.

In Roman days it was possible to ford the river close to the present site of London Bridge. There was an alternative crossing at Brentford, but as soon as the lower route had been secured it became the more frequented, and the ford was replaced by a bridge. The mouths of the Walbrook and the Fleet provided harbours adequate for the limited needs of Roman times, for most cross-Channel shipping then made for Lympne, Dover, Richborough, or Reculver. Roads from these ports converged on Canterbury, whence Watling Street ran to London. A town was laid out inside defensive walls, including the hills on which the Tower and St. Paul's now stand, and coinciding roughly with the eastern two-thirds of the City.

Legions were detailed to construct roads radiating west, northwest, north and northeast from London, and the Roman Londinium became the effective focus of civil government in the province of Britannia, but it was by no means as pre-eminent at that time as it is today. St. Albans, for instance, remained an autonomous town—a political experiment of the emperor Claudius. The municipal independence of St. Albans was, in some degree, a measure of the strength of the forest barrier between that town and London.

Significantly enough, the Roman town at St. Albans adjoined a conquered British capital, which had formerly been located at near-by Wheathampstead. Both sites lie in the Chalkland belt, along which the Icknield Way, avoiding the forests both of the London Basin and of the clay vales to the northwest, ran to Salisbury Plain. It was on the margin of Salisbury Plain that Winchester emerged, towards the end of the Dark Ages, as the capital of Wessex.

London's rise to the status of national capital could scarcely have been foretold in the Dark Ages. For a long period there was no English nation: separate kingdoms—Kent, Wessex, East Anglia, Northumbria, Mercia, and others—rose, expanded, and engaged in war. Some were extinguished by absorption, some by conquest, and some by Viking and Danish invasion. In the long run the most successful was Wessex, whose kings were able to recover the Danelaw in the 10th century and to reign over a united England, but, even in Wessex, the king and the court moved from place to place, so that the centre of legislature and administration shifted from one royal estate to another. Similar practices were followed by the Danish kings who ruled from 1016 to 1042, and the names of several towns appear in the records of the time as temporary centres of royal power.

There is little in the obscure Dark-Age history of London to suggest a conscious rivalry with Winchester. Even with the help of Domesday Book, it is impossible to make satisfactory comparisons of the sizes, urban strength, and urban consciousness of 11th-century English towns.[1] Judged by the number of moneyers, however, London, Winchester, and York were among the principal towns at the time of the Conquest, and London was a busy port carrying on a vigorous trade with near-by ports of the Continental mainland. Its history during the Dark Ages had not been wholly one of stagnation.

Although so little is known of pre-Domesday London, it is clear that civic administration had developed in the town to a most unusual degree. The burgesses were so powerful that William I concluded a treaty with them as a means of securing control of the flourishing town, which gained still more in importance from the building of the Tower,

[1] Domesday Book lists about seventy places with borough status, additional to boroughs on royal, ecclesiastical, and aristocratic estates, but is known to omit mention of certain towns which existed at the time of the survey.

Montfichet's Tower, and Bayard's Castle. The political connection with the Continent doubtless did much for London under the Normans: the significance of the situation of the town, on the nearest large estuary to Europe, was beginning to reveal itself. London never had merchant gilds, presumably because civic affairs were regulated strongly enough to make controls on trade unnecessary, and the already cosmopolitan town presumably profited from its commercial freedom. Its supremacy as a port appears in the tax records of 1204, when London merchants paid more than the merchants of any other English port.

The strongly centralised government of the Tudors was based on Westminster, the ancient royal centre eventually to be engulfed by London. London itself, with 75,000 inhabitants by 1500, had long been growing under the impetus of its own size, and by 1550 had secured 80 per cent of the country's external trade. The momentum which had carried it so far had already become independent of any advantages derived from its site or from its situation in its region. As the capital of a united country, and later of a united empire, it was to experience growth unaffected by its regional or by its national situation.

Physical Expansion and Functional Change

Within the Metropolis, however, qualities of site continued to be influential. When the growth of London is mapped by stages (Fig. 28:4), an immediate connection can be perceived between form and quality of the ground on the one hand, and mode and direction of growth on the other. Physical extension has been accompanied by functional change, the various early Londons indicated in Fig. 28:4 corresponding roughly to the distinctive areas of today.

The population of 75,000 in 1500 had become 150,000 or more by Elizabethan times; a century had sufficed to double the number of inhabitants. As the map shows, late-Tudor London was spreading along the north bank of the river, reaching out both to the east and to the west. Bankside settlement stretched from the Tower through Wapping to Shadwell. The Inns of Court already existed west of the City, and the area between the Strand and Holborn had been built-up. That is to say, late Tudor London included those areas which at the present time contain concentrations of business houses and newspaper offices, as well as parts of the existing West End. Buildings on Whitehall linked the Strand with the immediate surroundings of Westminster Abbey.

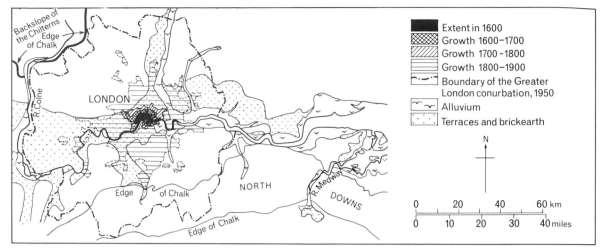

FIG. 28:4. Stages in the growth of London

On the south bank, Southwark lay at the far end of London Bridge, still the only bridge over the Thames at London, and a ribbon of buildings ran along the south bank of the river as far as Rotherhithe. The flood-plain alluvium further downstream had been empoldered and was in use as cattle pasture, but both London and Southwark stood on patches of terrace above the level of floods.

By the early 1700s, the ribbon-building reaching out from the City had become continuous town. Southwark was consolidating itself in between the roads which radiated southward, and Lambeth marshes were being drained, but the most marked extension had taken place towards the west, on the north bank, where building had reached the Tyburn, and Westminster Bridge built in 1738 testified to the growth of London on the upstream side. The whole of the area which is now called the West End had been built over by 1725, but the site of Hyde Park remained in pasture.

By 1800 London had a population of a million. Hyde Park, Green Park, and St. James's Park indented the fringe of a London which had caused to swell, and was fast uniting with, Chelsea, Paddington, Somers Town, Islington, and Bethnal Green. Streets and buildings extended continuously from Watling Street to the lower end of the Lea. Building by this time was clearly associated with gravel terraces, for London was large enough to abut on land of varying quality. The terraces had been first settled, for they alone could supply ground-water, and it was across the terraces that continuous building kept on spreading. By the end of the Napoleonic Wars, the settlement of South-

wark was merging with Walworth and Kennington, and Blackfriars bridge linked the western end of the City with the South Bank. The main port area remained below London Bridge, which set a limit to shipping by its narrow arches. Early 19th-century London thus included what are now recognised as the central districts. Tottenham Court Road, Oxford Street, Piccadilly, Whitehall, Shoreditch, and Whitechapel Road were all built-up; Soho, Mayfair, Westminster, and Spitalfields had emerged as recognisable divisions.

The pace of growth and of internal change increased as the 19th century drew on. The specialised functional areas of today could not have emerged unless houses had been converted to, or replaced by, shops and offices, and conversion and replacement could not have occurred if residents had not moved out. Large numbers of people could not have slept in the suburbs and worked in the centre without the aid of public transport. The huge 19th-century extension of London was, therefore, made practicable by advances in engineering.

Steam railways built during the 19th century do not cross inner London: the termini at Paddington, Marylebone, Euston, St. Pancras, and King's Cross lie roughly on the edge of London as it was in 1800. Lines from the east were able to penetrate the City, and four lines from the south cross the Thames to north-bank termini. Since the radial lines belonged to competing companies, no ring-railway was constructed, and, in any case, the suburban services were needed mainly to move people inwards and outwards to and from the centre, which acquired omnibus services and electric railways. The earliest electrified lines were partly exposed and partly underground, but the later tube railways run wholly through tunnels beneath central London, emerging to the surface only on the outskirts. Tunnelling continued well into the present century, its costs being kept down by the character of the London Clay, which allowed tunnels to be cut accurately and quickly; and it was renewed in the 1960s with the construction of the Victoria Line.

Land drains, installed—or at least begun—in the 19th century, enabled dense building to invade the outcrops of London Clay. But even when surface water is drained off, the clay is still liable to shrink when dry and to swell when wet; it makes a poor foundation for buildings, and numbers of the houses constructed upon it are liable to cracking. The extending tentacles of London spread preferentially across sandy and gravelly deposits, along the roads which themselves kept as far as possible to dry ground, but the spaces between the roads were built over as the fringing suburbs struck deeper and deeper into the country. Thus by 1900 the Greater London Conurbation had come into being, containing some 6 million inhabitants.

The achievements of 19th-century civil engineering in London included great improvements to the systems of water supply and sewage disposal, without which London could scarcely have grown so large. In a sense, the installations were the outcome of the needs of the time, but in another sense they were typical products of new industrial techniques. Piped water greatly speeded the settlement of clayland. On the terraces it superseded supplies from shallow wells, which were much contaminated and great spreaders of disease. Only in the 19th century did London shake itself free of the epidemics by which it had been troubled for so long.

The rise of consolidated authorities was almost inevitable in the circumstances of the 19th century, but was also a sign of characteristic changes in public service and administration. The Metropolitan Water Board was not actually established until 1902, when the century had turned, and the Port of London Authority came into being in 1908. Their formation amounted to a recognition of the unity of the port and of the Conurbation. By 1900, the sprawling town was consolidating itself by infilling many of its vacant spaces. In the early years of the 20th century, the population of Greater London increased no more rapidly than that of England and Wales as a whole. But although the impetus which had produced an enormous conurbation, with an enormous number of inhabitants, was dying away, people were still moving out from the centre, and the town continued to spread

physically. The functional characteristics of its inner districts became more and more strongly defined. During the inter-war period there was another spell of rapid increase in numbers, due mainly to migration, which helped to bring about the spread of suburbs. Very many estates of semi-detached houses came into being at this time, setting an architectural pattern which is now typical of many residential districts throughout the country.

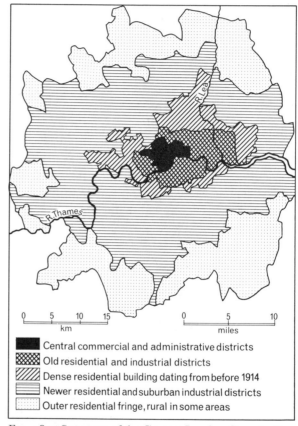

FIG. 28:5. Structure of the Greater London Conurbation

Five main divisions of the Conurbation have separated themselves out from one another (Fig. 28:5). The metropolitan centre of commerce, finance, and government—the City, the West End, and Westminster—has a very low density of resident population. The old residential, industrial, and dockside areas, developed in the late 18th and early 19th centuries, and corresponding in part to the East End, tend to suffer from urban blight, their houses sliding into disrepair and whole districts declining in social esteem. The third division includes high-density housing built in the late 19th and early 20th centuries. Some parts of this division have also gone downhill—Victorian and Edwardian houses, designed for large families and their servants, have commonly been subdivided into flats or simply let by rooms. The suburban ring includes the homes of half the people of the Conurbation, besides patches of older building where former outlying settlements have been engulfed, and belts of industry, especially of light industry located alongside trunk roads. Finally there comes the outer fringe, distinguished by low-density housing. Like the main suburban ring, this division experienced invasion by housing in the inter-war period, and in the post-war years some of its open spaces have been taken for estates of council houses. The 20th-century pattern of development has followed that of former times. London has thrust vigorously outwards on the outgoing routes, and after some delay the intervening gaps have been filled in.

Docks, Port Trade, and External Passenger Traffic

The dock system is largely the product of 19th-century engineering, although the 20th century has brought some notable additions and improvements. The need for docks arose from the high tidal range of the estuarine Thames, and from the congestion prevailing on the wharf-lined river. Each group of docks is located on the inside of a bend in the channel—that is, on the lobe of a meander, on flat ground underlain by alluvium and London Clay, and not greatly built-over (Fig. 28:6). Dock entrances could be made both on the upstream and the downstream sides of the systems (Plate 81). Two expectable tendencies can be noted in the development of the docks—the extension of docks further and further down the river, and a downstream increase in the size of basins. A certain specialisation in types of cargo is also detectable.

The London and St. Katharine Docks, on the north bank adjoining the Pool, adjoin the City.

Dating mainly from the first half of the 19th century, they specialise in handling cargoes of tea, fruit, wine, and wool; large quantities of general cargo are also dealt with. The site of this group of docks was already enclosed by continuous building when construction took place, and the quays are not rail-served. The Surrey Commercial Docks, on the opposite side of the Lower Pool, are scarcely better placed in relation to railways. This group, the outcome of 250 years of piecemeal development, handles much imported timber, especially from the Baltic, in addition to general cargo.

The West India and Millwall Docks are located on the Isle of Dogs, and the East India Dock by the confluence of the Lea. The elements of this group were completed at dates ranging from 1802 to 1870. The system is rail-served, is well equipped to handle bulk imports of grain, sugar, and hardwood, and shares in the import trade in fruit. The East India Dock has lost the site of its Export Basin to a power station, and now concentrates on coaster-borne traffic.

The Victoria and Albert Docks were opened in 1885 and 1880, and the King George V Dock was added to the group in 1921. The combined group of Royal Docks, occupying an extensive site between Gallions Reach and the mouth of the Lea, includes the largest collective sheet of impounded dock water in the world. The rail-served quays and transit sheds receive meat, grain, tobacco, and fruit among the cargoes imported from Commonwealth countries, the Americas, and the Far East. It is mainly by traffic through the Royal Docks that the Port of London acts as an inlet and outlet for the whole country.

Tilbury Docks were opened in 1886. Rail services were generously provided, but road access was limited, all road transport at the time of construction being horse-drawn. In later years the road

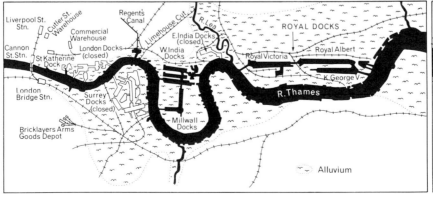
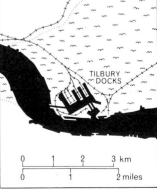

FIG. 28:6. The dock systems of London

PLATE 81. The West India Docks, looking upstream.

system has been improved, and more than half the import tonnage is now distributed by road. Enlargements have been carried out to allow Tilbury Docks to accommodate big ships, and trade is bound to increase in response to the construction of the Dartford–Purfleet tunnel under the Thames, dock extension, the building of a grain terminal, provision for container traffic and for roll-on roll-off transhipment, plus improved road access—all accomplishments of the 1960s. Tilbury Docks are designed for transit, providing no warehouses. Export cargoes include a wide range of manufactures; among the imports are the products of Australasia, the Indian sub-continent, and the oilfields which export from the Persian Gulf. Tilbury became London's nearest passenger port when the floating landing-stage was built in 1930; vehicle ferries connect it with termini on the European mainland.

The airports of London compete very strongly for passenger traffic, not only with Tilbury, but also with Harwich, Southampton, and packet stations on the Channel coast. London Airport is located on a wide expanse of flat terrace, east of the lower Colne and between the diverging roads to Staines and Slough. The second main terminal, at Gatwick, is rail-served. For some years Luton and Stansted served as supplementary or diversionary airports, and diversions on some occasions took passengers as far afield as Prestwick in Scotland. Existing plans, notwithstanding the serious suggestion of one geographer that a third terminal should be developed in Hyde Park, are for a third main field at Foulness, on the northern shore of the lower Thames Estuary.

London as an Industrial Region

Of the 4½ million workers in Greater London, fewer than 1 million are employed in manufacturing industry, but the proportion so employed is not much less than that in England and Wales as a whole. London takes its proportionate share in the metal and engineering trades, in timber-milling, in woodworking, and in the processing of foodstuffs, and has a high proportion of workers in garment-making, paper-milling, and printing and publishing. There is a great attraction to light industry in the huge local market offered by London, and London's industrial development in the inter-war period took place partly at the expense of the depressed industrial regions of the coalfields.

The downstream spread of docks was accompanied by the location on the lower river of industry which needs raw material in bulk—oil refining, sugar refining, timber-milling, and cement-making. In the Conurbation generally, however, industry is very widely scattered. Certain concentrations can be identified—the clothing and furniture industries in the East End, the modern electrical industries on radiating trunk roads and on the North Circular Road—but industry has not become as strongly localised as have service functions.

Industrialisation of the metropolitan area, relying heavily on the burning of fossil fuels, has significantly altered the local climate, creating for London a heat island of the sort familiar in many large urban areas (see bibliography: Chandler). Also, the Thames, used as a common sewer, became shockingly polluted. However, the Clean Air Act of 1956, progressively implemented to prevent the generation of smoke, has promoted a marked cleaning of London's air, a reduction in smog (now almost a thing of the past), and a reduction also in fog and cloud. Simultaneously, the control of discharge of industrial effluents by the Port of London Authority has meant a cleaning-up of the river itself. Wild birds, unknown in the London metropolitan area, have come back to rejoin the adjusted starlings and pigeons, and fish are once again invading the Thames.

Present Status and Future Prospects of the Metropolis

The Greater London Conurbation, as officially defined for census purposes, is remarkably self-contained. Of its 8 million people, fewer than 100,000 live in the Conurbation and work outside it; some 250,000 live outside it but come in to work. Most of the daily movement takes place within the limits of the Conurbation, with more than 1 million travelling daily between the central districts and the suburbs (Plate 82).

While Greater London has great advantages as a market, port town, and supplier of labour, it suffers undeniably from serious congestion. Attempts to build suburban houses on the edge of the surrounding country have defeated their own object, by converting country to suburb, and the definition of a Green Belt round the metropolis has not entirely arrested expansion (Plate 20). The building of new towns—at Stevenage, Crawley, Hemel Hempstead, Harlow, Welwyn Garden City, Hatfield, Basildon, Milton Keynes, and Bracknell—constitutes a kind of leapfrogging of London over the Green Belt. London outspill estates includes numbers of sites well outside the London Basin (see bibliography), while individual firms have migrated to places not only in the Midlands but also in Southwest and Northwest England, South Wales, and Central Scotland. Three main forces seem to drive the out-movement: congestion of transport (although this is rarely mentioned), shortage of space, and shortage of labour force. Although the metropolis continues to exert physical pressure on its borders, diminishing population densities in some at least of its residential districts plus ever-intensifying land-use competition have checked and even slightly reversed demographic growth and industrial expansion.

In consequence, with official encouragement and aid, numbers of London concerns, including office operations, have been migrating, and continue to migrate, whether to peripheral areas or to some

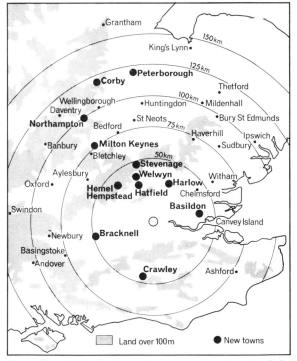

FIG. 28:7. Colonisation of south-eastern England by outposts of Metropolitan London

PLATE 82. London commuters jostle to board one of the few trains home during the nationwide go slow by the railway unions, April 1972.

PLATE 83. The beginning of vertical expansion—post-war flats at Roehampton.

other region. A perceptible result is to construct a new and enlarged Southeastern Region, on which sundry authoritative planning reports agree (see bibliography), delimited roughly by the Wash–Solent line of a former geographical generation, but usually excepting East Anglia. On the scheme of regional subdivision used in this book, the Southeast Region includes the London Basin, the Hampshire Basin, Southeast England, and part of the South Midlands Scarplands. As shown in Fig. 28:7, the metropolis is in fact directly affecting the future, growth, and economic activity of numerous places within a radius of 160 km (100 mi.). This is already the part of Britain with the strongest base of wealth (see bibliography: Rawstron and Coates;

Coates and Rawstron): it could well develop into an homogenised, very highly urbanised Southeast highly stocked with footloose industry.

Meantime the skyline of London has greatly changed in response to the redevelopment of areas devastated by bombing in World War II and to redevelopment in general (Plate 83). The most ambitious building project announced as yet is the fixing of a drop-gate barrier across the lower Thames, to remove the risk of flooding from the central estuary, including parts of Central London. In view of the occasional storm surges in the North Sea, plus the continuing slow geological subsidence of the estuarine area, this project seems wholly worthwhile.

APPENDIX
New Towns

	Date of designation	Population	
		End 1967	Ultimate
Great Britain:			
Stevenage	1946	61,700	100/105,000
Crawley	1947	63,700	75,000
Hemel Hempstead	1947	67,900	80,000
Harlow	1947	75,800	80,000
Aycliffe	1947	18,000	45,000
East Kilbride	1947	57,000	100,000
Peterlee	1948	20,000	30,000
Hatfield	1948	24,700	29,000
Welwyn	1948	44,300	50,000
Glenrothes	1948	23,700	75,000
Basildon	1949	75,000	140,000
Bracknell	1949	28,300	60,000
Cwmbran	1949	41,700	55,000
Corby	1950	47,500	80,000
Cumbernauld	1955	23,000	70,000
Skelmersdale	1961	16,000	80,000
Livingston	1962	7,200	100,000
Telford	1963	22,000	90,000
Redditch	1964	29,000	90,000
Runcorn	1964	28,800	90/100,000
Washington	1964	21,400	80,000
Irvine	1966	27,000	85,000
Milton Keynes	1967	40,000	250,000
Peterborough	1967	81,000	175,000
Newtown	1967	5,000	13,000
Northampton	1968	131,000	220,000
Warrington	1968	127,000	205,000
Northern Ireland:			
Craigavon	1965	41,000	150,000
Antrim	1966	7,000	30,000
Ballymena	1967	20,000	70,000

Source: Central Statistical Office

Chapter 29

Conclusion

DRASTIC changes in national and local economy and land-use, with associated change in the visible landscape, have been described in the foregoing chapters. Although the pace of change seems greater now than it has ever been before, the appearance of speed may be due in part to the difference between the limited perspective of the present day and the long, leisured vistas of history. It is difficult from this distance to appreciate the feelings aroused by Dark-Age invasions, by the Conquest, by the Black Death, by depopulation of medieval villages, by the Civil War, by parliamentary enclosure, by the French Revolutionary and Napoleonic Wars, by early industrialisation, by the Great Famine of Ireland, or by the agricultural depression of the late 19th century. To the people directly involved, and to many contemporary observers, these events must have seemed as vital and urgent as anything occurring today. On the other hand, very many of the processes which affected the geography of the British Isles before 1914 were initiated, and carried out, at some level lower than the national. Economic activity and its geographical distribution, the relationship between the people and the land, evolved for many centuries by natural selection. Only with the emergence of numerous nation-states in the 19th and 20th centuries, and with their involvement in world war, did national influence, control, and direction come to be thought necessary, useful, and inevitable.

In its external relations, the United Kingdom today is a single unit—affected as a whole by the interplay of world politics, by the political development of the Commonwealth, and by halting and dubious advance towards some kind of European unity. For many internal purposes, also, it is a single unit, and the trend towards a strongly centralised government has, during the inter-war and post-war periods, been very marked. Internal stresses, however, have not been entirely resolved. Among the former Celtic lands of the north and west, most of Ireland has detached itself from the United Kingdom. Movements of independence in Cornwall, the Orkneys, and the Shetlands—variously complicated by appeals for union with Brittany, Denmark, the Faroes, Iceland, and Norway—are small symptoms of the sort of feeling which is quite powerfully expressed by demands for increased control by Wales and Scotland over their own affairs. Whatever may happen in the future, it can at least be said that the past has not sufficed to anglicise the uplands of the west and north.

On the regional scale, as on the national, an historical view tends to minimise the swift drama of past change. The rapid rise—and equally rapid decline—of iron-manufacture in the Black Country and in South Wales lose their immediacy by belonging to the past. Region-wide conversion of agriculture in Southwest England and in East Anglia, having been accomplished, are accepted with scarcely a question. Scarcely a region, however, fails to record some mode of transformation during the last hundred, fifty, or even twenty years. The market-gardening and resort trade of coastlands in the south, the tourist industry of North Wales, the Lake District, and the Scottish Highlands, the threat to Scottish coal-mining, the decline in exports of coal and cotton, the rise of mechanical engineering—all, on the historical time-scale, are recent developments, separated by very few years from the establishment of industrial estates, the building of nuclear power stations, and the driving of motorways across the Midlands.

The most recent changes, and changes now in progress, loom large because they are close, and seem uncertain because their outcome is still not fully known. Without some scale of measurement, it is impossible to make a direct comparison between present and former rates of change. Every age of rapid technical development has been acclaimed as a climax—usually as a climax of progress, whatever that may mean—but it is undeniable that, during the 20th century, thermal, mechanical, and electrical power have been applied more widely and more effectively than ever before.

A direct result has been to increase mobility. Despite difficulties of congestion, travel is easier and swifter than in previous centuries. Increased real incomes make travel possible for a large fraction of the community, and daily journeys to work and annual journeys on holiday are now customary. Personal mobility for purposes of business and pleasure has increased. Internal migration, however, has been somewhat handicapped in the postwar period by the housing shortage; it is a sign of the times that successive national governments have made themselves responsible for the promotion and control of building-campaigns.

Social mobility—the possibility of moving on the social scale—has increased during the 20th century. However greatly the ethics of social classification may be deplored, people in practice apply their own criteria, often basing them on occupation. The increase in social mobility therefore amounts to increased occupational mobility—an increased chance for children to lose or gain occupational and social status by choosing—or being forced into— occupations different from those of their parents.

Although internal migration is beset by difficulty, occupational change is in practice often accompanied by a change of residence. The resulting redistribution of people, and the nation-wide effects of national newspapers and broadcasting, might be expected to reduce the contrasts between one region and another. Additional factors likely to work in the same direction are the dispersion of industry and of administration—a dispersion made possible by road transport and electric power. Dispersion of industry is already reflected in the new life injected into old towns, in the construction of new towns, and in the variety introduced into areas where industry has hitherto been uniform. The very fact of dispersion, however, demonstrates that centralising tendencies do not operate unopposed. The industrial pull of the coalfields, already weakened, can be expected to weaken further in the future. Moreover, new industries—such as the overlapping groups of petro-chemical and synthetic fibre industries—set whole new series of problems in location. Rising industrial output, rising consumption, and increase of population all encourage deliberate planning; for purposes of planning, large parts of the country, or even the whole country in some contexts, are taken as the fundamental unit.

Southeast England, for instance, is calculated to increase its population from $17\frac{3}{4}$ million to $21\frac{1}{4}$ million by 1980. Greater London has its own Council; Southampton–Portsmouth, Bletchley, and Newbury are all intended to undergo massive expansion, and Ashford, Ipswich, Northampton, Peterborough, Swindon, and Stansted are all to grow fast.

It need not be concluded, however, that differences among regions will become so blurred as to disappear. Quite apart from enduring physical contrasts, there are local loyalties, and some regional loyalties, which are dynamic enough not merely to persist but also to grow stronger. Local consciousness, if not regional consciousness, seems likely to continue in full force.

Although traditional dialects, with their distinctive vocabularies, are dying out it is quite possible that local and regional accents are becoming more and more specialised and distinctive with the passage of time. Broadcasting not only makes allowance for regional accents, but also demonstrates their great variety. It may well be significant that Lancashire and Yorkshire speech are distinguishable by accent, that the Liverpool area has developed its own accent within Lancashire, and that the Black Country, in the course of industrialisation, produced an accent all of its own. The pace and direction of the growth of local accents is impossible to gauge, but general observation reinforces the historical study of language in suggesting that regional developments on diverging lines are likely to take place. In this way, at least, contrasts between regions may well be enhanced. Customs, like speech, are slow to change, and can also display divergent trends. The southern limit of Rugby League football or of the custom of taking high tea are real social boundaries. Only detailed anthropological study could show where such boundaries should be drawn, to what extent they coincide with boundaries of other kinds, where lie the limits between contrasted accents, and where regions are thought, by their inhabitants, to end.

It may be doubted if people in general have any strong regional consciousness, beyond a vague sense of loyalty to their home town, their home area, or their home county. In any event, regional consciousness is very difficult to assess because of its subjective, subconscious, and emotional nature. In direct contrast, a very clear result emerges from recent studies—namely, that large towns tend to secure for themselves a service area, which is quite well marked-off from the adjacent service areas of neighbouring towns. The greatest towns, however, serve areas which include their smaller neighbours, some becoming regional capitals. It has repeatedly been suggested that the present administrative sub-division of the United Kingdom—a product of the Dark Ages and the Norman Conquest—should be revised on regional lines, giving practical expression in the work of administration to the effective status of regional capitals. Here, again, is a tendency opposed to centralisation on the national level.

In the towns themselves, as in the surrounding countryside, old and new are intermingled. It is fashionable with some today to show sentimental regard for railways and for Victorian architecture; but fascinating as these works of the 19th century may be, they form no more than one group of the products of the past. In every town and in every region, structures of diverse periods are to be seen. New in their day, and the expression of change in progress, they have been preserved by the forces of anti-change. Wherever old and new alike are combined in a unified scene—even when the unity is one of repeated variety—and wherever the activities of the people are subject to some localised influences, there a distinctive geographical character can be identified. So long as such a character can be perceived on a regional scale, regional geography will continue to serve its purpose of description, definition, assessment, and interpretation.

Bibliography

THE works listed below range widely in character, scope, and purpose. The statistical publications have provided much of the source-material for the foregoing chapters. Some of the text-books contain detailed accounts of single topics; others—particularly those intended for the general reader—are both wider in scope and generally lighter in treatment. Ease of reading, however, need imply neither deficiency of content nor over-simplification; slight and discursive books of a topographical kind have been rigidly excluded, and the works named are recommended as being both sound and up-to-date. Some of them provide most useful reviews of subjects linked with, but distinct from, geography.

The articles listed for the regional chapters have been selected to give recent accounts of varying aspects of regional life. With few exceptions, they have appeared in the *Advancement of Science*, the handbooks published by the British Association for annual meetings, *Economic Geography*, *Geography*, the *Geographical Journal*, *Geographical Studies*, the *Geographical Review*, the *Proceedings of the Geologists' Association*, the *Scottish Geographical Magazine*, or the *Transactions of the Institute of British Geographers*. Numerous works on Ireland appear in *Irish Geography*; the *East Midland Geographer* is among the university publications dealing with a particular area.

As far as possible, given works are cited under one head only, in order to keep the lists down to reasonable length. The main exceptions are those books or articles which deal with a certain subject in relation to more than one region. On the other side, statistics of agriculture, population, employment, and industry do not appear under the regional heads, although part of the regional text relies heavily upon them.

The recommended maps are either on the scale of 1 : 63,360 or on that of 1 : 25,000. Sheet-numbers for the 1 : 63,360 maps of Great Britain refer to the Seventh Series. Sheets of the 1 : 25,000 map are not named by the Ordnance Survey, but names have been added below in order to help identification. Generally speaking, the recommended 1 : 63,360 sheets provide as typical a sample as possible of a whole region, while the 1 : 25,000 sheets illustrate single important aspects.

PART ONE

1. LIVELIHOOD AND LAND USE

Central Statistical Office: *Annual Abstract of Statistics*. London: H.M.S.O.
Central Statistics Office: *Statistical Abstract of Ireland (annual)*. Dublin: Stationery Office.
Statesman's Yearbook.
Ulster Yearbook. Belfast: H.M.S.O.
Whitaker's Almanack.

2. THE NATURE OF THE LAND

E. H. Brown, *The Relief and Drainage of Wales*. Cardiff: University of Wales Press.
G. H. Dury, *The Face of the Earth*. Penguin Books.
G. H. Dury, 'Diversion of Drainage by Ice'. *Science News* 38, 1955.
W. G. Fearnsides and O. M. B. Bulman, *Geology in the Service of Man*. Penguin Books.
J. F. Kirkcaldy, *General Principles of Geology*. London: Hutchinson.

D. L. Linton, 'The Delimitation of Morphological Regions'; in *London Essays in Geography* (ed. L. D. Stamp and S. W. Wooldridge). London: Longmans, Green.

D. L. Linton, 'Problems of Scottish Scenery'. *Scot. Geogr. Mag.* 47, 1951.

C. R. Longwell and R. F. Flint, *Introduction to Physical Geology*. New York: Wiley.

J. A. Steers, *The Sea Coast*. London: Collins.

J. A. Steers, *The Coastline of England and Wales*. Cambridge: University Press.

J. A. Steers, *The Coastline of Scotland*. Cambridge: University Press.

A. E. Trueman, *Geology and Scenery*. Penguin Books.

A. K. Wells and J. F. Kirkaldy, *Outline of Historical Geology*. London: Murby.

3. CLIMATE, VEGETATION, AND SOILS

Air Ministry, Meteorological Office, *Climatological Atlas of the British Isles*. London: H.M.S.O.

S. R. Badmin, *Trees in Britain*. Penguin Books.

W. G. V. Balchin, 'The Nation's Water Supply'. *Geog.* 42, 1957.

British Forestry Commission: reports and other publications. London: H.M.S.O.

C. P. Burnham, 'The Regional Pattern of Soil Formation in Great Britain'. *Scot. Geogr. Mag.* 86, 1970.

T. J. Chandler, 'Climatology Applied in the Service of Man: A Symposium'. *Adv. Sci.* 13, 1957.

G. H. Dury, 'Weather, Climate, and River Erosion in the Ice Age'. *Science News* 33, 1954.

H. L. Edlin, *Trees, Woods, and Man*. London: Collins.

R. Geiger, *The Climate Near The Ground*. Harvard: U.P.

S. Gregory, 'Accumulated Temperature Maps of the British Isles'. *Trans. Inst. Brit. Geog.* 1954.

S. Gregory, 'Regional Variations in the Trend of Annual Rainfall over the British Isles'. *Geogr. Journ.* 122, 1956.

S. Gregory, 'The Contribution of Uplands to the Public Water Supply of England and Wales'. *Trans. Inst. Brit. Geog.* 1954.

F. K. Hare, *The Restless Atmosphere*. London: Hutchinson.

C. E. Hubbard, *Grasses*. Penguin Books.

G. Kimble and R. Bush, *The Weather*. Penguin Books.

H. H. Lamb, 'Britain's Changing Climate'. *Geogr. Journ.* 133, 1967.

G. Manley, *Climate and the British Scene*. London: Collins.

J. D. McLay, 'The Work of the Forestry Commission in South West Scotland'. *Scot. Geogr. Mag.* 85, 1969.

A. A. Miller, 'The Use and Misuse of Climatic Resources'. *Adv. Sci.* 13, 1956.

W. H. Pearsall, *Mountains and Moorlands*. London: Collins.

W. Pennington, *The History of the British Vegetation*. London: E.U.P.

J. C. Rodda, 'Rainfall Excesses in the United Kingdom'. *Trans. Inst. Brit. Geog.* No. 49, 1970.

Sir John E. Russell, *The World of the Soil*. London: Collins.

A. G. Tansley, *Britain's Green Mantle*. London: Allen & Unwin.

W. B. Turrill, *British Plant Life*. London: Collins.

4. THE PATTERN OF PEOPLING

J. H. Andrews, 'Some Statistical Maps of Defoe's England'. *Geog. Studies* 3, 1956.

M. Ashley, *England in the Seventeenth Century*. Penguin Books.

M. Beresford, *History on the Ground*. London: Lutterworth Press.

M. Beresford, *The Lost Villages of England*. London: Lutterworth Press.

S. T. Bindoff, *Tudor England*. Penguin Books.

V. G. Childe, *Prehistoric Communities of the British Isles*. Edinburgh: Chambers.

G. Clark, *Prehistoric England*. London: Batsford.

R. G. Collingwood, *Roman Britain*. Oxford: U.P.

H. C. Darby, 'The Clearing of the English Woodlands'. *Geog.* 36, 1951.

H. C. Darby (ed.), *An Historical Geography of England and Wales before 1800*. Cambridge: U.P.

R. A. Donkin, 'The Cistercian Order and the Settlement of Northern England'. *Geog. Review* 59, 1970.

E. Ekwall, *The Concise Oxford Dictionary of English Place-names*. Oxford: Clarendon Press.

H. J. Fleure, *A Natural History of Man in Britain*. London: Collins.

H. L. Gray, *English Field Systems*. Harvard: U.P.

J. and C. Hawkes, *Prehistoric Britain*. London: Chatto and Windus.

W. G. Hoskins, *The Making of the English Landscape*. London: Hodder & Stoughton.

A. R. Myers, *England in the Late Middle Ages*. Penguin Books.

Ordnance Survey: *Place Names on Maps of Scotland and Wales*.

S. Piggott, *British Prehistory*. Oxford: U.P.

S. Piggott and K. Henderson, *Scotland Before History*. Edinburgh: Nelson.

J. K. St. Joseph, 'Air Photographs and Archaeology'. *Geog. Journ.* 105, 1945.

D. M. Stenton, *English Society in the Early Middle Ages*. Penguin Books.

D. Whitelock, *The Beginnings of English Society*. Penguin Books.

5. AGRICULTURE FROM 1700

F. A. Barnes, 'The Evolution of Salient Patterns of Milk Production and Distribution in England and Wales'. *Trans. Inst. Brit. Geog.* 1958.

R. H. Best and A. G. Champion, 'Regional Conversions of Agricultural Land to Urban Uses in England and Wales, 1945–67'. *Trans. Inst. Brit. Geog.* No. 49, 1970.

J. B. Caird, 'The Making of the Scottish Rural Landscape'. *Scot. Geogr. Mag.* 80, 1964.

Central Statistics Office: *Statistical Abstract of Ireland (annual).* Dublin: Stationery Office.

H. C. Chew, 'Fifteen Years of Agricultural Change'. *Geog.* 43, 1958.

J. T. Coppock, *An Agricultural Atlas of England and Wales.* London: Faber & Faber.

J. T. Coppock and A. M. Coleman, 'Land Use and Conservation'. *Geogr. Journ.* 136, 1970.

Department of Agriculture for Scotland: *Agricultural Statistics, Scotland (annual).* Edinburgh, H.M.S.O.

Lord Ernle, *English Farming Past and Present.* London: Heinemann.

Ruth Gasson, 'The Changing Location of Intensive Crops in England and Wales'. *Geog.* 51, 1966.

H. L. Gray, *English Field Systems.* Harvard: U.P.

D. B. Grigg, 'An Index of Regional Change in English Farming'. *Trans. Inst. Brit. Geog.* 1965.

D. A. Hill, *The Land of Ulster.* Belfast: H.M.S.O.

S. R. Jones, *English Village Homes.* London: Batsford.

Land Utilisation Survey of Great Britain: *County Reports.* (These Reports, dealing chiefly with the inter-war period, are now mainly of historical interest. Numbers of them, however, contain useful summaries of geology, climate, landform, and agricultural history.)

Ministry of Agriculture and Fisheries: *Agricultural Statistics, England and Wales (annual).* London: H.M.S.O.

T. O'Riordan, 'Spray Irrigation and the Water Resources Act, 1963'. *Trans. Inst. Brit. Geog.* No. 46, 1970.

C. S. Orwin, *A History of English Farming.* Edinburgh: Nelson.

H. Pakington, *English Villages and Hamlets.* London: Batsford.

J. H. Plumb, *England in the Eighteenth Century.* Penguin Books.

L. D. Stamp, *Man and the Land.* London: Collins.

L. D. Stamp, 'Wartime Changes in British Agriculture'. *Geogr. Journ.* 109, 1947.

L. D. Stamp, *The Land of Britain: its Use and Misuse.* London: Longmans, Green.

E. K. Teather, 'The Hedgerow: an Analysis of a Changing Landscape Feature'. *Geog.* 55, 1970.

A. R. Wannop, 'Scottish Agriculture'. *Scot. Geogr. Mag.* 80, 1964.

M. Williams, 'The Enclosure and Reclamation of Waste Land in England and Wales in the Eighteenth and Nineteenth Centuries'. *Trans. Inst. Brit. Geog.* No. 51, 1970.

6. THE RISE OF INDUSTRY

T. S. Ashton, *Iron and Steel in the Industrial Revolution.* Manchester: U.P.

H. L. Beales, *The Industrial Revolution, 1750–1850.* London: Frank Cass.

G. D. H. Cole, *Introduction to Economic History, 1750–1950.* London: Macmillan.

W. H. B. Court, *A Concise Economic History of Britain.* Cambridge: U.P.

H. C. Darby (ed.), *An Historical Geography of England and Wales before 1800.* Cambridge: U.P.

K. G. T. McDonnell, D. C. Coleman, and S. Pollard, *A Survey of English Economic History.* London and Glasgow: Blackie.

P. Matoux, *The Industrial Revolution in the Eighteenth Century.* London: Jonathan Cape.

J. U. Nef, *Cultural Foundations of Industrial Civilisation.* Cambridge: U.P.

J. H. Plumb, *England in the Eighteenth Century.* Penguin Books.

A. Redford, *Labour and Migration in England, 1800–1850.* Manchester: U.P.

Wilfred Smith, *An Economic Geography of Great Britain.* London: Methuen.

L. D. Stamp and S. H. Beaver, *The British Isles.* London: Longmans, Green.

D. Thomson, *England in the Nineteenth Century.* Penguin Books.

7. COAL AND INDUSTRIAL POWER

British Iron and Steel Federation: *Annual Statistics.*

Central Electricity Authority: *Reports and Accounts (annual).* London: H.M.S.O.

Central Office of Information: *Nuclear Energy in Britain.* London: H.M.S.O.

Central Statistical Office: *Annual Abstract of Statistics.* London: H.M.S.O.

Central Statistics Office: *Statistical Abstract of Ireland (annual).* Dublin: Stationery Office.

Colliery Yearbook.

W. H. B. Court, *Coal—History of the Second World War.* London: H.M.S.O. and Longmans, Green.

J. H. Dunning and C. J. Thomas, *British Industry, Change and Development in the Twentieth Century.* London: Hutchinson.

P. R. Mounfield, 'The Location of Nuclear Power Stations, &c.' *Geog.* 46, 1961.

R. C. Estall, 'The Problem of Power in the United Kingdom'. *Econ. Geog.* 34, 1958.

P. E. Kent, 'North Sea Exploration—a Case History'. *Geogr. Journ.* 133, 1967.

N. Lansdell, *The Atom and the Energy Revolution.* Penguin Books.

M. R. Luckas, 'Recent Developments in the United Kingdom Oil Industry'. *Geog.* 50, 1965.

National Coal Board: *Annual Report and Statement of Accounts.* London: H.M.S.O.

J. E. Nef, *The Rise of the British Coal Industry.* London: Routledge.

North of Scotland Hydro-electric Board: *Annual Report and Accounts.* Edinburgh: H.M.S.O.

E. M. Rawstron, 'Changes in the Geography of Electricity Production in Great Britain'. *Geog.* 40, 1955.

T. M. Thomas, 'Recent Trends and Developments in the British Coal Mining Industry'. *Econ. Geog.* 34, 1958.

Sir Arthur Trueman (ed.), *The Coalfields of Great Britain.* London: Edward Arnold.

Ulster Yearbook, Belfast, H.M.S.O.

8. THE AGE OF STEEL

G. C. Allen, *British Industries and their Organization.* London: Longmans, Green.

British Iron and Steel Federation: *Annual Statistics.*

British Iron and Steel Federation: *A Simple Guide to Basic Processes in the Iron and Steel Industry.*

British Iron and Steel Federation: *A Simple Guide to Finishing Processes in the Iron and Steel Industry.*

British Iron and Steel Federation: *Britain's Iron Ore Resources.*

British Iron and Steel Federation: *The Location of the British Steel Industry.*

British Iron and Steel Federation: *The World's Iron Ore Supplies.*

W. R. Jones, *Minerals in Industry.* Penguin Books.

B. S. Keeling and A. E. G. Wright, *The Development of the Modern British Steel Industry.* London: Longmans, Green.

G. Manners, 'Transport Costs, Freight Rates, and the Changing Economic Geography of Iron Ore', *Geog.* 52, 1967.

J. E. Martin, 'Location Factors in the Iron and Steel Industry'. *Trans. Inst. Brit. Geog.* 1957.

D. C. D. Pocock, 'Stages in the Development of the Frodingham Ironstone Field'. *Trans. Inst. Brit. Geog.* 1964.

P. C. D. Pocock, 'Britain's Post-War Iron-Ore Industry'. *Geog.* 51, 1966.

E. M. Rawstron, 'Three Principles of Industrial Location'. *Trans. Inst. Brit. Geog.* 1958.

H. C. Roepke, 'Movements of the British Iron and Steel Industry, 1720 to 1951'. *Urbana*, Ill.: U. of Illinois Press.

Statistical Summary of the Mineral Industry (annual). London: H.M.S.O.

A. Street and W. Alexander, *Metals in the Service of Man.* Penguin Books.

K. Warren, 'Recent Changes in the Geographical Location of the British Steel Industry'. *Geogr. Journ.* 135, 1969.

T. I. Williams, *The Chemical Industry.* Penguin Books.

9. TRADE, TRANSPORT AND COMMUNICATION

J. H. Appleton, 'Some Geographical Aspects of the Modernisation of British Railways'. *Geog.* 52, 1967.

S. H. Beaver, 'Ships and Shipping: the Geographical Consequences of Technological Progress'. *Geog.* 52, 1967.

J. Bird, 'Traffic Flows to and from British Seaports'. *Geog.* 54, 1969.

R. N. E. Blake, 'The Impact of Airfields and the British Landscape'. *Geogr. Journ.* 135, 1969.

Board of Trade: *Annual Statement of the Trade of the United Kingdom.* London: H.M.S.O.

Central Statistical Office: *Annual Abstract of Statistics.* London: H.M.S.O.

Central Statistics Office: *Statistical Abstract of Ireland* (annual). Dublin: Stationery Office.

R. T. Foster, 'Pipeline Development in the United Kingdom'. *Geog.* 54, 1959.

P. N. Grimshaw, 'The U.K. Portland Cement Industry'. *Geog.* 53, 1968.

C. Hadfield, *British Canals.* London: Phoenix House.

Lloyd's Register of Shipping: *Annual Summary of Merchant Ships Launched.*

Ministry of Transport and Civil Aviation: *Report of the Committee of Inquiry into Inland Waterways* (Cmnd. 486, 1956). London: H.M.S.O.

F. W. Morgan, *Ports and Harbours.* London: Hutchinson.

A. C. O'Dell, *Railways and Geography.* London: Hutchinson.

J. A. Patmore, 'The Contraction of the Network of Railway Passenger Services in England and Wales, 1836–1962'. *Trans. Inst. Brit. Geog.* 1964.

K. R. Sealy, 'The Siting and Development of British Airports'. *Geogr. Journ.* 133, 1967.

K. R. Sealy, *The Geography of Air Transport.* London: Hutchinson.

L. D. Stamp, 'Britain's Railway Policy'. *Geogr. Journ.* 131, 1965.

Statesman's Yearbook.

Ulster Yearbook. Belfast: H.M.S.O.

H. D. Watts, 'The Inland Waterways of the United Kingdom in the 1960s'. *Econ. Geog.* 43, 1967.

Whitaker's Almanack.

10. POPULATION

I. Carruthers, 'A Classification of Service Centres in England and Wales'. *Geogr. Journ.* 123, 1957.

Census Reports for England and Wales, Ireland, Northern Ireland, Scotland.

J. B. Fleming and F. H. W. Green, 'Some Relations between Country and Town in Scotland'. *Scot. Geogr. Mag.* 68, 1952.

T. W. Freeman, *The Conurbations of Great Britain.* Manchester: Manchester U.P.

E. M. Hubback, *The Population of Britain.* Penguin Books.

A. J. Hunt (ed.), 'Special Number of Population Maps of the British Isles'. *Trans. Inst. Brit. Geog.* No. 43, 1968.

H. R. Jones, 'A Study of Rural Migration in Central Wales'. *Trans. Inst. Brit. Geog.* No. 37, 1965.

H. R. Jones, 'Migration Within Scotland'. *Scot. Geogr. Mag.* 83, 1967.

H. R. Jones, 'Migration to and from Scotland since 1961'. *Trans. Inst. Brit. Geog.* No. 49, 1970.

P. N. Jones, 'Some Aspects of the Changing Distribution of Coloured Immigrants in Birmingham, 1961–66'. *Trans. Inst. Brit. Geog.* No. 50, 1970.

C. M. Law, 'The Growth of Urban Population in England and Wales'. *Trans. Inst. Brit. Geog.* No. 41, 1967.

G. C. K. Peach, 'Factors Affecting the Distribution of West Indians in Great Britain'. *Trans. Inst. Brit. Geog.* No. 38, 1966.

R. H. Osborne, 'Internal Migration in England and Wales, 1951'. *Adv. Sci.* 48, 1956.

P.E.P. Report: *World Population and Resources.* Distributed by Allen & Unwin.

A. E. Smailes, 'The Geography of Towns'. London: Hutchinson.

G. P. Wibberley, 'Some Aspects of Problem Rural Areas in Britain'. *Geogr. Journ.* 120, 1954.

J. D. Wood, 'Scottish Migration Overseas'. *Scot. Geogr. Mag.* 80, 1964.

PART TWO

11. INTRODUCTION TO PART TWO

H. E. Bracey, 'A Rural Component of Centrality Applied to Six Southern Counties in the United Kingdom'. *Econ. Geog.* 32, 1956.

Central Statistics Office: *Statistical Abstract of Ireland (annual).* Dublin: Stationery Office.

J. T. Coppock, 'The Relationship of Farm and Parish Boundaries'. *Geog. Studies* 2, 1955.

Department of Agriculture for Scotland: *Agricultural Statistics, Scotland (annual).* Edinburgh: H.M.S.O.

G. H. Dury, *Map Interpretation.* London: Pitman.

G. H. Dury and J. A. Morris, *The Land from the Air.* London: Harrap.

F. H. W. Green, 'Community of Interest Areas in Western Europe'. *Econ. Geog.* 29, 1953.

G. H. T. Kimble, 'The Inadequacy of the Regional Concept'. In *London Essays in Geography* (ed. L. D. Stamp and S. W. Wooldridge). London: Longmans, Green.

D. L. Linton, 'The Delimitation of Morphological Regions'. In *London Essays in Geography* (ed. L. D. Stamp and S. W. Wooldridge). London: Longmans, Green.

Ministry of Agriculture and Fisheries: *Agricultural Statistics, England and Wales (annual).* London: H.M.S.O.

A. C. Montefiore and W. M. Williams, 'Determinism and Possibilism'. *Geog. Studies* 2, 1955.

O. H. K. Spate, 'How Determined is Possibilism?' *Geog. Studies* 4, 1957.

12. THE REGIONS OF IRELAND

A View of Ireland. British Association.

Belfast in its Regional Setting. British Association.

Central Statistics Office: *Statistical Abstract of Ireland.* Dublin: Stationery Office.

J. K. Charlesworth, *The Geology of Ireland.* Oliver & Boyd: Edinburgh and London.

R. Common (ed.), *Northern Ireland from the Air.* Belfast: Queen's U.P.

D. J. Dwyer, 'The Peat Bogs of the Irish Republic'. *Geogr. Journ.* 128, 1962.

E. Estyn Evans, *Irish Heritage.* Dundalk: Tempest.

T. W. Freeman, *Ireland: its Physical, Historical, Social and Economic Geography.* London: Methuen.

T. W. Freeman, 'The Prospect for Irish Agriculture'. *Geogr. Journ.* 120, 1954.

D. A. Gillmor, 'Cattle Movements in the Republic of Ireland', *Trans. Inst. Brit. Geog.* No. 46, 1969.

J. P. Haughton, 'The Social Geography of Dublin'. *Geog. Review* 47, 1947.

J. H. Johnson, 'Studies of Irish Rural Settlement'. *Geog. Review* 48, 1958.

J. H. Johnson, 'Population Changes in Ireland, 1951–61'. *Geogr. Journ.* 129, 1963.

A. J. P. McCarthy, 'The Irish National Electrification Scheme'. *Geog. Review* 47, 1957.

T. McEvoy, 'Forestry in Ireland'. *Adv. Sci.* 14, 1958.

Sean O'Faolain, *The Irish.* Penguin Books.

J. A. Soulsby, 'The Shannon Free Airport Scheme: a New Approach to Industrial Development'. *Scot. Geogr. Mag.* 81, 1965.

L. Symons (ed.), *Land Use in Northern Ireland.* London: University of London Press.

J. R. Tarrant, 'Recent Industrial Developments in Ireland'. *Geog.* 52, 1967.

Ulster Yearbook. Belfast: H.M.S.O.

Recommended maps: Ordnance Map of Ireland, 1:63,360.
Sheets 43 (with parts of sheets 31 and 42)

(Manor Hamilton), 105 (with part of sheet 114) (Galway), 110 (Edenderry), 139 (Arklow), 145 (Limerick), 166 (Clonmel), 188 (Youghal), 192 (Glengarriff).
Ordnance Survey of Northern Ireland, 1 : 63,360, Popular.
Sheets 7 (Belfast), 11 (The Mourne Mountains).

13. WALES AND THE WELSH BORDER

J. A. Andrews, 'Chepstow: a Defunct Seaport of the Severn Estuary'. *Geog.* 40, 1955.
R. Beard, 'Changing Patterns of Employment in the Forest of Dean'. *Geog.* 56, 1971.
E. G. Bowen (ed.), *Wales: A Physical, Historical, and Regional Geography.* London: Methuen.
E. G. Bowen, *The Settlement of the Celtic Saints in Wales.* Cardiff: U. of Wales Press.
British Regional Geology: *North Wales.* London: H.M.S.O.
British Regional Geology: *South Wales.* London: H.M.S.O.
British Regional Geology: *The Welsh Borderland.* London: H.M.S.O.
H. Carter, *The Towns of Wales.* Cardiff: U. of Wales Press.
H. Carter and G. Rowley, 'The Morphology of the Central Business District of Cardiff'. *Trans. Inst. Brit. Geog.* No. 38, 1966.
H. W. E. Davies, 'The Development of the Industrial Landscape of Llanelly'. *Geog. Studies* 4, 1957.
H. W. E. Davies and D. F. Hagger, 'Recent Industrial Changes in South Wales'. *Adv. Sci.* 18, 1961.
M. Davies, *Wales in Maps.* Cardiff: U. of Wales Press.
Wyn Griffiths, *The Welsh.* Peguin Books.
G. M. Howe, *Wales from the Air.* Cardiff: U. of Wales Press.
G. M. Howe and P. Thomas, *Welsh Landforms and Scenery.* London: Macmillan.
G. Humphrys, 'The Journey to Work in Industrial South Wales'. *Trans. Inst. Brit. Geog.* No. 36, 1965.
H. R. Jones, 'A Study of Rural Migration in Central Wales'. *Trans. Inst. Brit. Geog.* 1965.
G. R. Jones, 'Some Medieval Rural Settlements in North Wales'. *Trans. Inst. Brit. Geog.* 1953.
G. Manners (ed.), *South Wales in the Sixties.* Oxford: Pergamon Press.
J. Oliver, 'The Wetness of Wales. Rainfall as a Factor in the Geography of Wales'. *Geog.* 43, 1958.
W. H. Pearsall, *Mountains and Moorlands.* London: Collins.
The Cardiff Region: British Association Handbook.
G. H. Thomas, 'The New Iron Ore Terminal at Port Talbot' *Geog.* 54, 1969.

J. G. Thomas, 'Some Enclosure Patterns in Central Wales'. *Geog.* 42, 1957.
J. G. Thomas, 'The Geographical Distribution of the Welsh Language'. *Geogr. Journ.* 122, 1956.
T. M. Thomas, 'Wales: Land of Mines and Quarries'. *Geog. Review* 46, 1956.
D. G. Watts, 'Changes in Location of the South Wales Iron and Steel Industry 1860–1930'. *Geog.* 53, 1968.

Recommended maps: Seventh Series sheets 116, 129, 154.
1 : 25,000 sheets [part of Anglesey], SO53 [Hereford], SS69 [Swansea].

14. THE SCOTTISH HIGHLANDS

British Regional Geology: *The Grampian Highlands.* Edinburgh: H.M.S.O.
British Regional Geology: *The Northern Highlands.* Edinburgh: H.M.S.O.
British Regional Geology: *The Tertiary Volcanic Districts.* Edinburgh: H.M.S.O.
J. R. Coull, 'The Economic Development of the Island of Westray, Orkney'. *Scot. Geogr. Mag.* 82, 1966.
Department of Agriculture for Scotland: *Types of Farming in Scotland.* Edinburgh: H.M.S.O.
F. Fraser Darling, *Natural History in the Highlands and Islands.* London: Collins.
W. A. Hance, 'Crofting in the Outer Hebrides'. *Econ. Geog.* 28, 1952.
K. R. Lea, 'Hydro-electric Power Generation in the Highlands of Scotland'. *Trans. Inst. Brit. Geog.* No. 46, 1969.
Moray McLaren, *The Scots.* Penguin Books.
A. S. Mather and D. Smith, 'Moray Firth Development'. *Geog.* 56, 1971.
R. Millman, 'The Marches of the Highland Estates'. *Scot. Geogr. Mag.* 85, 1969.
R. Millman, 'The Landed Properties of Northern Scotland'. *Scot. Geogr. Mag.* 86, 1970.
A. C. O'Dell, 'Highlands and Islands Developments'. *Scot. Geogr. Mag.* 82, 1966.
A. C. O'Dell and J. Mackintosh (eds.), *The North-east of Scotland.* Aberdeen: Central Press.
W. H. Pearsall, *Mountains and Moorlands.* London: Collins.
I. M. L. Robertson, 'Changing Form and Function of Settlement in South West Argyll, 1841–1961'. *Scot. Geogr. Mag.* 83, 1967.
D. Turnock, 'Hebridean Car Ferries'. *Geog.* 50, 1965.
D. Turnock, 'Lochaber: West Highland Growth Point'. *Scot. Geogr. Mag.* 82, 1966.
D. Turnock, 'Glenelg, Glengarry and Locheil: an Evolutionary Study of Land Use'. *Scot. Geogr. Mag.* 83, 1967.
D. Turnock, 'Regional Development in the Crofting Counties'. *Trans. Inst. Brit. Geog.* No. 48, 1968.

H. Walton, 'Climate and Famine in Northeast Scotland'. *Scot. Geogr. Mag.* 68, 1952.

D. P. Willis, 'Population and Economy of Fair Isle'. *Scot. Geogr. Mag.* 83, 1967.

Recommended maps: Seventh Series sheets 19, 37, 40. 1:25,000 sheet NS26 [Elgin].

15. CENTRAL SCOTLAND

N. I. Beckles, 'Textiles and Port Growth in Dundee'. *Scot. Geogr. Mag.* 84, 1968.

British Regional Geology: *The Midland Valley of Scotland*. Edinburgh: H.M.S.O.

R. H. Campbell, 'Scottish Shipbuilding; its Rise and Progress'. *Scot. Geogr. Mag.* 80, 1964.

J. R. Coull, 'Modern Trends in Scottish Fisheries'. *Scot. Geogr. Mag.* 84, 1968.

P. Crabb and I. Douglas, 'Water Resources Management in South West Perthshire'. *Scot. Geogr. Mag.* 86, 1970.

Department of Agriculture for Scotland: *Types of Farming in Scotland*. Edinburgh: H.M.S.O.

P. Green, 'Some Planning Problems of a Large Burgh: Hamilton–Clydeside'. *Scot. Geogr. Mag.* 83, 1967.

H. R. Jones and D. C. D. Pocock, 'Some Economic and Social Implications of the Tay Road Bridge'. *Scot. Geogr. Mag.* 82, 1966.

J. H. Jones and C. B. Marshall, 'The Longannet Power Station'. *Geog.* 53, 1968.

A. G. Kinniburgh, 'New Developments in Clydeport'. *Scot. Geogr. Mag.* 82, 1966.

P. D. McGovern, 'The New Towns of Scotland'. *Scot. Geogr. Mag.* 84, 1968.

D. R. MacGregor, 'A Survey of the Social and Economic Effects of the Forth Road Bridge, &c.'. *Scot. Geogr. Mag.* 82, 1966.

R. Miller, 'The New Face of Glasgow'. *Scot. Geogr. Mag.* 86, 1970.

D. C. D. Pocock, 'Economic Renewal: the Example of Fife'. *Scot. Geogr. Mag.* 86, 1970.

C. J. Robertson, 'Locational and Structural Aspects of Industry in Edinburgh'. *Scot. Geogr. Mag.* 74, 1958.

C. J. Robertson, 'New Industries and New Towns in Scotland's Industrial Growth'. *Scot. Geogr. Mag.* 80, 1964.

Scientific Survey of Southeastern Scotland: British Association Handbook.

P. J. Smith, 'Glenrothes: some Geographical Aspects of New Town Development'. *Scot. Geogr. Mag.* 83, 1967.

J. M. Soons, 'Landscape Evolution in the Ochil Hills'. *Scot. Geogr. Mag.* 74, 1958.

The Glasgow Region: British Association Handbook.

W. H. K. Turner, 'The Concentration of Jute and Heavy Linen Manufacture in East Central Scotland'. *Scot. Geogr. Mag.* 86, 1966.

W. H. K. Turner, 'The Growth of the City of Dundee'. *Scot. Geogr. Mag.* 84, 1968.

K. Warren, 'Locational Problems of the Scottish Iron and Steel Industry Since 1760'. Pt. 1, *Scot. Geogr. Mag.* 81, 1965; Pt. 2, *Scot. Geogr. Mag.* 81, 1965.

R. V. Welch, 'Immigrant Manufacturing Industry established in Scotland between 1945 and 1968, &c.'. *Scot. Geogr. Mag.* 86, 1970.

Recommended maps: Seventh Series sheet 60. 1:25,000 sheet NS98 [Grangemouth].

16. THE SOUTHERN UPLANDS AND THE BORDER COUNTRY

British Regional Geology: *Northern England*. London: H.M.S.O.

British Regional Geology: *The South of Scotland*. Edinburgh: H.M.S.O.

R. Common, 'The Geomorphology of the East Cheviot Area'. *Scot. Geogr. Mag.* 70, 1954.

Department of Agriculture for Scotland: *Types of Farming in Scotland*. Edinburgh: H.M.S.O.

J. B. Fleming and F. H. W. Green, 'Some Relations between Country and Town in Scotland'. *Scot. Geogr. Mag.* 68, 1952.

W. H. Pearsall, *Mountains and Moorlands*. London: Collins.

Scientific Survey of Southeastern Scotland: British Association handbook.

J. Tivy, 'Reconnaissance Survey of Certain Hill Grazings in the Southern Uplands'. *Scot. Geogr. Mag.* 70, 1954.

Recommended maps: Seventh Series sheet 69. 1:25,000 sheet NU00 [Rothbury].

17. THE LAKE DISTRICT, THE ISLE OF MAN AND THE PENNINES

T. H. Bainbridge, 'Population Changes over the West Cumberland Coalfield'. *Econ. Geog.* 25, 1949.

British Regional Geology: *Northern England*. London: H.M.S.O.

British Regional Geology: *The Pennines and Adjacent Areas*. London: H.M.S.O.

E. Davies, 'Treens and Quarterlands. A Study of the Land System of the Isle of Man'. *Trans. Inst. Brit. Geog.* 1956.

R. H. Kinvig, 'The Isle of Man and Atlantic Britain: a study in historical geography'. *Trans. Inst. Brit. Geog.* 1958.

R. Lawton, 'The Economic Geography of Craven in the Early Nineteenth Century'. *Trans. Inst. Brit. Geog.* 1954.

W. H. Pearsall, *Mountains and Moorlands*. London: Collins.

W. E. Richardson, 'Temperature-differences in the South Tyne Valley, near Alston, Cumberland'. *Weather* 9, 1954.

A. E. Smailes, 'The Lead Dales of the Northern Pennines'. *Geog.* 21, 1936.

M. M. Sweeting, 'Erosion Cycles and Limestone Caverns in the Ingleborough District'. *Geogr. Journ.* 115, 1950.

Recommended maps: Seventh Series sheets 82, 84, 111. 1 : 25,000 sheets NY45 [Carlisle], NY63 [North Pennines], SK05 [South Pennines].

18. THE LANCS.–CHESHIRE PLAIN AND ITS INDUSTRIAL BORDERS

British Regional Geology: *The Pennines and Adjacent Areas.* London: H.M.S.O.

Department of Economic Affairs, *The North West.* London: H.M.S.O.

R. C. Estall, 'Industrial Change in Lancashire and Merseyside'. *Geog.* 46, 1961.

Manchester and its Region: British Association handbook.

M. E. Marker, 'The Dee Estuary: its progressive Silting and Salt Marsh Development'. *Trans. Inst. Brit. Geog.* No. 41, 1967.

Merseyside: British Association handbook.

R. Millward, *Lancashire: The History of the Landscape.* London: Hodder & Stoughton.

J. Salt, 'The Motor Industry on Merseyside'. *Geog.* 53, 1968.

E. S. Simpson, 'The Cheshire Grass-Dairying Region'. *Trans. Inst. Brit. Geog.* 1957.

A. Taylor, 'The Relation of Crop-distribution to the Drift Pattern in Southwest Lancashire'. *Trans. Inst. Brit. Geog.* 1955.

K. L. Wallwork, 'The Cotton Industry in North West England: 1941–61.' *Geog.* 47, 1962.

Recommended maps: Seventh Series sheets 101, 109. 1 : 25,000 sheet SJ52 [Wem].

19. THE INDUSTRIAL NORTHEAST OF ENGLAND

A Physical Land Classification of Northumberland, Durham, and Part of the North Riding of Yorkshire. Newcastle-upon-Tyne: The North East Development Association.

British Regional Geology: *Northern England.* London: H.M.S.O.

A. A. L. Caesar, *A Survey of Industrial Facilities of the North East Region.* Newcastle-upon-Tyne: Reid & Co.

G. H. Daysh and J. S. Symonds, *West Durham. A Study of a Problem Area in North Eastern England.* Oxford: Basil Blackwell.

N. R. Elliot, 'Hinterland and Foreland as illustrated by the Port of Tyne'. *Trans. Inst. Brit. Geog.* No. 47, 1969.

Industrial Estates. Cheltenham and London: J. Burrow, for North Eastern Trading Estates.

Scientific Survey of Northeastern England: British Association handbook.

Recommended maps: Seventh Series sheet 78. 1 : 25,000 sheet NZ52 [Tees Estuary].

20. THE INDUSTRIAL REGION OF THE WEST RIDING

J. H. Appleton, 'The Railway Network of Southern Yorkshire'. *Trans. Inst. Brit. Geog.* 1956.

British Regional Geology: *The Pennines and Adjacent Areas.* London: H.M.S.O.

G. B. D. Gray, 'The South-Yorkshire Coalfield'. *Geog.* 32, 1947.

E. Lipson, *A Short History of Wool and Its Manufacture.* London: Heinemann.

M. J. Mortimore, 'Landownership and Urban Growth in Bradford, &c.'. *Trans. Inst. Brit. Geog.* No. 46, 1969.

H. Rees, 'Leeds and the Yorkshire Woollen Industry'. *Econ. Geog.* 24, 1948.

Sheffield and Its Region: British Association handbook.

Recommended maps: Seventh Series sheet 96. 1 : 25,000 sheet SK49 [Rotherham].

21. THE SCARPLANDS OF EASTERN ENGLAND

British Regional Geology: *East Yorkshire and Lincolnshire.* London: H.M.S.O.

British Regional Geology: *The Pennines and Adjacent Areas.* London: H.M.S.O.

H. C. Chew, 'Fifteen Years of Agricultural Change'. *Geog.* 43, 1958.

K. C. Edwards, 'Changing Geographical Patterns in Lincolnshire'. *Geog.* 39, 1954.

G. E. Fussell, ' "High Farming" in the North of England, 1840–1880'. *Econ. Geog.* 24, 1948.

M. Kirk, 'The Vale of York: The Evolution of a Landscape'. *Geog.* 40, 1955.

D. L. Linton, 'The Landforms of Lincolnshire'. *Geog.* 39, 1954.

R. F. Peel and J. Palmer, 'The Physiography of the Vale of York'. *Geog.* 40, 1955.

H. Thorpe, 'Some Aspects of Settlement in County Durham'. *Geog.* 35, 1950.

H. D. Watts, 'New Industrial Building in East Yorkshire 1946–62'. *Geog.* 50, 1965.

Recommended maps: Seventh Series sheet 105. 1 : 25,000 sheet SE97 [Vale of Pickering].

22. THE MIDLAND TRIANGLE AND ITS NORTHERN BORDERS

S. H. Beaver, 'The Potteries, a Study in the Evolution of a Cultural Landscape'. *Trans. Inst. Brit. Geog.* 1964.

Birmingham and Its Regional Setting: British Association handbook.

British Regional Geology: *Central England.* London: H.M.S.O.

British Regional Geology: *The Pennines and Adjacent Areas.* London: H.M.S.O.

T. J. Chandler, 'Communications and a Coalfield: a study in the Leicestershire and South Derbyshire Coalfield'. *Trans. Inst. Brit. Geog.* 1957.

Department of Economic Affairs, *The East Midlands Study*. London: H.M.S.O.

Department of Economic Affairs, *The West Midlands*. London: H.M.S.O.

G. H. Dury, 'Drainage Diversion by Ice'. *Science News* 38, 1955.

W. G. Hoskins, *Leicestershire: the History of the Landscape*. London: Hodder & Stoughton.

B. L. C. Johnson, 'The Distribution of Factory Population in the West Midland Conurbation'. *Trans. Inst. Brit. Geog.* 1958.

E. R. Rawstron, 'Some Aspects of the Location of Hosiery and Lace Manufacture in Great Britain'. *East Midland Geographer*, No. 9, 1954

M. B. Stedman and P. A. Wood, 'Urban Renewal in Birmingham, An Interim Report'. *Geog.* 50, 1965.

M. J. Wise, 'Some Factors Influencing the Growth of Birmingham'. *Geog.* 33, 1948.

Recommended maps: Seventh Series sheet 131.
1:25,000 sheet SK51 [Loughborough].

23. SCARPLANDS OF THE SOUTH MIDLANDS

S. H. Beaver, 'The Development of the Northamptonshire Iron Industry, 1881–1920'. In *London Essays in Geography* (ed. L. D. Stamp and S. W. Wooldridge). London: Longmans, Green.

British Regional Geology: *Bristol and Gloucester District*. London: H.M.S.O.

British Regional Geology: *Central England*. London: H.M.S.O.

British Regional Geology: *East Anglia*. London: H.M.S.O.

British Regional Geology: *London and Thames Valley*. London: H.M.S.O.

Department of Economic Affairs: *The East Midlands Study*. London, H.M.S.O.

H. P. R. Finberg, *Gloucestershire*. London: Hodder & Stoughton.

E. W. Gilbert, 'The Industrialisation of Oxford'. *Geogr. Journ.* 109, 1947.

W. R. Mead, 'Ridge and Furrow in Buckinghamshire'. *Geogr. Journ.* 120, 1954.

Ministry of Housing and Local Government: *Northampton, Bedford, and North Bucks Study*. London: H.M.S.O.

W. L. Sargant, 'The Pattern of the Anglo-Saxon Settlement of Rutland'. *Geog.* 31, 1946.

D. I. Scargill, 'Metropolitan Influences in the Oxford Region'. *Geog.* 52, 1967.

The Oxford Region: British Association handbook.

Recommended maps: Seventh Series sheet 144.
1:25,000 sheet SP81 [Aylesbury].

24. EAST ANGLIA AND THE FENLANDS

M. A. Arber, 'Dust-storms in the Fenland around Ely'. *Geog.* 31, 1946.

British Regional Geology: *East Anglia*. London: H.M.S.O.

H. C. Darby, *The Draining of the Fens*. Cambridge: U.P.

E. E. Day, 'The British Sea Fishing Industry'. *Geog.* 54, 1969.

Department of Economic Affairs: *East Anglia, A Study*. London, H.M.S.O.

R. E. Dickinson, 'The Town Plans of East Anglia. A Study in Urban Morphology'. *Geog.* 19, 1934.

G. J. Fuller, 'Geographical Aspects of the Development of Boston (Lincs.) between 1700 and 1900'. *East Midland Geographer* 2, 1954.

G. E. Fussell, ' "High Farming" in the East Midlands and East Anglia'. *Econ. Geog.* 27, 1951.

W. W. Williams, 'An East Coast Survey: Some Recent Changes in the Coast of East Anglia'. *Geogr. Journ.* 122, 1956.

Recommended maps: Seventh Series sheets 124, 125.
1:25,000 sheets TF22 [Spalding], TM45 [Aldeburgh].

25. SOUTHWEST ENGLAND

J. R. Blunden, 'The Renaissance of the Cornish Tin Industry'. *Geog.* 55, 1970.

British Regional Geology: *Southwest England*. London: H.M.S.O.

H. C. Chew, 'Fifteen Years of Agricultural Change'. *Geog.* 43, 1958.

A. Downes, 'Farming the Fortunate Isles'. *Geog.* 42, 1957.

G. E. Fussell, ' "High Farming" in Southwestern England, 1840–1880'. *Econ. Geog.* 24, 1948.

J. C. Goodridge, 'The Tin-Mining Industry: a Growth Point for Cornwall'. *Trans. Inst. Brit. Geog.* No. 38, 1966.

E. Johns, 'The Surveying and Mapping of Vegetation on some Dartmoor Pastures'. *Geog. Studies* 4, 1957.

W. L. D. Ravenhill, 'The Settlement of Cornwall during the Celtic Period'. *Geog.* 40, 1955.

A. H. Shorter, 'The Site, Situation, and Functions of Exeter'. *Geog.* 39, 1954.

Recommended maps: Seventh Series sheet 186.
1:25,000 sheet SX97 [Teignmouth].

26. THE BORDERS OF THE WEST COUNTRY, THE HAMPSHIRE BASIN AND ITS BORDERS, THE CHANNEL ISLANDS

A Survey of Southampton and its Region: British Association handbook.

Bristol and its Adjoining Counties: British Association handbook.

British Regional Geology: *Bristol and Gloucester District*. London: H.M.S.O.

British Regional Geology: *The Hampshire Basin and Adjoining Areas*. London: H.M.S.O.

Channel Islands: Committees for Horticulture and for Agriculture and Fisheries in Jersey and Guernsey. Reports and Special Publications.

G. M. Davies, *The Dorset Coast*. London: Adam & Charles Black.

G. H. Dury, *The Channel Islands* (Report of the Land Utilisation Survey of Great Britain).

L. E. Taverner, 'Changes in the Agricultural Geography of Dorset, 1929–1949'. *Trans. Inst. Brit. Geog.* 1955.

F. Walker, 'Economic Growth on Severnside'. *Trans. Inst. Brit. Geog.* No. 37, 1965.

M. J. Williams, 'Drainage Activity in the Somerset Levels Since 1939', *Geog.* 49, 1964.

Recommended maps: Seventh Series sheets 165, 179. 1:25,000 sheets ST95 [Vale of Pewsey], SU11 [Fordingbridge].

27. SOUTHEAST ENGLAND

J. A. Andrews, 'The Development of the Passenger Ports of Southeast England'. *Geog.* 35, 1950.

British Regional Geology: *The Wealden District*. London: H.M.S.O.

I. D. Margary, *Roman Ways in the Weald*. London: Phoenix House.

Ministry of Housing and Local Government, *The South East Study*, 1961–1981. London: H.M.S.O.

W. H. Parker, 'Settlement in Sussex, 1840–1940'. *Geog.* 35, 1950.

B. W. Sparks, 'The Denudation-chronology of the Dip-slope of the South Downs'. *Proc. Geol. Assoc.* 60, 1949.

G. S. Sweeting, 'Wealden Iron Ore and the History of its Industry'. *Proc. Geol. Assoc.* 55, 1944.

S. W. Wooldridge and F. Golding, *The Weald*. London: Collins.

Recommended maps: Seventh Series sheet 172. 1:25,000 sheet TQ72 [Rye].

28. THE LONDON BASIN

J. Bird, *The Geography of the Port of London*. London: Hutchinson.

Board of Trade, *The Movement of Manufacturing Industry in the United Kingdom 1945–65*. London: H.M.S.O.

British Regional Geology: *London and Thames Valley*. London: H.M.S.O.

Central Statistical Office, *The New Towns of Britain*. London: H.M.S.O.

T. J. Chandler, *The Climate of London*. London: Hutchinson.

R. Clayton (ed.), *The Geography of Greater London*. London: George Philip.

B. E. Coates and E. M. Rawstron, 'Regional Incomes and Planning 1964–65', *Geog.* 52, 1967.

J. T. Coppock, 'Changing Arable in the Chilterns, 1875–1951'. *Geog.* 42, 1957.

J. T. Coppock, 'Land-use Changes in the Chilterns, 1931–1951'. *Trans. Inst. Brit. Geog.* 1954.

Department of Economic Affairs, *East Anglia, A Study*. London: H.M.S.O.

Department of Economic Affairs: *The East Midlands Study*. London: H.M.S.O.

P. Hall, *London 2000*. London: Faber & Faber.

J. R. James and others, 'Local Government Reform in England, etc.'. *Geogr. Journ.* 136, 1970.

D. E. Keeble, 'Industrial Decentralisation and the Metropolis, etc.'. *Trans. Inst. Brit. Geog.* No. 44, 1968.

J. E. Martin, *Greater London*. London: Bell.

Ministry of Housing and Local Government, *Northampton, Bedford, and North Bucks Study*. London: H.M.S.O.

Ministry of Housing and Local Government, *The South East Study*, 1961–1981. London: H.M.S.O.

Ministry of Housing and Local Government, *Strategic Plan for the Southeast*. London: H.M.S.O.

F. J. Osborn and A. Whittick, *The New Towns*. London: Leonard Hill.

Port of London Authority (Port of London Authority handbook).

E. M. Rawstron and C. E. Coates, 'Opportunity and Affluence', *Geog.* 51, 1966.

M. J. Wise, 'The Role of London in the Industrial Geography of Great Britain'. *Geog.* 41, 1956.

M. J. Wise, 'The Future of Local Government in England, etc.'. *Geogr. Journ.* 135, 1969.

S. W. Wooldridge and G. E. Hutchings, *London's Countryside*. London: Methuen.

Recommended maps: Seventh Series sheet 160. 1:25,000 sheet SU 86 [Aldershot].

29. CONCLUSION

P. Archer (ed.), *Social Welfare and the Citizen*. Penguin Books.

Britain and Europe: Economist Intelligence Unit Ltd., London.

J. A. C. Brown, *The Social Psychology of Industry*. Penguin Books.

M. Chisholm, 'Must We All Live in South-east England?' *Geog.* 49, 1964.

G. D. H. Cole, *Local and Regional Government*. London: Cassell.

G. Connell-Smith, *Pattern of the Post-war World*. Penguin Books.

J. H. Dunning and C. J. Thomas, *British Industry, Change and Development in the Twentieth Century*. London: Hutchinson.

P. S. Florence, *Industry and the State*. London: Hutchinson.

T. W. Freeman, *Geography and Planning*. London: Hutchinson.

L. L. Goodman, *Man and Automation*. Penguin Books.

C. D. Harbury, *The Industrial Efficiency of Rural Labour*. Cardiff: U. of Wales Press.

Ministry of Housing and Local Government, *The South East Study*, 1961–1981. London: H.M.S.O.

A. E. Moodie, *The Geography Behind Politics*. London: Hutchinson.

P.E.P. Report: *Growth in the British Economy*. London: Allen & Unwin.

W. J. H. Sprott, *Human Groups*. Penguin Books.

G. Williams, *Economics of Everyday Life*. Penguin Books.

M. J. Wise and others (13 articles), 'This Changing Britain'. *Geog.* 49, 1964.

FURTHER TEXTS

I. C. McIntosh and C. B. Marshall, *The Face of Scotland*. Oxford: Pergamon Press.

J. B. Mitchell (ed.), *Great Britain: Geographical Essays*. Cambridge University Press.

Nelson's *Regions of the British Isles* (in progress: various authors).

L. D. Stamp and S. H. Beaver, *The British Isles*. London: Longmans, Green.

J. A. Steers (ed.), *Field Studies in the British Isles*. London: Nelson.

J. A. Wreford Watson and J. B. Sissons (eds.), *The British Isles*. London: Nelson.

Index

Page references in bold refer to Figure pages and those in italics refer to plates.